Justice Denoted

Recent Titles in
Bibliographies and Indexes in Popular Culture

Humor Scholarship: A Research Bibliography
Don L.F. Nilsen

The Comic Art Collection Catalog: An Author, Artist, Title, and Subject Catalog of the Comic Art Collection, Special Collections Division, Michigan State University Libraries
Randall W. Scott, compiler

Animation, Caricature, and Gag and Political Cartoons in the United States and Canada: An International Bibliography
John A. Lent, compiler

Comic Books and Comic Strips in the United States: An International Bibliography
John A. Lent, compiler

Comic Art of Europe: An International, Comprehensive Bibliography
John A. Lent, compiler

Robert Benchley: An Annotated Bibliography
Gordon E. Ernst, Jr., compiler

Comic Art in Africa, Asia, Australia, and Latin America
John A. Lent, compiler

The Frankenstein Film Sourcebook
Caroline Joan ("Kay") S. Picart, Frank Smoot, and Jayne Blodgett

Comic Art of Europe through 2000: An International Bibliography, Volumes I and II
John A. Lent

Justice Denoted

The Legal Thriller in American, British, and Continental Courtroom Literature

Compiled and Edited by
Terry White

Foreword by Michael A. Kahn

Craft Notes by novelists, authors/lawyers, and trial attorneys, such as Neil Albert, William Bernhardt, William Deverell, Linda A. Fairstein, David M. Fuqua, Frances Fyfield, John Gerald Gleeson, John Wesley Hall, Parnell Hall, Roderic Jeffries, Jonnie Jacobs, Stephen Jones, Michael A. Kahn, Nancy Kopp, Albert J. Krieger, Bonnie MacDougal, Philip Michael Margolin, Margaret Maron, Mary Grace O'Brien, Lisa Scottoline, Robert L. Shapiro, Grif Stockley, and Michael E. Tigar

Bibliographies and Indexes in Popular Culture, Number 9

PRAEGER

Westport, Connecticut
London

Library of Congress Cataloging-in-Publication Data

Justice denoted : the legal thriller in American, British, and continental courtroom literature / compiled and edited by Terry White ; foreword by Michael A. Kahn.
p. cm.—(Bibliographies and indexes in popular culture, ISSN 1066–0658 ; no. 9)
Includes bibliographical references and index.
ISBN 0–313–30301–0 (alk. paper)
1. Legal stories—Bibliography. 2. Legal stories—History and criticism. I. White, Terry, 1952– II. Series.
Z5917.L3J87 2003
[PN3448.L4]
016.80883′9355—dc21 2003048802

British Library Cataloguing in Publication Data is available.

Library of Congress Catalog Card Number: 2003048802
ISBN: 0–313–30301–0
ISSN: 1066–0658

First published in 2003

Praeger Publishers, 88 Post Road West, Westport, CT 06881
An imprint of Greenwood Publishing Group, Inc.
www.praeger.com

Printed in the United States of America

The paper used in this book complies with the Permanent Paper Standard issued by the National Information Standards Organization (Z39.48–1984).

10 9 8 7 6 5 4 3 2 1

Contents

Epigraphs

"What kind of man are you? You have sat here and voted guilty along with everyone else because there are some theater tickets burning a hole in your pocket."

--George Voskovec (Juror No. 11) to Paul Hartmann (Juror No. 7) in Reginald Rose s *Twelve Angry Men*

"Every person who comes through my door wants one of two things: either they want me to take something away from somebody else or they want me to keep somebody from taking something away from them."

--Kemp Scales, Attorney-at-Law, Titusville, PA

He who goes to law holds a wolf by the ears.

--Robert Burton, *Anatomy of Melancholy*

Woe unto you also, ye lawyers! for ye lade men with burdens grievous to be borne, and ye yourselves touch not the burdens with one of your fingers.

--*Luke* (11.46)

"The first thing we do, let's kill all the lawyers."

--Dick the Butcher in *II Henry VI* (Act 4. sc. 2) by William Shakespeare

"Why does a hearse horse snicker/ Hauling a lawyer away?"

--Carl Sandburg's "The Lawyers Know Too Much"

"The lawyers know a dead man's thoughts too well."

--Carl Sandburg, quoted as title of Carolyn Wheat's *Dead Man's Thoughts*

The lawyer's truth is not truth, but consistency, or a consistent expediency.

--Henry David Thoreau "On the Duty of Civil Disobedience"

Sanctus Yves erat Brito
Advocatus sed non latro
Res miranda populo

{St. Ives was a Breton,
a lawyer but no thief—
An astonishment to the people.}

The one great principle of the English law is to make business for itself. There is no other principle distinctly, certainly, and consistently maintained through all its narrow turnings.

--Charles Dickens, *Bleak House*

"How can a man be guilty at all? We are all of us men, one as much as the other."

--K.'s exclamation at the end of Kafka's *The Trial*

And so the Assistant Public Prosecutor does not get annoyed about him; he is only annoyed at the stupidity, which puts such a person in the position of district judge.

--Kafka, from the fragment *The Assistant Public Prosecutor*

The jury system puts a ban upon intelligence and honesty, and a premium upon ignorance, stupidity, and perjury.

--Mark Twain, *Roughing It*

The hungry judges soon the sentence sign,/ And wretches hang that jurymen may dine.

--Alexander Pope *The Rape of the Lock*

Justice without force is powerless; force without justice is tyrannical.

--Pascal *Pensées*

After all, a criminal lawyer is not concerned with facts, he is concerned with probabilities. It is the novelist who is concerned with facts. . . the lawyer does not, cannot be expected to go further than to show what the ordinary man would most likely do under presumed circumstances.

--Richard Hughes, *A High Wind in Jamaica*

The love of justice in most men is only the fear of suffering injustice.

--La Rochefoucauld, *Maxims*

Eye for an eye, tooth for a tooth, hand for a hand, foot for a foot.

--*Exodus* 21.24

"There is a point beyond which even justice becomes unjust."

--Sophocles, *Electra*

"Let justice be done, though the heavens fall."

--Lord Mansfield quoting a favorite maxim *Fiat justitia et ruant coeli* in *Rex v. Wilkes* (1768)

Then Pilate said to Him, "Do you not hear how many things they testify against you?" But he answered him not one word, so that the governor marveled greatly.

--*Matthew* 27.13

"Let the jury consider their verdict," the King said, for about the twentieth time that day.
"No, no!" said the Queen. "Sentence first--verdict afterward."

--Lewis Carroll, *Alice's Adventures in Wonderland (Through the Looking-Glass)*

"Virginians! I did not ask for quarter at the time I was taken! I did not ask to have my life spared. The Governor of the State of Virginia tendered me his assurance that I should have a fair trial. But under no circumstances will I be able to have a fair trial. If you seek my blood, you can have it at any moment, without this mockery. I've had no counsel, I have not been able to advise with anyone. I know nothing about the feelings of my fellow prisoners, and I am unable in any way to attend to my own defence. . . .There are mitigating circumstances that I would urge in our favor, if a fair trial is to be allowed us, but if we are to be forced with a mere form, a trail for execution, you might spare yourselves that trouble."

--John Brown (qtd. in *The Trial of John Brown*, Leonard Ehrlich)

No freeman shall be arrested, or detained in prison, or deprived of his freehold, or outlawed, or banished, or in any way molested; and we will not set forth against him, nor send against him, unless by the lawful judgment of his peers and by the law of the land.

--*Magna Carta*

"I have perhaps some shallow spirit of judgment;/ But in these nice sharp quillets of the law, Good faith, I am no wiser than a daw."

--Shakespeare *Henry VI*, Part 1

"Are you going to hang him *anyhow*--and try him afterwards?"

--Mark Twain, *Innocents at Home*

"There is but one law for all, namely, that law which governs all law, the law of our Creator, the law of humanity, justice, equity--the law of nature and of nations."

--Edmund Burke, *Impeachment of Warren Hastings*

"If the law supposes that," said Mr. Bumble, "the law is an ass."

--Charles Dickens, *Oliver Twist*

Lawyers, I suppose, were children once.

--Charles Lamb

The law, in its majestic equality, forbids the rich as well as the poor to sleep under bridges.

--Anatole France

Injustice is relatively easy to bear; what stings is justice.

--H. L. Mencken

TO: Johnnie Cochran
FROM: Michael Schneider [Alan Dershowitz's associate]
DATE: February 9, 1995

We had an interesting tip…says that the prosecution's theory [in the O.J. Simpson trial] is based on two Perry Mason stories by Erle Stanley Gardner: 1) The Case of the Howling Dog!!! And 2) The Case of the Buried Clock. This might be useful as a reference in a closing argument: although the prosecution would have you believe that this is The Case of the Howling Dog, real life is not like Perry Mason novels, etc.

--*American Tragedy: The Uncensored Story of the Simpson Defense,* by Lawrence Schiller and Michael Willwerth (New York: Random, 1996), 369.

Litigant, *n.* A person about to give up his skin for the hope of retaining his bones.

--Ambrose Bierce, *The Devil's Dictionary*

Foreword: Legal Thrillers: True Facts versus True Fiction

Michael A. Kahn

"What's the deal with all you lawyers writing novels?"

I hear the question often — at book signings, at cocktail parties, and even during courtroom recesses.

Some of those asking have a fairly straightforward technical query in mind, namely, why do lawyers have success writing novels? That answer has always seemed fairly obvious. The skills of a good trial lawyer are similar to the skills of a good novelist. Both must take a diverse cast of characters and use them to weave a compelling and believable story of human conflict. While their audiences may differ — a reader for the writer, a jury for the lawyer — both must find a way to captivate and ultimately convince their audience of the credibility of the story. The author who fails loses his readers. The lawyer who fails loses his case.

But others who ask the question about lawyers writing novels seem to be seeking an answer beyond the merely technical. They wonder why any trial lawyer would devote so many hours to the pursuit of happiness outside his profession. Why, they wonder, would Scott Turow, John Grisham, Philip Margolin, Lisa Scottoline and other courtroom warriors turn to fiction? The glib answer — to get rich — is the wrong answer, since most novelists earn royalties that, when divided by the time they spend writing their books, equate to less than minimum wage. No, something else is going on, and we attorney-authors know what it is.

When you handle real lawsuits by day and write imaginary ones at night, you find yourself mulling over the difference between fact and fiction in the realm of legal thrillers. Take the recent motion picture *Erin Brockovich*, for example. Although the film opens with the claim that it's based on a true story, anyone familiar with the real case or the demands of Hollywood knows that this Julia Roberts vehicle is far more an homage to the Wonder Bra than an accurate depiction of real events.

Which is no criticism of the movie. Some of us seek our truths in facts — in newspapers and Sunday morning talk shows and history books and various compilations of hard data. Others seek truth in fiction. Some folks want to know the circumference of the sphere; others prefer to hear the music of the spheres. That the facts got reshaped in the creation of *Erin Brockovich* is hardly surprising. It's been happening since at least the time of the *Iliad*. After all, Homer was a poet, not a war correspondent.

John Norwich's recent *Shakespeare's Kings* assesses how closely the Bard's historical plays correspond to English history. Not surprisingly, Norwich concludes that Shakespeare made crucial changes in the "true stories" to make the plays more dramatic. So what? If I want factual truth, I'll go to the grungy version of Richard III in the history books. If I want artistic truth, I'll go to Shakespeare's version.

Which brings me back to legal thrillers. Although an actual courtroom may seem an ideal battlefield for the drama of good versus evil, thousands of litigants every year discover what most trial lawyers learn early in their careers: a courthouse is not the best place to find closure or anything approaching aesthetic coherence.

Just think of the outcomes of some our celebrated real courtroom thrillers, starting with the O. J. Simpson case — a double-murder that began as a modern American "Othello" and ended as a modern American farce with contradictory verdicts and an uncollectible damage award against a creep who might just resume his search for the killer of his children's mother if he ever tires of playing golf and chasing models young enough to be his daughters.

Or look at the impeachment trial of President Clinton, that grand rendezvous with history that quickly deteriorated into a partisan mud-wrestling match over whether a married man's efforts to conceal his adulteries constituted the type of a high crime and misdemeanor our Founding Fathers had in mind. Hardly any artistic resolution there.

Or read some of the harrowing tales in *Actual Innocence*, which details how the government regularly botches capital murder prosecutions. Where is the closure when 87 prisoners on death row — one out of every seven sentenced to die in the 24 years since resumption of executions in this country — had their convictions overturned by exonerating evidence, most after spending years in prison?

And thus the answer to why lawyers write novels is one that every trial lawyer learns from experience. An author has something a trial attorney can only dream about: total control. As one of my short stories, "The Bread of Affliction," opens:

> 'I know a former trial lawyer who gave it up to write courtroom thrillers. He claims he prefers the fictional kind because he gets to control the judge, the lawyers, the witnesses and, best of all, the outcome.'

That's the key. Whether you are judge, lawyer, litigant or juror, the real courtroom will rarely if ever deliver the aesthetic pleasure most of us crave. Reality and art may superficially resemble one another, but their differences are profound and permanent. There was a real Hamlet, and he lived and died in Denmark, but he and his story no more resemble Shakespeare's version than O. J.'s resembles Othello. So if you're looking for the equivalent of *Hamlet* or *Othello* in a courtroom thriller, turn off *Court TV* and head over to the fiction section of your local library or bookstore for some of the works discussed in this fine book. Two of my favorites are here:

Bleak House by Charles Dickens. This is the greatest novel by one of the greatest of English novelists. It's also a dead-on satire of lawyers and the Byzantine legal system of London. Dickens tells the story of several generations of the Jarndyce family who wait in vain to inherit money from a disputed fortune in the lawsuit of *Jarndyce v. Jarndyce*, a massive case that has dragged through decades of convoluted legal maneuvering. This legal thriller features one of the greatest opening chapters in English literature.

Billy Budd by Herman Melville. Like Dickens, Melville was fascinated by lawyers and the legal process. His "Bartleby the Scrivener," narrated by a Wall Street lawyer, remains one of the eeriest short stories in American literature. Unlike Dickens, though, Melville toiled in obscurity and died penniless after spending his final two decades working as a customs inspector. His executors found among his papers a manuscript entitled "Billy Budd, Foretopman." It was first published a quarter of century later, after the rediscovery of his long out-of-print *Moby Dick.* Those who persevere through some of the early digressions in this extraordinary novella will find themselves treated to one of the great courtroom scenes in literature, set aboard the 19th-century warship *Indomitable*, where the chaste young Billy stands trial for the murder of the evil Master-at-Arms Claggart.

Acknowledgments

Of all thanks I must render, my wife Judy gets the first. Thanks very much to Michael Kahn for his incisive (and *pro bono*) preface. Jon Breen's bibliography was a real inspiration for me to do likewise. For typing assistance and Internet tracking, I thank this able campus staff: Pam Urch, and Stacy Morris. Many thanks to Kim Cook of the Kent Ashtabula Library for his tips on thrillers and to staff assistant Susan Hazlinger for flawlessly processing two thousand books throughout the state system. Others helped with contributions, such as Marsha J. Valance, one of many helpful subscribers to *Dorothy L.* And to Tara Rose I give heartfelt thanks for formatting this manuscript. Dr. James T. Sabin of Greenwood must be thanked for accommodating my requests for time.

My deep appreciation must also be expressed to Elizabeth in Columbus for getting this project over a near-fatal computer virus three years ago, and to two stalwarts of the computer lab: Jim Walts and Stephen Kellat for helping me wrestle with that spawn of Satan, my office computer. Finally, most sincerely, to Margaret M. Zarriello, the best of researchers and friends these many years.

To D. F. in North Little Rock: your chain letter from lawyers planted the seed that started this 5-year project. It is heartening to believe that they too believe we all need, as Gerry Spence wrote, "love and luck." Thanks much more for the friendship over the last twenty-five years. I do gratefully acknowledge those authors, reviewers, trial attorneys, public defenders, prosecutors, judges and novelists who took time out from practices and their writing to fill out my questionnaires and provide this text with their fine commentary in **Craft Notes**.

Terry White
Ashtabula, Ohio
July 7, 2003

Special thanks to: Neil Albert, William Bernhardt, Harland W. Braun, Vincent Bugliosi, Paul DePasquale, William Deverell, Linda Fairstein, David Fuqua, John Gerald Gleeson, Amy Gutman, John Wesley Hall, Parnell Hall, Lizzie Hayes, Frances Hegarty, Jonni Jacobs, Roderic Jeffries, Stephen Jones, Michael Kahn, Harriet Klausner, Albert J. Krieger, Bonnie MacDougal, Phillip M. Margolin, Margaret Maron, Bonnie McDougall, Mary Grace O'Brien, the O'Shaughnessy sisters, Pamela and Mary, Wendy Putnam Park, Mark Seiden, Lisa Scottoline, Robert L. Shapiro, Grif Stockley, David L. Strauss, and Michael E. Tigar.

Introduction: The Legal Thriller and the Modern Courtroom Drama

Terry White

The thriller is an extension of the fairy tale. It is melodrama so embellished as to create the illusion that the story being told, however unlikely, could be true.

--Eric Ambler, qtd. in *Writers on Writing*. (Sel. Jon Winokur, Philadelphia: Running, 1986, 30.)

Judge Weaver, one of courtroom drama's most serenely capable characterizations of jurisprudence, in an offhand moment describes "the fascinating pageant" of what lies behind a murder trial to Paul Biegler, defending attorney, in *Anatomy of a Murder*: "I am endlessly fascinated by the raw drama of a murder trial, of the defendant fighting so inarticulately for his freedom . . . of the opposing counsel--those masters of overstatement, flamboyantly fighting for victory . . . of the weathervane jury swaying this way and that, of the judge himself trying his damnedest to guess right and at the same time preserve a measure of decorum."[1]

One of the great ironies of courtroom drama is that there is often so very little of it--that is, the actual dramatics of the courtroom itself. It is as if the real thing, with its ponderous movement through the legalese of centuries of Anglo-Saxon precedent, cannot render the emotional response to justice so basic to its purpose.

Today many readers and some publishers consider courtroom thrillers, whether noted as "courtroom dramas" or "legal thrillers," to be a distinct genre of mystery; in fact, one major publishing house distributes a bi-monthly newsletter which considers the legal thriller a distinct genre in its cataloguing but finds it troublesome because not every legal thriller is a "mystery"; one recent issue, for example, notes that there are many other more traditional mysteries in which the sleuth is a lawyer.[2]

Why, then, should the legal thriller be culled from the domain of mystery proper? Why have it at all as a separate entity? One possible answer lies in Judge Weaver's earlier remark to Paul Biegler, defending Lieutenant Manion for the murder of his wife's rapist: "I am a rabid fan of murder trials, a fan just as hopeless in my way as those hordes of panting and painted harpies out there who are jamming our sessions" (291). Unkind and politically incorrect though the Judge is, he is right: there is something endlessly fascinating in a courtroom where life is at stake that nothing can compare to it. Justice may or may not be done. A guilty defendant may go free, a recalcitrant jury may set its heels and render a nullification verdict. Justice may never be done but the heavens will never fall because of it. A murderer on the witness stand will never collapse, fainting into the arms of the brilliant cross-examiner. We know this is the formulaic stuff of many a Perry Mason--and many a modern legal thriller as well--but we nonetheless crave the explicit, dogmatic, and final rendering of justice, which is always fiction's task, never life's.

Nothing else in a story-world is so ideal for the collision of raw emotion and sublimated, precisely-controlled utterance as a well-orchestrated trial with its defendants, plaintiffs, lawyers, judge and jury all figuring in an "unpredictable" denouement. I urge the reader to sample the **Craft Notes** commentary to glean the insights of the many lawyers, novelist-lawyers, and judges who have thought longest about the symbol of the courtroom to a modern society. Those who have practiced the law as well as the novelist's craft speak of their dual roles and the challenges to make the law less abstract without sacrificing verisimilitude to the reader's appetite for sensationalism.

The Modern Courtroom Novel

It is tempting, by dint of his sheer output, to call the novels of Erle Stanley Gardner, that one-man Perry Mason factory, a hub of the modern legal-thriller from whose spokes radiate all directions of the modern legal thriller today, but that is short-sighted. Gardner's output is commendable but not a beginning--as Scott Turow's *Presumed Innocent* was a recent resurgence in the legal thriller's long history--but there is not likely to be a Golden Age of the legal thriller. For one thing, such would have to define the legal thriller to exclude Shakespeare's *Measure for Measure* and *The Merchant of Venice*, which plays belong to the history of the courtroom "dramatic" thriller as much as Gardner's canon does. Although I am including a smattering of European literature, such as Camus' *The Stranger*, Kafka's *The Trial*, and Balzac's *Cesar Birotteau*, I make no pretensions to completeness and wish that I could have extended continental Europe's geography far enough to include Dostoevski. Ben Drew Kimpel, magnificent teacher from the University of Arkansas, not only made me aware of the holes in my education but began me on the way to filling them.

The lines of the modern thriller stretch back centuries. Witness the gothic tale with its antecedents in *The Castle of Otranto* through Stoker's *Dracula* to Poe, King, Barker, et alia today. No definition is always apt, for some works must elude capture. Note that "law-related" as a criterion would bring us to accept Aeschylus' *The Eumenides* as well as *The Song of Roland* and *The Nibelungenlied* right up to Heinrich Böll's *The End of a Mission* and Joyce Carol Oates' *Do with Me What You Will*. Some winnowing, of course, must be done to keep from being overwhelmed by the sheer numbers. Admittedly, I have poached lightly on *noir* or hardboiled turf for some books because heated exchanges in the halls of justice by lawyers in Armani suits with attache cases is not, by definition, what constitutes a "thriller," or is that what readers crave in fictional suspense; besides, as a compiler, I had to go where the literature beckoned. I would prefer to err on the side of being too liberal in selection. Readers should always be trusted as the final arbiters, and though lawyers grind their teeth at jurors in charge of so weighty a thing as justice, we must all concede to the common view that readers will know what they like and why they like it in their fiction. The legal thriller will find its own equilibrium. There must always be new developments to keep any genre from stultifying.

The Trial in Courtroom Fiction

What of the trial itself as apotheosis of justice? Time in court is almost always a guarantee of entry here but rarely is it a guarantee of quality writing. Why courts and trials are so often incidental to the "courtroom thriller" is a mystery of its own. To see either as a criterion would preclude the very best of legal fiction and deny it its special privilege to roam beyond the marble halls of justice. Fortunately, it is not an issue because Grif Stockley, Scott Turow, John Grisham, Phillip Margolin, Lisa Scottoline, Bonnie MacDougal, the O'Shaughnessy sisters, Gini Hartzmark, and Margaret Maron always put their protagonists into the maw of the justice system--even when bullets and knives are whistling about their lawyers' heads. Therefore, it seems reasonable to consider, rather than time spent in a courtroom, time spent to effect justice for a good cause, even a cause that fails, by using the law for that purpose.

The protagonist is almost always an attorney or officer of the court, but of course lawyers must and do predominate although there is a respectable slew of judges, jurors, legal investigators, paralegals or various minions of some lawyer like private eyes rounding out the protagonist list. Lawyers, we know, do often hire private investigators far more out of a sensible division of labor than that they do not want to sully the firm's reputation with grubby sleuthing. Occasionally, a lawyer herself is the declassé member of the firm with such tasks relegated to her–Frances Fyfield's Sara Fortune and her employer Ernest Matthewson are examples of both found throughout the bibliography. We readers do not care, however, for we follow our sleuths wherever they go in the cause of effecting their own sorts of justice for their own reasons, so long as the novel is artistic, unified, and interesting and the character is worth the following.

In legal fiction, it almost always will end right. When Paul Biegler wins his case, he goes to claim a lawyer's fee from the defendant he has saved from the gallows or worse--for Lieutenant Manion, a life behind bars. But both husband and wife are gone like thieves in the middle of the night. No fee, no heartfelt thanks or clap on the back for a job well done, just gone. Biegler's companion in law Parnell McCarthy, another sage of the novel, urges him to forget Manion, to leave him to the "squalid prison of *himself* (though frequently inspired by the eloquence of mash whiskey), "'helpin' bastards and angels alike', between whom, always remember, Lady Justice has never distinguished'" (511). A more colloquial version of "leave her to heaven," no doubt, but withal a fine and final sense that justice, ultimately, will be done and Lady Justice's scales may tip from time to time, but she will find their point of balance.

For lack of a better term, it is equilibrium that the courtroom thriller strives for in contrast to the culpability of the whodunit. Mean rooms rather than mean streets or mean hearts will always matter more to the sleuthing protagonist of the courtroom drama. The track of Chandler-Hammett-Cain is well-trod and not at all threadbare if you like the jazzed-up patois of James Ellroy, but legal-thriller fans find it less enticing to follow two-fisted heroes. We live, a philosopher once said, in a most litigious age, and there is no moral high ground to choose between as there once used to be in an age before moral relativism, MTV, and the WWF rowdies who are good guys once week and bad the next. Besides, the select combat between modern courtroom warriors is intellectually liberating. Paul Biegler and Claud Dancer, or if you prefer, Mason and Hamilton Burger, do not exactly tip the scales of cosmic justice, but what they do is exciting stuff for the common citizen in the grip of the law. When we get, as Judge Weaver puts it, a good intellectual dogfight between lawyers--"flamboyantly fighting for victory, for reputation, for more clients, for political advancement" (291)--we are fortunate to behold a well-made skirmish. Like those unclassical harpies the judge unkindly refers to, we believe that the law can be made to serve us too--solve our problems, get us our just deserts, or keep other people from stripping from us our property and even our lives if only we too could work as hard, as late, and as smart as Judge Knott, Rachel Gold, Kate Milholland, Kali O'Brien, or Nina Reilly.

The Lawyer as Hero

"The lawyer is, thus, at once a literary theorist. At the same time, the lawyer is also engaged in rhetoric; the use of language in order to effect power."[3] Writers, whether practicing or retired lawyers, do not choose lawyers as protagonists without an eye toward this concept of power even if the lawyer herself is in retirement (Susan Wittig Albert's China Bayles, to name only one of many), in disrepute (Barry Reed's alcoholic Frank Galvin, George V. Higgins' guilty-by-association Jerry Kennedy or Neil Albert's disbarred Dave Garrett). The profession of law is never an irrelevancy to the plot, even when lawyers are burnouts (and there are numerous burnouts to behold in this bibliography, almost as if it were a precondition to an enlightened sensibility). No other profession is so well suited to both tranquillity of purpose and violence. I speak of plot verisimilitude as much as anything. (Some lawyers sharply disagree in **Craft Notes**.) Cops, detectives, and private eyes wallow in the one, rarely see the other; academics sniff with disdain at the idea of serving clientele, although medical doctors are worth a glance as candidates for thriller-heroism, they too much invest themselves in the technology of healing and suffering within their own cloistered field; besides that, medicos make great villains (witness the many malpractice novels noted in here). With or without the courtroom itself, it means something to be a lawyer in a mystery fiction. Detectives are, of course, so thick on the ground that one usually divides them into officers of the law or private investigators. The entire tribe is accommodated with the exception of the *soi-disant* cozies, that aberration of true mystery, that every fan should despise from the soul. The idea that husbands and wives pursue murderers and crooks is anathema to common sense. They are not recognized here. The lawyer exists happily between the extremes of outright criminal investigation (many do, none should) and performing by proxy the need for citizens to administer the basic tenets of ninth-century Anglo-Saxon law in a modern courtroom with all its byzantine convolutions and twists of recondite language. John Grisham has been commercially rewarded but not appreciated for finding the formula that works within the David-Goliath motif. Real lawyers must defend, not pursue, their psychopathic clients, but as the novels of William Diehl attest, the lines can sometimes blur so successfully that the line between the psychological suspense and the legal thriller merge in each other's wake. Robert Tanenbaum's Butch Karp will often leave his sanctum in the New York City Criminal Courts division to search for Marlene Ciampi, the love of his life, who does indeed go in pursuit of psychopaths, rapists, and men who beat up women. Exceptions to that premise sometimes boost sensationalism out of a lackluster plot, but such gimmickry is always eschewed by the best writers, and we readers will be generous when we see our favorite protagonists put themselves in harm's way. Any list will show a sliding scale between *noir* and the domestic cozy variety; unfairly, perhaps, I think of William G. Tapply's Brady Coyne and his genteel sleuthing for his wealthy Boston clientele. But think of their numbers and possibilities among this small sampling and the reader will undoubtedly find the "right" amount of violence needed to whet the appetite: Judith van Gieson's Neil Hamel, Michael Nava's Henry Rios, Linda Fairstein's Alex Cooper, Tanenbaum's spatting couple, the O'Shaughnessy sisters' Nina Reilly, Turow's Sandy Stern, and so forth. By the way, the **Series Characters** appendix will reveal their names, creators, and locales of their practices.

The contemporary fictional lawyer is as often as not a woman like Michael Kahn's Rachel Gold or Frances Fyfield's Helen West or Sarah Fortune or any of Lisa Scottoline's tough, sassy women of law because we subscribe to the notion that testosterone does not fight evil (brains fight evil), but what reader does not like to see courage in action no matter the gender? John Wesley Hall, veteran of 200 trials, calls it "zeal" in his **Craft Notes** commentary—the most necessary item of a trial lawyer's gear. It seems very odd to make the fact of the court house a mere accessory of this kind of mystery fiction, but such is actually the case.

All good mystery fiction reflect us and our times. Most lawyers themselves will admit they are not heroic in the traditional epic sense but they are able to prosecute and defend for justice's sake with equal ardor. It does not seem especially heroic to winkle out a legal solution to a problem from the arcana of Blackstone, but Arthur Train's Squire Mason is able to batter foes into apoplectic submission with his finessing of legal points. That he had to be reformed toward a more palatable kind of protagonist says something about this need for the law to be benevolent toward the common folk. Arthur Miller once said of his famous Salesman's very unheroic nature in "Tragedy and the Common Man," that

> the common man [is in no way] debarred from such thoughts or such actions. Seen in this light, our lack of tragedy may be partially accounted for by the turn which modern literature has taken toward the purely psychiatric view of life, or the purely sociological. If all our miseries, our indignities, are born and bred within our minds, then all action, let alone heroic action, is obviously impossible.[4]

The courtroom is our symbol of the flowering of such possibilities of action, although we rarely circumscribe it by calling it justice. The legal sleuth is out there in the tumult, away from the office, even though their creators know that drudgery is ninety-five percent of the job. Law schools have been traditionally quickest to incorporate literature courses into the curriculum because of the latter's obvious usefulness to the craft of law.

When I widened the scope to get in as many books and works as possible, I realized there might be a clouding of what it is that makes this kind of fiction definable. It is, I believe, more compelling and attractive a form of mystery than the current stodge of murder mysteries being cranked out to "cozy," "malice domestic," and serial-killer formulas. What, then, makes the lawyer heroic? It obviously must mean that the protagonist-lawyer, who is often an accessory to the criminal investigation, must put herself at risk. She or he must be able to risk more than the social embarrassment of misconstruing a legal technicality in front of a veteran trial judge. The timeless concept of justice itself is no more in evidence in a typical suspense thriller than in the legal novel. Bad guys get off; innocence does not always prevail. The wag who opined that the law is not about justice, that it is about lawyers is ever so right--and wrong. Lawyers, love 'em or hate 'em, are us. What they do affects us all and the quality of our lives in particular. It is not just that they hold back the wolves of anarchy from our gates but that they attempt to reconcile us to the disparity between ideal justice as we want it and real justice as we invariably get it in a courtroom of law. Despite the blunt wedge I use to divide the flock of suspense thrillers out there, thrillers more than other kinds of literature beguile us with a need to see justice accomplished because we want to see evil punished more than we want to see good rewarded. No one complains about wealthy people being wealthy, but nothing infuriates the common citizen more than to see the rich get away with their crimes. Today more than ever, the courts matter to society as former Supreme Court nominee Robert H. Bork suggests by asserting that our judicial system is not working: "[L]aymen rarely have a complete understanding of what is taking place and those lawyers who do, by and large, become cynically accepting of a system that they do not admire but have learned how to work, or at least to live with."[5] The legal thriller of the near-future will make more inroads into the legal system's failures as our age becomes more litigious.

A Last Sidebar with the Reader

I make no apologies for the eclectic nature of the bibliography. The reader will find mostly novels, but I include short-story collections (a *sine qua non* of Horace Rumpole), teleplays, filmed adaptations of plays and novels, film scripts, and one or two oddities, such as self-published novels via the vanity press or the Internet. The legal thriller is so rich a subgenre of the traditional, well-made mystery that it goes forward in all directions even while it erases some of its past traces: the Harlequin-romance, the Christian mystery, science fiction, fantasy, hardboiled, novels of manners (the underrated Auchincloss comes first to mind). The shapeshifting of the whodunit is one of the pleasures of the elastic legal thriller, in fact, whether one prefers the locked-room mystery to the *noir*, whether stabbing with knives or with tongues--all are grist for the courtroom thriller's mill.

Secondly, I list films, scripts, and novels by the writer's original name where possible rather than as by a pseudonym. Many authors, of course, worked on scripts of their books, but the principle of selection here is based on the idea that a film is a collaboration, whether it is faithful to the author's words or not. The classic *Twelve Angry Men* by Reginald Rose ought not to be left out on the reasoning that, because it is not a novel, it should not be included here. The same goes for novelizations after the fact, and though these are commercial ventures meant to capitalize on the popularity of a film or a TV series, the rationale is the same.

Though I enjoyed Jon Breen's allotting a percentage of courtroom time in *Novel Verdicts*, I found that my interest flagged when I attempted to do the same. His are the better critical annotations and judgments on many works briefly noted here, particularly Erle Stanley Gardner, Arthur Train, and Henry Cecil. But as even he concedes about Gardner's great creation, fictional lawyers rarely appear in court. To be sure, there are outstanding works in both novel and dramatic form that require the courtroom's service, such as *Inherit the Wind* or *The Caine Mutiny* (novel and play), there is a real dearth of courtrooms (or jury-rooms) in the legal thriller still. Eden Phillpotts' *The Jury*, *Anatomy of a Murder*, *Twelve Angry Men*, Dreiser's *An American Tragedy*, *To Kill a Mockingbird* and a very few others have not been supplanted despite the lawyer-protagonists unleashed after the Grisham-Turow phenomenon of the late-1980s. Some writers, of course, render courtroom drama extremely well. The fact is that most do not--or disdain it altogether. One remembers some courtroom scenes vividly in books like *To Kill a Mockingbird*, where Atticus Finch tricks Ewell by tossing him keys to see which hand he'll use, yet those moments are rare. I have asked lawyers many questions about law and justice in and out of the courtrooms. It is a curiosity that lawyers who write novels do not spend an inordinate amount of time in court; they obviously know something. For some lawyer-novelists, in fact, it seems an Achilles heel and one feels the pages becoming leaden as the obligatory courtroom appearance announces itself as an intrusion in a plot that did not need it. No doubt, there are authors of legal fiction who defer to the law and avoid betraying their ignorance of proper procedure; it is easy for a lawyer to catch out the amateurs fumbling around in their arena. I trust that the reader will find plenty of amusing, ironic, or interesting sidelights on the craft of legal thrillers from some of its finest practitioners in **Craft Notes**.

I therefore remain content to allow this enfeebled principle of selection to stand: lawyers, men and women, all shapes, sizes, and sexual predilections are welcome here just as long as they provide more than a foil's service to a detective in the investigation. The gate is barred to any novel, drama, or story where there is either no use of the law or lawyers or courtroom protocol, whether in passing or in plot-driven necessity; also, where the lawyer is incidental to conflict resolution or plot (though lawyers necessarily outnumber others, the fact of a lawyer is not an indispensable criterion). The list of the excluded, however, is not long because lawyers who write or novelists who write "legal thrillers" might borrow from the Ed McBain police procedural or the Hammett-Chandler tradition but they keep within the courtroom's purview. I have grudgingly admitted a few private eyes so long as they are ex-lawyers like Vic Warshawski or they are in a conflict over a legal issue or involved with legal characters in some important way (often a will contest). The problem of pseudonyms requires consistency. I include works under real names as a first choice, though the pen name is commonplace; this risks a pettifogging nicety but avoids arbitrary choices of selecting. Wherever real names are problematic, I have used common sense--take, for example, Ed McBain, born Salvatore Lombino, famed author of the 87th Precinct series; his legal name is Evan Hunter, under which he has penned the Matthew Hope lawyer series. Readers will find Hunter, Evan cross-referenced to McBain, Ed.

References

[1] John Donaldson Voelker [Robert Traver, pseud.], *Anatomy of a Murder* (New York: St. Martin's, 1958) 291-92.

[2] "Let Us Define Our Terms," *Murder at the Flatiron Building* [St. Martin's Press] Oct. 1996: n. pag.

[3]Ian Ward, "Legal Fiction: Law in the Novels of Nineteenth-Century Women," rev. of *Adversaria: Literature and Law*, by E. J. Hintz, T. Anderson, and A. McGillvray, eds. (Winnipeg: U of Manitoba P, 1994) *Journal of Legal History* 17.2 (1996): 191.

[4] Arthur Miller, "Tragedy and the Common Man," *The Theatre Essays of Arthur Miller*, ed. and introd. Robert A. Martin, fwd. Arthur Miller (New York: Viking, 1998) 5-6.

[5]Robert H. Bork, foreword, Max Boot, *Out of Order: Arrogance, Corruption, and Incompetence on the Bench* (New York: Basic, 1998) v.

Legal Thrillers: A to Z Bibliography

A

1. Aarons, Edward S[idney]. *The Defenders* Greenwich, CT: Fawcett-Gold Medal, 1961. London: Jenkins, 1962. Aaron's reputation is based on the success of the popular paperback *Assignment* series that spawned several dozen titles featuring CIA agent Sam Durell of "K" section, some of which were written by Aarons' son Will after his father's death in 1975. Aarons novelizes the Reginald Rose television series about the Prestons, a father-son lawyer team who work a pair of cases with more sleuthing than courtroom action. The screenplay by Rose (orig. title *The Defender*) was first produced by CBS as a *Studio One* performance on 25 February and 4 March 1957 in which the lawyer and son defend a delivery boy against a murder charge and featured actors Ralph Bellamy, Steve McQueen, Martin Balsam, and William Shatner. E. G. Marshall played Lawrence Preston in the Emmy-winning TV series of this title that ran from 1961 to 1965. He also made two (Paramount, 1997) video-to-TV movies *The Defenders*: *The Payback* and *Choice of Evil* before his death in August 1998. The former is the better in which Beau Bridges plays Preston's son Don and Martha Plimpton his granddaughter M. J. The case concerns Michael Lane, an outraged father who kills his daughter's paroled rapist. (*See* Rose's entry for his most famous teleplay, *Twelve Angry Men.*)

2. Abarbanell, J. R. [Jacob Ralph]. *The Heart of the People A Picture of Life As It Is Lived Today*. Boston: Clark, 1908. The Recorder (Judge) of the Court of General Sessions of New York City utters these grim words in the opening sentence: "Prisoner at the bar, what have you to say why sentence of death should not be imposed on you?" (1). John McQuillan is found guilty of first-degree murder and sentenced to electrocution in Sing Sing. A blue-blooded scion named Harold Armytage helps McQuillan escape from the Tombs before the sentence can be carried out and disguises him as one of his black servants at the Armytage mansion. Declared legally insane at his trial, Harold scoffs at the legal system and prepares for the plot twist of a case of switched identities involving a mysterious figure who goes about as a populist preacher known by the cognomen Soggarth Arroon.

3. Abella, Alex. *Final Acts.* New York: Simon, 2001. Charlie Morell is a Cuban lawyer and writer on voodoo cults who is framed in a multiple murder. He is defended by Rita Carr.

William Shatner as the examining magistrate. All three acts take place in the chambers of the Juge d'Instruction of Paris. Paul Sevigne's first case is a murder in which a parlor maid shot her lover Miguel, the chauffeur of a rich family they were both employed by. She claims that, as they quarreled in the Rolls Royce, a shot came from behind her and struck her lover; then she fainted and was discovered naked with the pistol in her hand.

5. Acheson, Edward. *Red Herring*. New York: Morrow, 1932. [Retitled *Murder by Suggestion,* London: Hutchinson, 1933]. Danny Farnham is a small-potatoes beat reporter with a yen to write a novel about "the perfect crime." He becomes so taken with the idea that he robs the Hartland bank of $70,000 and kills a night watchman.

6. Ackroyd, Peter. *The Trial of Elizabeth Cree: A Novel of the Limehouse Murders*. London: Sinclair-Stevenson, 1994. New York: Doubleday-Talese, 1995. Ackroyd is an acclaimed biographer of T. S. Eliot and Charles Dickens, a distinguished novelist whose *Hawksmoor* won the Whitbread Prize and *Chatterton* was short-listed for the more prestigious Booker Prize in 1987. Besides poetry and criticism, his penchant for the historical novel of fact and fiction wrapped about major or minor historical personages is self-evident from his other titles, such as *The Great Fire of London* and *The Last Testament of Oscar Wilde.*

"Lambeth Marsh Lizzie" is the moniker attached to the narrator in her youth, a miserable existence of poverty and religious sadism inflicted on her by her deranged mother. Discovering her talents as a comic "patterer"and stage actress of the music hall circuit about London in the latter half of the nineteenth century, the narrator joins Dan Leno's troupe of performers and acquires a reputation. During the summer of summer of 1880 a series of grisly murders are being committed in the seedy Limehouse district. Such real figures as Karl Marx and novelist George Gissing intersect with the plot's main action through their use of the Reading Room of the British Museum and are even suspected of involvement by the police investigating these murder-mutilations; the popular press feeds the local frenzy by naming the suspect as the work of a *golem*, a man-made monster of Jewish folklore. The title derives from the putative murder of Lizzie's husband, a reporter of means who courts her and takes her off the stage and who later dies of arsenic poisoning. The trial scenes, like the shifts in point of view to an omniscient author, are suspenseful intercalary chapters of witness interrogations that seem to have little to do with the horrific murders, for we have a confessional diary from the perpetrator, but are cleverly wrought delays that bring all these characters, actions, and motivations to a stunning conclusion.

7. Adams, A. K., ed. *Favorite Trial Stories: Fact and Fiction*. New York: Dodd, 1966. Of the 18 stories (6 are nonfiction), only Gardner's and Benét's were printed in Blaustein's *Fiction Goes to Court.* Irving S. Cobb's

"Words and Music"; Erle Stanley Gardner's "The Case of the Irate Witness" (*see* Blaustein); Arthur Train's "The Meanest Man"; O. Henry's "The Whirligig of Life"; Stephen Vincent Benét's "The Devil and Daniel Webster"; Vincent Starrett's "The Eleventh Juror"; Agatha Christie's "The Witness for the Prosecution"; Charles Dickens' "The Memorable Trial of Bardell against Pickwick"; Rafael Sabatini's "The Night of Charity"; Jack London's "The Benefit of the Doubt." Melville Davisson Post's "Naboth's Vineyard" features one of Uncle Abner's finest courtroom moments, and Bret Harte's "Colonel Starbottle for the Plaintiff" gives readers a legal figure worthy of Mark Twain.

8. Adams, Frederick Upham. *The Bottom of the Well.* New York: Dillingham; London: Upham, 1906. Praised in his day, unreadable now, the author of this courtroom tale mixes ingredients of the day, such as switched identities, surprise discovery, a conspiracy of strikers, grandiose courtroom speech, low characters, and a romantic love interest to defy every tenet of craft in plot construction since Poe. Fourteen men stand trial for the murder of manufacturer Amos Buckingham. The prosecution must prove they are anarchist plotters known to have conspired at a resort called The Well to effect the nefarious deed.

9. Adams, J. Orville. *The Cruiser: A Romance of the Idaho Timber Land Frauds.* Spokane, WA: Adams, 1909. The decision over one squatter's right to his claim is the centerpiece of this novel of intrigue in which a small band of men led by the villainous Waterson attempt to take over valuable Idaho timber land. The whole community is affected by the outcome of the battle between two well-matched lawyers. The young lawyer opposing the claimant utters the famous Triple-I objection in one of the earliest uses of the expression popularized by Perry Mason's aversary Hamilton Burger.

10. Adams, Samuel Hopkins. *Sunrise to Sunset.* New York: Random, 1950. London: Long, 1951. The title refers to the twelve-hour day imposed by a mill owner on his workers. Based on a true, unsolved crime in Rhode Island and relocated to Troy, New York in the 1830's, the plot involves a romance between the owner of Eureka Mill's wife, a former mill girl herself, and Guy Roy, a cousin of the owner. When a dead mill girl's body turns up on Sadler's Island, victim of a botched abortion, the estranged husband is charged on flimsy evidence and tried for her murder.

11. Ainsworth, W. H. [William Harrison]. *Guy Fawkes.* London: Bentley; New York: Nafis, 1841. Philadelphia: Barrow, n.d. Ainsworth is the author of well-researched historical romances and this is evident in the hefty tome of the infamous Gunpowder Plot during the reign of James I. Fawkes, of course, would lend his name to posterity as the arch conspirator of this failed attempt to blow up the king along with peers and minions, which "monstrous act" would lead the oppressed Catholics of England to open rebellion. It was

Fawkes who was found in the vault beneath Parliament House "with touchwood and matches in his belt." Ainsworth's hefty tome gives short shrift to the trial scene in the Star Chamber; however, lightening the pedestrian style of the author's courtroom summary--in which each of the eight conspirators utters his last words before the jury retires and, in a single sentence, returns to announce the guilty verdict--is the romantic figure of the haggard but defiant Fawkes himself, who like Milton's great hero-rebel Satan of *Paradise Lost*, that seventeenth-century's greatest work, is magnificent in his failure and his refusal to serve a hated lawful authority. Ainsworth later authored *Star Chamber* (London: Routledge, 1854).

12. Albert, Neil. *Appointment in May*. New York: Walker, 1996. Albert's style and characterizations resemble the classically laconic hard-boiled fiction of Hammett and Marlowe. Both he and his wife are practicing attorneys who reside in quiet Lancaster County among the Amish, although Albert is originally from Oregon. He has been writing since the age of thirteen, he says, and confesses that he felt lucky to get his first novel, *The January Corpse*, published in hardcover after taking out a year to read modern fiction to see what was being bought and read. His reading is eclectic and ranges from the traditional mystery (Ross Macdonald, Les Roberts) to the middlebrow intellectual (Updike, Roth, Richard Ford) to the quirky and esoteric (Isabelle Allende, Henry James). Though his series character belongs to hard-boiled fiction, private eye David Garrett deserves his special status here; his disbarment for taking his wife's law exams has him doing private investigation work in Philadelphia and across Pennsylvania and the compiler's excuse to include one of the best modern stylists of the genre. A recent work is a nonfiction true-crime work about a local case. (*See* Mr. Albert's commentary in **Craft Notes**.)

13. _____. *Burning March*. New York: Dutton, 1994. Dave returns to his old law office at the behest of the firm's accounting officer; however, she is burned to death in a suspicious fire in her apartment before she can speak to him. Garrett is asked by one of the partners to investigate the death.

14. _____. *Cruel April.* New York: Dutton, 1995. Dave's girlfriend, married Kate McMahan, does not arrive on her scheduled Miami flight to Philadelphia. When Kate's baggage is claimed by someone else, he knows she is in serious trouble. To extricate her from the drug ring that has ensnared her, he binges on diet pills and a four-day, sleepless quest to extricate her. Optioned for television.

15. _____. *The February Trouble.* New York: Walker, 1992. In the heart of Amish country in Lancaster County, Dave finds trouble in the form of sabotage to Uncle Chan's, a Chinese fast-food franchise owned by Bruce Chadwick, but it turns into more than detergent put into the wonton soup when Anne Chadwick, the owner's wife disappears and Anne's friend Nancy Saunders is killed. Dave's investigation uncovers laundered mob money behind a phony ransom demand and more trouble, but it also introduces him to iron-pumping Kate McMahan, his soon-to-be lover.

16. _____. *The January Corpse.* New York: Walker; Markham, Ontario: Allen, 1991. A case of disappearance involving a lawyer with mob clientele. Dave has only the weekend to gather evidence affirming Daniel Wilson's death seven years prior when he was ambushed in a car with his sister Lisa. Dave soon learns why a Philadelphia private investigation outfit has abandoned the case to him when it appears that the lawyer may have rigged his own disappearance and absconded with a hundred thousand dollars of the Philly mob's cash. A memorably titillating denouement.

17. _____. *Tangled June.* New York: Walker, 1997. This sixth Garrett mystery sends the disbarred lawyer in search of his own roots. Albert alternates narrators in this one by rotating Garrett and his transsexual secretary Lisa Wilson, a former lover, in alternating chapters. Dave discovers he is not his mother Barbara's son and he and Lisa go to California to find his real parents. In a 1998 Amazon.com interview, author Albert professes that each of his novels is a coming-to-terms with a particular demon—"chemical, sexual, familial, whatever."

18. Albert, Susan Wittig. *Chile Death: A China Bayles Mystery.* New York: Berkley Prime Crime, 1999. Albert's first novel *Thyme of Death* was nominated for the Agatha and Anthony awards. She gave up her posts as university administrator and English professor; she holds a doctorate from the University of California at Berkeley and resides in the Texas hill country northwest of Austin with her husband Bill. Together they write late-Victorian mysteries under the *nom de plume* Robin Paige (they wrote more than 60 young-adult novels between 1986-1991). The China Bayles series qualifies for courtroom bibliography by virtue of the fact that her protagonist is a 40+ retired criminal lawyer from Houston and litigator who maintains her law credentials but not her practice. That mere fact does not ensure her inclusion as lawyer-

protagonist; however, because the lawyer eventually supersedes the herbalist in the sleuthing department and on occasion she will uncover or argue some point of law to assist the denouement. China owns an herbal shop in a small Texas town called Pecan Springs, "halfway between Austin and San Antonio," the denizens of which must rival Detroit in murders per capita. Bayles cohabits with ex-cop Mike McQuaid, who desires marriage and stability for his young son Brian. Each novel brings China into semi-serious debate over surrendering her independence to this man and settling down to domestic life. The herbal motif is the author's passion as well as a gimmick, for the China Bayles homepage offers seeds for sale, recipes, histories of her signature plants, and planting advice.

Jerry Jeff Cody is one of the judges in the annual Cedar Choppers Chili Cook-Off, but someone knew him and hated him well enough to spike some chili with peanuts, knowing the allergic reaction would kill him. McQuaid is recovering from a shooting during his Texas rangers stint, so the burden of sleuthing falls mostly on China's shoulders, and she discovers that Jerry Jeff had plenty of secrets he wanted hidden.

19. _____. *Hangman's Root: A China Bayles Mystery.* New York: Scribner's, 1994. New York: Berkley, 1995. A well-known research scientist is found hanged in the midst of angry protests against his animal experimentation. Local biology professor Dottie Riddle becomes the prime suspect, but China does not believe a penchant for taking in stray cats is compatible with murder; she gets her a lawyer and goes sleuthing for the killer.

20. _____. *Lavender Lies: A China Bayles Mystery.* New York: Berkley Prime Crime, 2000. Greedy Pecan Springs developer Edgar Coleman is murdered just in time to preempt China's marriage to acting Police Chief Mike McQuaid; before they can tie the knot, they have to solve the crime.

21. _____. *Love Lies Bleeding: A China Bayles Mystery.* New York: Berkley Prime Crime, 1997. The *North American Gardener*'s review of this China Bayles mystery appreciates its author's use of "fascinating and accurate botanical references" for its rendering of the addictive herbs of this novel's plot. More than the consequences of marijuana, cocaine, and heroin use, however, is China's investigation of a Texas Ranger's suicide and her relationship with McQuaid. The signature herb is most apt: "[Love Lies Bleeding] was worn by knights to symbolize purity and truth; by the Renaissance (when it was used to treat venereal disease) it had become a symbol of corruption."

22. _____. *Mistletoe Man.* New York: Berkley, 2000. The ninth Bayles is light on violence and heavy on whimsy. China ties the knot with McQuaid and opens a tea room with friend Ruby; however, the man of the title is China's herb supplier for the coming holiday season and now Pecan Springs' latest murder victim.

23. _____. *Rosemary Remembered: A China Bayles Mystery.* New York: Berkley, 1995. When Rosemary Robbins, Pecan Springs town accountant and China's look-alike, is found dead in the front seat of McQuaid's truck, he believes the killer is Jake Jacoby, an ex-convict who had once threatened him. Meanwhile, China is putting on an herbalist conference at the local resort hotel when her co-owner Jeff Clark disappears on a fishing trip. It turns out that he had been Rosemary's lover. China has her own suspicions that include an abusive ex-husband and former clients and, armed with an Ouija board and spirit channeler Sheila, she uses a séance to summon the spirit of Lo Que Sabe as clues. Then Brian, McQuaid's son, disappears while his father is off in Mexico chasing Jacoby.

24. _____. *Rueful Death: A China Bayles Mystery.* New York: Berkley, 1996. China and Maggie, friend and former nun, embark on a religious retreat at St. Theresa's monastery in the Texas Hill Country, where the nuns grow rocambole garlic for a living. The peaceful convent life has been disrupted by poison-pen letters and arson fires of late, and it culminates in the murder of the mother superior, for which China has discovered a motive: converting St. Theresa's into a posh conference center will make someone much money.

25. _____. *Thyme of Death: A China Bayles Mystery.* New York: Scribner's, 1992. China is weary of big-city Houston politics and office backstabbing, so she retreats after the manner of Voltaire's advice and cultivates her own garden in the form of an herbal shop in Pecan Springs, TX. An old friend is found dead and the investigation points away from suicide toward murder when China discovers a stash of love letters. Two series characters are introduced in this Agatha- and Anthony-nominated first novel: ex-cop Mike McQuaid (who becomes her lover) and redheaded Ruby Wilcox, owner of the New Age shop next door to China's.

26. _____. *Witches' Bane: A China Bayles Mystery.* New York: Scribner's, 1993. China's best friend Rita, owner of the herb shop next door and a harmless flake enamored of New Age thinking, invites China to attend a tarot card session along with several educated women from Pecan Springs and the university. Bad timing, however, because exsanguinated animals found in the ritualized killings of Santeria create gossip about the women by a bible-thumping preacher. When one of these iconoclastic women with a penchant for wearing black and growing poisonous herbs affiliated with black magic is found with her throat slit after a Halloween Wiccan ceremony, the gossip mongers are lathered into a frenzy of accusations against the women as Satanists and witches. Worse yet, Rita is implicated in the murder.

27. Aldrich, Thomas Bailey. *The Stillwater Tragedy.* Boston: Houghton, 1880; Edinburgh: Douglas, 1886. This one proved popular enough to be

reprinted with illustrations by Jefferson Press of Boston and New York in 1908, the year after his death. The author of *Prudence Palfrey*, *Marjorie Daw*, *The Queen of Sheba*, and numerous poetry collections was also editor of the *Atlantic Monthly* and will best remembered for his *The Story of a Bad Boy* (1869), an autobiographical tale for children. Aldrich's story involves a murder plot set in the rustic New England town of Stillwater. Old Lemuel Shackford is found murdered in his own house in Welch's Court and his young kinsman Richard is the town gossips' prime suspect.

28. Aldridge, James. *A Sporting Proposition.* Boston: Little; London: Joseph, 1973. A small town in Australia is divided over the ownership of a wild pony. Scott Pirie is a thirteen-year-old roughneck of a Huckleberry Finn whose beloved Welsh pony Taff is all he cares about. When the town's richest citizen domesticates an identical pony to pull a carriage built for his crippled daughter, young Scotty takes and hides the pony in the outback, and it becomes a matter for the local magistrate. The narrator's nonconformist father expertly defends the accused boy and sets up a contest as a public event for the town to witness which child the pony will choose to belong to. This is one of those rare initiation novels for all ages, for it takes no cloying backward glance at childhood innocence; neither does it exploit the sentimentality of Josie Eyre's polio, nor wink at Pirie's hard-nosed poverty. Aldridge shows his young protagonist-narrator learning about life and justice in the serio-comic courtroom's "sporting proposition." A second novel is *The Untouchable Juli* (London: Joseph, 1975; Boston: Little, 1976)

29. Alexander, Bruce. *Blind Justice.* New York: Putnam's, 1994. Alexander's historical novels feature the sleuthing skills of blind jurist Sir John Fielding (1721-80). Young Jeremy Proctor narrates the tales of the late Sir John, founder of the Bow Street Runners (ancestors of Sir Robert Peele's "bobbies"), half-brother to jurist and novelist Henry, and magistrate of the Bow Street Court known for his exactitude of judgment and refusal to suffer fools gladly yet withal a compassionate man "who discharged more prisoners than he sent on for trial"(2). Proctor first comes before the magistrate as a boy in 1768 on a trumped-up charge of theft and gradually becomes his eyes, then ultimately Sir John's amanuensis for these tales of detection. His idolatry is leavened by the boy's naïveté in the story world. Other characters assist to provide levity, for example, fellow lawyer James Boswell from Edinburgh, boon companion to Dr. Johnson, diarist, and frequenter of tarts, recklessly discusses his clap at dinner with a visiting ship's surgeon. Aside from small-debt matters and disputes between merchants in busy London, Sir John's major case involves profit taking from a South-Sea Bubble company (The Island Company) precipitated by Lord Goodhope's killing.

30. _____. *Death of a Colonial.* New York: Putnam's, 1999. Sir John is summoned to the home of the Lord Chief Justice where he meets various

dignitaries gathered as a secret cabal to discuss a matter of succession before the House of Lords but mainly to protect the King's interests in acquiring the fortune of a man Sir John condemned to the gallows. A North American colonial named Lawrence Paltrow has claimed succession rights and he laid claim to the Laningham title and fortune.

31. _____. *Murder in Grub Street.* New York: Putnam's, 1995. Thirteen-year-old Jeremy assists the magistrate in a sensational murder case involving the slaughter of printer Ezekiel Crabbe, his entire family, and two apprentices at his home in Grub Street. Found at the scene of the crime waving a bloody axe is a demented poet called John Clayton. Another cameo appearance by Dr. Johnson.

Others in the series published by Putnam's include *Jack, Knave, and Fool* (1998); *Person or Persons Unknown* (1997); and *Watery Grave* (1996).

32. Allen, Grant. *Miss Cayley's Adventures.* New York: Knickerbocker [Putnam's]; London: Putnam's, 1899. A "modern" woman disdains a teaching career and goes off around the world with all of two pence in her pocket, falls in love with an Englishman, returns to save her beau from a nefarious plot involving a forged will, one she had typed for the wealthy uncle. Her testimony on the stand is twisted by the QC to expose her as a scheming adventuress. The century-old racism of the buffoonish nemesis of the hero shows the evolutionary progress of the Anglo-Indian conflict and makes a silent comment about England's struggle with multiculturalism as evidenced in films like *My Beautiful Laundrette* and *My Son the Fanatic.*

33. Ambler, Eric. *The Schirmer Inheritance.* New York: Knopf, 1953. Ambler is one of the greats of espionage literature. This novel enters here for its lawyer-protagonist's quest to find the lost heir to an American fortune among the displaced peoples of post-WW II Europe.

34. Amiel, Joseph. *A Question of Proof.* New York: Crown, 1993. Dan Lazar is hated by the Philadelphia DA's Office because he has a habit of springing guilty scum from the justice system with his whiz bang lawyering skills, so when a charge of bribery is leveled, it is given serious attention; the second plot-strand mixes him into a murder case because he has been having sex with the widow of a newspaper publisher, recently dead of blunt-force trauma to the back of the head. She is the prime suspect in the murder of her husband.

35. Anderson, Maxwell. *Winterset: A Play in Three Acts.* New York: Dramatist's Play, 1935; rev. 1946. Anderson's poetic melodrama is about a youth named Mio who returns to the New York waterfront to avenge his father's death, executed for a murder in a payroll robbery committed by a thug named Trock Estrella but tried and executed because he was an foreigner and an anarchist. The film (RKO, 1936) earned grudging praise but most agree that it does not translate to the screen. Dir. Alfred Santell. Writ. Anthony Veiller. Perf.

Burgess Meredith, Eduardo Ciannelli, and Paul Guilfoyle.

36. Anouilh, Jean. *Poor Bitos* [*Pauvre Bitos*]. Trans. Lucienne Hill. London: French, 1964. The playwright who specializes in illusiveness and role-playing after the fashion of Pirandello sets up a cast of patrician partygoers in an old chateau. Invited also is a heartless and humiliating prosecutor named Bitos, the reincarnation of Robespierre (scene-changing recreates the French Revolution).

37. Ard, William. *Hell Is a City*. New York: Rinehart, 1955. Jamie Cãlyero shoots a corrupt vice cop in a Brooklyn flophouse to protect his sister. Ard's main shamus Timothy Dane takes an assignment for a crusading editor of a newspaper. The maneuverings of crooked cops and polls to obfuscate the truth is darkly fascinating, but crime writer/editor Francis M. Nevins deplores the flimsy trial sequence and says that the book could have been a masterpiece "were it not for a grotesquely bad denouement" (qtd. in *Twentieth Century Crime & Mystery Writers* 29). His death from cancer at 37 silenced a writer who eschewed the slickly popular Spillane treatment of *noir* to follow the nobler Hammett-Chandler tradition.

38. Arkwright, Richard. *The Queen Anne's Gate Mystery*. London: White, 1889. 2 vols. Rpt. New York: Arno, 1976. Harry Collingwood is accused of poisoning his wife with strychnine. George Pen Owen is Harry's school chum and the book's narrator who with wife Lady Geraldine try to save him. Harry's arraignment in Westminster police court has him poorly defended by pompous Joseph Barclay. The Old Bailey trial is summarized and a second, albeit with different defendant, lacks any verisimilitude.

39. Arnold, Catherine. *Due Process*. New York: Signet, 1996. Lawyer Karen Perry-Mondori is a Florida defense attorney. She defends accused murderer Jack Palmer, accused of rape and murder; he insists he is being framed. Widow Caroline deFauldo claims the motive was jealousy. As the trial date approaches, another death occurs.

40. _____. *Imperfect Justice*. New York: Signet, 1997. Perry-Mondori takes on mob boss Angelo Uccello's case when his safe is discovered by feds to contain a huge amount of cocaine. Perry-Mondori believes the mobster's story that the drugs were planted, and she soon finds evidence that a conspiracy of DEA, CIA and FBI agents. She also discovers the truth about her real father.

41. _____. *Wrongful Death*. New York: Signet, 1999. Perry-Mondori's brother is found dead of a bullet in the head, an apparent suicide. But Karen knows her brother, a highly valued US senator, would not consider that option--that is, until a scandalous video blackmail tape surfaces. Her latest incorporates the medical mystery with genetic research--in *Class Action* (1999), a homeless

man is found dead, the killer and the son turn a simple *pro bono* case for Perry-Mondori into a conspiracy trial.

42. Arnston, Harrison. *Deadly Evidence.* New York: Harper Paperbacks, 1993. Novelization of the script by Brad Mirman of the MGM/UA 1992 film *Body of Evidence*, starring Willem DaFoe, Joe Mantegna, Ann Archer and Madonna. A lawyer defends a woman accused of killing wealthy, elderly Andrew Marsh--by sexing him to death after she has conveniently had herself written into his will. It is thin in characterization and is influenced, at least in the trial sequence, by Agatha Christie's *Witness for the Prosecution.*

43. Arrighi, Mel. *The Death Collection.* New York: Popular, 1975. San Franciscan Arrighi began on stage in off-Broadway productions, summer theater, and touring companies. A transplanted New Yorker, he is both novelist and dramatist, and has written for television with journalists, writers, actors, and artists as characters. One series character, however, is lawyer Harrington, a Manhattan attorney and a guy who is frequently visited by the screw-up fairy. His saving grace is that he is a better detective than lawyer. He once took a case of a youth accused of murdering someone while on an acid trip. Harrington (no first name) solved the case without going to court. The 37-year-old army vet and graduate of New York University Law School (Class of '54) is a lifelong resident of Greenwich Village (*Detectionary* 50).

Detectives Romano and Dench arrive in Harrington's office one day and announce he is under suspicion of murdering one of his own clients: bohemian painter Matthew Stokes, whom Harrington once defended in a breach-of-contract suit against the painter's own dealer, an art gallery owner who was selling Stokes' best work at cut-rate prices.

44. _____. *Freak-Out.* New York: Putnam's, 1968. Harrington's debut novel has him being evicted for non-payment of rent, failing to establish a regular clientele, losing his last 10 cases, and having a girlfriend who writes pornography for a living--yet she spurns his advances. He is contemplating bumming a loan from girlfriend Willoughby Bunker to pay his back office rent when a fresh case arrives: young Ken Sadler believes he killed a girl named Wanda while he was tripping on acid.

Ashford, Jeffrey, pseud. *See* Jeffries, Roderic G[raeme]. . . .

45. Aubert, Rosemary. *The Feast of Stephen.* Bridgehampton: Bridge Works, 1999. Canadian author Aubert, criminologist and poet, has a series character, Ellis Portal, who is a disgraced judge and narrator of his stories. The second Ellis Portal mystery sees the former judge back on skid row among the Toronto homeless. He agrees to help Tootie Beetes, street name Queenie, discover who murdered her friend Melia. A second plot commences right after in which Judge Stoughton-Melville, a law-school mate, calls him in a rooming

house to ask if he will find his wife Harpur, missing from the Riverside Institute.

46. _____. *Free Reign.* Bridgehampton, NY: Bridge Works, 1997. Ellis discovers a severed hand with an insignia ring while working in his hidden garden; the hand leads him to a well-connected, downtown attorney and a conspiracy involving a halfway house for pregnant teenaged girls and the sale of fetal tissue.

47. Aubrey-Fletcher, Henry Lancelot. Henry Wade, pseud. *The Evidence of You All.* London: Constable, 1926. New York: Payson, 1927. A police tale about the death of a financier; the suspect and defendant in the Old Bailey trial is the victim's male secretary, who also happens to be engaged to the daughter.

48. Auchincloss, Louis. *Diary of a Yuppie.* Boston: Houghton, 1986. Literary critic Alfred Kazin describes the career canon of Louis Auchincloss in a single sentence: "When it comes to the minute social differences and unexpected human conflicts that can be the life of fiction, there is simply no one else like him." High praise when one considers that he and his more than forty works of fiction have for their depiction of Manhattanites so often been likened to predecessors Henry James and Edith Wharton. Of the middlebrow characters and climbers whose lives intersect with his privileged clans and the socially ambitious circles of various founding families and their businesses and law firms, one sees F. Scott Fitzgerald, J. P. Marquand linked to these greater literary icons in reviews and critiques of Auchincloss' work. There are those, too, who dismiss him, unjustly, as the chronicler of East Coast snobbery and elitism.

The most admired novel of manners, however, is still *The Rector of Justin* about an octogenarian headmaster-founder of a New England Episcopal boys' school. Not surprisingly, Auchincloss has authored critical studies of both James and Wharton--the two with whom he has been most frequently compared. Since his retirement from law in 1986, he has turned out much nonfiction; two recent works: *The Style's the Man: Reflections on Proust, Fitzgerald, Wharton, Vidal, and Others* (Boston: Houghton, 1994) and *The Man behind the Book* (Houghton, 1996). He attended Groton, Yale, graduated from the University of Virginia Law School, and maintained a law practice with Hawkins, Delafield & Wood, a blue-chip Manhattan firm while writing throughout an almost half-century, a spate uninterrupted except for duty in Navy Intelligence and as a gunnery officer (1941-45). He was elected to the National Institute of Arts and Letters and is a past president of the Museum of New York City, received an honorary doctorate from NYU in 1974 and the New York State Governor's Art Award. Auchincloss does not write lawyer fiction in the popular sense. He writes novels of manners about characters in moral crises that occasionally intersect with the legal profession or formal justice. His Tower, Tilney & Webb is one of the most famous literary firms in fiction. Unlike Henry James, who creates convoluted centers of consciousness to delineate inner struggles,

Auchincloss' style is one of economy and ironic wit. He always understood (as he once criticized the Victorian George Eliot for her seminal failure in this regard) that a novelist must be an *entertainer*. If he is like James, it is in his subtle exploitations of ambivalence--characters at cross purposes with their own desires or conventional morality. Intrigues, power struggles, and polite discourse across polished tables in high-rises overlooking the Manhattan skyline combine to form his singular postage stamp of fictional territory, nor does Auchincloss apologize for turning his focus almost exclusively on America's Mayflower set. Never in Auchincloss' fiction do we hear the stentorian rhetoric of courtroom fiction, never a Perry Mason performing last-minute courtroom drama in behalf of a client; seldom even is there more than a whisper of actual courtroom theatrics in the great volume of his work. A courteous man, Auchincloss defends his microcosm in *A Writer's Capital* against the critics who decry its smallness and see merely snobbery: "But not only was it not small numerically, it was open-ended. One could, if one wanted, meet almost anybody in it" (17). Many prominent legal and literary figures were friends and acquaintances of his family, such as John W. Davis, Judge Learned Hand, and Arthur Train. Auchincloss said of his literary debt to the law: "I think it is a profession ideally married to the writing because both deal with the written word and an emphatic need for probing and analyzing" (Gelderman 191). His major novels and some collected short works dealing with the law are noted here.

Robert Service of *Diary of a Yuppie* focuses upon a typical kind of Auchincloss character in or out of law--a man determined to succeed at all costs, although he commits no crimes. This one has rightly been compared most to Fitzgerald's Jazz Age classic *The Great Gatsby*. Service is also a precursor of the corporate raiders of the coming decade with their double-crosses, swindles and takeovers. He believes that senior partners "invoking the ideals of the past while garnering the profits of the present" are mere hypocrites. The law, for Service, is a game with rules that you must play with meticulous attention to the boundaries. Ethical considerations are inconsequential, and there is no more moral opprobrium attached to a lawyer caught crossing the line than being "offside in football." This razor-sharp, thirty-two-year-old lawyer has bigger goals than an imminent partnership in a big New York law firm in mind. Service's "perfect" marriage to the graceful and intelligent Alice is no match for the ardor of his corporate drive, and it certainly pales beside his explosive affair with Sylvia, whose naked ambition matches his own and whose social connections provide the ultimate bridge to the pinnacles of success.

49. _____. *The Embezzler*. Boston: Houghton, 1966. Guy Prime is one of the more colorful of the author's tribe of villains who exceed mere crassness or mercenary ambitions of the climbers and schemers to become a financial criminal. This is Guy's record to posterity, a vindication of his fall and an *apologia* for his claim to infamy as the man who brought down the Stock Exchange. Guy eventually does turn over his story to Rex Geer, his closest friend and then to Angelica, his wife. We follow his sordid path from his bright

law firm days to the ultimate portrait of an embittered old man who succumbed to paltry greed.

50. _____. *Fellow Passengers.* Boston: Houghton, 1989. A collection of 10 character portraits beginning with "Aunt Mabel" and "Aunt Lou Haven." The majority are personal reminiscences with varying temporal settings, although the three legal stories are linked to the apprenticeship days of first-person narrator Danny Ruggles, either beginning his law career with Arnold & Degener ("Orlando Hatch") or in the post-Navy resumption of his legal career interrupted by a three-year stint at becoming a professional writer.

51. _____. *The Great World and Timothy Colt.* Boston: Houghton, 1956. Timmy Colt returns from his Navy duty to the law firm of Sheffield, Knox, Stevens, & Dale where he resumes his practice in corporate law under the tutelage of senior partner Knox, a wise, moral man and virtual replication of the later Tilney. In this apprenticeship novel, Colt is caught in a Manichaean vice between good and bad angels. Knox is the lawyer whom he admires for all that is good in legal practice; unctuous Sheridan Dale is the estates expert, an amoral second-rater with ambitions. When Knox dies, Tim comes entirely under the wing of Dale and his nephew--a vile, arrogant businessman attempting a complex corporate merger. As Colt rises in the firm, gaining wealth and prestige along with the attentions of a beautiful woman, he casts off wife and early ethical scruples in a self-destructive spin. When the nephew attempts to cheat his siblings, Colt faces his ultimate moral choice--and fails to disclose the information. Colt, like his fictional mentor and real-life creator, loves the "abstractness of the practice of law."

52. _____. *I Come as a Thief.* Boston: Houghton, 1972. This novel reflects a typical Auchincloss theme: some people are masochistically, unconsciously bent on their own self-destruction. Tony Lowder is the able and good-looking grandson of an Irish immigrant who prospered as a contractor and left behind a family that has been running downhill--except Tony, who has a promising future in politics as Special Assistant to the Regional Director. He has married the only child of an old, correct New York family. His wife tolerates his affair with the wealthy Joan Conway, his mistress before his marriage. With an acute drop in the marketplace comes a pressure for more money. Tony's dilemma is a reflection of what happens to the inner experience as well as the surface relationships of these sophisticated people when the agony of temptation, not resisted, makes its way into the center of their lives. Part III contains a rare excursion into court for Auchincloss as Tony testifies in a criminal trial against the two Mafiosi as part of his own bribery plea bargain.

53. _____. *A Law for the Lion.* Boston: Houghton; London: Gollancz, 1953. Eloise Dilworth is married to a lawyer who works for her uncle's law firm. Eloise's mother, the family black sheep owing to her dissolute life as a

European, becomes the catalyst that forces Eloise to confront her own unhappy marriage to her ambitious but impotent husband. Eloise nearly consummates an affair with a popular war novelist but is exposed by her husband as an adulterer and is thus dragged through the mud and into divorce court. She ultimately, however, rejects her newfound lover and husband--hoping to reconcile--as she asserts her own independence and individuality in a conclusion as reminiscent of Ibsen's Nora as one of James' stronger women. This novel was, according to Auchincloss biographer Gelderman, written while the author underwent psychoanalysis.

54. _____. *The Partners.* Boston: Houghton, 1974. Distinguished New York firm Shepard, Putney & Cox is living on faded glory and the guiding force of one senior partner, Beekman ("Beeky") Ehninger. Beeky once saved his firm from decline and must now talk his old friend and partner Hubert Cox into merging with Sloane & Sidell. There is a subplot involving Ehniger's museum activities and a Uriah heap-like character with a nefarious forgery scheme that does little to add drama. As always, it is Auchincloss' narrow world of old money confronting modern values--or valuelessness. Beeky is the son of a rich mother and a socially ambitious father; he carries a Victorian sense of honor into his transactions, yet is not without ridicule, especially in his marital situation (the wife of one associate refers to him as "a sublimated faggot"). Beeky resembles two other senior partners elsewhere--Henry Knox and Clitus Tilne--for his genuine love of the legal profession.

55. _____. *Powers of Attorney.* Boston: Houghton, 1955. Many familiar characters from Tower, Tilney & Webb are back in this collection of a dozen. More gems of irony along with Auchincloss' wistful charm for exploiting the anecdotal, especially when it concerns one of his favorite themes: those blue bloods from the bygone Gilded Age like the dowager Miss Shepard in "The Ambassador from Wall Street"or Bayard Kip, a junior partner lost in remembrance of quaint gentility in an age without morals ("The Deductible Yacht"). Auchincloss has a depth of feeling for his characters that shows his true range. "The 'True Story' of Lavinia Todd," about the deserted wife of the hard-driving Chambers Todd, is still modern in an age of feminism. Auchincloss defies those who say the short story is exclusively the property of the young because nearly every story is a middle-aged epiphany. Characters often lose themselves in the tide of new developments or chicanery from elemental human emotions; some lucky few rediscover a new sense of themselves and go on. Some stories are clearly dated: big Harry Reilly, considered too "Irish" and brash to be given an appointment as partner, is rescued from himself at the end of "The Mavericks" in a manner reminiscent of a Doris Day film--except for the business of aborting Harry's child from a weekend liaison; even that scandal cannot doom his newfound relationship with Clitus Tilney's charming daughter Fran. Shortly before his death, Auchincloss was asked to write an updated teleplay for a PBS production and gave up after

several months, protesting that it was impossible to update a pregnancy's shock value from the mid-1950's to today's times.

56. _____. *The Romantic Egoists.* Boston: Houghton, 1952. Of the 8 stories contained, 6 are boyhood reminiscences like "Billy and the Gargoyles" or non-legal tales like "Wally"; however, two are among his finest: "The Legends of Henry Everett," about a great lawyer's parting speech to a young colleague and "The Great World and Timothy Colt," a story that Auchincloss developed into a full-length novel. The latter part of the Montherlant inscription to this collection expresses the essential Auchincloss: "*Ils traversent la guerre et les révolucions sans avoir vu une seule fois un cadavre, sans savoir comment cela est fait. Incurablement préservés, et bourgeois malgré eux.*"

57. _____. *Second Chance: Tales of Two Generations.* Boston: Houghton, 1970. In this collection of a dozen stories, two plots cohere about legal characters. In "The Cathedral Builder," John Lancaster, the miserly founder of the law firm in which the narrator clerks, attempts to impose his twenty millions and his mad will onto a cathedral construction project that has obsessed him all his life; in "Second Chance" the lawyer-narrator undertakes the divorce proceedings for his sister-in-law Rebecca, although her husband is one of his oldest friends.

58. _____. *Skinny Island: More Tales of Manhattan.* Boston: Houghton, 1987. This dozen stories has a single legal tale: "The Senior Partner's Ethics." Young Brendan Boss is apprenticed to a senior partner in his firm who works for a single client, a bank; one day, however, he uncovers evidence that this man has suppressed in litigation involving the bank, and he must make a moral choice whether to abet the violation of ethics or expose it in court.

59. _____. *Tales of Manhattan.* Boston: Houghton, 1976. Only the middle section of this collection of tales of Manhattan society life concerns the law. "Arnold & Degener, One Chase Manhattan Plaza" features members of a distinguished law firm, whose members write about one another, especially Lloyd Degener, and themselves and the society they live in. Auchincloss focuses on one man, a senior partner and one of those typical dry, impersonal men to the world but romantics to themselves who fuse legal fiefdoms out of a founder's dynastic vision but are often regarded by others as men "of no accessories, no appendages, no stray bits or loose ends."

60. _____. *Three Lives.* Boston: Houghton, 1993. This collection of novellas consists of three first-person narratives. The second is "The Realist." Alida Vermeule is a Barnard undergraduate and granddaughter of a robber baron who meets her husband-to-be when he takes her family's case to keep her favorite aunt's will from giving all her property to an unscrupulous lawyer named Stern. Alida's tale is less about that than it is an *apologia* of her life

against her liberated middle-aged daughter's accusation that she, like the women of her social class and circle, had no independence. Alida's spirited record is her proof that she was an opportunist, a capable manipulator behind the scenes, and the guiding force of her brilliant husband's law career. This is one of the best examples of Auchincloss' most subtle spin-off themes from his WASP chronicles--how "unliberated" women, specifically, the wives of the early twentieth-century power brokers of upper-crust New York influence the social and economic worlds portrayed. He comes closer to James here than Wharton, but he does not invoke mental access to his characters to compel greater recognition from critics for this quietly profound achievement. Jonathan Yardley, Pulitzer Prize critic and contributor of the *Washington Post Book World*, dissents in one earlier novel: "[The women of *The Book Class*] get affectionate and clear-eyed tribute . . . Auchincloss never manages to make the reader care about them; they never seem to matter, to be of real consequence . . . A late-published novel, *The Dark Lady*, seems to bear this out (1977). Ivy Trask, a 55-year-old woman and fashion editor of a New York magazine called *Tone*, struggles "to preserve the ideal of a woman's role as a pioneer in art and elegance through the worst of the Depression and now, in 1937, seemed moderately sure of survival" (3). The word *Depression* is a loaded pistol in the sentence, but Auchincloss remains coolly indifferent to its reverberations.

61. _____. *A World of Profit*. Boston: Houghton, 1968. Some of the worst reviews Auchincloss ever received were aimed at this book, which is the record of the greedy Shallcross family of Long Island and the fast rise and fall of a securities lawyer named Livingston. Seemingly based on the shady Wall Street dealings of Edward M. Gilbert, a businessman who misappropriated funds and absconded to Brazil in the mid-1960s, the novel evolved out of "The Money Jugglers," one of the stories in *Tales of Manhattan*; it offers a large theme in which, according to an Auchincloss interview later that year, the world has become morally confused to the point that "there is no accepted code of what is right and wrong, [where] marital infidelity, financial fraud, even violence have become acceptable" (qtd. in Gelderman 165). The Shallcrosses are enamored of young Jay Livingston, brilliant securities lawyer and parvenu, who offers them the means to recoup their dwindling family fortune. Auchincloss has a classical view of such machinations and provides a modern sense of fate, for it will invariably end in a summoning of the three sisters of revenge: bankruptcy, a broken marriage, and an indictment.

62. Avallone, Michael (Angelo), Jr. *Stag Stripper*. New York: Midwood, 1961. It was inevitable that somewhere in the vast output of the writing machine that Michael Avallone is he would mention a trial somewhere in one of his 200 mysteries, thrillers, and unclassifiable cross-pollinations that bring the total output to around 1,000 across the genre of fiction. Creator of both *U.N.C.L.E.* series, the deservedly popular Ed Noon private-eye novels, and the novelizations from *Hawaii 5-O* through the *Partridge Family* to popular films like *Friday the*

Thirteenth, Part 3, he is a self-professed child of the pulps and an American phenomenon.

B

63. Bahr, Arthur W. *Certifiably Insane*. New York: Simon, 1999. Renowned attorney Kate Newhouse is known for defending women clients on the battered-women syndrome, but this case is different: police officer Janice Jensen was found in the middle of a bloodbath, nonchalantly eating grapes, as her cop-husband lay shot in the eyes and head, her baby stabbed to death. Kate assembles her defense team of best friend and forensic scientist Simon Rose and a media darling.

64. Bailey, F[rancis]. Lee. *Secrets*. New York: Stein, 1978. London: Melbourne, 1979. One of America's premier defense attorneys since his defense of Dr. Sam Sheppard authors this novel about trial attorney Michael Kilrayne, himself charged with murder in a Boston courtroom. The prosecution tries to prove murder in the absence of a corpse, vanished socialite Sarah Hansen. Evidence presented by the prosecution includes videotape of the alleged victim's sex life, in which the legs and torso of one of her sex partners are said to be "consistent with the legs and torso of Mr. Kilrayne."

65. Bailey, H. C. [Henry Christopher]. *The Garston Murder Case* [British title: *Garstons*]. New York: Doubleday; London: Gollancz, 1930. By 1941, Bailey had published 19 mysteries featuring a pair of sleuths, 14 of them with protagonist Reggie Fortune, a throwback to the Dorothy Sayers-style of detection, and an ongoing delight to those who favor the puzzle of mystery fiction. With gray-eyed lawyer Joshua Clunk, however, he found an interesting creation to break the mold because the portly lawyer is a bible-spouter, "chirruping sacred music," a genteel scalawag, but a first-class criminal lawyer who can solve crimes while Inspector Bell and Scotland Yard bark up the wrong trees. Bailey was educated at the City of London and Corpus Christi College, Oxford. Besides his mysteries, he was a drama critic and correspond who worked through WW II for the London *Daily Telegraph*. On two occasions, Fortune and Clunk would appear in the same novel: *The Great Game* (London: Gollancz; Garden City, NY: Doubleday, 1939) and *The Wrong Man* (Garden City, NY: Doubleday; London: Macdonald, 1946).

Clunk becomes tangled in the affairs of the Garston family, munition manufacturers. He must connect the vanishing of a chemist, worthless stolen jewelry, and the elderly matriarch's strangling murder.

66. _____. *Mr. Clunk's Text* [British title: *The Veron Mystery*]. New York: Doubleday; London: Gollancz, 1939. A wealthy and disliked farmer in the small village of Tanmoor signs his will leaving everything to a young woman nobody knows and dies. His housekeeper disappears and is found dead

with broken glass in her dress. Just before her death, she had written a letter to Joshua Clunk asking for his services. A fire in the gorse reveals a body and a small bottle. Clunk's intrusion into the case brings him up against Inspector Bompas.

67. _____. *Nobody's Vineyard: A Joshua Clunk Story* [British title: *Dead Man's Shoes*]. Garden City, NY: Doubleday; London: Gollancz, 1942. A homeless, 16-year-old boy named Gussage disappears one night from his village, last seen on a bluff overlooking the sea. The body turns up with the boy's face half-destroyed, and a publican with a reputation for smuggling is implicated in the paper as the last to see him alive. After seeking out Clunk for help, the lawyer sniffs out a real-estate development scheme and a motive for homicide in a falling out among greedy plotters.

68. _____. *Orphan Ann* [British title: *The Little Captain*]. Garden City, NY: Doubleday; London: Gollancz, 1941. Mollie Morn was shot in the head and left beside the cottage of Captain Davy. He and his manservant, Buller Noy, are the prime suspects, but Clunk knows there is more to the case than Inspector Bell suspects, and in fact it begins in a hellish home for unwed mothers near exclusive Penley called Martha's Home for Girls and ends in blackmail and espionage secrets involving the Admiralty's firm of Peppard-Hayton.

69. _____. *The Sullen Sky Mystery.* New York: Grosset; London: Gollancz, 1935. Josh Clunk's new client is Isaac Terry, owner of a garage in the village of Waldon, who once did a stretch in Borstal prison. Fearing persecution by the police because of his record, he asks for Clunk's help, but Clunk immediately suspects something else lies behind his client's request and is not disappointed when a prominent citizen of Waldon is found murdered near Sandhaven by a couple on an outing to the seashore.

More Clunks by Doubleday/Gollancz: *The Twittering Bird Mystery* [British title: *Clunk's Claimant*] (1935); *The Queen of Spades* [British title: *Slippery Ann*] (1944); *The Red Castle Mystery* [British title: *The Red Castle*] (also London: Lock, 1932); *Shrouded Death* (also London: Macdonald, 1950). A pair of Clunk-Fortune novels: *The Great Game* (London: Gollancz; New York: Doubleday, 1939) and *The Wrong Man* (London: Macdonald; New York: Doubleday, 1946).

70. Baker, Daniel. D.B., pseud. *The Guiltless Cries and Warnings of the Innocent: against Injustice, Oppression, Cruelty, False-Swearers, Envious Men, and Such Like Witnesses, Arisen Up against a Plain Man, or, A Living and True Witness Condemned, through Want of Sound (yet through Just) Judgment: Together with the Unequal and Unreasonable Proceedings of Humphry Wildey, Mayor, and Edward Solley, and Robert Sollers, Aldermen, and Justices of the City Worcester, As May Plainly Appear by What Followeth, besides the Unjust*

Sufferings of the Guiltlesse . London: R Wilson, 1660. Baker's diatribe defends his Quaker beliefs in that wonderfully prolix and allegorical style that would survive into the fiction of Nathaniel Hawthorne and the first stirrings of American literature on the New England coast of the nineteenth century. Baker, albeit writing what purports to be autobiography rather than fiction, in the final decade of the Interregnum (his publishing date marks the return of Charles II and the opening of London theater to the delightful decadence of the Restoration comedy), is authoring a narrative with the essential ingredients of a modern-day courtroom drama: a "crime" has been committed, the perpetrator(s) must be found, nefariousness must be sanitized in the light of justice restored. The title, literally, says it all, but the author adds a few more words for good measure as "servant, witness, and prisoner for the elects sake."

71. Baldacci, David. *Absolute Power.* New York: Warner, 1996. Before full-time writing from his home in Virginia, the author had worked as a corporate and trial attorney in Washington, DC. Baldacci's first novel is an amalgam of police procedural, legal novel, and spy-thriller. Despite the mixed genres, a very successful one (Baldacci's writing skills are first-rate but uneven); the minor characters are as interesting as the major ones, but the welter of improbable coincidences stretches credulity at times. Capitalizing on the success of his first effort, he turned out two more suspense thrillers without lawyers and with a falling off in writing power. *Total Control* (Warner, 1997) is about a woman whose life is turned upside down when her husband, reported dead in a fiery plane crash, is investigated by the FBI for the bombing of that plane in which he was supposedly killed. *The Winner* (Warner, 1997) features LuAnn Tyler, a tough single mother from Appalachia who is blackmailed to conspire with a brilliant psychopathic killer to win the New York lottery. His fifth novel (*Saving Faith*, 1999) mixes the staples of his earlier suspense works and his legal thrillers with an FBI investigation involving a renegade deputy director of the CIA named Robert Thornhill, attempting a blackmail scheme to force Congress to reinstate the CIA back to its glory days.

An insipid public mask hides a cruel, womanizing President, who crosses paths with an aging burglar named Luther Whitney in the midst of a bedroom romp with the wife of a political crony. The main plot connects the major characters to the White House when Luther is in the act of burgling a rich Virginia house he had been casing at the very moment that the philandering First Man shows up with the wife of rich and powerful Walter Sullivan. The thief secretes himself in a recessed vault behind a secret mirror while the drunken President is about to have sex with Christine Sullivan. Things go wrong when the oafish Richmond gets rough; a fight ensues, he slugs her and she is just about to plunge a letter opener into him when two Secret Service men enter and shred her brains with two slugs from their weapons. Luther escapes and contacts an old friend for help, Jack Graham, the ex-fiancé of his daughter, now a Virginia Commonwealth prosecutor. Jack was once an idealist about the law until Kate Whitney rejected him; now Jack is fighting his conscience for attempting to ensconce himself in the capital's biggest law firm by marrying the daughter of one of its wealthiest clients--a firm which just happens to represent the interests of billionaire Sullivan, the man who wants to see his wife's killer get real justice; furthermore, he has an international assassin on a two-million-dollar contract plus $100,000 per diem to see that that is exactly what will happen.

The film (Columbia/Castle Rock, 1997) starred Gene Hackman, Scott Glenn, Ed Harris, and Clint Eastwood; the latter also directed with scripting done by veteran screenwriter-author William Goldman, who must have accommodated an aging star's ego to produce a film based on a book so that it would betray only the merest relationship to the former.

72. _____. *The Simple Truth.* New York: Warner, 1998. Mike Fiske and Sara Evans DC lawyers and colleagues. Sara, however, is clerking for a Supreme Court justice. A 25-year-old murder comes to light when convicted murderer named Rufus Harms smuggles out a letter to the Supreme Court from his Virginia prison protesting his innocence. Then people connected to him begin to die, including Mike Fiske, whose brother is a former cop and asks Sara for help in investigating. Baldacci comments on his choice of title in an online interview: "[T]he older I get I can't find simple truth anywhere, and I do look for it. I live near Washington, DC, the capital city of spin. Truth does not rule here, perception does. The concept of truth is merely who gets out one set of facts first." He is currently working on a network television series and another thriller.

73. Ball, Doris Bell [née Collier]. Josephine Bell, pseud. *Easy Prey.* London: Hodder; New York: Macmillan, 1959. Ball (more familiar to readers as Josephine Bell) was born in Manchester, educated at Cambridge, and then became a University College Hospital of London physician. She created numerous sleuths in her more than 40 crime novels, such as Amy Tupper, Dr. David Wintringham, Dr. Henry Frost, and Scotland Yard Inspector Steven Mitchell (who appears in other series novels). She closed her medical practice at 57 and continued to write full-time until she was 85. Her legal series character is Claude Warrington-Reeve, a London barrister, featured in this novel and the two below. This one concerns an embezzled estate, multiple murders, blackmail, and a corrupt family lawyer playing a wife against her sister.

74. _____. *A Flat Tyre in Fulham* [US title: *Fiasco in Fulham*]. London; New York: Macmillan, 1963. Barrister Hugh Mellanby entices employer Warrington-Reeve into assisting an investigation when a body turns up in the boot of a stolen Jaguar turns up after an aborted armed robbery. The car belongs to Sir John Drew, uncle of his fiancée Belinda.

75. _____. *A Well-Known Face.* New York: Washburn, 1960. Jane Fuller wants to file desertion against her husband, missing for three years,

because of his failure to impregnate her. The day she enters Warrington-Reeve's office to file the papers is the day Dr. Roger Fuller he is found dead in their Didington home.

76. Ballard, W. T., and Norbert Davis. Harrison Hunt, pseud. *Murder Picks the Jury.* New York: Mystery House, 1947. A former prosecuting attorney drops out of society after convicting the wrong man and sending him to death; after mistreatment by officials in Vale City, he vows revenge on the town--until he meets a woman in town whose father is about to go on trial for murder.

77. Ballinger, Bill S[anborn]. *The Law.* New York: Warner, 1975. Based on a made-for-TV film in which the main character is LA public defender Murray Stone, defending one of four men accused of the torture-murder of a professional football player. Judge Rebeccah Fornier is notable as a hugely biased, incompetent jurist. (*See* Oliansky, Joel, and William Sackheim).

78. _____. *Not I, Said the Vixen.* New York: Fawcett, 1965. Cyrus March, an LA lawyer too fond of booze, prepares to defend Ivy Lorents, who reminds him of his lost beauty Beatrice. Lorents does not deny shooting Arthea Simpson in her apartment; she claim she mistook Arthea for a burglar. The prosecution, however, says she murdered her lover to prevent her fiancé from learning of her lesbian affair.

79. _____. *The Tooth and the Nail.* New York: Harper; London: Reinhardt, 1955. A nameless defendant goes on trial in New York for the hatchet-murder of his chauffeur. The defendant is supposed to have burned the body in a furnace; a tooth from his mouth becomes key evidence.

80. Balzac, Honoré de. *César Birotteau* [Trans. of *Histoire de la Grandeur et de la Decadence de Cesar*] Trans. Frances Frenaye. Oxford: Clarendon, 1909; New York: Juniper, 1955. The important French author and proponent of realism with a painstaking emphasis on the mundane and unemotional penned dozens of novels with a few centering on the courtroom and, generally, its inability to dispense justice. Balzac was himself a lawyer but never practiced, thanks to a mistress' support. He wrote *The Chouans*, his first novel, hiding from creditors after a disastrous business venture in 1825. He thereby initiated one of the most powerful trends in naturalism-as-literature via his preface to *Comédie Humaine* (1842).

Other Balzac novels with minor courtroom interludes or legal matters include: *Cousin Pons*, *Pére Goriot*, *An Historical Mystery*, *The Gallery of Antiquities*, *Lost Illusions, Scenes from a Courtesan's Life, Ursule Miroët*, *Lucien de Rubempré*, *The Lesser Bourgeosie*, *Gobseck*, *Colonel Chabert*, *A Commission in Lunacy*, *The Last Incarnation of Vautrin*, *A Start in Life,* and *The Marriage Contract.*

81. Banning, Margaret Culkin. *The Iron Will.* New York and London: Harper, 1936. A *Bildungsroman* featuring a youth, iron mining and a trial in Minnesota that consumes the entire 239-page novel. Marshall Crinton is defense counsel for the Greysolon Mining Company of Duluth, fighting the state the state of Minnesota, which is suing for unpaid taxes.

82. Banville, John. *The Book of Evidence.* London: Secker; New York: Scribner's, 1989. Born in Wexford, Ireland, Banville had six books published and recognized before this one, which was short-listed for the Booker Prize in England. Now a Dubliner, he is literary editor of *The Irish Times.* Freddie Montgomery is a bad hat, a lousy son and husband, a 38-year-old expatriate and one-time scientist who spends all his time in shot-and-beer bars. On his return to Ireland, he steals a painting that has become an obsession for him, but the sordid escapade ends in a murder. His lawyer tells him to plead down to manslaughter. The blackly comic narrative is Freddie's brief to himself, not a real confession, but a psychic plunge to the core of his murderous self just short of stream-of-consciousness.

83. Barbour, A. Maynard. *That Mainwaring Affair.* New York: Grossett, 1900. Formulaic melodrama with staple ingredients: the murder of Hugh Mainwaring, the lost will, the discovery of the old will, and the rightful heir's timely appearance at the trial.

84. Bardin, John Franklin. Gregory Tree, pseud. *The Case against Myself.* New York: Scribner's, 1950. London: Gollancz, 1951. The wife of a Broadway gossip columnist is accused of poisoning her husband's mistress. Fledgling lawyer Bill Bradley defends her with the help of psychiatrist Noel Mayberry. Sidenote: the narrative is a mélange of different points of view from the lawyers and judge through jurors to witnesses, suspects, and defendant. Bradley and Mayberry return in *The Case against Butterfly* (Scribner's, 1951).

85. Baring-Gould, Sabine. *The Broom-Squire.* New York: Stokes, 1895; London: Stokes, 1896. An infant girl is abandoned by her sailor father and raised in a tavern where she meets and is rescued from the gutter by a wealthy farmer named Jonas Kink. When he is murdered, she is sent to trial--without evidence. The prosecutor seeks death for the young mother on no firmer grounds than her relationship to the deceased: "Remember that a wife guilty of the murder of her husband, who is allowed to run free, encourages all others, possibly even your own, to rid themselves of their husbands . . ." (313).

86. Barlow, James. *The Burden of Proof.* London: Hamilton; New York: Simon, 1968. The brutal life and criminal career of Vik Daken, East London thug, apprehended with three other felons in a botched heist. The courtroom scene is spread over two chapters and is curiously inept with summary lists of

evidence against the perps interspersed with dialogue from Crown prosecutors.

87. _____. *Term of Trial.* London: Hamilton, 1961. New York: Simon, 1962. An English teacher in an unnamed Midlands industrial city anguishes over cowardice during the war and fails to realize that a 15-year-old student is in love with him. Realizing her intentions after a school trip to the Continent, he rejects her; she lies about him, and he finds himself indicted in Magistrate's Court on a charge of indecent assault. A real-life verdict concludes the courtroom verdict of the novel.

88. Barmby, Cuthbert. *James Cope: Confessions of a United States District Attorney.* New York: New Amsterdam, 1899. Nineteenth-century legal treatises wrapped within a detective story.

89. Barre, Michael. *The Case against the Andersons.* New York: Delacorte, 1983. Fifteen-year-old Maggie Anderson is at a Philadelphia boarding school while her parents are in England. She talks a sympathetic staff member, who is romantically involved with a young lawyer, into filing suit against her parents. The parents bring in their own lawyer and the case goes to court. It is less about a mystery or courtroom action (although well done) than it is about the psycho dynamics of parental love and neglect, and a teenager's maturing.

90. Barrett, Margaret, and Charles Dennis. *Given the Crime.* New York: Pocket, 1998. Susan Given heads NYC's Asset Forfeiture Unit with a fearless mob-busting reputation, yet she finds time to be a mother to her Salvadoran-born daughters. The routine changes drastically during a headline-making case when she confronts a corpse, a vindictive colleague at work, and a paranoid, soon-to-be ex-husband.

91. Barron, Stephanie. *Jane and the Unpleasantness at Scargrave Manor: Being the First Jane Austen Mystery.* New York: Bantam, 1996. Barron has summoned Jane Austen from her grave as the effete icon of academics to refurbish her as a period sleuth--with modest success. Although these historical mysteries are not actually courtroom dramas, historian and author Barron has seeded them with exactitude regarding the background of early nineteenth-century British custom and legal practice (a caveat: this erudition comes with footnotes). In this novel, Jane, invited to a ball to celebrate her friend Isobel's forthcoming marriage, gets embroiled in the business of the death of the Earl of Scargrave, a much older man. The death of Scargrave and the subsequent murder of Isobel's maid ensure that the 22-year-old wife and deceased's nephew, Fitzroy, Viscount Payne, with whom she is alleged to be in love, are subsequently arraigned by the House of Lords and tried for murder of a peer of the realm. Bantam published the second Jane Austen mystery the following year: *Jane and the Man of the Cloth.* Another recent one is *Jane and the*

Stillroom Maid (2000).

92. Barth, John. *The Floating Opera.* New York: Doubleday, 1967. Originally published by Appleton in 1956, this revised version restores the original ending, but it would not have mattered, for Barth is one of the most overrated of postmodernist writers. He is here because his central character is a lawyer who dabbles in legal matters, or as Todd Andrews says of his career in the first chapter, he has been "confined since 1920 mainly to legal briefs and *Inquiry*-writing" (1). There is no plot to speak of, and like all his novels, a fashionable questioning of values replaces craft and storytelling. Writes the last great pre-millennium critic Martin Seymour-Smith, "[Barth] is ingenious, clever, admirable--and a crushing bore" (45).

93. Barton, Fredrick. *With Extreme Prejudice.* New York: Villard, 1993. New Orleans English professor Barton writes about a grieving widower, Mike Barnett drifting through an alcoholic haze until he returns home to find his wife's law files ransacked; then he discovers missing papers pertaining to her crowning achievement as a lawyer--*Grieve v. Retif* before the Supreme Court, a case that obsessed her long after she won. Soon, he discovers the obvious: her death was not an accident.

94. Basso, Hamilton. *The View from Pompey's Head.* New York: Doubleday, 1954. Young lawyer Anson Page returns from his practice in Manhattan to his native Southern town of Pompey's Head to investigate case of misappropriation of funds. The newly deceased and much-respected editor of novelist Garvin Wales stands accused of withdrawing thousands from the royalties earned by Wales. The film exploits the love interest between Page and his old sweetheart (TCF, 1955; British title: *Secret Interlude*). Dir. and writ. Philip Dunne. Perf. Richard Egan, Dana Wynter, and Cameron Mitchell.

95. Batten, Jack. *Crang Plays the Ace.* Toronto: Macmillan, 1987. Batten's series character is lawyer and jazz buff Crang of Toronto, Ontario (no first name). The author graduated from Toronto Law School, still lives there, but has abandoned law for writing both fiction and nonfiction from everyday law for Canadians through sports history to legal biography and forensics. His recent DNA study is *Mind over Murder: DNA and Other Forensic Adventures* published by McClelland of Toronto. The Crang novels are fast, fun, and wryly entertaining.

Crang picks up a case from his friend Tom Catalano, a litigator at the powerhouse legal firm of McIntosh, Brown & Crabtree. Matthew Wansborough, holder of seven directorships, wants to know why a firm he invested $300,000 in called Ace Disposal--and merely, he says, to help a black-sheep cousin of the family gain a vice presidency with minority interest in the firm--is suddenly making much more money than it ought under a majority investment group headed by aggressive, evasive Charles Grimaldi.

Wainsborough suspects the books are cooked and wants Crang to nose out the fraud to avoid scandal.

96. _____. *Riviera Blues.* Toronto: Macmillan, 1990. Crang takes an "assignment" from his ex-father-in-law to search out a family member affiliated with Swotty Whetherhill's wealthy trust company; it seems he sent his cousin a facetiously mocking postcard that has the older man concerned. Crang and girlfriend Annie are going to Monaco and agree to swing over to Cannes to check out Jamie Haddon's welfare and arrive just in time to see his broken body lying on the ground from a rooftop fall. The mystery involves a homosexual liaison and a missing optical disk worth millions. Another pair of Crangs is *Blood Count* (1991) and *Straight No Chaser* (1987), the latter about a jazz pal named Dave Goddard, who wants Crang to tail a man who is tailing him.

97. Beach, Rex E. *The Spoilers.* New York: Collier's, 1905. Adventure author Beach writes of two Alaskan miners who strike gold in Nome, but their mine is held in receivership by a court action brought by a claim jumper, a "spoiler," and Judge Stillman, a corrupt "politician [who] had by now absorbed all the richest properties in the district and worked them through his hirelings" (120). Some two-fisted action interrupts the Judge's moral turpitude and brings his lovely niece into the arms of one of the heroes.

98. Bean, Gregory. *Grave Victory.* New York: St. Martin's-Dunne, 1998. Bean's fourth outing for series character Harry Starbranch, Victory, Wyoming police chief who comes to the aid of friend and town-council ally Cassie Buchanan. Her son Carl has been sentenced to death for the murder of a research assistant at a nearby agricultural college.

99. Becke, Louis, and Walter Jeffrey. *First Fleet Family.* New York, London: Macmillan, 1896. This novel will suffice as a representative of a slew of such romantic, post-Walter Scott novels involving the adventures of historical figures ranging from young men who go soldiering or to sea through rogues and their scrapes with the law to a variety of transported villains, naives, and ne'er-do-wells. Most, like this one, express their exotic flavor in their title or subtitles that teem with nouns or names, such as Macmillan's 1897 announced fare: *The Men of the Moss-Hags* by S. R. Crockett, author of *The Raiders*. Or *A Set of Rogues*, detailing in its lengthy subtitle the "*Faithful Confession of Christopher Dutton*," by Frank Barrett; and, more akin to Becke and Jeffrey's historical narrative here, Walter Raymond's *In the Smoke of War*, a Cromwellian saga of Roundheads versus Cavaliers. These were the pulp thrillers of their times as fictionalized biography, although the editors claim to base the narrative on the papers of a real William Dew. Young William, in the time of King George III, decides to engage in a smuggling adventure with a friend from his seacoast village; the end result is capture by the King's revenue officers and, instead of Newgate Gaol or transportation, the local squire, who of course is also the legal

magistrate, allows the lad to go soldiering as a Marine, where adventures in New South Wales beckon.

100. Becker, Stephen. *A Covenant with Death.* New York: Atheneum, 1964. London: Hamilton, 1965. Native New Yorker Becker was educated at both Harvard and Peking University and done several translations from the French as well as novels and biography (Marshall Field III in 1964). A young and inexperienced judge narrates this story of a beautiful adulterous wife's murder in the small town of Soledad City in the American Southwest of 1923. The dialogue is very crisp and can shift from the colloquial through the *noirish* to the erudite in a passage. Judge Lewis' decision in chapter 16 is a magnificent example of trial by court.

Bell, Josephine, pseud. *See* Ball, Doris Ball Collier. . . .

101. Bellow, Saul. *Herzog.* New York: Viking, 1984. The lawyer Simkin is one of Moses Herzog's betrayers in this, one of the early Chicago laureate's novels of personal and cultural decline and death. The courtroom scenes Herzog witnesses are analogs for his own sexual guilt. The decline of the law seems to disgust the author, for he witnesses corruption and links it to a trial scene involving the homosexual Aleck-Alice, a male prostitute. The judge and the prostitute are linked when Aleck-Alice says to him that "your authority and my degeneracy are one and the same" (228).

102. Benjoya, Mitchell. *Final Judgment.* Chicago: Contemporary; Pickering, Ontario: Beaverbooks, 1978. Isadore Jacob Leavitt is a Boston attorney who fights hard and successfully in court for his clients: the first is Dubois, a black pimp accused of helping gang rape and beat a young white woman; another is a Charlestowner named O'Connor accused of robbing a bank and killing a guard. Leavitt's courtroom skills ensure victory, but when he learns of their guilt, he hires a hit man to have both killed. Although the plot is more suited to true crime than fiction, Benjoya shows he can work the same side of Boston's streets as Higgins.

103. Benke, Patricia D. *Cruel Justice.* New York: Avon, 1999. Benke is a California Appellate Judge. San Diego Chief Assistant DA Judith Thornton has much on her plate in this third novel: she buries her mother and best friend dying of lymphatic cancer, stomps out sexual harassment in the workplace, works to free an innocent man accused of molesting his own daughter, and tries to get her own daughter to soccer practice on time, where, additionally, Coach Gareth is the budding love interest.

104. _____. *False Witness.* New York: Avon, 1996. Assistant DA Judith Thornton risks her life among gangbangers and taggers, seeking a witness to the murder of William Franklin Threadgill. Gui Colon is a former "tagger," now a

mural artist, who sees a man crush Threadgill's head in with a huge rock at the base of a retaining wall in a wealthy canyon suburb of San Diego.

105. _____. *Guilty by Choice.* New York: Avon, 1995. Notes Jon Breen that it "sticks admirably to the legal issues and eschews the rather obvious woman and/or child in jeopardy situation it could easily have fallen into" (*Year's 25 Finest*, xvii). Niki Crawford, a park service employee, sees a man walking a little girl to the river in the rain and later discovers that the Kelly Solomon in the newspapers, the little girl found in the San Diego River, must have been she, but Crawford does not come forward. When the case against Bobby Engle begins to unravel, an eyewitness to the crime is the only hope of a conviction.

106. Bennett, Arnold. *Buried Alive.* London: Chapman; Garden City, NY: Doubleday, 1908. Never appreciated for his genuine comic sensibility, especially by the effete crowd of the Bloomsbury circle, this stalwart of the early twentieth-century novel of realism and naturalism (*The Old Wives' Tale* (1908), *Clayhanger* (1910), and *Riceyman Steps* (1923)), writes a whimsical tale of a reclusive painter Priam Farll, whose manservant Henry suddenly dies. Farll is mistaken at the door for his deceased servant and soon a distant relative arrives to displace him from his own home. The trial scene at the end is to restore Farll to his rightful identity.

107. Bensink, Beau, and Sharon E. Doyle. *Amanda Donohoe: Shame II: The Secret.* (Paramount, 1995). Kay Lenz plays Diana Caddell, former DA in LA, who agrees to help out a small-town law practice and assist in the defense of Gilbert Rawlins in a capital murder case; the problem is twofold: Rawlins' own mother does not want to admit her son could be insane and her courtroom antagonist is both a believer in capital punishment as well as her love interest. Dir. Dan Lerner. The film is based on an Australian film *Shame* (Metro/Barron, 1987), itself hailed in *Halliwell*'s as a "[p]owerful indictment of male bonding and aggression" (671). In it, a female lawyer (Deborra-Lee Furness) uncovers a serial-rapist in a small town. Dir. Steve Jodrell. Writ. Beverly Blankenship and Michael Brindley. Perf. Tony Barry, Simone Buchanan, and Gillian Jones.

108. Benson, E. F. [Edward Frederic]. *The Blotting Book.* London: Heinemann; New York: Doubleday, 1908. Two lawyers entrusted with £30,000 of young Morris Assheton's estate embezzle the lad's money as he is about to come to his majority, lose most in various investments and stock options; then, to avoid detection, Mr. Taynton frames him for the murder of his partner by forging a letter on a blotting book: "You damned brute, I will settle you" (226).

109. Bentley, Barbara. *Mistress Nancy.* New York: McGraw, 1980. The notorious case of infanticide among the bluebloods is diminished to a soap opera of FFV's and their scandalous gossip. The record is that Richard Randolph was accused of murdering the child produced by him and his sister-in-law Nancy,

later to be wife of Gouverneur Morris, chief drafter of the US Constitution. Patrick Henry defends in "Trial" of the novel's courtroom section, acerbically demolishing witnesses, whereas the youthful John Marshall, Henry's co-counsel, is largely missing in action. (*See* Walz, Jay and Audrey Walz.)

110. Bentley, Phyllis. *Inheritance.* London: Gollancz; New York: Macmillan, 1932. Bentley writes of machines and men in the Yorkshire valleys of West Riding in the last century. The Oldroyds are a powerful manufacturing family in the Ire Valley of 1812 Yorkshire, a time when Luddism is rife in West Riding. Old Mr. Oldroyd is murdered and three Luddites are charged and tried in York.

111. _____. *Modern Tragedy.* London; New York: Macmillan, 1934. A textiles mill in West Riding of Yorkshire faces crises from within and without during the post-war economic depression of the mid-twenties throughout Yorkshire. Trade unionists arrange a hunger march and two men responsible for the financial success of the mill fiddle the books to mislead shareholders and are ultimately brought to trial.

112. Berman, Richard. *Hostile Witness.* New York: Avon, 1994. Police arrest an innocent man when a congressman dies of a suspicious heart attack and who had had a previous confrontation with the dead man. Defense attorney David Cohen investigates the congressman's enemies to save his client.

113. _____. *Unjust Death.* New York: Avon, 1995. David Cohen's first client after quitting as a Brooklyn ADA is small-time burglar LeVander Jefferson, but he has a big problem because he is being fingered for the murder of a white woman after an eyewitness sees him breaking into the Gladstone house.

Bernard, Diane, pseud. *See* Levitt, Diane. . . .

114. Bernhardt, William. *Blind Justice.* New York: Ballantine, 1992. Bernhardt debuted in 1992 with *Primary Justice*, an immediate bestseller, written after graduation from the University of Oklahoma's law school. He adds (almost) annually to the *Justice* series, which features trial attorney Ben Kincaid. One other non-Kincaid courtroom novel is noted here: a rite-of-passage novel called *The Code of Buddyhood* in 1992 and bears comparison to Scott Turow's apprenticeship novel *One L.* Bernhardt professes that his writing and legal practice are complementary: "Writing fulfills certain artistic urges that legal practice often does not, and legal practice can be satisfying in an immediate, tangible way that writing is not" (*CA*). One year later, he was voted one of the top 25 young lawyers in the US. In 1997, he was honored as an inductee of the Oklahoma Writers Hall of Fame and is currently director of Tulsa's Arts and Humanities Council. Bernhardt's Kincaid is like Perry Mason in that he is as

much sleuth as lawyer; however, he possesses none of Perry's swagger and is burdened by the triste of the disillusioned good man who sees the law as much an obstacle as a friend. "I enjoyed writing Ben Kincaid from the first day he crawled into my brain," says Bernhardt in a 1998 *Murder on the Internet* interview. However, he adds, "I'm a much better lawyer."

Ben Kincaid leaves corporate law to set up his own practice and reluctantly agrees to defend a friend framed for murder before a judge that he knows despises him.

115. _____. *Cruel Justice.* New York: Ballantine, 1996. Novel number five in the Kincaid series opens with the protagonist's career hanging by a thread that links a decade-old murder at a country club to a grisly string of sex-murders of boys. A feeble-minded caddie is brought to trial ten years after the crime and defended by Ben in a case that blends upper crust society Tulsa with the drug world.

116. _____. *Dark Justice.* New York: Ballantine, 1998. Ben goes to Washington State to escape courtroom burnout and do a book signing promo for his first novel but instead becomes embroiled in a vicious fight between loggers and environmental activists (Green Rage) when a lumberjack is murdered, and the accused is a man who wants Ben as his trial attorney because Kincaid had won an acquittal for him in a homicide case six years earlier. Ben faces tough-as-nails Granville ("Granny") Adams in a courtroom battle.

117. _____. *Deadly Justice.* New York: Ballantine, 1993. Kincaid, in need of money, is hired by a large company as in-house counsel. When one of the firm's lawyers is killed, Kincaid is given a week to exonerate himself or take the rap.

118. _____. *Double Jeopardy.* New York: Ballantine, 1995. Called homage to Hitchcock, this one is about mistaken identity in Dallas that sends an innocent man fleeing the law (a non-Kincaid novel).

119. _____. *Extreme Justice.* New York: Ballantine, 1998. Bored with his life and swearing to quit law practice, Kincaid passes time tickling the ivory at Uncle Earl's Jazz Emporium; then the murder of jazz singer "Cajun Lily" sends him back into arms of justice. The cops finger Ben's friend Earl Bonner for the crime, the owner and one-time lover of the deceased, who once did time for murdering a man whose face was frozen in a rictus grin of death--the same look on Lily's face when she came crashing through the ceiling of his nightclub during the anniversary celebration.

120. _____. *Legal Briefs: Stories by Today's Best Legal Thriller Writers.* New York: Doubleday, 1998. Editor-author Bernhardt's introduction to this collection poses an intriguing question: "If everyone hates lawyers so much,

why are they buying our books?" Bernhardt's "*What We're Here For*" is his contribution to this collection, all of which except Grisham's and Margolin's are previously unpublished. The other 10 other stories include Grif Stockley's "The Divorce," about a husband-wife pair of con artists who attempt to victimize Jake Page in a sex scandal; a badly rhyming anti-Clinton piece called "Poetic Justice" by Steve Martini; "Stairwell Justice" by Jay Brandon (an amusing look at courtroom reality in that most cases are settled before trial); Richard North Patterson contributes "The Client"; Michael A. Kahn's "Cook County Redemption," a comic gem of characterization with a delicious legal comeuppance for the villain; Phillip Margolin's "The Jailhouse Lawyer," in which a lawyer-novelist talks to a radio talk-show host about a defendant who outmaneuvered the legal system; "Voir Dire" is about jury-tampering in a mob trial by Jeremiah Healy; John Grisham's 1994 "The Birthday," and "Roads" by Philip Friedman, an aging lawyer's private reckoning with capital punishment. Lisa Scottoline is the lone woman lawyer-author paying homage to males split between careers and families in the comic "Carrying Concealed," which story rounds out the collection.

121. _____. *The Midnight before Christmas: A Holiday Thriller.* New York: Ballantine, 1998. A child of divorcing parents is kidnapped by the father, and he must be rescued before Christmas Eve.

122. _____. *Naked Justice.* New York: Ballantine, 1997. The first black mayor of Tulsa is Wallace Barrett, a former football hero, is the prime suspect in the murders of his wife and their two daughters. Better than the O. J. Simpson trial knock-off it resembles.

123. _____. *Perfect Justice.* New York: Ballantine, 1993. Bernhardt was inspired by his involvement with Klan Watch, a division of the Southern Poverty Law Center, for the genesis of the plot of Kincaid's fourth appearance, which is also a sequel to *Deadly Justice* and winner of the Oklahoma Book Award. Primarily about racism in the form of hate crimes against Coi Than Thien, a Vietnamese settlement in the Ouchita Mountains of Arkansas, where Ben assumes the defense of white supremacist Donald Vick, member of ASP (Anglo-Saxon Patrol). The plot mixes politics and hate mongering with a surprise ending that disappoints.

124. _____. *Primary Justice.* New York: Ballantine, 1991. Kincaid leaves the DA's office to work for Raven, Tucker & Tubb, a gray-pinstripe law firm in Tulsa but finds corruption in the form of hush money offered to buy him off as in-house counsel for a big corporation embezzling money.

125. _____. *Silent Justice.* New York: Ballantine, 2000. Ben breaks a personal oath to avoid all civil cases--mainly because they are not civil and a poor defendant cannot get justice. In this heartbreaking civil case reminiscent of

the bestseller and true case by Jonathan Harr's *A Civil Action* (Random, 1995) in which families sued a powerful corporation for polluting its town's drinking water. Ben takes on H. P. Blaylock Industrial Machinery Incorporated and its arrogant CEO. He faces ruthless Charlton Colby, top-gun litigator of his one-time employer and a judge who has too much sympathy for big business and too little for the eleven devastated families suing because their children drank toxically contaminated water and died. Bernhardt unfortunately adds a serial-killer subplot.

126. Berry, Carole. *The Letter of the Law.* New York: St. Martin's, 1987. New York: Berkley Prime Crime, 1995. Narrated by Bonnie Indermill, 36-year-old office manager of the New York City law firm of Ely Sneed, Kellogg & Petit about one Friday in which one of the lawyers, Albert Janowski, fails to show for a client meeting. He turns up shot to death in a seedy hotel and the investigation leads to a case of internal blackmail.

127. Besant, Walter [Sir]. *The Orange Girl.* London: Chatto; New York: Dodd, 1899. A little bit of *Candide* in the plotline as a young man of good family is kicked out of his home to make his way in the world with little to protect him except his fiddle and poetic sensibilities; the novel opens in Newgate Gaol with frequent visits to the King's Bench and the infamous prison along the way. An unscrupulous lawyer named Probus plots with one of the youth's relatives to prevent financial ruin to a counting house by having the succession fall to the evil relative, but to circumvent the law of primogeniture, the pair must ruin the youth by making him a patsy for their scheme--or have him hanged at Tyburn Hill. Two more Besants mixing civil or ecclesiastical law with history and romance are *St. Katharine's by the Tower* (London: Chatto, 1892; New York: Harper, 1891), and *For Faith and Freedom* (New York: Harper, 1889), the latter about the succession of the Stuarts (1603-1714) with a pair of chapters in Book 3 devoted to the Bloody Assizes and Judge Jeffreys.

128. _____, and James Rice. *The Chaplain of the Fleet.* London: Chatto, 1900. Besant, wildly popular in his day, was another inheritor of the Walter Scott mantle of historical and romantic adventure, but he had a knack of combining the eighteenth-century picaresque masters like Smollett and Fielding with his lush narratives. Sixteen-year-old Kitty Pleydell is entrusted by her father's will to his dissolute brother, also a man of the cloth except that he proudly bills himself "The Chaplain of the Fleet" among all the so-called Fleet parsons. In the Rules of the Fleet, a district of London sacrosanct from ecclesiastical law which requires that banns be published prior to the marriage ceremony, Doctor Shovel marries anybody and everybody without delay, providing his fee of a single guinea is met (Fleet marriages were stopped by the Marriage Act of 1753. Kitty (a combination of Richardson's Clarissa and Pamela) is coerced by her uncle into marrying a besotted Lord Chudleigh and later nobly offers to release him from what would be an odious obligation.

129. Bessie, Alvah. *Bread and a Stone.* New York: Modern Age, 1941. London: Swan, 1948. Follows a murder case of Ed Sloan, an ordinary working stiff with a family and a past criminal record, who is arrested, indicted, and found guilty of murder for the stick-up murder of a mill operator. Even the wife is perplexed about her husband's mental state unsure whether he might be a psychopathic liar. Intersperses newspaper accounts, legal documents, letters from various people, such as counsel for the defendant to his wife after the verdict and various points of view to uncover the motive for murder and legal justice. Culminates in legal briefs arguing the death-penalty decision versus the evidence for life imprisonment. Interesting.

130. Betti, Ugo. *Corruption in the Hall of Justice* [*Corruzione al Palazzo di Giustizia*]. New York: Vanni, 1961 Ed. and Introd. Vincent Luciani. The premier Italian playwright after Pirandello, Betti invokes the concept of, or the search for, justice in all his plays. He studied law and received his degree in 1914, volunteered at the outbreak of the war and was taken prisoner at the infamous Caporetto retreat. From 1931 on, he served as a judge in Rome's Fascist courts. Although he wrote other than serious drama, it is for his 25 plays he will be known, all of which concern tortured souls and their search for expiation. Like Kafka's character K., his protagonists are obsessed with the problem of justice and human responsibility. This play is acknowledged as his masterpiece; it is about a crime within a courthouse. A tribunal orders an investigation in which retiring Chief Justice Vanan is entreated by his daughter Elena to profess his innocence and name the guilty colleague. The major characters are superbly delineated from the fragile Elena through the nefarious Judge Cust to the wryly-sardonic Judge Croz. A good introduction to Betti is *Three Plays on Justice: Landslide, Struggle till Dawn, The Fugitive* (San Francisco: Chandler, 1964).

131. Bickel, Mary [Dupuy]. *Brassbound.* New York: Burt, 1934. [Rpt. as *The Trial of Linda Stuart*, London: Hamilton, 1935]. Ethelinda Stuart is on trial for murdering her fiancé just before their wedding. Stanley Wilmott, the prosecuting attorney, tries to prove that she loved another man, Scott Barclay.

132. Bier, Jesse. *Trial at Bannock.* New York: Harcourt, 1963. Ex-con Earl Stacey pleads not guilty to murder one, although he admits to shooting Floyd Gehringer in the back six times. Lawyer Ira Hart, who narrates much of the tale to colleague Julius Grubb, must convince a Wyoming jury that his client was kidnapped from his Denver home by Gehringer and feared for his life.

133. Binkley, Anne. *What Shall I Cry?.* New York: Harcourt; London: Gollancz, 1968. Opens on the eighth day of Claudelia Johnstone's trial for the murder of her lover Harry Scythe and ends with her getting 15 years at Tahachapi Woman's State Prison.

134. Bishop, Paul. *Chalk Whispers.* New York: Scribner's, 2000. Bishop is a veteran LA cop-turned-writer, and much like another well-known author from the retired LA ranks, pens police procedurals. A tortured, murdered black call girl is given low priority until the victim's identity establishes her as a prominent child-advocate attorney and daughter of a judge nominated for a seat on the California Supreme Court.

135. Black, David. *The Confession.* (Franchise-Sterling Home Entertainment, 1995). Black's script adapts a 1966 novel (*see* Sol Yurick) and emphasizes the lawyer's, rather than the father's, moral dilemma, although Kingsley gives another standout performance as the aggrieved parent whose son dies of neglect because attending personnel at the hospital where he rushes his dying child see him as another statistic. When the vengeful father goes on a killing spree "to honor his son's memory," Baldwin, an attorney ambitious for the DA's office, is the one assigned to get a not-guilty plea from Fertig; it is he who must square his own conscience in the light of Fertig's admonition to his lawyer: "It is not hard to do the right thing . . . it is hard to know what the right thing is." Dir. David Jones. Perf. Alec Baldwin, Ben Kingsley, Amy Irving.

136. Black, William. *Highland Cousins.* London: Low; New York: Harper, 1894. In Duntroone village, Jess McLean's highland cousin Barbara get legal experience of Scots law when she is accused of shoplifting and is brought before the Pleading Diet in Chapter 42. The diet is the equivalent of a preliminary hearing and an "agent" is the equivalent of a trial lawyer or barrister.

137. Blackmore, R. D. [Richard Doddridge]. *Lorna Doone.* London: Dent; New York: Dutton, 1908. Introd. Ernest Rhys. Blackmore was educated at Exeter College, Oxford, and called to the bar but unable to pursue a legal career because of his health. A legacy enabled him to grow fruit in orchards and write novels. Lorna Doone, subtitled *A Tale of Exmoor*, was his third (1869) and most popular novel. In Oxmoor, Devonshire during the late 17th century, John Ridd, yeoman, loves Lorna Doone of the powerful, rogue clan of Doones, who violate the law, corrupt the king's counselors, and have their way with the farmers, miners, and tradespeople of Exmoor in the shire of Somerset. A series of long-standing grudges-to-be-settled commence with a warrant against one of them.

138. Blackstock, Terri. *Evidence of Mercy.* Grand Rapids, MI: Zondervan, 1995. Blackstock, a former pulp-romance producer for Harlequin and Silhouette, has a legal-thriller series character in Gulf Coast lawyer Lynda Barrett. Her lawyer is often a foil for a conflict that enables Blackstock to profess her Christian message. The great Flannery O'Connor did this to no one's dismay, but Blackstock manufactures transparent plots, simple characters, and stilted

dialogue to encumber the message. Barrett of St. Clair, Florida takes rich, arrogant Jake Stevens for a test flight in her Piper, a luxury she can no longer afford. But someone has sabotaged the plane, nearly killing them both.

139. _____. *Ulterior Motives.* Grand Rapids, MI: Zondervan, 1996. Barrett has a minor role here as the lawyer for a scorned woman's ex-husband, accused of murdering his former employer. Sharon Robinson takes up her ex's cause, shelters his hostile wife and children in her own home while Detective Tony Banks handles the sleuthing and becomes enamored of the noble soul of the former Mrs. Robinson. Two others where law and morality clash are *Justifiable Means* (Zondervan, 1996) about Melissa Nelson, a rape victim, and her psychopathic stalker; and *Newpointe 911* (Zondervan, 1998), the second book of that title about Louisiana firefighters.

Blake, Nicholas. *See* Day Lewis, C[ecil]. . . .

140. Blaustein, Albert P., ed. *Fiction Goes to Court.* New York: Holt, 1954. Blaustein's collection of eighteen stories is dated, the majority fall between the period of the wars in publication dates, but there are some comic gems here. Blaustein's editorial principle of selection is to allow some of the top-ranked Anglo-American legal scholars, lawyers, trial attorneys, and politicians to choose their favorite stories about the law. The result is a mix of classic tales, and "modern" narratives. Vintage tales from Arthur Train, Irvin S. Cobb, and Melville Davisson Post balance literary heavyweights like Faulkner and John Galsworthy. Erle Stanley Gardner (both a selector and the selectee of Hollywood celebrity attorney Jerry Geisler) rounds out the collection with "The Case of the Irate Witness." The classic Stephen Vincent Benét tale "The Devil and Daniel Webster" is the choice of playwright Elmer Rice, whose greatest plays of the twenties (*The Adding Machine* (1923) and *Street Scene* (1929)) overshadow three of his own dramatic works about law: *Counsellor-at-Law*, *On Trial*, and *For the Defense*. Another who abandoned the law for the arts and earned a Pulitzer in his field is librettist Oscar Hammerstein II (Marc Connelly's "Coroner's Inquest"). Other selectors include a Who's Who of American post-WW II American politics: Sen. Estes Kefauver (Irwin Shaw's "Triumph of Justice"), Speaker Sam Rayburn (Richard Harding Davis' "A Wasted Day"), Adlai Stevenson (choosing a brief comic story "The Negotiable Cow" from A. P. Herbert's collection *The Uncommon Law*); then-Vice President Richard Nixon chose Train's comic tale "The Dog Andrew"). Also included: Supreme Court Associate Justice Tom C. Clark (Ruel McDaniel's "Coroner De Luxe"), Chief Justice Fred Vinson, Harvard legal patriarch Samuel Williston, and William J. ("Wild Bill") Donovan of the CIA's precursor, the OSS (James Reid Parker's "All the Little Jokers"). The British are also represented by A. A. Milne ("The Barrister," selected by John J. McCloy) and by Lord High Chancellor Gavin Turnbull Simonds ("The Blushing Beginner and the Bearded Juryman" by "O," pseudonym of Theo Mathew).

141. Blum, Bill. *The Face of Justice.* New York: Onyx, 1998. Blum was co-counsel in two landmark death-penalty appeals in California (six total as counsel of record) and is currently an administrative law judge in Southern California. Defense attorney David Nova's former client Randy Sturgis, a sociopath who might have gotten the death penalty, has just been released on a technicality. He kidnaps a federal judge and taunts Nova into finding him.

142. _____. *The Last Appeal.* New York: Onyx, 1997. Five years earlier defense attorney Peter Harrigan lost his family in a car accident during the first death-row appeal for double-murder defendant Harold Ashbourne. Now it is the last appeal before his client goes to the gas chamber when a surprise witness turns up who might hold proof of his client's innocence. Harrigan and Jozie Guzman attempt to retrace his client's primary alibi, Henry Debray, and other members of the radical Saviours environmental group on the night of the murders.

143. _____. *Prejudicial Error.* New York: Dutton, 1995. Blum's skill is evident from the first few pages of this first novel: an ironic cast of mind that enables him to turn the seemingly buffoonish character into a man that most readers empathize with easily, a concise style that paints in the Los Angeles urban milieu and its courtroom nucleus of characters in sharp, pithy strokes. Not all critics agree: Phil Crome, writing for the 20 May 1966 *Mystery Zone Review Page* on the Internet calls it all stereotype strung together with time-honored set pieces: "a transparent plot, two-dimensional characters, BORING legal procedure . . ."

John Solomon, once the hotshot of the Major Trials Division for the Los Angeles District Attorney's Office, has fallen on hard times; he is chasing one hundred dollar fees to evict tenants and made himself a local joke among the legal circuit for his liquid lunches. But now he has a chance to redeem himself because politically ambitious Howard Ainsworth, former rival and now chief prosecutor, has made a backroom deal to get him appointed defending counsel for one Juan Thomas, a lowlife gangbanger and alleged shooter of a vice cop outside the notorious Mustang Club. After a humiliating prelim (Solomon has been picked to fail), he learns how far he has fallen. Not the least of his discomfiture is owing to his sudden encounter with one of the prosecution's witnesses: Officer Mary Delgado, the woman with whom he had an affair two years earlier that cost him his career. What for Solomon begins as an opportunity to pick up a county paycheck becomes an obsession as he lifts the lid on a ring of cocaine, corrupt cops and kickbacks that stretches from a sleazy strip joint to the halls of justice.

144. Bohjalian, Chris. *Midwives.* New York: Harmony, 1997. In 1981 Reddington, Vermont, a midwife is arrested and tried for murder when she saves a baby during an ice storm. Later, her assistant claims the mother was alive

when the baby was cut out during the Cesarean.

145. Bok, Curtis. *Backbone of the Herring.* New York: Knopf, 1941. Born in Wyncote, Pennsylvania in 1897, Bok withdrew from Williams College in 1917 to enlist. After the war, he returned to school, graduating from the University of Virginia Law School. In 1936 he became Judge of the Orphans Court of Philadelphia and in 1937 became President Judge of the Court of Common Pleas No. 6. More like a novel in structure, this one spends much time in the Judge's courtroom as well as away with scenic dialogue and a rounded portrait of the Judge's family life. In *Booker v. Booker,* a husband charges a wife with desertion and the Judge himself takes her deposition from the witness stand.

146. _____. *I, Too, Nicodemus.* New York: Knopf, 1946. The books of Judge Bok are not exactly novels, although case histories are always prominent. But these invariably act as plot devices for the judge to hang introspections about law and justice, personal philosophizing, moral or legal quibbles, and various kinds of memorabilia filtered through the experiences of Judge Ulen, a composite figure described here as "a judge who had no great scholarship or dignity or wit, but a concern to be kind and patient" (4).

147. _____. *Star Wormwood.* New York: Knopf, 1959. This book adds the usual tatterdemalion of musings but the tone is far weightier in Judge Ulen's court this time. The trial features a grisly murder by a mentally unstable Roger Haike, rapist-murderer of a sexually precocious teen, burns the body in a furnace and eats a bit of the cooked arm through sheer aberrant impulse.

148. Böll, Heinrich. *End of a Mission.* New York: McGraw, 1986. Trans. Leila Vennewitz [*Ende einer Dienstfahrt,* Köln-Berlin: Kiepenheur, 1966]. Böll, like laureate Günter Grass, is one of the best European post-moderns. His prose is dryly laconic yet with a compelling cumulative power. *Billiards at Half-Past Nine* and *Clown* are among his most popular works, although the latter is markedly existentialist in thesis and scope; neither concerns his usual subject--the recovery of Germany from the Nazi debacle. (His appraisal of the *Wirtschaftswunder* (Germany's "economic miracle") is, according to critic Seymour-Smith, acute and penetrating (66). This novel concerns a father-son pair of cabinetmakers from a small village. Johann and Georg Gruhl are apprehended watching a jeep burn from a punctured gas tank and charged with property damage and public mischief in the Birglar County court of Judge Dr. Alois Stollfus. The conviction and light sentence are noted in the first few pages, but what is not revealed is motivation for the crime from a host of character and expert witnesses, public statements, newspaper accounts and the recorded observations of dozens of characters.

149. Bonnet, Theodore. *Dutch.* Garden City, NY: Doubleday, 1955.

London: Allen, 1956. A 400+ page rambling tale of various locals who cluster about a tavern near San Francisco in which the owner has discovered he has an original Rembrandt on the wall. One of the characters is a boozy lawyer; another is the bar owner's daughter witnesses a robbery and cop killing in which an Hispanic youth named Raymond Dirigo is apprehended, indicted, tried, and executed in a pair of chapters.

150. Borden, Mary. *Action for Slander.* New York: London: Harper, 1937. In private life Mary Borden (Mary Turner Spears) was Lady Spears, wife of Major General Sir Edward Spears, who brought de Gaulle out of Nazi-occupied France in 1940. She herself was awarded the Croix de Guerre and Legion of Honor from France for wartime services. The *London Times* called her novels "[i]ntelligent, resourceful, accomplished"; a socialite, she narrowed her novels to that strata. Her pseudonym was Bridget MacLagan.

QC Sir Quentin Jessops addresses the jury thusly in the opening pages: "Did Major Daviot cheat at poker on Saturday evening the 26th of October, 1929, in the country house of Sir Bernard Roper?" (5). The answer to this nonburning question will be found almost 300 pages later. The film (London, 1937) adapted from her novel, however, assembled a stellar cast for its time. Dir. Tim Whelan. Writ. Ian Dalrymple. Perf. Clive Brook, Ann Todd, Margaretta Scott, Arthur Margetson, and Ronald Squire.

151. _____. *You, the Jury.* New York; London: Longman, 1952 [British title: *Martin Merriedew*]. A brother and sister from the village of Crabbe form a close friendship with an iconoclastic lad from the same village named Martin Merriedew. Years later, he is tried for treason because, as a male nurse in the Italian campaign in Libya (enlisted as a conscientious objector), he attempted to persuade wounded German and English soldiers to quit fighting.

152. Borgenicht, Miriam. *Undue Influence.* New York: St. Martin's, 1989; Toronto: Worldwide, 1990. Lydia Ness works for a high-powered attorney because she wants the good life that a Legal Aid lawyer cannot have. Her boss saddles her with a high-profile rape case in which young Pamela Howells is a rape-murder victim and her new client, she believes, is innocent with an airtight alibi. So why does she feel like the lawyer bamboozled by her own client?

153. Borneman, Ernest. Cameron McCabe, pseud. *The Face on the Cutting Room Floor.* London: Gollancz, 1937. New York: Gregg, 1981. Its publishing history is more interesting than its tale of double-cross and murder. Told in first-person *noir* style, the putative author, Cameron McCabe, disappears on page 248 before the book's conclusion, having confessed to the murder of a girl found lying in her own blood on the floor of a studio editing ("cutting") room. A multi-page sequence is devoted to McCabe's *pro se* defense, each point articulating why he could not have committed the crime. A long epilogue by A. B. C. Müller, acquaintance of the narrator, gives the reader a literary exegesis of

McCabe's ms., serving as his epitaph as well as discoursing on Hemingway, James Cain and Joyce and full of quotations, all of which are pedantically sourced in a bibliography. The book, apparently, would not go away, so the author was tracked down by Julian Symons after the Gollancz edition of 1974 as being one Ernest Wilhelm Julius Bornemann, a well-published (but not, as noted, in mystery fiction) Austrian professor from Salzburg University.

154. Botein, Bernard. *The Prosecutor.* New York: Simon, 1956. As a New York State prosecutor, Botein had a distinguished record as an investigator and prosecutor during the 1930s. He has authored texts on trial law and courtroom procedure: *Trial Judge* (New York: Simon, 1952) and *The Trial of the Future* (with Murray A. Gordon, New York: Cornerstone: 1965). Edgar Bailey is a ruthless young Assistant DA, who uses his father's connections to the DA's office to further his career. Mainly, the novel is less about the rise and fall of an ambitious prosecutor than it is Justice Botein's exposé of the dangerous intertwining of democratic processes within a big-city DA's office and its politics of venality and greed.

155. Boulle, Pierre. *Face of a Hero.* New York: Vanguard, 1956. Trans. Xan Fielding. Boulle's *Bridge over the River Kwai* earned him international popularity. This one is about a Provençal public prosecutor, Jean Berthier, who witnesses the accidental drowning death of a village girl in the River Rhone on an outing with his girlfriend. Public pressure mounts to convict a local scapegrace for what is believed to be her murder. To keep silent would require him to seek the death penalty for the despised youth. Another legal thriller by Boulle in an American translation: *The Executioner* (New York: Vanguard, 1961) in which a traveler in a Chinese city is told a bizarre tale of a court executioner named Chong who poisons seven condemned men in the moments before he cuts off their heads and is himself tried and sentenced to death.

Bowen, Marjorie, pseud. *See* Long, Gabrielle Margaret Vere Campbell.

156. Bowen-Judd, Sara. Mary Challis, pseud. *Burden of Proof.* New York; Toronto, Worldwide, 1982. This is the first of her 4-book series-featuring attorney Jeremy Locke.

157. _____. *Crimes Past.* New York; Toronto: Worldwide, 1980. A Jeremy Locke mystery.

158. _____. *And Shame the Devil.* London: Collins, 1967. New York: Holt, 1972. Writing under her most famous *nom de plume* Sara Woods, Bowen-Judd produced 48 novels (each with a Shakespearean title) featuring suave barrister Antony Maitland, war-wounded veteran with an Intelligence background. She used her experience in a solicitor's office and practiced her craft almost exclusively from the Christie-Sayers side of the fence with aplomb

and skill to make the formula work time and time again. Thoroughly English, she wrote her mysteries from her residence in Nova Scotia (critics are right to suggest that London remains a vague city for that reason). Gillian Rodgerson quotes her in saying, "I write crime novels with a legal background because the law has always interested me" (qtd. in *Crime and Mystery* Writers 1105). Although Maitland's physical heroics are generally compacted into a furiously implausible five minutes toward the end, there are suspenseful moments when the villains turn their sights on the sleuthing Maitland creeping up on them with guile and deductive skills, although it is all a bit too déclassé for frumpish Uncle Nicholas. Even though John Mortimer's better-known barrister has surpassed Antony in fame in recent times, for many readers, Antony Maitland, his wife Jenny, and uncle (Sir Nicholas Harding) are the British equivalent of a certain law office in Los Angeles penned by Erle Stanley Gardner. Their weaknesses are strikingly similar: Mason and his entourage have the same conversations in book after book; we do not know what they think. Antony's small circle is as unrevealing of inner depths of characterization and despite Woods' intimating at psychological turmoil, we never feel that Maitland is capable of any kind of emotional response. His wife is pure cardboard. Woods used the Margaret Leek byline to produce an early 1980's 3-book series featuring Stephen Marryat, another English attorney.

Maitland makes the first of several visits over many novels to the grim Yorkshire industrial town of Arkenshaw. His brief requires defending two police officers, Sgt. Fred Duckett and Constable James Ryder, accused of wrongful arrest by two Pakistani immigrants, one a journalist and the other a med student, who had just been acquitted of burglary.

159. _____. *Away with Them to Prison.* London: Macmillan; New York: St. Martin's, 1985. Antony and Uncle Nicholas agree to defend two salesmen accused of murdering a protection-racket victim in North London. The men accuse two Scotland Yard officers of demanding extortion money.

160. _____. *The Bloody Book of Law.* London: Macmillan; New York: St. Martin's, 1984. A journalist is accused of burgling the jewels of family friend Denise Thurlow. After successfully defending the case, Maitland is afterward suspected by Superintendent Briggs of suborning perjury--and then murdering his own client.

161. _____. *Bloody Instructions.* London: Collins; New York: Harper, 1962. The first novel in the Maitland series has Antony going to the office of an elderly solicitor and finding the inoffensive old gentleman murdered. The police believe a hotheaded actor named Joseph Dowling did it. Sir Nicholas is enlisted as defense counsel with Antony assigned the job of tracking down the real killer. The courtroom duel between the two seasoned veterans is Woods at her best.

162. _____. *Cry Guilty.* New York: St. Martin's, 1981. Maitland acts as

Assisting Prosecuting Counsel, side by side with courtroom foe Bruce Halloran against allies Kevin O'Brien and Derek Stringer, so that he can cross-examine three defense witnesses, one of whom might have killed Alan Kirby, a client who had been arrested on a charge of stealing a Rubens. Antony is searching for the identity of the ringleader of a gang of art thieves in this sequel to the non-courtroom *Weep for Her* (1980). In the case of Louise Chorley, an adulterous wife who has admitted to shooting her husband David, Antony finds a connection to the art thieves he has been seeking.

163. _____. *Dearest Enemy.* London: Macmillan; New York: St. Martin's, 1981. Leonard Buckley and wife Victoria are beloved on the London stage as the elderly "Perfect Couple"; Leonard is convinced Victoria is trying to kill him. Then on-stage during the opening-night performance of *Done in by Daggers*, Victoria is murdered. Antony defends the husband.

164. _____. *Done to Death.* London: Macmillan, 1974; New York: Holt, 1975. Jenny is visiting crime writer Emma Anstey in the Yorkshire village of Burton Cecil as a ruse to placate Chris Conway, fearful his old aunt is going to commit suicide but afraid to confront her directly with the letter that he is convinced was typed on her typewriter. While sleuthing, she uncovers shocking events in the quiet town that include suicide, counterfeiting, and vicious accusations from poison pen letters, and is herself in danger when she gets too close to the truth behind a blackmail and forgery scheme.

165. _____. *Enter a Gentlewoman.* London: Macmillan, 1982; New York: St. Martin's, 1982. Antony and his uncle are set to become courtroom adversaries in a divorce action. Beautiful, sexy Elizabeth Coke seeks a divorce from her respectable solicitor husband, alleging "exceptional depravity" against him in a letter to friend Primrose Ross in which she claims to be coerced into having sex with another man while her husband witnesses the action (based on the Adelaide Bartlett case of a husband's murder in a love triangle in which the older husband approved the cuckoldry). Antony represents husband Edward in a counter suit libel action against his wife. Two murders occur before closing arguments, including Elizabeth's. Despite the steamy possibilities, a routine Woods novel.

166. _____. *Enter the Corpse.* New York: Holt, 1973; London: Macmillan, 1973. Nearly eighty, the old reprobate godfather of Roger Farrell is released from prison. Maitland had once saved Farrell's life by sinking the *Savannah*, which "Uncle" Hubert had been using stolen goods as ballast for smuggling abroad. Maitland finds himself in the middle of the hunt for the hidden gold bullion he is rumored to have squirreled away.

167. _____. *Exit Murderer.* London: Macmillan; New York: St. Martin's, 1978. Antony goes to Chedcombe to work on a case with Vera Langhorne, who

will accept Sir Nicholas' proposal at the end of the novel. A man Antony had encountered briefly six years before in a diamond-smuggling case brings him back to Northdean when diamond smuggling erupts there again.

168. _____. *The Ghost of an Idea.* London: Toronto: Worldwide, 1981. The third of four Jeremy Locke novels.

169. _____. *An Improbable Fiction.* London: Collins, 1970. New York: Holt, 1971. Lynn Edison, the sister of a deceased actress whose death the coroner called a sleeping-pill suicide, uses a weekly program to defame the character of celebrity Paul Granville by accusing him of murder on national television. He sues for libel, and Antony defends her, and as the author's formulaic fiction goes, ends up murdered with his accuser the prime suspect. The improbable in Woods' fiction is not of course in the inevitability of the murderer being exposed, least-likely suspect or no, but invariably it is in the killer confronting Maitland, gun in hand, and explaining the crime and its motives like the nemesis in a James Bond novel who laboriously explains the reasons why Bond must die.

170. _____. *The Healthy Grave.* Toronto: Worldwide, 1980. A Stephen Marryat novel.

171. _____. *The Law's Delay.* London: Macmillan; New York: St. Martin's, 1977. Two murders intertwine when Ellen Gray's father is convicted of murdering his wife and lover after returning from the war. The daughter is convinced he was innocent because of a poem inscribed by her mother on the fly-leaf in Palgrave's *Golden Treasury*, yet she is herself found with a handgun in the chambers of murdered stockbroker John Wilcox, the key prosecution witness in her father's trial twenty years before. Maitland, skeptical, gets her acquitted in the first half of the novel, then seeks the killer's identity in the second half.

172. _____. *Let's Choose Executors.* London: Collins, 1966. New York: Harper, 1967. Vera Langhorne makes her series debut as a practicing barrister-at-law in the West Midland town of Chedcombe; she brings Antony into the defense of solicitor's clerk Fran Gifford, prime suspect in the poisoning death of elderly Alice Randall, who had changed her will to favor Gifford shortly before her death.

173. _____. *The Lie Direct.* London: Macmillan; New York: St. Martin's, 1983. John Ryder is charged under the Official Secrets Act (and incidentally accused of bigamy) with the passage of state secrets to a Soviet agent, Dr. Boris Gollnow, who later defects and exposes Ryder. Ryder claims he was set up; then, during the trial his wife is arrested for the murder of Winifred Paull, wife number two. Maitland's climactic confrontation with one witness is less like a

cross-examination, says Jon Breen, than a "conversation about the evidence in the case" (200). He further notes that an unusual Maitland novel is the 1983 *Call Back Yesterday* about reincarnation and no courtroom scenes.

174. _____. *Murder's Out of Tune.* London: Macmillan; New York: St. Martin's, 1984. Maitland is back in provincial Arkenshaw defending local actor Richard Willard, accused of hiring someone to kill his estranged wife.

175. _____. *Naked Villainy.* London: Macmillan, 1986; New York: St. Martin's, 1987. London: Macmillan; New York: St. Martin's, 1987; Boston: Hall, 1988.

176. _____. *An Obscure Grave.* London: Macmillan; New York: St. Martin's, 1985. Antony is entreated to defend a young man from Chedcombe, Oliver Linwood, accused of suffocating a two-week-old infant. The investigation leads him to a connection among three dead babies from this small village.

177. _____. *Past Praying For.* London: Collins; New York: Harper, 1968. It opens in the Old Bailey in 1957. Maitland is Bruce Halloran's junior in the murder prosecution of Camilla Barnard, accused of the shotgun killing of her husband, Richard. Cut to 1965: Barnard is now accused of the arsenic poisoning of second husband Oliver, the cousin of the first. Harding defends at Northdean Assize Court with Vera Langhorne (subsequently Lady Harding) as his junior.

178. _____. *Proceed to Judgement.* London: Macmillan; New York: St. Martin's, 1979. Woods' most familiar opening: Antony and Jenny at home listening to a barrister entice him into a seemingly hopeless case. This time it is Kevin O'Brien, QC, with a story about a pair of alleged lovers charged with murdering the woman's husband by replacing his insulin with morphine. Kate Johnstone is charged along with family physician Dr. James Collingwood with the murder of her husband Douglas. Jon Breen aptly calls it a "Perry Mason written by C. P. Snow" (198). This one was published in an omnibus volume edited by Walter J. Black along with novels by William Haggard and Hugh Pentecost (Roslyn, NY: Detective Book Club, 1980).

179. _____. *Serpent's Tooth.* London: Collins, 1971. New York: Holt, 1973. Maitland defends 17-year-old Joe Hartley of Arkenshaw village, one of 13 foster children of Alfred and Agnes Baker. An office boy employed by solicitor Chris Conway's firm, he does not deny clubbing his foster father to death with a poker, nor does anyone seriously doubt that he did it. Breen labels this anomaly a whydunit instead of a whodunit (196).

180. _____. *A Show of Violence.* London: Macmillan; New York:

McKay, 1975. Antony returns to the Yorkshire city of Arkenshaw, where he is briefed by solicitor Chris Conway in the defense of a 13-year-old runaway named Tommy Smith, accused of stealing three Holbein miniatures and then of beating Alfred Neale to death. Neale had taken the boy in and discovered the Holbeins under Smith's mattress.

181. _____. *Tarry and Be Hanged.* London: Collins, 1969. New York: Holt, 1971. Maitland had gotten Dr. Henry Langton acquitted when he was accused of murdering his wife Ruth and burying her in his garden. Over a year later, another body is dug up in a clump of the doctor's favorite shrubbery, and this woman has also been garrotted with a Venetian-blind cord. Antony's sleuthing exposes a bizarre serial-murder scheme.

182. _____. *They Love Not Poison.* London: Macmillan; New York: Holt, 1972. Also Yorkshire-based, *They Love Not Poison* is about witchcraft and set in 1947 and thus a prequel to the rest of the series, Antony not yet become a barrister. ("One of Woods' best novels," opines Breen, "although it is without courtroom action" (195)).

183. _____. *They Stay for Death.* New York: St. Martin's, 1980. Maitland makes another sortie to Chedcombe village; this time at the behest of his aunt, who informs him of the mysterious circumstance of three elderly, well-off patients of the Restawhile Hotel all dying close together. Village gossips have wagged tongues before, Maitland knows, but this time there is reason to suspect: a fourth patient dies while he is on the scene investigating, and the post mortem concludes it to be homicide, not natural causes.

184. _____. *A Thief or Two.* London: Macmillan; New York: St. Martin's, 1977. Malcolm Harte is a young jeweler's assistant accused of stealing gems and murdering employer George DeLisle. Woods adopts a boilerplate "cozy" plot in featuring a crime scene consisting of a weekend house party complete with rich guests, a butler, and a corpse.

185. _____. *This Little Measure.* London: Collins, 1964. Roddy Gaskell is grandson of shipping magnate Roderick Gaskell, "The Pirate King." A codicil to old Roderick's will bequeaths to son Andrew "the problem of the Velasquez," which painting appears to be stolen, and when the father of Roddy dies from ingesting an exotic poison from Nepal, Roddy--back from a trip there--is accused. Sir Nicholas Harding defends in this one while Antony sleuths, and turns up critical forensic evidence to confront the killer on the witness stand in true Perry-Mason style.

186. _____. *Though I Know She Lies.* London: Collins, 1965. New York: Holt, 1972. Sir Nicholas defends Barbara Wentworth, accused of poisoning her sister. Maitland enters his uncle's case as consulting detective rather than

barrister.

187. _____. *Trusted Like the Fox.* London: Collins, 1964. New York: Harper, 1965. A photographer is tried in 1962 for alleged treason committed twenty years before while working under the name Guy Harland as a famed biologist's assistant. His treachery effected a deadly biological experiment carried out by the SS on a Polish city's water supply. Maitland defends, in his first case since taking silk. Breen praises lavishly: "This is one of the most extensive trials in Woods' novels, with much detailed testimony and shifting points of view, and one of her very best" (194).

188. _____. *A Very Good Hater.* Toronto: Worldwide, 1981. The final of the 4-book series featuring London barrister Jeremy Locke.

189. _____. *Villains by Necessity.* London: Macmillan; New York: St. Martin's, 1982. Antony defends a shopkeeper and supposedly-reformed felon accused of burglary. The client claims he returned to old habits to foil a protection racket. Arnold's climactic trial follows the murder of a tenant of the house.

190. _____. *Yet She Must Die.* London: Macmillan, 1973. New York: Holt, 1974. Jeremy Skelton, a writer of mysteries, stands accused of strangling his wife Lydia in circumstances that seem parallel to the Julia Wallace case (a nylon scarf), which case Skelton was researching for his next book. Maitland, summoned to Chedcombe by barrister Vera Langhorne, does the sleuthing while Uncle Nicholas defends in court.

A Stephen Marryat tale: *Voice of the Past* (Margaret Leek, pseud., Toronto: Worldwide, 1981). She also uses the Leek pseudonym for *We Must Have a Trial* (Worldwide, 1980).

Other Woods' novels published by Macmillan of London are noted by date only with US (or other) publishers included with years in parentheses:

Call Back Yesterday (1982; St. Martin's, 1983); *The Case Is Altered* (1967; Harper, 1967); *Defy the Devil* (1984; St. Martin's, 1984); *Enter Certain Murderers* (London: Collins, 1966); *Error of the Moon* (1963; Avon, 1986), *Knavish Crows* (Toronto: Worldwide, 1981, 1971); *Knives Have Edges* (London: Collins, 1986; Holt, 1968), *Malice Domestic* (Avon, 1986, 1962); *Most Deadly Hate* (1986; St. Martin's, 1986), *Most Grievous Murder* (St. Martin's, 1982); *My Life Is Done* (1976; St. Martin's, 1976); *Nor Live So Long* (St. Martin's, 1986; Boston: Hall, 1987); *Put Out the Light* (1985; St. Martin's, 1985); *The Taste of Fears* (London: Collins, 1963; rpt. as *The Third Encounter*, New York: Harper, 1963), *This Fatal Writ* (1979; St. Martin's, 1979), *Weep for Her* (1980; St. Martin's, 1980); *Where Should He Die?* (St. Martin's, 1983); *Where There's a Will*, by Anne Burton, pseud. (Toronto: Worldwide, 1980), and *The Windy Side of the Law* (1965; Harper, 1965).

191. Bramble, Forbes. *The Strange Case of Deacon Brodie.* London: Hamilton, 1975. New York: Coward, 1976. Deacon Brodie was the eighteenth-century Scotsman and gentleman-thief that Stevenson used for his classic portrait of the war between good and evil in the soul. Not a medico but a cabinetmaker, William Brodie allegedly got to try out his own trap-door-operated gallows after his crime spree ended in a brief trial and confinement in Tolbooth prison. Bramble is a London- educated American and author of plays performed at London University.

Brand, Christianna, pseud. *See* Lewis, Mary Christianna Milne. . . .

192. Brandon, Jay R[obert]. *Afterimage.* New York: Pocket, 2000. Native Texan and San Antonio author Brandon is one of many lawyers-turned-writers; however, the difference between him and the others is that he began both careers simultaneously. He told an interviewer for *CA* that he had despaired of a writing career and so entered law school (he has a master's in creative writing from Johns Hopkins). While at the University of Houston (J. D., 1985), he published his first novel within the month of being admitted to the bar. *Fade the Heat*, in 1990, introduced his series character San Antonio DA Mark Blackwell, but he had already begun his writing career with suspense thrillers, such as *Tripwire* (Bantam, 1987). He practiced law out of the San Antonio DA's office and was a staff attorney at the Court of Appeals. His practice includes family and criminal law. He left a cyberspace note on *Amazon.com* to say that he picked up Chris Sinclair and his lover Dr. Anne Greenwald right after *Angel of Death* because he enjoyed their characters and wanted to delve into their relationship immediately (he is currently working on a third book about the pair, one that explores a mystery from Anne's past).

Sinclair recognizes the forensically reconstructed face of his former wild college lover in the countenance of a 14-year-old murder victim, found in a shallow grave outside San Antonio. He finds the girl's mother, Jean, but there is something wrong--namely, she did not report her daughter missing, and she seems to be involved in her murder, the prime suspect being one Raleigh Pentell, a corrupter of youth and drug supplier to a band of aimless, thieving teens, including Clarissa, Jean's older daughter, now missing.

193. _____. *Angel of Death.* New York: Forge, 1998. Sinclair believes an African-American community leader committed a double homicide, and he uses a legal loophole to get a conviction. Malachi Reese, however, has a strike force of fanatics to get revenge against Sinclair for putting him on death row; it starts with the killing of Sinclair's protege in the DA's Office. Reviewer Dick Adler notes: "You may not like either Sinclair or Reese very much at the end, but you'll come away understanding why the law can go only so far in bringing people together."

194. _____. *Defiance County.* New York: Pocket, 1996. Galilee, TX, is

just south of metropolitan Houston, but Kelsey Thatch, a young assistant DA from Austin, is brought in as special prosecutor because the local DA has family ties in Galilee's sensational double-murder-kidnaping case involving the town's leading family. Lorrie Blystone and her husband have been murdered and their infant daughter taken right out of her crib. Alice Beaumont, owner of the town's one successful business, wants Billy Fletcher, her own factory manager and prime suspect, brought to trial.

195. _____. *Fade the Heat.* New York: Pocket, 1990. Blackwell confronts a professional and personal nightmare when his son is accused of rape in this Edgar-nominated novel.

196. _____. *Local Rules.* New York: Pocket, 1995. Lackluster plotting mars this one in which San Antonio lawyer Jordan Marshall is coerced by a small-town judge into acting as attorney at a hearing for a local youth, young Wayne Orkney, charged with the attempted murder of his best friend Kevin. What Jordan does not know is that the entire town wants to see the boy convicted because he is also suspected in the battering death of Jenny Fecklewhite, the town's darling.

197. _____. *Loose among the Lambs.* New York: Pocket, 1993. His sixth novel has DA Mark Blackwell running for re-election while prosecuting a highly-regarded legal colleague in a sordid child-molestation case.

198. _____. *Rules of Evidence.* New York: Pocket, 1992. Black lawyer Raymond Boudro routinely defends black clients, cynically plea-bargaining them through the justice system when he locks horns in the courtroom with a white detective named Stennet in a case of racial profiling involving a black client in the crime-heavy east side of San Antonio. Soon, however, he finds himself taking on the white detective as a client when a black named Gordon Frazier is found beaten to death in an east-side alley. When a witness at the station house points to the vice cop at his desk as the man he saw beating a black man where the body was found, deceives discover Stennet's prints on the gun located near the victim's body.

199. Breen, Jon L., introd. *The Year's 25 Finest Crime and Mystery Stories.* 5th annual ed. Ed. Staff of *Mystery Scene*. New York: Carroll, 1996. Breen (*Novel Verdicts*) summarizes the year's notable achievements in mystery fiction during 1994-95. Selections favor *noir*ish themes and styles as well as women authors. Grittier selections by Scotsman Ian Rankin, Britisher Susan B. Kelly and that outstanding British espionage-fiction author Julian Rathbone ("Of Mice, Men and Two Women") are singularly. Old (American) pros like William F. Nolan and Edward D. Hoch ("The Hudson Chain") are included with newcomers on both sides of the water. One selection, "The Judge's Boy," by Jean B. Cooper, deserves mention here as an award-winning legal tale about a

corrupt old judge on the Carolina coast and his "boy," Ray Ford, also a lawyer and beholden to the old man. The judge asks Ray to retrieve his black lover, Tablue James, from a nearby island and the $200,000 she stole from him.

200. Brennan, John N[eedham]. Haggard. John Welcome, pseud., ed. *Best Legal Stories.* London: Faber, 1962 Welcome's edition includes a few classics. Agatha Christie's "The Witness for the Prosecution" and Louis Auchincloss' "The Great World of Timothy Colt" [sic] mixed with Dickens' "Bardell v. Pickwick," Maupassant's "A Fair Exchange," John Galsworthy's "The Juryman," and Henry Cecil's "Painswick v. Gloster." Welcome's modern selections include the great Irishman Frank O'Connor's farcical "Legal Aid," Somerset Maugham's "The Happy Couple," featuring an irascible judge and Michael Gilbert's solicitor-forger in "Mr. Portway's Practice." The reader will find two less-known stories by Robert D. Q. Henrique's court-martial tale ("No Arms No Armour") and E. Œ. Somerville and Martin Ross' comically poignant "An Irish Problem" about a pair of neighbors in litigation over a sheep. Cyril Hare's "Murderer's Luck," the editor claims, is rescued from its magazine obscurity. (Hare is the pseudonym of Alfred A. G. Clark.)

201. _____. *Go for Broke.* London: Faber; New York: Walker, 1972. The Oxford graduate, war veteran, solicitor in a Wexford, Ireland firm, and citizen of the world turns his passions for gambling, steeple chasing and world travel to use in this Flemingesque spy novel in which series spy Richard Graham--*bon vivant* and devotee of fox hunting, races, and cardplaying like his creator--sees a solicitor to file a slander suit in response to a charge of cheating at cards by oafish villain Eric Vaughan. There is a brief courtroom scene in the denouement. Welcome also authored 20 books, evenly split between nonseries novels and nonfiction, including *Cheating at Cards: The Cases in Court* (1963).

202. Breslin, Catherine. *Unholy Child.* New York: Dial, 1979. London: Sphere, 1981. Self-described as an "explosively sensational story of law, medicine, religion, and sex," a pregnant nun gives birth and is later indicted for murdering her infant, found in a waste basket with the nun's panties stuffed in its mouth. The other female lead is Meg Gavin, a tough Twin Cities reporter who fascinated with Sister Angela Flynn and her mental state. The trial sequence comes late (page 430) but is effective.

203. Brill, Stephen. *Late Last Night.* (Screenland/Scanbox Asia Pacific-Danmark, n. d.) Released in 1999, this farce-comedy is piffle with an old plot. A staid family man loses all when his wife kicks him out, so he goes on a night of wicked fun escorted by a mentor familiar with Hollywood's underbelly. Emilio Estevez plays the Century-City entertainment lawyer, Steven Weber is the companion. Brill wrote and directed.

204. Brooks, Vivian Collin. Osmington Mills, pseud. *Trial by Ordeal.*

London: Bles; New York: Roy, 1961. Special Branch Detective Baker probes further into an arson-murder after the defendant, a previously convicted arsonist, pleads not guilty. An interesting point of difference between British and American law is pointed up by the inspector to a woman suffering from post-partum depression: "The first twelve months of motherhood is legally recognized as an exceptional period of stress. . . " (249).

Brown, Carter, pseud. *See* Yates, Alan G. . . . .

205. Brown, Herb. *Presumption of Guilt.* New York: Fine, 1991. Brown was a Columbus, Ohio trial lawyer until 1987 when he was elected to the Ohio Supreme Court Justice. In his second novel, he writes from the point of view of a gifted child named Charles, who is injured anally when playing a sexual game with two older girls; when his hysterical mother discover his bloody underpants and interrogates him, Charles is coerced into a series of lies that will put an eighteen-year-old neighbor boy on trial. Charles has a nervous breakdown while testifying, the accused abuser commits suicide after the court proceedings, and the final portion of the book brings the principals together at the wedding of the girl who hurt him.

206. _____. *Shadows of Doubt.* New York: Fine, 1994. Harvard Law grad Kathleen Sullivan is suddenly contacted by her birth mother, who tells her that she has a degenerative disease; this knowledge, however, enables her to befriend a half-sister, who is going through a rough marriage with an abusive husband. When the husband dies because of a hair dryer shoved into his bath, Kathleen agrees to defend.

207. Brown, J. E. [John Edward]. *Incident at 125th Street.* Garden City, NY: Doubleday, 1970. Three punks hassle an old man at the 125th Street train station in New York. A Good Samaritan comes to his aid, and one of the youths is accidentally knocked over a rail and later dies of his injuries. Because the witnesses refuse to come forward (until the end), there is the chance that the man, Martin, will be arraigned by the district attorney for manslaughter. Told from a variety of internal points of view (except Martin's) beginning with the managing editor of a paper.

208. Brown, Katharine Holland. *The Father.* New York: Day, 1928. London: Heinemann, 1929. brown was from Alton, Illinois and a Phi Beta Kappa graduate of the University of Michigan. A Massachusetts abolitionist sells his land and printing press to take up the cause in Illinois, where his path crosses with Springfield citizen, Abraham Lincoln, a hard-working defense lawyer who takes the son's case after a young man is found dead following a thrashing given by the son.

209. Brown, Sandra. *The Witness.* New York: Warner, 1995. Brown is a

popular writer of over a dozen bestsellers. This unorthodox legal thriller does feature a lawyer and courtroom action, but its author draws from staples of other genres, oddly mixing horror and romance especially, to stitch this bizarre novel together. The characters are either stock (clannish hillbillies; evil head of a racist organization called the Brotherhood; sluttish woman having an affair with husband) or ridiculous (fat, sexually promiscuous best friend of the protagonist); a wounded, sensitive male, who somehow juggles a profession in psychology with the US Marshal's Service, and despite amnesia, falls in love with the heroine who kidnaps him and beguiles him with a story that they are husband and wife). All of it swirls around an even more improbable plot of the female lawyer who assumes a name from a dossier so that she can leave a high-powered law firm to serve justice in Prosper, South Carolina, and who must flee the racist evildoers with her newborn and kidnaped escort in tow once the brotherhood deems her unworthy of joining their conspiracy.

210. Brown, Zenith Jones. Leslie Ford, pseud. *The Girl from the Mimosa Club.* New York: Scribner's; London: Collins, 1957. She used other pseudonyms (Brenda Conrad, David Frome) and produced a 16-book series about career soldier Colonel John Primrose and a Georgetown widow. A Californian, she was a teaching assistant at the University Washington with specialties in English, Greek, and philosophy. In New York she became an editor for *Dial* and served as a correspondent for the Air Force during WW II in England.

Johnny Brayton is a fledgling lawyer whose first assignment is to plead the strippers arrested from the sleazy Mimosa Club all guilty, pay their fines, and get them into taxis. When his own socialite mother is accused of murder, Brayton's relationship with one of the girls becomes a factor Enoch Chew exploits in his defense in the trial.

211. _____. *Trial by Ambush.* New York: Scribner's, 1962. [Rpt. as *Trial from Ambush*, London: Collins, 1962]. The best man and law school roommate of an alcoholic Baltimore scion is accused of raping his friend's fiancee two days before the wedding. Enoch Chew is the flamboyant defense attorney who destroys her testimony on cross. Jones Brown wrote her medical thrillers under the pseudonym Brenda Conrad.

212. Budd, John. Julian Prescot, pseud. *Both Sides of the Case.* London: Barker, 1958. Young Julian is now an articled clerk in his Uncle Chandos' law office about to serve his 5-year apprenticeship. Most of the cases are domestic involving divorces, paternity suits, and conveyancing clients with an occasional encounter with a malefactor in the course of his legal errands.

213. _____. *The Case Continued.* London: Barker, 1959. Julian Prescott's story as fledgling solicitor is picked up after *Both Sides of the Case.* Now as a real lawyer, he learns to deal with his first set of clients and is exposed to the

vagaries of human nature at odds with the law. Legalities range from a larcenous juvenile named Duke with his doting mother through an irate alderman in a paternity suit to various gambling and tax-evading offenders.

214. _____. *Case for Court.* London: Barker, 1964. Two lawyers are featured in this overlapping series of five tales embedded in the novel's plot: Major Matheson is a self-important, established, and petty-minded barrister who spends as much time boasting of his feats in pubs as he does in courtroom bravura; when a young, war-decorated newcomer bests the older advocate in a licensing hearing, the peevish Matheson becomes the implacable enemy of Weld, and their feud is duly recorded by the sapient narrator known simply as Prescot, also a solicitor. The legal maneuverings are outstanding and far superior to many a more popular author of legal novels. However, author "Prescot" gives us a thoroughly entertaining and informative look at English law through the major's buffoonery and his antagonist's analytically precise lawyering skills in a small, anonymous English city. The feud ripens with each case from "sheep worrying" against an Alsatian dog through a charge against a vindictive poison-pen writer to a jewelry store robbery-with-violence, and a final murder case, in which a pair of caretakers are accused of killing for gain the wealthy and elderly woman.

215. _____. *Case for Hearing.* London: Barker, 1963. Mr. Wallace Sambrook is a cunning rogue of a burglar with many enemies in the police and criminal ranks, especially one overworked detective-inspector named Drax, who would like to see his foe standing in the dock. They get their wish, but the quarry proves elusive, as narrator Prescot follows the housebreaker's antics with an amused eye.

216. _____. *Case for the Accused.* London: Barker, 1961. The Prescot law offices have added an assistant solicitor, Graham, by name, who takes over the matrimonial client list for the narrator and who is guided through the intricacies of law and human nature. Prescott also deals with his own caseload that includes a fence, an office nuisance named Miss Spurge, whose accusations against a pub redound to her discredit when she is arrested for driving while under the influence, and various sorts of civil or criminal mischief that culminate in the successful verdict against a man who had kicked at a dog's head and been assaulted by its owner. Two more are *Case for Trial* (1962) and *The Case Re-Opened* (1965).

217. _____. *Case Proceeding.* London: Barker, 1960. Although Prescott alludes to a racier client list that includes homosexuals and pornographers, it is the wryly amusing case with regional flavor that still succeeds. His first case is a farmer whose bull got into a neighboring farmer's field and despoiled seventeen of the man's prize heifers by impregnating them with his inferior stock. A case of defalcation ensues and then Prescot agrees to do a stint in the

matrimonial files section for vacationing colleague Mr. Magnus.

218. Buffa, D[udley]. W. *The Defense.* New York: Holt; Markham, Ont., Canada: Fitzhenry, 1997. Buffa practiced criminal law in Portland, Oregon and won acquittals for his first 15 clients. He has a Ph. D. from the University of Chicago and now lives in Walnut Creek, California. His protagonist Joseph Antonelli is a defense attorney without scruple when it comes to defending guilty clients: "I never lost a case I should have won, and I won nearly all the cases I should have lost" (1). He takes a case involving lowlife Johnny Morel indicted for raping his 12-year-old stepdaughter, but the case grows complex when the mother of the victim pleads for her husband. Important to Antonelli's moral development is the subplot of his old friend and mentor Judge Leopold Rifkin.

219. _____. *The Prosecution.* New York: Holt, 1999. Attorney Joe Antonelli earns his series status in this second thriller; this time, however, he is a special prosecutor, appointed by Judge Horace Woolner, in the case of Chief Deputy DA Marshal Goodwin, accused of killing his wife. A second case involves the Judge's wife Alma and a murder.

220. Bugliosi, Vincent, and Ken Hurwitz. *Shadow of Cain.* New York: Norton, 1981. Famed Manson prosecutor's first novel favors the prosecution--no surprise, according to Jon Breen who adds that Bugliosi's novel, along with Henry Denker's *Outrage*, begins the shift in emphasis away from the defense in courtroom fiction and even compares the central character to Sinclair Lewis' Elmer Gantry; however, this Gantry (Raymond Lomak) is no religious quack, for he is every inch a cold, multiple murderer, allegedly born again and rehabilitated twenty years after his crime. Inexplicably but in far-fetched Hollywood style, Bugliosi has Lomak take a job as director of a group of charities for an aging cowboy star who owns a football team. Only the psychiatrist who routinely sees Lomak knows how close to cracking he really is. Two murders occur and Lomak is back on trial. Breen's praise is apt: "The trial scenes are expertly done, highlighted by a brilliant summation by the defense lawyer, for once not on the side of the angels. Though some saw this book as a brief against the parole of Charles Manson, which in part it well may be, it is also a good novel" (13). (*See* Mr. Bugliosi's definition of *guilt* and *innocence* in the **Lawyers' Lexicon**.)

221. _____, with William Stadiem. *Lullaby and Good Night.* New York: NAL, 1987. Bugliosi's collaborator on this one is a Harvard law grad and New York Bar member who has authored three books, practiced law on Wall Street, written for the Hollywood film industry. Bugliosi, of course, will be linked to Manson, but his record of 105 out of 106 felony jury-trial convictions (with nearly 1,000 felony cases) is the real legacy of his 8-year career in the LA DA's Office; recently, he has cut back his private practice for the lecture and writing

circuit. This novel is based on a Jazz-Age sex scandal in New York City. Young Emily Stanton comes to the big city looking for fame on the stage but finds marriage to Warren Matthews, a Tammany Hall politico. He becomes abusive, she flees, finds herself the victim of a frame-up masterminded by her husband to gain custody of their child. As hostess at Texas Guinan's speakeasy, she makes connections with celebrities like Polly Adler, Judge Joseph Crater, Arnold Rothstein, and even Mayor Jimmy Walker. Her plot to get evidence to expose the city's machine to get her child results in a sensational murder trial.

222. Bullard, Linda McKeever. *Shades of Justice.* New York: Dutton, 1998. Gwen Parrish is one of Houston's most successful African-American lawyers with an ambition to become judge, but she has to move cautiously through the minefields of politics and race to achieve that goal.

223. Bullett, Gerald. *The Jury.* London: Dent; New York: Knopf, 1935. Enthralling from the opening conversation in a Soho restaurant between cynical journalist Mark Perryman and his friend's wife to the concluding reminiscence of the 34-year-old architect-husband. Three sections move the reader from the crime (the poisoning of Daphne Strood) to the individual jurors. The second is a transcript of the trial itself, and the final part ("The Twelve Debating") focuses on the deliberations, with flashbacks from several jurors' lives. The final revelation brings into sharp focus the discrepancy between courtroom justice and the truth. Jacques Barzun calls this one of the "greatest of those trial books that focus on members of the jury" (qtd. in Breen 13).

224. Bulwer-Lytton, Edward [Edward George Earle Lytton, first Baron Lytton]. *Eugene Aram.* London: Colburn; New York: Harper, 1832. This handsome young socialite of the early Victorian period was a Byronic figure known across Europe; in fact, he had been Lady Caroline Lamb's lover for a time (Byron's inamorata) and was once offered the throne of Greece, a country Byron died for. Born Edward Bulwer, a general's son, he graduated from Cambridge in 1826, married Rosina Wheeler the next year in what became a notoriously turbulent marriage and served in parliament from 1831-41 and again from 1852-66. He was raised to the peerage in 1866 as first Baron Lytton of Knebworth. His historical dramas were full of romantic splash and survived into the next century, especially *Richelieu* (1838). His one popular, but not best, novel is *The Last Days of Pompeii* (1834), which capitalized on the wide popularity of the historical romances being written by contemporary Sir Walter Scott.

Eugene Aram, according to the author's later Preface (1840), was based on the crime of a convicted killer, who once resided in York Prison for abetting the robbery and murder of a citizen. His notoriety stemmed from the fact that he was not by nature a criminal, but a studious and self-taught teacher, who wanted to pursue scientific studies with the proceeds of his crime (the victim was a noted scoundrel). Bulwer-Lytton was fascinated by the motives of such a man as Dostoevsky would be later in *Crime and Punishment*, when an impoverished student kills a worthless pawnbroker and fails to use the money the crime was conceived for. W. T. [William Thomas] Moncrief (1794-1857) produced a stage version *Eugene Aram, or, St. Robert's Cave* for the Surrey Theatre in 1832 and a printed but unpublished version exists of an American stage version by William Espy (1852-1908) in 5 acts (New Orleans: A. S. Collins, 1874).

225. _____. *Night and Morning.* Leipzig: Tauchnitz, 1843. Philip Beaufort could not declare his marriage to Catherine Morton, a mere trades woman, for fear that his immensely rich uncle would disinherit him. After the uncle's death, his brother Robert, "with a face of smiles and a heart of ice" (22), refuses to acknowledge Catherine's claim to the estate or her children's legitimacy. She and her husband attempt to regain the inheritance in a lawsuit despite missing witnesses and the parish registry itself missing from the Welsh parsonage.

226. _____. *Paul Clifford.* London: Routledge, 1830; New York: Harper, 1835; Philadelphia: Lippincott, 1868. Clifford is the long-lost son of William Brandon, the judge who sentences a young felon to death for participating in the highway robbery of a nobleman, and at the moment of the youth's appearance before him in court, recognizes him as his son. Father and son exchange long soliloquies in which Bulwer-Lytton's professed purpose to attack the sanguinary criminal code of England--and its unwitting partner, the vicious cycle of prison incarceration--is made clear. As the author says in a preface to the 1840 edition, the novel is "a loud cry to society to amend the circumstance--to redeem the victim. It is an appeal from Humanity to Law."

227. Bunn, T. Davis. *The Great Divide.* New York: Doubleday, 2000. When his children and wife die in a car crash, attorney Marcus Glenwood resigns and moves to a small North Carolina town; he is hampered by lawyers in his own firm but finds himself immersed in the case of a couple's child missing in China.

228. Burgess, Anthony. *A Clockwork Orange.* New York: Norton, 1963. Even Burgess was shocked at the success of the novel and laments that posterity will know him for this work more than any other of the dozens of novels and nonfiction works. Note on the American edition of 1986: Stanley Kubrick's jazzy film (GB/Warner-Polaris, 1971) inspired the book's huge commercial success, but the American edition he based his script on was without the twenty-first chapter, in which Alex reverses his destructive ways and, bored with mindless violence, seeks creation. Sincere or not to the book's premise of youthful brutality and sudden reform, the English (European) texts generate different responses owing to this truncation by an indifferent New York publisher. Fifteen-year-old Alex and his droogs (gang members) are out bashing heads and destroying lives and property in this grim and sleazy futuristic tale

narrated in Alex's polyglot of Cockney slang and pidgin Russian until Alex finds himself betrayed, apprehended, and sentenced for murder and rape. He elects to go for "Reclamation Treatmer.t" rather than serve out his sentence and becomes good by way of behavior-modifying pharmaceuticals rather than free will.

229. Burke, Alan Dennis. *Dead Wrong.* New York: St. Martin's, 1990 . A divorced contractor begins an affair with a woman and winds up a patsy in an immigrant-smuggling scheme. The novel opens with the narrator asking his lawyer-cousin to defend him against a charge of murder.

230. _____. *Getting Away with Murder.* Boston: Atlantic-Little, 1981. A reporter is implicated in the murder of his editor's wife.

231. Burke, James Lee. *Cimarron Rose.* New York: Hyperion, 1998. Burke, a hard-boiled mystery writer, offers a lawyer protagonist in Texas attorney Billy Bob Holland, who has an illegitimate son Lucas Smothers, who grew up abused by his stepfather. Fearful he might have killed his girl in a drunken blackout during an outing with a gang of rich hellions calling themselves East Enders, he is arrested for the murder and defended by Holland. The book-page editor of the *Rock Hill Herald* [South Carolina] notes: "Over 280 pages of fighting, beatings, assaults, unrelenting hatred, wrapped up at the end as neat[ly] as any 30-minute sitcom."

232. _____. *Heartwood.* New York: Doubleday, 1999. Rich, corrupt businessman Earl Dietrich is invites Billy Bob to a luncheon with various big shots, but a call later from Dietrich smells like an insurance scam; he tells Holland one of his laborers, Wilbur Pickett, stole an heirloom watch and $300,000 in bearer bonds from his safe while his wife's back was turned . Then a man in jail on a drunk and disorderly tells Holland that Pickett called him after the theft to ask bout unloading the bonds. Holland knows the informant once had rogue CIA connections as a mercenary pilot and was linked to another shady Dietrich operation.

233. Burnett, Frances Hodgson. *In Connection with the De Willoughby Claim.* New York: Scribner's, 1899. In the Carolina mountains where he took refuge, "Big Tom D'Willerby," a 300-pound, good-natured descendant of the wealthy Judge De Willoughby seeks his claim against the government for his father's estate for the sake of his nephew and adopted daughter, a couple in love.

234. Burton, Sarah, and Judith Holland. Hannah Wakefield, pseud. *Cruel April.* London: Women's Own, 1996; New York: St. Martin's, 1997. The authors, a former editor and practicing attorney, relocated to London in the early 1970s. The flyleaf inscription notes that Hannah Wakefield was educated at Tufts and Berkeley, but the degrees belong to Holland. Burton was New York City born and educated and qualified as a solicitor the year she moved to

London (1972). Then she worked for Seifert, Sadeley, and Williams but since 1990 has been legal officer for the Greenpeace's London headquarters. Their series character, Dee Street, is an American lawyer who also came to England in the early 1970's disillusioned by the violence and politics of her home country. She settles in, although never quite Anglicized, and despite a long-running affair with medico named David Baker. Dee, ever the introspective doubter and her own most ruthless critic, finds the initiative to separate from her prestigious firm, Samuelson Stevens, to go out on her own with Suze, a girlfriend from Yorkshire, who plays foil character and occasional alter ego as much as friend. Although the Wakefied novels have been lauded as being part of the new wave of feminist sleuths, Linda Semple avers Dee's capers to be more in the espionage line of the thriller (*Crime and Mystery Writers* 1053).

In this one, Dee is trying to avoid a public falling out with her friend Janey Riordan, who has just located an important witness for an upcoming murder trial; however, Janey does not want to pay her lawyer's considerable fee for services rendered. When Riordan is murdered, Dee becomes the prime suspect.

235. _____. *A Woman's Own Mystery* [British title: *A February Mourning]*. London: Women's Press, 1990; New York: St. Martin's, 1991. Dee awakens to a bad day getting worse by the minute: her client Gillian Shiraz is proving difficult by missing a court hearing in a bitter custody suit over her daughter. Dee averts disaster by parrying the ex-husband's lawyer's accusation of the mother's unfitness owing to her lesbianism; her home pregnancy test shows positive, although her 5-year relationship with Baker is on the rocks, she dislikes the new office associate, and a phone call just comes in about the missing Shiraz: she has been charged with manslaughter in the murder of Annie Murphy, a woman giving shelter to the mother and daughter after the separation. An adaptation was broadcast on BBC Radio 4.

236. _____. *The Price You Pay.* London: Women's Own, 1987; New York: St. Martin's, 1990. David Baker, after a hiatus of several years, comes back into Dee's life with a simple request: he and his journalist wife Amanda need wills made out to fulfill an insurance requirement to enable him to establish a hostel for young schizophrenics. The plot involves one of Baker's patients, Carlos, who had assaulted a bartender in a pub, and was subsequently incarcerated in a state hospital by his sister to prevent his deportation back to Chile. The plot thickens when Amanda later confesses to Dee that she made omissions in the will that she does not want her husband to know about and such admissions, if come to light, will threaten her life. Soon after, she and Baker's patient are found in bed with bullets in their heads.

237. Busch, Frederick. *Closing Arguments.* New York: Ticknor, 1991. New York: Fawcett-Columbine, 1993. Professor Busch holds Colgate's Fairchild Professor of Literature chair. He resides in Sherburne, New York,

with his family. Mark Brennan is an upstate New York lawyer suffering from post-traumatic stress disorder; his marriage is already shaky when he takes on a *pro bono* case of a young woman accused of murdering her lover in bed and finds himself enthralled by her sadomasochistic plunge.

238. Busch, Niven. *The San Franciscans.* New York: Simon, 1962. Saga of a family dynasty in 1949 - 1950 San Francisco; the clan is headed by banker Charlie Yarnum--more precisely, by Yarnum's wife Laura, who inherits the fortune left by her late husband, as we learn in the book's opening. She is left to fight for her husband's reputation and money against the younger generation of Yarnums; quitclaims and threats of lawsuits are bandied between her and the more covetous of the family, but marriage, not the courtroom, resolves the strife in this too-well-mannered tale.

239. Butterworth, W. E. [William Edmund] III. *The Court-Martial.* New York: Signet, 1962. Philadelphia attorney Gregory Fitts goes to Wetzlar, West Germany, to defend an old friend, Chief Warrant Officer Joseph Watson, who is accused of murdering his mistress. Fitts and Watson's wife were once lovers. Breen finds the court martial skillful but discovers two extraordinary details about this novel worth noting: it contains an unusual amount of swearing in during the preliminaries from counsel through court reporters to interpreters, and it appears to be one of the earliest mass market books "to make free use of the most popular taboo four-letter expletives" (14).

C

240. Cable, Mary. *Avery's Knot.* New York: Putnam's, 1981. Cable's novel is based on a real-life New England murder case in 1832 in which The Reverend Ephraim K. Avery, a Methodist minister of Bristol, Rhode Island, is accused of the strangulation murder of a pregnant mill girl, Sarah Mariah Cornell of Fall River, Massachusetts. Much dialogue, obviously an authorial creation, surrounds the magistrate's hearing in Bristol and Avery's trial in Newport. A cameo is offered to Jeremiah Mason, Daniel Webster's law partner, who appears for the defense and makes a summation for the defense.

241. Cain, James M[allahan]. "*The Baby in the Icebox*" *and Other Short Fiction.* New York: Holt, 1981. Ed. Roy Hoopes. Roy Hoopes brings together selections from Cain's early magazine publishing days. Among the sketches, dialogues, and short stories is a short novel sold to *Liberty* for $4,000 in 1938 (Cain had by then achieved fame as a novelist), originally titled *Money and the Woman* and later *The Embezzler.* The tale concerns a man working for a Baltimore insurance company who mortgages his house to enable a woman to return money to a bank and then later tries to protect her from indictment for altering the company's records and embezzling during his testimony to the grand jury.

242. _____. *The Butterfly*. New York: Knopf, 1947. At his death in 1977, Cain was considered one of the major hard-boiled writers of his time along with such stellar *noir*ists as Hammett and Chandler. He graduated from Washington College in 1910, taught journalism at St. John's College and later wrote, in addition to the novels he is famous for, political commentary. His trademark is ordinary people, middle class, who get swept into violence as a result of passion. He claims an epiphanic moment occurred when he, along with an enthralled nation, listened to the courtroom testimony of Roxy Stimson, whose husband was mired in the infamous Teapot Dome Scandal. As the divorced wife of a man who worked for Attorney General Henry Daughtery, Cain says, "her manner of speech during the senate hearings of 1924 'burst on the country like a Fourth of July rocket' [that] electrified the country and the literary world" (qtd. in Roy Hoopes, pref., *The Baby in the Icebox* (New York: Penguin, 1984, 87). His major novels are *Double Indemnity* and *The Postman Always Rings Twice* (*See* below). Another tale of tangled relationships as Jess Tyler, denizen of the Appalachian coal-mining country, receives a surprise visit to his log cabin from his grown daughter Kady with a butterfly birthmark. Jess goes to court twice as a result of his obsessive interest in her (she wears a butterfly tattoo). The first time is on a disorderly conduct charge resulting from a bar fight and later for incest. A unsolved murder also occurs.

243. _____. *Galatea*. New York: Knopf, 1953. London: Hale, 1954. Cain goes back for *Postman* seconds here: ex-pug Duke Webster gets involved with the obese wife of a restaurant owner in Upper Marlboro, Maryland, helps her lose weight, falls in love with her . . . and you can guess the rest. Webster is then charged with the husband's murder in a disappointing trial scene, which Jon Breen says, "rings as falsely as the Hollywood ending that follows" (16).

244. _____. *The Magician's Wife*. New York: Dial, 1962. London: Hale, 1963. Another go-round for the *Postman* plot with the difference that the culpable couple are not first blamed for the spouse's murder: executive Clay Lockwood and Sally Alexis, wife of a magician-heir, plot his death in a traffic accident; instead, the magician's assistant is accused. Breen laments: "It seems the presence of an extended trial scene in a Cain novel is a bad sign. This fairly late example of his work is truly dreadful, tin-eared and flat" (16).

245. _____. *The Postman Always Rings Twice*. New York: Knopf, 1934. Naturalism comes roaring out of Thomas Hardy's Wessex, transplanted to California, in this *noir* classic involving adulterous sex and murder. Cora Smith Papadakis's affair with drifter Frank Chambers leads to the murder of her Greek husband. Passion is replaced by cowardice, drunkenness, a fatal automobile accident, and the eventual execution of Chambers. Performed as a two-act opera with music by Stephen Paulus and libretto by Colin Graham (Valley Forge, PA: European American Music, 1982).

246. Caine, Hall. *The Deemster.* New York and London: Appleton, 1897. Caine had a fascination for the Manx character, its language, laws and customs. The frontispiece of this edition (Manx edition) shows a church and nearby Tynwald Hill, the ancient Mount of Laws on the Isle of Man. The Deemster is the appointed lawmaker of the island and he administers what are called Breast Laws--that is, the laws of his own breast (making). The title is conferred upon land-rich Thorkell Mylrea of eighteenth-century Ballamona, a mean-spirited, ambitious man who shares law on the island along with the Bishop of Man. When the Deemster's son Ewan is murdered, a nephew and son of the Bishop, Dan Mylrea, is accused of the crime and brought to trial.

247. Camus, Albert. *The Stranger* [*L'Étranger*, Paris: Gallimard, 1942.] Trans. Stuart Gilbert. New York: Knopf, 1946. This serious existentialist, a self-described "atheistic humanist," is one of the greatest and most influential thinkers, writers, and philosophers of the twentieth century. James M. Cain's hard-boiled style is deemed a critical influence on Camus' own style in this, his greatest novel of the philosophy of existentialism, in which a simple man of Algeria, who loves sunlight and water, Meursault, is condemned to death and refuses to accept the consolation of an afterlife. The trial in the book's second half leads to the protagonist's execution. (Meursault's "crime," however, is failing to cry at his mother's funeral and only technically for the shooting of the Arab). A philosophical novel second only to Voltaire's *Candide* in greatness.

248. Canavor, Frederick. *Rape One.* Seattle: Madrona, 1982. Canavor is a former Assistant DA prosecutor of King's County's violent crimes and had been a CID investigator charged with the security of Emperor Haile Selassie. His novel opens with a serial rapist' vicious attacks on various women near Central Park and moves through the investigation to the trial itself, but the innocence or guilt of Billy Waterman is subordinated to the courtroom combat of opposing counsels, both of whom are veterans in exploiting the criminal justice system's chinks and flaws to score their points in trial and manipulate the jury.

249. Cannon, Taffy. *Class Reunions Are Murder.* New York: Fawcett-Crest, 1996. Series character Nan Robinson, LA attorney, flies to Spring Hill, Illinois, for her twenty-year class reunion and becomes involved in the murder investigation of the class slut.

250. _____. *A Pocketful of Karma.* New York: Carroll, 1993. New York: Ballantine, 1995. Nan Robinson is an attorney-investigator for the State Bar of California. In her first outing, she goes in search of her missing secretary Debra LaRoche following a trail that takes her from Hollywood to a crackpot spiritualist movement in the Malibu hills called the Past Lives Institute.

251. _____. *Tangled Roots.* New York: Carroll, 1995. New York:

Fawcett-Crest, 1996. Second book in the series featuring California attorney Nan Robinson. Robinson learns that her brother-in-law is arrested for the murder of the scion of a flower-growing dynasty, ruled by a patriarch named Angus. The gun in evidence was the brother-in-law's and the motive is obvious: Shane Pettigrew had had an affair with Nan's younger sister.

252. Carcaterra, Lorenzo. *Sleepers.* New York: Ballantine, 1995. The author has maintained this work as factual autobiography, although the film (Warner, 1996) starring Brad Pitt, Dustin Hoffman, Robert De Niro, and Kevin Bacon as a nasty Sean Nokes ends with a disclaimer by New York State denying that there ever was such a boys' reformatory as Carcaterra claims in the Wilkinson School for Boys where he and his three friends were brutalized and sodomized in--or that such a homicide case as Michael engineered to lose against friends Tommy and John ever occurred; the latter are members of the notorious New York gang called Westies who murdered one of their tormentors in a New York Irish bar. This is primarily a coming-of-age story of four friends from Hell's Kitchen in the 1960's with a dark twist that ends in a courtroom. "Shakes" is author and narrator Carcaterra, who--along with friends John, Michael, and Tommy--grows up in the Irish-Italian enclave of Hell's Kitchen where they learn the values of the street and run errands for neighborhood godfather King Benny. When the boys play a prank on a hot-dog vendor that results in a terrible accident to an innocent citizen, they are sent to a reformatory upstate where they are systematically tortured and sexually abused by guards led by one sadistic Sean Nokes, who years later is recognized at his meal in a westside bar by John and Tommy, unconvicted killers and drug users. Michael, now a lawyer and assistant DA, contrives to lose the case by scripting the defense strategy to save his friends despite the fact that the entire neighborhood knows and actively conspires with him.

253. Carr, Caleb. *Angel of Darkness.* New York: Random, 1997. Carr's bestseller *The Alienist* (1994) inspired this return to murder and abnormal psychology in its infancy. Set in Lower Manhattan where the author grew up, the novel is told by a journalist dying of tuberculosis in 1919 about a notorious murder case 22 years earlier (the reader will think of Susan's Smith's drowning-murder of her two children in South Carolina). Libby Hatch is a mother who claims that "a lunatic Negro" assaulted her while she was riding home with her three children in a wagon one night and, when she fought him off, he shot at them, killing Matthew and Tommy Hatch. In the trial scene Clarence Darrow, rushing in to defend the grieving mother from Chicago, is opposed by Manhattan alienist Dr. Kriezler, whose theory and expert testimony it is that the mother killed her own children and an ongoing investigation, using new forensic science, implicates her in this shooting and the killing of at least six other children.

254. Carr, John Dickson. *Below Suspicion.* New York: Harper, 1949.

London: Hamilton, 1950. Honored with a Grand Master in 1962, Carr primarily used the bylines Carter Dickson and Carr Dickson besides his own name in a writing career that spawned 70 mystery novels besides a dozen other genre and nonfictional works (he once used the *nom de plume* Roger Fairbairn for an historical novel). Though an American, his four principal detectives are either French (*juge d'instruction* Henri Bencolin), Irish (barrister Patrick Butler), or English (the bibulous Dr. Gideon Fell--modeled on G. K. Chesterton--and Sir Henry Merrivale a.k.a "H. M"). Occasionally, Butler and Fell combine forces, as in *Below Suspicion.* Carr is most English in technique; he favors the intellectual puzzle, the misdirection or attention drawn skillfully away from the guilty party. The crimes are always intricate even when antic farce is introduced, the clues there to be "read" right, and even his detectives are fooled, sometimes by passion (handsome Butler, for instance) or vanity--but not for good, even if the guilty are acquitted through the acumen of Butler in court. Justice always prevails. A sampling token number of Butlers and Merrivales are found below.

Butler is a flannel-tongued barrister who claims to prefer guilty clients. In this one, mixing cult-poisonings and Satanism, the lawyer defends pretty nurse-companion Joyce Ellis on a charge of poisoning her elderly and hypochondriacal employer, Mildred Taylor. Another is *Patrick Butler for the Defense* (Harper, 1956).

255. _____. *Death Turns the Tables* [Retitled as *The Seat of the Scornful*, London: n. pub., 1941]. New York: Harper, 1941; rpt. New York: International Polygonics, 1985. This Gideon Fell opus "[b]egins with a powerful sentencing scene," according to Francis Nevins, "though lacking [in] trial action" (qtd. in Breen 17). In its alternative title, the novel is republished in a Dr. Fell omnibus (London: Hamilton: 1959). John Edward Lypiatt beats his wife to death in a jealous rage and despite the jurors' verdict of guilty with "a strong recommendation to mercy" (615), the judge sentences him to die.

256. _____. *It Walks by Night.* New York: Harper, 1930; London: Hamilton, 1976. While a college student at Haverford College in Pennsylvania, Carr had begun experimenting in short-story form with his first series detective, the flamboyant Parisian Henri Bencolin. Bencolin's cases are always variations of the locked-room murder and lack the finesse of his later books. This impossible murder involves a man found dead in a gaming establishment; the mystery? All the entrances were being watched, yet he is found inside, beheaded. Complete with floor plan and lurid prose: "The head itself stood in the centre of the red carpet upright on its neck; it showed white eyeballs and gaped at us with open mouth in the low red light" (25).

257. _____. *The Judas Window.* New York: Morrow; London, Heinemann, 1938. Sir Henry Merrivale is another detecting creation of the author's with his own endearing Rumpolian eccentricities. Merrivale also gently

caricatures Sir Winston Churchill in some of his social indifference, but it is as a master of closed-door mysteries that readers know him. The "Old Man" appeared in 23 sleuthing adventures beginning with *The Plague Court Murders* in 1934 and ending with *Fear Is the Same* (New York: Morrow; London: Heinemann, 1956). Though a barrister (as well as a doctor of medicine with an ancient family baronetcy), Merrivale is qualified less by slovenly grammar or appearance than by his ingenuity for detecting solutions from seemingly implausible circumstances. In this novel, Avory Hume is found dead in a locked room, stabbed with an arrow. James Answell, who is found unconscious with the body is the prime suspect. Merrivale, though fifteen years out of harness, accepts the brief to defend Hume in the Old Bailey trial.

258. Carr, Robyn. *New York: Mind Tryst.* New York: St. Martin's, 1999. Features a Colorado woman lawyer protagonist.

259. Casey, John. *The Half-Life of Happiness.* New York: Knopf, 1998. Casey was educated at Harvard Law and the University of Iowa. His *Spartina* won the National Book Award in 1989. He is currently Professor of English at the University of Virginia. This is no legal thriller in any sense, although it is about a lawyer Mike, his wife Joss, and their daughter in Charlottesville, Virginia. If you crossed John Cheever with John Updike, you would get this kind of domestic fiction. There is a snippet of trial action (Mike is occasionally in court), but the real power is in the writing as Mike sees himself a middle-aged man in the middle of a "flyapart life"(252).

Cashman, John, pseud. *See* Davis, Timothy F. T. . . . .

Caudwell, Sarah, pseud. *See* Cockburn, Sarah. . . .

260. Cauffiel, Lowell. *Marker.* New York: St. Martin's, 1997. Alcoholic Michigan judge Nelson Connor renders justice while drunk. Then ex-con Lawrence Gary and a criminal sidekick blackmail the judge. A sobered judge decides to go after the blackmailers instead of pay up.

261. Champion, David. *Celebrity Trouble: A Bomber Hanson Mystery.* Santa Barbara, CA: Knoll, 1997. A case of child sexual abuse for the flamboyant trial lawyer, "Bomber" Hanson. Champion uses son Tod, a failed composer and second-tier lawyer, as narrator of the novels. He stutters in the presence of his famous father (whose appearances are limited in contrast to the son) and acts as gofer. Champion's characters are wooden and the plots thin. His first novel is *The Snatch* (Santa Barbara, CA: Knoll, 1994) about an LA cop and South Central gangbangers in a convoluted, wacky case of kidnaping.

262. _____. *The Mountain Massacres: A Bomber Hanson Mystery.* Santa Barbara, CA: Knoll, 1995. Bomber takes on local opposition when DA Webster

Arlington Granger III indicts Bart O'Neil for the murder of Alf Ritchie--for killing O'Neil's three dogs. Champion's unfortunate reliance on the paper-thin observations of son Tod produce such teeth-gritting cerebrations as this one, after the seductive wife of the deceased leaves the witness stand: "I thought I noticed a touch of moisture in the judge's eye. I know my eyes were far from dry. For truly, who can resist an attractive damsel in distress?" (95).

263. _____. *Nobody Roots for Goliath: A Bomber Hanson Mystery.* Santa Barbara, CA: Knoll, 1996. Hanson's son Tod initiates a smoking case for his swashbuckling lawyer-*père* when a poor North Carolina farmer named Zepf with 12 daughters sues T. S. Armstead, "purveyors of fine tobacco." The MacGuffin is a search for a mole inside the tobacco company who will testify, but the courtroom scene at the end is amateurish; the dialogue is flat, and the father-son personality extremes are droll but unamusing.

264. _____. *Phantom Virus.* Santa Barbara, CA: Knoll, 1999. Merilee Scioria leaves a series of motley crew of lovers in her wake after her mysterious death of an undiagnosed virus; her rich father wants Bomber to sue the doctor for malpractice.

265. Chandler, David. *The Ramsden Case.* New York: Simon, 1967. Loosely based on the murder of three civil rights workers in Mississippi during the 1960s. Thomas Ramsden and an idealistic young woman are tried for the first-degree murder of Deputy Sheriff Willie Joe Martin, a boyhood acquaintance of Ramsden, and the man Ramsden suspected was responsible for the murder of four young civil rights workers found buried in a junkyard. During a struggle with Martin, Ramsden shoots him.

266. Chappell, Helen. *Dead Duck.* New York: Fawcett-Gold, 1997. A snow goose decoy is the weapon used to kill Judge Findlay Fish, but most people are more concerned about the condition of the rare antique. Reporter Hollis Ball is in town covering the story of Watertown, Maryland's annual Decoy Jamboree when the murder thrusts her into the middle of events, including a ghostly haunting by her deceased husband. Ball and her ghost-husband first appeared in *Slow Dancing with the Angel of Death* (Fawcett-Gold, 1996).

267. Chase, Carol. Kate Charles, pseud. *Appointed to Die.* New York: Mysterious, 1993. Midwesterner Chase, born in Cincinnati, Ohio, and educated in Illinois and Indiana, lives in Bedford, England. Her Anglican administrative experience has lent itself to a 5-book, cozy/ecclesiastical mystery series that qualifies for inclusion because one of her pair of sleuths is a solicitor. David Middleton-Brown and artist Lucy Kingsley are hired by a charismatic priest named Gabriel Neville, being blackmailed in *A Drink of Deadly Wine* (London: Headline; Mysterious, 1991).

268. _____. *The Snares of Death.* London: Headline, 1992; New York: Mysterious, 1993. A devout young man is defended by Middleton-Brown for the murder of the charismatic and controversial new vicar of St. Mary the Virgin. Other Headline-St. Martin's titles: *A Dead Man Out of Mind* (1995) and *Evil Angels among Them* (1995).

269. Chase, Linda, and Joyce St. George. *Perfect Cover.* New York: Pocket, 1997. Chase and St. George's debut novel is a fine police procedural with a protagonist who works out of the Special Prosecutor's Office. Tina Paris's unit goes after corrupt politicians and law-enforcement officials with Mafia ties. Half-Italian, half-Puerto Rican, she works undercover on three cases: a rotten street cop named Eddie Calvert; a ward politico and his State Supreme Court father believed to be mobbed up; and finally, a sadistic rapist who sends boasting faxes.

270. Chastain, Thomas. *Perry Mason in the Case of Too Many Murders.* New York: Morrow, 1989. The first continuation of Erle Stanley Gardner's Perry Mason series. Mason is hired by a woman accused of shooting her husband after the husband shoots a man in a bar.

271. Chatterton, Ruth. *The Betrayers.* Boston: Houghton, 1953. London: Harrap, 1954. Celia Mills, a Senator's wife and a liberal trial lawyer, becomes involved in the defense of nuclear physicist Michael Prescott, who is the target of a rabble-rousing Senator Floyd Glavis. Her own husband chairs the subcommittee investigating the scientist, and when Prescott is indicted for contempt of Congress by refusing to appear, she undertakes his successful defense in the trial and almost sacrifices her marriage; however, later, there are unanswered questions that make the case more complex than she had first believed.

272. Chevalier, Haakon. *For Us the Living.* New York: Knopf; London: Secker, 1949. Arrogant, philandering Steve Callahan, a superintendent of labor on a ranch in the San Joachim Valley of 1929, is found murdered in his hotel suite in San Francisco, his wife Germaine next to him unconscious from Amytal poisoning. First, she is tried for the murder and then eight years later radical labor organizer Angelo Parenti, who had once opposed Callahan as representative of the company's interests, is put on trial.

273. Christie, Agatha [Dame]. *The Mysterious Affair at Styles.* London: Lane, 1920. New York: Dodd, 1927. The grand dame of mystery fiction, Christie's skill with plotting variations in the genre enabled her to set her mark in courtroom fiction with a mere few works in the total output. Her short story "Witness for the Prosecution" is one of the most famous adapted as play or film; however, she rarely wrote trial sequences. Her first novel sees John Cavendish

charge in the Old Bailey with the poison murder of his stepmother Emily Inglethorp. The defendant's barrister Ernest Heavywether appears briefly, and Hercule Poirot solves the crime outside court.

274. _____. *Sad Cypress.* London: Collins; New York: Dodd, 1940. Elinor Carlisle stands in the dock for the poison-murder of wealthy, elderly Mary Gerrard. A flashback resets the narrative; a trial sequence concludes with Hercule Poirot becoming the defense's crucial witness.

275. _____. *Witness for the Prosecution.* New York: Dell, 1932. Much anthologized and deservedly famous work of one of the world's best known authors of any genre, which despite its sensational and melodramatic plot is believed to be based on a real case. Its brevity in short-story or dramatic form (20 pp.) and compactness of characterization belie its shrewd portraiture of the psychology of a defense lawyer (Mr. Mayherne) and his defendant (Leonard Vole), whom he acquits in a way that surely no courtroom has ever seen. Billy Wilder's 1957 script and film for London and American audiences alternatively (UA, 1957) is an homage to this version in dramatic form. With brilliance all around mixing suspense with the comedic in Charles Laughton's portrayal of Mayherne as an irascible and ailing barrister defending accused murderer Tyrone Power in his final completed film. Laughton's wife Elsa Lanchester plays the bossy nurse and, best of all, is Marlene Dietrich's gimmicky performance as gigolo Power's *inamorata*, the title character. The final scene of vindication is Wilder's melodramatic contribution to Christie' own, a pure Hollywood ending. Christie (Mary Clarissa, née Miller) received her Order of the British Empire in 1971, five years before her death. The best-known version is by French (New York and London) in 1954; in the previous year she had adapted her story for the theater (Nottingham and London).

276. Churchill, Winston. *Mr. Crewe's Career.* New York, London: Macmillan, 1908. Best known for *Richard Carvel*, Churchill's novel here is about a lawyer father and a prodigal son. The boy's spirit sends him out West but he returns to practice law in Ripton, New York, with his father, who happens to be the legal representative for the powerful and unscrupulous Northeastern Railroads. The son takes a case for one Humphrey Crewe, local bigwig and aspiring politician, against the railroad because of internal injuries suffered by one of his expensive horses.

277. Clark, Alfred Alexander Gordon. Cyril Hare, pseud. *He Should Have Died Hereafter.* London: Faber, 1958. [Rpt. as *Untimely Death*, New York: Macmillan, 1958]. A point of English inheritance law turns this tale. Primogeniture is the ancient law of oldest sons inheriting from their fathers but a son can be "barred in his entail" and a father can leave his estate to whom he chooses. Francis Pettigrew is out riding on the Oxmoor heath when he sees a dead man. This dead man will become a very peripatetic corpse before the

novel is through as lawyers must debate the exact day and manner of his death to determine which of two male cousins will inherit the Gorman estate.

278. _____. *Tragedy at Law.* London: Faber, 1942. New York: Harcourt, 1943. Clark was a barrister and later county court judge, who was educated at Rugby and New College, Oxford, where he took a first in modern history. Called to the bar in 1924, he practiced for 15 years. One of three novels featuring series sleuth Francis Pettigrew, a middle-aged minion of the British circuit court system. The major plot of this one involves High Court Justice William Barber, who is involved in a minor road accident in which Pettigrew is himself one of the passengers. The injured man, Sebastian Sebold-Smith, wants £15,000 pounds or he will ruin the Judge's reputation.

279. Clark, Douglas. *Roast Eggs.* London: Gollancz; New York: Dodd, 1981. Scotland Yard detectives Masters and Green must solve the crime while court is in recess and before defendant James Connal resumes the stand on cross examination; he is on trial for the arson-murder of his wife, and the case against him is weak. Breen notes: "It's a pure intellectual puzzle for readers nostalgic for R. Austin Freeman, Freeman Wills Crofts, J. J. Connington, and their Golden Age colleagues. . . . As in other Clark novels, his pharmaceutical expertise comes into play" (27-28).

280. Clark, Mary Higgins. *Let Me Call You Sweetheart.* New York: Simon, 1995. A prosecuting attorney is waiting in the plastic surgeon's waiting room to hear news of her injured daughter when she notices two women with familiar faces and is shocked to realize where she has seen one of the faces before: Suzanne Reardon was the victim in the "Sweetheart Murder Case." baffled why plastic surgery patients are made to resemble a murder victim, and against advice, she investigates the 11-year-old case. Meredith Baxter played the attorney in the 1997 telefilm *Mary Higgins Clark's Let Me Call You Sweetheart.*

281. Clark, Walter van Tilburg. *The Ox-Bow Incident.* New York: Random, 1940. Wrongly demoted to cowboy-novel status, Clark's tale of Western rope justice is an outstanding, perhaps great, American novel; it is undoubtedly a searing look at frontier justice miscarried, which Hollywood respected beautifully through its depressing conclusion. When rustlers kill a man on the range and flee into the Sierras, a posse gathers to pursue and rides up on three men. They hang them after a night of deliberation and later discover their error. Though Croft is a sensitive narrator and Gil an interesting character, Judge Tyler is more than a stock character or, as he seems, comic relief; the men resent him as a representative of the law's unreliability. The film (TCF, 1943) teamed scriptwriter Lamar Trotti with veteran director William Wellman and starkly realistic performances by Anthony Quinn as the Mexican traveler and Henry Fonda as the conscience-haunted cowboy-narrator of Clark's novel. The

British film title is *Strange Incident.*

Many cowboy novels deserve mention for their use of the theme of justice; some well-known ones are W. R. [William Riley] Burnett's *Bitter Ground,* Charles O. Locke's *The Hell-Bent Kid* (Norton, 1957), Richard Poole's *Gun Vote at Valdoro*, Ned Conquest's *The Gun and Glory of Granite Hendley* (Doubleday, 1969), Todhunter Ballard's *West of Justice* [as by John Hunter] (Houghton, 1954); The *Sheriff of Tombstone*, Ernest Haycox' *Trail Town* (Dell, 1941), Charles Portis' *True Grit* (Simon, 1968), Elmore Leonard's *Valdez Is Coming* (Greenwich, CT: Fawcett, 1970), and Oakley M. Hall's *The Warlock* (Viking, 1958). *Valdez Is Coming* was turned into a Burt Lancaster film (UA, 1970); *Trail Town* and *True Grit* were films as well. Harold Shumate drafted the screenplay for the former (1945) and John Wayne parlayed George's Majestic Lounge (U of Arkansas) graduate Portis' novel of a little girl desiring to avenge her murdered father's death, and partnered with aging, hard-drinking US Marshal Rooster Cogburn, into one of his most famous screen roles.

282. Clarke, Anna. *We the Bereaved.* Garden City, NY: Doubleday, 1982; New York: Charter, 1988 . Harry Johnson is a London solicitor summoned to a hospital in Sussex to see elderly Miranda Porlock, a woman he barely knows. She hands him her will in an envelope, dies shortly thereafter, and Harry discovers that he is named beneficiary of her house. he knows that somehow this is connected to his wife's hit-and-run death just months ago.

283. Clemens, Samuel Langhorne. Mark Twain, pseud. *The Tragedy of Pudd'nhead Wilson, and the Comedy of Those Extraordinary Twins.* Hartford, CT: American, 1894. [Rpt. as *Pudd'nhead Wilson*, London: Chatto, 1894]. In Dawson's Landing in 1830 Missouri, struggling lawyer David ("Pudd'nhead") Wilson pursues a hobby of collecting fingerprints. Roxana, a 15/16 white slave owned by leading citizen Judge Driscoll, is caring for two virtually identical babies, her own son and the judge's. She switches babies only to watch her boy grow up a callow, mean-spirited youth as the favored boy. Years later, a pair of Italian "Siamese" twins, the Tocci brothers, are put on trial for the stabbing murder of the judge. Wilson's closing argument and demonstration involve the pioneering science of fingerprinting. Twain's ironic tale is an early detective fiction, and unfortunately it provides fodder for us to deplore nineteenth-century racism. Twain's greatness as a writer, humorist, and moralist is that he was able to satirize race laws of his own time when Jim Crow laws were being rigorously enforced and lynchings were blistering the moral landscape of America. Its charming humor ensures it will outlast the political correctionists of our times. Witness: the Cleveland Playhouse premiered Murphy Guyer's adaptation of Twain's novella under the title *The Emancipation of Valet de Chambre* between April and May 2000 adding a narrator, former slave Youth Griffin, which character , Associate Director Guyer says, would restore humor back to the story.

284. Clouzot, Henri-Georges. *Les Inconnus dans le Maison.* (French, 1941). The Continental production is based on a mystery in which a barrister defends his teenaged daughter from a murder charge. Dir. Henri Decoin. Perf. Raimu, Juliette Faber, and Jacques Baumer. (*See* Simenon, Georges.)

285. Cobb, Irvin S. *Back Home.* New York: Doran, 1912. Cobb's stories about Judge William Pitman Priest, Kentucky arbiter and Civil War veteran, are regionalist local color, light on trial action, but worth re-reading, says Jon Breen. Three of these ten of Cobb's first collection get into Judge Priest's western Kentucky courtroom. In "Five Hundred Dollars Reward," the judge manipulates justice for a defendant who shot a bully in a family feud. In "Words and Music," the judge himself is a witness for the defense in Tennessee trial of Breck Tandy in the killing of a county clerk. The judge regretfully sentences a fellow vet to two years "at hard labor" in an assault case for shooting fellow countian Virgil Settle ("When the Fighting Was Good" 171). Scanty courtroom action in his novel *Alias Ben Alibi* (New York: Doran, 1925) about a newspaper editor's career. There is brief trial time in another short novel *Judge Priest Turns Detective* (Indianapolis: Bobbs, 1937). This was a star vehicle for Will Rogers in John Ford's *Judge Priest* (Fox, 1934) with Dudley Nichols adapting Cobb for the screen. Ford remade the film of the wise and controversial Kentucky judge (Republic, 1953) with Laurence Stalling scripting stories from Cobb. Considering it his favorite film, Ford changed the title to *The Sun Shines Bright.* Many regulars appear. Perf. Charles Winninger, Arleen Whelan, John Russell, Stepin Fetchit, and Milburn Stone.

286. Cockburn, Sarah Caudwell. Sarah Caudwell, pseud. *The Shortest Way to Hades.* London: Collins, 1984; New York: Scribner's, 1985. Often compared to Dorothy Sayers for her erudition (she graduated in Classics from Aberdeen and read law at St. Anne's College, Oxford), Caudwell mixes murder with mirth in a few novels that have become an acquired taste admired for barbed wit and literate comedy. Caudwell practiced law in the legal section of Lloyd's Bank Trust Division. She was the daughter of novelist Claud Cockburn and the original of the Sally Bowles character from *Cabaret* (based on Christopher Isherwood's *Goodbye to Berlin*--in real life, actress and journalist Jean Ross). The narrator of Caudwell's work is an epicene Oxford medieval law professor Hilary Tamar, and the stories that Tamar tells concern five young Lincoln Inn barristers headed by a disorganized but intelligent young woman named Julia, a Gauloise-smoking barrister herself, with a propensity for mischief or serious trouble. Praised by friends for her wit, erudition, amusing eccentricity (she smoked a pipe), and loyalty, the author died of cancer in her London home on 28 January before *The Sybil in Her Grave* went to press. A cult figure in America despite a mere 4 novels, she has been translated into Swedish and Japanese. The *London Times* obituary noted an amusing anecdote of this novel: while preparing for novel, she was seen staring at a block of flats near a towpath by Barnes Bridge. A passerby asked her if anything was wrong. She

replied: "Do you think, if you pushed someone from the top of that building, you could be sure of it being fatal?"

One member of the Galloway family refuses to sign off on a complex trust arrangement so that a £5 million estate will not accrue £3 million in taxes unless she is paid for her signature on the rearranging of the trust. The recalcitrant cousin dies suddenly and Hilary's "nursery" of Lincoln Inn barristers gather to confer. Is it murder?

287. _____. *The Sibyl in Her Grave.* New York: Delacorte, 2000. Caudwell died before the book came out, ending the urbane career of her Oxford legal historian and mentor to her nursery of London barristers Cantrip, Selena, Julia and Ragwort as well as sending the question of Hilary's gender into perpetuity. Julia's Aunt Regina makes a fortune but has a problem with taxes that requires Tamar's intercession. However, this subplot plot is connected to one featuring the disreputable psychic counselor named Isabella del Comino, who flounces into the quiet village of Parsons Haver and disrupts life there–until her abrupt death.

288. _____. *The Sirens Sang of Murder.* New York: Delacorte; London: Collins, 1989. Caudwell's third effort, a saga of international intrigue mixing witchcraft, international tax law, and sex, gained the prestigious Anthony Award for Best Novel. Caudwell's preparation for this novel took her to the Channel Islands, the Caymans, and Monaco in search of locations where accidents might happen.

289. _____. *Thus Was Adonis Murdered.* New York: Scribner's, 1981; Harmondsworth, Middlesex, Eng.: Penguin, 1982. P. G. Wodehouse meets Henry James in this intellectual whodunit featuring a group of esthetes and barristers who sit about coffeehouses amusing themselves with the sparkling wit of their own conversation. Hilary is in London researching medieval law when one of the group, tax specialist Julia Larwood from the office next door, becomes the prime suspect in the murder of her one-time lover, an afternoon tryst with a fellow art lover traveling in her Venice tour group. Tamar reads Julia's letters to the group who interject commentary and cleverness while Tamar works analytically to save her.

290. Coe, Charles Francis. *Pressure.* New York: Random, 1951. A mob mouthpiece in an anonymous big city confesses, between sips of whiskey and his scribbling pen, his tale of how his greed caused him to slip into the hands of the Outfit.

291. Coel, Margaret. *The Dream Stalker.* New York: Berkley-Prime Crime, 1997. *The Dream Stalker* is concerned with corporate greed, radioactive-waste disposal and the effects on the Arapaho residing inside the reservation. Coel has a 5-book Native American series character in Vicky Holden, an

attorney for the Arapaho tribe of the Wind River Indian Reservation in Wyoming. Vicky has a foot in both camps but moves easily between the Arapaho and the white world, although she is sometimes rebuffed by tribal peers for thinking like a *ho:xu'wu:ne'n* [white woman].

292. _____. *The Eagle Catcher.* Niwot, CO: U of Colorado P, 1995; New York: Berkley Prime Crime, 1995. Arapaho tribal chairman Harvey Castle is found murdered in his tipi; his nephew is the prime suspect.

293. _____. *The Ghost Walker.* New York: Berkley Prime Crime, 1996. Series character Father John O'Malley, Jesuit priest and head pastor at St. Francis Mission, finds a body wrapped in tarp in a ditch during a snowstorm. When he returns with police, the body is gone. The investigation leads to the disappearance of Marcus Deppert, convicted drug dealer, and the murder of his girlfriend. Father John is concerned that Vicky's drug-addicted, rebellious daughter Susan is implicated in murder and might be the next victim.

294. _____. *The Lost Bird.* New York: Berkley Prime Crime, 1999. Vicky just concludes a successful defense of Sam Eagle Hawk in his wrongful termination suit, when two matters commence almost simultaneously: Hollywood actress Sharon David wants Vicky to find her biological parents because she believes she might have been adopted after her mother, a resident of the Wind River Reservation, gave birth to her, and the other is even more urgent: she hears that Father John has been shot dead on the reservation. A man driving Father John's red pickup was killed, but it was Joseph, and the BIA cops and sheriff's office want to keep it quiet to lay a trap for Sonny Red Wolf and his activist followers.

295. _____. *The Story Teller.* New York: Berkley Prime Crime, 1998. Vicky is summoned to Denver by a tribal elder because of a valuable missing artifact: a one-of-a-kind ledger book of the Arapaho people's history has gone missing, and it is worth millions to an unscrupulous collector. Vicky learns that a student died mysteriously while doing research on the ledger. Father John assists her investigation. Her latest is *The Spirit Woman* (Berkley, 2000).

296. Cohen, Bruce. *Mistrial.* A 1996 teleplay and HBO production about a cop-killer who is about to walk away from the murder of two police officers while the detective who brought him and put him on trial is himself indicted after an accidental shooting. Disgusted at justice run amok, Det. Steve Donohue (Bill Pullman) pulls his gun and takes the judge and jury hostage after the cop-killer is declared free by the court. Perf. Robert Loggia and Blair Underwood.

297. Cohen, Larry with Andy Wolk. *The Defenders: Choice of Evil.* (Paramount, 1997) This straight-to-video film and another (*See The Defenders: Payback*) began a short-lived lawyer series based on the Prestons from the

Reginald Rose teleplay and 1960's TV series. E. G. Marshall (with a year to live) is featured in both, but the cases involve nephew and granddaughter in lieu of the original lawyer son. Beau Bridges and Martha Plimpton perform in both films with Marshall. In this one Jack Casey is an investigative journalist with powerful enemies in the police department that ensure his wrongful conviction of murder. In *Payback*, the trio work on the case of a man who confesses to a lethal act of revenge. Director Andy Wolk is also credited as coauthor of the teleplay.

298. Cohen, Octavus Roy. *Danger in Paradise.* New York: Macmillan, 1945. Cohen churned out dozens of pulp novels from hard-boiled to comic, but never distinguished himself in plot or characterization to last, and he was as inept at duplicating British dialect as a black man's speech, but that never stopped him. Lawyers, trials, and grand juries are frequently mentioned but he shied away from attempting courtroom scenes. In this mainstream mystery, Howard Lawton has been stealing from his business partner at Lawton & Robbins when the man is shot to death by the firm's secretary; he stands to benefit from the insurance, but he cannot be sure a jury will see him as innocent, so he arranges to stand trial; his get-out-of-jail card is her written confession if he is not acquitted. One of his humourous novels, totally politically incorrect, is *Florian Slappey Goes Abroad* (1928) that features, in addition to the main character, lawyer J. Caesar Clump (rpt. Freeport, NY: Books for Libraries, 1970).

299. Collins, Max Allan. *Damned in Paradise.* New York: Dutton, 1996. The Muscatine, Iowa resident scripted the Dick Tracy comic series from 1977 to 1993 and has authored the Nathan Heller historical thrillers, of which 7 have received Shamus nominations. On leave from the Chicago P. D. and heading for Hawaii, Heller meets Clarence Darrow and agrees to assist him in a sordid case on the islands involving a socialite's rape and the subsequent trial of the defendants. Accused of the revenge murder of the islander who raped Thalia Massie are the husband and mother of the victim, along with two Navy men.

300. Collins, Tess. *The Law of Revenge.* New York: Fawcett, 1977. Currently living and writing in San Francisco, where she shares her apartment with a Siamese cat named Bathsheba, Tess Collins is the granddaughter of a coal miner, raised in the southeastern Kentucky town of Middlesboro. She graduated from the University of Kentucky with a degree in journalism and was the recipient of the John Yeager Scholarship and Oswald Award for creative writing. After graduating, and with $500. of unspent scholarship money, she decided to leave Kentucky and struck out for San Francisco in 1978, where she became the literary manager for the Curran Theatre, which features Broadway productions.

A San Francisco lawyer is called back to her Appalachian roots to defend her brother from Contrary, Kentucky, charged with murdering the town's leading executive. Alma Mae Bashears is also forced to revisit her girlhood nightmare of a gang rape. The prosecutor, in fact, is the one responsible for her rape.

301. Collins, Wilkie. *The Law & the Lady.* 3 vols. London: Chatto, 1875. Bride Valeria Brinton marries older Eustace Woodville and is beset by a series of eccentricities and events that perplex her about her new husband. At the end of the first volume, she discovers that his real name is Macallan and that he was tried for poisoning his first wife, but a Scottish jury rendered a Not Proven verdict, freeing him but tainting his good name. In volume two, Valeria reads the text of the trial.

302. Collison, Wilson. *The Murder in the Brownstone House: From the Records of a Young Lawyer.* New York: McBride, 1929. The narrator opens with his first-person account of the trial about to begin in which he is defending young patrician Jerry Belden in New York City's Supreme Court for the murder of May Marnes, "[j]ust one more of Manhattan's flashy and parasitic gold-diggers" (6).

303. Colum, Padraic. *Castle Conquer.* New York: Macmillan, 1923. Historical romance between a Francis Gillick, returning to his clan's village near Dublin and Brighid Moynagh, and his indictment as one of the "moonlighters" accused of murdering the father of Mountford Wolfe. The peculiarities of trial in Ireland are summarized with their Anglicized and Norman variations, seemingly as if being explained to Brighid, a witness for Francis, testifying that they were together during the night of the murder.

304. Colver, Anne. *Theodosia, Daughter of Aaron Burr.* New York: Farrar, 1941. Her famous father's trial, after his arrest in Virginia, covers only a single chapter and is mere summary by Theodosia with the emphasis on the important names in attendance.

305. Colvin, Kelly. *Hear That Train Blow!.* A Novel about the Scottsboro Case. New York: Delacorte, 1970. The book is a self-described documentary novel which uses court records for the witness examination scenes of Alma Buford and Virginia Cooley, two sexually promiscuous young white women riding the trains and alleging rape by six of nine black youths from Scottsboro, Alabama, in 1931 ("Days of Judgment" 59-151). The bulk of the novel is devoted to the aftermath of the trial and its national repercussions. An outstanding made-for-TV courtroom drama was produced a few years later in 1976: *Judge Horton and the Scottsboro Boys.* Dir. Fielder Cook. Perf. Arthur Hill, Vera Miles, and Lewis J. Stadlen.

306. Comstock, Harriet T[heresa]. *Smothered Fires.* London: Heinemann; New York: Doubleday, 1924. A New York judge sentences a woman named

Mary Carlin to five years on a manslaughter charge for murdering her married lover in his apartment. After the sentencing, she summons the judge to her cell to confess why she killed him--and the judge suddenly recognizes his castoff wife Kathleen from long ago, spurned because of his belief that their newborn child was the dead man's from her previous attachment to him.

307. Condon, Richard. *The Venerable Bead.* New York: St. Martin's, 1992. According to Smith and White, Condon did not begin his writing career until the age of 42 (161). Condon was a past master of suspense--for examples, the cynical *The Manchurian Candidate* (1959), to name his best-known--and the *Prizzi* trilogy (*Prizzi's Honor*, 1982; *Prizzi's Glory*, 1988; *Prizzi's Money*, 1994). This is one of his final satirical novels, impossible to summarize for its sheer zaniness. Protag is Leila Aluja, an Iraqui-American, lawyer, lobbyist, film star, and counterespionage agent. The MacGuffin involves a search for a secret yogurt formula.

308. Connelly, Michael. *The Concrete Blonde.* New York: St. Martin's, 1997. Harry Bosch, a tough LA cop in Robbery/Homicide, is hunting the Dollmaker, a serial killer who preys on women in the sex industry. Harry confronts the man, kills him when he makes a sudden move; later evidence proves the man to be the Dollmaker. Connelly's novel alternates between Harry's civil trial for the shooting and police procedural.

309. Conroy, A. L. *Storefront Lawyers.* New York: Bantam, 1970. In this novelization of creator David Karp's TV series, a trio of idealistic, young law graduates join a white-shoe firm on the condition that it will bankroll them so that they can give free legal service to the indigent. One of their first clients is a man who shoots a prominent citizen, although he had never seen the man before, saying the victim stole his house.

310. Cook, Robin. *Harmful Intent.* New York: Berkley, 1990. Dr. Jeffrey Rhodes loses Patty Owen in the delivery room after giving her Marcaine to help her pain. In the criminal trial afterward, a nurse testifies seeing him give himself an IV injection but did not know that it was paregoric to ward off flu symptoms; the doctor's history of addiction to a painkiller works against him at the trial and he loses. Beneath the medical jargon, there is a mystery about a killer who used tainted Marcaine on another victim, which proves Rhodes was not "operating under the influence," but he must solve the crime as a fugitive to do the sleuthing to exonerate himself.

311. Cook, Thomas H. *The Chatham School Affair.* New York: Bantam, 1996. Cook is a two-time, Edgar-Award nominated author of 13 novels and 2 true-crime books. Chatham is a tiny seacoast town in 1926, when Elizabeth Channing, a young art teacher, arrives to begin her career at elite Chatham School, dedicated to turning arrogant boys from good families into moral young

men. Channing is an exotic ingredient into this mix and what results is scandal, suicide, murder, and a sensational trial. Seven decades later, the bodies are buried, but the questions about what happened are still unanswered.

312. Cooper, I. S. [Irving Spencer]. *It's Hard to Leave When the Music's Playing.* New York: Norton, 1977. The trial of Professor Daniel Carter, who admittedly euthanized his best friend and musician Luigi Morello, dying of ALS. The Q & A is good with prosecutor Grant trying to tear into the motive of behind Carter's choice to deny heroic efforts and unplug the respirator, yet it is coldly delivered by the doctor on the witness stand, despite his repetition of his friend's dying wish expressed in Italian and unconsciously rendered by the doctor on the witness stand as he relives the moment. The book's clear didactic purpose is to make a case for doctor-assisted suicide in terminal illnesses at a patient's request.

313. Cooper, James Fenimore. *Chainbearer*; or, *The Littlepage Manuscripts.* New York: Burgess, 1845; New York: Townsend, 1860; Grosse Point, MI: Scholarly, 1968. The three novels by America's foremost novelist of his time noted here are this litigious author's attempt to explain and justify the patroon system to his countrymen, or at least to those upstate New Yorkers who were dominated by the powerful clans of Schuylers and Van Renssellaers. Collectively the trilogy is called "The Littlepage Manuscripts" written to defend the powerful landowning families (a complete antithesis to the democratic "Leatherstocking Tales"). *The Chainbearer* (1845) is the second novel narrated by Cornelius Littlepage's son Mordaunt and set in the days of the Revolution. The title refers to the surveyor whose task it is to bind up the wilderness in marketable lots. Cooper's claim is that the wealthy had a right to their profits because they took on the dangers of the wilderness against great odds and won.

314. _____. *The Redskins,* or, *Indian and Injun: Being the Conclusion of the Littlepage Manuscripts.* New York: Burgess, 1846; Putnam's, 1896. The concluding book is set during the Anti-Rent War of the mid-1840's during which farmers protested the right of the patroons to enforce antiquated and feudal rights over them. The armed uprising was considered by Cooper to be the essential American question of the day rather than slavery. Mordaunt's grandson Hugh narrates but the narrative voice is Cooper's and it often becomes merely a shrill diatribe against the majority of American citizens and especially toward the worst of those "marauders, the anti-renter" (iii).

315. _____. *Satanstoe*; Or, *The Littlepage Manuscripts: A Tale of the Colony.* New York: Burgess, 1845. 2 vols. The trilogy opens with the narration of Cornelius Littlepage, who describes his founding of his estate in the wilderness at Mooseridge. Praised as an almost perfect novel, it avoids the litigiousness and hectoring that would replace Cooper's art of storytelling as he felt himself alienated from his fellow Americans and their views.

316. _____. *The Ways of the Hour.* New York: Putnam's; London: Bentley, 1850. Young Mary Monson is charged with arson and murder in the town of Biberry, Duke's county, New York, where two charred skeletons are found in the ashes of their burned house. She is defended by lawyer Tom Dunscomb. Cooper abandons his story to lambaste the public for consistently violating sound legal principles and individual rights. He spews out every indictment simmering in his craw for the last twenty years in an almost nonstop series of lectures interrupted by his own narrative.

317. Cooper, Kent. *Anna Zenger, Mother of Freedom.* New York: Farrar, 1946. Cooper's homage to Anna Zenger in this novelized biography uses notes of the court trial published by Zenger himself, German-born printer in the generation preceding the Revolutionary War, accused of seditious and libelous printings defaming the King's lawful representatives.

318. Corman, Avery. *Kramer versus Kramer.* New York: Random, 1977. On the surface a well-written drama about a child-custody case, but its timeliness in bringing into brighter focus the idea of sacrificing fathers who bond with sons and then fight mothers for custody makes this a cultural landmark. The film, especially, is "catnip to the emotion-starved masses," deplores *Halliwell's Film Guide* (568), which yet garnered Oscars for Best Picture, Director (Robert Benton), Best Actor (Dustin Hoffman) and Supporting Actress (Meryl Streep). Corman is also an award-winning documentarian. Ted Kramer's battle with ex-wife Joanna over the custody of son Billy while his professional career wanes is told in the brittle and edgy style of modern minimalists like Raymond Carver and Amy Hempel.

319. Cose, Ellis. *The Best Defense.* New York: HarperCollins, 1998. Award-winning *Newsweek* reporter Cose is one of America's important writers of race relations, affirmative action and gender issues in the workplace issues. His prestigious career includes journalism for *Time* and the *New York Daily News*. Recent books are *Color-Blind* (1998) and *Affirmative Action and the Dilemma of the Qualified* (1996). He also edited a collection of twelve African-American writers in *The Darden Dilemma* (1997), about the inner conflicts of black prosecutors between loyalty to the black community and the law they must enforce, a law which sends multitudes of blacks to prison as a solution to social problems other than crime.

His first fictional novel concerns a killing triggered by affirmative action when a white computer-training expert loses his job to an Hispanic and guns him down as soon as the takeover company announces its diversity policy that will cost him his job. John Wisocki hires Felicia Fontaine, a black defense attorney, as his defense counsel, and though she is a savvy woman and rising media star, she is also impatient with the victimology of the disadvantaged; soon, she gets grief from the black community and is mobbed by various white characters and forces rallying around her client. The obligatory antagonist-as-ex-flame is Mario Santiago leading the prosecution's case in the fireworks trial. Reviewers praise Cose's skill in subordinating the political issue of affirmative action to the complex characters enmeshed by it.

320. Coughlin, William J[eremiah]. *Day of Wrath.* New York: Delacorte, 1980. Coughlin wrote more than legal thrillers and his unusual publishing history includes both political romance and mainstream fiction, as well as solidly built crime novels. His series character, lawyer and recovering alcoholic Charley Sloan, with his career and sobriety in balance, shows endurance. Coughlin began his writing career almost accidentally because he was a lawyer and judge in Detroit. He received a University of Detroit law degree in 1953, went to work for the Wayne County Prosecutor's Office and most recently held the title of US Law Judge for the Social Security Administration in Detroit from 1973 until his death in 1992. He first wrote a nonfictional account of his legal experiences but found no market until a British firm asked him for fiction. He responded with a story about an unethical attorney named Stoney Walsh in a spoof called *The Widow Wondered Why* (1966) and followed it with a second Walsh tale *The Dividend Was Death.* Next came *The Destruction Committee*, which was also published in the US. *The Grinding Mill* (London: Harrap, 1973) bombed, and a few years would pass before his next attempt, but he had found his author's niche. *The Stalking Man* was pure suspense thriller about a detective's search for a maniac (Delacorte, 1979). A mainstream novel tinged with romance and mixing politics, academics, and the legal profession is *No More Dreams* (A &W, 1982). His "real money," as he called it in *CA*, would come in the eighties with two books noted below, and the Charley Sloan books, popular with readers and critics. Cancer struck in the summer of 1991; he died the following spring. *Day of Wrath* is a suspense thriller about the kidnaping of eleven judges by a terrorist.

321. _____. *Death Penalty.* New York: HarperCollins, 1992. Coughlin did not have to go farther than downtown Detroit's Wayne County Circuit Court for the plot of this one: Dr. Jack Kevorkian, a frequent visitor to that court house until his conviction, sentence, and internment in the spring of 1999 for his most recent euthanasia killing, is fictionalized as Miles Stewart, M. D., the infamous medico the newspapers call the "Angel of Death," who helps wealthy, terminally ill patients to die and is now Charley's new client, a circumstance which gives Sloan gets a chance to redeem his career from the brink of disbarment; there is also a case involving an extortion scam that implicates a reputable judge who happens to be an old friend and mentor.

322. _____. *The Heart of Justice.* New York: St. Martin's, 1995. Written prior to his death in April 1992, Coughlin penned a final tale of courtroom justice and domestic fiction both about Paul Murray, of Irish immigrant background, now a federal judge who must rule on a corporate merger between

business gurus Crandell and Valentine that comes too close to home, for his new, wealthy wife is being betrayed by a favorite uncle looting from the family trust fund to make the merger bid.

323. _____. *Her Father's Daughter.* New York: Putnam's, 1986. A family saga of the Sidney Sheldon sort centering around flamboyant Victoria Van Horn, a lawyer who inherits her powerful father's corporation. In a subplot, her Congressman lover gets her arrested on a drug charge after he had attempted to rape her while high on cocaine.

324. _____. *Her Honor.* Judge Kathleen Talbot is newly appointed to the bench and finds herself at the center of a high-profile euthanasia case even while she is being accused of taking her own father off life support; she also finds herself attracted to the defense attorney.

325. _____. *In the Presence of Enemies.* London: Sidgwick, 1989; New York: St. Martin's, 1993. Jake Martin's blue-chip firm saddles him with a will contest in a small town in Upper Michigan. He lets the decedent's wealthy widow seduce him, gets fired over his conduct, and is opposed by the state's best attorney in a longshot courtroom battle.

326. _____. *The Judgment.* New York: St. Martin's-Dunne, 1997. Coughlin's posthumous novel has Motowner Charley Sloan working two cases: one involving big-city politics as he defends the Detroit police commissioner from charges of embezzling one million dollars; the other involves him via his girlfriend, Detective Sue Gillis, who is working on a serial-murder case that involves child murders in a bizarre manner--after killing them, the murderer cleans their bodies and puts them inside plastic wrapping so that they can be laid out in the snow like sleeping angels.

327. _____. *Shadow of a Doubt.* New York: St. Martin's, 1991. Sloan is in small town in Michigan to defend ex-lover Robin Harwel's stepdaughter, accused of murdering her own multimillionaire father. Charlie, seduced by both, must battle the politically motivated DA as well as prove the girl's innocence.

328. _____. *The Twelve Apostles.* New York: Putnam's, 1984. The intrigues and scandals of a powerful New York law firm and its ravenous crew of unethical lawyers.

329. Cowan, Sada. *Bitter Justice.* Garden City, NY: Doubleday, 1943. London: Gifford, 1946. Young Dr. Pedro de Corona is in love with the wife of his benefactor and colleague, Dr. Gordon Sterling. He forms a liaison with an exotic Broadway dancer named Lolita, whose murder results in his indictment and trial. About half the book is devoted to the trial, and in a most melodramatic

fashion, Patricia Sterling announces she has kept her trial lawyer credential up-to-date and decides to take on Pedro's defense against savvy prosecutor Dane Markham. The climax is when she puts her own husband on the stand for cross.

330. Cox, Anthony Berkeley. Francis Iles, pseud. *Malice Aforethought.* London: Gollancz; New York: Harper, 1931. A cynically humorous tale of a dapper little doctor with a detestable wife, whom he poisons with *bacillus enteritidis* and is brought to trial. A brief excerpt is found in Michael Dibdin's edition of *The Vintage Book of Classic Crime*, pp. 311-21 (Picador, 1993; Black Lizard, 1997).

331. _____. Anthony Berkeley, pseud. *Trial and Error.* London: Hodder; Garden City, NY: Doubleday, 1937. The civil trial of Lawrence Todhunter for the murder of Jean Norwood in the Old Bailey. What makes the case so unusual (a private prosecution for murder) is that another man, Vincent Palmer, is awaiting execution for the same crime and that the prosecution's case rests mainly on the defendant's self-accusations.

332. Cozzens, James Gould. *By Love Possessed.* New York: Harcourt, 1957. Cozzens prefers the law above all professions because it epitomizes the fullest use of reason and offers many contrasts with irrationality that his characters face. Arthur Winner is a mid-fifties lawyer whose life is chronicled in fewer than 50 hours with a multitude of challenges that are easy to summarize but impossible to explain. The novel must be read, especially if one prefers the weightier lawyer-protagonist novels of Auchincloss and Turow. Some of the complexities are legal but all are emotionally profound on Winner's psyche and within his circle of family and friends--for example, young Ralph Detweiler's rape charge and Winner's sister's devotion to the boy. Another: Noah Tuttle is his law partner, a much-admired man, who (Winner discovers) has been embezzling trust funds for many years.

333. _____. *The Just and the Unjust.* New York: Harcourt, 1942. London: Cape, 1943. Abner Coates is a young Assistant DA on the verge of deciding to enter politics in the story of a small-town murder trial of big-city criminals. The setting is a small town in Pennsylvania called Childerstown. The case itself, a gang kidnaping of a narcotics dealer, is "the most boring ever to have a whole novel devoted to it," according to Jon Breen (29), but part of Cozzens' purpose is to expose how much dullness there is in courtroom preparation for even a sensational trial. Fortunately, Judge Coates is less bland than his son. A secondary case involves a high-school teacher accused of taking photos of his students naked.

Craddock, Charles Egbert, pseud. *See* Murfree, Mary Noailles. . . .

334. Craig, Georgiana Ann Randolph. Craig Rice, pseud. *Eight Faces at*

Three [Running title: *8 Faces at 3*]. New York: Simon, 1939. A combination of booze and barbiturates ended the life of this colorful mystery writer, publicity agent, producer, and novelist who created series characters like Bingo Riggs and Handsome Kusak. She also ghost wrote for Gypsy Rose Lee and George Sanders. She earned fame and praise for one series character especially--rumpled lawyer and Chicagoan, John J. Malone, who in this tale teams up with friend and press agent Jake Justus and eccentric heiress Helene Brand to discover who killed a vicious dowager and why the murderer then made up the beds in the victim's house and stopped the clocks at three. In an uncollected tale by Rice titled "His Heart Could Break" (1943), Malone goes to see a client on death row in the Illinois State Prison because he has uncovered some exculpatory evidence; however, he arrives too late--the man has hanged himself.

335. _____. *Having Wonderful Crime.* New York: Simon, 1943; Cleveland, OH: World, 1944. Young newlywed Dennis Morrison awakens in a strange hotel room on Fifth Avenue with the Justuses and Malone with a hangover and no memory of the night before except that he had gone on a bender and abandoned his bride somewhere. Preparing to return, police hammer at the door and inform him his new wife is dead, lying decapitated in bed.

336. _____. *My Kingdom for a Hearse.* New York: Simon, 1957. The "little lawyer" is summoned to the Delora Deanne cosmetics company and discovers that "she" is really several women, each of whom provides an anatomical part of the image of the lovely model known to the public as Delora Deanne. Hazel Swackhammer ("I am also Delora Deanne") shows Malone newspaper clippings about the composite model's appearance at night clubs around town and then she shows him a box with suede gloves inside of which are a pair of "slender graceful, ringless, and even now, lovely" hands (9).

337. Crawford, F[rancis]. Marion. *Sant' Ilario.* London and New York: Macmillan, 1889. Sequel to *Saracinesca* (the Saracinesca are one of Rome's great houses) in this tale of rival cousins vying in a lawsuit for titles and lands left by their great-grandfather during the turbulent days of Garibaldi. The protagonist is a painter named Anastase Giouache who intrudes himself into the affairs of Giovani Saracinesca and the antagonist Arnoldo Meschini, murderer of Prince Montevarchi.

338. Cray, David, pseud. *Bad Lawyer.* New York: Carroll, 2001. Hotshot criminal defense lawyer who threw it away for booze and cocaine wants back in the limrelight, and he thinks he has it now in a media-hot case of Thelma Barrow's daughter Priscilla--a white woman who killed her black, abusive husband. What begins auspiciously turns bad when two of his roommates are killed by men looking for $450,000 in drug money that Priscilla is supposed to have ripped off.

339. Creasey, John. [Michael Halliday in Britain, Kyle Hunt in the United States, pseud.]. *Alibi.* New York: Scribner's, 1971. His death in 1973 ended a writing career so prolific that Michael Avellone might be the only writer to come within hailing distance of it. Granted, this voluminous production earned him the mockery of some critics who saw him more as a business than a serious author—"Syndicate C" was one appellation from a reviewer in the *New York Times Book Review*, but the *Spectator* across the Atlantic was kinder, calling his output "an incredible forty-year, six-hundred book feast . . . [for] his fans." Creasey wrote under 24 pseudonyms, male and female, created several mystery, romance, and espionage series but rarely ventured beyond formulaic crime drama into courtroom fiction in all of his 560 novels. According to Smith and White's 1995 *Cloak and Dagger Fiction*, his best work was in that genre, and he is credited by no less an expert than Julian Symons with "pioneer[ing]" the modern-day police procedural (176).

The Roger West series is one of his more competent ones, for Creasey rarely gave more than his usual fortnight to the penning of any novel. Considered "the best-known policeman in England," Chief Superintendent Roger ("Handsome") West is in court the day one of his cases is arraigned in a routine preliminary hearing. Suddenly, a young woman is allowed to offer an alibi to the accused, who is charged with assault for smashing an electric guitar over the head of another man. She claims she was in bed with him--and two others!--when the incident occurred. West's investigation will land him in a sexual blackmailing bind with this same blonde when his digging into her past goes beyond drug- and sex orgies to reveal a conspiracy involving prominent members of business and Parliament plotting a coup against the government of England itself.

340. _____. *Sly as a Serpent.* London: Hodder; New York: Macmillan, 1967. Brian Callard, who is dominated by his mother, snaps under the strain and strangles her. Dr. Cellini believes he can get Callard off with a unique self-defense plea.

341. _____. *Too Good to Be True.* London: Hodder; New York: Macmillan, 1969. Justin Gray, a man of rigid ethical standards, refuses to agree when his three partners in a realty firm want to acquire valuable land cheap from Mrs. Pantanelli, a wealthy and senile elderly woman. When she is poisoned, Justin is accused by eyewitnesses, and the beautiful client who could provide his alibi has disappeared. Dr. Emmanuel Cellini makes only a second appearance to help sort things out. "A hopelessly old hat [ending] in 1910, let alone 1969," says Breen archly (31).

342. Crockett, S. R. [Samuel Rutherford]. *The Gray Man.* New York: Harper, 1896. Romance about Scots history during the turbulent reign of "King Jamie" (James VI, 1567 - 1625) in which a mysterious "Gray Man" is witnessed by the narrator at the murder of Thomas Kennedy of Culzean. The trial of John

Mure, the alleged Gray Man, and his son James occurs at the High Court of Justiciary in Edinburgh with the king himself not only in attendance but scribbling and passing notes to the court justices during the proceedings.

343. Cronin, A. J. [Archibald Joseph]. *Beyond This Place.* London: Gollancz; Boston: Little, 1953. First published serially in *Collier*'s under the title *To Live Again.* Paul Burgess, a youth on the threshold of a teaching career, is told by his mother that his father, believed dead, is the murderer of a young woman who had threatened to expose her pregnancy; in a lurid scandal, Rees Mathry, the father of Paul, is serving out his life sentence in Stoneheath after being reprieved from the death penalty. The son investigates, finds new evidence, and reopens the case.

344. Cuomo, George. *Trial by Water.* New York: Random, 1993. Cuomo's eighth novel is built around a father's relationship to his son and his own to a married woman he is seeing. A prom-night fracas at the lake between two boys, rivals for the same girl, results in the drowning deaths of two teenagers and a courtroom prosecution for the protagonist's son Brian.

Curtis, Richard, pseud. *See* Touster, Irwin . . . .

D

345. Daley, Elizabeth. *The House without the Door.* Harrisburg, PA: Military Serv. Pub., 1942. Admired by Agatha Christie, Daley wrote a series of classic whodunits based on her New England sleuth Henry Gamadge, manuscript expert. Gamadge brings his skills to bear upon a case involving the heirs of Curtis Gregson, a respectable Connecticut lawyer, whose death from an overdose of morphia had occurred three years prior and whose wife was tried and acquitted of his murder. Now she claims that there have been four attempts on her life.

346. Daley, Robert. *Tainted Evidence.* New York: Warner, 1993. Another Wambaugh-like tale by Connecticut author Daley of two cops and an ambitious prosecuting attorney. In the Three-Two in Harlem, vicious drug dealer Lionel Epps is cornered by Officers Barone and Muldoon in a shootout. The sudden death of the DA vaults ambitious Karen Henning into position to be elected DA if she can put the scumbag away. It seems a slam-dunk but defense counsel Justin McCarthy proves a formidable courtroom adversary.

347. Daly, Conor. *Buried Lies.* New York: Kensington, 1995. Conor's series character is another one of those disenchanted lawyers who forsake legal practice for another pursuit. Kiernan Lenahan becomes a professional country club pro in Westchester County, NY. Although Daly's narrative is studded with the finer points golfing for the enthusiast, and the sleuthing is sometimes

stretched to accommodate it, his style is richly descriptive.

348. _____. *Local Knowledge.* New York: Kensington, 1995. Lenahan becomes the prime suspect in the murder of Milton Country Club's one-third owner and founder when the body of Sylvester Miles is found in a pond that Lenahan ordered dragged for golf balls. Another Lenahan outing with a Florida setting is *Outside Agency* (Kensington, 1997).

349. Dane, Clemence, pseud., and Helen Simpson. *Enter Sir John.* London: Hodder; New York: Cosmopolitan, 1928. Actress Martella Baring is accused of the fireplace-poker murder of the wife of actor-manager Gordon Druce. Sir John Saumarez, cinema idol, attends her trial. A second Sir John novel, *Re-Enter Sir John* (Hodder, 1932) gets into court very briefly.

350. Daniels, Harold R. *The Accused.* New York: Dell, 1958. London: Deutsch, 1961. Massachusetts college teacher Alvin Morlock is on trial for the murder of his wife Louise; told via transcripts alternating with flashbacks. "An efficient piece of storytelling," applauds Breen, "but the courtroom scenes are a procedural disaster, reading more like a TV trial than a real one" (32).

351. Daniels, Norman. *Arrest and Trial.* New York: Lancer, 1963. A novelization from a short-lived TV series starring Ben Gazzara as the investigative officer and Chuck Connors as defense counsel. One executive is tried for the attempted murder of another executive, the latter having beat out the former for the CEO spot.

352. _____. *The Missing Witness.* New York: Lancer, 1964. Two trials: the father of a retarded baby who died in surgery and the surgeon for murder. The surgeon, who claims he did not euthanize the infant, then sues the police for slander.

353. _____. *Shadow of a Doubt.* New York: Fawcett-Gold Medal, 1961. London: Muller, 1962. A high-school science teacher sees a man leaving a vacant house next door to his Westwood, California, home. When a ten-year-old girl is found there raped and murdered, Griffith becomes key witness in the case against a prominent citizen. The book seems to promise a big capital felony trial but does not deliver in the second half, which is just as well, argues Breen, for there is "so much in-court conversation among the central characters it's a wonder the judge doesn't shut them up" (34).

354. Dannay, Frederick, and Manfred B[ennington]. Lee. Ellery Queen, pseud., ed. *101 Years' Entertainment: The Great Detective Stories, 1841-1941* [alt. title *To the Queen's Taste*]. Boston: Little, 1941; rpt. 1943. A massive tome of mostly pure detection but Melville Davisson Post's "The Doomdorf Mystery," with Uncle Abner appearing alongside Squire Randolph, is to be

noted here.

355. _____. *The Bizarre Murders.* Philadelphia: Lippincott, 1962. Contains: *The Siamese Twin Mystery*, *The Chinese Orange Mystery*, and *The Spanish Cape Mystery.*

356. _____. Ellery Queen, pseud. *Calamity Town.* Boston: Little; London: Gollancz, 1942. Fans of Ellery Queen still appreciate the classical, fair-play whodunits penned by this pair of authors, Brooklyn-born cousins, whose real names are Daniel Nathan and Manford Lepofsky. Among them is veteran thriller writer Edward Hoch, who says: "The solutions are often brilliant, dazzling displays of the least-suspected-person technique at its most ambitious" (qtd. in Jakubowsky 75). Queen was the last of the classical detectives. In the 1930s Dannay and Lee worked under studio contracts and edited *Mystery League* magazine, and from 1941, *Ellery Queen's Mystery Magazine* (Dannay credited as the more active); they wrote the Queen radio series from 1939-48 and co-founded the Mystery Writers of America. The cousins intended to retire from writing after *The Finishing Stroke* (1958) but a final cluster of Queens were published 5 years later with *A Fine and Private Place* (1971) coincident with Lee's death from a heart attack.

Queen is that gentlemanly writer (of his own cases) and amateur detective, who remains an amorphous figure throughout his long, caper-solving series (wears good suits, has "devastatingly" silver eyes, seems more attracted to women as he ages; the first Queens showed him to be a *fin-de-siècle* dandy, doffed in tweeds and affecting a pince-nez, scoffing at his father, Inspector Richard Queen, whose connections to police investigation give Ellery *carte blanche* at crime scenes. Hoch claims that Queen was at his best in his middle period during the forties "when he was equally adept at solving a small-town poisoning (*Calamity Town* [1942]) and tracking a big-city serial killer (*Cat of Many Tails* [1949])" (Jakubowsky 75). Queen's habit is to leave his Manhattan office (he writes there), and as a result of his father's work in police investigations, intercepts police investigations with his perfect solutions to the crime without managing to ruffle a dark hair of his handsome head or perturb the egos of professional cops as do Holmes and Poirot. Very few Queen mysteries get inside the courtroom because they are boilerplate examples of classic detection. The compilers of *Detectionary* aver:

> The 'author' has the distinction of being one of the most important personalities in the history of detective fiction. Not only is Ellery Queen, the detective, one of the most famous characters in literature, but the magazine that bears his name is the most important and successful of its type. As an anthologist, Ellery Queen is without peer, his taste unequalled. . . . Indeed, Ellery Queen clearly is, after Poe, the most important American of mystery fiction. (90)

Jim Haight is accused of poisoning his sister, although the poison was apparently intended for Haight's wife. This was the first of Queen's Wrightsville novels, published as an omnibus (Boston: Little, 1956).

357. _____. *Double, Double* [alt. title: *The Case of the Seven Murders*, New York: Pocket, 1958]. Boston: Little; London: Gollancz, 1950. Ellery receives strange newspaper clippings from Wrightsville. The town miser dies and leaves a fortune to a beloved, impoverished doctor, who promptly announces the building of a new hospital with the money. Then a pair of stranger events, duly noted in the local paper and anonymously sent along: a wealthy businessmen, turned beggar by his own imprudence dies, then the town drunk meets a violent end. Ellery fathoms a dark secret of his idyllic New England town: people are dying like the nursery rhyme: *Rich man, poor man, beggar man, thief . . .*

358. _____. *The Dragon's Teeth* [alt. title: *The Virgin Heiress*, New York: Pocket, 1954]. New York: Stokes; London: Gollancz, 1939. Ellery's partner Beau Rummell, himself a lawyer at loose ends, brings Queen a case involving a millionaire named Cadmus Cole, a reclusive who lives aboard ship; he hires the detective to investigate an impending case, one that might make it impossible for him to hire a detective later--namely, his own murder.

359. _____. *Ellery Queen's Big Book.* New York: Grosset, 1938. The first Queen omnibus.

360. _____. *Ellery Queen's Mystery Parade.* New York: Cleveland: World, 1944. All detection tales but a pastiche by Jon L. Breen worth noting titled "The Austin Murder Case," in the style of S. S. Van Dine with Philo Vance and DA John F. X. Markham combining skills to solve the murder of a musical comedy star.

361. _____. *Face to Face.* New York: NAL; London: Gollancz, 1967. Lorette Spanier is tried for the murder of thirties singing star Gloria Guild.

362. _____. *The Fourth Side of the Triangle.* New York: Random; London: Gollancz, 1965. Millionaire Ashton Mckell and his wife are accused of murdering a fashion designer. Their son Dane is subsequently arrested after the parents are cleared. Ellery is hobbled from a skiing accident and plays a lesser role in this one.

363. _____. *The Glass Village.* Boston: Little; London: Gollancz, 1954. In a tiny New England village called Shimm Corners, one of its most famous citizens is beaten to death with a poker and a drifter named Josef Kowalczyk accused. To avert a lynching, Judge Shinn presides over a phony trial riddled with procedural errors to satisfy First Selectman Hube Hemus, leader of the

angry townspeople who want to avenge Aunt Fanny Adams' murder. Queen does not appear in this one or in *Cop Out* (Cleveland: World; London: Gollancz, 1969).

364. _____. *Halfway House.* New York: Stokes; London: Gollancz, 1936. Bigamist Joseph Gimball maintained households in New York and in Philadelphia (as Joseph Wilson); he used a house in Trenton, New Jersey to change identities, so when he is found stabbed to death there, his Philadelphia wife is tried in Mercer County Courthouse. When Queen's testimony fails to help her defense, she is found guilty; then Queen must find the real killer to save her from death row.

365. _____. *The Hollywood Murders.* Philadelphia: Lippincott, 1957. Includes *The Devil to Pay*, *The Four of Hearts*, and *The Origin of Evil.*

366. _____. *The New York Murders.* Boston: Little, 1958. Contains *Cat of Many Tails*, *The Scarlet Letters*, and *The American Gun Mystery* [alt. title: *Death at the Rodeo*] (New York: Triangle, 1933; London: Gollancz, 1951).

367. _____. *QED: Queen's Experiments in Detection.* New York: NAL, 1968; London: Gollancz, 1969. Short-story collection. "Miracles Do Happen" gives a glimpse of Ellery's profession as he takes a wife's case for a husband accused of murdering a moneylender in his office when the note was called in too soon.

368. _____. *There Was an Old Woman* [alt. title: *The Quick and the Dead*, New York: Pocket, 1954]. The old woman of the title is Mrs. Cornelia Potts, shoe manufacturing heiress, who accompanies her Harvard lawyer and son Thurlow into the Supreme Court building for a slander action. When the judge dismisses the case, a scuffle with reporters occurs on the sidewalk, and Ellery, accompanying his own father on an unrelated case, is induced by the family lawyer to meet the son and deflect him from buying a gun but ultimately finds himself being coerced into acting as second in the code of the duello for Thurlow.

369. _____. *The Tragedy of X.* New York: Viking; London: Cassell, 1932. The first of four novels about Drury Lane is also the first to do so. It features a deaf, retired actor based on William Gillette, Sherlock Holmes portrayer, and is "one of the finest pure detective novels of the thirties" (Breen 147). In New York's Criminal Courts Building, stockbroker John O. DeWitt is tried before Judge Grimm for the murder of Charles Wood, killed when thrown from a ferry. (The novel's principal murder is the poisoning of Harley Longstreet while he rides a streetcar.) DA Bruno "viciously assailed" DeWitt on cross, but no testimony is quoted. Breen also notes that *The Tragedy of Z* (1933), a later Drury Lane novel, includes a 7-page summarized trial.

Lippincott of Philadelphia published an omnibus Drury Lane series in 1961: *The X, Y, Z Murders*. Some additional Queen omnibuses and novels noted below.

370. Darden, Christopher, with Dick Lochte. *The Trials of Nikki Hill.* New York: Warner, 1999. Darden made his reputation with LA prosecutor Marcia Clark opposed to the Dream Team in the O. J. Simpson trial and published his account of it (as did several other principals). His first attempt at fiction features a melodramatic, courtroom-less tale of a savvy black woman attorney who is assigned the case of Jamal Deschamps, a gangbanger in the wrong place at the wrong time. Cops caught him in an alley, where he was evading Crazy Eights gangsters in South Central LA, having just pulled the diamond ring off the finger of a naked white female's corpse in the alley's dumpster. Not just anyone, the woman is Maddie Gray, celebrity tabloid TV personality, and the case immediately becomes front page.

371. Davidson, David. *The Quest of Juror 19.* Garden City, NY: Doubleday, 1971. Davidson has a long history in television and journalism. He once interviewed 2,500 Bavarian Germans about life under Hitler and produced several award-winning dramas and documentaries. His novel is less legal thriller than a mainstream novel of midlife crisis in the style of John Cheever or John Updike, although it opens in court as the reader meets Mark Robling performing his civic duty. The daily menu of crime inspires him to thoughts about confronting the problems in his life, such as a recalcitrant son and a treacherous colleague upon whom he begins to plot a crime of his own.

372. Davidson, Louis B., and Eddie Doherty. *Captain Marooner.* New York: Crowell, 1952. Introd. William McFee. Lawyer Davidson's hobby of researching maritime piracy cases and scanning the logs of old sailing vessels for criminal activity resulted in this tale based on a mutiny aboard the *Globe* in the 1800s. Captain Worth is one part Ahab and two parts Bligh, who flogs his men and loves whale oil as if it were gold. His ship rescues sailor Joe Thomas adrift on the ocean and then, branding him a Jonah, maroons him on a desert isle. At the end of the novel, Thomas is tried for the hated captain's murder.

373. Davies, Jonathan. *Given in Evidence.* London: Hodder, 1996. A drug-smuggling operation comes before the British courts.

374. Davies, Rhys. *The Black Venus.* London: Heinemann, 1944. New York: Howell, Soskin, 1946. Whimsical account of the eighteenth-century Welsh custom of "courting in bed." Olwen Powell, a beautiful young woman whose father owns much land, is summoned to a hearing by church elders and neighbors; she has her village in an uproar because she takes several lovers without marriage in mind under the ancient custom that was originally meant to prove a woman's fertility rather than sexual compatibility.

375. Davies, Valentine. *Miracle on 34th Street.* New York: Harcourt, 1947. The novel that produced the wholesome classic film about the trial of Macy's Department Store Santa, threatened with being committed because he believes himself the real Santa Claus. George Seaton, director, won an Oscar for adapting Davies' novel. Perf. Edmund Gwenn, John Payne and Maureen O'Hara.

376. Davis, Christopher. *Philadelphia.* New York: Bantam, 1994. Davis novelizes John Nyswaner's screenplay in this Hollywood-topical story of a Philadelphia lawyer working for an old-line firm; just as he is at the threshold of making partner he discovers he has AIDS and is fired, ostensibly over a missing case file, but in fact because of his disease. He hires Joe Miller, a personal-injury litigator who gets his clients from slick TV ads, to get justice. The TriStar 1993 film starring Tom Hanks and Denzel Washington (playing Miller) was directed by Jonathan Demme.

377. Davis, John Gordon. *Unofficial and Deniable.* New York: HarperCollins, 1999. Cosmopolitan Davis was born in Rhodesia (Zimbabwe) educated in Pretoria at the University of South Africa, worked as a miner in Ontario before returning to the law as a Crown Counsel in Rhodesia prior to independence. He held the same position in Hong Kong. He and his Australian wife divide their time among three places: on a farm in Spain, in Africa, and aboard his yacht. Jack Harker is an ex-South African military intelligence officer who does not want to risk exposure by the Truth and Reconciliation Commission in 1994 established after independence. He and his wife disappear aboard his yacht but a month later he is on trial for murder in a Florida courtroom. A recent novel, *The Year of Loving Dangerously*, has courtroom elements and is set in the tense days prior to the Chinese government's reclaiming of Hong Kong in 1999.

378. Davis, Lindsey. *Time to Depart.* New York: Warner, 1998. Ancient Roman investigator Marcus Didius Falco finally gets his man in this seventh book of the series--notorious criminal Balbinus Pius, but the archcriminal invokes a law to preclude his execution by hanging and goes into exile.

379. Davis, Rankin. *Abuse of Process.* New York: Berkley, 1997. A courtroom sketch artist is the only one convinced of the guilt of a truck driver in a 5-year series of murders in the London area.

380. _____. *Hung Jury.* New York: Berkley, 1999. The Attorney General for England and Wales is prosecuting a high-profile murder case. Alex Parrish is the lone juror holding out for a not-guilty verdict. A subplot involves the brother of the Prime Minister, who is notified by terrorists that his brother has been abducted, the very brother who is prosecuting the case. If England frees

the defendant, they'll free Sir Edward Haversham.

381. Davis, Robert P. *The Divorce.* New York: Morrow; London: Hale, 1980. A look at a modern, messy divorce with a sidebar on the legal action that follows in the wake of a marriage gone awry. The participants are an educated, wealthy husband and wife from fictional upscale Menlo Park, Connecticut, who so mismanage their marital relationship (to the delight of their scandalized contemporaries) that the judge terminates the couple's parental authority and orders their arrest for perjured testimony. Davis claims the account is real, and adds a legal document for verisimilitude, but it is less shocking today it must have seemed to its original audience.

382. Davis, Timothy Francis Tothill. John Cashman, pseud. *The Cook-General.* New York: Harper, 1974. London: Hamilton, 1975. Based on an 1879 murder case: Kate Webster, a pitiless Irish servant, is accused of murdering and dismembering her elderly employer, Julia Thomas.

383. _____. *The Gentleman from Chicago: Being an Account of the Doings of Thomas Neill Cream, M. D. (M'Gill) 1850-1892.* New York: Harper, 1973. The subtitle's reference to the infamous Neill (Cream) case, a doctor who poisoned his victims, is slanted toward sensationalism, but the book is a creditable exercise in imagining a killer's view of his past. Consisting of three parts with the first being his own account of his warped childhood in Quebec between 1850-76; the second covers his experiences in Britain, Canada, and back in the US. Part 3 includes a synopsis of his trial and imprisonment (1881-89) in Joliet's Illinois State Prison and concludes with the a medical professional's commentary on the case and the man's sanity.

384. _____. *Kid Glove Charlie.* New York: Harper, 1978. An oft-arrested burglar enjoys attending others' trials and cheering them on. Two brothers in Manchester go on trial for a constable's murder while "Kid Glove" Charlie roots for their acquittal. He himself is on trial in the Old Bailey is for the attempted murder of another constable. A magistrate's hearing follows in Sheffield, where Peace is charged with the murder of his former mistress' husband, and he is later put on trial in a Leeds Assize for the same charge. Charles Frederick Peace was a legendary Victorian criminal (1832 - 1879).

385. Day Lewis, C[ecil]. Nicholas Blake, pseud. *A Tangled Web.* London: Collins; New York: Harper, 1956. Poet laureate (1968) Lewis authored 20 mysteries, 16 of which feature Oxonian Nigel Strangeways.

386. Deal, Borden. *The Advocate.* Garden City, NY: Doubleday, 1968. John Bookman is a small-town lawyer in sleepy Tupelo in the Deep South. His political ambitions were wrecked a few years earlier by an inopportune comment on integration before the cameras; his marriage is rocked by a liaison

and illegitimate child. His court cases are briefly summarized, the first dealing with his out-of-court defense of an 18-year-old sadistic rapist from a well-to-do family and the other concerns a testator's will disputed sanity and an attempt by a political rival from the gubernatorial campaign to blacken Bookman's name over a charge of undue influence.

387. Deaver, Jeffery Wilds. *Mistress of Justice.* New York: Doubleday, 1992. Former journalist and Wall Street attorney Deaver has authored five novels and garnered an Edgar nomination for *Manhattan Is My Beat* (1989). This novel offers a paralegal sleuth and part-time jazz musician, Taylor Lockwood, who is hired by trial lawyer Mitchell Reece, a member of a blue-chip Wall Street firm. Reece wants Lockwood to find out who stole a 25 million-dollar promissory note he was holding in a forthcoming corporate litigation out of his own office files before his reputation, and the client, is ruined.

388. De Felitta, Frank. *Audrey Rose.* New York: Putnam's, 1975. London: Collins, 1976. Bill and Janet Templeton lose their daughter Audrey Rose in a fiery car crash. A man named Elliott Hoover claims their daughter Ivy is the reincarnation of his daughter. Breen calls it a "second-rate horror novel" with "[o]verwrought trial action" (35). The film of this title (UA, 1977) is described as a spiritualist thriller.

389. De La Ramée, Louise. Ouida, pseud. *Under Two Flags.* Philadelphia: Lippincott, 1877. A lot of sand and fury mostly about derring-do among the chausseurs d'Afrique, but here is yet another novel built around the law of primogeniture and a brother's betrayal of another. In this case, Bertie Cecil is the elder brother and a peer stripped of his legal inheritance by a scheming sibling.

390. De Vere, Edward [7th Earl of Oxford]. William Shakespeare, pseud. *The Merchant of Venice.* Glenview, IL and Brighton, Eng.: Scott, 1973. Scholars locate this great comedy in the Earl's second period between 1594 and 1598. It belongs here because it includes a lawsuit and trial as well as the memorable soliloquy on the "quality of mercy." Portia, who in the crossdressing fashion of Shakespeare's strong female leads, presides over the case by imitating a lawyer named Balthasar to render justice. In finding for Shylock, the despised moneylender, however, Portia allows him his penalty contract: a "pound of flesh" to be taken from Antonio, who had guaranteed the contract for an even harsher anti-Semite--fellow Venetian shipping entrepreneur, Bassanio. Failing to sway him with her speech, Portia tells Shylock that he may have his pound of flesh from any part of Antonio he prefers but that he may not take not one single drop of blood along with it--or his own life will be forfeit. Andrew C. Emerson, Indianapolis attorney, muses that Shakespeare's play might be the origin of the British rule of damages: loser pays winner's costs plus attorney's fee. Other notable plays with lawyers and the law include *Hamlet*

(Rosencranz and Guildenstern) *King Lear*, *Measure for Measure*, *Othello*, *Richard II*, and A *Winter's Tale*.

391. Defoe, Daniel. *The Fortunes and Misfortunes of the Famous Moll Flanders, & c. Who Was Born in Newgate, and during a Life of Continu'd Variety for Threescore Years, besides Her Childhood, Was Twelve Year a Whore, Five Times a Wife, Twelve Year a Thief, Eight Year a Transported Felon in Virginia, at Last Grew Rich, Liv'd Honest, a Died a Penitant.* London: Dent; Rutland, VT: Tuttle, 1982. Since publication in 1772, Defoe's great novel has leaped its picaresque fences to become the starting point of the modern novel. The difference between Moll's record of her life as a serial bigamist, thief and female rogue of the eighteenth century is that, as a woman on her own like John Cleland's Fanny Hill (whose "memoirs" are begun the same decade), she is more than the surface verisimilitude of what she records. Defoe's anti-romantic and very busy pen ensured her place in the literature of his time and ours. Moll's repentance is not sham but neither is it for the betterment of the moral rectitude of the reader, as she says--that is incidental to the intimate details and realism of Moll's record of her adventurous and sexually liberated life amid the marital romps and thieving capers she faithfully confesses to. One episode lands her back to her birthplace in Newgate Gaol as she is brought before the magistrates and sentenced to Virginia. Filmmaker Jim Sheridan's *Moll Flanders* is a stylish version, produced in 1996, and starring Robin Wright.

392. Deighton, Len. *Violent Ward.* New York: HarperCollins, 1993. An odd comic gem from one of the best espionage thriller authors of the last century. In fact, Smith and White consider him one of the three great espionage novelists of our times along with Eric Ambler and Ted Allbeury. (John le Carré, pseud., limps home a distant fourth). Deighton briefly used the Southern California locale in one of his Bernard Samson trilogies, but this time the protagonist is a devious criminal lawyer named Mickey Murphy, whose clients are even shadier. One of whom is a dangerous, self-made millionaire, Zach Petrovich, married to Murphy's boyhood sweetheart; the lawyer has to find out why he is the prime suspect in a brutal killing.

393. DeMille, Nelson. *Gold Coast.* New York: Warner, 1990. The title refers to the North Shore of Long Island where lawyer-narrator John Sutter lives. His new neighbor and soon-to-be client is underworld boss Frank Bellarossa, who claims that US Attorney Alphonse Ferragamo is trying to frame him for the execution murder of a drug cartel associate in order to get the Columbians to murder him, he claims, because of a personal vendetta stemming from a courtroom incident several years ago.

394. _____. *Word of Honor.* New York: Warner, 1985. Former Vietnam vet Ben Tyson has led a good life, albeit with a rocky marriage, since the war. Now 16 years after the war, someone from Ben's unit has leaked a secret with

the dire result that a Vietnam journalist brings to the public in the form of a bestselling expose about an atrocity committed in a Hue hospital in 1968 against wounded and dying men. The book alleges soldiers from Lieutenant Tyson's command are responsible. The Army responds to public pressure and court-martial him. DeMille was himself a lieutenant in Vietnam.

395. Denker, Henry. *A Case of Libel.* New York and London: French, 1964. Denker's play is based on the book *My Life in Court* by Louis Nizer. Dennis Corcoran, a foreign correspondent, sues a New York columnist named Boyd Bendix for libel. Corcoran is smeared as a "drunken, immoral, yellow-bellied degenerate who tried to give us the impression that he was a fearless war correspondent" (13). Robert Sloane, trial attorney, makes a stirring summation in the third act.

396. _____. *A Place for the Mighty: A Novel about Superlawyers.* New York: McKay, 1973. Broadway playwright-novelist Denker writes a dialogue-driven plot revolves around a disturbed black assassin, Midgely Grove, of a liberal Supreme Court Judge when court is in session; much of the novel is ponderous and dated, but there is an anticipation of the kind of jury nullification verdict in the promised second trial, in which the book's protagonist and co-counsel, idealist Scott Ingramm, casts off the spell of radical chic politics. Lincoln Winkler, whose grandstanding, self-aggrandizing politics caricatures the late William Kunstler's style, is determined to exploit the case for all its worth despite his co-counsel's advice that a plea of insanity is the right way. It toys with the Doctrine of Social Inevitability (Winkler's summation on pp. 348-52), trendy but unwarranted by the conflicts. Other Supreme Court killings occur in Edward Linn's *The Adversaries* (1973) and John Grisham's T*he Pelican Brief* (1992).

397. _____. *Doctor on Trial.* New York: Morrow, 1992. Variation on Denker's previous malpractice book with striking similarities: in this one, Kate Forrester is the doctor being sued by the powerful man. Claude Stuyvesant's 19-year-old daughter dies in an emergency room of a New York hospital. Dr. Forrester was in charge but unable to make a diagnosis when Claudia Stuyvesant was brought in by her mother with complaints of fever and abdominal pain.

398. _____. *Judge Spencer Dissents.* New York: Morrow, 1986. Denker's conservatism about social issues finds venting in the character of innovative Judge Harry Spencer of the Circuit Court of Appeals in St Louis. The issues: Busing, Affirmative Action, Comparable Worth, and Bi-Lingual Education. Judge Spencer is a Harry Truman kind of homespun jurist-philosopher who enrages his colleagues by dramatizing court cases to expose the tyranny of liberalism run amok in the US. For example, he orders his decision in a lawsuit on bi-lingual education printed in Spanish in the *Law Journal* to show his disapproval, although he supported the actual case for it; in another instance, he

is accused of sexism by the Women's Bar Association because he orders a female lawyer to wear a bra in court.

399. _____. *Labyrinth.* New York: Morrow, 1994. New York murder trial involving multiple personality.

400. _____. *My Son, the Lawyer.* New York: Crowell, 1950. The career of David Brown through college, law school, and clerkship to a fledgling practice during the tough days of the Depression. Brown's shady partner Nudelson gets him involved with bribery of a state liquor authority inspector because he needs money for his mother dying of cancer. The novel is hijacked en route by Mama, who badgers her son incessantly about everything. When he says he wants to abandon law to write for a WPA project, she erupts in her best Jewish-mother *shtik*: "Write? You're *meshugah*? Crazy altogether? Who's giving you chances to write?" (150).

401. _____. *Outrage.* New York: Morrow, 1982. A man's daughter is raped and murdered, but the perpetrator goes free on a technicality. The father hunts down and executes his daughter's murderer. His young defender cannot get him to cooperate on an insanity plea because he insists on being tried. The trial is followed from *voir dire* to deliberation. Breen applauds this one, despite its being a polemic to catch the shifting winds of popular opinion.

402. _____. *The Physicians: A Novel of Malpractice.* New York: Simon, 1975. Powerful John Stewart Reynolds sues Metropolitan General Hospital and one of its neonatal staff, Dr. Christopher Grant, for malpractice alleging that phototherapy treatment of his infant grandson's jaundice resulted in a smaller head size and severe retardation.

403. _____. *This Child Is Mine.* New York: Morrow, 1995. Child custody case of *Manning v. Salem.* The principals of the action tried by the Family Court judge, Judge Judson Hart, the plaintiffs, Lori Adams and Brett Manning, natural parents versus the defendants Bill and Christine Salem, adoptive parents of two-and-a-half-year-old Scotty Salem.

404. Denton, Kit. *The Breaker.* Sydney and London: Angus and Robertson, 1973. New York: St. Martin's, 1981 [subtitle: The Novel behind Breaker Morant]. The real Harry Morant and Peter Hancock were executed by firing squad of Cameron Highlanders at Pietersburg on 27 February 1902. These Australian officers and a third man (sentenced to life on the Isle of Wight) were court-martialed by the British Army for murdering prisoners during the Boer War. Since then, no Australian soldier has been tried on a capital charge by a British Army Court. The book was inspired by a conversation with Harry ("Breaker") Morant, who according to the book was "a horseman, poet, soldier, and, perhaps, murderer of civilians" (n. pag.). Denton based his novel on two

years of research and court records, although the British government would not provide several essential documents. The film by South Australian Film Corporation in 1980 received an Oscar nomination for the screenplay. Dir. Bruce Beresford. Writ. Jonathan Hardy, Bruce Beresford, and David Stevens. Play by Kenneth Ross. Perf. Edward Woodward, Jack Thompson, and John Waters.

405. Derleth, August. *Sentence Deferred.* New York: Scribner's; London: Heinemann, 1939. Forensic evidence comprising a charred corpse, dental evidence, and two different bullets in the skull of dead banker Henry Hornly result in two defendants being tried separately for his murder while Judge Peck observes from the gallery until it is time for him to reveal the murderer's identity. Derleth suffers by comparison, imputes Breen, for his gimmickry and the novel is more notable as a regional period piece, "giving a strong feeling of the problems of the Depression era" (37).

406. _____. *Sign of Fear.* New York: Loring, 1935. London: Newnes, 1936. Judge Ephraim Peck appears for the defense in this tale from the Wisconsin author's Sac Prairie saga of detective novels. Archeologist Christopher Jannichon returns to his home in Prairie du Chien because of a series of postcards with veiled threats.

407. Dershowitz, Alan M. *The Advocate's Devil.* New York: Warner, 1994. Knicks starting point guard Joe Campbell is accused of raping Jennifer Dowling, a charge he denies by claiming consensual sex. His lawyer Abe Ringel secures a not-guilty verdict despite some disturbing evidence against his client that suggests he needs to rape to overcome his impotence. Abe is then horrified to discover that his own 18-year-old daughter is dating Campbell and plans to "seduce" him as a birthday present to herself. A decent courtroom thriller and first novel from the famed Harvard law professor who has defended Claus von Bulow, Mike Tyson. He recently authored the *Abuse Excuse* (1994), an attack on the sob stories and cop-outs offered by criminal clients nowadays. In aligning himself with the Simpson trial, Dershowitz cast off his reputation as an outstanding Constitutional lawyer for a mess of pottage--the aura of TV glitz surrounding Simpson's pop-up Dream-Team lawyers. The serious issue debated in the epilogue is whether a lawyer should breach the lawyer-client privilege, something Dershowitz notes the American Bar Association is currently considering in its rules of lawyer confidentiality. A nonserious sidebar occurs midway through the Campbell rape trial when penis size evidence is debated by opposing counsel. ABC aired its televised version as a Sunday Night Movie, starring Ken Olin as Ringel, on 5 October 1997.

408. _____. *Just Revenge.* New York: Warner, 1999. Max Menuchen's family was slaughtered in a Lithuanian forest, and he promised his dying grandfather he would fulfill the old man's last word: "'*Nekema*!'" [Revenge!]

(46). Amazingly he discovers the Nazi leader living in 'retirement as a Boston car mechanic but dying of pancreatic cancer. He consults Harvard-trained lawyer Abe Ringel for advice, but the Justice Department's Office of Special Investigations turns them down because Marcellus Prandus will certainly die before deportation proceedings can work through the courts. Washington lawyer Seth Bloom admires the book for its powerful philosophical undertones and complexity (Prandus loves his grandchildren too) but regrets that Dershowitz took time away to take potshots at his detractors from the Dream-Team episode (*Legal Times* 29 Nov. 1999: 29).

409. Deverell, William H[erbert]. *Dance of Shiva.* Toronto: McClelland, 1984; New York: Bantam, 1985. Canadian lawyer born March 4, 1937 in Regina, Saskatchewan, he received his LL.B. from the University of Saskatchewan in 1962. He was a partner and trial attorney with a Vancouver firm from 1964 until 1979, when writing took over his career. Besides his memberships in several mystery-writing associations, Deverell is also a past chair of the Criminal Justice Section of the Canadian Bar Association and a founding member of the British Columbia Civil Liberties Association. He has authored a true-crime work based on his defense of a man accused of killing his elderly female employer during a luxury cruise (*Fatal Cruise: The Trial of Robert Frisbee*, McClelland, 1991). He also scripted *The Button Man*, a CBC pilot for the very popular CBC-TV series *Street Legal.* His novels are praised by critics for clear prose, sense of humor, and gift for characterization. He splits time between Costa Rica and Pender Island off the coast of British Columbia. (*See* Mr. Deverell's comment in **Craft Notes**.)

Brian Pomeroy's legal firm (Pomeroy, Macarthur, Brovak and Sage) is introduced in this novel and will return in *Kill All the Lawyers.*

410. _____. *High Crimes.* Toronto: McClelland, 1979; New York: St. Martin's, 1980. Drawn from a trial in which the author was counsel, the novel concerns Newfoundland history in which eighteenth-century Irishmen, escaped indentured servants and impressed sailors, became a clan of rogues and smugglers headed by Peter Kerrivan. The novel is about drug smuggling, Columbian narcotics bosses, CIA and DEA agents with Mounties in opposition to the traffickers and their minions, among whom is the dashing Peter Kerrivan, Newfoundland's modern version of his famous namesake, betrayed by a friend in a bad dope bust. Judge Tilley dissects a Toronto lawyer named Peddigrew for sport but then turns on Inspector Mitchell of the RCMP to throw the case out of court and free the smugglers.

411. _____. *Kill All the Lawyers.* Toronto and New York: Random, 1994. Someone is taking Dick the Butcher's line from de Vere's *Henry the Sixth*, Part II, seriously and lawyers with sleazy clients are being executed in Vancouver one after another. First is Arthur Besterman, reformed alcoholic and criminal lawyer; then Brian Pomeray is almost killed after defending eco-terrorists.

412. _____. *Mindfield.* Toronto: McClelland, 1989; Latham, NY: British American, 1990. Dr. Gregor Satorius is in a Montreal courtroom facing tough *séparatiste* and civil rights lawyer Sarah Paradis, who has brought a lawsuit on behalf of brain-damaged clients, all of whom claim to have been victims of Satorius' CIA-sanctioned experiments at his clinic in the 1970s.

413. _____. *Needles.* Toronto: McClelland; Boston: Little, 1979. Taking a break from his legal practice to work 15 hours a day at his manual typewriter paid off in the $50,000 First Novel Award from his publishing house (McClelland & Stewart/Seal) and the following year the Periodical Distributors Association of Canada Award. Foster Cobb is a Crown prosecutor in Vancouver working a murder case against notorious Dr. Au Pang Wei, tong leader of a heroin syndicate run out of Hong Kong. The case looks good for Cobb, but he has a serious problem: he himself is a steady heroin addict.

414. _____. *Platinum Blues.* Toronto: McClelland, 1989; Latham, NY: British American, 1990. In the *New York Times Book Review,* Marilyn Stasio says this novel offers "hilariously pointed observations on the legal chicanery and artistic horn-swoggling that goes on in the record industry; also praised in the Toronto *Globe and Mail* for its crisp dialogue and good trial scenes" (qtd. in *CA*). Oliver Gulliver is a small-town lawyer in Fool's Gold, California, when his daughter brings home a burned-out Canadian rocker named C. C. Gilley. Gilley's love ballad to the daughter is now a big hit worth millions, and Gulliver sees the golden opportunity of a lifetime in suing the music moguls for pirating the tune.

415. _____. *Street Legal.* Toronto: McClelland, 1995. The novelization of the popular series syndicated "from Russia to Abu Dhabi," according to its proud author's note. The fledgling Toronto law firm of Robinovitch, Barr, Barr, Tchobanian takes a variety of cases that range from hate-literature law to defending a man accused of serial murder to a Frenchman arrested for triple murder in a drug war. The major focal character is the second Barr, née Connor, wife of the first Barr.

416. _____. *Trial of Passion.* Toronto: McClelland, 1997. A new look from the author, although the opening is typically sensational. Kimberley Martin, young, nude, smeared with red lipstick, crying hysterically, beats on the door of a retired Anglican bishop in the middle of the night in West Vancouver. Full of middle-aged triste and Rimbaud or Virgil quotations is Arthur Beauchamp, who will defend his friend Jonathan O'Donnell, Dean of Law at the University of British Columbia, charged with raping that young woman.

417. Dewlen, Al. *Twilight of Honor.* New York: McGraw, 1961. London: Longman, 1962. Owen Paulk is appointed by the court to defend a drifter

accused of killing Jess Hutcherson, a Texas Panhandle town's leading citizen. Owen is one of those disenchanted trial attorneys who has had an acquitted client go out and murder (his young wife dying adds to his despair). Now he is faced with a difficult defense and little help except from an elderly lawyer and his young, beautiful daughter. The case concerns a murder in the Texas Panhandle when old Jess Hutcherson is killed by a pair of hitchhikers; a twist occurs when the 17-year-old female turns on her boyfriend, alleging she was raped--and promptly claims the reward money. Despite what sounds like an egregious piling on of stereotypes, this novel elicits comparison to the Big Trial novels, especially one set in the Upper Peninsula of Michigan, *Anatomy of a Murder*. The astute Breen ranks it very high among legal thrillers: "The case is one of the most throughly presented, from jury selection through eloquent closing arguments through verdict, in all of fiction" (38). Judge James A. Sharman is nothing like Voelker's somber Judge Harlan Weaver, however, but he is a delightful morsel of characterization in his own right, prone to surreptitious reading of issues of the *National Geographic* when his cases dawdle and notorious for grunting, gesturing, and mugging toward trial lawyers and witnesses when his cases are exciting.

418. Dias, Dexter. *Error of Judgment.* London: Hodder; New York: Mysterious, 1996. Dias is a British barrister, whose books mixes taut psychosexual suspense with courtroom drama. As a British barrister, he could be likened to an American civil liberties lawyer whose practice is built around clients disadvantaged by discrimination or poverty. He authored various political and legal pieces before meeting Ruth Rendell while he was defending in a murder trial in 1993. She encouraged him to write fiction.

On Christmas Eve, Will Turner walks into a Queensway brothel with a claw hammer. He confesses to murder but is suffering from amnesia and cannot identify himself or his victim. Barrister Nick Downes, with psychological and obsessive problems of his own and a 12-year relationship with Sally Fielding, his lover and courtroom foe, coming to an end, finds himself consorting with whores and making the beast with two backs with Liz Turner, his client's wife. The murky plot notwithstanding, this novel packs a sinister psychological wallop.

419. _____. *False Witness.* London: Hodder; New York: Mysterious, 1995. Tom Fawley is a lawyer without an ideal left: "All those fancy words, the ones with the capital letters, like Justice and Mercy, just made me feel like vomiting into my wig box" (13). His current client is a suave little man who might be a monster: Richard Kingsley faces a Bill of Murder for knifing 16-year-old Molly Summers 43 times, and despite Fawley's advice to plead down to manslaughter on a diminished capacity defense, wants to fight it in court claiming to have an alibi in one Philip Templeman, about whom he knows almost nothing. Another gripping legal thriller from a brilliant writer.

420. _____. *Rule of Law.* London: Hodder; New York: Mysterious, 1998. A secret camp of the Holocaust surfaces when a British millionaire, ex-cabinet minister and former Army major, Simon Montford, goes on trial for murder in the first war-crimes trial since Nuremburg. Dan Beckett is the reluctant prosecutor.

421. Dibden, Michael, ed. *The Vintage Book of Classic Crime.* New York: Vintage, 1997. Dibden's collection, first published by Picador (New York, 1993), is wide-ranging within "classic" crime genre, from the puzzle to the procedural, and cuts a broad swath across time and country to include excerpts of some legal thrillers, such as Raymond Postgate's *Verdict of Twelve*, Cameron McCabe's *The Face on the Cutting Room Floor*, *Malice Aforethought* (Francis Iles, pseud.); and *We, the Accused* by Ernest Raymond.

422. Dickens, Charles. *Bleak House.* London: Bradbury, 1853. Lawyers abound in Charles Dickens' fiction; he is peerless among authors in the nineteenth century and comparable to Russia's Dostoevsky for world greatness. Collectively, a number of lawyers and cases exist in *Oliver Twist* (1838), *Nicholas Nickleby* (1839), *The Old Curiosity* Shop; Barnaby *Rudge* (1841), *David Copperfield* (1850), *Hard Times* (1854), *Little Dorrit* (1857), and *Our Mutual Friend* (1865). It is, however, in *Bleak House* that Dickens does his most scathing work in satirizing the machinations of the law and its blighting of justice in Victorian England. His legal minds, solicitors and barristers, range from slightly disreputable family solicitor like Mr. Tulkinghorn in this novel or Mr. Vholes to an outright nefarious minion of the law in Sampson Brass. These men symbolize the law's aggravation of social and personal injustice. As he had done in attacking the Poor Laws, London slums, workhouses, and crime-schools like Fagin's in *Copperfield*, he takes on the law's majesty in the form of the Court of Chancery and the never-to-be-resolved *Jarndyce v. Jarndyce* inheritance case. (It actually is when a will is discovered; however, the law's slow grinding has consumed the entire fortune by then.) Tom Jarndyce blows his brains out in frustration; his heirs and cousins go to court, bicker with one another or--as in the instance of Sir Leicester and Lady Dedlock of Chesney Wold--hire Tulkinghorn to follow up their suit to claim the wealth before it can be dissipated in court costs.

Two other Dickens novels that feature trial scenes are noted below. (*See* also **Series Characters** for some of Dickens' best-known lawyers and cases.) Sidenote on American editions: Boston, New York, and Philadelphia, to name only the major cities of publication, published pirated editions of Dickens' novels as soon as they came out in London. (Dickens published with Chapman and Hall until 1846; thereafter he went with Bradbury and Evans before returning to Chapman in 1859.) Dickens complained of this unfair practice in *American Notes* (1842) and unsuccessfully campaigned to stop American publishers from depriving English authors of royalties.

423. _____. *The Posthumous Papers of the Pickwick Club.* London: Chapman, 1837; Philadelphia: Carey, 1838. Like all Dickens novels that first saw print in serialized magazine form, the adventures of the Pickwick Club, an assortment of characters surrounding Samuel Pickwick and benevolent Sam Weller, with names like Augustus Snodgrass, Alfred Jingle, and Mr. Wardle, expound upon a variety of contemporary topics from their various jaundiced or comic viewpoints. A pair of chapters in the published version of the novel under this title by Chapman a year afterward have Mr. Pickwick being sued by his former landlady, Mrs. Bardell, for breach of promise in one of literature's most delightful trials. Frank Spinney adapted *Bardell versus Pickwick* as a libretto in two acts in 1881 with songs by T. H. Gem and music by Spinney. The New York title page of an undated edition by Black is worth repeating: *The Pickwick papers; the posthumous papers of the Pickwick club being a faithful record of the perambulations, perils, travels, adventures, and sporting transactions of the corresponding members; edited by Boz./by Charles Dickens, with illustrations by Robert Seymour, Hablot Knight Browne* (*'Phiz'*).

424. _____. *A Tale of Two Cities.* London: Chapman, 1865; New York: Collier, n. d. The 1865 edition is illustrated by H. K. Browne, who alone or with George Cattermole, created memorable images of the many figures and scenes in Dickens. Dickens published in 1859 his historical novel of the French Revolution (assisted by Thomas Carlyle's research), which details the trial for treason and the execution of Sydney Carton who utters his immortal words as he sacrifices himself for Darnay on the guillotine: "It is a far, far better thing that I do, than I have ever done; it is a far, far better rest that I go to, than I have ever known" (418).

Dickson, Carter, pseud. *See* Carr, John Dickson . . . .

425. Diehl, William. *Primal Fear.* New York: Villard, 1993. Diehl is a veteran thriller writer who capitalizes on current international sensationalism with drug-running, macho cops and federal investigators (his CIA operatives graduate from the James Bond school of espionage) to have produced several bestsellers since 1988, including *Sharky's Machine*, *Hooligans*, *Thai Horse*, and *The Hunt.* The plots tend to be formulaic and carried by dialogue with just enough technothriller research to convince the casual reader. Moreover, his turning to the courtroom thriller has been equally successful and auspicious. Although the flaws are no longer in weaponry research but in legal points, he has created in Martin Vail, a macho legal eagle with a surrounding cast of oddball assistants.

Aaron Stampler insists he did not kill the much-admired Archbishop of Chicago, though caught with a bloody knife at the scene. He admits to participating in paid sex with another pair of street teens for the Archbishop's voyeuristic sexual pleasure. Cocky lawyer Martin Vail and his team defend babyfaced Stampler. Richard Gere's portrayal of Vail is overshadowed in the film (Paramount, 1996) by Academy-Award nominee Edward Norton as the shy, stammering altar boy.

426. _____. *Reign in Hell.* New York: Ballantine, 1997. Mary Frances Wilkens praises Diehl's third outing with Martin Vail as "top-notch," saying his creator "has finally hit his stride in this fine blend of legal, political, and psychological thrillers" (*Booklist* 15 Sept. 1997). Vail's reputation as Illinois' winningest attorney makes him the perfect candidate for a top-secret case the President is bringing against a radical militia called the Sanctuary, posing as a Christian organization. Having just convicted several top-level state government officials for corruption and racketeering, Vail, himself a legal whiz on the RICO statute, is AG Margaret Castaigne's recommendation to the White House. Soon, however, Vail uncovers disturbing facts about Sanctuary's guerrilla-warfare-trained membership under General Joshua Engstrom: his religiously fanatical militia attacked an Army convoy in Montana and he has a deep hatred for the President Pennington. More: crafty psycho Aaron Stampler appears again as a radio fundamentalist preacher.

427. _____. *Show of Evil.* New York: Ballantine, 1995. In the quiet, religiously repressed community of Gideon, Illinois, a wife and mother of a newborn is found in her home murdered and sexually mutilated. What enemies could Linda Barbour, wife and mother of an infant son, have had? The community believes Satanism is involved because a coded inscription had been written in blood on her head--the same kind of code left on Bishop Rushman's head in *Primal Fear* when Vail defended a psychotic killer with a murderous killer named Roy inside his head. Now chief prosecutor for Cook County, Vail and his Wild Bunch (*see* **Series Characters**) are busy with two cases: one involves a man who claims to have killed his wife in self-defense; the other develops when three bodies are found in the city dump. When the Barbour murder turns up, Vail is confronted with Aaron Stampler yet again, but Stampler has been isolated and confined for ten years in the maximum-security state mental institution.

428. Dinneen, Joseph. *Underworld U.S.A.* New York: Farrar, 1956. London: Cassell, 1957. Dinneen's foreword is an unbiased summation of his views of the legal system of crime and punishment, with its odd mix of jurists, lawyers, and juries in opposition to society's colorful rogues, as he has witnessed it as a long-time Massachusetts crime reporter. The novel purports to be a synopsis of those observations of the flaws of the system as it filters through the criminal career of one Carlton ("Fingers") Tolland of the Prohibition Era. Toward the end, Tolland wins an unexpected acquittal in court because the jury responds to the judge's contempt for the US attorney bringing the FBI's case against Tolland rather than the evidence.

429. Disney, Dorothy Cameron. *Explosion.* New York: Random, 1948.

Tax lawyer Harbison Greer's family is involved in a murder investigation when his sister-in-law's house on a quiet residential street in Washington, DC explodes and her body found inside among the debris; however, it is determined that she died of carbon monoxide poisoning and that someone had rigged the explosion to cover the crime. It soon appears that a motive is found in her recently changed will.

430. Doctorow, E. L. [Edgar Lawrence]. *The Book of Daniel.* New York: Random, 1971. The author received a National Book Award nomination for his third novel, a fictionalized historical account of the relationship between executed Communists Julius and Ethel Rosenberg and their children, one of whom, Daniel, reflects the traumatic story of his parents' trial and execution for giving away nuclear secrets to the Soviet Union without the polemic of their guilt or innocence involved.

431. Dodge, Constance W. *In Adam's Fall.* Philadelphia: Macrae-Smith, 1946. An historical novel of Salem witchcraft that opens after the protagonist's suicide: Damaris Horn is betrayed by her own relatives and scandal-mongering villagers. Her appearance before Judge Stoughton and the tribunal is a mere couple of pages.

432. Doherty, P. C. [Paul C.]. *A Tournament of Murders: The Franklin's Tale of Mystery and Murder As He Goes on Pilgrimage from London to Canterbury.* New York: St. Martin's, 1997. The third pilgrim tale (*An Ancient Evil*, 1994 and *A Tapestry to Murders*, 1996); this one opens in 1356 and is narrated by young Richard Greenele, squire to Sir Gilbert Savage. Richard, on the knight's orders, is seeking lawyer Hugo Coticol, who will give him information on the deaths of his parents. He and two companions arrive in Colchester, a plague-stricken town, to discover Coticol is dead. there is, however, a letter from Sir Robert Greenele revealing that he had been framed for murdering two noble friends, imprisoned, and condemned to die.

433. _____. *The Mask of Ra.* New York: St. Martin's-Minotaur, 1999. Doherty writes historical sleuthing tales with an admixture of law or the courts from widely different time periods. An Oxford scholar, he now lives in Essex and is rumored to be the creator of the new Anna Apostolou series. He has used several pseudonyms (C. L. Grace, Paul Harding, Ann Dukthas, and Michael Clynes). He has two Hugh Corbett tales from King Edward I (1272-1307). He has also used the period of Richard III (1452-85) for another. Also by the author: *Satan's Fire*, 1996 (another Hugh Corbett mystery); *The Fate of Princes* (Hale, 1990); and *The Assassin in the Greenwood*, 1994. One of his other detectives is a high priest, Amerotke, Chief Judge of Thebes, from the period of a century after the rise of the New Kingdom, a period of great court intrigue as well as development in the reign of Tuthmosis II (1479 BC). He returns victorious in battle to Thebes (Doherty maintains the Greek name). Before he

can share a mystical secret with his young bride, he is poisoned by an adder. Amerotke investigates, walking a tightrope in a power struggle between Queen Hatusu and Grand Vizier Rahimerre. The sequel, *The Horus Killings* (2000), begins in the reign of Queen-Pharoa Hatusu (orig. Hatshepsut) after her purge of the enemies in court. When several high priests are murdered, Amerotke is summoned to investigate.

434. Dohrman, Richard. *Vonda Rosegood.* New York: Harper, 1965. London: Transworld, 1966. If Erskine Caldwell and Al Capp were to have collaborated, it might read something like this novel. The title character is a cross between Aimee Semple Macpherson and Daisy Mae, and there is a murder trial alluded to in which the faith healing Vonda was indicted for killing a an older man who kept $2,000 in his freezer.

435. Dold, Gaylord. *The Devil to Pay.* New York: St. Martin's, 1999. Former criminal defense attorney Dold creates a nightmare for his wealthy San Franciscan lawyer Jack Darwin, facing financial ruin, thanks to his free-spending, soon-to-be-ex-wife. Jack is befriended and defended by lawyer David Avila, when wife Karla sues for divorce, charging him with sexual brutality. Then cops begin to look closely at Darwin as a suspect in a series of rape-murders, and when his own lawyer seems to be operating from dubious motives, Darwin moves to save his both life and his career. Darwin's first novel is *Schedule Two* (St. Martin's, 1996).

Dominic, R. B., pseud. *See* Latsis, Mary, and Martha Henissart. . . .

436. Donahue, Jack. *The Lady Loved Too Well.* New York: McGraw, 1978. Harlan Cole's defendant is author Cornelia Sherry, accused of the steak-knife murder of her lover.

437. _____. *Pray to the Hustlers' God.* New York: Reader's Digest-Crowell, 1977. Attorney Harlan Cole's client is a mobbed-up John Heywood in a case arising from the beating death of a Houston basketball coach and an attempt to fix the NBA playoffs.

438. Dooling, Richard. *Brain Storm.* New York: Random, 1998. Dooling has two previous novels that mark out lawyers as figures of interest but do not zero in on lawyer-protagonists in the fashion of more popular contemporaries like Grisham or Turow. His *White Man's Grave* (New York: Picador, 1995) was a finalist for the National Book Award in 1994 about an Indianapolis bankruptcy attorney whose world is shattered when his Peace Corps son disappears in the jungles of Sierre Leone. His debut novel *Critical Care* (Morrow, 1992) is a black comedy about doctors, hospitals, and lawyers. In his third novel, a judge assigns a copyright lawyer to defend a hate-crime murder suspect. Joe Watson, however, is a computer researcher, not a trial lawyer,

content with his lackluster work searching databases and playing violent computer games. Because federal Judge Whittaker Stang had once read Watson's undergraduate article on hate crimes, he appoints him chief counsel for a white skinhead accused of killing a black poet and painter. Praised for his mix of dry humor and zesty characterizations, Dooling was once a practicing attorney at Bryan Cave in St. Louis.

439. Doppler, William Bryant. *To Catch a Trone.* 1999. Offline. <http://www.rural.escape.ca/angling_north/fiction.trone.htm>. A 460,000-word unpublished mystery featuring Sincerity Ward and her troubles with the law, one large bipedal animal, and a backwoods family known as the Trones, keepers of the Trone Promise. Ward, a biker chick rebelling against her wealthy parents, is implicated in a jurist's murder on the day she is scheduled for transport to a juvenile facility. She pleads not guilty in the shooting death of Justice O'Reilly.

440. Douglas, M. S. [Marjory Stoneham]. *Road to the Sun.* New York: Rinehart, 1952. The backdrop of the story is the displacement of poor farmers when the Miami Canals were dug in Florida and the dynamiting of the dikes by some angry farmers whose crops were destroyed. One hardscrabble farmer, HampYandell, is killed in his field by Jason Horne. Henry Clay Hooker defends the young husband of the shotgun-murder in the long trial sequence of the novel's midsection.

441. Downing, Warwick. *A Lingering Doubt.* New York: Pocket, 1993. A Marine Corps sergeant during the Korean War, Downing attended the University of Wyoming and did graduate work at San Francisco State College (now University), 1957-60. Since 1970, he has been affiliated with the law firm Clanahan, Turner, Downing & Knowlton. Downing's fiction favors lawyers who are part of the National Association of Special Prosecutors.

Jack Bard, a veteran defense lawyer and a man of strong liberal principles, defends Drusus Church, a young black man who has a past as a gangbanger is accused of murdering a thug of a drug dealer.

442. Doyle, Arthur Conan [Sir]. *Micah Clarke.* London: Longman; New York: Harper, 1889. Historical novel about a youth born in 1664 near Portsmouth and who becomes ensnared by the Duke of Monmouth's cause against Catholic James II. One chapter is devoted to the summary executions by hanging of the rebels, confined in an enclosure and led *en masse* to their deaths after a mock trial. Clarke is one of a dozen spared the rope and fated for deportation to the New World.

443. Dratler, Jay J. *The Pitfall.* New York: Crown, 1947. Lurid little tale told in the first-person by a successful, married Hollywood scriptwriter, who lets a cop friend talk him into making a play for a woman in his behalf. He does but falls in love with her himself. Muddled by a pill-popping habit, the narrator

shoots the jealous husband, a career burglar, when he confronts him at home. During the trial, the cop plays an incriminating tape of the two adulterous lovers in her flat with the narrator's threats to kill the husband before he can tell the wife of the affair.

444. Dreiser, Theodore. *An American Tragedy.* New York: Boni, 1925. London: Constable, 1926; Cambridge, MA: Bentley, 1978. An undisputed classic of courtroom fiction about 21-one-year-old Clyde Griffiths, on trial for the drowning of his poor, pregnant girlfriend just as he is about to marry socially prominent Sondra Finchley (disguised in trial references as Miss X). Dreiser based his naturalistic novel on the real trial and conviction of Chester Gillette, who in 1906 was convicted and later executed for the murder of girlfriend Grace Brown. "Every florid word of the lawyers' speeches to the jury rings true. Most testimony is summarized, until the very detailed account of the defendant's time on the stand, one of the most elongated and harrowing examinations in all trial fiction" (Breen 39-40). The clash between opposing counsels Jepson (defense) and Mason (prosecutor) is delicious courtroom drama and Judge Oberwaltzer has to find them both in contempt at one point in the trial combat (740-41).

445. Drury, Allen. *Advise and Consent.* Garden City, NY: Doubleday, 1959. Twenty years of covering Washington politics provided correspondent Drury with the fodder to convert into fiction. *Advise and Consent* was his first effort and one that garnered the Pulitzer that year to be followed by a spate of novels that have all focused on the machinations of Capitol Hill. Drury, like the politically conservative Fenimore Cooper in the last century, has drawn the ire of liberal reviewers who see his proselytizing and his anger toward Beltway politicos as overwhelming his artistry and that, even when he has exciting plots, he will stop the action to let his mouthpiece-of-the-moment take over and soliloquize *ad nauseum.* Three of his political novels by Doubleday--he published steadily until 1995 (*A Thing of State*, Scribner's, 1995)--with either legalities or lawyers never far from the plotline are *Capable of Honor* (1966), *Decision* (1983), and *Preserve and Protect* (1968). *A Shade of Difference* (1962), sequel to *Advise and Consent*, focuses on the efforts of an African colony to break free from English rule in the arena of the United Nations. Loring Mandel adapted Drury's Pulitzer-Prize winning novel for the stage with Ed Begley, Richard Kiley, and Kevin McCarthy in key roles.

In the near-future, a controversial selection for Secretary of State sets off a firestorm of activity among many senators who fear the nominee's views regarding the Soviet Union. Their efforts to block the appointment go beyond political maneuvering and lead to blackmail, suicide, and even the death of the President.

446. Duffy, James. Haughton Murphy, pseud. *Murder & Acquisitions.* New York: Simon, 1988. Reuben Frost is a retired Wall Street lawyer, married to a former ballerina, and chair of the National Ballet Company. His creator

lives in Manhattan with his wife and is a partner in a Wall Street law firm.

447. _____. *Murder for Lunch.* New York: Simon, 1986. Graham Donovan, a senior partner at Chase & Ward, falls to the floor dead during a meeting with senior partner Arthur Tyson and Executive Partner George Bannard. Bannard solicits Frost's help with the funeral arrangements and tidying up Donovan's desk; it quickly leads to a murder investigation when Frost accentually discovers that the dead man had drunk contaminated water, and with that, a motive and prime suspect emerges: it was an open secret that Donovan had been having an affair with Anne Singer, wife of the colleague who heads contract negotiations for Latin American ventures and is a former CIA agent.

448. _____. *Murder Saves Face.* New York: Simon, 1991. A woman associate of Frost's former law firm is found strangled in the law library, and he is called back to help find the murderer. Clues surface in fax transmissions and computer files.

449. _____. *Murder Takes a Partner.* New York: Simon, 1987. The artistic director of the ballet company Frost chairs as director is killed in a way to make it seem a street mugging. Frost's wife aids in the sleuthing.

450. _____. *Murder Times Two: A Reuben Frost Mystery.* New York: Simon, 1990. The host of the Frosts' literary soiree is killed in a way to implicate all the members of the group, including Frost and Cynthia.

451. _____. *A Very Venetian Murder.* New York: Simon, 1992. The Frosts are staying at the Cipriani when they are cajoled into investigating an attempt on the life of a famous fashion designer named Gregg Baxter, who discovered that his insulin bottle had been tampered with; then three days later, he is killed in what the authorities describe as a murder resulting from an *omosessuale* encounter, Baxter being an active gay male with a penchant for quick liaisons. One more Frost: *Murder Keeps a Secret* (1989).

452. Duke, Winifred. *Skin for Skin.* London: Gollancz; Boston: Little, 1935. Neither whodunit nor whydunit, this novel purports to be a psychological thriller, but as an analysis of a killer's motives, it fails. Walter Blanche is a nondescript, middle-aged man leading a respectably drab life when he decides to kill his wife. He batters her to death, attempts to fool the police, is indicted, tried, found guilty, and sentenced to die at the Salchester Assizes. But he is freed when the case is overturned on appeal and wryly discovers that his life with Blanche was not so bad a thing.

453. Dumas [pére], Alexandre. *The Count of Monte Cristo* [*Le Comte de Monte-Cristo*, Paris: Lévy, 1884]. One of the world's best-known books but appreciated in its time as much for its realism as its fantasy elements; in the style

of the day, it was a *roman de moeurs*, or novel of manners, and its theme is one of Dumas' strongest: the sins of fathers are visited upon their sons' heads. It was sreialized and completed in 18 volumes in 1846, but the book's structure is divided into three, each opens on a precise date and place. The first, *Marseille*, concerns the short-lived happiness of 19-year-old first mate Edmund Dantés, who delivers a letter to the island of Elba for his dying captain, and brings his ship safely to port. He pays his debts and prepares to marry his fiancée. Two envious rivals send a letter denouncing him to the King's Prosecutor; he is seized and interrogated by the Assistant Prosecutor, M. Noirtier de Villefort (whose own father had been the addressee of what was a letter to Bonapartists). Dantés is then sent off to 14 years' confinement in Château d'If.

Dumas lived in a litigious age, and he was a frequent visitor to the law courts as either defendant or plaintiff (and on at least one occasion as duelist resulting from a lawsuit). The political and historical intermix with fact and fantasy, but a staple of plot elements make these notable for their uses of intrigue (secret, stolen, or forged documents are often the catalyst), and counterplotting among characters of high and low importance occasionally raises the specter of legal authority. These works are especially notable for mention, owing to their author's cycles of historical works during France's turbulent centuries, particularly the seventeenth: *The Black Tulip* [*La tulip noire*, ser. 1850], *Marguerite de Valois* (*La Reine Margot*, ser. 1845; opens as drama in Théâtre Historique, 1847), *Twenty Years After* [*Vignt Ans Aprés,* ser. 1845; this is the sequel to his most famous novel, *Les Trois Mousquetaires*, ser. 1844).

454. Dumaurier, Daphne. *Mary Anne.* London: Gollancz; Garden City, NY: Doubleday, 1954. Du Maurier's book is a well-researched tribute to her great-great grandmother, the notorious Mary Anne Clarke, who died in 1852. She led a scandalous life in her day with memoirs and published letters that tarnished the reputation of one of the royal family's blackest sheep, the Duke of York, whoremonger, gambler, and embezzler of the King's exchequer. Clarke went one letter too far, however, publishing a letter that damned Right Honourable William Fitzgerald, Chancellor of the Irish Exchequer, M. P. of Ennis, of--among other base activities--siring and causing the death of his own bastard; she pled guilty on the advice of her attorney, was sentenced to nine months.

455. Dunbar, Anthony P. [Tony]. *City of Beads.* New York: Putnam's, 1995. Dunbar graduated from Brandeis and Tulane University School of Law. He worked with civil rights organizations in the South (he coauthored a nonfiction book on migrant farm workers and a humanitarian award for another: *Our Land Too* (Pantheon, 1971). He was also director of Southern Prison Ministry 1972 - 1978. His protagonist is "Tubby" Dubonnet, who combines a raffish charm with enough lawyering skills to get by in novels packed with local color and whimsy. Although he has lost his zest for the law, Tubby stays with it

because it pays the bills, particularly his alimony to ex-wife Mattie, and he has much to do to keep her and their three daughters free of various scrapes and entanglements while serving the parade of odd clients crossing his office threshold. Here, the *bon vivant*, ex-college wrestler and divorced lawyer must reckon with shadowy, high-powered casino owners and powerful businessmen unhappy about his environmental lawsuit and some unhappy druglords peeved because Tubby's girlfriend shot and killed a drug dealer.

456. _____. *The Crime Czar.* New York: Dell, 1998. Tubby, as usual without clients, agrees to help friend Judge Al Hughes in his re-election campaign; meanwhile he simmers over the shooting of his friend Dan and crosses paths with a prostitute named Daisy, whose boyfriend was killed when she refused to work for the local crime boss.

457. _____. *The Crooked Man.* New York: Putnam's, 1994. Tubby's menage of clients is as colorful as ever: a plastic surgeon who refers his own patients to Tubby so they can sue him, one of whom is a transvestite entertainer with a skin condition allegedly caused by Dr. Feingold. Into this mix enters Darryl Alvarez, a nightclub manager caught unloading fifteen bales of marijuana from a shrimp boat. When he is murdered, Tubby realizes that the blue gym bag Alvarez had given him shortly before his death is a million dollars' worth of trouble.

458. _____. *Lucky Man.* New York: Dell, 1999. When office sex leads to murder, rape, and possibly suicide, Tubby becomes the target of a moralistic, crusading prosecutor.

459. _____. *Shelter from the Storm.* New York: Putnam's, 1997. Dubonnet confronts big-time criminal Willie "Rue" LaRue in town for a planned heist at the First Alluvial Bank; the caper is scheduled for Mardis Gras eve, when the holdup will be assisted by the confusion of streets packed with partying revelers.

460. _____. *Trick Question.* New York: Putnam's, 1997. Tubby is involved in a medical mystery that focuses on cryogenics, specifically the frozen head of one Dr. Valentine, a famous researcher; when a custodian opened a closet-sized door of the prestigious Moskowitz Memorial Lab one morning, the frozen body fell to the floor and the head flew off.

461. Duncan, Thomas W[illiam]. *Ring Horse.* Garden City, NY: Doubleday, 1940. Nauseatingly warm-hearted tale of law professor Paul Reese recounting his Iowa youth and his friendly involvement with an unemployed circus clown, Dan Gilpin, and his horse Wild Fire. The secondary love interest is supplied by Betty Canfield, daughter of the county attorney. The author is addicted to inscrutable oxymoron: "He laughed without mirth," "His manner was at once formal and informal" (172).

462. Dunne, Dominick. *Another City, Not My Own.* New York: Crown, 1997. Dunne, whose own daughter was murdered, covered the O. J. Simpson trial and wrote a series of reports for *Vanity Fair.* The book which resulted from the trial is a melange of fact and fiction, narrated by a Maileresque alter ego he calls Gus Bailey, who crosses paths with dozens of celebrities and notorious personages in presenting this slice of Americana. Bailey incorporates fictional meetings, such as with Andrew Cunanan, the murderer of jet-set designer Gianni Versace. Dunne exposes what he considers the rift between blacks and whites after the trial and claims that Simpson set race relations in this country back to the days of Rosa Parks and 1955.

463. Dunne, John Gregory. *Dutch Shea, Jr.* New York: Simon-Linden; London: Weidenfeld, 1982. John ("Dutch") Shea is a criminal lawyer with a practice consisting of lowlifes like his current client, a massage-parlor operator. The novel is formless and consists mainly of Shea's sardonic or bitter recriminations toward himself all mixed in with Catholic guilt and his daughter's murder by an I.R.A. terrorist bomb.

464. Dürrenmatt, Friedrich. *A Dangerous Game* [*Die Panne*: *Ein Hörspiel.* Zürich: Arche, 1961]. Trans. Richard and Clara Winston. Dürrenmatt was a Swiss who wrote novels, plays, and criticism in German. He is considered a brilliant failure as a playwright because his dramas fail to carry off their themes. He was a "slick polemicist" (Seymour-Smith 147) as a critic and believed, as he wrote in "Problems of the Theatre," an essay delivered in 1954 that comedic art can be successful only if it remains *gemütlich*; art that is dangerous, or one that exposes the senselessness and hopelessness of the world, will be avoided by the public. Stock figures of a judge and public prosecutor conclude this short novel, *eine noch mögliche geschichte*, says the subtitle wryly about an average man named Alfredo Traps, employee of a textile firm. One of his detective novels is *The Judge and His Hangman* [*Der Richter und Sein Henker*], trans. Therese Pol, New York: Berkely, 1958).

465. _____. *The Marriage of Mr. Mississippi* [*Die Ehe des Herrn Mississippi*, Zurich: Verlag, 1957]. London: Cape, 1964; New York: Grove, 1964. Trans. Michael Bullock. Florestan Mississippi is the Public Prosecutor of a comedy that is three parts Shavian, one part-Kafka with a dash of Molière. Amidst the gunfire of a revolutionary battleground, Mississippi proposes to Anastasia, whose husband has just died by her poisoning hand. He courts and kills her in the same way with poison-laced coffee, spouting nonsense about "planting the red flag of justice in the midst of the tottering edifice of the world" (118).

466. Dyer, George. *The People Ask Death.* New York: Scribner's; London: Heinemann, 1940. Austin Scarborough is a member of the San Francisco Board

of Police Commissioners; he has been shot at the Thermopylae Club pool, and clues point to *Times* reporter Persen "Buzz" Drake. Drake's fellow members of the Catalyst Club (six amateur criminologists featured in other Dyer novels) try to prove his innocence against the machinations of a rival paper and a politically ambitious DA. Idealistic, young trial lawyer Richard Victor defends Drake and exploits a classic situation of the legal thriller: he stalls while awaiting the arrival of the missing key witness. Ludicrously dated thriller interspersed with reproduced photos and sensational headlines of Drake in hospital, prison, conferring with lawyer, etc.

E

467. Eberhardt, Michael C. *Body of a Crime.* New York: Dutton, 1994. Eberhard used his experience as defense attorney in the longest running US murder trial to result in an acquittal. Sean Barrett, young trial lawyer with a passion for defense, is assigned a "no-body" case. A former athlete is implicated in the disappearance of his girlfriend--a fight at the beach was witnessed--but the woman's body is missing.

468. _____. *Witness for the Defense.* New York: Onyx, 1998. Hunter Dobbs is a San Francisco public defender with a bad marriage, an inebriated judge and a witness willing to perjure himself in a murder case going from bad to worse when he is accused of suborning perjury. A colleague, Sarah Harris, offers him hope: she will represent him before the California Bar, providing that he defend her friend up on a kidnapping charge.

469. _____ with John Tullius. *Against the Law.* New York: Dutton; London: Penguin, 1995. A populist politician is implicated in the assassination of Hawaii's governor, a killing that is marked with ancient warrior rituals. The DA's office arrests the movement's leader Peter Maikai and assigns Dan Carrier to prosecute, but not only is the case technically flawed but Maikai was the only real father he has ever had. When Maikai collapses and dies during his preliminary hearing (angry Judge Shimada has to call the room to order and clear the courtroom after disturbances), Carrier launches his own investigation with the help of Maikai's daughter Lily.

470. Eberhart, Mignon G. *Hunt with the Hounds.* New York: Black, 1950. Opens with the conclusion of Judd Baily's trial for murdering his wife in rural Bedford; his acquittal means the investigation into Ernestine's murder resumes.

471. Eckert, Allan W. *The Court Martial of Daniel Boone.* Boston: Little, 1973. Eckert added to letters and other known documents with some valuable research from the Cincinnati Historical Society to fill in gaps in the trial sequence of a little-known occurrence in the life of the great frontiersman. Captain Boone was court-martialed in 1877 (and pled guilty) to six related

charges of leading Indians into the Boonesborough encampment and making his men lay down their arms in a surrender to the Indians but denied his actions were treasonable.

472. Edgley, Leslie. Robert Bloomfield, pseud. *Vengeance Street.* Garden City, NY: Doubleday, 1952. Mark Bennett is a metallurgist selected for jury duty and the lone holdout for a guilty verdict in the case of a murdered girl's trial. A failed bribery attempt results in a hung jury and new trial for obvious killer Dean Whalen. Then Mark's son is killed by the man who had attempted to bribe him in the first trial; other deaths follow, including the foreman and Bennett's wife. The police and DA of San Rico seem indifferent to the murders multiplying from the trial.

473. Edwards, Martin. *All the Lonely People.* London: Piatkus, 1990; New York: Norton-Foul Play, 1991. Debut novel of Harry Devlin, a solicitor in Liverpool like his creator, praised in the London *Times* for its "pungent Mersey whiff." Lawyer Harry Devlin has made both novel and short-story appearances, especially in *Ellery Queen's Mystery Magazine* and *Bella.* Most recently, a short story "With a Little Help from My Friends" appears along with a Rumpole story ("Rumpole at Sea") in the anthology *Murder on Deck!: Shipboard and Shoreline Mystery Stories*, ed. Rosemary Herbert (Oxford, 1998). Another is "The Case of the Suicidal Lawyer" in the *Mammoth Book of New Sherlock Holmes Adventures*, ed. Mike Ashley (Carroll, 1998). Edwards read law at Balliol College, Oxford and became a partner at Mace & Jones in 1984; his published writing mixes light essays in various reviews alongside legal writing that includes books on law as, for instance, *Understanding Computer Contracts* (London: Waterlow, 1983) and *Understanding Dismissal Law* (1984).

474. _____. *Eve of Destruction.* London: Piatkus, 1996; New York: Norton-Foul Play, 1998. Devlin's case begins with a teenaged car thief, who stumbles upon a ghastly triple murder in a deserted conservatory; one of the victims is the adulterous wife of another client. The husband had tapes of her unknown lover for use in a divorce suit shortly before the killings. An earlier novel is *Yesterday's Papers* (1994).

475. _____. *I Remember You.* London: Piatkus, 1993. Harry seeks a connection between reluctant clients in danger. First is tattoo artist Finbar Rogan, who is the victim of arson and then a car bombing. The other is Rosemary Graham-Brown, who is too eager to leave a luxurious home behind and immigrate to Spain.

476. _____. *Suspicious Minds.* London: Piatkus, 1992. In Harry Devlin's second outing, the solicitor searches for the wife of his best friend and most important client, Jack Stirrup. Stirrup's daughter and boyfriend are the next to disappear; meanwhile he is courting the enigmatic Valerie Kaiwar, a barrister.

Egan, Leslie, pseud. *See* Linington, Elizabeth. . . .

477. Eggleston, Edward. *The Graysons.* New York: Century, 1887. Edinburgh: Douglas, 1888. The 1910 reprint includes author's preface from the 1888 edition alleging the genesis of the tale of rustic trial lawyer Abraham Lincoln's defense in a murder trial in an old neighbor's story "received about 1867" (n. pag.). Inexperienced Abe Lincoln defends good-hearted youth Tom Grayson, on trial for shooting rival George Lockwood. (Sidenote: one of the earliest examples of the stock situation of a killer confessing from the witness stand.)

478. _____. *The Mystery of Metropolisville.* New York: Judd, 1873. Eggleston is deservedly forgotten despite his preface's pompous claim to contribute "to the history of American civilization" (7). Chapter 39 is entitled "Trial," but in fact is the grand jury's arraignment of one of Metropolisville's citizenry, Albert Charlton, for post-office theft involving a land warrant. Amusingly, his attorney Conger tries to get him to plead insanity, and failing that bizarre tactic, advises his client to plead guilty "to relieve [him] of the responsibility" of trying the case at all (247).

479. Ehrlich, Jack. *The Chatham Killing.* New York: Pocket, 1976. Wry, sardonically narrated masterpiece of a Western that surpasses *True Grit*'s Rooster Cogburn for its portrait of a tough sheriff, who operates barely within the law in a vast and wild country. John J. Savage is the narrator of the Chatham killing, set down in the post-1890's Wyoming. The incident about a murder years earlier: 17-year-old Kathy Sturgess, daughter of cattle baron Stuart, who will later stand trial for killing his range enemy, Jacob Chatham, is found in a hayloft in a post-coital position with twenty stab wounds. Judge Nathan Guinness, Harvard-educated, sent out to the territories to try Sturgess, is an hilarious portrait of the eccentric, almighty judge until proud Savage puts him in his place with a lesson about treating men with respect (73-74).

480. _____. *Court Martial.* New York: Pyramid, 1959. Johnny Riggo faces court martial as a result of a vindictive general, whose daughter he had tried to run off with and marry in Mexico. Lieutenant "Ric" Richter defends the Airman despite his singular lack of legal training.

481. Ellis, Kenneth M. *The Trial of Vivienne Ware.* New York: Grosset, 1931. Written as a radio drama about the murder of millionaire architect Damon Fenwicke and the trial of socialite Vivienne Ware for the crime. Dolores Divine has a walk-on part as star witness for the prosecution when someone hurls a knife at her as she makes her way to the witness stand.

482. Ellis, Peter Berresford. Peter Tremayne, pseud. *The Subtle Serpent: A*

Celtic Mystery. New York: St. Martin's, 1996. P. Berresford Ellis is a Celtic scholar (from Coventry, England), author of more than 30 novels of biography and history, and writer of historical mysteries featuring Sister Fidelma, a legal advocate of the 7th century. The preface, or "Historical Note," accompanying the Fidelma novels explains the important Brehon Laws to which Fidelma, as the daughter of a king, would serve in the capacity of advocate of these laws of *Fénechas* ("land tillers"). The laws governing Ireland at this time, as distinct from the romanized Anglo-Saxon laws across the sea were extraordinarily liberal to women in the so-called Dark Ages, and as far as women's rights are concerned, Sister Fidelma had a parity with males in the seventh century of her time. In fact, the absence of primogeniture itself is significant. This story is a traditional whodunit built around a dead body. The headless corpse of a young female is hauled up from a well by the bucket rope attached to her ankle; in her bound hands are the symbols of the two faiths warring for dominance in remote southwestern Ireland that suggest this to be a pagan-inspired killing (Christianity had not yet eradicated the old ways of belief). Sr. Fidelma, an advocate of the Brehon Laws, is sent to investigate the crime.

Others in the St. Martin's series: *Absolution by Murder* (1994), *Suffer Little Children* (1997), and *Shroud for the Archbishop* (1995).

483. Ellsberg, Edward. *Mid Watch.* New York: Dodd; London: Heinemann, 1954. Ensign Victor Cushing, a Naval Academy graduate, chafes under duty aboard the hulk *Manhattan*, especially now his wife is expecting in a difficult childbirth. When a series of mishaps occur belowdecks to put the ship in grave danger, he disobeys the Chief Engineer's orders. During his court martial, his judge advocate attacks the word *lawful* in Charge III of the regulations to show that Cushing's disobedience was not in violation of that criterion. (Sidenote: see pp. 208-11 for the difference between a *nolle prosequi* plea in a civilian versus in a navy court.)

484. Endore, Guy. *Methinks the Lady.* New York: Duell, 1945. London: Cresset, 1947. Part 1 is written by Mrs. Spence Gillian from prison before and during her murder trial. Her lawyer pleads her not guilty by reason of insanity, but she is found guilty, although the proceedings are drastically interrupted by the suicide of Judge Barmaine. Part 2 comprises the dialogue of three "alienists" appointed by the court to examine Mrs. Spence.

485. England, George Allen. *The Alibi.* New York: Grossett; Boston: Small, 1916. Bank employee Walter Slayton engineers a heist at his Powhatan Bank in New York City and incriminates innocent, guileless fellow employee Arthur Mansfield of the robbery and the murder of a cashier. Mansfield is sentenced to life at hard labor in Sing Sing after a brief trial in which his defense attorney can muster no exculpatory evidence at all. His escape and search for his arch-enemy is the focus of the second half of the novel.

486. Erckmann, Emile, and Alexander Chatrian . *The Polish Jew: A Romantic Moral Drama in Three Acts* [Juif Polonaise. Trans. from the French of Messrs. Erckmann and Chatrain [sic] by Henry L. Williams.]. New York: De Witt, 1872. A curiosity as a legal thriller of its era from collaborators in former Alsatia; it involves a prosperous innkeeper who, fifteen years earlier, had murdered a Polish traveler for his gold and burned the body in a lime kiln. Following his daughter's nuptials and much drinking to the newlyweds, he dreams he is on trial for that murder. The president of the court summons a mesmerizer to unlock the details of the crime upon which his success is founded--a hypnotic state within a dream that ultimately induces terror and a heart attack. A popular play of the time called *The Bells* was based on this work.

487. Evelyn, John Michael. Michael Underwood, pseud. *Adam's Case.* London: Hammond; Garden City, NY: Doubleday, 1961. Early Series character Adam Cape is briefed to prosecute Frankie Young on a charge of "wounding with intent"; his wife Carole is the victim and she later turns up dead, a strangled murder victim fished out of the North London Canal. Feeling responsible for her death, Cape investigates. Simon Manton also enters the case after her murder.

488. _____. *The Anxious Conspirator.* London: Macdonald; Garden City, NY: Doubleday, 1965. Solicitor Roger Elwin is assigned to represent Tony Dayne, a confidential informer who was mistakenly arrested in one of Simon Manton's raids on a forgery ring. Dayne, however, refuses to be released after arrest, fearing the gang's revenge.

489. _____. *Anything but the Truth.* London: Macmillan, 1978. New York: St. Martin's, 1979. Ian Tanner is charged with killing a pal by running him down in a stolen car. The judge in the case, his first Old Bailey case, discovers a conflict of interest soon after the trial commences because his son is employed by the stolen car's owner, a figure with ties to mobsters. Young copper Patrick Bramley is on temporary assignment for the investigation. Breen calls prosecutor Bruce Ridge "one of the most breathtakingly incompetent advocates in fictional annals" (177).

490. _____. *The Crime of Colin Wise.* London: Macdonald; Garden City, NY: Doubleday, 1964. The title character is a corrupt TV repairman who plans the perfect murder for novelist Geoffrey Goodwin. Wise goes through the criminal justice system, but is assisted by insider Inky Pooler.

491. _____. *Crime upon Crime.* London: Macmillan, 1980. New York: St. Martin's, 1981. Tony Ching is a homosexual prostitute found strangled and his liaisons with a West Middlesex Crown court judge all point toward a blackmail motive; a career criminal named Arthur Kedby stands accused and is

defended by Rosa Epton, now a partner at Snaith and Epton.

492. _____. *Crooked Wood.* London: Macmillan; New York: St. Martin's, 1978. Series characters Nick and Clare Attwell investigate the murder of solicitor Stanley Fulmer despite the fact that an alleged professional hitman is in the Old Bailey dock for the crime.

493. _____. *Death in Camera.* London: Macmillan; New York: St. Martin's, 1984. A Runnymede Crown Court justice falls to his death from a balcony during a photo session at opening ceremonies as a result of a poison pellet fired from the row of photographers; a nephew becomes chief suspect and Rosa Epton's client. "Heavier carnage," observes Jon Breen, "than in most Underwoods" (180).

494. _____. *Double Jeopardy.* London: Macmillan; New York: St. Martin's, 1981. Rosa Epton defends Toby Nash, a man she falls for at a New Year's Eve party, on a charge of raping Tricia Langley. Langley is murdered while Nash is out on bail, and Rosa becomes his alibi.

495. _____. *False Witness.* London: Hammond, 1957. New York: Walker, 1961. Derek Yates is an employee of the local paper mill and fiancé of Jennie Rawlins, the daughter of the mill owner and High Sheriff of Seahaven, first Assize town on the Coastal Circuit. Yates claims he was robbed in the park of the firm's payroll. Barrister Jeremy Harper, himself in love with Jennie, is a witness at his trial. When a murder occurs in the Clerk of Assize's Office after Yates is convicted and sentenced, Superintendent Simon Manton of the Yard is called in.

496. _____. *Goddess of Death.* London: Macmillan; New York: St. Martin's, 1982. Rosa Epton represents Philip Arne's brother, charged with an almost archaic vagrancy law ("loitering with intent to commit an arrestable offense") as he lurked in close proximity to a classic Rolls-Royce. Before his trial in Shepherd's Bush Magistrate's Court, however, Philip is murdered by a blow from a bronze statuette of an Indian goddess, and it appears looks as though the brother is responsible.

497. _____. *Hand of Fate.* London: Macmillan; New York: St. Martin's, 1981. Brutish, wealthy businessman Frank Wimble plots to kill his wife, bury her in the woods, and marry his mistress. A dog turns up a severed hand with the wife's wedding ring on one fingers, but the police cannot build a thorough prosecution with nothing else but Wimble's adulterous history. Hackneyed but the time spent in the jury room amid the to-and-fro of debate sparkles.

498. _____. *Lawful Pursuit.* London: Hammond; Garden City, NY: Doubleday, 1958. Detective Constable Roy Cordari goes underground to solve

an extraordinary series of bail-jumping cases when the sixth fails to appear for his hearing in West End Magistrate's Court. Defendant Alexander Burfa's disappearance leads all the way to Algeria. Simon Manton must be called in to wrap it up.

499. _____. *Menaces, Menaces.* London: Macmillan; New York: St. Martin's, 1976. Light, amusing fare that mixes in solid police procedural as Henry Sipson defends himself on charges of trying to extort £10,000 from a bingo company. Then a second crime with the identical *modus operandi* occurs while he is in prison. Nick and Clare Attwell, now married, so the sleuthing.

500. _____. *Murder on Trial.* London: Hammond, 1954. New York: Washburn, 1958. Evelyn's first legal thriller has a commonplace middle-aged senior clerk John Pinty preparing for jury duty in the Old Bailey. He is seated as foreman in the trial of William Edgar Tarrant charged with murdering Constable David Moss. Then Tarrant is shot at the moment of making his way to the witness box "shot through the heart" (23). He had promised to make startling revelations the day before--next Pinty vanishes and immediately becomes the prime suspect of the Yard's youngest Detective Chief Inspector, Simon Manton.

501. _____. *Murder with Malice.* London: Macmillan; New York: St. Martin's, 1977. Nick Attwell is suspended on a charge of soliciting a bribe from a 17-year-old murder suspect and son of a TV celebrity. Breen notes that another Attwell novel published later that year, *The Fatal Trip*, has brief courtroom action in the first chapter.

502. _____. *A Party to Murder.* London: Macmillan, 1983. New York: St. Martin's, 1984. A gossip-loving staff member of the Grainfield Prosecuting Solicitor's Office is found clubbed to death at the annual Christmas party. Newly appointed Chief Prosecuting Solicitor Murray Riston's ex-lover, Caroline Allard, another legal staff member, is charged. Her old law-school friend Rosa Epton represents her.

503. _____. *A Pinch of Snuff.* London: Macmillan; New York: St. Martin's, 1974. Brian Tanner, steward at the Blackstone Club, conspires to steal the club's famous snuff-box collection. When his contact is murdered, he finds himself accused. Rosa Epton, the young female lawyer who stars in Underwood's recent fiction, makes her debut as assistant to solicitor Robin Snaith.

504. _____. *The Silent Liars.* London: Macmillan; Garden City, NY: Doubleday, 1970. When George Dimitriu, a successful businessman, is murdered, Chris Laker is charged, yet he had no prior connection to the victim. Chief Inspector Adams investigates in the victim's native Rumania.

505. _____. *Smooth Justice.* London: Macmillan; New York: St. Martin's, 1979. In Bloomsbury Magistrate's Court, hated Donald Ferney is known by a newspaper sobriquet as the "kindly" magistrate, but when the court's elderly usher is found clubbed to death outside the magistrate's private entrance, it is widely believed Ferney was to be the intended victim.

506. _____. *A Trout in the Milk.* London: Macmillan, 1971. New York: Walker, 1972. James Geddy is defending racketeer Frank Manion on multiple felony charges when his young apprentice barrister, Robin Appleman, is found stabbed to death sitting in Geddy's chair in chambers. The Old Bailey trial proceeds with the denouement revealing a variety of twists and turns of delayed information, such as the possession of a photograph of a young murdered Swiss girl.

507. _____. *Victim of Circumstance.* London: Macmillan; New York: St. Martin's, 1980. A two-part novel with much court action: in the first, schoolmaster John Farndon professes an intent to kill his wife Monique. The second part features the case of *Queen vs. Farndon.*

Other Underwoods without an American publisher are numerous. These are published by Hammond: *Death on Remand* (1956), *Arm of the Law* (1959), *Cause of Death* (1960). The following were published by Macdonald: *The Case against Philip Quest* (1962), *Girl Found Dead* (1963), *A Crime Apart* (1966), *The Man Who Died on Friday* (1967), *The Man Who Killed Too Soon* (1968), *The Shadow Game* (1969) and *Shem's Demise* (1970). A final Hammond novel is *Murder Made Absolute* (Hammond, 1955; Washburn, 1957).

F

508. Fabre-Luce, Alfred. *The Trial of Charles de Gaulle.* New York: Praeger, 1961. Fictional trial of the real leader. (*See* Van Rjndt, Philippe.)

509. Faherty, Terence. *Deadstick.* New York: St. Martin's, 1991. Faherty is no failed seminarian, like his creation Owen Keane, a researcher for a Boston law firm. The Indiana native resides in Indianapolis and has a second, non-legal, series featuring Scott Elliot. The Keane mysteries are more psychological than suspense mysteries. Other tales published by St. Martin's include *Die Dreaming* (1995), *Live to Regret* (1992), *The Lost Keats* (1993, the prequel), *The Ordained* (1997), and *Prove the Nameless* (1996).

Fair, A. A., pseud. *See* Gardner, Erle Stanley . . . .

510. Fairstein, Linda. *Cold Hit.* New York: Scribner's, 1999. Awarded in 1991 by the American Bar Association as one of twenty recipients of the Outstanding Young Lawyers, Fairstein is currently regarded nationally as an

authority on violence against women (she prosecuted the notorious Preppy Murder case as chief of the Sex-Crimes Unit for the New York District Attorney's Office and has been Deputy Chief of its Trial Division since 1981). She served on Governor Cuomo's Task Force on Rape, 1989-92; President Clinton's Violence against Women Advisory Council in 1995, and authored *Sexual Violence: Our War against Rape* (Morrow, 1995). Highly regarded as an unswerving, dedicated public servant and with more than 25 years in as a prosecutor, she told an interviewer for *CA* that writing about her experiences "is an extraordinary opportunity to inform readers about the criminal justice system and to entertain at the same time." (*See* Ms. Fairstein's commentary in **Craft Notes**.)

The cold hit of the title refers to a computer match of a DNA sample from a recent rape with evidence from an older crime. With series characters mike Chapman and Mercer Wallace, Alexandra ("Alex") Cooper, Assistant DA in charge of Manhattan's Sex Crimes Unit, works two cases simultaneously: a serial rapist who has emerged from the shadows again and two homicides connected to fine arts being sold on the black market.

511. _____. *Final Jeopardy.* New York: Scribner's, 1996. Alex wakes up to her own obituary. Isabella Lascar--her tall, blonde, actress and friend--has been found shot in the head while hiding out at Alex's Cape Cod summer home to avoid a stalker. Because she was there and driving a rental car in Alex's name, police assumed she was the victim (the face was unrecognizable). However, she might well have been intended as the victim of a psycho from her past. The case takes another turn when the police discover that she and Isabella shared the same lover.

512. _____. *Likely to Die.* New York: Scribner's, 1997. Since Isabella's death in *Final Jeopardy*, Alexandra has been going through the motions until she is named to head the investigation into the savage murder of renowned neurosurgeon Dr. Gemma Dogen of the Manhattan Medical Center, found sexually assaulted and stabbed in her office. One psychotic seems a prime suspect. Worse yet: a series of underground tunnels connects the psychiatric hospital to the teaching college and the hospital so that numerous vagrants had access to the doctor's office. But the investigation also turns up numerous suspects, enemies the doctor herself made in her work.

513. Fallon, Ann C. *Blood Is Thicker.* New York: Pocket, 1990. The first book in this traditional mystery series about Dublin solicitor James Fleming. The lawyer is in Kilmartin, County Wexford, to meet three sisters to make funeral arrangements for their elderly deceased brother, but all is not as it might appear: the sisters are not grieving, there is a fortune to be inherited, and the brother was murdered by a knife to his chest with evidence pointing to sister Violet as the killer.

514. _____. *Dead Ends.* New York: Pocket, 1992. Fleming is visiting a country inn in County Sligo when a death occurs requiring his sleuthing skills. More Fallons by Pocket: *Deadly Analysis* (2000), *Hour of Our Death* (1995), *Potter's Field* (1993), and *Where Death Lies* (1991).

515. Fane, Anthony. *The Wycliffe-Pepin Case: 'Double Shooting at Merrile Court.'* New York: Poe, 1931. Straightforward (i.e., back-to-front, classic mystery) whodunit, but the lead sleuths comprise a trio of Basil Torrens, DA Boland, and Dr. Fletcher, the M.E. The crime: a well-known banker is found dead slumped over his *inamorata* with a suicide-pact note nearby.

516. Farjeon, J[oseph]. Jefferson. *The Judge Sums Up.* London: Collins; Indianapolis: Bobbs, 1942. Justice Unwin is meticulously summing up the case and evidence against the accused, Peter Gaskell, for the wilful murder of Walter Drake over a young woman. Suddenly, he reels back in a swoon--but now because of illness. He has seen something that now calls the entire case (and the obviousness of Gaskell's presumed guilt) into question. The first two-thirds of the novel ("Talk") is entirely transcript of the court record.

517. Farris, Michael P. *Guilt by Association.* Nashville, TN: Broadman, 1997. Farris is an attorney, founder and President of the Home School Legal Defense Association and former General Counsel for Concerned Women for America; he has authored books on Christianity and the law and appeared for *Nightline* interviews and debated on *Crossfire* in opposition to the National Education Association and the ACLU. The plot revolves around violence against an abortion clinic in a small-college town in Washington State and defense attorney Peter Barron. After protesting in front of an abortion clinic turns violent (an infiltrator is hired by the clinic's owners to escalate the conflict), the clinic burns to the ground and Suzie O'Dell, a college student on the group's pro-life board, is charged with murder and arson. Barron made a first appearance in *Anonymous Tip* about Gwen Landis and her 4-year-old son Casey battling a legal system set in motion by a faceless, nameless accuser.

518. Fast, Howard. *Conceived in Liberty: A Novel of Valley Forge.* New York: Simon; London: Joseph, 1939. Fast wrote 23 mysteries under the pseudonym E. V. Cunningham and 35 under his real name with a total more than 80; he was once blacklisted during the McCarthy era. The court martial of three men for desertion and murder while serving under General ("Mad Anthony") Wayne, Washington presiding over the tribunal, in the dark days of Valley Forge. Fast does very well with the gritty realism of the men's predicament and the interrogation by defense lawyer Hamilton of a swashbuckling cavalry officer who brought the charges.

519. _____. *The Trial of Abigail Goodman.* New York: Crown, 1993. Abigail Goodman is a 41-year-old mother and professor of Women's History at

Hilden University. With two grown children and a successful career, she decides to terminate her third pregnancy; the problem is that, in this future, abortion is a capital offense. The problem with the novel's treatment of abortion is that, like the author's surname, it is all about cardboard characters in what Abigail calls "the war on women" (256); men are either nasty or sweet "little boys" in this war and thus the book cheapens its cause.

520. _____. *The Winston Affair.* New York: Crown, 1959. London: Methuen, 1960. Captain Barney Adams, Harvard Law grad and first in military law at West Point, is assigned to defend racist Army lieutenant Winston who admits to murdering a British sergeant in the Far East because "He had to die," God having ordered him to do it (68).

521. Faulkner, William. *Intruder in the Dust.* New York: Random, 1948; London: Chatto, 1949. Lucas Beauchamp, a black man, is found with a Colt pistol in his pocket hunched over the body of Vinson Gowrie in Faulkner's Yoknapatawpha County. The town wants to lynch and burn the proud, stiff-necked old man. Loquacious lawyer Gavin Stevens wants to plead him guilty to satisfy the bloodlust of the mob and the Gowrie clan. Faulkner would return to this theme of a black man persecuted by mob violence in a subtler way in one of his greatest novels. Joe Christmas is indicted for the murder of a white woman, his benefactress, in *Light in August* (Random, 1932) with the question of race and identity mixed up in a murder mystery that still leaves readers guessing whodunit.

522. _____. *The Mansion.* New York: Random, 1959; London: Chatto, 1961. Faulkner conceived this book to be the final chapter of work begun in 1925; it concludes the saga of the Snopes clan (*The Hamlet*, 1940; *The Town*, 1957). It opens with Mink Snopes, cousin of Flem, the leader of the tribe and a symbol of the new, ruthless and grasping Southerner, hearing the judge pronounce him guilty of the murder of Jack Houston.

523. _____. *Requiem for a Nun.* New York: Random, 1950; London: Chatto, 1953. Fifty-year-old Gavin Stevens, "more like a poet than a lawyer" (49), is defending Nancy Mannigoe, drunkard, domestic servant, and casual prostitute, for strangling to death one of the two white children of Gowan and Temple Stevens she was nursing. Gowan's drunkenness years ago caused Temple--then Temple Drake, spoiled sorority girl--to be raped by the brute Popeye in *Sanctuary*; she was kidnapped for a month in a Memphis whorehouse. It was presented as a three-act play at the John Golden Theatre in New York City on 28 January 1959 adapted by Ruth Ford and directed by British filmmaker Tony Richardson. Published as a play (Random, 1959). Camus also translated the play.

524. _____. *Sanctuary.* New York: Modern Library, 1931; New York:

Random, 1958. The trial scene in this so-called potboiler written in 1929 and published in 1931 is probably the most lurid piece of writing Faulkner did, yet its many revisions belie that it was written strictly to make money, which Faulkner wrote in the misleading Introduction to the Modern Library edition of 1932, calling it "a cheap idea. . . conceived to make money" (rpt. Editors' Note, *Sanctuary*, New York: Vintage, 1987, 337). Gavin Stevens smokes a corncob pipe like a country lawyer but is Harvard-educated and a Phi Beta Kappa to boot. He has a wild shock of white hair, a lively, thin face and practices law in the same way that he plays chess with his moves planned in advance (*Detectionary* 103). Though he, and almost every major character Faulkner ever wrote of, is mentioned from novel to novel, Stevens has a major role here in which a spoiled sorority girl named Temple Drake is out for a night of fun with her boyfriend. When they stop to buy whiskey from a bootlegger in the country, their paths cross with the psychopathic misfit Popeye who, unable to rape her because of his impotence, violates her with a corncob and keeps her hostage (Stevens, defending the bootlegger, holds the bloodied article aloft during the sensational trial). Gavin Stevens appears throughout the six stories collected in *Knight's Gambit* (New York: Random, 1949; London: Chatto, 1951; *see* Foote, Horton).

525. Faust, Frederick Schiller. Max Brand, pseud. *Destry Rides Again.* New York: Dodd, 1930. London: Hodder, 1931. Faust used 19 pen names in a career cut short by his death at 51. His fiction during the twenties was mostly under the Max Brand pseudonym, and he wrote thousands of slick pieces for the pulps including novels and serials. Richard W. Etulian notes in his introduction to the Gregg Press edition (Boston, 1979) that this, Brand's best known western, was serialized in 6 installments as "Twelve Peers" in *Western Story* magazine beginning February 1, 1930 (v). Harrison Destry is a rebellious youth of Wham framed by his best friend Chester Bent and convicted by twelve jurymen because they want to rid the town of him. He returns and exacts revenge on half his "peers" with guns, fists, and wits by the first half of the book; in effect, this is another western in which the town and its corrupt or indifferent citizenry, not the gunslinger, is the real villain.

526. _____. *Dr. Kildare's Trial.* New York: Dodd, 1942. London: Hodder, 1931. Young Doctor James Kildare arrives upon a traffic accident with bodies strewn about and administers aid to a Miss Courcy with broken bones in her leg, after cuffing her across the face to silence her and stripping away her clothing. His trial for malpractice is tepid despite the histrionics of the prosecutor.

527. Feegel, John R. *Autopsy.* New York: Avon, 1975. Feegel, a lawyer and pathologist, scores an Edgar with this meticulously detailed procedural about attorneys, morticians, and autopsy surgeons. The plot concerns a Florida tomato grower Myrl Caton, who is found shot to death in his Connecticut motel

room. Following a sloppy investigation, the widow brings suit challenging the suicide verdict by citing a Florida law that says an insured who commits suicide to enrich a beneficiary must allow for a two-year waiting period before collecting.

528. Ferber, Edna. *Cimarron.* Garden City, NY: Doubleday; London: Heinemann, 1930. The film (RKO, 1930) won Best Picture, a big sprawling early talkie. Prod. William LeBaron. Perf. Richard Dix, Irene Dunne, and Estelle Taylor. Its remake in 1960 by MGM with Glenn Ford in the lead as Yancey Cravat was panned as "flabby" and unnecessary (*Halliwell's* 146). Based on the Cravat family settling the Oklahoma prairie town of Osage. A courtroom scene midway with eloquent, dashing, half-intoxicated Cravat making a defense speech for the Fallen Woman of the town, gambling-hall proprietor and madame Dixie Lee.

529. Fielding, Henry. *The History of the Life of the Late Mr. Jonathan Wild, the Great, by Henry Fielding; to Which Is Added the Life and Actions of Jonathan Wild, by Daniel Defoe.* New York: Knopf; 1926. Introd. Wilson Follett. Two treatments by two of England's greatest novelists of the same man for different purposes--and yet not. The historical Jonathan Wild was tried and hanged at Tyburn on 24 May 1725 for being what today we might call a Washington lobbyist. He acted as intermediary between criminals and their victims, and because he had so flourished and achieved such notoriety in his day for "selling" back stolen goods to victims that his execution spawned a flood of broadsheets, ballads, homiletics, pamphlets, and "true' accounts of his life. Defoe's *True and Genuine Account of . . . the Late Jonathan Wild* was Fielding's own chief inspiration, but he had other than his predecessor's aim--that is, Defoe's own specialty to capitalize on a sure thing like the salaciousness of a debauched criminal's life. First serialized for publication in 1743, it was deemed a transparent attack on the arch-politician of his era, Sir Robert Walpole, which it was, of course, as the Great Man, thinly disguised as the "thief-taker" Wild. But Fielding always goes beyond his sole subjects into the universal traits marking all humanity--in this case, corruption and greed--to castigate politicians of Walpole's ilk. Contemporary John Gay had produced the long-lived *Beggar's Opera* in similar vein. Not much by way of lawyers or trials in any case amid the wit, burlesque, and sheer brilliance of eighteenth-century prose. In the same year Greenberg (New York, 1926) brought out an edition with John Macy writing the introduction.

530. _____. *Tom Jones.* Harmondsworth, Eng: Penguin, 1968. Ed. R. P. C. Mutter. Fielding's masterpiece was published February 28, 1749 and still has enough to qualify for a half-dozen genres. Himself a lawyer, admitted to the bar in 1740, Fielding was appointed Justice of the Peace for Westminster and then Middlesex. His symbol of justice and benevolence bears the name Allworthy, the squire who raised the infant Tom to young manhood on his country estate.

Being the local magistrate, Allworthy first sends servant and self-confessed mother of Tom, Jenny Jones, out of the county when her illegitimate birthing is detected by Allworthy's vindictive sister Bridget. He also presides at the trial of the schoolmaster Partridge, whose shrewish wife forces him to confess to being the father of the foundling. Squire Allworthy later sentences Tom's pregnant beauty Molly Seagrim to a House of Correction for a similar crime, but he intervenes. Tom himself faces a magistrate in Book XVI, when he is victimized by Lord Fellamar. A minor character is the lawyer Dowling, in the employ of Allworthy. a trial during his journey when he is a in Performed at the Theatre Royal in Covent Garden as a comic opera in 1769 by Joseph Reed. John Osborne scripted the film for motion picture (*Tom Jones: Film Script.* Ed. Robert Hughes. New York: Grove, 1964). Joan Macalpine adapted it for a three-act play in 1966 (London: Evans, 1966).

531. Fielding, Joy. *Missing Pieces.* New York: Doubleday, 1997. Family therapist Kate Sinclair's half-sister JoLynn announces her plans to marry Colin Friendly, a man on trial for the murder of 13 Palm Beach women.

532. _____. *Tell Me No Secrets.* New York: Morrow, 1993. Chicago DA Jess Koster, reeling from a bitter divorce and the unexplained disappearance of her mother, finds herself harassed by an anonymous tormentor. It is less formulaic when it deals with the criminal justice system's difficulties in prosecuting rape as well as with the terrors and frustrations of independent single women.

533. Fields, Bert. D. Kincaid, pseud. *The Lawyer's Tale.* New York: Turtle Bay-Random,1992. Hollywood attorney Harry Cain, dubbed the "Sunset Bomber" for his litigation skills, manages several cases from murder through blackmail to malfeasance involving a famed director's missing film--all while his beloved wife perishes slowly from cancer. Unfortunately for the reader, the pseudonymous LA attorney-author's writing is flamboyantly puerile and pedestrian, as witness Cain's reflection on the plane arriving at LAX: "Before [his wife], girls had been 'the enemy,' a prey on whom to use any tactic leading to bed" (5).

534. _____. *The Sunset Bomber.* New York: Linden, 1986. The first Harry Cain outing as litigator among the rich and shameless of Hollywood's elite.

535. Finder, Joseph. *High Crimes.* New York: Morrow, 1998. Author of spy-thrillers with a techno slant, Finder's third thriller combines military courtroom drama with a government conspiracy about an unassuming Boston broker named Tom Chapman whose prints are run by the police investigating a routine burglary; they discover he is really Sgt. Ronald Kubik, an Army deserter wanted for the murder of 87 civilians--the entire village population of La Colina

in El Salvador in 1985. Chapman admits to his Harvard law-prof wife Claire that he is Kubik but argues that he is the Army's scapegoat; in fact, he says, Army Chief of Staff William O. Marks is his former commanding officer who ordered the slaughter and the cover-up. She enlists the help of court-martial attorney Charles O. Grimes III and the military assigns a new grad terry Embry to defend. Currently being scripted for the film. Another Finder international suspense novel falls within the legal-thriller purview: *Extraordinary Powers* (Ballantine, 1993), wherein the narrator is an intellectual property rights specialist working for the blue-chip Boston firm of Putnam & Stearns, a CIA "outside" law firm, one that performs legitimate services without violating the Agency's charter.

536. Fish, Robert L. *The Murder League.* New York: Simon, 1968. London: NEL, 1970. Comic novel of three elderly British writers, each a co-founder of the Mystery Authors' Club, form a murder-for-hire organization. Sir Percival Pugh defends one of the trio in the death of a charity executive. Two more Murder League novels, *Rub-a-Dub-Dub* (1971) and *A Gross Carriage of Justice* (1979).

537. _____. *Trials of O'Brien.* New York: Signet, 1965. Based on the Peter Falk TV series--Daniel J. O'Brien, a trial attorney with a wide underworld acquaintanceship with small-time criminals, defends a safecracker.

538. _____ with Henry Rothblatt. *A Handy Death.* New York: Simon, 1973. London: Hale, 1975. Billy Dupaul was the Mets' most valuable bonus baby 8 years ago, but he blew his career by getting drunk and shooting a man; now while Dupaul serves his time in Attica, the DA decides to up the charges to murder one because bullet fragments worked their way into the victim's brain and he dies. Billy's lawyer Hank Ross sees something fishy--not in the DA's unprecedented legal move but in the facts surrounding the original investigation.

539. Fitzmaurice, Eugene. *Circumstantial Evidence.* New York: Jove, 1978. The Pennsylvania murder trial of surgeon Paul Oslo.

540. Fitzsimmons, Cortland. *No Witness!.* New York: Stokes, 1932. An arson fire is investigated by the Nassau County DA's Office, led by Henry Whitpur and his "star detective" Tom Gavin. The fire reported by a Mrs. Daller, who is shot at by persons unknown while talking to Gavin. A body found in the fire could be the remains of her husband George, who disappeared the night of the fire.

541. Flannagan, Roy. *County Court.* Garden City, NY: Doubleday, 1937. London: Heinemann, 1938. A Virginia farm wife is on trial for the murdering her husband at the instigation of a character known to the folks of Juliaville as a mental defective but to her and others, Captain Jinks is a prophet with healing

powers.

542. Fletcher, J. S. [Joseph Smith]. *The Middle Temple Murder.* New York: Grosset, 1919. Whodunit about an editor for a London paper, Frank Spargo, who becomes interested in the murder of man from New South Wales, John Marbury, found bludgeoned from behind near Middle Temple Lane; the only clue is a scrap of paper found on the dead man with a solicitor's name written on it. The solicitor claims that Marbury had wanted to see him about diamonds and during the coroner's inquest, an M. P. named Aylmore grudgingly acknowledges small financial dealings with the deceased twenty years ago.

543. Flood, John. *Bag Men.* New York: Delta, 1998. The body of Father Sedgwick is found on a runway of Boston's Logan Airport on New Year's Day, 1965. Not found with his corpse are 4,000 communion hosts blessed by the Pope and intended for the faithful in the first English-language mass in America. Ray Dunn, a young DA, but also the son of a corrupt cop, gets the case.

544. Flowers, R. Barri. *Damning Evidence.* iUniverse.com. 2000. An Internet legal thriller about a middle-aged lawyer raising two teens after the death of her husband. Kate del Graten is an Assistant DA of Portland, Oregon with an office nemesis in Jerrod Wessler, trying to beat her out for the top spot in the Homicide Bureau. When her son is indicted for murdering a young couple, she asks her husband's law partner, and current lover, to defend him against Wessler.

545. Foley, Tom. *Measuring Lives.* New York: Barricade, 1996. A murder investigation set in Naples, Florida with a plot involving a conspiracy over a trust fund.

546. Follett, James. *Crown Court.* London: Barker, 1977. New York: St. Martin's, 1978. Martin Janssen has a dying wife, creditors hounding him, and is summoned for jury duty at Fulchester Crown Court where the formidable Mr. Justice Sinclair Vice presides; Martin barely endures three cases, including a murder trial, when a terrorist and his henchmen take over the courtroom. Powerful, succinct characterization makes this one of the best of its kind.

547. Folsom, Allan. *Day of Confession.* Boston: Little, 1998. Santa Barbara novelist and screenwriter Folsom's second novel comes up with an international cast of characters much in the manner of his first (*The Day after Tomorrow*, Boston: Little, 1994). LA entertainment lawyer Harry Addison goes to Rome to retrieve his younger brother's body after a bus explosion; but Vatican and Italian police intercept him and inform him that his brother, Father Daniel Addison, was a prime suspect in the murder of Rosaria Parma, Cardinal Vicar of Rome. Even more, a special task force set up by the Italian Ministry to investigate the assassination, known as *Gruppo Cardinale*, has put him in the

crosshairs as his brother's accomplice in a vast conspiracy that involves hundreds of thousands of Chinese lives in a terrorist plot.

548. Foote, Horton. *Tomorrow.* New York: Dramatist's Play, 1963. One of the most adapted of Faulkner's works. The author himself included a screenplay in *Knight's Gambit.* Horton also adapted Faulkner's short story as a teleplay and film in 1985. Faulkner's original story was published in the Saturday Evening Post of 23 November 1940. Horton's TV play was aired live on CBS' *Playhouse 90* on 7 March 1960 and followed with a taped performance on 18 July 1961. Foote's film version was released in 1972 with Robert Duvall's brilliant lead performance. All versions are faithful to the main plot in which juryman Stonewall Jackson Fentry, a worn-out hill man from Frenchman's Bend cannot vote to acquit farmer Bookwright for the murder of "swaggering bravo" Buck Thorpe, child of the pregnant, abandoned girl he had saved and fallen in love with many years before.

549. Foote, Mary Hallock. *John Bodewin's Testimony.* Boston: Ticknor, 1885. The legal issue of the title is that, in the 1870's of the Arkansas River valley, ruggedly proud John Bodewin, original surveyor of the Eagle Bird mine before its purchase by the current owner, declines an offer by him of $5,000 to testify in court.

550. Foote, Shelby. *Follow Me Down.* New York: Dial, 1950. London: Hamilton, 1951. Civil War historian Foote adopts multiple points of view like another Mississippi writer to tell the story of a devout Mississippi farmer, who spends three weeks on a deserted island with young Beulah Ross and then kills her. His insanity defense is offered by Parker Nowell. Foote gives us an inside panorama of Luther Eustis' trial, from the court clerk in the first chapter to Nowell's late in the book.

551. Footner, Hulbert. *The Whip-poor-will Mystery.* New York: Harper, 1935. [Rpt. as *The New Made Grave*, London: Collins, 1935]. Weir Lambert is editor of the *Kent County Witness*, a small-town weekly in the South; he seeks the girl who placed an anonymous personal ad to "Whip-poor-will" in his classifieds. He finds Leila Cowdin, helps her bury her father's body, and winds up codefendant on a murder charge. Breen urges readers to avoid this one: "The circuit-court trial before a three-panel judge and jury is a singularly boring one, and the young couple's soppy romance is nearly as hard to take as the book's egregious racism" (45-46).

552. Forbes, Esther. *General's Lady.* New York: Harcourt, 1938. London: Chatto, 1939. The final third of the novel deals with the arraigning of a pair of accused lovers, Morganna Milroy, wife of General Milroy, and the man accused of shooting the general in the chest, Alan Brann (in reality, Lieutenant Alwyn Brandon, deserter from His Majesty's Expeditionary Forces).

553. _____. *Mirror for Witches*. Boston: Houghton; London: Heinemann, 1928. The real title is a beaut: *A Mirror for Witches in Which Is Reflected the Life, Machinations, and Death of Famous Doll Bilby, Who, with a More Than Feminine Perversity, Preferred a Demon to a Mortal Lover. Here Is Also Told How and Why a Righteous and Most Awfull* [sic] *Judgment Befell Her, Destroying Both Corporeal Body and Immortal Soul.* Boston: Houghton, 1928. Rpt. 1963; Chicago: Academy, 1985

554. Ford, Jeremy. *Murder Laughs Last.* New York: Bouregy, 1956. London: Ward, 1959. Despite the flamboyant plotline, the book is nearly all Q & A and courtroom action. Hank McGrath is the best crime reporter in New Jersey until his sister is murdered in a framed suicide and no one will print his story. He swears revenge against Dr. Stephen Carr, dentist and reputed crime-syndicate head, the man responsible. Carr is brought to trial for another crime--the murder of William Harris III, All-American halfback. McGrath attends Carr's trial awaiting the verdict.

Ford, Leslie, pseud. *See* Brown, Zenith Jones. . . .

555. Ford, Paul Leicester. *The Honorable Peter Stirling and What People Thought of Him.* New York: Holt, 1907. Harvard-educated, New York City attorney Peter Stirling begins his career with a case about a doctored can of milk that killed tenement children to political campaigning against the Tammany machine to his founding of his law firm Stirling, Ogden and Rivington. From its first printing in 1894, this puzzlingly popular novel went through 51 "editions" (printings) by the time Holt printed its version.

556. Forrest, Arthur. *The Biddle Boys and Mrs. Soffel: The Great Pittsburgh Tragedy and Romance: With Full Description of Their Lives and Crimes* . Baltimore: Ottenheimer, 1902. Forrest was a journalist who based his pulp novel on the true case of Edward and John Biddle and the romance of one brother with the wife of the warder, Mrs. Peter K. Soffel, that led to their escape from a Pittsburgh jail. (*See* Nyswaner, John.)

557. Forrest, Katherine V. *Murder by Tradition.* Two series characters in the detective genre, Kate Delafield, a homicide cop and closet lesbian, and homophobic partner investigate a multiple stabbing murder at a restaurant called The Tradition in which the victim had picked up another man in the bar the previous night. Kate's partner writes it off as a simple gay killing, but Delafield proves that the real murderer enjoys killing homosexuals. Kate is also afraid she will be exposed during the trial of the killer in the second half of the novel, such knowledge about her would, she believes, destroy her career in the LAPD.

558. Forrest, Williams. *Stigma.* New York: Crown, 1957. London:

Redman, 1959. The court martial of Sergeant Abel Bliss for murder, misconduct as a prisoner and maltreating prisoners in an encampment during the Korean War.

559. Forster, E. M. [Edward Morgan]. *A Passage to India.* London: Arnold; New York: Harcourt, 1924. Not a legal thriller by any means, yet more than a novel of divergent and clashing cultures inasmuch as it depicts the racism and colonialism of the English in turn-of-the-century India. Dr. Aziz is a refined, cultured man who makes the acquaintance of three newcomers to India, and a ripening friendship with them, especially with Cyril Fielding, the narrator. One of the trio, Miss Adela Quested accuses Dr. Aziz of sexually assault her during a visit to the Marabar Caves, but then recants at a sensational trial. Seymour-Smith calls it "a beautiful and poetic novel, incomparably superior to its predecessors; it outweighs everything else achieved by Forster . . ." (172). Like Alan Paton's *Cry, the Beloved Country*, it remains one of the books that belong to the world.

560. Forster, R. A. *Character Witness.* New York: Kensington-Pinnacle, 1997 . When a wife tries to claim the estate of her dead ex-husband for the life insurance, the judge challenges the attorney to prove the man was not a suicide.

561. _____. *Keeping Counsel.* New York: Zebra, 1996. New Mexico attorney Tara Linley is bound by attorney-client privilege in her defense of her best friend's lover, but Bill Hamilton is a dangerous psychopath of a client.

562. _____. *The Mentor.* New York: Kensington-Pinnacle, 1998. LA attorney Lauren Kingsley prosecutes an elusive terrorist organization called Independent Militia responsible for the bombing of an IRS building downtown and a rash of bombings across the country. Her mentor, Judge Wilson Caufield, is assigned the case, and the US Attorney's Office, playing politics, figures that giving Lauren the assignment to plead before this judge will get a sticky problem with search-and-seizure ruled in their favor. While Lauren builds her case, FBI investigator Eli Warner discovers a reason to investigate the judge himself, despite his known integrity. Then the judge turns up dead.

563. Fox, Gardner F. *Witness This Woman.* New York: Fawcett-Gold Medal, 1959. London: Muller, 1961. A Westchester County, New York, rape case prosecuted by a politically ambitious Assistant DA David Kirwan; defending the accused is the fiancée.

564. Fox-Davies, A C. [Arthur Charles]. *The Testament of John Hastings.* London: Long, 1911. John Hastings is found guilty of shooting a barmaid and is hanged. His will funds an investigation to clear his name. Barrister Ashley Tempest prosecutes the case in this espionage thriller.

565. Franzos, Karl Emil. *The Jews of Barnow.* New York: Arno, 1975 [Trans. M. W. Macdowall. Pref. to the American ed. Barnet Phillips]. The Austrian Franzos' stories date from the 1870s and all seem keenly unsympathetic to the Eastern Jews, in one way or another. "What Franzos describes is Jewish life pent up in some Galician town," writes Barnet in the preface (vi). Though intellectually superior to the peasants who can brutalize them in an instant, his stories indict them for their Talmudic fanaticism and secretive rituals that keep them isolated in the rigid orthodoxy of their faith. The final story, "Nameless Graves," concerns the Jewish practice of excommunication or *cherem*, invoked by the rabbi against a beautiful innkeeper's daughter because she hid her long golden hair instead cutting it as demanded by custom on her marriage day. After a series of miscarriages and acts against the family, the rabbi is sentenced by an Austrian magistrate for crimes against the husband or his business, the Jewish community rallies around him even more. He also wrote *The Chief Justice* [*Das Präsident*] (Erzählung, Breslau: Trewendt, 1884).

566. Frederic, Harold. *The Damnation of Theron Ware.* Cambridge: Belknap-Harvard U P, 1960. Ed. Everett Carter. Never recognized with the generation of naturalist writers like Stephen Crane as a major writer, the novel keeps Frederic's small fame alive. Much as had done as a husband and father in life, Frederic creates a character whose damnation is a result of a sexual fall, but it is also a fall into knowledge: scientific, religious, and esthetic (Carter xviii). This text follows the first American edition (Chicago: Stone, 1896). Theron, as a young Methodist minister, consults lawyer Levi Gorridge in his law office to see if he can obtain a higher wage than his Quarterly Conference allows him and his wife. In Chapter 25, Gorridge engages in a dispute with the Reverend Ware that further erodes his reputation within his pastorate.

567. Fredrickson, Michael. *A Cinderella Affidavit.* New York: Forge, 1999. Michael Chin is arrested for murdering a police officer in Boston's Chinatown during a drug raid. Frederickson's novel is built around one of the most shattered and abused of disciplinary rules for lawyers: Rule 6-101: the ethical injunction against "failing to act competently." Chin's lawyer Sarah Kerlinsky files a motion to have the police disclose their informant, which request would normally be routinely denied at a suppression hearing (thus, the success of so-called Cinderella affidavits, which are all finery but no substance--in other words, lies). When three of the four men arrested in the apartment below Chin's cut deals with the state against Chin, there is a rush to find the snitch, Danny Li, who turns to inexperienced corporate lawyer Matthew Boer for help. Boer is a litigation associate at prestigious Boston firm Daphnis & Clooney.

568. Freedman, J. F. *Above the Law.* New York: Dutton, 2000. Freedman is a Santa Barbara resident and a film and television director. Luke Garrison, a mix of idealism and lawyerly pragmatism, returns when Northern California DA

Nora Ray, an old friend, asks for his help in a case reminiscent of the ATF disaster in Waco; this time, the cowboys of the DEA are involved when, at the US AG's instructions to take reclusive kingpin Juarez alive, they storm the compound in a botched raid that leaves three agents dead. The subsequent investigation is a stonewalled coverup that Garrison as Special Prosecutor must break through to get the truth to put a complex case together and go to trial.

569. _____. *Against the Wind.* New York: Viking, 1991. Santa Fe defense attorney Will Alexander, a boozer and womanizer, is defending Lone Wolf and three members of an outlaw biker gang accused of murdering and mutilating a gay doper in the desert.

570. _____. *The Disappearance.* New York: Dutton, 1998. Former Santa Barbara DA Luke Garrison looks back on a hotshot career of ruthless ambition that haunts him in the Northern California woods where he sees repentance--especially for one case that sent an innocent man to death. Now, three years after leaving office, Judge Ferdinand De La Guerra asks Luke to defend Joe Allison, a suspect in the abduction-murder of a 14-year-old Emma Lancaster. In seeking a second chance at reclaiming self-worth, Luke finds himself believing that either his client did it or he is hiding something as bad.

571. _____. *Key Witness.* New York: Dutton; London: Penguin, 1997. Wyatt Matthews is an LA corporate attorney who yearns for courtroom action and finds it when he takes a sabbatical from his firm to do *pro bono* legal aid. The case he is assigned guarantees it: an 18-year-old black male has been charged in a series of rape-murders about to become a media firestorm with Matthews and client Marvin White in the middle. Helena Abramowitz' opening statement (368-72) and cross of expert witnesses, Det. Marlow (378-88) and the crossing colloquy by her and Matthews of the county coroner Dr. Ayala (388-90; 390-401) is worthy of Traver's *Anatomy of a Murder.*

572. Freeman, R[ichard]. Austin. *The Eye of Osiris.* London: Hodder, 1911. [Rpt. as *The Vanishing Man*, New York: Dodd, 1912]. An Egyptian scholar presumed dead has left a bizarre request in his will: he must be buried in a certain parish churchyard or his brother will forfeit his inheritance. But a cousin files an application in probate to have himself declared legal heir to the estate. Breen calls this a fine detective novel "with an especially interesting murderer" (47-48) and Freeman an undervalued writer with Dickensian skill at creating secondary characters.

573. _____. *For the Defence: Dr. Thorndyke.* London: Hodder; New York: Dodd, 1934. Barrister Thorndyke's client is painter Andrew Barton, on trial for his own murder because the body found at the base of a cliff and battered beyond recognition is actually his cousin, whose place he had taken.

574. _____. *The Jacob Street Mystery.* London: Hodder, 1942. [Rpt. as *The Unconscious Witness*, New York: Dodd, 1942]. Lotta Schiller is a woman vanished with a will left behind that might not be legitimate; this final Dr. Thorndyke novel argues its case and answers its questions in probate court.

575. _____. *The Red Thumb Mark.* London: Collingwood, 1907. New York: Newton, 1911. Freeman's first novel featuring Dr. John Evelyn Thorndyke, specialist in medical jurisprudence is narrated by the obtuse Dr. Jervis. Chapters 15 and 16 are devoted to the trial of Reuben Hornby for stealing diamonds from a rich South African entrusted to his uncle, a diamond merchant and owner of Hornsby's of London. The bloody thumb print is major evidence in the case.

576. Frey, Stephen W. *The Takeover.* New York: Dutton, 1995. Andrew Falcon is the newest partner at Wall Street's Winthrop, Hawkins, whose work in the mergers-and-acquisitions department earns him a staggering million-dollar bonus. When he informs the firm founder and his mentor Granville Winthrop that he intends to quit so that he can bankroll his own software company, the old man retracts the bonus and kicks him out. Thereafter, Falcon and he are enemies with a multimillion-dollar fee at stake if he can outmaneuver Winthrop and his nefarious committee known as the Sevens in a high-stakes corporate merger. Princeton, NJ resident Frey is a vice president of corporate finance at Westdeutsche Landesbank in Manhattan.

577. Frieder, Patricia. *Signature Murder.* New York: Bantam, 1998. Chauffeur Teddy Bellasandro is the prime suspect in the brutal murder of his employer, Isadora Stanton. Lawyer Matty Donahue had recommended Bellasandro to the irascible and elderly woman, even though he had done time for a murder with similar traits. The police and DA consider the case a slam-dunk.

578. Friedman, Philip. *Grand Jury.* New York: Fine-Dutton, 1997. Friedman was born in New York and raised in Yonkers but attended Cal-Berkeley and Stanford before returning to complete his education with a *Juris Doctore* from New York University School of Law. He received the American Jurisprudence Award for his work in copyright law. He majored in mathematics through graduate school before settling on the law. With three international bestsellers to date, his writing career took off with *Rage* (New York: Atheneum, 1972), a noncourtroom tale about Army helicopters accidentally releasing a nerve gas as they fly over a rancher and his son camping out; the father takes bloody revenge when his son dies. Friedman scripted his novel for the film (Warner, 1972, dir. and starring George C. Scott). Following his 1979 CIA spy-thriller *Termination Order* and almost a decade in film and TV work, he thereafter probes legal issues in the contemporary world without the minutiae of legal technicality or jargon that can glaze a reader's eyes. Not only is he one of

the many writers who practice law but his work combines law and film in areas related to the protection of authorship and motion picture production. The novels after *Rage* invariably get into the courtroom and make even trial preparation a dramatic part of the novels.

The title belies the sleuthing that dominates this massive (almost 700 pages) tome, which one reviewer slams as a "tar pit" after an excellent opening depiction in the first few chapters of the flawed jury system in America in which jurors are more motivated by stupidity and bias than idealism. Two grand jurors, both professionals, become involved with each other as a prosecutor presents a drug-conspiracy case against two elderly and distinguished residents of New York's Chinatown, the Engs. The basic implausibility is that Susan Linwood (Chinese-American) and David Clark violate the most basic tenet of a grand jury and discuss the case in progress.

579. _____. *Inadmissible Evidence.* New York: Fine, 1992. Friedman's second courtroom drama spent fifteen weeks on the *New York Times* paperback bestseller list. Manhattan Assistant DA Joe Estrada's ambition propels him into a major homicide case involving the retrial of a rich real-estate developer; it is not only a front-page, rape-murder case that will cover him in publicity but media allegations of racism inflame its notoriety because minority group leader Roberto Morales is the man charged with killing his young, beautiful mistress.

580. _____. *Reasonable Doubt.* New York: Fine, 1990. New Yorker Michael Ryan, a former federal prosecutor, defends his pregnant, ex-daughter-in-law Jennifer Kneeland Ryan, in the murder trial of his son Ned. He assumes her guilt, despises her but takes her case in the interest of his unborn grandchild. Ryan's research in the task of finding a possible killer and his trial preparation earned kudos from critics.

581. Frost, Barbara. *Innocent Bystander.* New York: Coward, 1955. Marka de Lancey is an NYC lawyer who calls in a criminal law specialist to defend her client, Gregory Trefani, an Italian musician, accused of the morphine poisoning of nightclub singer Trixie Maxon. Unfortunately, according to Breen, the 17 pages of trial action itself are "inept," "unconvincing," and "TV-ish" (49).

Fyfield, Frances, pseud. *See* Hegarty, Frances. . .

G

582. Gaboriau, Émile. *File No. 113* [alt. title: *The Blackmailers: Dossier No. 113*]. New York: Lovell, 1883; Boston: Little, 1899. Trans. George Burnahm Ives. Thieves make their way into Parisian banker M. André Fauvel's office and steal 350,000 francs. Cashier Prosper's examination by the magistrate consists entirely of three witnesses giving hearsay evidence or downright gossip to have him charged with the crime.

583. Gadol, Peter. *The Long Rain.* New York: Picador, 1997. Distracted by the breakup of his marriage, small-town lawyer and winemaker Jason Dark hits and kills a teenaged boy while driving recklessly. When a car thief confesses to the crime, Dark attempts a partial atonement by defending the man *pro bono.*

584. Gaghan, Stephen, writ. *Rules of Engagement.* Dir. William Friedkin. Prod. Richard D. Zanuck and Scott Rudin. Story James Webb. Perf. Samuel L. Jackson, Tommy Lee Jones, Guy Pearce, Anne Archer, and Ben Kingsley. Paramount, 2000. The Article 32 court martial of Colonel Terry Childers, a 30-year veteran, and his defense by Vietnam buddy (Jones), wounded in combat and who later became, by his own admission at retirement, "a weak lawyer" with a drinking problem for the Marines. Childers is being tried in Camp Lejeune, NC, for the massacre of 83 Yemeni citizens for a rescue action at the American embassy in Sana à when he gave the order to fire on "unarmed" protesting citizens. Gaghan won an Oscar for adapting the script of *Traffic* based on the British series.

585. Gaines, Ernest J. *Of Love and Dust.* New York: Dial, 1967. Born on a Louisiana plantation, Gaines worked the fields throughout his childhood, moving to California and completing a degree at San Francisco State and then winning a Wallace Stegner Fellowship to Stanford. Sydney Bonbon is a brutal, simple man working as overseer of a plantation with a black woman and white wife; he is goaded into killing a young black worker named Marcus for lusting after his black woman with a scythe-blade, and though a hearing is mentioned in the final chapter, he leaves without a trial fearing Cajun justice for flouting its unwritten race laws.

An unofficial court is convened in another Deep-South novel by Gaines. In *The Red Cock Crows* (Macmillan, 1944), a black preacher named Scofield is brought before a vigilance committee on the charge of inciting a slave insurrection; though fictional, the novel is based on "happenings" in the now-vanished town of Livingston, Mississippi in 1835. (*See* Styron, William).

586. Gaither, Frances Ormond. *Double Muscadine.* New York: Macmillan; London: Joseph, 1949. Tennessee-born Gaither wrote of Mississippi and here invades Faulkner's territory without invading the talent to retail the effects on the characters of the fictional town of Waverley of a family slave's trial in the Oxford court house circa 1850's; Aimée, being the family cook on the plantation of Kirk McLean, stands accused of putting arsenic in the tea, killing one of the family. Much of the novel intersperses courtroom D & A. The author claims the story is based on a real case from the Supreme Court of Mississippi.

587. Galsworthy, John. *Over the River.* London: Heinemann, 1933. [Rpt. as *One More River*, New York: Scribner's, 1933]. The final Forsyte Chronicles

volume focuses on *Corven v. Corven*. Sir Gerald, left by wife Clare in Ceylon, is bringing a divorce action on grounds of her adultery with a younger man, whom she had met on the return trip to England.

588. _____. *The Silver Spoon.* London: Heinemann; New York: Scribner's, 1926. *The Forsyte Saga*, spanning 9 volumes and covering London high society in the twenties, earned the author the Nobel in 1932. Galsworthy was "depthless" but honest, writes Seymour-Smith, and "grotesquely overvalued" by his own generation (179), although his plays *Strife* (1909) and *Justice* (1910) are good social criticism. In *The Silver Spoon*, Fleur Mont, the daughter of Soames Forsyte, is the defendant in a libel suit. Defense counsel's aim is to attack the status quo of sexual permissiveness and immorality, Galsworthy's ultimate subject in the chronicles but not one that he penetrates, for it is merely to look at its sleaze from the insider's point of view.

589. Gann, Ernest K[ellogg]. *The Magistrate.* New York: Arbor; Markham, Ont., Canada: Fitzhenry, 1982. Tale of Judge Julian Hickock's moribund life on and off the bench. The trial of a pornographer drags along the narrative without being remarkable.

590. _____. *Of Good and Evil.* New York: Simon; London: Hodder, 1963. Separated by sections of morning, noon, afternoon, and evening, the novel details the workings of law-enforcement in a big, anonymous city. Thoughtfully pessimistic Judge Thomas Brownell is one of the recurring characters.

591. Gardner, Erle Stanley. A. A. Fair, pseud. *All Grass Isn't Green.* New York: Morrow; London: Heinemann, 1970. Gardner was born in Malden, Massachusetts, the son of a mining engineer who, like his world-famous creation, became a lawyer. He said of his early days as a student at Valparaiso University in Indiana and of one of his professors, "I learned more law there in a period of three or four weeks than I ever learned anywhere in anything like the same amount of time" (Morton 80). An altercation with another professor nearly sent him to jail and got him expelled. (Gardner, a boxer in his teen years, who roamed the Klondike with his father, claims he slugged this professor.) He began novel writing in the early 1930's with *The Case of the Velvet Claws.* He was still writing for and very much influenced by the pulps with their gritty realism, magazines and fanzines such as *Black Mask*, *Clues*, *Detective Fiction Weekly*, and *Dime Detective* were tough-minded reflections of a hard, dirty Depression-era mentality and Mason was a fighter capable of twisting the law and threatening his opponents and clients alike. On occasion he wrote under a *nom de plume* (besides the Charles J. Kenney noted here, he had used Charles M. Green in the 1920's and later Robert Parr and Kyle Corning; the last-named is similar to a fledgling lawyer character Gardner tried out dating from *Black Mask* days--6 stories appeared between 1932-33 about Ken Corning, an idealist who fights corruption in "York City" and who is assisted by an able secretary,

Helen Vail, a Della-Street prototype). During this time he created a lawyer named Peter Wennick, who like the early Masons also had a touch of the hardboiled about him in the classic *noir* and *Black Mask* fictional style of the thirties. Wennick, however, was a mere law clerk for an important "West Coast" law firm. After forty years of Mason novels, however, Gardner's lifetime output would be so staggering that prolific John Creasey alone bears comparison in number and rival Mickey Spillane a much-distant second in sales (Mundell n. pag.). "He went on to attain the distinction of being the 'top-selling author' in the world, an estimated 310,910,603 copies as of January 1, 1979, with translations into twenty-three languages including such exotic tongues as Tamil and Urdu . . ." (Fugate 13). After 1933, Gardner was a self-employed writer and never looked back, often dictating as many as four Masons at one time.

For all their slickness, Mason novels do not go out of print. By 1977, it could be claimed by *Detectionary*'s compilers that not a single one had yet (70). One reason is offered by the author himself, who said that justice is done in his books. The average person's life is full of confusion, and seeing someone get into and out of trouble is enormously satisfying. In 1962 Gardner was recognized as a Grand Master by the Mystery Writers of America; he had won an Edgar for Best Fact Crime for *The Court of Last Resort* in 1952). Only the active New Yorker Michael Avallone today seems to be within striking distance of Gardner's 146 novels, more than 80 featuring the supersleuth lawyer Perry Mason. Deduct another 29 of that total under the pseudonym A. A. Fair for the Bertha Cool-Donald Lam mystery duo, minus 9 that feature California DA Doug Selby and with a flock of lesser sleuths, not counting Wennick--such as lawyer-con man Lester Leith, Gramp Wiggins (whose daughter is married to Dan Duryea, DA of Santa Delbarro County, CA), ex-lawyer Terry Clane, Sheriff Bill Eldon, Paul Pry, and Sidney Zoom--you have a writer who almost singlehandedly defined the courtroom thriller as the public knows it, this despite all the clichés, banalities, and improbabilities. Gardner's skillful plot handling and his incisive characterization make the Mason novels both readable and laudable today. An interesting sidenote is offered by film critic Leonard Maltin about the lack of continuity in the part of the famed attorney by Hollywood in the years before the Raymond Burr TV series and films stabilized his portrait more akin to the Gardner version on the page. Warren Williams first held the role, "but the screenwriters kept changing their minds about the way Perry should be portrayed. He was definitely flashier than [Gardner's Mason], but in *The Case of the Lucky Legs* (Warner, 1935), he's portrayed as a constant tippler (à la Nick Charles) and in *The Case of the Curious Bride* [Warner, 1935], he's positively giddy" (1028). Ricardo Cortez attempted the role in 1936 in *The Case of the Black Cat* (Warner; retitled *The Case of the Caretaker's Cat*). When the long-running CBS series ended in 1966, Monte Markham and Sharon Acker played Perry and Della in the short-lived *The New Adventures of Perry Mason* (1973). Two telefilms from 1987 are *The Case of the Sinister Spirit*, in which Perry defends a publisher accused of murdering a writer at a haunted hotel featured Robert Stack opposite Raymond Burr, and *The Case of the Scandalous*

Scoundrel. Fans know Mason's career chapter and verse down to the exact dimensions of his LA office in the Central Utilities Building at Central and Clark Streets and even to the quirks of the various judges he practices before, even though the details of Mason's personal life remain scant. (*See* Frank Robbins' "The World of Perry Mason" in **References**.)

Rich Milton Calhoun asks the B. Cool Detective Agency to look for a missing writer and is subsequently indicted for murder in a drug-smuggling scheme. In this last novel to be published in Gardner's lifetime, and though a very poor book, Jon Breen lauds the author for a lifetime's achievement and finds even his flaws to be virtues. "He was spotting killers in the courtroom and spreading around the three '*I*'s' to the very end" (85).

592. _____. *Beware the Curves.* New York: Morrow, 1956. London: Heinemann, 1957. John Dittmar Ansel claims to be a writer and engages Lam & Cool to locate a man named Endicott for copyrighting purposes because the man had told him a great story in Paris six years ago that Ansel would like to use. Lam immediately discovers two things: the client is no writer and his physical description had been given to the police by a cabdriver, including the fact that he carried a gun in his briefcase, before being dropped off at an address in Orange County that happened to be the home of one Karl Carver Endicott, wealthy citizen of Citrus Grove and murder victim. When the client and the Elizabeth Endicott, widow of the decedent, attempt to take out a marriage license in Yuma, Arizona, the police arrest them and put Ansel on trial for murder. Gardner's foreword in this one is an emotional appeal to society and penologists to implement what we call nowadays shock probation for youthful felons; he deplores the hardening of first-time offenders given minimum sentences of one year in Nevada penitentiaries: "When the prison doors first clang shut on such a young man, when he first realizes the horror and degradation of prison life, when he is plunged into an existence of men deprived of women but not of sex. . . there is a feeling of revulsion and horror" (n. pag.)

593. _____. *The Bigger They Come.* New York: Morrow, 1939. [Rpt. as *Lam to the Slaughter*, London: Hamilton, 1940]. Bertha Cool, unflatteringly described as 165 pounds of potatoes in a sack with "bulldog jaw," glittering, greedy eyes and a sailor's vocabulary, is the founder of a private detective that takes aboard the bantamweight but brainy Donald Lam, a lawyer serving indefinite suspension from legal practice, in a long-running series involving capers and clients similar to the ever-durable Mason series; however, the emphasis on the Lam-Cool episodes plays off their caricatures for comic effect: he with his wily, Mason-like deductive powers yet possessing an eye for curves and cleavage; she with her tacky jewelry and greedy eye for the client's fee. In later novels, Bertha becomes less obese but no less profane, albeit her slang is harmless by today's standards ("Fry me for an oyster"). Despite their obvious resemblance to the Mason novels in plot, character, style, and even the occasional legal hairsplitting, the Gardner-Fair subterfuge lasted for years,

although Mason fans immediately suspected the connection. Lam gave Gardner a freer hand in some senses that he might have felt lacking in his craft. Donald is as close to the hardboiled as Gardner cared to get, but he is more human than Perry and does get a free hand with the ladies once in a while despite his and his author's prudish attitude toward sex, which observation is not to suggest that Donald is Perry's libidinous alter ego. The flirtatious minxes in the Lam-Cool novels are the same bimbos, to borrow old slang, that they are in the Mason books. Gardner apparently chafed under the unyielding rectitude of Mason regarding women and, perhaps, Della Street's ubiquitous presence would always ensure Perry never really had much chance to see what women were like outside the office. Bertha, on the other hand, is a caricature of a gray-haired grandmother with a salty tongue; she gains or loses weight from novel to novel (the authors of *Detectionary* claim she is "mammoth" at over 200 pounds (27). But Bertha is never much more than a foil character to her ingenious, reticent junior partner. Her shy, efficient secretary is Elsie Brand.

One last point: the plots in the Lam-Cool books are very similar to the Mason novels but they must on occasion hang fire while Donald works out his next move. This is good storytelling, and today's readers of serial fiction should wonder why it is that so many first-person narratives are loaded with impossible detail in which characters tell themselves things that no person tells him-, herself in real life. Gardner understood craft. A sample of the 29 Lam-Cool novels is included here because sleuthing, with a rare foray into a legal technicality, is the priority.

Lam is given a first assignment, seemingly simple: serve papers on one Morgan Birks for client Sandra Birks, estranged wife. Morgan's murder will give Donald an ironic chance to prove the claim that got him suspended from practicing law: he can get away with murder. Gardner himself maintained that, at the time, it was a completely legal way to achieve the perfect murder. Filmed for television by CBS in 1955.

594. _____. *The Case of the Amorous Aunt.* New York: Morrow, 1963. London: Heinemann, 1969. Mason hurries to a motel in Calexico to save a Boston client's rich aunt from "a Bluebeard," according to Della (3). The niece believes Montrose DeWitt intends to kill the smitten woman, but it is the aunt who tells Perry she saw him clubbed to death beside the road but is charged with his murder by ambitious Baldwin L. Marshall.

595. _____. *The Case of the Angry Mourner.* New York: Morrow, 1951. London: Heinemann, 1958. Mason is vacationing in a mountain cabin in Bear Valley when the distraught mother of 21-one-year-old Carlotta Adrian consults him. The daughter claims to have left playboy Arthur Cushing after rebuffing his advances, but the mother found him dead with a bullet hole in his chest and broken glass, including her daughter's compact, all over. Acting to save her daughter, she cleaned up the cabin, and now finds herself facing a preliminary hearing. The dead man's father brings in high-priced legal talent to assist the

local DA. The triple-I objections fly in an exciting courtroom denouement.

596. _____. *The Case of the Baited Hook.* New York: Morrow; London: Cassell, 1940. Mason takes a retainer from a mysterious man who visits him at night with a woman in a mask in tow and agrees to handle any legal matter for the woman once she identifies herself to him. Mason discovers the man to be a wealthy architect immediately but later learns the woman is the estranged wife of businessman Albert Tidings, who is one of the trustees of a young woman's property; she is being introduced into high society as Russian-born nobility by a Mrs. Trump and is about to marry a wealthy man. Mrs. Trump accuses him of fraud and wants him removed, which removal occurs while Tidings sits in his car--with a bullet--in a case of double blackmail and murder. Grosset via Morrow added this one to *Sulky Girl* and *Silent Partner* in its *The Erle Stanley Gardner Triple Decker.*

597. _____. *The Case of the Beautiful Beggar.* New York: Morrow, 1965. London: Heinemann, 1972. The title's beggar is sweet, naive Daphne Shelby, niece of elderly Horace Shelby, declared *non compos mentis* by action of his half-brother Borden Finchley; the conservatorship hearing puts his million-dollar estate into the hands of the greedy Finchleys in "a conspiracy," Perry as *amicus curiae* tells the niece, "as old as the hills" (28). She is afterward indicted for the murder of Ralph Exeter, a friend of the Finchleys. The Detective Book Club edition (Black, 1987) adds a Lam-Cool mystery: *Up for Grabs* (1964).

598. _____. *The Case of the Bigamous Spouse.* New York: Morrow, 1961. London: Heinemann, 1967. A children's encyclopedia saleswoman discovers her best friend's husband is living under the assumed name of Gillett. When he is found shot to death at the estate of George Belding Baxter, she is accused. Mason and Burger argue *res gestae* before Judge Laporte at trial.

599. _____. *The Case of the Black-Eyed Blonde.* New York: Morrow, 1944. London: Cassell, 1948. Diana Regis is paid to read to wealthy Jason Bartsler, but stepson Carl Fretch accuses her of theft and assaults her. Then Regis is charged in a preliminary hearing with the shooting murder of her roommate Mildred Danville, a dead ringer for her, found lying in the mud with a bullet in her brain. Series characters Assistant DA Drumm and Sgt. Holcomb reappear after a long absence, and in the latter's case, with no love lost for the "wise guy" lawyer who, he says, got him kicked off the homicide squad.

600. _____. *The Case of the Blonde Bonanza.* New York: Morrow, 1962. London: Heinemann, 1967. Dianne Alder is a gorgeous blonde from Bolero Beach, adding 12 pounds to her diet to model fashions for the plus-sized woman in what Mason calls "the damnedest contract [he has] ever read" (20). Mason attempts to nose out the background of her contract with Harrison T. Boring, the modeling agency's president. When Boring is found bludgeoned in a room

at the Restawhile Motel, Alder becomes the prime suspect, and Mason defends her in a Riverside County prelim.

601. _____. *The Case of the Borrowed Brunette.* New York: Morrow, 1946. London: Cassell, 1951. Mason uncovers an impersonation plot when he spies a series of identical brunettes in dark dresses and furs standing on street corners--one of whom, Eva Martell, has been recruited to take the place of Helen Reedley, temperamental and estranged spouse of Orville Reedley, for the ostensible purpose of maintaining a lease on an apartment in Reedley's wife's name. The man hiring the brunettes is later found shot in the apartment and Mason is called to testify before a grand jury and grilled by the amateurish Harry Gulling from the DA's office.

602. _____. *The Case of the Buried Clock.* New York: Morrow, 1943. London: Cassell, 1945. In this atypical novel, Mason is not introduced until thirty pages into the narrative and is present at the scene of the murder. A returning vet finds embezzler Jack Hardisty shot to death in a mountain cabin; the angry decedent's wife Milicent is arrested. Near the cabin is a buried alarm clock (on sidereal time that almost misleads Mason) used to establish an alibi.

603. _____. *The Case of the Calendar Girl.* New York: Morrow, 1958. London: Heinemann, 1964. Mason goes often to court, defending two different clients on the same murder charge: contractor George Ansley consults Mason about a traffic accident he is involved in with model Dawn Manning. Ansley is then accused of murdering a photographer.

604. _____. *The Case of the Careless Cupid.* New York: Morrow, 1968. London: Heinemann, 1972. A widow in her fifties consults Mason for the purpose of getting legal advice about exemplary damages accruing from an act of slapping a man's face. The man in question has been following her for weeks. Behind Selma Anson's question, however, is the accusation of arsenic poisoning in the crab salad her husband "lapped up" at a family cookout; the relatives of her future husband want to see her convicted. Mason opts for trial by judge.

605. _____. *The Case of the Careless Kitten.* New York: Morrow, 1942. London: Cassell, 1944. Helen Kendal's kitten almost dies from a dose of strychnine. Helen's wealthy Uncle Franklin Shore resurfaces (by telephone) after vanishing years earlier. Then Henry Leech, a go-between who was supposed to take Helen to her uncle, is found shot to death in his car. Jon Breen calls this "one of the best pure detective novels [Gardner] ever wrote" (60).

606. _____. *The Case of the Caretaker's Cat.* New York: Morrow, 1935. London: Cassell, 1936. Miser Peter Laxter, who died in a fire, guarantees a perpetual job of caretaker of his estate and a home for life to his 65-year-old caretaker in his will, but Sam Laxter, the major beneficiary, claims he is not

obligated to the man's Persian cat. Two more murders follow: the caretaker is strangled and Ethel DeVoe, possessor of dangerous knowledge, is clubbed with a blunt instrument. Both Mason and Della Street become witnesses for the prosecution in a convoluted plot that is powered, according to Jon Breen, by a "MacGuffin of hidden money and diamonds [which is]. . . elaborate enough for any Golden Age detective story practitioner, and the key clue is a good one" (54).

607. _____. *The Case of the Cautious Coquette.* New York: Morrow, 1949. London: Heinemann, 1955. Mason, performing rarely as a personal-injury lawyer, seeks witnesses to the hit-and-run accident that left his young client with a broken hip. After a newspaper ad produces two suspect vehicles, he becomes intrigued with the murder of chauffeur Hartwell L. Pitkin, found shot to death.

608. _____. *The Case of the Counterfeit Eye.* New York: Morrow; London: Cassell, 1935. Peter Brunold's collection of glass eyes includes bloodshot ones for the day after a binge. When one is stolen and replaced with a fake, he intuitively fears he is to be framed for murder. Then millionaire Hartley Basset is found murdered with a bloodshot glass eye in his clenched fist, he and the dead man's widow are charged. Perry Mason appears before his first prelim, but the novel carries vestiges of the hardboiled school—for example, Mason, impersonating a window washer to get around a detective at Sylvia Bassett's door: "You poor little fool, were you trying to take a run-out powder/" (154). Debuting here also is courtroom foe Hamilton Burger.

609. _____. *The Case of the Crimson Kiss: A Perry Mason Novelette and Other Stories.* New York: Morrow, 1971. London: Heinemann, 1975. After Gardner's death, stories written for the pulps surfaced in collections of his shorter works. The title story is one of two Mason short novels written for *American* magazine in the June 1948 issue. Fay Allison is accused of the poisoning murder of Carver C. Clements, found dead in his apartment with red lipstick marks on his forehead. Mason questions a prosecution expert testifying to numerous fingerprints Fay left in the apartment. One of the 4 stories included is "Fingers of Fong," a throwback to his days as a pulp writer and fledgling lawyer defending Chinese citizens in Oxnard, California. A non-courtroom Mason short novel heads a subsequent collection, *The Case of the Crying Swallow* (Morrow, 1971), in which playboy-sportsman Claude L. Winnett asks the lawyer to trace his missing wife of a month. The three stories reprinted with this feature Lester Leith, Sidney Zoom and amateur sleuth Jerry Bane in "The Affair of the Reluctant Witness," reprinted from 1949. Both short novels were included in a book-club edition of *The Case of the Cautious Coquette* (1949).

610. _____. *The Case of the Crooked Candle.* New York: Morrow, 1944. London: Cassell, 1947. When a client rear-ends a sheep truck, Mason gets

involved in the affairs of the Skinner Hills Karakul Company. He later represents a father and daughter on charges of murdering Fred Milfield by a blow to the head. Says Breen: "Jacques Barzun and Wendell Hertig Taylor recommend this Mason above all others to enthusiasts of formal detection: there is much fascinating technical testimony . . ." (61).

611. _____. *The Case of the Curious Bride.* New York: Morrow, 1934. London: Cassell, 1935. New bride Rhoda Montaine seeks Mason's advice (feigning to be seeking counsel for a friend) in what begins as a *corpus delicti* matter involving first husband Gregory Moxley believed dead in a plane crash. She is now married to Carl Montaine, a spineless man with a wealthy father and a former drug habit. The motive for murdering a con man is supplied by the grilling Mason gives Montaigne in the divorce-action deposition (281-83).

612. _____. *The Case of the Dangerous Dowager.* New York: Morrow; London: Cassell, 1937. The film *Granny Get Your Gun* (Warner, 1940) was inspired by this one. Matilda Benson describes herself to Mason as "a hardbitten old hellion," who drinks, swears, and smokes big cigars; she also liked the way he handled "that howling dog case" (3). She wants him to pay off Sam Grieb, one of the shady characters who run a gambling ship anchored beyond the pier; he holds her granddaughter Sylvia's gambling debts, about $7,000 worth of paper. Opens with a facsimile of the concluding page (275) of *The Case of the Stuttering Bishop*, published in September of the preceding year.

613. _____. *The Case of the Daring Decoy.* New York: Morrow, 1957. London: Heinemann, 1963. Oil executive Jerry Conway opens the paper to read a half-page ad smearing him and requesting shareholders of California & Texas Global Development & Exploration Company to send in their proxies to Gifford Farrell. Conway summons Mason when he thinks he has been framed in some kind of badger game by a mysterious phone caller giving her name as Rosalind.

614. _____. *The Case of the Daring Divorcee.* New York: Morrow, 1964. London: Heinemann, 1969. Thanks to Gertie's love of chocolate creams and romance novels, Mason does not get a good description of the woman claiming to be Adelle Hastings and in danger; she left her purse and gun behind in his office when he returns from a luncheon conference. The gun might have killed her husband Garvin Hastings. Gardner used a real trick from his lawyering days when he filled the courtroom with Chinese to confuse a policeman on the stand asked to identify his client. A similar trick works in a lineup of women wearing dark glasses to foil Lt. Tragg's attempt to get Gertie to identify Mason's client.

615. _____. *The Case of the Deadly Toy.* New York: Morrow, 1959. London: Heinemann, 1964; rpt. Cambridge, MA: Bentley, 1981. Retitled from its original serial publication in *The Saturday Evening Post* as *The Case of the Deadly Grandpa,* the novel opens with the scandalous divorce of Mervin

Selkirk; at issue is 7-year-old son Robert Selkirk, center of a pending custody battle between divorcing parents. Norda Allison, Selkirk's fiancée, breaks up with him over the boy's treatment by the father and is accused in a preliminary hearing of murder when he is found shot to death at a golf course. Burger fires off numerous objections, including the Triple-I, citing hearsay, when Mason asks a most relevant question about young Bobby discharging a gun found under his pillow.

616. _____. *The Case of the Demure Defendant.* New York: Morrow, 1956. London: Heinemann, 1962. An abridged version of this was published in *The Saturday Evening Post* under the title *The Case of the Missing Poison.* While treating a young woman for "guilt," Dr. Logbert P. Denair puts her under with a combination of truth-serum drugs and tape records her. Nadine Farr shocks him by confessing to poisoning her uncle. Although not her real uncle, she had been staying with Mosher Higley at the time of his death. During her subsequent murder trial, Perry displays Gardner's avid love of forensics by tripping up the doctor on his own turf. Higley's coronary thrombosis was triggered by potassium of cyanide with much ado in the cross over its telltale "odor of bitter almonds" (200). Gardner exposes the real murderer in the denouement via a babbling husband's sordid tale of greed and Judge Ashurt brings the gavel down "on that note of complete and utter moral degradation" (237).

617. _____. *The Case of the Drowning Duck.* New York: Morrow, 1942. London: Cassell, 1944. Rancher John L. Witherspoon fears his daughter Lois is about to marry the son of a murderer, so asks Mason to study the transcript of an 18-year-old murder trial to assess the defendant's guilt.

618. _____. *The Case of the Drowsy Mosquito.* New York: Morrow, 1943; London: Cassell, 1946. Gardner combines some favorite props in this one about family greed over mining shares and arsenic poisoning as Mason investigates the murder of Banning Clarke.

619. _____. *The Case of the Dubious Bridegroom.* New York: Morrow, 1949. London: Heinemann, 1954. Mining executive Edward Garvin is charged with murdering his first wife Ethel when she is found with a bullet hole in her left temple sitting in her car near Oceanside, CA. Mason goes up against an unworthy foe in the change of venue. San Diego County DA Hamlin L. Covington is "angry and flustered" throughout his opening speech, to which Mason objects frequently. Another note of distinction to this otherwise entertainingly playful number is that it contains Perry Mason's shortest opening statement--says the cheerful lawyer archly, standing before the jury: "He can't prove it" (162). Reissued by Ballantine in pbk. in 1997.

620. _____. *The Case of the Duplicate Daughter.* New York: Morrow,

1960. London: Heinemann, 1965. Muriell Gilman, a former juror in a case Mason defended, consults him about her father's sudden disappearance. He reappears but is accused of strangling a private detective in his shop and pushing her car over a cliff.

621. _____. *The Case of the Empty Tin.* New York: Morrow, 1941; London: Cassell, 1943. Mrs. Arthur Gentrie is a neat housewife who finds a shiny tin can in a corner of her cellar. In it are numbers stamped in code. When a man and his housekeeper go missing from the house next door, the boarder upstairs, an old man named Elston Karr, who used to run guns up the Yangtze for a Shanghai outfit, calls Mason to protect him from the unwanted publicity that the police investigation will bring because he fears retaliation from old enemies.

622. _____. *The Case of the Fabulous Fake.* New York: Morrow, 1969. London: Heinemann, 1974. In the foreword, Gardner praises Orange County criminologist Jack Cadman for his forensic skills with the "new" blood-alcohol testing. Disregarding his two posthumous novels, this is the last Mason. Diana Douglas, charged with the shooting murder of a blackmailer, is defended by Perry, who shows more masculine energy than is usual: "I'm vicious myself . . . when some pimp starts shoving a woman around" (141).

623. _____. *The Case of the Fan Dancer's Horse.* New York: Morrow, 1947. London: Heinemann, 1952. Mason and Della find a fan-dancer's costume in a car involved in an accident; he advertises to find the owner, with stage name Cheri Chi Chi, but several claimants think that a prize gelding is meant by the ad's reference to "certain property." A rancher found executed by a Japanese sword, with a piece of ostrich feather in the wound, implicates the owner.

624. _____. *The Case of the Fenced-In Woman.* New York: Morrow, 1972. London: Heinemann, 1976. This is the first of two posthumous Mason novels left behind in Gardner's "pending file" at the time of his death in 1970, which, according to the publisher's note, is lacking in "final-draft polishing." Morley Eden consults Mason when Vivian Carson has a barbed-wire fence put up, dividing his house and grounds in half, and moves in, claiming half the house and lot are hers. Eventually the two become codefendants in the stabbing murder of her estranged husband Loring, whose body is found "just on the other side of that fence" (65), the accusation being they conspired to steal securities hidden on the property. Reissued by Ballantine in 1995. (*See The Case of The Irate Witness* for a third posthumous Mason.)

625. _____. *The Case of the Fiery Fingers.* New York: Morrow, 1951. London: Heinemann, 1957. Gardner leavens this one with moments of humor in a plot featuring nurse consulting Mason about how to prevent a patient from being murdered by her husband; she is accused of petty larceny of costume

jewelry on trumped-up charges and the evidence of fluorescent powder. In the second trial, Victoria Braxton is accused of the arsenic poisoning of her sister.

626. _____. *The Case of the Foot-Loose Doll.* New York: Morrow, 1958. London: Heinemann, 1964. Mildred Crest picks up hitchhiker Fern Driscoll, fresh from San Diego but escaping from a young man who first picked her up because "he turned out to be a wolf" (10). When she is killed in an accident, Mildred assumes her identity (she is reeling from the perfidy of her fiancé Robert at the time); she then becomes a suspect in her own murder, but goes to trial for the ice-pick murder of blackmailer Carl Harrod.

627. _____. *The Case of the Fugitive Nurse.* New York: Morrow, 1954. London: Heinemann, 1959. Mason receives a sentence of contempt of court from Judge Telford in a complex plot involving the golddigging widow of a wealthy surgeon whose plane goes down in a Utah desert; within 24 hours Steffanie Malden, "dripping mink and diamonds," hires Mason to go to the doctor's love nest he shared with his chief nurse and office manager, locate the safe, and extract the money her husband had been salting away--it seems the IRS had been badgering the doctor prior to his death, convinced that as much as $100,000 had been secreted from records. Mason, however, walks into a trap, finds himself accused of stealing the loot, while the scheming widow herself is accused of murder when a drugged whiskey flask is found in the wreckage.

628. _____. *The Case of the Gilded Lily.* New York: Morrow, 1956. London: Heinemann, 1962. Businessman Stewart G. Bedford must pay $20,000 blackmail after his whirlwind courtship and marriage to younger Ann Roan; it seems she's guilty of insurance fraud for pawning jewelry and claiming it stolen. He pays up or the scandals magazines get the mug shots and proof.

629. _____. *The Case of the Glamorous Ghost.* New York: Morrow, 1955. London: Heinemann, 1960. Olga Corbin Jordan hires Mason to get her black-sheep half-sister Eleanor out of her latest predicament to save the family honor—dancing in a near-nude state in a public park before two witnesses. But her real problem is that her alleged husband Douglas Hepner, a government informant on jewel smuggling, was shot to death in that park the same night.

630. ____. *The Case of the Golddigger's Purse.* New York: Morrow, 1945 (Armed Services Edition, 1945). London: Cassell, 1948. Begun in Yucatan and finished in Colombia, the book concerns Sally Madison's attempt to wheedle money from wealthy Harrington Faulkner for pet-shop employee Tom Gridley, afflicted with tuberculosis; he has developed a cure for the gill disease afflicting goldfish-collector Faulkner's rare Veiltail Moor Telescopes ("the Fish of Death"). When Faulkner is found murdered, a broken fish bowl and several dead goldfish lying in the vicinity of the body, Madison is charged. Mason represents her in the prelim. Also published in a trio along with Margery

Allingham and Ngaio Marsh for the Detective Book Club by Black. (Sidenote on Marsh: She wrote the 1975 script for the British series *Crown Court*.)

631. _____. *The Case of the Green-Eyed Sister.* New York: Morrow, 1953. London: Heinemann, 1959. Sylvia Bain Atwood consults Mason because of a blackmail attempt on her sick father. J. J. Fritch purportedly possesses a tape recording implicating Ned Bain in a bank robbery, but Sylvia's sister Harriet is later accused of murdering Fritch with an ice pick. "The preliminary hearing is one of Gardner's longest non-stop courtroom scenes . . ." (Breen 68).

632. _____. *The Case of the Grinning Gorilla.* New York: Morrow; New York: Black, 1952. London: Heinemann, 1958. Mason defends Josephine Kempton, accused of the carving-knife murder of Benjamin Addicks, who had been involved in psychological experiments on simians, but the apes prove a red herring. Mason deduces an insane wife in the background whom the millionaire could not divorce. Mason opens with a sidebar on his profession: "A couple generations ago . . . lawyers were stuffy people. They thrust a hand inside their coats while they declaimed oratorically. Busts of Blackstone adorned their offices. Then came a new and more flippant generation . . . [who] resented the stony-faced dignity of the old boy" (3).

633. _____. *The Case of the Half-Wakened Wife.* New York: Morrow, 1945. London: Cassell, 1949. Parker Benton invites all concerned parties to an oil-lease transaction of an island, Mason and Della included, for a cruise on his yacht; the lawyer's client is Jane Keller, selling to the millionaire. Scott Shelby, however, owns the lease and is blocking the sale; when he disappears overboard, his wife Marion is accused of his murder. Mason's hunch that Shelby has salted away large sums of money, ducked out and framed his wife briefly backfires, and he winds up in a defamation-of-character suit against him and Paul Drake. He is even fired by the wife (189), a fact which causes Della to throw herself into the lawyer's arms. Another rarity is the appearance of Jackson, Mason's research assistant, "a genius at uncovering the exact needle he wanted from the haystack of legal decisions" (15).

634. _____. *The Case of the Haunted Husband.* New York: Morrow; Cleveland: World, 1941; London: Cassell, 1942. Before he became boringly respectable, Mason was able to sound human, as he does here in a rare moment giving vent to a thoughtful disquisition on life and death: "We can only see from birth to death. The rest of it is cut off from our vision" (189-91). The plot only seems typical, moreover: Stephane Olger, tired of her chiseling and scheming boss, tosses her waitress apron and adopts her middle name Claire to hitchhike to Los Angeles and a career in film; is involved in an accident with a drunken, sexually aggressive male driver; he disappears and leaves her at the wheel to face charges of felony theft auto and drunk driving.

635. _____. *The Case of the Hesitant Hostess.* New York: Morrow, 1953. London: Heinemann, 1959. A penniless drifter is on trial for robbing rich widower Rodney Archer, alibied by nightclub proprietess. Mason investigates her link to the garrote-murder of Daphne Howell.

636. _____. *The Case of the Horrified Heirs.* New York: Morrow 1964. London: Heinemann, 1971. Virginia Trent, a former legal secretary who knew Mason from her past association, calls him to defend her when she is picked up at the airport for narcotics trafficking (the drugs were planted in her baggage). That case is separate from the main plotline in which a childless, wealthy Lauretta Trent calls Baxter to meet her because Baxter had witnessed her will ten years before. Mrs. Trent is murdered on the way (her car is run off a cliff and the body is not recovered); again, Baxter is implicated in a frame-up. Trent was a woman with a heart weakened by poisoning attempts; she also had two sisters and brothers-in-law living with her--all eager to inherit. Deputy DA Jerry Caswell, opposing Mason, twice utters the Triple-I objection in court.

637. _____. *The Case of the Howling Dog.* New York: Morrow, 1934. London: Cassell, 1934. One of the earliest and best Masons that includes a complete jury trial. Arthur Cartwright wants the lawyer to make a will leaving money to a neighbor, Mrs. Clinton Foley, and he wants to complain about Mr. Foley's barking dog, an old police dog. Mason detests this kind of practice, but when Cartwright sends him ten $1,000 bills as a retainer, he changes his mind. Arriving for an appointment with Foley, Mason discovers man and dog shot dead. Mason is grilled under hot lights by police nemesis Sgt. Holcolmb in Chapter 9. His hypothesis of the crime to the jury in Chapter 21 is a classic.

638. _____. *The Case of the Ice-Cold Hands.* New York: Morrow, 1962. London: Heinemann, 1968. Mason and Della go to the races with instructions to cash five pari-mutuel tickets if client Nancy Banks' Dough Boy comes in. Nancy is soon accused of murdering Marvin Fremont, who had worked for her brother Rodney, a gambler and embezzler. Fremont was found shot at a motel, packed in dry ice to confuse the forensics. Burger offers the brother immunity if he will testify against his sibling.

639. _____. *The Case of the Irate Witness.* New York: Morrow, 1972. London: Heinemann, 1975. The title piece of this posthumous collection is singular for being a short story (it is followed by three short Mason novels without trial action). Mason's fishing trip is interrupted for the defense of Harvey Corbin, accused of robbing the Jebson Commercial Company.

640. _____. *The Case of the Lame Canary.* New York: Morrow; Grosset; London: Cassell, 1937. It starts like a Chinese wedding in the T'ang dynasty--complicatedly. Rita Swaine and caged canary are in the lawyer's office where she tells him a story between sobs about a sister Rossy being sued for divorce by

husband Walter, who married her for her money and recently denies having taken $10,000 from his wife to invest in his business; he is suing her boyfriend (the married sister's ex-boyfriend) on the grounds of alienation of affection because of letters from the wife to the former boyfriend and one back to her from him urging divorce. Although he is courting Rita now, he used to handle her investments and is convinced Walter is stealing from her. The canary enters by way of an accident--literally, in front of the house while Rita was clipping its toenails and being visited by Jimmy Driscoll, the second-hand boyfriend. Police have his name and he will be called as a witness to the accident; thus, Walter has proof that the boyfriend was in his house without his consent.

641. _____. *The Case of the Lazy Lover.* New York: Morrow, 1947. London: Heinemann, 1954 . Mason receives a check for $2,500 in his morning mail from a woman who has run off with her daughter's boyfriend, a man who is an important witness in a lawsuit. Mason's mysterious client is Lola Faxon Allred; that check is soon to be followed by another, which proves to be a forgery. Allred is charged with the murder of her husband, but is herself found dead in a wrecked car. Walter J. Black produced an issue in the same year as Morrow and Ballantine reissued in pbk. in 1997.

642. _____. *The Case of the Lonely Heiress.* New York: Morrow, 1948. London: Heinemann, 1952. A nurse who had cared for wealthy George P. Endicott stands to inherit a fortune, which she plans to give her beautiful daughter, appropriately named Marilyn Marlow; the inheritance is contested by the family on the grounds of a witness to the will's signing. When this woman is murdered, Mason sets out to find the killer. Two unusual items to note: one is the sheer comic relief of character Robert Caddo, sleazy publisher of a lonely hearts magazine, and his big blonde harridan of a wife; the other is the opening delay in which the nurse's daughter poses as an heiress to entice the deceased's family into revealing their plans. Black, Inc. produced an edition the same year for the Detective Book Club.

643. _____. *The Case of the Long-Legged Models.* New York: Morrow, 1958. London: Heinemann, 1963. Stephanie Falkner inherited majority stock in a modest Las Vegas casino from her father Glenn, an unsolved murder victim six months ago. A mysterious syndicate tried to pressure the other stockholders into selling but a man named George Casselman manages to intervene and buys off the other frightened shareholders and now wants to buy her stock. Falkner wants Mason to represent her in the sale but not at a nominal figure; she also wants the lawyer to help her bring her father's killers to justice. When Casselman winds up with a bullet hole in his chest, she is brought to trial.

644. _____. *The Case of the Lucky Legs.* New York: Morrow; London: Harrap, 1934. J. R. Bradbury is a retired banker from Cloverdale who wants to make a case of fraud against a Hollywood promoter. Frank Patton comes to

town representing a motion-picture company and an advertising gimmick that involves a contest search for The Girl with the Lucky Legs. Patton sells the idea to the chamber of commerce, which in turn gets local merchants to sell scrip to the public on profits to be earned from the film. Bank stenographer Marjory Clune wins the contest, leaves town for fame and glory but stays missing after the ruse is exposed.

645. _____. *The Case of the Lucky Loser.* New York: Morrow, 1957. London: Heinemann, 1962. An anonymous young woman calls Mason to ask him to sit in on People versus Balfour that morning "and draw conclusions" (3). Ted Balfour is accused of hit-and-run manslaughter of an unidentified victim. He is convicted but subsequently accused of murdering the same man by shooting. Mason argues with the double-jeopardy rule before Judge Cadwell at the *habeus corpus* hearing by citing numerous precedents (71).

646. _____. *The Case of the Mischievous Doll.* New York: Morrow, 1963. London: Heinemann, 1968. One of Gardner's favorite ploys is the double and the mixed-identity resulting from it. A woman demands to show Mason her appendectomy scar to prove her identity because she fears she is being groomed to double for "the madcap heiress of Montrose," the spoiled and impulsive Minerva Minden. Minden eventually is the one who goes to trial for murdering a private detective; she is also suspected of killing her would-be impersonator.

647. _____. *The Case of the Moth-Eaten Mink.* New York: Morrow, 1952. London: Heinemann, 1958. A waitress vanishes without explanation, leaving behind a mink coat. Restaurateur Morris Alburg asks Mason's advice, but soon he and another waitress are accused in a preliminary hearing of the murder of a blackmailer. Sidenote: Most of the Perry Mason TV series episodes were not based on the Gardner books; however, the hour-long pilot filmed in 1957 (though not the first episode to be telecast) was adapted from this one.

648. _____. *The Case of the Musical Cow.* New York: Morrow, 1950. London: Heinemann, 1957. Breen notes that this is the last of the Mason novels *not* to feature a series character (66). Dog trainer Rob Trenton is on vacation in Europe and inadvertently becomes mixed up with dope smugglers. When narcotics agent Harvey Richmond is murdered aboard a houseboat, Trenton is fingered as the prime suspect.

649. _____. *The Case of the Mythical Monkeys.* New York: Morrow, 1959. London: Heinemann, 1965. Gladys Doyle is secretary-companion to novelist Mauvis Niles Meade, a kind of woman novelist coyly derided by mouthpiece Mason as a purveyor of "smooch, seduction and smut" (25). Doyle's car breaks down on a mountain road, and she is given shelter for the night by a handsome man identifying himself as John at a cabin in Pine Glen

Canyon. In the morning she finds a dead man on the floor of the cabin, not John.

650. _____. *The Case of the Negligent Nymph.* New York: Morrow, 1950. London: Heinemann, 1956. Mason defends a client met under unusual circumstances: he is surveying the property of an millionaire's mansion from a canoe when he sees her fleeing. Dorothy Fenner has taken from the house a bottle containing a message about the death of Minerva Danby, drowned from the rich man's yacht a few months earlier. Mason goes to court twice: first for her bail-bond hearing on charges of jewel theft; then in a jury trial for murdering the millionaire.

651. _____. *The Case of the Nervous Accomplice.* New York: Morrow, 1955. London: Heinemann, 1961. Gardner's plot begins to sound like a Danny Kaye film: Mrs. Enright A. Harlan hires Mason to buy stock in a real-estate investment company to make a nuisance of himself at a director's meeting for the purpose of attracting her amorous husband Enny back to her and away from Roxy Claffin, client and girlfriend. The murder of millionaire George C. ("Daddy") Lutts in a deserted house in the company's development project supersedes the levity.

652. _____. *The Case of the One-Eyed Witness.* New York: Morrow, 1950. London: Heinemann, 1956. Myrtle Fargo is accused of stabbing her husband to death. Crucial witness for the prosecution is Mrs. Newton Maynard, who appears on the stand with one eye bandaged.

653. _____. *The Case of the Perjured Parrot.* New York: Morrow; London: Cassell, 1939. Fremont Sabin's widow and son are intent on destroying each other over the will because of a question of the will's dating and the time of death. The parrot of the title enters as an instance of a favorite Mason courtroom gambit involving evidence-switching during a coroner's inquest to baffle the prosecution--in this case, a parrot found near the murdered recluse that curses like a drunken sailor. A Ballantine reissue in 1998.

654. _____. *The Case of the Phantom Fortune.* New York: Morrow, 1964. London: Heinemann, 1970. Business executive Horace Warren offers Perry $500 to attend a dinner party with Paul Drake posing as a caterer to identify a fingerprint that might belong to a servant or guest who is possibly blackmailing Warren's wife. Perry ends up defending Warren in a preliminary hearing on a charge of shooting the wife's former employer, a man with a dubious character, who is found dead in a deserted storeroom. Mason's cross of a firearms expert (192-95) shows that Gardner did not yet understand the science of ballistics well enough.

655. _____. *The Case of the Postponed Murder.* New York: Morrow,

1973. London: Heinemann, 1977. The final Mason courtroom thriller, originally published three years after the death of Gardner, must have been written decades earlier because of its hardboiled remnants, all expunged when Mason later became respectable. Most experts date it back to his *Black Mask* days as a fledgling writer. Mae Farr is the client, posing as her sister Sylvia, who is accused of the shooting-murder of womanizing Penn Wentworth aboard his yacht.

656. _____. *The Case of the Queenly Contestant.* New York: Morrow, 1967. London: Heinemann, 1973. Ellen Adair won a beauty pageant at 18, but she disappeared to have the baby of rich Harmon Haslett out of wedlock. Her right-of-privacy concern collapses with the real issue being the scheme she concocted with a childless couple to have them raise the boy and his right to inherit Haslett's millions. When "diabolically clever" Agnes Burlington, blackmailer and nurse who witnessed the birth, is murdered, she tells Mason not to argue circumstantial evidence, which the lawyer promptly does and solves the crime in the prelim--despite the reasonable objections of chief trial deputy Stanley Dillon. The Detective Book Club edition comes with a Lam-Cool novel published the year prior, *Widows Wear Weeds.*

657. _____. *The Case of the Reluctant Model.* New York: Morrow, 1962. London: Heinemann, 1967. Collin Durant is being sued for libel and slander by art dealer Lattimer Rankin because a painting Rankin sold to Otto Olney was purportedly not a work of a French painter with the fantastic name Phellipe Feteet. The case evolves into murder when Rankin's witness to the slander, Maxine Lindsay, a young art student, is accused of shooting Durant.

658. _____. *The Case of the Restless Redhead.* New York: Morrow, 1954. London: Heinemann, 1960. Mason is in court observing the trial of waitress Evelyn Bagby, accused of jewel theft. Mason gives her nervous young lawyer Frank Neely advice on crossing an eyewitness that gets her acquitted and the two later collaborate in a preliminary hearing when she is accused of shooting actor Steve Merrill, second husband of a movie star.

659. _____. *The Case of the Rolling Bones.* New York: Morrow, 1939. London: Cassell, 1940. In a complex plot involving a shakedown scheme and double identities, the niece of millionaire Alden Leeds is opposed by greedy family members who have whisked the old man off to a sanitarium. Mason files a *habeus corpus* writ; then he later defends him in a preliminary hearing on a murder charge. Gertie, the romance-reading switchboard operator, appears.

660. _____. *The Case of the Runaway Corpse.* New York: Morrow, 1954. London: Heinemann, 1960. Myrna Davenport tells Mason her husband Ed, believed dying in a motel room, has left a sealed note in his office accusing her of poisoning him and another relative, Hortense Paxson. After the husband is

reported to be dead, Mason opens the envelope, finds only blank pages, and reseals it. Mason cleverly gets hearsay into evidence at the trial before Judge Siler while his courtroom adversary in Fresno, Talbert Vandling, a courtroom adversary, heaps praise upon Mason for solving the case.

661. _____. *The Case of the Screaming Woman.* New York: Morrow, 1957. London: Heinemann, 1963. John Northrup Kirby tells Mason that he picked up a girl carrying a gas can on a deserted road and took her back to her car--except that it was missing. He is later accused of murdering the surgeon Dr. Phineas Lockridge Babb, who uttered Kirby's name before he died. Burger gets skewered by his own witness on the stand, and Mason utters the Triple-I (134).

662. _____. *The Case of the Shapely Shadow.* New York: Morrow, 1960. London: Heinemann, 1966. Janice Wainwright, secretary of Morley Theilman, delivers a suitcase under mysterious circumstances--blackmail, she thinks. When she is accused of shooting Theilman to death at an abandoned mountain site, Mason defends her in a jury trial.

663. _____. *The Case of the Shoplifter's Shoe.* New York: Morrow, 1938. London: Cassell, 1939. Virgina Trent seeks help for her well-to-do Aunt Sarah, a shoplifter. The case, however, is not about kleptomania but a missing cache of diamonds and murder when the aunt's shoe is found stained with the victim's blood. Rpt. in pbk. by Ballantine in 1998.

664. _____. *The Case of the Silent Partner.* New York: Morrow, 1940. London: Cassell, 1941. Carlotta Faulkner Lawley and her sister Mildreth own a chain of flower shops, the former sister afflicted with a heart ailment and a gambling-addicted husband with control of her stock certificates. A competitor acquires the small holding of the firm's third director. Mason and Tragg play their cat-and-mouse game more than usual in this one and in a moment of pique, the lawyer attacks the long-suffering, straight-man cop for refusing to see the plot to induce a heart attack in Millie's sister: "You're responsible for your share of it--and look at Loring Churchill. That smug, beetle-browed, bookish nincompoop will nag her to death" (254).

665. _____. *The Case of the Singing Skirt.* New York: Morrow, 1959. London: Heinemann, 1965. Cigarette girl and novelty singer Ellen Robb works in a corrupt town called Rowena. When she refuses to cooperate with her employer in a card-cheating scam, she is fired under the pretext that she looted the till. She is later charged in a preliminary hearing with the murder of Nadine Ellis, wife of a gambler who lost money at the club, found in a drifting yacht off catalina Island with "two bullet wounds in the body" (112). Mason, according to Breen, cites an unusual number of "intriguing appellate decisions. . . .The ending brings a nice irony in the strained Mason/Burger relationships" (75).

666. _____. *The Case of the Sleepwalker's Niece.* New York: Morrow; London: Cassell, 1936. Edna Hammer retains Mason because she is worried about her uncle Peter Kent's potentially violent sleepwalking episodes. Kent will go on trial for the murder of his half-brother P. L. Rease, supposedly having mistaken him for business partner in one of his sleepwalking episodes. Hamilton Burger is at his wit's end from beginning to end of this long courtroom sequence in which Judge Markham overrules all the D. A.'s objections to Mason's testing his theory. The air is thick with Triple-I's from both adversaries, and at one point, baffled by Mason's querying a prosecution witness, Burger says: "I think that question is plainly incompetent, irrelevant and not proper cross-examination" (264).

667. _____. *The Case of the Spurious Spinster.* New York: Morrow, 1961. London: Heinemann, 1966. Half-blind, crippled Amelia Corning is owner of Corning Mining, Smelting, and Investment company; secretary Susan Fisher is Mason's client in a case involving a shoe box full of $100 bills and discrepancies in the accounts. Then two elderly ladies in wheelchairs claim to be the absentee owner Mrs. Corning, and finally a murder by letter opener of the operator of the Mohave Monarch mine.

668. _____. *The Case of the Stepdaughter's Secret.* New York: Morrow, 1963. London: Heinemann, 1968. Harlow Bissinger Bancroft, a self-made millionaire, consults Mason when he discovers his stepdaughter Rosena Andrews, on the verge of her marriage to a man from a family on the social register, is being anonymously blackmailed about her father's criminal past.

669. _____. *The Case of the Stuttering Bishop.* New York: Morrow, 1936. London: Cassell, 1937. Bishop William Mallory of Sydney, Australia, consults Mason about a drunk-driving accident in Orange County that resulted in a manslaughter charge 22 years ago. Suspecting him a phony because of his stutter, Mason has Drake trace the bishop to his hotel, where he is discovered in his room beaten unconscious. The chain leads to a woman who drove the car in that 1914 accident and was then victimized by her wealthy father-in-law Renwold C. Brownley, who wanted to destroy his son's marriage. When Mason confronts the vindictive millionaire with her story of a child by Oscar Brownley, raised by adopted parents in Australia, he rebuffs Mason and accuses the lawyer of conspiring with "an adventuress" to replace his granddaughter with an imposter; soon after, Brownley is found with five bullets in him in a car driven off a pier. Donald Woods played Mason in the film (Warner, 1937).

670. _____. *The Case of the Substitute Face.* New York: Morrow; London: Cassell, 1938. Society matron Mrs. Carl Newberry and her husband meet Mason and Della, returning from Hawaii on an ocean liner. Mrs. Newberry suspects her husband is cheating her, and his sudden death exposes a

stuffed money belt. Mason defends Anna Moar, accused of murdering her husband.

671. _____. *The Case of the Sulky Girl.* New York: Morrow, 1933. London: Harrap, 1934; rpt. Philadelphia: Triangle, 1944; Leyden, MA: Aeonian, 1976. Twenty-three-year-old, hot-tempered Frances Celane's inheritance is held in trust by her uncle, punctilious Edward Norton, a stickler who will dispense the estate to charity if she marries before 25. She asks Mason to help her keep her money and marry. She is, in fact, married to Rob Gleason and being blackmailed. Norton is seen clubbed to death by "a man swinging a club" (65), and she and Gleason are charged with the crime. As Breen and Van Dover note, this is not the first Mason but it is the first with the kind of courtroom confrontation and theatrics for which Mason/Gardner will become famous. Secretary Della Street and private-eye Paul Drake are not yet situated in the Mason retinue but some characters and types will appear and reappear with those names that Gardner admitted to coining from telephone directories in spoonerism fashion, reversing names and letters. Hamilton Burger's forerunner, Assistant DA Claude Drumm, and assistant Frank Everly appear as foe and friend to Mason in court. (*See* **Series Characters** for a list of the most recognizable or interchangeable members of the Mason family.)

672. _____. *The Case of the Sun Bather's Diary.* New York: Morrow, 1955. London: Heinemann, 1961. Mason's client, Arlene Duvall, calls for help from the Remuda Golf Club's fourteenth hole claiming her clothes (camper and car) have been stolen while she was sunbathing nude.

673. _____. *The Case of the Terrified Typist.* New York: Morrow, 1956. London: Heinemann, 1961. Before disappearing from her office, Mae Wallis leaves two diamonds stuck to the underside of her desk with chewing gum. Mason is retained to defend Duane Jefferson, a partner in a gem firm, which happens to be in the same building as Wallis' office, on a charge of killing a smuggler. Breen praises this one for the clever way Perry extricates himself from "a loser's ignominy," for this was Gardner's attempt to placate those readers who had begged him to allow Hamilton Burger to win just once: "Though we all know Perry Mason never defends a guilty client, the jury delivers a guilty verdict, and the only question is how (not whether) Perry will show it didn't really happen and rob Burger of his victory" (71). On October 17, 1963, a TV Mason episode aired, 'The Case of the Deadly Verdict," in which the lawyer "loses" at a murder trial against Burger (William Talman) after client Janice Barton (Julie Adams) is convicted and sentenced to the gas chamber. Rated No. 51 in *TV Guide*'s "100 Greatest Episodes of All Time" (June 28 - July 4 1997).

674. _____. *The Case of the Troubled Trustee.* New York: Morrow, 1965. London: Heinemann, 1971. The trustee of the title is Kerry Dutton, who

reinvested some trust funds that the law might call defalcation. A subplot revolves around his interest in blonde Desere Ellis, fiancée of a man named Fred Hedley, who wants to endow a trust fund for political thinkers. Gardner's characterization of Hedley as a beatnik in the Woodstock era, with speech sprinkled with slang like "goof" and "cool," bungles verisimilitude of diction.

675. _____. *The Case of the Vagabond Virgin.* New York: Morrow, 1948. London: Heinemann, 1952. A gossip columnist threatens to blackmail a businessman who helped out 20-year-old Veronica Dale, a girl running away from a dreary life in a small town. The executive hires Mason to get her, charged with vagrancy, out of jail. But when he is charged in a preliminary hearing with the murder of his partner, the baby-faced Dale is the key witness.

676. _____. *The Case of the Velvet Claws.* New York: Morrow; London: Harrap, 1933. The Perry Mason series begins with the boilerplate from which very little would change over the decades. Gardner, on a similar but less morbid track as Poe, believed in the helplessness of a beautiful woman in need of rescue, which often translates to the colloquialism "with a lot of curves." But a personal problem, such as a recalcitrant relative or spouse or a social embarrassment, nearly always escalates into murder with the arrows of guilt pointing at the innocent client. Gardner, a self-made man when that ideal was uncritically accepted by a majority of society, "related to them immediately when he met them and represented them uncritically when he came to place them in his fictions . . . but rarely slipped into the obtrusive homiletics of Horatio Alger" (Van Dover 19).

Here, a woman consults Perry about an embarrassing situation: she had attended a party at the Beechwood Inn without her husband's knowledge in the company of a politician. A robbery occurs, the police investigate, take down names. The woman is subsequently blackmailed or her name will appear in a scandal sheet called *Spicey Bits* along with the politician's. Mason learns that the magazine will take bribes and that its hidden owner is a reputable businessman, George Belter. After failing to coerce Belter to withhold his client's name from publication, he sees the wife of the publisher on his way out the door: Eve Belter, his client under a false name.

677. _____. *The Case of the Waylaid Wolf.* New York: Morrow, 1960. London: Heinemann, 1965. A stenographer for an engineering company is being sexually harassed by her boss, Loring Lamont. She intends to file civil or criminal charges, but Lamont turns up murdered at the lodge where he had taken her.

678. _____. *The Case of the Worried Waitress.* New York: Morrow, 1966. London: Heinemann, 1972. Waitress Katherine ("Kit") Ellis "buys" Mason's usual table at his midtown restaurant because she wants advice about her aunt Sophia's miserly behavior: the aunt studies newspapers for grocery

bargains, but eats little food and also passes herself off as a blind pencil peddler yet keeps hatboxes at home stuffed with fifties and hundreds. Right after her consultation with Perry, the niece is accused of stealing the stash. Mason goes easy on Lt. Tragg on the stand and shakes hands with Burger in the finale. The Detective Book Club reprint (Walter J. Black, Inc.) in the late 1980's (Roslyn, NY) comes with a Lam-Cool mystery *Cut Thin to Win* and the A. A. Fair pseudonym "exposed," although the ruse had long since been known.

679. _____. *The Count of Nine* [Running title: *9*]. New York: Morrow, 1958; London: Heinemann, 1959. Another foreword on the theme of rehabilitation of convicts except that it is society's apathy Gardner laments. The novel has the detective agency of Cool & Lam involved with a client who pays them to keep gatecrashers out of his socialite parties. But big-game hunter and curio collector Dean Crockett the Second has had a second jade Buddha and blowgun stolen from his last party. Donald recovers the blowgun, secreted in a flagpole, and then discovers the client in his penthouse office lying on the floor with a dart buried to the hilt in his neck.

680. _____. *The D. A. Breaks a Seal.* New York: Morrow, 1946. London: Cassell, 1950. Major Selby is in Madison City on furlough, but his DA job has been taken back by his old enemies. Sylvia Martin meets him at the depot, where he sees people wearing white gardenias, including lawyer Carr. Later he goes to a crime scene with Sheriff Brandon--he, Sylvia and Inez remain his only real allies in the series--where he detects the odor of almonds at the death of a hotel guest. Selby then assists Inez in a case where wealthy Eleanor Preston's will is being contested on the grounds of undue influence by her companion whose heir stands to inherit (both women conveniently die in a car crash); despite her past, she appears respectable, thanks to a makeover by her lawyer, A. B. Carr.

681. _____. *The D. A. Breaks an Egg.* New York: Morrow, 1949; London: Heinemann, 1957. The novel opens with Selby wearing his halo and professing his integrity to the new power-hungry owner of *The Blade*. Selby then investigates two seemingly unrelated crimes to find the connection and a solution. Carr's wife is interrogated about Daphne Arcola, a girlfriend from Windrift, Montana; another woman from the same city, Rose Furman, is believed to be the corpse discovered with a stab wound in the back in the park; Carr's wife and Daphne had once been "party girls" for a dude ranch out there. The other is a case of burglary that implicates the wife of Horace Lennox staying at the Lennox home in Madison during the burglary on the same night as the killing.

682. _____. *The D. A. Calls a Turn.* New York: Grossett, 1943; Morrow, 1944; London: Cassell, 1947. An intoxicated man calling himself Carleton Grines calls the sheriff's office and tells them to come get him, that he is driving

a stolen car, and that he wants to be picked up. When Selby and Sheriff Brandon arrive on scene, they witness a car crash caused by Grines veering left of center coming down the hill. A little sleuthing convinces them the accident was a set-up and the man was dead inside the car. The victim turns out to be Desmond Billmeyer, a highly successful, popular and aggressive businessman with a past that involves an amnesiac episode with "a burning building," according to a helpful caller (60).

683. _____. *The D. A. Calls It Murder.* New York: Morrow; London: Cassell, 1937. The D. A. series, as the 9 novels featuring Doug Selby came to be called, began with this. In mid-December 1935, the editor of *Country Gentleman* magazine offered Gardner $10,000 to produce an "acceptable" protagonist for a book-length series. Gardner turned in the final installment of *The Thread of Murder* one month later; it was retitled and the Doug Selby series was born with the final volume, *The D. A. Breaks an Egg*, appearing in 1949. of course, the relationships among principal characters are stereotypes, but in some ways Gardner was experimenting: Sheriff Rex Brandon is an older version of Paul Drake, a cardboard figure at his best, but against the younger, more emotional Selby, the older and more experienced Sheriff becomes an interesting foil in a way that Drake could not. The love (or emotional) relationships between Doug and the two women, Sylvia Martin and Inez Stapleton, have potential far beyond the inert Mason-Della Street one, but neither yields much depth. Alphonse B. Carr ("Old ABC") is a far better Hamilton Burger-style courtroom nemesis, however: "Carr is in some ways Gardner's revenge on Mason; he is a Mason with an unlocked id. Mason exercises his exciting lack of scruples on behalf of his innocent clients; Carr merely extends his unscrupulousness to include his choice of clients" (Van Dover 77-78).

684. _____. *The D. A. Cooks a Goose.* New York: Morrow, 1942; London: Cassell, 1943; Philadelphia: Blakiston, 1946. Doug Selby in a case of switched babies, a dead miser who turns out to be wealthy, a missing mother, and a misplaced will. D. A. Selby receives a call from a frightened woman at a bus station demanding protection for her baby. The baby is left behind, allegedly the child of the woman who claimed to be estranged wife of Ezra Grolley, recently deceased citizen of Madison City's. Doug and Sheriff Brandon soon discover more than that at the notoriously reclusive miser's ranch: thousands of dollars stuffed into coffee cans at his ranch; a second discovery soon follows: Mrs. Grolley's dead body. A hit-and-run accident on a mountain road near Grolley's place leads the homicide investigation to Doug's courtroom nemesis, Old ABC himself. Carr is representing the woman whose baby was killed in that accident not far from Grolley's place.

685. _____. *The D. A. Draws a Circle.* New York: Morrow, 1939. London: Cassell, 1940. Most of the Doug Selbys do not get into court, Jon Breen notes, as a result of the basic difficulty in plotting a courtroom drama and

a whodunit in which the prosecutor is the protagonist (57). The plot here involves a nude corpse, apparent victim of a gang killing, found near the house where unwelcome stranger A. B. Carr, Doug's future archfoe and a shady character, has recently bought an expensive house. The body shows two almost coincidental bullet holes, suggesting a different gun's bullet. Selby focuses attention on an unhappy woman suspected of engineering her husband's death in a car crash and her crippled father. Two series characters appear: ex-rancher and Sheriff Rex Brandon and police chief Otto Brandon, aptly described by Breen as "one of the stupidest cops in detective fiction" and whose questioning by Carr "ranks among Gardner's funniest cross-examinations" (Breen 57). NBC adapted it for television in 1971.

686. _____. *The D. A. Goes to Trial.* New York: Morrow, 1940. London: Cassell, 1941. A hostile grand jury returns a quick indictment, forcing a trial in which Selby opposes Inez Stapleton. It commences with a tramp found on a railway trestle outside of town, apparently struck by a train. But the dead man has a connection with the shady accountant for a lumber mill.

687. _____. *The D. A. Holds a Candle.* New York: Morrow, 1938; London: Cassell, 1939. The attorney-detective's second outing as Madison County DA. He takes on a shakedown racket cleaning out a young, drunk-driving gambler named Stapleton with a wealthy father; the case begins with a hitchhiker turning up dead in a cabin with a gun in his hand and a note pinned to his body.

688. _____. *The D. A. Takes a Chance.* New York: Morrow, 1948; London: Heinemann, 1956. Doug cracks a case involving the murder of a woman named Eve Dawson in a blackmail scheme involving documents linking the mayor of Las Alidas with a paving graft. A. B. Carr, himself implicated in covering up the investigation, bails out one of the party girls linked to the dead woman's scheme, flies her to Tijuana and marries her so that neither can testify against the other.

689. _____. *Double or Quits.* New York: Morrow, 1941; London: Hale, 1949. Lam and Cool get into a legal battle with an insurance company over double indemnity because a client dies under mysterious circumstances.

690. _____. *Give 'Em the Ax.* New York: Morrow, 1944. [Rpt. as *An Axe to Grind*, London: Heinemann, 1951]. Donald returns to the B. Cool Detective Agency after Naval service, but he is hampered by bouts of malaria. Best scene, according to Jon Breen, is the in-office taking of Bertha's deposition and this: "A sharp lawyer's devastating cross-examination provides a prime specimen of Gardner's witness-stand Q-and-A" (84).

691. _____. *Kept Women Can't Quit.* New York: Morrow, 1960; London:

Heinemann, 1961. Gardner's foreword in this Lam-Cool outing speaks to one of his favorite themes--the rehabilitation of convicts. This one is typically unvarnished mystery *sans* courtroom action or legal antics from clever Donald. Just a curvaceous cutie named Hazel Downer who claims to be looking for her highrolling bookie husband, missing with $50,000, which figure coincidentally happens to be half the unrecovered swag from a daylight armored-car heist involving one of the robbers and Hazel's phone number at the precise moment the cops bagged him. What no-nonsense police sergeant Frank Sellers wants of the bantam sleuth and his corpulent partner is an explanation why the woman had the Lam-Cool office number on her in the first place.

692. _____. *This Is Murder.* New York: Spivak; New York: Morrow, 1935. London: Methuen, 1936. Sam Moraine, advertising executive, becomes involved in the ransom-kidnapping of Ann Hartwell and is the prime suspect in the murder of a local figure involved in shady politics. Because DA Phil Duncan is both a friend and man distrusted by Eaton Driver, foreman of the grand jury seeking an indictment against Morraine and suspicious of the town's corrupt political machine, Moraine is permitted to question witnesses about documents related to the murder of Peter Dixon.

693. _____. *Traps Need Fresh Bait.* New York: Morrow, 1967; London: Heinemann, 1968. Donald goes undercover for a man calling himself Barney Adams and claiming to represent the investigations division of the Continental Divide Insurance and Indemnity Company of New Mexico. He wants Donald to pose as a man who will answer an ad in the paper requesting witnesses to a recent car accident for a reward. Donald at first believes Adams is a shill for a group of bigger insurance agencies pooling resources and hoping to expose a con game in which witnesses are suborned to perjure themselves. Through a chance meeting with a beautiful young woman, alone, broke in the big city, and willing to perjure herself for the advertised $300, he discovers there is much more behind the ad and murder is one of the outcomes. Donald must save the girl and avoid the cops.

694. _____. *Try Anything Once.* New York: Morrow, 1962. London: Heinemann, 1963. Client Carleton Allen protests innocence by claiming he was with another woman at the motel the night that Assistant DA Ronley Fisher died of a suspicious fall into a swimming pool. He wants Donald Lam to take his place the next night, pretending to be the customer sought by the police. In a later courtroom scene, Lam supplies lines to the prosecutor to help Fisher's replacement convict a pair of lovers for the murder of the wife.

Lastly, there is the Ellery Queen edition of Gardner's lesser-known lawyer, the cunning and crooked Lester Leith: *Erle Stanley Gardner's The Amazing Adventures of Lester Leith* (New York: Davis, 1980; Dial, 1981). Trial lawyers, not always among the most avid of Mason fans, say that Perry Mason became respectably middle class by the mid-1950's and because of the

Supreme Court's liberalism of the 1960's obviating the need for flashy lawyering in courtrooms, Mason himself would become obsolete. Gardner once mystified a police witness on the stand by trooping dozens of Chinese merchants with exchanged identities in front of him. Yet a few Gardners still ought to be acknowledged as among the best where some courtroom gimmickry prevails before it became a thing of the past.

695. Gardner, John. *The Sunlight Dialogues.* New York: Knopf, 1972; London: Cape, 1973. Gardner, a medieval scholar of repute, attempts a Joycean homage with an inspired lunatic called the Sunlight Man, arrested for painting the word *Love* on two lanes of highway. What Joyce did with the ambulatory Bloom in Dublin or the dreaming Finnigan by the side of the River Liffey does not work in Batavia, New York in the sixties. Gardner first composed fiction in his grandmother's law office. The Honorable Arthur Hodge, Sr., is one member of a large legal/political family populating this overly stuffed and pretentious tome.

696. Garfield, Brian Wynne. *Death Sentence.* New York: Evans, 1975. Garfield is a prolific author of slick thrillers but his *Death Sentence* and *Death Wish* were the inspiration for the Charles Bronson (as Paul Kersey) action films that began with the title film (Paramount, 1975) and continued through *Death Wish 5: The Face of Death* (TCF, 1993). When Paul Benjamin's wife and daughter are ruthlessly attacked in their New York apartment by thugs--the wife dies, the daughter becomes a vegetable--the cops and courts are powerless to bring him justice, so the former conscientious objector becomes an urban vigilante killer stalking the dirtbags of, first, New York City and then Chicago. Here Irene Evans, Chicago prosecutor, is both love interest and important character in the novel.

697. Gathje, Curtis. *A Model Crime.* New York: Fine, 1995. Gathje's uncle Stephen Butter once revealed to him over Thanksgiving dinner that he himself had been a suspect in a notorious tabloid crime involving a famous model in New York City in 1937 because he had been the last one to see lovely Ronnie Gedeon alive. That conversation led to this fictionalized account, which intersperses the tabloid accounts and photos along with cameos by some of the personalities of the day, such as Walter Winchell, Adela Rogers St. John, and Dorothy Kilgallen. Veronica Gedeon was murdered on Easter morning along with her mother and a boarder named Frank Byrnes. In the trial, Robert Irwin is defended by famed criminal lawyer Sam Leibowitz.

698. Geller, Shari P. *Fatal Convictions.* New York: Harper, 1998. Some of the San Fernando Valley's most despised human beings, criminal child molesters, are being killed by a vigilante fed up with the criminal justice system's failure. With wicked humor and deadly aim, the unidentified killer sets out to right the wrongs inflicted on the innocent. Everyone from DA Rebecca

Fielding through a pedophile-in-drag to treatment-center directors are under suspicion. Oakwood Center's court-appointed clients continue to die grisly deaths while Fielding's enemies in the DA's Office try to indict her for the killings.

699. Gemmette, Elizabeth Villiers, ed. *The Law in Literature: Legal Themes in Short Stories.* New York: Praeger, 1992. With Bernhardt's *Legal Briefs* (1998), Shapiro and Garry's 1998 anthology (*see* Shapiro, Fred R.), and this collection of 39 legal tales, the long hiatus between anthologies is broken thrice in one decade. Shapiro's collection overlaps Gemmette with a few identical works, but between them they replace *Fiction Goes to Court* 1954 and *Favorite Trial Stories* (1966). (*See* Blaustein, Albert P. and A. K Adams.) Gemmette includes some of the earlier standards (absent Arthur Train) like Davisson Post and Reid Parker, but she subsumes tales under various rubrics of justice (human and extra-legal, if not exactly divine) to include Japanese and Continental writers. Although justice arrives in the denouement of the majority and, as noted, is often well beyond the courtroom's purview, Gemmette is imaginatively capricious in choosing--for example, Kafka's "In the Penal Colony" and Poe's "The Pit and the Pendulum" are headed under *Capital Punishment.* Elsewhere she is more traditional, as for instance in her trial-lawyer stories: Bret Harte's "Colonel Starbottle for the Plaintiff" and Irwin Shaw's "Triumph of Justice." Susan's Glaspell's archly feminist "A Jury of Her Peers" resurfaces (*see* Glaspell, Susan), but many are either resurrected after long silence or collected as legal fiction for the first time, including the Shiga Naoya's "Han's Crime" and Ryunosuke Akutagawa's "In a Grove," Robert O'Neil Bristow's "Beyond Any Doubt" and Paul Lawrence Dunbar's "The Lynching of Jube Benson." It is a wide-roaming but estimable anthology showing forth a rich perspective of literary trends ranging from nineteenth-century traditional realists and naturalists (Tolstoy, Scott, Balzac, and Maupassant) through allegorists and surrealists like Hawthorne and Kafka to the science fiction of Asimov and Vonnegut to the metafiction of Barthelme's "Some of Us Had Been Threatening Our Friend Colby." No courtroom boundaries are elastic enough to include Prosper Mérimée's tale of the Corsican vendetta, "Mateo Falcone," or, to name another son naive to the world's hardness, the young protagonist in Willa Cather's "Paul's Case." There is, even so, such delightful *savoir faire* in choices like Thurber's "The Catbird Seat" (humorous exemplar of the legal concept of *mens rea*) that the reader remains oblivious to actual courts of law and what a legal story is.

700. Genberg, Ira. *Reckless Homicide.* New York: St. Martin's, 1998. Genberg, an Atlanta trial attorney, features a pair of brothers in his first legal thriller. Charlie Ashmore, reeling from his daughter's death by fire caused by a flammable perfume, and taking Seconal to sleep, begs his brother to help him get his pilot's job back. Michael, despite a conflict of interest because he is Brandon Air Lines' legal counsel, agrees but then finds he has to suppress his

brother's positive drug test by pulling strings. Two months later, Charlie's plane crashes, killing 120 people; the autopsy corroborates what the black box flight recorder suggests from Charlie's slurred speech: he was flying under the influence of a lethal dose of barbiturates. When Michael's role in clearing Charlie to fly is discovered, he finds himself indicted for reckless homicide and pinned to the wall with the very precedent he used to win his brother's suit against the perfume manufacturer. Wes Lukowsky, writing in *Booklist* (Jan. 1, 1998), is enthusiastic about *Reckless Homicide*, calling it "the best debut in the legal-thriller field since Turow's *Presumed Innocent* . . ."

701. Gerber, Albert. *The Lawyer.* New York: World, 1972. Follows the life and career of Roger Grayson, Philadelphia lawyer, from childhood through law school to attorney; two court cases are detailed: the first is an abortion trial in which he earns an acquittal for the defendant and in the second he defends a prostitute accused of murdering a police sergeant.

702. Ghráda, Máiréad Ní. *On Trial: A Play* [*An Triail.* Trans. Máiréad Ní Ghráda]. Dublin: Duffy, 1966. The play was first produced in Irish at Damer Hall, Dublin, on 22 Sept. 1964. It was then translated and produced at the Eblana Theatre on 19 March 1965. A desperate young mother with an out-of-wedlock infant commits suicide by putting her head and her child's in an oven and turning on the gas. In a mock-trial sequence are family members, employer, social worker, and others deemed responsible by the Counsel for the Defence.

703. Gide, André, and Jean-Louis Barrault, adapt. *The Trial.* By Franz Kafka. Trans. Jacqueline Sundstrom and Frank Sundstrom. London: Secker, 1950. The laureate's adaptation sensationalizes Joseph K.'s alienation one final step further with a knife plunged into his heart by an anonymous minion of the court--an appropriate ending for the author, who was a critic, diarist, novelist, playwright, prose-poet, and Nobel winner in 1947 and whose art plays in shifts between the extremes of a Christian symbolism and a Nietzschean abyss. (*See* Kafka, Franz).

Gilbert, Anthony, pseud. *See* Malleson, Lucy Beatrice. . . .

704. Gilbert, Michael F[rancis]. *Blood and Judgement.* London: Hodder; New York: Harper, 1959. Gilbert was once legal advisor to the Shah of Bahrain and since 1952 has been partner at Trower, Sull & Keeting in London. He is a graduate off the law school of the University of London (LL. B. with honors, 1931). He served in the Royal Horse Artillery in North Africa. He has over 20 novels that span police procedurals, espionage, and even romance in a 40-year writing career.

Rosa Ritchie, wife of an escaped prisoner, is found on the bank of a reservoir by two youths. Boot Howton, successor to her husband's criminal territory, is accused of her shooting murder. Young Scotland Yard detective

Patrick Petrella follows his instincts about the case in opposition to supervisor Superintendent Chris Kellaway.

705. _____. *The Crack in the Teacup.* London: Hodder; New York: Harper, 1966. A young solicitor finds himself in a campaign against racketeering that involves a local council, the press, and the public.

706. _____. *Death Has Deep Roots.* London: Hodder, 1951. New York: Harper, 1952. A young Frenchwoman is charged with the knife-murder of a British Resistance hero.

707. _____. *Death of a Favourite Girl.* London: Hodder, 1980. [Rpt. as *The Killing of Katie Steelstock*, New York: Harper, 1980]. A London TV celebrity returns to her small-town home to attend a dance; her murder provokes a national reaction to find and convict the killer.

708. _____. *The Dust and the Heat.* London: Hodder, 1967. [Rpt. as *Overdrive*, New York: Harper, 1967]. Oliver Nugent builds a drug and cosmetics firm after the war. The trial is a civil case, Mallinson Pharmaceutical Supplies vs. Quinn and Nicholson, involving Nugent's anticipating a perfume called Lucille with a bathroom product called Loo-Seal.

709. _____. *Flash Point.* London: Hodder; New York: Harper, 1974. A mainstream novel with interesting characterization. Christopher Martingale is asked by his supervisor, who is head of the Professional Purposes Section of the Law Society, to look into the most recent complaint by member Jonas Killey; it looks to be a nothing matter, typical of the oft-complaining lawyer and in this case reflects his personal vendetta against Will Dylan, head of one of the merging unions back then. However, what began as an investigation of a technical point in a case of the amalgamation of two unions in 1965, and Martingale's assignment is simply "to get this bloody man off our neck" (6).

710. _____. *Smallbone Deceased.* London: Hodder; New York: Harper, 1950; London: Hodder, 1966; New York: Garland, 1976. Fifty Classics of Crime Fiction, 1900-1950, Ser. Gen. eds. Jacques Barzun and Wendell H. Taylor. At the redoubtable firm of Horniman, Birley, and Craine, a large metal deed box with a compressor lid to keep the papers airtight is found to contain the body of Marcus Smallbone, a fellow trustee of the firm's founder Abel Horniman, garroted by a length of picture wire, and packed into the box as long as 8 weeks prior to discovery.

711. _____. *"Stay of Execution" and Other Stories of Legal Practice.* London: Hodder, 1971. Little courtroom action in these 13, but "Mr. Portway's Practice" is a gem and "The Blackmailing of Mr. Justice Ball" is about a trial over a will. "Murder by Jury" echoes a recent trial of a man who strangled his

wife while he was asleep. "The System" refers to the legendary founder of a law firm Abel Horniman, but he is given two different partners in *Smallbone Deceased.* The final story is the title story, virtually a short novel that begins in court with the death sentence Harry Gordon for murdering actress Janine Mann. Gilbert writes in the preface about that story: "[It occurred] to me how little the law has changed [regarding black-market crimes] . . . when *Stay of Execution* was written it was still possible, though uncommon, to be hanged for murder" (6).

712. Gilbert, W[illiam]. S. [Sir], and [Sir] Arthur Sullivan. *Trial by Jury.* New York: Random, n.d. The Modern Library edition of *The Complete Plays of Gilbert and Sullivan*, edited by Bennett Cerf *et alia*, includes the delightful sendup of jurisprudence *Trial by Jury*, first performed at the Royalty Theatre in 1875.

713. Giles, Kenneth. *Death and Mr. Prettyman.* London: Collins, 1967; New York: Walker, 1968; rpt. 1984. A respected lawyer from Kent is murdered in the Inns of Court during a peasouper. Inspector James sorts through a variety of eccentric suspects.

Gill, B. M., pseud. *See* Trimble, Barbara M[argaret]. . . .

714. Ginnes, Judith S. Paige Mitchell, pseud. *Love Is Not a Safe Country.* New York: Dutton; London: Barker, 1967. An illiterate black man, Hickory Peavey, is on trial for slitting a white man's throat. New York Jewish lawyer Adam Hill goes South to try the case but is severely injured and dies while fellow defense attorney Con Norton fills in; the dead man's daughter, in love with hill, testifies for Peavey on the stand.

Giroux, E. X., pseud. *See* Shannon, Doris. . . .

715. Glaspell, Susan. *Trifles* in *Plays by Susan Glaspell.* Ed. and introd. C. W. E. Bigsby. Cambridge: Cambridge U P, 1987; 1916. Glaspell was a founder of the Provincetown Players. Her best-known play is a feminist critique of a woman's role is couched within a whydunit rather than a whodunit. George Henderson, County Attorney, along with Sheriff Peters and farmer Hale stumble around the house where a wife has strangled her husband in his sleep because she could not bear her wretched life a moment longer. Mrs. Peters and Mrs. Hale solve the crime by seeing in the accumulation of the details that the men miss out of male arrogance the explanation why Mrs. Wright killed her husband in his sleep: justice, in other words, for smothering her life and vitality.

716. Glickman, James. *Sounding the Waters.* New York: Crown, 1996. Glickman studied creative writing with Robert Penn Warren and Steinbeck scholar Jay Parini, among others, finds much of the master's influence in this

tale of a lawyer, Ben Shamas, who gets by with long hours at his practice so that he can avoid thinking about his dead daughter and his failed marriage. When his best friend asks him to run his senatorial campaign, it puts him in close contact with the wife Laura, Ben's first love, and exposes him to the ruthless tactics of a blackmailing opposition.

717. Gloag, Julian. *A Sentence of Life.* London: Secker; New York: Simon, 1966. Publisher Jordan Maddox is visited by Surrey police who inform him that an employee of his, June Singer, had been murdered in what looks like a *crime passionnel.* He is shocked to discover that police are building a circumstantial case against him because the victim was murdered with his scarf.

718. Godwin, William. *Things as They Are; or the Adventures of Caleb Williams.* London: Crosby, 1794. New York: Rice, 1795; New York and London, Penguin, 1988. Godwin was a radical philosopher important to that transitional period between the dying Age of Reason and the beginnings of Romanticism. Shelley was his most significant follower but Coleridge and Wordsworth were also involved. On one level it is a psychological novel as Caleb Williams attempts to fathom the secret of his master Squire Falkland. On another, it is an anti-law (or anti-government) treatise inspired when two of Godwin's closest friends were arrested by the William Pitt government during the "Treason Trials" following the suspension of *habeas corpus* on 12 May 1794. Squire Falkland is tried at the beginning and end of the book for the murder of Tyrrel. Tyrrel's own son and a tenant are tried for the crime and executed; a peasant is tried for a crime similar to Falkland's. Williams, Falkland's secretary, witnesses his conduct during this trial (Falkland presides as Justice of the Peace), and is himself framed to divert suspicion. He is tried on charges of theft, escapes, and is tried twice more. Then in the climactic courtroom scene, Falkland is induced to lay bare his soul and confess. A broken man, he is later brought before a magistrate "fatigued and almost destroyed" (330). Caleb is often a tiresome, self-justifying prig but the novel maintains its power in the sections devoted to sleuthing.

719. Goethe, Johann Wolfgang [von Goethe]. *Fairy Tales, Short Stories, and Poems by Johann Wolfgang von Goethe.* Ed and Trans. John W. Thomas. New York: Lang, 1999. Ser. 1. Germanic Lang and Lit. Vol 190. One of the selections is a tale called "The Lawyer" about an elderly merchant married to a young beautiful wife who leaves her at home and allows her to take a lover in his absence, providing she choose one with prudence and avoid the town dandies. She chooses a young lawyer who tells her that, if she will assume one half of his vow of self-denial and abstinence from all pleasures, they will hasten their day of dalliance. The self-abnegation, however, brings the woman to a higher plane of monastic existence and she foreswears all pleasure from then on and thanks the lawyer for enlightening her. We do not hear what the lawyer thinks.

720. Goldman, Lawrence Louis. *Judd for the Defense: The Secret Listeners.* New York: Paperback Library, 1968. Based on characters from the television series and built around themes of student-teacher relationships, drug abuse.

721. Goldsmith, Oliver. *The Vicar of Wakefield[:A Tale Supposed to be Written by Himself*]. Boston: Heath, 1900. Ed. William Henry Hudson. Reprinted from the fifth edition (1773-74), the last that Goldsmith saw through the press. The memoirs of the good and guileless Dr. Pimrose reflect the Johnson circle's fetish for argumentative and philosophical prose on subjects like the essential condition of human nature or natural law, the nature of good and evil, that which brings happiness or effects misery, etc. Goldsmith's classic tale belongs here because of the chapters devoted to the inhumane English penal system, which made felons of debtors and hanged unfortunates as well as criminals under brutal capital punishment laws. The denouement presents the vicar's son George, bloodied and shackled, meeting his father in jail and facing such a fate for issuing a formal challenge to the corrupt son of Sir William Thornhill, author of the family's misfortunes.

722. Gollomb, Joseph. *New York.* New York: Macmillan, 1928. Melodrama centered around the stabbing murder of gimlet-eyed Judge Robert Craigin, foe to the criminal element of New York City.

723. Golub, Aaron Richard. *The Big Cut.* New York: St. Martin's, 2000. Attorney Johnny Ocean gets involved with the gangs in Chinatown, Manhattan, when he takes a case of sisters-in-law battling over a multimillion-dollar estate.

724. Goodchild, George, and Bechhofer Roberts. *The Dear Old Gentleman.* London: Jarrolds, 1935. New York: Harper, 1936; London: Hamish, 1970. The narrator is summoned to sit on the jury to try Margaret Sampson for the murder of Bessie McIntosh. She is found in the basement of a house in Southridge Terrace with her head battered in. The Scottish trial differs markedly from the English, which begins with speeches by counsel for the Crown and for the defense. There are no coroners' inquests; a preliminary enquiry is initiated by the Procurator Fiscal, the official responsible for authorizing arrests. "Instead, [trial] begin[s] with the hearing of all the evidence. The prosecution [Advocate Depute] calls its witnesses, which the other side may cross-examine. Then the defense calls its evidence. Only after all the witnesses have been heard do the lawyers offer their arguments" (15).

725. _____. *The Jury Disagree.* London: Jarrolds, 1934. New York: Macmillan, 1955 . The jury deliberate the case of a mild-mannered man on trial for murdering his wife. As the novel opens, the case against John Tanner has concluded, and a jury of ten men and two women retire to deliberate the verdict.

Each chapter is focused around one member of the jury. (*See* sidenote to Aarons, Edward S.)

726. Gordon, Arthur. *Reprisal.* New York: Simon; London: Hamilton, 1950. Reporter Joe Melady is on a story in Hainesville, Georgia, covering the trial of three white men accused of beating a black youth to keep him quiet about the "Hainesville Massacre," in which four black citizens had been killed in racially motivated mob violence the year before. Melady is convinced that this racist town is a real story and attempts to write it.

727. Gorman, Edward. *The Day the Music Died.* New York: Berkley Prime Crime, 2000. Gorman is a writer, editor, and anthologizer of mystery fiction. He has several series character, one of which is lawyer Sam McCain. The novel is set in 1958 and McCain is working for Judge Whitney; the day after he returns from the last Buddy Holly concert (although Holly and the Big Bopper died on 3 Feb. 1959), he finds the murdered wife of Judge Whitney's nephew Kenny, and when Kenny commits suicide, everyone believes it was a murder-suicide affair, but McCain finds more with his sleuthing--abortion, murder, and jealousy--in the repressed era of the 1950s.

728. _____. *Senatorial Privilege.* New York: Forge, 1997. DA Amy McGuire investigates the brutal murder of a teenaged girl; the case is complicated by politics and pressure when a much-admired and powerful black US Senator wants the investigation ended with a local youth's conviction.

729. _____. *Wake Up Little Susie: A Mystery.* New York: Carroll, 2000. Sam McCain is asked by Judge Whitney to investigate the death of the former district attorney's ex-wife.

730. _____. *Will You Still Love Me Tomorrow?: A Sam McCain Mystery.* New York: Carroll, 2001. Gorman's Sam McCain's series is continued. He is a new lawyer in Black River Falls, Iowa, in the midfifties. His new girlfriend is pregnant and her father is an outspoken liberal, fired in the aftermath of the McCarthy hearings. Then her father is murdered on the eve of USSR Premier Nikita Kruschev's state visit to town.

731. Goss, Herbert I. *T. Thorndyke*[,] *Attorney-at-Law: The Romance of a Young Lawyer.* Boston: Clark, 1907. Amiable, slow-moving tale addressed to the "Gentle Reader," as being the narrative of one Theophilus Thorndyke, 27-year-old lawyer newly set up in Berlin, Coos County, New Hampshire; he recounts the events of the past 20 years from his arrival. The narrator acknowledges at the outset that no "black-hearted, thorough-going villain" will be found in his pages (6). His first real case is Griffin v. Glen Manufacturing, about a laborer seeking to recover for a broken ankle suffered at work, but the real conflict is in "our hero's" attempt to win the daughter of cranky Judge

Pillsbury for his bride.

732. Gotti, Victoria. *The Senator's Daughter.* New York: Forge, 1997. The Teflon Don's daughter's first novel features Taylor Brooke, attorney, assigned to defend a young black man accused of clipping Joseph Sessio, union boss. Stalked throughout by a murderous ex-husband and falling for the dead man's son Michael, Brooke is wondering whom to trust amid an investigation of corruption in the DA's office. Gotti followed this with *I'll Be Watching You* (Crown, 1998), an overplotted suspense thriller.

733. Grafton, C. W. [Cornelius Warren]. *Beyond a Reasonable Doubt.* New York: Rinehart, 1950. London: Heinemann, 1951; New York: Garland, 1976. Fifty Classics of Crime Fiction, 1900-1950, Ser. Gen. eds. Jacques Barzun and Wendell H. Taylor. Born of a missionary family in China in 1909, Grafton earned a literature degree from Columbia and at his brother's urging turned to law for a career. Barzun and Taylor were enamored of this selection (Grafton had two previous hardboiled mysteries) for its powerful first-person narrative and because of the use of an unusual courtroom strategy, its "diabolical innocence" (n. pag.). The Commonwealth of Kentucky puts the narrator on trial for his life in the spring of 1940 for the murder of his brother-in-law Mitch Sothern; his *pro se* defense concludes with the jury's return of a verdict in a few minutes of deliberation.

734. _____. *The Rope Began to Hang the Butcher.* New York: Farrar, 1944. London: Gollancz, 1945. David Matthews, missing for seven years, returns to his hometown at the very moment a case is before Judge Widgett's courtroom in Calhoun County, Kentucky, over property rights that would favor plaintiffs and relatives Jerome and Lucella Matthews in the absence of a will. His return is short-lived, literally, because he is murdered, but the body might not be that of David Matthews, and the lawyer-narrator is convinced that David and Jerome are the same person.

735. Grafton, Sue. *"I" Is for Innocent.* New York: Holt, 1992. Grafton's series character is private investigator Kinsey Millhone, but this novel is a legal case divided into three sections. The first third is the prosecution's case and background; the second third is the defense; and the final third is courtroom cross-examination and rebuttal. Hotshot lawyer Lonnie Kingman is trying to bring a civil action against David Barney to keep him from enjoying the profits from his wife's murder, being that Kingman had failed to get a conviction five years ago. Now as the statute of limitations is about to expire, Millhone agrees to take over the investigation.

736. Graham, Winston. *The Merciless Ladies.* London: Ward, 1944; New York: Doubleday, 1980. Graham authored the Poldark novels. Set in the 1920s, Paul Stafford, born into poverty, has becomes a successful portrait painter of

high-society women he sleeps with. He is sued for libel by one of his subjects over the painting *Diana Marnsett* by the subject.

737. _____. *Take My Life.* London: Ward, 1947. Garden City, NY: Doubleday, 1967. Nick Taylor is an ex-Guards captain committed to the Old Bailey for trial charged with murdering an ex-lover, whom he meets unexpectedly in London after the war. His opera-star wife ventures to Scotland to prove his innocence. Made into a Hitchcock-style film (GFD/Cineguild, 1947) with Graham and Valerie Taylor collaborating on the script.

738. _____. *The Tumbled House.* London: Hodder, 1959. Garden City, NY: Doubleday, 1960. An adulterous liaison between a journalist and the wife of a man from a distinguished family erupts in a libel case designed to destroy the cuckold's reputation. Roger Shorn, the plaintiff, publishes a piece accusing Donald Marlowe's distinguished father of plagiarizing another's work. He is in turn slandered in his club and the case is brought before the Queen's Bench.

739. Grant, Charles. *Stories of Naples and the Camorra.* London and New York: Macmillan, 1897. The final novella of these linked stories about the lawless association of bandits operating in Naples is "Domenico," the bastard son of a prominent member of the Camorrists. Camorra justice and Italian legal justice operate independently throughout these tales but in this last about a youth who grows up under Camorra tutelage and acquires a fierce reputation, the enmity between him and his half-brother culminates in one's murder and the other's imprisonment over a plot to gain hidden treasure from the father, himself a victim of Domenico's revenge.

740. Grant, Susannah. *Erin Brockovich.* (Universal, 2000). The title figure is a trash-talking, twice-divorced mother of three with a deep cleavage who takes a menial clerical job at the LA law office of a struggling attorney. Then she uncovers something wrong in the real-estate records of a *pro bono* case where Pacific Gas & Electric have polluted the water and caused numerous maladies for the people living in that area. Co-executive producer Carla Shamberg heard the story at the chiropractor's office she shares with Brockovich, who was at the time working for LA lawyers Masry & Vititoe. In the real case, 600 plaintiffs settled for $333 million from P.G. &E. Dir. Steven Soderbergh. Perf. Julia Roberts (Oscar), Albert Finney, and Aaron Eckhart.

741. Grant-Adamson, Leslie. *Lipstick and Lies.* London: Hodder, 1998. Crime and suspense writer Grant-Adamson plays the psychological thriller angle here also in a tale about a lawyer Gillian Spry, who investigates botched criminal investigations. She investigates the Rita Morden affair, in which an adulterous wife of the fifties was strangles and her lover hanged for it. The daughter of the murdered woman, Anna, recounts part of the crime from her perspective as both adult and 8-year-old witness to researcher Spry.

742. Gray, A. W. [Albert William]. by Sarah Gregory, pseud. *The Best Defense.* New York: Signet, 1999. Albert William Gray is a native Texan, resides in Fort Worth, a former professional poker player with stints at the Binnion World Championship and jazz musician. The six-foot-six Dallas lawyer is called Bino (short for *Albino*) because of his white hair, but the name derives from his father, the deacon, honoring an old-time Baptist circuit rider. Bino's office staff includes Dodie [Dora Annette] and Horace ("Half-a-Point") Harrison, the ex-bookmaking son of a gambler father. Gray has authored two fine non-fiction true-crime books: *The Cadet Murder Case* and *Poisoned Dreams*. He has a second legal-thriller series about brainy, sexy Texas attorney Sharon Hays (under the *nom de plume* Sarah Gregory).

In this one, Hays enters one of those trial-by-television spotlights when bad-boy actor David Spencer is found murdered in a motel room. The accused is fugitive Darla Cowen, who also happens to be a longtime friend, now client, of Sharon herself.

743. _____. *'Bino.* New York: Dutton, 1988. Bino's seedy client's death is linked to a prominent Texas politician's assassination and an FBI probe. Bino's jaundiced view of his own profession: "The law's a pile of shit. . . The whole justice system is like the biggest, festering stack of dog crap you ever saw. . . with a bunch of flies buzzing around it. And us lawyers are the flies carrying off our own little pieces of shit, back to the nest . . . "(59).

744. _____. *Bino's Blues.* New York: Simon, 1995. Bino gets involved in three predicaments at one time: he's involved with flashy Houston lawyer Rusty Benson accused of wife murder; a blues singer who might be connected to the dead wife, a federal sting that could be meant for him because he exonerated Dallas cop Tommy Clinger. Add a hired gun with a neatness fetish to the mix.

745. _____. *Capitol Scandal.* New York: NAL-Signet, 1999. Attorney Hays is assigned the defense of a Texas congressman accused of murdering an intern he was sleeping with.

746. _____. *In Defense of Judges.* New York: Dutton, 1990. Gray delayed writing the sequel to *'Bino*, he told *CA*, because he did not want to be known as a one-trick pony. Of his series character Bino Phillips, he says: "I think Bino's a pretty swell guy, but I don't want him for my alter-ego." Bino here fights the syndicate, FBI, and a psychopath intent on murdering his son.

747. _____. *In Self-Defense.* New York: Signet, 1995. Sharon Hays' case involves Midge Rathermore, the teenage daughter of a Texas millionaire; she stands accused of hiring a pair of teenaged assassins to kill her father. Sharon herself is all the while being stalked by a sadistic killer she once helped to put away.

748. _____. *Killings.* New York: Dutton, 1993. Bino Phillip's client is fingered as drug kingpin who sells to Dallas University students. The two alibi witnesses are missing, one the victim of a sexual serial predator who exsanguinates his victims.

749. _____. *The Man Offside.* New York: Dutton, 1989. Ex-pro footballer Rick Bannion runs errand for a Dallas bail bondsman to make ends meet. He agrees to help a former lover and her husband Jack Brendy, also a former Cowboy an entrepreneur who was caught in a government dope sting. The Brendys' lawyer is slick, groomed Fred Cassell, who sends Bannion on a fool's errand to locate Skeezix, doper lowlife and government stooge.

750. _____. *Prime Suspect.* New York: Dutton, 1992. Lackey Ferguson contracts with rich Percival Hardin to build a bathhouse, and while visiting the house in the course of negotiations to get an advance, he rebuffs Hardin's sexy wife. The wife is murdered hours afterward by a psychopathic ex-con, and Lackey is accused.

751. _____. *Public Trust.* New York: Signet, 1997. Another strong tale for series protagonist and Dallas attorney Sharon Hays. In this one, she has to believe a convicted rapist's word that the DA railroaded Raymond Burnside onto death row because of his father-in-law's clout, which translates into her opposing the leading candidate for governor in a courtroom battle. Hays is a tough woman and a tender mother, good at detection but better at courtroom maneuvering, especially when her opponents are tough Texans with more macho swagger than courtroom sense. One more is *Public Interest* (1995).

752. _____. *Shares.* New York: Simon, 1996 . Ex-cop Frank White returns to Dallas after serving his term in California for shooting a black man whose father was a local councilman. He is promptly mixed up with two very different women: a dorm mother at the posh Riverbend School for Girls and Darla Bern, sexy ex-con who wants to trap him into participating in a kidnapping scheme.

753. _____. *Size.* New York: Dutton, 1988. Sizemore F. Brandon is "Pecos Jimmy" Fontenot's lifelong companion; "Size" moves his lips as he reads the Fifth Amendment his lawyer gave him on a scrap of paper to respond to the federal prosecutor's questions about his relationship to Fontenot during the grand jury. But Fontenot's lawyer points out that he is facing thirty years on RICO charges and all that stands between him and that sentence is his hulking bodyguard, a happy-go-lucky, card-playing brute who knows where all the bodies are buried.

754. Graziunas, Daina, and Jim Starlin. *Predators* [Orig. title *Thinning the*

Predators]. New York: Warner, 1996. Unusual reversal of lawyer-protagonist in this tale of a lawyer whose family is killed by a serial killer at the moment he suffers a fall in an elevator, which accident leaves him with psychic gifts enabling him to track his family's killer and pursue a new career as a hunter of psycho killers. The story stays ludicrous right through the happy-ending conclusion.

755. Green, Anna Katharine. *Hand and Ring*. New York: Putnam's, 1883. London: Ward, 1884. Brooklyn-born Green (married name Rohlfs) lived most of her life in Buffalo. She is one of the names of detective fiction that should not be forgotten. Often compared to Poe and Wilkie Collins, she borrowed techniques of atmosphere and ratiocination from both and spun cleverly plotted tales of deduction years before Sherlock Holmes upstaged all contenders in the deductive (actually, inductive) crime-writing market. Book 3 concerns the trial of Craik Mansell, accused of killing a Sibley, New York widow with an axe; the chief witness against him is the woman he courted but who refused to marry him.

756. _____. *The Leavenworth Case: A Lawyer's Story*. New York: Burt, 1878; New York: Putnam's, 1878; London: Routledge, 1884. Series character Ebenezer Gryce, New York detective, is featured in this crime tale told in the first person by a junior partner in the firm of Veeley, Carr & Raymond; it concerns the shooting murder of an old client of the firm, Mr. Leavenworth, shot in the head while he sat in his own library. In *The Chief Legatee* (New York: Authors and Newspapers Assoc., 1906), a lawyer has a minor role in a story about a bride who runs away from her groom shortly after the ceremony and asks her lawyer to draw up a will. Collier of London published it three years later under the title *A Woman of Mystery*.

757. Green, George Dawes. *The Juror*. New York: Warner, 1995. Green's first novel, *The Caveman's Valentine*, earned an Edgar. This second novel concerns the trial of mob boss Louie Boffano and Juror 224, Annie Laird, a young mother, and sculptor of boxes you have to reach under to feel with your hands. Boffano's paid killer is called the Teacher, a suave and sophisticated psychopath, hired to coerce her vote in the trial. The Teacher subtly moves in on her fears and devotion to son Oliver and becomes obsessed with controlling her. The Columbia Pictures film starred Alec Baldwin and Demi Moore.

758. Green, Tim. *Outlaws*. New York: HarperPaperbacks, 1997. Cody Grey, player for the Texas Assassins, is arrested for the murder of an IRS agent out to get him. Madison McCall reluctantly takes him on as a client and finds herself becoming a target.

Greenberg, Martin Harry. *See* Olander, Joseph D. . . . .

759. Greene, Ward. *Death in the Deep South.* New York: Stackpole, 1936 London: Cassell, 1937. Crime-and-courtroom story of college professor Robert Hale in a small business college when pretty coed Mary Clay is murdered and found in an elevator shaft at the college; at first, black janitor Tump Redwine is accused, and a confession beaten out of him, but then suspicion shifts to the Yankee teacher, who is indicted by an ambitious DA named Andy Griffen and brought to trial amid a frenzied town in a lynch-mob atmosphere.

760. Greenleaf, Stephen. *Beyond Blame.* New York: Villard, 1986. Both Greenleaf and his lawyer-protag are non-practicing attorneys. John Marshall Tanner actively dislikes the profession, based on the judicial system's relentless and fatal persecution of one of his clients, and thus practices the private investigator's craft from his San Francisco office. Tanner reflects upon the law's mixed blessing in *Book Case* (noted below) about his five years of lawyering:

> As introduced in law school . . the law was a decidedly mixed blessing--stimulating intellectually but daunting psychologically; exciting philosophically yet intimidating pedagogically; august in the abstract and slimy in too many of its earthly manifestations. (79)

His creator's reasons are more personal than philosophical. Greenleaf says that he wrote his first Tanner awaiting his bar exam, but a writer's workshop turned him altogether from the law. The well-traveled author was born in Washington, DC, grew up in Idaho, where he took his bar exam, did a tour in Vietnam, and has lived since in San Francisco, Portland, Seattle, but currently resides in Ashland, Oregon. Greenleaf intersperses his narrative with facsimiles of legal material, such as legal depositions, a judge's instructions to the jury. His trial scenes are good theater without overplaying the denouement *a la* Perry Mason.

761. _____. *Book Case: A John Marshall Tanner Mystery.* New York: Morrow, 1991. Tanner's publisher friend gives him a manuscript to read; his assignment is to find the author of "Homage to Hammurabi," a manuscript purportedly written by a man in prison convicted of a crime he did not commit. Tanner instead discovers one mystery within another that begins with a sex scandal at prestigious Sebastian School, where grades were inflated to get the sons and daughters of the rich into the nation's best colleges; it culminates with the beating murder of the author-whistleblower.

762. _____. *The Ditto List.* New York: Villard, 1985. Seriocomic novel of D. T. Jones, a divorce lawyer for abused, abandoned and hard-luck women in San Francisco, who has a gay male secretary he cannot afford and a Catholic judge who hates him and fiddles with the docket to avoid him. Two of his cases involve a naive but decent country girl recently married to an oafish husband and the other, a more upscale version, is helped by Jones in an unorthodox

manner by setting up a gay-male sting to keep the wife from losing everything in a divorce.

763. _____. *Ellipsis.* New York: Scribner's, 2000. Tanner's 16th outing. He signs on as bodyguard to a bestselling romance writer to protect her during her tour (she has been receiving death threats).

764. _____. *False Conception: A John Marshall Tanner Mystery.* New York: Pocket; New York: Penzler, 1994 [/A John Marshall Tanner Novel]. Tanner is doing background checking on a surrogate mother for a wealthy couple when she disappears.

765. _____. *Flesh Wounds.* New York: Scribner's, 1966. Tanner agrees to search for a missing model, the future stepdaughter of his ex-lover Peggy Nettleton.

766. _____. *Grave Error.* New York: Dial, 1979. Tanner is hired to investigate a husband's infidelity by a beautiful woman; she does not want documentation, however, because his reputation as a national consumer advocate might lead to scandal or even blackmail.

767. _____. *Impact.* New York: Morrow, 1989. Two lawyers, their lives and loves, California tort reform, all intersect over a plane crash near San Francisco, in which each is representing different parties in lawsuits against the government and the airlines industry. Alec Hawthorne is a superstar aviation attorney, but Keith Tollison is an ex-civil rights lawyer scratching out a living defending drunk drivers in Altoona. His high-school buddy Jack Donohue (and the man he is cuckolding with wife Laura) bring the lawyers together. Jack was one of the flight victims but his adulterous companion was traveling under an assumed name when the plane went down, and there are not enough body parts to assemble to recognize her. During the trial, Tollison asks Laura about the state of her marriage before the crash.

768. _____. *Past Tense.* New York: Scribner's, 1997. Tanner's friend Lieutenant Charlie Sheet explodes with acts of vigilantism around San Francisco. Tanner seeks to stop the violence by getting at the core of his friend's repressed memories.

769. _____. *Southern Cross.* New York: Morrow, 1993. Tanner's friend, Seth Hartmann, is a civil rights lawyer from Charleston and the target of a white-supremacist group calling itself The Alliance for Southern Pride.

770. _____. *Strawberry Sunday: A John Marshall Tanner Novel.* New York: Scribner's, 199. The recuperating shamus is pulled out of his depression (recovering from bullets fired by Charley Sleet in *Past Tense*) by migrant-

worker activist Rita Lombardi, recovering down the hall. Her murder sends him back into the fray.

The following are mostly Tanners: *Blood Type* (Morrow, 1992), *Death Bed: A Detective Story* (Dial, 1980), *Ellipsis* (Scribner's, 2000), *Fatal Obsession* (Dial, 1983), *State's Evidence* (Dial, 1982), and *Toll Call* (Villard, 1987).

771. Gregor, Manfred. *Town without Pity.* Trans. from the German [*Das Urteil* by Robert Brain]. New York: Random; London: Heinemann, 1961. Four soldiers stationed in a small German town after the war viciously rape 16-year-old Karin Steinhoff out swimming with her boyfriend. Captain Korneff defends at their military tribunal and, though loathing himself for it, skewers the poor girl on the witness stand with pointed questions, and in the end asks mercy for his guilty clients.

772. Grierson, Edward. *A Crime of One's Own.* London: Chatto; New York: Putnam's, 1967. Born in Bedford, England, educated at St. Paul's, London, and Exeter College, Oxford, Grierson practiced law for three years before enlisting. He finished the war a lieutenant-colonel with service in the Middle East. Donald Maitland is a Warmouth bookstore owner, who comes to suspect that one of his patrons is a courier for spies. He follows her home and enters her apartment the night she is murdered with an office paper-knife bearing his prints. He denies being there to his lawyer but his story falls apart during his trial for her murder.

773. _____. *The Massingham Affair.* London: Chatto, 1962. Garden City, NY: Doubleday, 1963. Grierson takes a case from the Northumberland dockets knows as the Edlingham Burglary from the end of the nineteenth century and transplants it Massingham on the moors. An elderly vicar and his daughter are the victims of two violent burglars in their rectory in 1891; two men named Milligan and Kelly are from a nearby village are found guilty and sentenced to life imprisonment. Justin Derry is now a solicitor from that same village and recalls the trial and the verdict. A visitor to his office inspires him to launch an investigation to prove the men innocent in the face of hostility from the villagers and his own fiancée.

774. _____. *Reputation for a Song.* London: Chatto; New York: Knopf, 1953; New York: Penguin, 1986. Rupert Laurence Anderson stands trial for the murder of his father in the County of York.

775. _____. *The Second Man.* London: Chatto; New York: Knopf, 1956. The plot is built around the case of *Regina vs. Maudsley*, as narrated by the barrister assisting new colleague Marion Kerrison in her defense of loutish John Maudsley, accused of murdering his elderly aunt for her jewels.

776. Grippando, James M. *The Pardon.* New York: HarperCollins, 1994. Jack Swyteck is the son of the Florida governor and a lawyer with a Yale law degree and a career with the Freedom Institute defending the kind of scum his father executes, especially his current client, a child-killing psychopath named Eddy Goss. Two years earlier, his father refused to hear his pleas to spare Raul Fernandez' life when Jack begged him to believe that he had had a conversation with, and proof from, the real killer just the night before. Grippando publishes mainly suspense thrillers (*The Abduction*, 1998; *Found Money*, 1999; *The Informant*, 1996) but is himself a trial lawyer in South Florida. Grippando's latest is *Under Cover of Darkness* (HarperCollins, 2000), a legal thriller involving serial murder in Seattle.

777. Grisham, John. *The Brethren.* New York: Doubleday, 2000. Many critics argue that Grisham's first novel, *A Time to Kill*--his only one to date to miss becoming a bestseller (sold only 5,000 copies)--is still his best. The enormous popularity belies (or may explain) facile characterizations, occasional improbable plots, and easy moral outrage, but there is no denying an innate cynicism toward the law's chief practitioners as a set of scoundrels out to make big money at the expense of ordinary, decent people. Born in Jonesboro, Arkansas in 1955, he studied accounting at Mississippi State but graduated from the law school at Ole Miss; he practiced for a decade with a specialty in both criminal defense and personal-injury litigation in Southaven, not far from the birthplace of the South's greatest novelist (Grisham collects Faulkner first editions), he splits time between Mississippi and a 204-acre estate outside Charlottesville, Virgina. Grisham was both a practicing attorney and a state legislator who arose at 5:00 a.m. every morning to finish his first novel. More than anyone, Grisham and Scott Turow breathed new life into the legal thriller after its post-Perry Mason decline. Grisham, in particular, exposed it to new legal possibilities as well as borrowing from the staple of suspense thrillers appropriate to the cynical, sensation-hungry nineties. Witness *The Chamber*'s opening sentence: "The decision to bomb the office of the radical Jew lawyer was reached with ease." Numbers do not lie: he is *the* rainmaker of courtroom fiction with 110 million books sold and translated into 34 languages--each Grisham novel sells 3 million hardback copies on average and the first of his 6 film adaptations (*The Firm*) grossed $270 million; ironically, *The Chamber* is his all-time bestseller at 3.17 million copies, whereas the film made a mere $27 million. His latest, *The Testament*, broke all personal records with a 2.8 million first printing--a second printing occurred the same week. The self-effacing, devout Baptist author told *Newsweek* in 1999: "I don't pretend it's literature. It's high-quality, professional entertainment."

Three former judges comprise the Brethren; they meet each day in the law library of the Trumble Prison where they are incarcerated to write briefs for fellow cons and collaborate on a moneymaker of a scam, but when it goes wrong, they have a new and powerful enemy on the outside who has a very long reach. Grisham notes of his most recent fiction, *A Painted House,* that "there is not a single lawyer, dead or alive, in this story."

778. _____. *The Chamber.* New York: Doubleday, 1994. Young Adam Hall is a familiar Grisham character: a green lawyer with ambitions, or as it has been often stated about a Grisham novel: David and Goliath go to court. As a hard-charging rookie lawyer with a big-bucks Chicago firm, and much against the advice of a senior member of the firm, he plans to take on a *pro bono* capital murder case. That case involved the Klan bombing of the home of radical Jewish lawyer Marvin Kramer in Greenville, Mississippi in 1967, which resulted in the death of his twin sons and his own maiming. After two mistrials, local Klansman Sam Cayhill was found guilty of setting the bomb and sentenced to death in 1981. Twelve years later, Hall believes there was an accomplice to the crime, but his real motive is personal: unrepentant racist Sam Cayhill is his own grandfather.

779. _____. *The Client.* New York: Doubleday, 1993. Worldly-wise, 11-year-old Mark Sway and his little brother are enjoying a Marlboro in a weedy lot outside Memphis when a black Lincoln pulls up. A suicidal New Orleans lawyer named Romey reveals to the older boy the reason for his wanting to die: his client, Benny ("The Blade") Muldanno will get him eventually. The Blade, he said, murdered a US Senator named Boyette and hid the body that everybody in America is searching for. Now that Mark knows, soon the killer will know about Mark. Separating them from a horde of mob hitmen and a team of federal agents with US attorneys in tow is a young, inexperienced lawyer named Reggie Love. Susan Sarandon and Tommy Lee Jones take the opposing leads in Joel Schumacher's 1994 adaptation.

780. _____. *The Firm.* New York: Doubleday, 1991. The "David" in this megaseller after his first book features naive-but-ambitious, Harvard Law grad Mitch McDeere, wooed by a gracious Memphis firm where everything--salary, billable hours, benefits--is over the top and partners "are multimillionaires by the age of forty-five." Mitch discovers the one flaw in the deal: this firm you do not leave, not alive anyhow. Then an FBI investigation plunges him into terror and intrigue, with no choice left him but to pit his wits and legal skills against the firm's deadly secret. The Sydney Pollack-directed film with Tom Cruise and Gene Hackman (Paramount, 1993) made some big changes from Grisham's convoluted plot. Yet veteran scriptwriter Robert Towne would comment, "It's a wonderful paranoid fantasy. All the horrible things you can imagine happening to you do happen."

781. _____. *The Partner.* New York: Doubleday, 1997. Patrick Lanigan, once a young partner in a thriving Mississippi law firm, watches his own his car burn with a body inside. Then he flees to the village of Ponta Por, Brazil. Why did he steal $90 million from his firm's offshore account before arranging his

own funeral? The answer is in the trial in Mississippi where the crime occurred, an answer his former partners fear will reveal the truth.

782. _____. *The Pelican Brief.* New York: Doubleday, 1992. Two Supreme Court justices have been assassinated in a single day. Darby Shaw, a young law student, prepares a brief for her lover-mentor on nothing more than a brilliant guess, which brief he passes on. But to the Beltway establishment, it is real dynamite that could blow the cover off the murders and the cover-up. When Shaw's professor-lover is murdered, she and the brief go underground. Julia Roberts' character alternates between whey-faced, simpering naïveté and slick cunning in the Alan J. Pakula film version, another blockbuster Grisham adaptation (Warner, 1993) with Denzel Washington as the tenacious reporter who enlists the runaway Shaw's help in cracking the conspiracy throughout the cat-and-mouse chase.

783. _____. *The Rainmaker.* New York: Doubleday, 1995. Young Rudy Baylor narrates his own tale; he's the typical young law student who is a month away from finishing his degree at Memphis State with a job lined up with a small Memphis legal firm and confident of finishing in the top half of his class. For his "Legal Problems of the Elderly" class, Rudy takes on two clients. One, Miss Birdie, is a colorful but lonely old woman who asks him to draft a multimillion-dollar will. The other is a case against an insurance company which refused to honor a policy involving a young man with leukemia. If Great Benefits had accepted the claim, Donny Ray Black could have been treated; instead, he is dying, and it is too late for help. His family wants to sue the insurance company. Weeks oefore his finals, Rudy discovers that his future employer has been taken over by a large corporate law firm and there will be no job for him as a result. As Rudy nears financial collapse--he is evicted, a process server and a lawsuit await him, he discovers that Donny Ray's insurance company is being represented by the very firm which took over his would-be employers. Coppola's film is outstanding because of John Toll's cinematography and brilliant casting with John Voight stealing the film as the silken-tongued, $1,000-per hour lawyer for the defense. "Bruiser" Stone (Mickey Rourke) as Rudy's flamboyant mentor and Danny DeVito as Stone & Lyman's paralegal (a frequent bar-exam failure and ambulance chaser) round out a cast of lawyer-sharks that put a halo around Baylor's head as he seeks justice for Donny Ray's family. An intensely strong supporting cast finds room for Danny Glover, Teresa Wright, Dean Stockwell, Virginia Madsen, and Roy Scheider in small roles that really shimmer.

784. _____. *The Runaway Jury.* New York: Doubleday, 1996. In January 1996, Grisham returned to the courtroom as a lawyer in the wrongful death suit of *King v. Central Illinois Railroad.* Grisham was phasing out his legal practice to devote himself to writing, but he agreed to take the case and won his client almost $700,000. In this novel, a huge tobacco-company case in Biloxi with

hundreds of millions of dollars at stake. What the tobacco lawyers fear most is a precedent-setting compensatory award, and they scrutinize every quirk and habit of the jury pool. One potential juror seems to have no secrets and no past--juror number fifty-six, Nicholas Easter, a seemingly nondescript, recent arrival to Biloxi.

785. _____. *The Street Lawyer.* New York: Doubleday, 1998. Yalie law grad Michael Brock is working his way up in Sweeney & Drake, a powerhouse firm with about half its 800 lawyers working out of its DC offices. A backbreaking work week and a failing marriage cannot deflect him from his ambition until he meets De Von Hardy, a Vietnam vet who takes Brock and eight colleagues hostage in a boardroom because of a grudge against his recent eviction, the evictor being one of the firm's clients. Having a .44 put into his face triggers a conversion in the lawyer's soul and he winds up at the 14th Street Legal Clinic, facing a huge man named Mordecai Green, the clinic's director, who offers him redemption in the form of charitable lawyering in behalf of the powerless: "You don't do it for the money," says Green. "You do it for your soul" (106). Gone is the edgy suspense readers of Grisham came to expect; in its place is sentimental maundering replacing a heartfelt cynicism about lawyers.

786. _____. *The Testament.* New York: Doubleday, 1999. Grisham, himself a generous, church-related visitor to Pantanal, the setting of this book, knows the region, the people, and the culture well. Troy Phelan is an mean, eccentric 78-year-old billionaire who wants to deprive his three ex-wives and their loathsome brood of his $11 billion estate. Nate O' Reilly, a 48-year-old, washed-up boozer of a litigator with two broken marriages and the IRS close behind, is despatched to the Brazilian wetlands in search of one of the heirs. But unlike Marlow finding a demonic Kurtz in the Congo, O'Reilly's trip down Brazilian rivers discovers no heart of darkness but the pure-souled Rachel Lane, a missionary without a trace of the Phelan family's money-hungry avarice. Grisham himself comments in a 1999 *Amazon.com* interview: "Through Rachel, Nate begins to see the futility of his blind pursuit of the American dream." Grisham originally had envisioned a full-blown conversion for Nate but wife and editor dissuaded him.

787. _____. *A Time to Kill.* New York: Island-Winwood, 1989. Grisham had been practicing law for three years in Southaven, Mississippi, when he stopped by the court house one day in 1984 and lingered in the gallery as a 10-year-old girl testified against the man who had raped her and left her for dead. Says Grisham in his web-page profile, "I never felt such emotion and human drama in my life. I became obsessed wondering what it would be like if the girl's father killed that rapist and was put on trial. I had to write it down." In Clanton, Mississippi, a 10-year-old black girl is viciously raped and beaten by two drunken locals. The girl's father, knowing there is no justice in Mississippi courts for a black, exacts street justice with his rifle right on the courthouse

steps. Jake Brigance, a young defense attorney, strives to defend the man in a town seething with racism and Klan-inspired publicity. Gene Siskel hated the Joel Schumaker film (despite Samuel L. Jackson's able performance as the factory-worker father) for its "gorgeous shots of Ku Klux Klan rallies to punctuate the film" (*TV Guide*, 7 July 1997).

788. Gross, Fred L. *What Is the Verdict?*. New York: Macmillan, 1944. Gross is a past President of the New York State Bar Association. His anecdotal narratives are fictionalized stories of courtroom experiences. His interest lies less in fictionalizing the storyworlds than in the legal texts, precedents, and precepts illustrated by these anecdotes--"None of the narratives which follow is a report of an actual lawsuit," he affirms (v). To that end, each narrative comes with its own set of commentary or law cases in the footnotes. Sample titles: "The Sleepwalker," "The After-Born Child," "An Absolute Divorce," "Negligence," and "A Judiciary Campaign."

789. Gruenfeld, Lee. *The Expert.* New York: Dutton, 1998. Rebecca Verona is an LA attorney who defends the Tera-Tech Integrated's president of charges of treason when the US indicts him and his Silicon Valley microchip company for selling advanced technology to the Chinese. It is more complicated than that, however, because the attorney prosecuting her client is David Zuckerman, the lover she left for the James Perrein, the computer-chip president. The expert of the title is a world-renowned microchip scientist about whom she has doubts.

790. _____. *The Halls of Justice.* New York: Dutton, 1996. Gruenfeld is the author of suspense thrillers like *Irreparable Harm*, 1993, and *All Fall Down*, 1994; he favors plots that revolve around terrorism and exotic technology. Diane Pierman, a Santa Monica attorney, and her twin sister are attacked and their assailant is brought to trial. For Sal Milano, Deputy DA, the case is one he cannot lose. But he underestimates his defense opponent and the trial ends with the attacker freed. The sisters, however, cannot let it go and they set in motion their own plan to correct the imbalance of justice.

791. Guterson, David. *Snow Falling on Cedars.* New York: Harcourt, 1994. Set on the small fishing island of San Piedro, fisherman is found dead aboard his drifting boat, and the sheriff's investigation concludes homicide. Kabuo Miyamato, a fisherman of Japanese descent, is arrested for the crime. (The book opens on the morning of trial, but only a handful of pages are devoted to it.) Guterson's major themes are nationalism, cultural diferences and the prejudice that evolves from them.

792. Guthrie, A. B. [Alfred Bertram], Jr. *Murders at Moon Dance.* New York: Dutton: 1943. Lincoln: U of Nebraska P, 1993. Introd. William Kittredge. Guthrie wrote his big book, The Big Sky, while on a Nieman

Fellowship at Harvard in 1944. Kittredge compares this traditional western with Clark's *Ox-Bow Incident* in the respect that both are "antimythological" tales (ix). The plot involves a woman's kidnapping and the good citizens of Moon Dance form a vigilante posse and raid neighboring Breedtown, comprising outcasts, outlaws, and Indians. They burn houses and beat several and almost lynch one. Old Judge LaFrance is Guthrie's mouthpiece for articulating the traditional values of the West and the Western hero, a two-fisted, gunslinging hero who cleans out the bad hombres and restores civil order: "What did the western man do? Do? Why, he fought them Indians, and he chased the outlaws out of the country or buried 'em in Boot Hill. He saw a job had to be done and he done it" (235).

793. Gutman, Amy. *Equivocal Death.* Boston: Little, 2001. Gutman is an honors grad of Harvard law School and a former Capitol journalist. She was founding director of the Mississippi Teacher Corps. She practiced four years in New York city before quitting to write her first novel. She now serves on the New York City Bar Association's Lawyers-in-Transition Committee. Just out of Harvard Law, Kate Paine is on the fast track at Samson & Mills, the nation's richest, most powerful firm. Assigned to assist the charismatic managing partner, Kate cannot believe her good luck, but with the murder of Madeleine Waters, a beautiful female partner, Kate's world begins to collapse. A mysterious warning from Waters hours before her death leaves Kate confused. Terrified she could be the next victim, she tries to unravel the mystery of her death and discovers that, beneath the velvet-smooth veneer of Samson & Mills, there is a legacy of abuse and betrayal.

H

794. Haggard, H[enry]. Rider. *Mr. Meeson's Will.* London: Blackett; New York: Harper, 1888. Meeson is a tyrant who runs his publishing house with ruthless disregard for others, and when a young woman author challenges his meager allowance to her after she produces a bestseller, his own nephew comes to her defense; he is fired, taken out of the will, and his two partners Addison and Rosco given his two millions. Then when a whaler collides with the ship he is sailing on, he is marooned in her company again and becomes so repentant that he writes a new will on her back and dies shortly after. The tattooed will and the question of the testator's sanity is later argued in probate court with the argument presented by Mr. Meeson's business partners as plaintiffs.

Hailey, J. P., pseud. *See* Hall, Parnell. . . .

795. Haining, Peter, ed. *Murder on the Menu.* New York: Carroll, 1991. The theme of each story involves combines food with fear--or, at least the element of detection is subsumed in the dynamics of eating and killing in some

manner. Besides a melange of poison-murder stories, there is "A Case for Gourmets" by British crime writer Michael Gilbert, featuring his series protagonist Detective Inspector Patrick Petrella that opens in magistrate's court. Gilbert, another lawyer before he turned writer, was once legal advisor to Raymond Chandler and drew up Chandler's will.

796. Hall, Oakley. *Warlock.* New York: Viking, 1958. Warlock is a mining town in the 1880s and its story devolves from the journals of one Henry Holmes Goodpasture, member of the Citizens Committee, a deputized posse. It is a stark and unromanticized look at law and lawlessness in violent days in the Southwest of America. The action centers around a new sheriff, a former gunslinger named Clay Blaisdell, whose year as marshal is chronicled in episodes of violence and killing that culminate in his trial for killing an innocent man. One of the book's peripheral characters is Judge Holloway, who runs his court with bible, rusty derringer, and a bottle of half-drunk whiskey. The Judge is given to bellowing out, "The law is the law!" during sentencing of malefactors and on serious occasions will deliver a profane harangue from the bench:

> 'The law is the law!' he panted. 'But there isn't enough of it to go around out here. So when we get a good man protecting this town from hell with its door open I am not going to see him choused and badgered and false-sworn and yawped at fit to puke by a one-legged old son of a bitch like you!' (151)

797. Hall, Parnell. *The Anonymous Client.* J. P. Hailey, pseud. New York: Fine, 1989. Actor-turned-screenwriter Hall is the creator of a pair of sleuths; among his screen credits is *C.H.U.D.* en route to cult-classic status among buffs. He also covered crime reporting as a freelancer with a specialty in murder trials. The protagonist is a cab-driving ex-actor with a law degree (he grew up worshiping Perry Mason) but not much practice. Steve Winslow is an actor-turned-lawyer with a single client and no desire for more because it would interfere with his answering Broadway cattle calls for small roles. One day he receives an envelope with ten $1,000 bills and an anonymous note requesting his services on retainer and tries to track him down. (Hall offers a wryly amusing lesson in political-correctness fanaticism in a message to *DorothyL* because a copy editor had zealously changed every masculine reference from the third chapter onward--i.e., "When you find the client, put a tail on him or her. Don't let the client out of your sight, but don't let the client know he or she's being tailed." The author sent a letter to *Armchair Detective* and included the missive on his web site. (See Parnell Hall's commentary in **Craft Notes**.)

798. _____. *The Baxter Trust.* New York: Fine, 1988.

799. _____. *Blackmail: A Stanley Hastings Mystery Novel.* New York: Mysterious, 1994. Hastings delivers money to a blackmailer for a client, but she is not in the photos he receives, nor is she especially interested when she gets

them back.

800. _____. *Juror: A Stanley Hastings Mystery Novel.* New York: Fine, 1990. Second series protagonist Stanley Hastings takes a dim view of the justice system when he has to serve as a juror in a civil case that leads to the murder investigation of one juror.

801. _____. *The Naked Typist.* New York: Fine, 1990. Big Russ Timberlaine hires Steve Winslow when he discovers that a special gun in his collection is missing and replaced by a fake. When the real gun turns out to be a murder weapon, and the victim himself killed in Timberlaine's mansion, Winslow has to counter the prosecution's case that Winslow himself abetted the crime. Winslow has recently reappeared in short-story form ("The Witness Cat") for one of the Martin H. Greenberg-Ed Gorman edited anthologies, *Cat Crimes Goes to Court.*

802. _____. *Suspense: A Stanley Hastings Mystery Novel.* New York: Mysterious, 1998. Much satire and spoofing of the vanity of writers and the nefariousness of publishers, agents, and publicists in this Hastings outing where he is hired by Maxine Winnington, wife of a bestselling author, to find out who is harassing her. A simple case of installing Caller ID on the phone becomes a murder investigation with Hastings the prime suspect.

803. _____. *Trial: A Stanley Hastings Mystery Novel.* New York: Mysterious, 1996. Hastings finds himself working "more or less" for accident-claims attorney Richard Rosenberg. He interviews clients, real and prospective, about legitimate, and not-so-legitimate damage claims (i.e., slip-and-fall scams). Other Stanley Hastings outings (*sans* subtitles): *Actor* (1993), *Detective* (1987), *Favor* (1988), *Movie* (1995), *Murder* (1987), *Scam* (1997), *Shot* (1991), *Stranger (1989)*, and *Strangler* (1989). (See Parnell Hall's commentary in **Craft Notes** for a brief synopsis of several Hastings novels with legal elements.)

804. _____. *The Underground Man.* New York: Fine-Dutton, 1990. In this Steve Winslow caper, two potential clients ask for his services: the first is a wealthy man who wants Winslow to defend his teenage son David Thorngood, accused of killing girlfriend Kathy Wade in rough sex. Winslow refuses the proffered $100,000 fee. The next is an unclean, unshaven man named Walsh who asks questions about rewriting his will, gets his answers and leaves without a word; when Walsh is burned to death behind a dumpster in what appears to be a modern-day instance of a wilding, Winslow agrees to defend the boy accused. Another under the Haily pseudonym is *The Wrong Gun* (New York: Fine-Dutton, 1992).

Halliday, Michael, pseud. *See* Creasey, John . . . .

805. Hamill, Denis. *Three Quarters* [*3 Quarters*]. New York: Pocket, 1998. Younger brother of Pete Hamill, *New York Daily News* columnist Denis Hamill writes a tough-talking thriller about a former street cop framed for his girlfriend's murder. The plot involves a police disability retirement scam and a sleazeoid gubernatorial candidate. A murdered prostitute is found with three mint-condition quarters in her fist. Then Bobby Emmett, ex-cop framed for his lover's murder, takes over the book. What puts it here is Bobby's delightful lawyer Izzy Gleason, who is on the skids and looking for a big case to put him back in the newspapers.

806. Hamilton, Bruce [Arthur Douglas Bruce Hamilton]. *The Brighton Murder Trial: Rex v. Rhodes.* London: Boriswood, 1937. Hamilton coyly notes himself as editor of this trial's record, which "took place" in Lewes, Sussex, in the next decade. The specter of Nazism across Europe gives the book its ominous feel. James Rhodes faces a possible death sentence for the hammer-murder of a high-ranking member of a political organization. The victim, Bertram Hayward, was a rabid "Jew-baiter" and member of the National Youth Movement, a fascist organization.

807. _____. *Let Him Have Judgment.* London: Cresset, 1948. [Rpt. as *Hanging Judge*, New York: Harper, 1948]. The trial of Sir Francis Brittain, accused of the poison-murder of a strange man found in his well, later identified as Robert Teal. Brittain is known locally as John Willoughby, a device to ensure his privacy but which prompt the police to arrest him owing to his "disappearance" the night the body is discovered in Brittain-Willoughby's garden well. Best scene is during the coroner's inquest when a retired schoolteacher juryman puts the prosecutor and authorities on the spot with his sharp questions about the investigation.

808. Hamilton, Patrick. *Rope.* New York: French, 1929 ; London: Constable, 1929 [alternate title: *Rope's End.* Constable published a third edition in 1935 and reissued a reprint in 1975 from this edition]. Two friends strangle a classmate and invite the boy's family and friends to dinner; the body is stuffed in the trunk that serves as a buffet table. The play was inspired by the infamous Leopold-Loeb 1920's Chicago thrill-murder. Director Hitchcock, using seamless, ten-minute takes in his first color film in 1948, created an interesting experiment, according to Leonard Maltin's *1997 Film & Video Guide*. (The film also starred James Stewart and Farley Granger.) Hume Cronyn adapted Hamilton's play with Arthur Laurents writing the script. Universal released the 1995 version for MCA Home Video. The Leopold-Loeb murder inspired the darkly fascinating *Compulsion* (TCF/Zanuck, 1959) with Orson Welles directing and playing the defense attorney (Clarence Darrow in real-life) for the two youths (Dean Stockwell and Bradford Dillman). Richard Murphy wrote the outstanding courtroom scenes for the script. Final note: Leopold-Loeb gave further inspiration in 1992 to yet another film--a low-budget but highly praised,

moody black-and-white film directed by Tom Kalin that added text about the climate of homophobia which figured into the jury's deliberations. (*See* Levin, Meyer.)

809. Hanshew, Mary E. and Thomas W. *The Riddle of the Frozen Flame.* Garden City, NY: Doubleday, 1920. In one of the most ludicrous violations of courtroom decorum ever penned, Hamilton Cleek of Scotland Yard bursts into Mr. Justice Grainger's courtroom just as the jury is about to return its verdict against Sir Nigel Merriton in the dock. He not only interrupts proceedings but takes over the courtroom marshaling witnesses to the fore, demonstrating his sleuthing skills all the while, and in finale clutches the shoulder of the guilty person--to the appreciation of the court and barristers, who have all been stunned into silent observation of these amazing eleventh-hour proceedings because, write the authors, "English law, which, unlike American practice does not allow counsel to becloud the issue with objection and technical argument" (256).

810. Hardwick, Elizabeth. *The Simple Truth.* New York: Harcourt; London: Weidenfeld, 1955. Rudy Peck is on trial in a Chicago courtroom for murdering his pretty girlfriend Betty Jane Henderson. A pair of married courtroom watchers from different backgrounds fall into a nonsexual relationship during the trial.

811. Hardwick, Gary. *Supreme Justice.* New York: Morrow, 1999. Detroit-born Hardwick became an attorney, worked as a screenwriter and moved up to executive producer of television programs. Hardwick's first novel featured black cops and street gangs in Detroit (*Cold Medina*, 1996); then he looked at the public prosecutor's office in *Double Dead* (1997). In this one, young US Attorney Marshall Jackson must use his street-smart, hardened con twin to help him in a sensational trial handed him when Supreme Court Justice Farrel Douglas was assassinated during his commencement speech at a Detroit law school. Radical activist Daisaya Mbutu is charged with the crime.

Hare, Cyril, pseud. *See* Clark, Alfred Alexander Gordon. . . .

812. Harness, Charles L. *The Catalyst.* New York: Pocket, 1980. Researchers and corporate politicians are in desperate competition over patent rights to a new wonder drug called Trialine being developed at a high-pressure chemical plant in Connecticut; in the middle is patent attorney Paul Blandford. Late in the book, Paul deposes witnesses Ashkettles Chemical Company in the case that, except for simultaneous transcripts via the computer, seems quaint in this courtroom setting of the future because all three deponents journey to the Patents Office to be physically present at the conference table.

813. _____. *The Venetian Court.* New York: Ballantine, 1982. Sci-fier

about a patents infringement case--except that in the 21st century, it is a capital offense. Ellen Welles is defended in court by Quentin Thomas, but the judge is to be Rex ("Spider") Speyer, a ruthless jurist inclined toward the plaintiff, Universal Patents, which is suing Welles' engineering firm for its use of Fiber K, a polymer conductant that Universal Patents claims as its own manufacture.

814. Harrington, William. *Partners.* New York: Seaview, 1980. T. J. (Tommy Jo) Brookover is a Houston lawyer in Harrison County lockup facing fraud charges in the manipulation of Futures Dynamic stock and fraud in the sale of Lago Aguila allotments. Worst of all is the murder charge for causing one of her partners to kill Benjamin Mudge. Socialite lawyer Lois Farnham Hughes meets her father for lunch right after she discovers how ruthless her client really is, but her father says, "Then you'll have achieved something with her acquittal. It's nothing to congratulate yourself on, after all, when you've won acquittal for an innocent person" (340).

815. _____. *The Power.* Indianapolis: Bobbs, 1964. [Rpt. as *The Gospel of Death*, London: Joseph, 1966]. Nelson ("Chunk") Conaway is prosecuting attorney in a rural southern Ohio community when the sheriff calls and asks him for a decision in the death of a woman. Chunk makes the call to prosecute an itinerant preacher named Rob Jones on a manslaughter charge because he advised one of his tent parishioners, Mrs. Phoebe Rinard, not to take her medicine.

816. _____. *Town on Trial.* New York: Fine, 1994. A small-town murder case assumes national prominence. Marietta Rheinlander is a New York socialite accused of killing her lover, a congressman, during a weekend tryst in West Virginia at his retreat. The trial is narrated by the presiding judge across the Ohio River in a fictional county. It begins with the reading of the indictment and stays the course through the jurors' deliberations. Harrington is an attorney, author of more than a dozen novels, a licensed pilot, and a resident of Cos Cob, Connecticut.

817. _____. *Trial.* New York: McKay; London: Barrie, 1970. A pair of elderly Italian immigrants, the Rovigos, are shot in their small Ma-and-Pa store in Cleveland, Ohio, by an armed robber; the wife dies, and young Johnny Hall is sentenced to death in a brief newspaper account and single-chapter summary of the trial itself. The real issue, however, is in the second half of the novel as the homosexual relationship and subsequent scandal of two police officers involved in the investigation is exposed to the newspapers. Veteran cop Lieutenant Clement Yacobucci tearfully confesses to his nonplused wife the truth of being a "fairy" and the lover of homicide captain of detectives, Paul Chichester.

818. _____. *Which the Justice, Which the Thief.* Indianapolis: Bobbs, 1963. London: Joseph, 1965. Harrington's novel is a gem. Ostensibly narrated

by a retired 92-year-old judge who presided for half a century in a small court on the Ohio River, it details one memorable case involving an armed robbery of a jewelry store by a man and his woman companion. But *State of Ohio vs. Roger Louis* (and *v. Ruth Gordon*) is not so memorable for its circumstances but for the judge's shrewd and canny observations on justice and the people involved in it--lawyers, judges, their clients and defendants, the families and courtroom observers that all together make up what we deem "justice"--and for his matter-of-fact verisimilitude of the case in its entirety from *voir dire* through verdict. We do not sympathize with either defendant, but when prosecutor Baumgartner interrogates Gordon about her sexual history, we see what justice in the courtroom really leaves out of the equation.

819. Harris, Elmer. *Johnny Belinda.* New York: Dramatists, 1940. Harris' three-act play is set on an island south of Newfoundland at the turn of the century. Deaf Belinda McDonald, referred to as the Dummy and later as an "immoral woman," is on trial in the final act for murdering Locky McCormick in revenge because, the Crown argues, he had exposed her illicit relationship to Dr. Jack Davidson.

820. Harris, Frank. *The Bomb.* Introd. John Dos Passos. New York: Kennerley, 1909; Chicago: U of Chicago P, 1963. The Chicago Haymarket Square Riot of 1886. The opening sentence: "My name is Rudolph Schnaubelt. I threw the bomb which killed eight policemen and wounded sixty in Chicago in 1886" (1). Harris' foreword in 1909 claims to "take all the facts just as they occurred" (5-6), but one must remember that this is Frank Harris, one of the greatest self-promoters in literature who, like Fitzgerald's Gatsby, created himself out of some Platonic ideal. He was American, then British, by turns, knew everyone who was anyone in literature--shook Walt Whitman's hand after a lecture (he said), visited Karl Marx (and was praised by the great man for his excellent German--he said), and was a friend and fellow socialist of Shaw, the witty Wilde and the serious Havelock Ellis. His real name is (possibly) James Thomas Harris and he was born in Galway, maybe, in 1856. Journalist, writer, huckster, moneygrubber, liar, seducer, *arriviste*, and man about town, any number of towns, he led one of the most exciting lives ever lived at any time. (Sidenote: When Illinois Governor John P. Altgeld heroically pardoned the two surviving anarchists, as yet unhanged after the trials, his political career was ruined.)

821. Harris, John. *Light Cavalry Action.* London: Hutchinson; New York: Morrow, 1967. A 20-year-old cavalry charge is refought in the law courts. Lieutenant-General Henry Prideaux, D. S. O., brings a libel action against his former subordinate officer, Major George Higgins. In 1919 British troops attacked Bolshevik forces in the Civil War in South Russia. The last charge of British horse cavalry at Dankoi, near Nikolovssk, is one of the Army's glorious feats. Higgins published a letter defaming his former superior officer alleging

that "General Prideaux (or Colonel Prideaux as he was then) was noticeably not among those present when he was wanted" (30).

822. Harris, John Norman. *The Weird World of Wes Beattie.* New York: Harper, 1963. London: Faber, 1964. Shy, immature Wes Beattie is charged with murdering his uncle Edgar, and the Toronto Crown Attorney's Office is claiming he did it for his inheritance. Pugnacious lawyer Sidney Grant becomes involved in what looks like an open-and-shut case against the boy, who is claiming some "mystery gang" is framing him in a conspiracy.

823. Harris, Larry M. *The Pickled Poodles: A Novel Based on the Characters Created by Craig Rice.* New York: Random, 1960. Jason Beck is an idolized television personality being blackmailed, but he tells Malone that the blackmail, ongoing for three years before he discover it, is being committed by a dead man. The poodles of the title are drunk and somehow an important clue. Harris brings back the rest of the cast in this homage, including Captain Daniel von Flanagan of Homicide, Max Hook, gambling czar, and Joe the Angel.

824. Harris, Richard. *Honor Bound.* New York: St. Martin's, 1982. A New York lawyer seeks justice outside the courtroom to bring justice in the shooting death of his friend.

825. Hart, Frances Noyes. *The Bellamy Trial.* Garden City, NY: Doubleday; London: Heinemann, 1927. Long Island socialites Stephen Bellamy and Susan (Mrs. Patrick) Ives are adulterous lovers on trial for eight days in Judge Carver's courtroom, both accused of murdering Madeleine, Bellamy's wife, when she caught them in bed, but their testimonies from the stand differ markedly. Hart and collaborator Frank E. Carstarphen adapted for the stage in a three-act play (French, 1932). Stilted but still exciting right from the opening courtroom gossip of spectators and reporters.

826. Harte, Bret. *Gabriel Conroy.* Hartford, CT: American; London: Warner, 1876; Boston: Houghton, 1882. Western regionalist Harte's tale of a gentle giant of a man, who began as a survivor of an emigrant party in the snowbound Sierras. In Book 7, Conroy is on trial for murder in One Horse Gulch. His childhood companion, Philip Ashley, now a San Francisco lawyer calling himself Arthur Poinsett, returns to help Mr. Maxwell with Conroy's defense. Then a familiar Harte character appears to help out the prosecution: Colonel Starbottle, that rhetorically splendid Southerner from Siskiyou, lavishes his small learning upon the jury in several pages to prove that Victor Ramirez was murdered by a knife wielded by the defendant over a claim. In fact, Conroy's own absent wife also appears to testify for Gabriel. Various impostures are exposed or already explained concerning the fraud practiced on Ramirez so that the charge is officially dropped in a *nolle prosequi.*

827. Hartzmark, Gini. *Bitter Business.* New York: Fawcett, 1995. Hartzmark has attended and holds degrees from the law and business schools at the University of Chicago, been an economics writer for textbooks in addition to her journalism for the big Chicago papers, the *Tribune* and *Sun-Times.* She is currently an Arizonan. Her series character is Katharine Anne Prescott ("Kate") Milholland, lawyer and heiress of a prominent but troubled Chicago family, works in the mergers and acquisitions department of one of Chicago's "most aggressive" law firms. She calls it "the locker room of the profession," but Kate holds her own in the male-dominated field of corporate law and manages to escape most of her family's demands. As much sleuth as lawyer, Kate is a smart, tough lawyer who will take chances for her clients. The rap on her creator is that sometimes fissures show in the structures--bad characters tend to be too bad and in diverting the arrows of guilt away from the guilty parties, she sometimes makes it too obvious whodunit.

In this third Kate Milholland outing, Kate agrees to a dying colleague's request to represent the Cavanaugh family business. But the family behind Superior Plating & Specialty Chemical Company is at odds with one another. Lydia, the youngest daughter and a head case among dysfunctional siblings, threatens to sell her share of the business and the elder daughter dies suddenly and mysteriously. Kate has to find the killer.

828. _____. *Dead Certain.* New York: Fawcett, 2000. Milholland versus a greedy health-care corporation.

829. _____. *Fatal Reaction.* New York: Ivy, 1992. The author herself annotates this one in the July 1998 (No. 47) *Murder on the Internet*: "Azor Pharmaceuticals [see *Principal Defense* below] is going broke searching for a new miracle drug, and a deal with Tokyo-based Takisawa Corp. is its only hope to stay in business. When the lead lawyer on the negotiation for Azor is found murdered, Kate Millholland finds herself drafted as the dead man's reluctant replacement. . . . [Kate] struggles to not just make the deal that will save the company, but also to maintain the perilously fine line she's drawn between her personal and professional relationships." A standard device for Millholland's adventures is uncovering secret affairs, lethal chemicals, and discovering the cold-blooded killer.

830. _____. *Final Option.* New York: Ivy , 1994. "Black" Bart Hexter, one of Chicago's most powerful and ferocious players in the futures market, is found dead behind the wheel of his Rolls Royce with two bullets in his head. Despite numerous candidates for the prime-suspect position, including wife, children, mistresses, employees, and clients, Kate herself is suspected on flimsy evidence.

831. _____. *Principal Defense.* New York: Ivy, 1992. Hartzmark's first novel garnered an Edgar nomination. Kate represents Azor Pharmaceuticals, a

multimillion-dollar high-tech company founded by her sometime lover, Stephen Azorini. When Azorini's niece Gretchen is found raped and murdered, corporate raider Edgar Eichel moves in for a hostile takeover bid, forcing Kate to move fast to find Gretchen's killer before Stephen's company is sandbagged by Eichel; moreover, complicating matters is Joey Azorini, a violent older brother who, unlike his respectable brother the doctor, is still mobbed up.

832. _____. *Rough Trade.* New York: Ivy, 1999. Millholland is called to the home of Beau Rendell in her capacity as deal lawyer because the owner of the Milwaukee Monarchs is under pressure to relocate to LA; the team is wracked by problems of insubordination among players, bad coaching, and financial problems. His sudden puts son Jeff on the spot because of a violent argument between father and son about moving the team.

833. Haseloff, Cynthia. *The Kiowa Verdict.* New York: Simon, 1999. Haseloff, a writer of western novels, is a descendent of a woman held captive by Indians. Her story is based on the historical trials of two Indian leaders, Satanta and Adoltay, who led raiding parties of Kiowa Indians in the Southwest that killed a group of teamsters and were brought to trial on separate days in Texas in 1871. They were defended by a former Indian fighter S. W. T. Lanham, whose trial motions alone survived.

834. Hatfield, Kate. *Drowning in Honey.* London: Transworld, 1995; New York: St. Martin's, 1996. Pampered housewife Melissa Wraxall is summoned for jury duty and shocked out of her complacency as she detects unnerving similarities in the case being tried of a man named Michael Beechan, who came home from work, fed his children, put them to bed and stabbed his spoiled wife Penelope in the chest seven times.

835. Hawkins, Dean. *In Memory of Murder.* New York: Caxton, 1939. Gage & Gage comprises Porter Gage and uncle, Judge Gage, in a small Southern town. The nephew takes on a case for the prominent Lyell family. Cora Lee Bethany is murdered after a country club dance and clues are left behind at reclusive Lucy Lou Lyell's estate.

836. Hawley, Cameron. *Cash McCall.* Boston: Houghton, 1955. Maude Kennard is the Assistant Manager of Hotel Ivanhoe in Philadephia, where entrepreneur Cash McCall maintains a suite and is believed to be the real owner. She goes to family friend and Main Line lawyer "Judge" Torrant for information about him that ultimately leads to a love interest between her and the mysterious millionaire. The lawyer, a bore with a pedigree and exclusive club membership, finds himself trying to prove conspiracy charges against Will Atherson and his battery of lawyers from Winston Conway, top firm employed by McCall's enemies.

837. Hawthorne, Nathaniel. *The Scarlet Letter.* Boston: Houghton, 1900. Hawthorne finished his masterpiece on 4 February 1850. The book opens with the sentence already passed upon Hester Prynne as she stands in public view upon the pillory scaffolding before the town's dignitaries and the gossiping rabble alike for the immorality all know well. Hawthorne disdains comment upon the severity of "the Puritanic code of law" (72), but Hester's fate could have been much worse in reality.

838. Hayes, Al. *The Gingerbread Man.* (US/PolyGram, 1999). Hayes' script of the story by John Grisham captures the paranoia that has become Grisham's signature. Robert Altman's film directs Kenneth Branagh as hotshot Savannah lawyer Rick Magruder, Embeth Davidtz, as the enchantress who seduces him with a story about a deranged father stalking her (played with facial expressions rather than words by the brilliant Robert Duvall) and Robert Downey, Jr. as Magruder's colorful investigator.

839. Hayes, Joseph. *The Deep End.* New York: Viking, 1967. Lawyer Adam Wyatt takes advantage of his English wife's absence to have a fling with a blonde pickup after taking in a film; then he discovers that she and her demented husband Wilby intend blackmail for his sexual romp, or they'll accuse him of raping her. Wyatt pays the $3,000 but the couple want more.

840. Healy, J. F. [Jeremiah F.]. *The Only Good Lawyer.* New York: Pocket, 1998. Healy is a Rutgers and Harvard law grad who spent 18 years as a professor at the New England School of Law. He began a mystery-writing career in 1984 with *Blunt Darts*, highly praised by the *New York Times* and has received almost a dozen Shamus nominations for his series about private eye John Francis Cuddy, Boston private eye, in the hardboiled tradition of Lew Archer. He is currently the North American Vice President of the International Association of Crime Writers.

Cuddy gets involved with lawyers here. First, the one who hires him to seek out a missing alibi for a racist client whose wife is divorcing him and whose wife's black lawyer winds up shot dead beside his BMW on a deserted road. Was the drunken woman passed out in the seat of the car the racist's wife? Was dead lawyer Woodrow Wilson Gant, famed for a *Boogie Nights*'-sized endowment and appetite for white women, the victim of a hate crime? Cuddy does not think so, but he cannot locate the alibi, a local Southie barfly who goes by the name Mickey Mantle.

841. Healey, Jeremiah. *The Stalking of Sheila Dunne.* New York: St. Martin's, 1998. Criminal defense attorney Sheila Quinn has a problem client, Arthur Ketterson IV, out on bail on a murder charge for strangling Jessica Giordano, the woman he was seeing; now he appears obsessed with Quinn to the point of stalking her. She has personal problems to go with him: her father is dying in a nursing home, the trial judge is harassing her, and a new lover has

entered her life.

842. Hegarty, Frances. Frances Fyfield, pseud. *Blind Date.* Chatham, Kent: Mackays; London: Bantam, 1998. Born in Derbyshire, Hegarty graduated *cum laude* from the University of Newcastle upon Tyne and uses her mother's name for the Helen West novels. Fyfield, like Sarah Fortune, one of her two solicitors, has worked for the British equivalent of a white-shoe firm, and like West, the other, has worked for the Crown Prosecution Service since 1975. Having begun her West series in 1988, she won the Silver Dagger Award for her third book featuring her Crown Prosecutor, who works out of her Mayfield office. Even beyond what legal expertise Fyfield's twenty years' experience in criminal law has given her, she is praised widely for her deftly acute psychological portraits of her homicidal and disturbed characters. Novels have been printed under her real name and two aliases. Some include *Deep Sleep* (New York: Pocket, 1991, a Silver Dagger winner); *Half Light* (London: Penguin; New York: Pocket, 1993), *The Playroom* (Pocket, 1991); *Let's Dance* (New York: Viking, 1995); and *Trial by Fire* (London: Heinemann, 1990). This novel earned both Edgar and Agatha Award nominations, as well as being a Rumpole Award winner, although it features no series character. The plucky resilience of the female protagonist and the cynicism of her policeman collaborator is a variation on a theme in the on-again, off-again relationship between series sleuths Helen West and Geoffrey Bailey--the boilerplate of Fyfield novels--a pair less volatile than American Tanenbaum's starcrossed lovers (Karp and Ciampi) but much more likeable.

Elisabeth Kennedy, sister of a murdered woman, devises a ruse to trap the murderer using a dating service, but the case is thrown out of court on the grounds of entrapment and she herself is badly scarred emotionally and physically by her attacker. (*See* Ms. Hegarty's commentary in **Craft Notes**.)

843. _____. *A Clear Conscience.* London: Bantam; New York: Pantheon-Random, 1994. As West and Bailey seek an equilibrium point in their own relationship, the Crown's case of a brother's murder, followed by an abusive husband's violent death from a bayonet thrust, puts West squarely into the psychologically tormented world of Cath Boyce, sister and wife of the dead men, victim of a sordid life of official neglect, incest, and beatings.

844. _____. *Not That Kind of Place.* New York: Pocket, 1990. West and Bailey are deepening their friendship begun in *A Question of Guilt* by a quiet sojourn in Branston village; however, murder intrudes when a hastily buried body is partially dug up by a fox in the woods. The prime suspect is local teacher Antony Sumner, who had been having an affair with the married woman and admits that when they parted in anger, he had struck her with his walking stick.

845. _____. *Perfectly Pure and Good.* London: Heineman, 1989; New

York: Pocket, 1990; Pantheon-Random, 1994. Beautiful, auburn-haired Sarah Fortune provides a body for men to lust for and then torture. She is a maverick lawyer at a London law firm where she will never make partner because she is too independent and is always assigned the losers, castoffs and duffers related to clients of the firm. In this, one of her most gothic tales of a twisted family, she is sent to a seacoast village to settle the Pardoe family litigation among quarrelsome siblings and a demented matriarch ("Mouse") and to effect a gentle separation between her and Malcolm, Matthewson's stepson, who saved her life in a previous novel. She meets Julian, an intense physician, a neurotic Edward a teenager Joanna in a place where her attacker drowned and his abused wife committed suicide.

846. _____. *A Question of Guilt.* London: Heinemann; New York: Pocket, 1988. West and Det. Superintendent Bailey combine to bring a conviction to a pair of murderers when a murderously single-minded, 46-year-old widow arranges for the killing of her solicitor's wife. The case against the actual killer is easy: we know who, how, and why on page 7. Stanislaus Jaskowski is coldblooded Eileen Cartwright's pawn in her plot to free Jim Bernard by killing wife Sylvia, but getting the widow will not be easy, and her demented wrath turns toward West as the case against her is being made.

847. _____. *Shadow Play.* London: Bantam; New York: Pantheon-Random, 1993. Petty criminal Logo is a nuisance to West but a figure of evil for the daughter who flees him. Also missing are case files against drunken drivers from West's office and both strands of the plot point to 19-year-old office clerk Rose Darvey, whose present is an attempt to find love and escape the past of an obsessively murderous father's incestuous love. The West-Bailey relationship is on the rocks on this novel.

848. _____. *Shadows on the Mirror.* London: Heinemann, 1989; New York: Pocket, 1991. Sarah returns sent to Merton-on-Sea where the body of a woman washes ashore; she is the wife of Charles Tysall, a man investigated by the Crown Prosecution Service for his insider trading and fraudulent activities, but as she will learn, he is also a man with a penchant for carving up and scarring the faces of redheads who displease him.

849. _____. *Staring at the Light.* London: Penguin, 1999; New York: Viking, 2000. Fyfield is the equal of Houstonian David L. Lindsey when it comes to the portrayal of aberrant characters but especially strong, suffering female characters. It begins with Sarah Fortune defending eccentric artist Cannon Smith, who has a sideline in illegal explosives and a vicious twin brother. She faces off in court against Fyfield's other series lawyer, Helen West, in a suit to confiscate Smith's house. This time, it is in a dentist's chair that she will experience horror at the hands of sometime lover William Davenport.

850. _____. *Undercurrents.* London and New York: Viking, 2001. Shy American Henry Evans met and fell in love with Francesca Chisholm while hiking in India ten years prior. He returns to London to seek her out and engages a solicitor, who tells him that she is still in prison for having confessed to, and been convicted of, the murder of her 5-year-old son.

851. _____. *Without Consent.* London: Penguin, 1996; New York: Viking-Penguin, 1997. Fyfield's prologues are deep incursions into psyches as well as harbingers of things to come. Rape in the legal, emotional, and psychological senses conjoin in shifting points of view that alternate rape victims with a killer's ratiocination and Bailey's speaking to West about a rape scenario involving a seventeen-year-old. The storyline commences with the hunt for the rapist-killer and the suspicious attention directed Bailey's womanizing best friend and fellow police officer, Detective Sgt. Ryan.

852. Hellman, Lillian. *The Children's Hour.* Four plays by Lillian Hellman. Introd. Lillian Hellman. New York: Modern Library, 1942. Hellman's and Dashiell Hammett's troubles in the heyday of McCarthyism are part of the public record. Hammett refused to identify donors to the bail bond fund of the Civil Rights Congress and went to jail in 1951. Hellman called that "sad, comic, miserable time in our nation's history" (*That Scoundrel Time*, 1976, 37). Her first big success was *The Children's Hour* (1934) about a libel suit brought by Karen Wright and Martha Dobie, owners of a private school for girls, against a woman named Tilford because her grandchild had accused them of having what Judge Potter called "sinful sexual knowledge of one another" (69).

853. Henry, Diane, and Nicholas Horrock. *Blood Red, Snow White.* Boston: Little, 1992. The writers, a husband-and-wife team from Virginia, have journalistic backgrounds. Alec Anton, successful corporate lawyer for a Wall-Street firm, falls for his divorced blonde neighbor, Lee Hastings, whose son is missing. But Anton soon discovers connections between the woman's son and the money-laundering case he is working on.

854. Hensley, Joe L. *Color Him Guilty.* New York: Walker, 1987. Hensley is a former 5th Judicial Circuit Judge and past President of the Indiana Judges Association. He retired in 1989. Educated at Indiana University, Hensley's law experience is wide: from private practice through the county prosecutor's office to a one-term stint as Indiana legislator before his circuit court responsibilities. Hensley the writer has an interesting series character in the crusading Don Robak who, despite the law practice in his Midwestern town (fictional Bington, Indiana), is really a private eye out of the Ross Macdonald mold. There is the same taciturn, self-effacing (and penurious) hero, the same physical attractions to gorgeous women that imply but never achieve consummation, and the same kinds of evil characters Lew Archer found himself grappling with in sunny California. What Robak's creator lacks, however, is the muscular clarity and

grace of Macdonald as he puts his character through his paces. What he does possess that makes him almost unique is the relentless exposure of small-town vice and criminality. He tears the cover off hypocrisy better than any *noir*ist around. In 1994, Hensley introduced in *Grim City* a second character and legal protagonist in Jim Carlos Singer of Grimsley City, Kentucky, a Mexican-American, occasional parole officer and judicial assistant.

Hensley's note tells the reader that he first wrote and published this story as the *Color of Hate* in 1960 (New York: Ace, 1960) and has updated it here without changing the essentials. A black man is accused of the rape-murder of a white woman, and it is Sam April's job to get the man a fair trial in a town seething with racial hatred.

855. _____. *Deliver Us to Evil.* Garden City, NY: Doubleday, 1971. Attorney Robak has a week to save the life of Tague Robbins, scheduled to die for killing his wife Janet. Her numerous affairs provided enough motive and no one in town including the DA seems to believe, or care, he was framed.

856. _____. *Fort's Law.* Garden City, NY: Doubleday-Crime Club, 1987. John ("Jack") Fort is an older, slightly rumpled version of Robak. He and partner Abe Sapenstein work out of a shotgun office overlooking the Ohio River in Scannelsville, Indiana. Fort's client is local rowdie, Jesse deAlter, an abusive husband and drug pusher accused of a class B felony dope charge, but the ambitious DA is pushing for a conviction on the murder charge of the aunt. The murder was presumably motivated by the hard-drinking aunt's will and public knowledge that she doted on her nephew.

857. _____. *Grim City.* New York: St. Martin's, 1994. Grimsley, City Kentucky, is a bitter home to Jim Carlos Singer, whose law practice is unable to get off the ground; his own father was a hit-and-run killing, never solved, and he had to take a job as parole officer and judicial assistant to make his rent. Lately, threatening letters have been pouring in just as he finds himself in the middle of a sensational trial. Shirley Kentner fascinates him and like him, she is a pariah in town, but could she be guilty of the torture-murder of her older husband?

858. _____. *A Killing in Gold.* Garden City, NY: Doubleday, 1978. Robak gets involved in the murder of a friend's uncle by way of a counterfeit collection of territorial coins.

859. _____. *Legislative Body.* Garden City, NY: Doubleday, 1972. Freshman legislator Robak is spending time in Capitol City investigating the death of a complex and devious colleague named Sloan Link, dead of defenestration.

860. _____, and Guy M. Townsend. *Loose Coins.* New York: St. Martin's, 1998. Lawyer Al Sears is a recovering alcoholic suspended from practicing law,

with a marriage in tatters and no income, so he does private investigative work as a clerk in a rare coin shop. Someone from his past makes an attempt on his life.

861. _____. *Minor Murders.* Garden City, NY: Doubleday, 1979. Cheryl Rettner is a 16-year-old Lolita who is accused of the knife-murders of her foster parents; complicating Robak's defense, and possibly his political future, is a religious fringe group led by a charismatic leader, who had ties to the slain Davidsons and is making his presence felt for reasons Robak will discover.

862. _____. *Outcasts.* Garden City, NY: Doubleday, 1981. Robak goes to Avalon to defend his cousin Sam Hunter, an ex-cop on trial for the murder of Sheila Wyman, a woman of dubious reputation found dead in the Grand Hotel.

863. _____. *The Poison Summer.* Garden City, NY: Doubleday, 1974. Mike Wright takes over the sensational Kate Powell defense when his father dies suddenly. She is on trial for the poison-murder of her rich, aging industrialist husband.

864. _____. *Rivertown Risk.* Garden City, NY: Doubleday, 1977. Amos Walker has been indicted for murdering his younger wife with a blunt instrument, and Judge Robak presides over the trial of a man he once admired; its outcome could affect his re-election.

865. _____. *Robak's Cross.* Garden City, NY: Doubleday-Crime Club, 1985. Robak is opposing hated courtroom enemy Herman Leaks, Bington county prosecutor, in a case of murder involving a husband, whom he once cuckolded, on trial for using a .38 derringer to end his faithless wife's life.

866. _____. *Robak's Fire.* Garden City, NY: Doubleday, 1986. Robak is summoned to Drewville near the Ohio border to assist his partners Jake and Sam in their hard-going case involving a death-benefits lawsuit over a pair of suspicious fires involving local businessman Avery Benjamin, who had a suspicious shopping-center fire occur during construction and was later burned to death at home. The town's citizenry from judge to jurors seem to be in collusion against the lawyers, who are acting for the insurance companies. The witnesses for Robak's side have disappeared. The first wife of Benjamin says that she saw her husband alive.

867. _____. *Robak's Firm.* New York: Garden City, NY: Doubleday, 1987. A collection of 15 short stories in which 3 feature Cannert, an old man dying of cancer bent on revenge ("Tourist," "Searcher," and "Finder"). "Trial," the second story, is among the best--about a pair of shrewd old lawyers on opposite sides of the table, who conspire to effect justice by outmaneuvering the legal machinery during a trial involving a murder among poker players.

868. _____. *Robak's Run.* New York: Doubleday, 1990. Robak draws Stanley Willetts, accused of using a sledge hammer on his wife's face. Willetts claims he is innocent and that his influential mother-in-law is railroading him.

869. _____. *Robak's Witch.* New York: St. Martin's, 1997. Robak is brought in to assist the defense in a case involving an herbalist rumored to be a follower of the pagan Wiccan faith; she is accused of poisoning her nephew and niece. Robak discovers that the victims had been tied to a messianic preacher with a sordid past and whose church has already condemned his client to death.

870. _____. *Song of Corpus Juris.* Garden City, NY: Doubleday, 1974. Robak has beautiful, sexy Mary Ann Moffat as a client who is accused of manslaughter in the shooting death of a political hanger-on of her former stepfather, town boss Joe Watts. Mary Ann, who blacked out in the struggle for the gun after taking a wild shot at Watts, believes Watts arranged to kill her mother in a car crash. Soon, Robak discovers how long a reach his political nemesis has as the pressure is put to him from all directions to get out of this case and the hints are not subtle: his office is ransacked and he is ordered to stand trial on trumped-up assault charges.

871. Herbert, A. P. [Alan Patrick]. *Holy Deadlock.* London: Methuen; Garden City, NY: Doubleday, 1934. A serio-comic novel about a man and wife who want, amicably, to divorce. John Adam is informed via telegraph by wife Mary (a stereotype of the flapper or loose woman that John Galsworthy leers at in his saga). The serious business is the requisite adultery required by British divorce law, a law that led to hundreds of phony adulterous liaisons in seedy Brighton hotels with a photographer on hand to capture the straying spouse *in flagrante delicto* to please the court's definition of a single spouse's unfaithfulness. John, amiably trying to accommodate his wife's desire to marry new beau Martin Seal because he himself wants to marry a school teacher, stages a mock seduction with a prostitute with measles. Mary is herself on the witness stand later for allowing "intimacies" in her hotel room with Martin but she too fails to convince the presiding jurist.

872. _____. *Uncommon Law.* Garden City, NY: Doubleday, 1933. London: Methuen, 1935. Hailey's compendium of bizarre law cases before the House of Lords is intended as "frolics" in jurisprudence with an attempt to correct as well as to entertain, but the comedic factor predominates as one aberrant opinion after another is rendered by characters that step from a Fielding or Smollett novel: Lord Lick, Lord Arrowroot, Lord Mildew, Lord Flake, Lord Sheep, etc. offer opinions before justices like Justice Wool, Justice Foot, etc. Sir Ethelred Rutt, KC, is a staple figure in many cases like *Rex v. Bloggs*, in which a boatman is charged with failing to send his children to school.

873. Herrick, Robert. *Waste.* New York: Harcourt, 1924. Sprawling story of an idealistic engineer who testifies at a Congressional hearing against the Great Western Power Company, but the interesting sections are fueled by the anti-Communism (Bolshevism) of the day. In a prevision of the McCarthy hearings of the fifties, intellectuals and foreigners are persecuted while reckless profiteering goes unchecked. Protagonist Jarvis Thornton reels forth mouth-filling, teary sentiments on every page. Lambasting the "radiating posterity," he cries over feckless Americans and society as "[a] mad world, and a squalid world, with its bare bones exposed indecently in the mud" (357).

874. Herrington, Rowdy. *A Murder of Crows.* Written and directed by Harrington for Franchise Pictures, and Sterling Home Entertainment allowed it to escape in 1998. The film stars Cuba Gooding, Jr., who produced and plays opposite Tom Berenger (Det. Cliff Dubose) as Lawton Russell, a successful lawyer who develops a conscience in mid-trial defending a rich lowlife played by Eric Stoltz and ends up disbarred. Down and out in Key West as a fishing guide, he meets a strange client calling himself Christopher Marlowe who "dies" and leaves a manuscript with him that Russell-Gooding promptly passes off as his own and sends to a publishing house, where it promptly becomes a bestseller. Then an inscribed copy of the book is sent to the New Orleans homicide cop, who promptly discovers that the five dead lawyers in the novel equate to five dead lawyers in reality, all murdered in exactly the ways described in the novel. Moviegoers should utter a resounding Triple-I objection to films like this that stagger from the implausible through the impossible to the inept.

875. Hesky, Olga. *Life Sentence.* Garden City, NY: Doubleday, 1972. The novel opens with John Waggoner pleading not guilty to a charge of murdering his father-in-law. Told in flashback and digression from the year previous when his wife Agnes dies, we see a bland clerk who has been a cipher all his life but used to order at work and home come unraveled when he has to fend for himself and care for his aged in-law.

876. Hichens, Robert. *The Paradine Case.* London: Benn; Garden City, NY: Doubleday, 1934. This is the one everybody leaves off the Hitchcock retrospective--for good reason. "This is the wordiest script since the death of Edmund Burke," wrote James Agee upon its release in 1947. Gregory Peck plays the barrister who falls in love with his client, a guilty woman. Production tyrant David O. Selznick was rewriting dialogue and sending it to the actors daily before the shooting. Hitchcock, it is alleged, was so fed up with Selznick's bullying by the man who had lured him from England that he took naps during the shooting. The acting by Peck and Alida Valli, Charles Laughton and Ethel Barrymore gives the stodgy script "gleaming treatment," avers *Halliwell's Film Guide* (779).

877. Higgins, George V. *At End of Day.* New York: Harcourt, 2000. Boston

College graduate of its law school, Higgins was an attorney and former prosecutor who knew both sides of the courtroom law well; his death in 2000 shortly after completing *At End of Day* is a loss for American literature as well as for the legal thriller. He formerly worked as an assistant attorney general for the Commonwealth before he ever made a literary splash with the gritty crime novel *The Friends of Eddie Coyle* (Knopf, 1971). The film two years later, directed by Peter Yates and starring Robert Mitchum as the ageing thug Coyle, was both a critical and popular success. Higgins carved his niche then held it with rhythmically biting dialogue, sometimes in the melodic Irish-American cadences of a Southie, sometimes in the urbane tones of a silver-tongued lawyer, despite profanity sometimes so banally brutal that it sounds like eavesdropping in a roomful of Tourette's Syndrome victims. But his Boston wiseguys, lawyers, and lowlifes reflect the broken rhythms and patois of the streets, an obscenely lyrical melody as it has not been heard since James M. Cain. Whether a Jerry ("Digger") Doherty or a Jerry Kennedy, these sound like real people and this is unquestionably our American tongue. At his death, Higgins had published more than 20 novels with varying amounts of courtroom-versus-street action. Having cut his teeth on literature first at Stanford with an M.A., he returns to his former love before law practice by teaching creative writing at Boston University. A recent non-legal work is *The Agent* (Harcourt, 1999) with the usual consummately disguised plotting and black belt in dialogue. Richard Dyer of the *Boston Globe* labels its plot "a screed against greed" as it exposes the cutthroat, sleazy world of sports agents.

878. _____. *Bomber's Law.* New York: Holt, 1993. The last novel by a great American writer features a familiar theme: a hunt to bring two crime kingpins to justice. Nicholas ("Frogman") Cistaro and his partner Arthur Mckeon a.k.a. McKeach are the center of an investigation by members of law enforcement, FBI, and the Boston US Attorney's Office.

879. _____. *A Change of Gravity.* New York: Holt, 1997. The Grand Jury of Massachusetts is seeking an indictment of the former chair of the State House Ways and Means Committee, although Daniel Hilliard has been out of state politics since 1984, driven from office by the scandal of marital infidelities. As Hilliard and Ambrose Merrion--his former campaign manager--talk, we are amazed to realize that this corrupt pol and his foul-mouthed factotum are better in some ways than the faceless bureaucracy attempting to bring them to justice.

880. _____. *A Choice of Enemies.* New York: Knopf; London: Secker, 1984. The plot begins with the Middlesex Grand Jury trial of Jean Dussault indicted on four counts of extortion but centers around the netherworld of Massachusetts political fund-raising and favor-fixing because what Dussault could say about labor racketeering could go right to the Speaker's doorstep.

881. _____. *A City on a Hill.* New York: Knopf; London: Secker, 1975.

Whores, lawyers, and lobbyists in Washington, DC, in the final year of the Nixon Administration collapse.

882. _____. *Defending Billy Ryan: A Jerry Kennedy Novel.* New York: Holt, 1992. The Jerry Kennedy novels are mainstream legal thrillers all. They have the assorted colorful lowlifes that Jerry defends but avoid the concentration of macho swagger of thug life of his earlier novels and the gentrified criminality of his Boston/Washington politicos. Even as Jerry's reputation grows, he cannot peel off the criminal barnacles that attach themselves to his caseload, and there are always interesting judges and prosecutors gunning for him as he battles for his largely worthless clientele. In this third Kennedy tale, Jerry is the only lawyer in Boston willing to act as defense counsel in the contract-fixing trial of a sleazy Commissioner of Public Works.

883. _____. *Dreamland.* Boston: Little; London: Secker, 1977. A very different look from Higgins. Compton Cable is the narrator--a staid, middle-aged, by-the-book lawyer working for the firm founded by his grandfather on Beacon Street and built up by his father. His mundane narrative duly records his partnership date in Wills, Cable, when and how many points he is awarded, etc., but in the main it is a record of facts and assumptions about his father that Compton does not want to refute but which the narrative voice ultimately does by exposing facts that do not jibe with the veneer of his life. For one, his father's OSS experiences as the control in a spy operation quite possibly make his Harvard companion Andrew a stepbrother, which could explain his father's supporting Andrew; further, Compton's wife's confronts him with her knowledge of his adultery with Dierdre, Andrew's future wife, and rocks the narrator's foundation of respectability even more.

884. _____. *Imposters.* New York: Holt; London: Deutsch, 1986. Billy Taves, the DA of Bristol County, drives 60 miles to see Mark Baldwin, an ex-reporter now wealthy publisher. Taves, a pol with a Portugese constituency, and Waspish Baldwin had once helped each other out in their professional capacities but now they need each other again to prevent a vigilante murderer from blowing the lid off an old scandal involving a homosexual killing that implicates both men. Joe Logan is awaiting trial for murdering Thomas Brutus, a man who had killed his wife and son. He does not believe, in Taves' words to Baldwin in the publisher's office, that "the system, which of course is guys like [him] . . . doesn't punish killers even when it knows who they are" (9). Taves wants Baldwin to send a reporter to find out what Joe Logan will say about their past guilt.

885. _____. *The Judgment of Deke Hunter.* Boston: Little; London: Secker, 1976. Borderline legal thriller but lawyers and a criminal court case give it the nod. Massachusetts State Police Corporal Deke Hunter works for Commonwealth Assistant DA Richard Shanley as an investigating officer; his

current case is an armed robbery one in which all but one of the villains are easily bagged right after the crime. Teddy Donnelly, however, requires more circumstantial evidence despite his trademark .45 in his fist inn the bank's film of the robbery.

886. _____. *Kennedy for the Defense.* New York: Knopf; London: Secker, 1980. "I have a client named Teddy Franklin. Teddy Franklin is a car thief" (1), so laconic an opening belies the colorful characters that sleazy Boston lawyer Jerry Kennedy ("not related to the bastards," he says (11), entertains in his office. Besides "Cadillac" Teddy, other cases include Emerson Teller and Donald French, respectively for oral sodomy and murder of a federal agent.

887. _____. *The Mandeville Talent.* New York: Holt, 1991. Corporate lawyer Joe Carey, bored with his high-paid career, agrees to relocate from Manhattan to a small town in Massachusetts to assist his wife's academic career at Mt. Holyoke. He digs into the background of her grandfather's suicide twenty years earlier. What he uncovers is a motive for murder that might explain his falling on his shotgun in the office of his bank: he had borrowed $500,000 to buy property from an unknown source. These shadowy mortgagers lay hidden beneath a layer of lawyers that Joe and a Defense Department investigator seek to expose.

888. _____. *Outlaws.* New York: Holt; London: Deutsch, 1987. The title of this one is beguiling--not outlaws in the usual sense of a Higgins' novel but intellectual outlaws, children of privilege who turn on the establishment, is meant. Says the former mentor of the radicals of the Ipswich Ensemble, Professor Neville Naisbitt, when his CIA funding is exposed: "Every generation has sacrificed its children. And every generation has strived to sacrifice its parents, or at least what they believe" (337). Detective John Richards recruits Special Assistant Attorney General Terry Gleason to help him solve a series of armored car heists from the 1970s in which no organized crime connection exists.

889. _____. *Penance for Jerry Kennedy.* New York: Knopf; London: Deutsch, 1985. Harry Mapes is a senior citizen and a lifelong career burglar that Jerry does not want cluttering up his caseload because he has an important case for a friend and client in the morning, but Judge Luther Dawes, with his Revolutionary-War pedigree, ignores the fact that Mapes once sued Kennedy and assigns him anyway. Another and later client is Calvin Beal, a man almost 30-years-old without a criminal record, who has gone ballistic and is as mean as a junkyard dog; he does not threaten Jerry with a lawsuit like Harry Mapes; he threatens to kill him if he does not defend him.

890. _____. *The Rat on Fire.* New York: Knopf; London: Secker, 1981. An ambitious attorney pulls strings to get the Massachusetts AG to pressure

Detective Lieutenant Inspector John Roscommon and Corporals Michael Sweeney and Donald Carbone to investigate fire marshals who take payoffs not to investigate arson jobs around Boston.

891. _____. *Sandra Nichols Found Dead.* New York: Holt, 1996. Criminal defense lawyer Jerry Kennedy returns when classmate and Judge Henry Lawler appoints him to handle the *Estate of Sandra Nichols vs. Peter Wade*, involving the civil case of a woman's corpse found decomposing in a field and her ex-husband, a rich man with motive, means and opportunity. Because the DA cannot find sufficient evidence for a criminal prosecution, Kennedy becomes *de facto* a prosecutor in a wrongful-death suit.

892. _____. *The Sins of Their Father.* New York: Holt; London: Deutsch, 1988. A collection of 14 short stories featuring the usual cast of Higgins characters from high to lowlifes with a sprinkling of politicos and squarejohns thrown into the mix. Two are about lawyers' conversations with each other or clients in a sly, ironic style: "Intentional Pass"and "Ducks and Other Citizens."

893. _____. *Wonderful Years, Wonderful Years.* New York: Holt; London: Deutsch, 1988. Higgins' eighteenth novel features some typical silver-tongued lawyers and the crisp dialogue he is famous for and the ususal upper- and lower-class characters on both sides of the law. The plot centers around a Justice Department case being built against Ken Farley, a shady Massachusetts contractor, for bribery and political corruption.

894. _____. *A Year or So with Edgar.* New York: Harper; London: Secker, 1979. Plotless, gossipy first-person narrative of Washington lawyer, Peter J. Quinn, about his college chum Edgar Lannin.

895. Hill, Frederick Trevor. *The Case and Exceptions: Stories of Counsel and Clients.* New York: Stokes, 1900 . Hill wrote a text on estates law and authored biographies of Civil War generals Grant and Lee; he also authored a biography of Lincoln (*Lincoln the Lawyer*, Century, 1906) as well as a nonfiction work on 8 law cases: *Decisive Battles of the Law* (Harper, 1907). His fiction, mainly published by Stokes, is not altogether out of print but fading fast: *The Minority* (1902), *The Accomplice* (Harper, 1905) and *The 13th Juror* (Century, 1913).

A dozen stories in the collection with a range of legal issues covered from murder to acquisitions and wills. The best is "An Abstract Story," involving a society girl named Thornton being courted by a young lawyer working in the narrator's office. His competition for Miss Thornton's affections is a newcomer to New York City and a wheeler-dealer named Reginald Forbes. Forbes is clearly the preferred beau to the "sallow-faced chit" of a lawyer-swain, according to the narrator, but when Forbes talks a girl into posing as his wife to effect a deed transfer for a big profit, the lawyer gets poetic justice. The lead story "Outside the Record" shows a man on trial for murder rising to the DA's bait and confessing murder, "I killed him in the same spirit as I would kill any dangerous beast" (13). Hill is an inferior Auchincloss but manages to bring us into the fraternity of lawyers the way his greater successor would do. Hill, unfortunately, does not know his limits and incorporates a terrible imitation of colloquialisms for his lower-class characters, nor is he above melodrama: one gun is drawn but no bullet is fired.

896. _____. *Tales Out of Court.* New York: Stokes, 1920. This collection of 16 stories still survives; it includes the first 7 about the law in subjects revolving around conflicts over forgeries and wills, but "The Woman in the Will" is a quaint look at an era when women lawyers were a rarity and suspect breed; "The Shield of Privilege" is about a streetwise burglar who consults a smarmy corporate lawyer for his defense, the latter's house being his last criminal entry. The best of Hill's novels is noted below.

897. _____. *The Web.* New York: Doubleday, 1903. Behind the prestigious law firm of Rutledge, Bailey & Nugent lies a viper's nest of chicanery and profiteering by the Coast & Gulf Railroad, but it is about to be exposed to the light by the pending lawsuit in the Frayer action against the Placento Company. Young lawyer David Maddox runs afoul of the conspirators in a divorce action by the wife of Richard Lorimer, one of the directors. Lorimer's murder and an attempt to frame Maddox at the Coroner's Inquest is the beginning of the unraveling of this complicated plot.

898. Hill, Reginald. *Killing the Lawyers.* London: HarperCollins; New York: St. Martin's, 1997. Hill is one of the most literate and witty of mystery writers with a his pair of opposite-natured inspectors in the Dalziel/Pascoe tandem, yet his erudition never interferes with his entertainment. This is a new series character, Joe Sixsmith, a black private-eye from Luton, England. Joe has problems with two lawyers: one verbally assaults him, the other physically. When some associates and partners of these two are attacked, the arrow points right at Sixsmith.

899. Hilliard, A. R. [Alec Rowley]. *Justice Be Damned.* New York: Farrar, 1941. London: Cassell, 1944. Although it opens with the second murder trial of *People versus Peabody*, in which Frank Peabody is on trial in Murdock County for shooting Marcus Eastman and dumping his body in Swift River. Less a courtroom thriller for all that than a riddle because laying a plot to catch a wife's murderer is the real purpose behind the narrator's reflections and motives. A second sleuthing mystery features Judge Manfred called *Outlaw Island* (1942); it opens with a letter from Attorney General Marcus Salter to Jerome Carver, DA of Murdoch County, enquiring of the disappearance of Margot R. VanPelt, whose stated intention was to arrive at her summer cottage on Outlaw Island,

Loon Lake.

900. Hoag, Tami. *Ashes to Ashes.* New York: Bantam, 1999. Kate Conlan left the FBI to become a witness advocate in the DA's office. When 16-year-old Angie DiMarco witnesses a crime, Kate must protect her by tracking down the serial killer.

901. _____. *Guilty as Sin.* New York: Bantam, 1996. Little Josh Kirkwood's kidnapping terrifies a Minnesota town. A reputable citizen stands accused of the crime, but when a second boy disappears, a frightened community demands to know whether the police have caught the wrong man. Assistant County Attorney Ellen North believes she is building a case against a guilty man who controls an accomplice from jail. The book's trouble is that Hoag can't make up her mind whether she wants to write a suspense novel or a romantic thriller (Jay Butler Brooks is the romantic and courtroom opposite); the investigation itself is reduced to a subplot with an unsatisfactory ending.

902. Holland, Josiah Gilbert. *Sevenoaks: A Story of Today.* New York: Scribner's, 1886. Mill owner Robert Belcher, a crass man who loves power and popularity in the village of Sevenoaks, is sued for half-a-million dollars in damages by decent Paul Benedict, alleging infringement of patent rights on machinery he designed.

903. Hooks, Nathaniel. *Town on Trial.* New York: Exposition, 1959. A white teenaged girl cries rape by a black man in a small Southern town. The usual redneck cast comes out of the woodwork once Anna Lee's accusation of Robert Brysom is public, but what becomes intense and brilliantly worked through a child's eyes in Harper Lee's hands is merely another clichéd situation. The trial is too brief and ends with a ludicrous flourish by the judge.

904. Horn, Stephen. *In Her Defense.* New York: HarperCollins, 2000. Frank O'Connell is a DC lawyer at a prominent firm who gives it up to become a public defender. His client is Ashley Bronson, a socialite charged with the murder of Commerce Secretary Raymond Garvey. She claims Garvey is responsible for her father's suicide. While O'Connell and his private investigator Walter Feinberg check out the background, they turn up more than the possibility of another perpetrator to toss to the jury: they see the shadow of the CIA itself behind the deed. Horn is a native New Yorker from the Bronx with an engineering degree from Rutgers University. He commanded an infantry company of the 101st Airborne rangers in Vietnam. As a prosecutor for the Justice Department's Civil Rights Division, he tried well-known cases, such as the Kent State shootings of 4 May 1970 by the Ohio National Guard and the Dr. King assassination. In an interview for *Amazon.com*, he was asked if the idea had been germinating for a long time. He replied: "No. The story arose naturally. I had an opening line and a closing line and a central twist based on

my experience at the Justice Department. I would write a bit, think about it, write some more and put it away. It was something to do when I had spare time" (*From the Publisher* 27 Aug. 00: 11 paras.).

905. Hornung, E. W. [Ernest William]. *Mr. Justice Raffles.* New York: Scribner's, 1909. Brother-in-law of Sir Arthur Conan Doyle, Hornung's A. J. Raffles was, according to the authors of *Detectionary*, the most popular figure in literature after Sherlock Holmes in turn-of-the-century England:

> Raffles is the greatest criminal in the literature of roguery. The famed 'Amateur Cracksman' is a gentleman, as comfortable in the society of England's wealthiest families as he is on the cricket field or at a burglar-proof safe. . . .Late in his career, however, Raffles aligns himself with the side of law and order, turning to the detection of crime. A bullet in the Boer War ends his life. (147-48)

Raffles must break into the law offices of Burroughs & Burroughs, "the strongest firm in England for a criminal case" (128) to prove a letter is a forgery and save a money-lender from ruin.

906. Hoster, Grace. *Trial by Murder.* New York: Farrar, 1944. London: Hammond, 1952. Vikingesque beauty Tor Sigmund goes on trial for the murder of her uncle. Motive: she stood to gain half-a-million when Martin Linder died. The evidence is circumstantial: her gun fired the fatal bullet and the shot came from below her balcony. Chadwick Wray conducts her defense as if he considers her guilty and has to be admonished by the judge in mid-trial for his behavior.

907. Howells, William Dean. *A Modern Instance.* Boston: Osgood; Edinburgh: Douglas, 1882; Bloomington: Indiana U P, 1977. Introd. George N. Bennett. Two Howells scholars (David J. Nordloh and David Kleinman) established the definitive text of the book most consider Howell's most important. The author wrote to his agent and publisher James R. Osgood on 18 February 1881 about the manuscript of this, his "divorce story" because Howells believed that the subject of divorce was long overdue in American literature; it was a subject "both great and simple," he wrote, but it must be treated "without *shadiness*" [his emphasis] and without ponderous homiletics because it is a question in American life "only less intense and pathetic than slavery" (qtd. in Bennett xix). Temperamental Bartley Hubbard brings a divorce action against his equally temperamental wife Marcia Gaylord. Chapter 37 includes the text of the plaintiff's letter filed in the Tecumseh, Indiana court house citing "abandonment and gross neglect of duty" (404).

908. Huebner, Frederick D. *Judgment by Fire.* New York: Fawcett-Gold Medal, 1988. Huebner says that he began writing twenty years ago after taking a

modern fiction class at Macalester College that included Graham Greene, Dashiel Hammett, and Raymond Chandler. His library today includes Jim Harrison, Scott Turow and Latin American fiction. Protagonist Matt Riordan is a Seattle private eye, a former lawyer (his creator is a Seattle lawyer and graduate of University of Washington's Law School). Riordan maintained his practice until Edgar-nominated *Judgment by Fire* (1988).

Riordan's friend Hugh Prokop owns a marine supply business. When a warehouse burns to the ground, the fire department finds a safe with a quarter of a million dollars in it and the dead body of Prokop's accountant.

909. _____. *Methods of Execution.* New York: Simon, 1994. Riordan's ex-girlfriend, an attorney, asks him to look into the defense of a death-row convict, a sexual sadist named Robert Polhaus, because she believes he was unjustly convicted in the murders of two prostitutes; in fact, she is murdered trying to find evidence to exonerate him and Riordan flies to Walla Walla to see Polhaus to convince the slimebag not to fire him and later argues before a judge his right to defend Polhaus.

910. _____. *Picture Postcard.* New York: Fawcett-Columbine, 1990. Riordan helps friend and art gallery owner Lisa Thayer when she assesses three of her grandfather's paintings as fakes. The irate gallery owner who sold them as genuine Lee Thayers threatens her with a lawsuit if she does not desist. Her famous grandfather had mysteriously died years earlier in a car crash, although his body was never recovered. One more Huebner: *The Black Rose* (1986).

911. Hughes, Rupert. *Stately Timber.* New York: Scribner's; London: Jarrolds, 1939. Tale of a young man in the days of the Massachusetts Bay Colony who rebels against the Puritan ethic of Boston and its welter of capital punishment laws, brandings, and boring of tongues for misdemeanors in the 1650s. Seaborn Fleet is brought up on charges by a grand jury for a host of offenses, including mutiny, sedition, and rebellion, but it is only in the merest charges of "revileing the Courts of justice and the magistrates in base & unworthy termes and Making quarrels & contentions among the People in a very perfidious manner with profane swearing and cursing" (490) that he is found guilty, imprisoned, and later ventures to London.

912. Hughston, Dana. *You Stand Accused!.* New York: Hillman-Curl, 1937. The entire novel is the trial of sweet, little Millicent Dawson and her lover, Ned Winters, a medical intern and Walter Dawson's attending physician, accused of the murder of her husband. Young Ned whimpers less about obtaining the cholera culture that killed the man than he does about the "harlot" in the witness chair "showing just a little more of her legs than was necessary" and who led him astray and dashed his dream of becoming a doctor (211).

913. Hugo, Victor. *Bug-Jargal, The Last Day of a Condemned Man, and*

Claude Guex . New York: Crowell, 1896. Trans. Arabella Ward. The first is an adventure tale about the slave revolt in San Domingo in 1791 and the third is a variant of *Les Misérables* in which the protagonist is a good and honest working man. The second is Hugo's anti-capital punishment piece, partially in dramatic form as was printed in the fourth edition. The preface is an appeal to judges everywhere to abolish capital punishment.

914._____. *Les Misérables.* New York: Carleton, 1863. Trans. Charles E. Wilbour. Jean Valjean enters prison in 1796 for breaking a pane of glass and stealing a loaf of bread; several prison escapes thereafter, and his sentence has swelled to 19 years. The old convict's life, transformed by goodness, pursued by Inspector Javert across barricades and through Parisian sewers to a ripe old age of quiet benevolence and goodness, comprises Hugo's most popular work, although the social commentary Hugo buries the story in is long forgotten.

915._____. *The Man Who Laughs* [*L'homme Qui Rit*]. London: Routledge, 1886; New York: Appleton, 1869. Trans. William Young. Gwynplaine, a boy who grows to manhood with a face disfigured into a grimace of laughter, follows his master Ursus, a vagabond-philosopher, to England in 1705 where he is seized by constables and escorted to Southwark jail under an old Norman arrest procedure called the law of silent capture. Hugo admires English law but uses every opportunity to justify the Gallic wisdom of French differences, as the edition published by Caldwell of New York notes: "In England they venerate the law so much that they never repeal any; but they save themselves from the consequences of this veneration by never putting these laws into execution" (105).

916._____. *Ninety-Three* [Running title: *'93*]. New York: Harper, 1874. Trans. Frank Lee Benedict. All about those bad boys of the guillotine--Robespierre, Danton, and Marat--in those last heady days of spring 1793 when France flew the tricolor flew against the world and, mostly, against Paris. The summary executions are cut-and-dried but there is the trial of Gauvain in the conclusion as he faces three citizens members of the all-powerful Committee of Public Safety and fills his mouth with noble sentiments of France and honor--before the tied vote to acquit or condemn is broken and his death sentence pronounced.

917. Huie, William Bradford. *Mud on the Stars.* New York: Fischer, 1942. London: Hutchinson, 1944. Pvt. Peter Garth Lafavor of Louisiana narrates his experiences from 1929 to 1942. The Scottsboro case is mentioned in conjunction with a case he covers for his paper in the pre-war years about a poor, ignorant black man who has consensual sex with a white woman but is tried and sentenced to death for rape. Huie is a wretched writer.

918. Hulme, Juliet. Anne Perry, pseud. *A Breach of Promise.* New York: Fawcett-Columbine, 1998. The vast majority of Anne Perry's admirers had no

idea her early life in New Zealand was itself the fascinating stuff of mystery until New Zealand filmmaker Peter Jackson's chilling *Heavenly Creatures* (Buena Vista, 1994) with Kate Winslet and Melanie Lynskey compelling as obsessive teenagers from different classes who inhabit a post-pubescent fantasy world peopled with "heavenly creatures." The film portrays how two sensitive girls' fatal attraction for each other ultimately led to the bludgeoning murder of the mother of Pauline Parker. The other girl would grow up to become a celebrated author of mystery fiction. London-born Anne Perry writes two acclaimed Victorian mystery series: Inspector Thomas Pitt and his wife Charlotte in the late nineteenth century (in 1996 *Pentecost Alley*, a sixteenth outing) and Inspector William Monk and nurse Hester Latterly in the 1850's just after the Crimean War. William Monk awakened in a hospital in the mid-1850s without memory loss of his own identity. Perry had lived for a time in Los Angeles and worked as a flight attendant, store buyer and property underwriter. She maintains an output of one per series per year from her home in a converted barn in Portmahomack, tucked away in the Scottish Highlands.

The plaintiffs in a breach of promise suit being tried in a London courtroom are the snobbish Lamberts, suing daughter Zillah's fiancé, architect Killiam Melville, who argues that he cannot marry her, although she is rich and wealthy. Melville's counsel, Sir Oliver Rathbone, turns to Monk and Latterly to find out why.

919.______. *The Silent Cry.* New York: Fawcett-Columbine, 1997. Leighton Duff, a respected solicitor, is found murdered in one of London's worst slums with his son beside him, barely alive. When a series of rape-beatings of prostitutes in the area suddenly stops, Monk believes he has found a connection between the Duffs and the crimes. It also appears that the boy has killed the father and is subsequently arrested to be tried for murder.

920.______. *Slaves of Obsession.* New York: Fawcett-Columbine, 2000. Monk and wife Hester travel to America; it is the beginning of the American Civil War at te Manassas battlefield. Wealthy London arms dealer Daniel Albertson is their host at a dinner party when violence erupts in the form of a ritual murder, two disappearances, and the theft of Albertson's weapons.

921.______. *A Sudden Fearful Death.* New York: Fawcett-Columbine, 1993. "Private enquiry agent" Monk is on two intersecting cases, after the plot threads have been unraveled. In the first, an attack has been made upon the sister of a genteel lady in their London summerhouse; the other is a murder of a nurse at a local hospital. This one sees Old Bailey trial action as well.

922.______. *Weighed in the Balance.* New York: Ivy, 1997. Princess Gisela, widow of an exiled German prince, brings a slander suit against her countrywoman, Countess Zorah Rostova, in a courtroom battle for accusing her of murdering her husband Prince Friedrich. Distinguished barrister Sir Oliver

Rathbone takes the countess' case with help from Monk and Latterly.

923. Hume, Fergus. *The Mystery of a Hansom Cab.* Melbourne: Kemp, 1886. London: Hansom Cab; New York: Munro, 1888. A Melbourne mystery man named Oliver Whyte is found dead in the back of a hansom cab on St. Kilda Road. Midway through, squatter Brian Fitzgerald is tried but found not guilty, thanks to an eleventh-hour appearance by an alibi witness. The remainder of the book follows a whodunit path to conclusion.

Hunt, Kyle, pseud. *See* Creasey, John . . . .

924. Hunter, Evan. [Legal name of Salvatore A. Lombino]. *Lizzie.* New York: Arbor, 1984.

Hurwitz, Ken. *See* Bugliosi, Vincent . . . .

925. Huston, James. *Balance of Power.* New York: Morrow, 1998. Clancy-like technothriller with the fighting between legal combatants as important as between the military. Terrorists highjack an American ship on the high seas and trigger an ambitious Speaker of the House to use military action, against the President's desire for retaliation, when an underling finds a loophole in the Constitution that allows Congress to issue a Letter of Reprisal--in this case, a US Navy battle group sent to punish the attackers. In the courtroom setting, a DC circuit court hears an emergency appeal by lawyers from both sides; the issue, of course, is whether Congress has the right to supersede the express desires of the Commander-in-Chief. The denouement is contrived, literally, right on the steps of the Supreme Court building as the convoy appears ready to strike.

926. Hutchins, A. S. M. [Arthur Stuart-Menteth]. *If Winter Comes.* Boston: Little, 1921. A gossipy solicitor named Hapgood, residing in quaint Penny Green records the lives and goings on of a respectable couple, Mark Sabre and his wife Mabel, citizens of Penny Green also with a furniture business in nearby Tidborough. The lawyer's chatty tone notwithstanding, Sabre faces the dire experience of his wife suing him for divorce on the grounds of adultery, naming her servant girl Effie. Shortly after this, Sabre is pursued to Brighton and summoned to a coroner's inquest back in Tidborough where the bodies of Effie and her infant have been discovered.

927. Hyland, William, Jr. *The Black Chamber.* Edmonton, Alberta: Commonwealth, 1995. Highland is a senior associate with Duke & Karikas in St. Petersburg. His derives from a rich legal background, for his father, now a professor at Georgetown's School of Foreign Service, had served as deputy assistant for national security affairs under presidents Nixon, Ford, and Carter. Hyland acknowledged that many of the characters in his first novel--as much espionage thriller as courtroom drama--come from people his father knew in

those three administrations.

The title is named for a fictitious covert Middle Eastern operation run by the government and, set in present-day Russia and the US, deals with a presidential assassination attempt. Commonwealth publicity manager Neil van Dyk lauds the book for the realism of its courtroom scenes.

I

928. Iannuzzi, John Nicholas. *Courthouse.* Garden City, NY: Doubleday, 1975. A summer in the life of the Criminal Courts Building of New York County, Manhattan. Marc Conte is a defense attorney who takes on the City Hall machine which grinds up defendants and prisoners in its maw (the Tombs is in the midst of a full-scale riot with mayor and media in a frenzy). A variety of cases occur over the summer in which Conte either bests the system with his superior knowledge or courtroom savvy; he uses his skill for the deserving and undeserving alike. Assistant DA Malone is his nemesis in the federal district case of a mafia thug named Patsy the Crusher.

929._____. *Part 35.* New York: Baron, 1970. Iannuzzi, a veteran attorney with a lengthy string of first-degree murder cases under his belt, writes with verve of the big city. Alessandro Luca, a 31-year-old Manhattan lawyer, is assigned a murder case and defends one of two Puerto Ricans charged in the shooting death of a cop. In a stacked-deck trial performance, Luca reads portions of the Q & A of the other defendant, Hernandez, to the jurors--completely exonerating his own client Alvarado and then rests his case without another word (452-56). The extraordinary deference to the intelligence of twelve random Manhattanites aside, it makes the legal chicanery of indicting and trying Luca's client altogether moot.

Iles, Francis, pseud. *See* Berkeley, Anthony . . . .

930. Iles, Greg. *The Quiet Game.* New York: Dutton, 1999. Arthur Lee Hanratty's request for a stay of execution was just denied and he faces lethal injection in Huntsville, Texas. He has a psychotic, white supremacist brother still out there gunning for the narrator who put his brother on death row. The story is much wider, however, than a mere action thriller; it is a superbly well written book about a good man--a grieving widower, a father, son, lawyer, and writer--searching for a decent life in a world confused by violence and racism. One of his problems arrives with him on his return to his boyhood home in Natchez, Mississippi: his father is being blackmailed for failing to report that an ex-con patient named Ray Presley killed a dangerous in-law at his suggestion.

931. Innes, Hammond. *Atlantic Fury.* London: Collins; New York: Knopf, 1962. Story of two brothers, one a painter and the other a soldier, and their connection to Laerg Island in the Outer Hebrides of Scotland. The officer

brother, masquerading as Major Braddock, evacuates troops off the island under adverse conditions at sea and is later court martialed in Edinburgh for the loss of life.

Innes, Michael, pseud. *See* Stewart, J. I. M. . . .

932. Irving, Alexander. *Deadline.* New York: Dodd, 1947. Standard whodunit with a coroner's inquest occupying a few pages in the middle. Pretty, 24-year-old Celia Jefferson has her skull bashed in at the advertising offices of Endicott Brothers. Her wisecracking supervisor, Peter Cleveland, speculates that any number of persons might have wanted to kill her because "Miss Jefferson was almost universally disliked" (123).

933. Irving, Clifford (Michael). *Final Argument.* New York: Simon, 1993. The Cornell-educated, biographer, convicted con artist, and expatriate novelist (last heard of in the mountains of Mexico) Irving has co-authored works of espionage fiction with Herbert Buckholtz under the pseudonym of John Luckless, but he is notorious with another collaborator (Richard Suskind) for attempting to defraud McGraw-Hill and Life of hundreds of thousands of dollars, purportedly paid to the reclusive billionaire Howard Hughes in exchange for the rights to his autobiography. The scam was finally exposed in 1972, despite persistent denials by both McGraw-Hill and Life, by Howard Hughes himself, who arranged an elaborate and fool-proof press conference with seven reporters via teleconference from his hotel hideout in the Bahamas. Irving, ever remorseless about his ingenious stunt, said after serving sixteen months of his two-and-a-half-year prison sentence: "If I had to do it all over again, I would do it all, with one difference. I would succeed" (*CA*).

A 12-year-old case haunts successful 48-year-old Ted Jaffe, who practices with a conservative law firm, because twelve years ago, he prosecuted and convicted a man who killed the wealthy husband of the woman he was sleeping with. The man now faces execution. Comes with a powerful courtroom cross in the denouement.

934.______. *Trial.* New York: Dell, 1990. Young Houston trial lawyer Warren Blackburn lied for a client and ended up with a year's suspension. He returns to court with two clients: a guilty rich woman who will walk and a poor innocent Mexican laborer facing the death penalty. When Warren demands the judge recuse herself in the case of Quintana, she threatens him with contempt; it degenerates to this: [Blackburn to Judge Parker]: "I'll nail your ass to the wall"; she fires back: "Fuck you, counselor" (211).

935. Isaacs, Susan. *Lily White.* New York: HarperCollins, 1996. Lily is a Nassau County defense attorney with a client named Norman Torkelson, a handsome con artist who bilks gullible women out of their money, but now is charged with the murder of one of his victims. The overwritten subplot involves

Lily's domestic life--parents, husband, younger sister--in a parallel domestic crisis.

J

936. Jackson, Felix with Gertrude Purcell, and Henry Myers. *Destry Rides Again.* Script of the Marlene Dietrich-James Stewart film (Universal, 1939). (See Faust, Frederick Schiller). Dir. George Marshall. Perf. Marlene Dietrich (Frenchy), James Stewart (Tom Destry), Charles Winniger (Wash Dimsdale), and Brian Donlevy (Kent).

937._____. *So Help Me God.* New York: Viking, 1955. Although he seems a pale and empty vessel as a heroic figure, Manhattan attorney Spencer Donovan's decision to defy a congressional investigative committee with a cynical agenda comes in the beginning of the backlash against the red-baiting McCarthyites when many political and artistic celebrities were still doing the Robert Taylor shuffle in front of Martin Dies and the House UnAmerican Activities Committee to the tune of "I sold you and you sold me." The accusations are hurled and printed; his friends and associates quickly drop away from the young lawyer, whose defense of Gordon Beckwood, "never indicted in a court of American justice" (9), triggers his resignation from Arbutt and Miles and sets him on a plan to retaliate against the committee hounding him with an FBI investigation in the novel's opening.

938. Jacobs, Harvey. *The Juror.* New York: Watts, 1980. A week in the life of juror Leon Drew, a middle-aged ad copywriter who, at first, resents his presence in the courtroom for the case of *Varnik v. City of New York*; then a series of droll sexual encounters with another juror change his mind about public service.

939. Jacobs, Jonnie. *Evidence of Guilt: A Kali O'Brien Mystery.* New York: Kensington, 1997. Jacobs is an ex-English teacher and San Francisco attorney now living in Piedmont, California. She says, "I'm the mother at school who gets elected to do whatever 'because I'm home all day.'" One of her series characters, lawyer Kali O'Brien defends Wes Harding, accused of killing a woman and her young daughter, while struggling to find purpose and make sense of her life. (*See* Ms. Jacobs' commentary in **Craft Notes**.) Jacobs has a second series character in amateur sleuth and single mother Kate Austen in three mysteries also published by Kensington: *Murder among Friends* (1995), *Murder among Neighbors* (1994), *Murder among Strangers* (2000), and *Murder among Us* (1988).

940._____. *Motion to Dismiss.* New York: Kensington, 1999. Kali's best friend has married a successful businessman--then one terrible misfortune after another occurs: she is diagnosed with cancer, her wealthy computer magnate husband is accused of raping a Bay Area single mother, and the rape victim falls from a balcony, making it a murder case. Kali grudgingly prepares a consensual-sex defense but searches for the truth despite a complication presented by her assisting counsel, a former lover named Marc Griffen.

941._____. *Shadow of Doubt.* New York: Kensington, 1996. Kali returns to her hometown of Silver Creek and while visiting married friends is told by the husband that he might need a lawyer; she never learns why because he dies soon after the conversation, and when incriminating photos turn up, wife Jannine Marrero is the prime suspect.

942. Jacobson, Alan. *False Accusations.* New York: Pocket, 1999. Jacobson is a chiropractor, qualified as a medical evaluator by the state of California, whose experiences as an expert witness lend veracity to the courtroom scenes, but the book as a whole fails as a psychological thriller. A wealthy orthopedic surgeon is accused of running down a young couple in a senseless, coldblooded hit-and-run. He has no alibi. A witness puts him at the scene. Furthermore, a woman from his past seems to have set up the double murder just for revenge.

943. James, George P. R. [George Payne Rainsford]. *Morley Ernstein; or, The Tenants of the Heart.* London: Sims, 1850; New York: Harper, 1852. 2 vols. Lachrymose, turgid tale of a priggish youth and his affairs. Replete with letters to and fro that show the long sweep of the English epistolary novel this late in the Victorian era. One set of letters passes between Ernstein and his guardian Hamilton over unpleasant tidings of Morley Court, the family estate. One of the estates sold to Morley's father concealed the entailment and the rightful heir can bring claim to the rents received over 30 years. Another is *The Woodman: A Romance of the Times of Richard III* (London: Newbury, 1849).

944. James, P. D. [Phyllis Dorothy]. *A Certain Justice.* London: Faber; New York: Knopf, 1997 [reissued pbk Ballantine 1998]. Famed British mystery author James sends her series investigator, now Commander Adam Dalgliesh, into a complex investigation of a series of murders that begin when London attorney Venetia Aldridge, who had just defended a youth accused of murder, is herself found dead. James is credited by *Twentieth-Century Crime and Mystery Writers* with pushing boundaries in procedural detective fiction and lauded for her gothic strain, but her series characters are taciturn and rarely concern themselves with courtroom justice or procedural law; perhaps (the editor speculates) James' forensic background precluded an interest in it, although her characters do talk much about justice (594-95).

945. Jecks, Michael. *The Last Templar.* London: Headline, 1995. The author resides in Dartmoor, Devon, where his novels are set. After 13 jobs in 13 years, Jecks abandoned a career in computer science (his studies were in

actuarial science), threw away his television set to write full-time and study medieval history. His series sleuth is Simon Buttock, bailiff, and his bailiwick is 14th-century Devon England. Two plots intersect in this debut novel. When Pope Clement orders the destruction by torture and the stake, one surviving knight vows revenge on their accusers. It begins with the mystery of a charred body inside a cottage with Sir Baldwin Furnshill assisting Buttock's investigation.

946. Jeffries, Roderic G[raeme]. *The Benefits of Death.* London: Collins, 1963. New York: Dodd, 1964. Jeffries' writing career began in the early sixties and now includes several dozens of straight mystery novels of the classic whodunit variety, usually with a murder victim and many suspects, and police procedurals (under several pseudonyms) that occasionally overlap with a few courtroom dramas--well over 100 books thus far; he likes to put characters on the stand at crucial moments toward the denouement. The Ashford books tend to involve normal, law-abiding citizens in extra-legal activities to save themselves. In the 1980s, he created a third series, Inspector Alvarez, who operates out of Majorca, where Jeffries resides for health reasons. A graduate of the University of Southampton, where he studied navigation (1942-43), a 6-year stint in the British Merchant Navy, and by then a barrister-at-law, Gray's Inn, during the fifties, Rodreric Jeffries is a perennial favorite and bestselling author especially under the Jeffrey Ashford *nom de plume.* He is widely adapted into film, television, radio, and audio cassette, and his novels are translated into 15 languages and published in 17 countries. (*See* Mr. Jeffries' **Craft Notes** commentary.)

947._____. *The Bitter Bite.* London: HarperCollins, 1995; New York: St. Martin's, 1996. Calvin Slade and Timothy Rees have been friends for years when Slade approaches Tim with a plan to threaten a confession out of a man named Burrell, known by CID to have raped their friend Penelope, but who has an airtight alibi. Tim watches in horror as Slade kicks Burrell and applies electric shock to his testicles to elicit a worthless confession; when the two friends are arrested, two things become clear: rich Calvin Slade's lawyer is going to implicate Tim at trial to get his client a lighter sentence and that Tim was set up.

948._____. *The Burden of Proof.* London: Long; New York: Harper, 1962. The book opens with the clerk calling for *Regina v. Ventnor*, in which Roger Ventnor of Chelsea, abandoning a sexually vivacious Margaret Stukeley for a wealthy fiancée, is charged by police with the girl's murder because she died trying to rid herself of her unwanted pregnancy; the pills were given to her by Roger, so the prosecution will argue.

949._____. *Consider the Evidence.* London: Long; New York: Walker, 1966; rpt. 1985. Detective Constable John Craig and Detective Sergeant Dusty Miller are friends as well as officers, but now Miller has been accused of manufacturing evidence in a warehouse robbery by planting a bloody glove and wiping down a cosh used to bludgeon a guard into a permanent state of brain damage. The reason: to nail a vicious career criminal named Haggard. If he is willing to save his friend, Craig is soon exposed to the same moral and legal risks of his friend in a plot that mixes perjured testimony, planted evidence and the jealousy of Haggard's prostitute-girlfriend. This early Jeffries' is one of his best for tight plot and characterization with depth.

950._____. *Dead Against the Lawyers.* London: Collins, 1965. New York: Dodd, 1966. Radwick Holter, a brilliant defense barrister admired and hated for his successes in the courtroom, is under suspicion of murder by Inspector Brock when a man is killed in Holter's Kent office--a solicitor who had business in Hertonhurst. The spin against the formula is that Jeffries' protagonist returns to his young wife, allured by her sexuality and his own weakness for her.

951._____. *An Embarrassing Death.* London: Collins, 1965. New York: Dodd, 1966. An executive is found guilty of the murder of his stenographer, a socially ambitious woman who posed for pornographic photos; when a new trial is ordered on a technicality, he undertakes a *pro se* defense, gets the dead woman's boyfriend to incriminate himself, and his lawyer steps in to clinch the acquittal.

952._____. *Evidence of the Accused.* London: Collins, 1961. New York: British Book Centre, 1963. Lauded as his most ingenious mystery yet, a wealthy socialite is murdered, and her lover and husband are put on trial for the crime; each man confesses during the other man's trial. Carol Simpson Stern, writing in *Crime and Mystery Writers*, calls the ending of this one "*a tour de force* which produces the real murderer and leaves him free, outside the reach of the law" (598).

953._____. *Forget What You Saw.* London: Long; New York: Walker, 1967. Harry Brissom, a lawyer, witnesses a hit-and-run; the driver is a man named Simon, whose criminal expertise is needed for a bank heist by mastermind Ray Kirkland. If Harry identifies Simon, the job falls through; ergo, the solution is to threaten Brissom through his fiancée Daphne--and anyone else who can put pressure on him to perjure himself.

954._____. *The Hands of Innocence.* London: Long, 1965. New York: Walker, 1966. Opens with mild George Krammer's capital murder conviction in a Kent courtroom for the brutal murder of two little girls, but his death sentence is commuted to life as the abolition of capital punishment in England nears. He escapes to prove his innocence and thereafter becomes a manhunt for a fugitive with Scotland Yard copper, Det. Insp. William Agar on the trail.

955._____. *Prisoner at the Bar.* London: Long; New York: Walker, 1969. Robert Bladen is a young lawyer in an English country town in love with Katherine Curson, who is trapped in a loveless marriage. They meet at a remote spot where the body of an elderly man is found and police request assistance from anyone known to be in that area at the time. Robert goes to the police and is immediately suspected, his liaison with Katherine exposed, and is before the bench at Denbrington Assize Court with not even his barrister believing he is innocent.

More Ashfords with trials or lawyer-protagonists: *Counsel for the Defense* (Long; Harper, 1961); *Exhibit No. Thirteen* (London: Collins, 1962 as by Roderic Jeffries); *Presumption of Guilt* (Long, 1984; St. Martin's, 1986); and *Twisted Justice* (St. Martin's, 1993). Two others that were retitled are *Enquiries Are Continuing* (London: Long, 1964. [Rpt. as *The Superintendent's Room*, New York: Harper, 1965]) and a later reprint of *Will Anyone Who Saw the Accident . . .* (Long, 1963; Harper, 1964) as *Hit and Run* (London: Arrow, 1976).

956. Jennings, John E[dward]. *Call the New World.* New York: Macmillan; London: Hamilton, 1941. Next to Valour Jennings first epic of the Revolutionary War from the 1750s to the Battle of Quebec (*Next to Valour*, Macmillan and Hamilton, 1939) is followed by a smaller saga of the War of 1812. A brave young cavalry officer is court martialed after the Battle of Baltimore when a cowardly Captain Creed reverses his orders.

957. Jesse, F[ryniwyd]. Tennyson. *A Pin to See the Peepshow.* London: Heinemann; Garden City, NY: Doubleday, 1934. Julia Starling and her younger lover Leonard Carr are on trial for the murder of her husband Herbert. Daughter of a clergyman and great-niece of Alfred, Lord Tennyson, Jesse was a novelist, playwright, and criminologist (Lawrence seems to have borrowed her theory of murderers and "murderees" for a conversation between Birkin and Gerald in *Women in Love*). She edited selections for the British Trial Series.

958. Jobson, Hamilton. *The Evidence You Will Hear.* London: Collins; New York: Scribner's, 1975. Thirty-six-year-old Peter Mellish, a drifter in the small town of Coolidge, is on trial for the abduction and murder of Angela Murray; her case bears a resemblance to the disappearance of three young girls' disappearance the year before. Mellish's alibi is a woman with whom he has been having an affair.

959. John, Katherine. *Murder of a Dead Man.* New York: St. Martin's, 1997. John has 3 stylish thrillers featuring Sergeant Trevor Joseph. This one features that surprising rarity in legal thrillers--a murdered lawyer. A vagrant's death in an English seaside town preoccupies Sgt. Joseph because the dead man on Jubilee Street is an attorney who died two years ago.

960. Johnson, Mike. *The Perfect Murder: A Thriller.* New York: French, 1989. Johnson's play features a suave villain named Nicko Brannock, whose plot to save his career as a prominent, unscrupulous defense attorney backfires when his manservant is caught attempting to steal an incriminating file resulting in the murder of his own fiancé instead of her aunt, the judge who was bringing disbarment proceedings against him.

961. Johnston, Mary. *Lewis Rand.* Boston: Houghton; London: Constable, 1908. Historical drama that covers the days of Aaron Burr's trial for insurrection against the United States; the protagonist of the title began as a frontier youth and reaches the height of becoming one of Virginia's foremost lawyers and eventual aspirant to the governor's mansion; however, he succumbs to black rage and jealousy when he meets his rival Ludwell Cary by accident and slays him.

962. Jon, Montague. *A Question of Law.* London: Macmillan, 1981. New York: St. Martin's, 1982. Steven Kale, QC, defends Dr. Christopher Stirling, indicted for rape in the Crown Court at Liverpool. One of the three victims has made a positive identification of his client.

963._____. *The Wallington Case.* London: Macmillan; New York: St. Martin's, 1981. Kale's first case is a defense of Lady Ann Wallington against a murder charge, but she refuses to say where she was on the night of the murder or support an alibi.

964. Jones, Douglas C. *The Court-Martial of George Armstrong Custer.* New York: Scribner's, 1976. London: Allen, 1977. Fantasy of the Boy General's trial for negligence on that Montana battlefield known as Little Big Horn. Low-keyed account faithful to known records. Custer is reticent on the stand (General Sheridan's volcanic temper never erupts) and except for a brief moment of stream-of-consciousness at the end, the narrative is without flourish; even Asa B. Gardiner, the trial judge advocate in this Manhattan setting, is restrained until the summation when he denounces the defendant as "a bragging, strutting, primping, preening peacock" (257).

Judd, Harrison, pseud. *See* Daniels, Norman . . . .

K

965. Kafka, Franz. *The Trial.* New York: Schocken, 1995. Trans. Edwin and Willa Muir. Intro. George Steiner. Although it has been reprinted and translated throughout the world since its original publication date in 1925 (*Der Prozess*), it remains a work of inexhaustible fascination and one of the seminal precursors of existentialism. Joseph K. (all Kafka's wretched protagonists are nerve-shot reflections of his own deep anxieties) awakens one day to discover he is to be tried, and the remainder of the book is a guilt-riddled descent into the

world of bureaucratic horror that will ultimately execute him. That acerbically brilliant critic of modern literature, Martin Seymour-Smith, recommends Walter H. Sokel's *Franz Kafka* (1966) and Günther Anders' *Kafka* (1960) as the best brief introductions to Kafka. Collected stories featuring the law or justice (he was trained in the law but hated it) are "In the Penal Colony," "The Judgment," and "The New Advocate." The BBC film adaptation of *The Trial* in 1992 was scripted from the novel by Harold Pinter.

966. Kahn, Joan, comp. *Trial and Terror.* Ed. and introd. Joan Kahn. Boston: Houghton, 1973. A mix of terror, *noir*, hardboiled, dark-humored, and traditional mysteries with a few nonfiction trials, such as "The Trial of Robert Wood" by Edward Marjoribanks (a Camden Town murder of a streetwalker-turned-wife). Irish circuit-court judge Kenneth E. L. Deale's "The Brothers," reprising *People v. Bernard Kirwan* (1943), and Dorothy Sayers' "The Murder of Julia Wallace," a critique of William Herbert Wallace's trial for his wife's poker-murder in 1931 and one of Sir Edward Marshall Hall's most famous old Bailey cases. Other samples: Balzac's "An Episode of the Terror," Flannery O'Connor's "The Comforts of Home,"Edgar Lustgarten's "The Victim," Dashiell Hammett's "The Farewell Murder." One legal story is "The March Assize"by Samuel Warren, lawyer and novelist. *Terror*, however, is existential as well as traditional, for selections range from E. T. A. [Ernest Theodore Amadeus] Hoffman through Kafka ("The Knock at the Manor Gate") to Sartre's little existentialist gem "The Wall."

967. Kahn, Michael A. *Bearing Witness.* New York: Forge, 2000. A routine age-discrimination lawsuit against Beckman Engineering (initiated by a friend of Rachel's mother) leads to a key witness' murder in her Cadillac. Beckman Engineering is a powerful St. Louis construction company used to raking in profits for over 40 years. Gold unearths 60-year-old secrets involving bribery, greed, and murder.

968._____. *The Canaan Legacy.* New York: Lynx, 1988; Signet, 1992 [title: *Grave Designs*]. Kahn is a trial lawyer and partner for a St. Louis firm. (*See* his commentary in **Craft Notes**.) A graduate of Amherst and Harvard Law, he also teaches media law at nearby Webster University. His Rachel Gold series is widely praised for wit, intelligence, and inventiveness, pawky humor, and much like her creator, she is a St. Louis native who began her career in a big Chicago firm and then returned home. The difference now is that Rachel has a private practice, whereas Kahn still does his civil litigation for Gallup, Johnson & Neuman. Rachel was touted in *Bookends* as "a heroine for the nineties." Though a full-time attorney by day and father of five by night, Kahn finds his time for writing at the end of the day from 10:00 p.m. to midnight.

The senior partner of Abbott & Windsor arrives at the hospital DOA. His death is embarrassing because he had been having sex with a prostitute from one of Chicago's expensive call-girl services at the time his heart gave out; however, the mystery commences with a codicil to his will: $50,000 is left for maintenance of a pet's gravesite, yet Graham Anderson Marshall III never owned an animal. Rachel, retained by Abbott & Windsor to investigate Wagging Tail Estates and its pet cemetery, uncovers a trail of extortion, murder, and sexual depravity. Kahn told *Amazon.com* that he wrote this novel on a dare from his wife. (*See Grave Designs* below.)

969.______. *Death Benefits.* New York: Dutton, 1992. Once again, Abbott & Windsor has an internally awkward matter in St. Louis for Rachel to troubleshoot. This time, managing partner Stoddard Anderson brings the whiff of scandal when his suicide invokes a technical difficulty. Shortly before his untoward disappearance, he had quadrupled the death benefits of his life insurance. Anderson's widow cannot collect unless it can be proven that he was *non compos mentis* at the time of his suicide. However, Rachel's sleuthing uncovers a more profound mystery surrounding some rare artifact called Montezuma's Executor that the late lawyer might have discovered and paid for with his life.

970.______. *Due Diligence.* New York: Dutton, 1995. Rachel Gold uses more sleuthing skills than courtroom talents to get to the truth of two murders, but even as she comes closer to finding the answers she seeks, powerful forces are at work to stop her, including a US senator with presidential ambitions.

971.______. *Firm Ambitions.* New York: Dutton, 1994. Rachel Gold's third outing has her defending her sister against a murder charge for killing an aerobics trainer named Andros, whose other talent is in seducing bored housewives, including Rachel's sister Ann, while he cases their houses for burglary.

972.______. *Grave Designs.* New York: Signet, 1992. [Orig. title *The Canaan Legacy*, New York: Lynx, 1988]. (*See* entry for *The Canaan Legacy*.)

973.______. *Sheer Gall.* New York: Dutton, 1996. Sally Wade, personal injury lawyer, hires Gold to sue her husband for assault and battery; she alleges that he is obsessed with bondage. Neville McBride, a high-powered lawyer in his own right, pleads innocent. Defense attorney Jonathan Wolf insists Neville is being framed. After Wade is murdered, found spreadeagled in bed, and the husband becomes the prime suspect, Rachel is appointed executrix of her estate and discovers unpleasant surprises about Wade. Rachel's sleuthing shows her a netherworld of corrupt cops, corporate bigshots, strip-club owners, whores, and computer nerds.

974. Kampf, Harold. *My Brother, O My Brother.* London: Chapman, 1953. [Rpt. as *When He Shall Appear*, Boston: Little, 1954]. Janek Lazar is a saintly man who appears in England preaching kindness and healing the sick. Janek,

an obvious Christ figure, is put on trial in London for blasphemy.

975. Kane, Harnett T[homas]. *New Orleans Woman: A Biographical Novel of Myra Clark Gaines.* Garden City, NY: Doubleday, 1946. London: Davies, 1947. Chronicles the life and legal battles of Myra Clark Gaines (1805-85), a woman who claimed descendancy (and inheritance) from Daniel Clark, one of New Orleans merchant princes and a man who owned about one-third of the city in his time. Kane consulted legal briefs and court records from the Louisiana State Bar Library through King's County, New York to the Supreme Court for his novelization.

976. Kane, Henry. *Decision.* New York: Dial, 1973. A wife-swapping novel of Staten Island couples who meet and partner off for sex with the predictable result that two will betray their mates and fall in love. What gets it in here is that two swingers, Kirk Conover and the wife of the surgeon Richard Ellsworth, both serve on jury duty in a murder trial and cultivate their relationship from there. Despite the soap-operaish nature of the book, the trial sequences are long and detailed with good Q & A.

977.______. *A Halo for Nobody.* New York: Simon, 1947. Kane was a lawyer and a pretty fair pulp writer (*Peter Gunn*, New York: Dell, 1960) in his time, albeit he stayed with the Hammett-Chandler tradition longer than most. This one is another anachronistic Hammett knockoff with tough-guy operative and series deceptive Peter ("Petie") Chambers mixed up with the Scalzi organization of mobsters, carefully protected from the law by slick mouthpiece Andrew Grant. One more Kane pulp with a legal angle features a rarity, a female private investigator named Marla Trent in *Private Eyeful* (New York: Pyramid, 1959). A convict brought to court to testify whips out a gun and blasts the prosecutor. Trent's client is accused of providing the gun, and she has to clear herself as well as the client.

978. Katkov, Norman. *Blood and Orchids.* New York: St. Martin's-Marek, 1983. A crime shocks 1930 Honolulu as the State brings its case against four innocent men in the rape-beating of an adulterous Navy man's wife, Hester Ashley Murdoch, in Judge Stanley Walker's District Court. Tom Halehone defends the accused.

979. Katz, Jamie. *Dead Low Tide.* New York: HarperPaperbacks, 1998. Dan Kardon is a Boston lawyer asked by two friends, the parents of 19-year-old Aaron Winters to find out how he died in the resort town of Wettamesett on the Massachusetts coast because the police seem reluctant to investigate.

980.______. *A Summer for Dying.* New York: HarperPaperbacks, 2000. Kardon's private practice is picking up, and with new girlfriend Jenny Crane, things are looking better. He adds two clients, cousins Jerome and Daryl Mann, who are involved in a lucrative, low-risk real-estate deal that is so good it attracts some dangerous types who want to muscle in on the deal. When the businessman Jerome turns up dead, the rich basketball-star cousin Daryl is fingered for the crime.

981. Katzenbach, John. *Hart's War.* New York: Ballantine, 1999. "I work incredibly hard at creating bad guys that have a resonance," says Katzenbach in an online interview. His interest in criminal behavior began after his graduation from Bard College in 1972, when he embarked on his first writing job as a reporter for *The Trenton Times.* He spent three years on the crime beat before becoming a court reporter at *The Miami Daily News.* "We had it all," he recalls, "murder, drug wars, terrorism." Katzenbach then moved on to Miami's *Herald*, where he began a second career as novelist. *In the Heat of the Summer*, about a young Miami reporter's involvement with a serial killer, was adapted for the screen in 1985 as *The Mean Season.* He subsequently wrote one true-crime thriller about a murdered Mimi boy but found the genre incompatible. Next, Katzenbach produced this novel.

When the only black POW is accused of murder in a German camp, another POW with a year of law school defends him.

982.______. *Just Cause.* New York: Putnam's, 1992. Young black male on Florida's death row is soon to be executed, but he persuades a liberal Harvard law professor to take his case. The 1995 film began well but the heavy hand of Sean Connery as executive producer, whose part as the lawyer becomes smarmy as well as silly, almost ruins it. Laurence Fishburne is fine as the tough cop and Ed Harries' psycho-killer showed range long before *Pollock.*

983.______. *State of Mind.* A brother, who is a professor of abnormal psychology (with a specialty in serial-killer behavior), and a sister who composes crosswords and cryptograms discover family secrets in their hunt for a serial killer.

984. Kaufelt, David A. *The Fat Boy Murders: A Wyn Lewis Mystery.* New York: Pocket, 1993. Kaufelt has authored other works, mainstream fiction mostly among his 11 novels, and is known for the 1973 CBS television movie *Six Months with an Older Woman.* A creative writing instructor at Upsala College in New Jersey, Kaufelt graduated with a degree in engineering from the University of Pennsylvania and has an MA degree from New York University. *Detecting Men* notes that he is co-founder of the Key West Literary Festival (142). He splits residences between Key West and Sag Harbor, Long Island. His series creation is real-estate lawyer Wynsome ("Wyn") Lewis, formerly of Manhattan and current resident of Wagg's Neck Harbor, New York.

This one features a secret society from a long-ago Catholic high school in Waggs Neck, whose members used to torment a sensitive boy named Jackson Hall, who is now an important artist; meanwhile the so-called Fat Boys are being murdered. Lewis detects among the many suspects that include relatives of the victims as well as Hall and unearths family skeletons in the process.

985._____. *The Ruthless Realtor Murders: A Wyn Lewis Mystery.* New York: Pocket, 1997. Wyn uses herself as bait to lure a serial killer of real estate agents into the open.

986._____. *The Winter Women Murders: A Wyn Lewis Mystery.* New York: Pocket, 1994. Sophie Comfort Noble's death by a fall down a flight of stairs has meant her feminist daughter Rhodie has taken over her mother's gala literary event for the "winter women" of Waggs Neck. Wyn's squiring one of the speakers involves her when the woman, an author of feminist romantic tripe but with a kinky sex life, is found dead in her bed, nude, with a garrote around her neck.

987. Kazan, Elia. *The Assassins.* New York: Stein; London: Collins, 1972. When an Air Force master sergeant kills his daughter's boyfriend in cold blood right in his house on base, the commanding officer assigns Gavin McAndrews to the defense with the caution that it would be better not to make it seem as if the service were protecting their man from justice. McAndrews attempts a defense that will, in effect, try the daughter's anti-establishment hippie friends as the real cause of the boy's murder.

988. Kazan, Nicholas. *Reversal of Fortune.* This 1990 Warner film earned a Best Actor for Jeremy Irons for his stunning performance as the calculating aristocratic Claus von Bülow, convicted of killing his socialite wife Sunny (played entirely in flashback by Glenn Close). Co-produced by Oliver Stone and based on Alan Dershowitz' non-fiction bestseller of the same title, Leonard Maltin's 1997 *Movie & Video Guide* describes it as "[t]easingly ambiguous, and one of the most strikingly structured narrative films ever made" (1113). Ron Silver plays real-life Harvard law professor Dershowitz, who orchestrates the acquittal of the enigmatic von Bülow.

989. Keeler, Harry Stephen. *The Amazing Web.* London: Ward, 1929. New York: Dutton, 1930. Keeler hammered out a couple dozen cheap pulp mysteries with bizarre plots. This one begins in New York where an advertisement asking for 1,200 men with suitcases is part of a plan to save Archibald Chalmers, Englishman and Chicago idol, from the electric chair in a first-degree murder charge. Cut to Brossville, Kansas, the morning of the trial of Lindell Trent for grand larceny, where her lawyer and beau is David Crosby, with all three months of being an attorney-at-law, and he too will be part of this web of circumstance.

990._____. *The Lavender Gripsack.* London: Ward, Lock, 1941. [Rpt. as *The Case of the Lavender Gripsack*, New York: Phoenix, 1944]. Elsa Cole is a spitfire attorney with a tough one for her first murder assignment. Judge Penworth orders her to take on the defense of a nameless "John Doe" charged with murdering a night watchman.

991._____. *The Sharkskin Book.* New York: Dutton, 1941. [Rpt. as *By Third Degree*, London: Ward, Lock, 1948]. Ogden Farlow has been falsely arrested for the murder of his friend Peter van Dervelpen, who disappeared from Niagara City, and the cops work him over to get a confession. He goes on trial at the end of the book.

992._____. *Ten [10] Hours.* New York: Dutton, 1937. Bizarre tale of a court martial; its purpose: a set-up to keep a bank president and Home Guard captain from absconding with one million dollars in embezzled loot. Three writers attending a convention in Austin are hired by a detective agency to play tramps, get themselves arrested for "espionage" (lighting a hobo campfire off the highway) and subsequently tried overnight by the Harleysburg, Texas, Home Guard in this ruse to catch a thief under the guise of a military tribunal charging three hoboes with lighting signal fires for espionage purposes. Sequel to an even more bizarre tale of Harleysburgians called *The Defrauded Yeggman.*

993. Keene, Day. *Seed of Doubt.* New York: Simon, 1961. London: Allen, 1962. Port Palmetto, Florida is treated to a *cause célèbre* in the paternity case of *Miller v. Miller*, in which the allegation is that May Miller, wife of charter-boat captain Eric, was impregnated by handsome psychiatrist Michael Kilgallen, whom she was seeing for counseling in Fort Lauderdale several times a month.

994. Kellerman, Jonathan. *Self-Defense.* New York: Bantam, 1995. A young woman juror in a long, difficult trial that releases possibly repressed memories. Psychotherapist Alex Delaware, series character, struggles to circumvent the conspiracy of silence surrounding her.

995. Kelley, Leo P. *Cimarron and the Hanging Judge.* New York: NAL, 1983. After sailing on salt-water vessels, Kelley docked in New York and took a degree from the New School of Social Research with a bachelor's in English and followed it up with a business career in marketing and advertising before quitting to write westerns and pulp novels. The Hanging Judge is Fort Smith, Arkansas' own notorious Judge Parker who sentences two-fisted, manly Cimarron to die by the rope. "He wondered idly which event--his conviction or his having shared Sarah Lassiter's bed--was considered to be the more heinous crime by the law-abiding citizens of Fort Smith" (182).

996. Kelly, Lelia. *False Witness.* New York: Kensington, 2000. Kelly is a former banker whose character is Laura Chastain, a lawyer at Prendergrast & Crawley, a top-notch Atlanta firm. She successfully defends a corporate client

in a rape trial and discovers she has a real taste for criminal trial work, even though her firm considers it demeaning for senior associates. Working as an ADA, Chastain assists in the prosecution of James Stanley for the murder of his wealthy wife Christie. Stanley is a prominent and powerful attorney who knows how to obstruct Chastain's investigation. Kelly's Laura has good depth and the author works out plausible plot developments without neglecting the courtroom detail.

997.______. *Presumption of Guilt.* New York: Kensington, 1997. When Jeff Williams, a cop charged with killing a suspected child molester in police custody, asks her to defend him, Chastain takes on what is sure to be a tabloid-frantic case because the dead suspect is black, the cop white. More than a brutality case with tabloid problems, for Laura uncovers illicit gun sales, blackmail, cover-ups, and even murder behind it.

998. Kelman, Judith. *After the Fall.* New York: Putnam's, 1999. Charlie Magill's life collapses around him when his son Danny is charged with raping a high-school friend. Although Danny claims Lisa initiated the activity and that the sex was consensual, there is evidence for the case to go to trial. The novel, however, explores the relationships within the family and the community as the court of public opinion finds the son guilty and the family suffers--friends and colleagues avoid them, therapist wife Jesse loses clients, and the school refuses to readmit Danny.

999. Kennedy, Douglas. *The Big Picture.* New York: Hyperion, 1997. This one, highly touted with big pre-release money, weaves in and around several kinds of the thriller genre, including legal, but writes a novel that reads like an Americanized Martin Amis or Ian McEwan. The author is an American, in fact, who has lived in London for the past 20 years. His protagonist is a Wall Street lawyer with an upscale Connecticut life with middle-aged *angst* and issues with a bullying father who does an extraordinary thing one day: he kills the photographer who is cheating with his wife, freezes the body, cuts it into pieces with a Black & Decker, smuggles the sections aboard a yacht; then he blows up the yacht with an explosives recipe gleaned from the Internet. Now, with the dead man's identity, he is ready to begin his life as the photographer he has always wanted to be (his hobby when not lawyering).

Kenny, Charles J., pseud. *See* Gardner, Erle Stanley. . . .

1000. Kerr, Baine. *Harmful Intent.* New York: Scribner's, 1999. It is a by-now familiar plot: three years after Peter Moss lost a malpractice suit against Dr. Wallace Bondurant, he is still struggling with the memories and filled with self-loathing. he takes the case of Terry Winter, a tough-minded woman dying of breast cancer, whom Dr. Bondurant had failed to diagnose correctly. His dream of revenge is short-lived because she disappears into Mexico, leaving him to face the opposition's powerful medical and legal forces hired by the insurance company.

1001. Kerr, James. *The Clinic.* New York: Coward, 1968. A gallbladder operation results in Louis Corti's death and surgeon Dr. Matthew Hatch in a lawsuit. During the very detailed civil case proceedings in a California court, Dr. Peter de Haan, a general practitioner at the Hatch Clinic, testifies against his colleague's indifference to the patient's deteriorating condition and is subsequently fired by the hospital board.

1002. Kiefer, Warren. *The Stanton Succession.* New York: Fine, 1992. Stanton Technologies is a successful engineering company with an abrupt opening for its CEO spot when the founder dies of a heart attack. A scrambling for the succession ensues from within. Among those vying, the founder's lawyer and the wife of a vice-president.

1003. Kijewski, Karen. *Kat Scratch Fever.* New York: Putnam's, 1997. The firm of a Sacramento lawyer who committed suicide during the Christmas season hires private detective Kat Colorado to find out why (that is, can anything come back on the firm?). Kat discovers blackmail; furthermore, she is hired by an elderly woman, also a victim of the blackmailer, to uncover the identity of the extortionist. Both victims had contributed to one charity; then records reveal other contributors being victimized.

1004. Kingsley, Henry. *Austin Elliott.* London: Macmillan; Boston: Ticknor and Fields, 1863; New York: Scribner's, 1894. Apprenticeship novel of an age of Whigs, Tories, and derring-do in which young Austin Elliott acts as second for Lord Charles Barty, and deeming himself slandered after rumors that Barty died fighting Elliott's duel, the 23-year-old protagonist tracks down one of the presumed libelers, Captain Hertford traveling on the Continent, and survives a duel with of honor with him. After his return to England, Elliott presents himself to the magistrates for sentencing. In 1846 there was a legal issue over a law about dueling based on one fought by Lord Cardigan and Captain Tuckett involving the conveyancing of property to avoid the law's confiscatory powers.

1005. Kleist, Heinrich von. *Michael Kolhaas.* Berlin: Grote, 1902; London: Macmillan, 1910. Adapt. and ed. F. W. Wilson. Though Goethe snubbed him in Weimar, Schiller admired him and if, as Goethe thought, there was too much of the trendy "Werther sickness" about the young dramatist, Kleist's own life's adventures (arrested as a spy twice) certainly bore out a rationale for melodrama and melancholy both. On 21 November 1811, he carried out the wishes of his friend Henriette Vogel, herself dying of an incurable disease, and ended his own suffering in body and mind by shooting her and then himself. The brigand, Hans *Kohlhase*, was a man who robbed and murdered out of a sense of justice; in fact, the novel's opening paragraph concludes: "*Das Rechts gefühl aber macht ihn zum Räuber und Mörder*" (1). Perceiving an injustice at the hands of the Elector of Saxony over billing him for the stabling of his horses, Michael Kohlhaas begins a stormy career of plundering the countryside in the year 1538 that won't end until 1540 with his capture in Berlin, conviction, and execution.

1006. Klempner, Joseph T. *Felony Murder.* New York: St. Martin's, 1995. Former Federal Bureau of Narcotics agent Klempner broke into the thriller genre with a pair of action bestsellers (*Felony Murder*, 1995; rpt. 2000 and *Shoot the Moon*, 1997). This one is about a labyrinthine murder and coverup involving New York's top-echelon law enforcement. Joey Spadafino is a homeless man being defended by criminal defense attorney Dean Abernathy for the fatal mugging of a popular police commissioner.

1007. _____. *Flat Lake in Winter.* New York: St. Martin's-Dunne, 1999. Klempner's second legal thriller features criminal defense lawyer Matt Fielder who wants to fade away from his past by handling small cases; he has even built himself a log cabin far from New York City. But Fielder is the lone "death qualified" lawyer in the Adirondacks and succumbs to the pleas to help out mentally defective Jonathan Hamilton, who has confessed to slashing his rich grandparents to death.

1008. Klingsberg, Harry. *Doowinkle, D. A.* New York: Dial, 1940. John Doowinkle, Assistant DA, is a bookish prosecutor with a fascination for astronomy. He knows the constellations and the names and habits of gangsters equally well, so when he is trying a petty case of a traffic accident involving Tony Scofati and the lawyer is big-time mob mouthpiece Roscoe Finch, Doowinkle keeps Judge Rowan on the bench and puts more pressure on his hunch to see what is really important behind this case.

1009. Kluger, Richard. *Member of the Tribe.* Garden City, NY: Doubleday, 1977. First-person account of Seth Adler, son of a Civil War lieutenant, who comes of age and learns the law (and experiences antisemitism) in Savannah, Georgia, amidst much prejudice in the late nineteenth century. In one instance, his legal mentor Eugene Venable is confronted by the wife of a Jew challenged to fight a duel with an expert marksman, a man named Supplee over a sailing incident at the local regatta. Venable replies to her request to make the sheriff intervene to save her husband's life: "Madame . . . No sheriff, to my knowledge, has ever interfered with a rape, a duel, or a lynching throughout the history of the state of Georgia" (111). The novel opens in 1913 with the narrator reflecting the day before a trial in which he will defend a Jew unjustly accused of murdering a gentile child. His grandson David closes the book from his perspective in 1976.

1010. Koestler, Arthur. *Darkness at Noon.* Trans. Daphne Hardy. New York: Macmillan, 1941. Born in Budapest in 1905, Koestler lived an intensely exciting life amid the greatest political forces and troubles of our time. Like his protagonist Rubashov (modeled on Bukharin) a loyal member of the "Party" until the 1930's, he left it in 1938, was arrested by Franco's fascists and sentenced to death. Reprieved, he fled to France, was arrested again for his politics, and later barely escaped the Nazis. His reportage, fiction, autobiographical and cultural writings are among the best of the century's. *Darkness at Noon* opens with the memorable sentence of a cell door slamming behind Rubashov, comprises three "hearings"--really torture-interrogations by Ivanov, the new wolfish party member loyal to "No. 1" (Stalin, of course)---and ends with his brief trial and execution in "The Grammatical Fiction," loyal to the Party killing him right to the end, Rubashov waits for the bullet in the neck still believing in the perfectability of humanity. Sidney Kingsley adapted to a three-act play for the stage, a Drama Critics Award winner, with Claude Rains in the starring role.

1011. Komie, Lowell B. *The Judge's Chambers and Other Stories.* Chicago: Academy, 1987. First collected from the ABA's *Student Lawyer* and a couple non-legal journals, the 9 tales of lawyers and the law were published by the American Bar Association in 1983 (Chicago) and then expanded to 13 in this edition. Some will be reminded of Auchincloss' lawyers for the motif of mutual opposition between material success and spiritual emptiness (more women lawyers enter this world), but Komie's strength lies in his incisive, often truncated narrative. This choppy syntax is at times overdone, but here are lawyers most lawyers and readers will recognize as belonging to our hard-driving, moneymad times. Among them are the opener "I Am Greenwald, My Father's Son," "The Christmas Party," "Mentoring," a neat gothic tale of a young woman lawyer spatting with her bullying lover from the same firm in which she tells him at their restaurant meeting she has just substituted the fetal afterbirth of her miscarriage for the sushumi he just ate; the title story, a trial lawyer's revenge on the stereotype of the judge with onset Alzheimer's.

1012. _____. *Legal Fictions: Short Stories about Lawyers and the Law.* Woodstock, NY: Overlook, 1992. Introd. Jay Wishingrad. Komie's hefty tome is divided by time and subject--for example, two sections parse the last American century from mid-nineteenth (some interesting selections here) to mid-twentieth--while others classify by humor or by the sheer range of stories about law, justice, and legalities in human affairs ("Other Voices, Other Countries"). There is a concerted effort to avoid the standards or the classically great, although Melville and Kafka are here as well as two of Auchincloss' best stories ("The Tender Offer" and "The Colonel's Foundation"). Komie finds room for Continental and non-European writers too. The reader will find lightweights like Garrison Keillor side-by-side with William Gaddis' densely titled "Szyrk v. Village of Tatamount et al., in the United States District Court, Southern District of Virginia, No. 105-87." Kafka, Nadine Gordimer, R. Sarif Easmon, Guiseppe Di Lampedusa ("Joy and the Law") occupy the same slot but by no means theme. His final five authors--Greene ("The Case for the Defence"), Karel Ĉapek ("The Clairvoyant"), Paul West ("General Bellomo"), John Mortimer ("Rumpole for the Prosecution"), and Isabel Allende ("The Judge's Wife")--make this a valuable and refreshing addition to the few collections of legal short fiction extant.

1013. Komroff, Manuel. *A New York Tempest.* New York: Coward, 1932. Based on the famous [Ellen] Jewett-[Richard P.] Robinson murder case of 1836 in New York City. Oliver Benson stands trial for the murder of the beautiful Jane Holden found throttled in a room on the second floor of a notorious boarding house for women, a place where innocent country girls become ripened courtesans in the wicked city.

1014. Kopp, Nancy. *Absent Witness.* New York: Onyx, 1999. Nancy Kopp grew up on a farm in southern Wisconsin and lives in Madison. She has a B.A. in history at the Univ. of Wisconsin-Whitewater and later graduated *magna cum laude* from its law school in 1983. She served a one-year term as law clerk to a Wisconsin Supreme Court justice, spent three years as an associate in the litigation department of a large law firm, and since 1987 has served as a Wisconsin Supreme Court Commissioner. She is currently at work on a novel tentatively tiled "Prejudicial Error," featuring Ann Monroe, an attorney whose fiancé abandons her just shy of the altar, and takes a hate-crime case in a small town.

Carrie is a thirtyish partner at Ramquist & Dowd, a Chicago firm, who takes on the painful case for the Buckleys, whose daughter Katherine was left in a "twilight" state after a hit-and-run accident eight months prior. The Buckleys have been told that their daughter is pregnant; they want the hospital held accountable, but they also want the baby brought to term.

1015. _____. *Acts and Omissions.* New York: Signet, 1994. Kopp said that she was inspired by two headline cases for this one: Kimberly Bergalis was a Florida woman who contracted AIDS because of her dentist. The other was notorious Ohio-born necrophiliac serial killer Jeffrey Dahmer. Megan Lansdorf is trying to make partner in her Chicago firm when she takes on a case of negligence involving a hospital and a woman who contracts AIDS from her doctor. The subplot features Det. Lieutenant Mike O'Reilly just weeks from retirement when he is assigned a serial-killer case. The link between them is that all the victims strikingly resemble Megan.

1016. _____. *With Intent to Kill.* New York: Signet, 1998. Following her divorce, 35-year-old Liz Stanfield decides she needs a change of scenery. She no longer wants to live or work in Milwaukee, even though she is employed by the biggest law firm in Wisconsin. She moves to the suburb of Oakwood and becomes Horicon County's Assistant DA. The idyll is shattered when police locate the murdered corpse of 4-year-old Jeremy Barker, battered to death from numerous blows. Her superior and lover Harry Washburn wants answers fast because of public furor over the monstrous crime and assigns the case to her.

1017. Korelitz, Jean Hanff. *A Jury of Her Peers.* New York: Crown, 1996. Liberal, idealistic public defender Sybylla Muldoon cannot convince her psychotic client, a Manhattan street person named Trent, to plead insanity after he was witnessed viciously slashing a young girl getting off her school bus. But the doctors at Bellevue discover an implant under his arm with time-release LSD. Now Muldoon is nibbling at the edge of a conspiracy that will stretch right to the Supreme Court and her own father's nomination. The wacky conspiracy notwithstanding, Korelitz beams a sharp light on a flawed jury system. Korelitz followed this with another courtroom thriller involving a case of a Vermont single mother, Heather Pratt for infanticide, titled *Sabbathday River* (Farrar, 1999).

1018. Koukos, Pamela. *Faithful Love.* Bethel, CT: Rutledge, 1995. As syrupy as the title sounds, love story of a prosecutor Candace Cameron falling for Corey Matthews, tough-guy cop who melts in her presence.

1019. Krich, Rochelle Majer. *Angel of Death.* New York: Warner, 1996. Barry Lewis is a civil rights lawyer, and a Jew, who is defending a neo-Nazi group's petition to parade in a West Los Angeles neighborhood on Hitler's birthday and has been under attack from the Jewish community when a car bomb kills him.

1020. _____. *Speak No Evil.* New York: Mysterious, 1996. Lawyers die like flies in this one as a serial killer stalks and murders three lawyers who all defended rapists. It begins with the death of bitchy attorney Madeleine Chase, a much-disliked, ambitious backstabber who thwarts the career of the protagonist and former classmate at UCLA Law School, Debra Laslow.

L

1021. Lachman, Charles. *In the Name of the Law.* New York: St. Martin's, 1988. Bizarre tale of Manhattan attorney Jimmy Janos, a defense lawyer who bypassed law school but subsequently sued New York under an obscure law that enables him to practice law without a diploma. His brilliance at the law as an autodidact is belied by his reputation as a small-time litigator with disreputable clients. Suddenly, Jimmy offers himself as defense counsel to three members of a South Bronx street gang known as the Sick Assassins, who allegedly broke into a hospital to kill a key witness to one of their crimes. Their savagery also resulted in the murders of a hospital physician and Emil Franks, esteemed professor of Columbia University Law School.

1022. Lachnit, Carroll. *Akin to Death.* New York: Berkley, 1998. Hanna

Barlow is an ex-cop and lawyer who teams up with her law-school study partner Bobby Terry in a new firm. Their first case seems harmless enough--formalizing adoption papers. However, a man bursts into the office claiming to be the baby's biological father, and when the lawyers look into the adoptive couple, what they find is deceit and evasion to their enquiries.

1023. _____. *A Blessed Death.* New York: Berkley Prime Crime, 1996. Hannah Barlow quits the police force to become a lawyer. The plot involves the murder of Maria Luz Duran and the attempt by the church to spread her miraculous healing powers and exploit the martyrdom to attract followers. But then two people disappear: a teenager allegedly healed by Duran disappears and the priest investigating her background for canonization.

1024. Laing, Alexander. *Jonathan Eagle.* New York: Duell; Boston: Little, 1955. An historical tale of a seafaring lad and his derring-do across several continents, especially the young America of the late eighteenth century. A brief trial scene, very well done, occurs late in the novel with the roguish hero of the title presenting a *pro se* defense against his enemies for occurrences involving piracy in the Madre de Dios Bay and for various acts of sedition. One specific charge: "Defendant had incited mobs to riot, in Parley's tavern, and upon the common pasture, in 1799" (333-34).

1025. Lambert, Mercedes. *Dogtown.* New York: Viking, 1991. Whitney Logan is a young LA attorney who sleuths with a Chicana prostitute named Lupe.

1026. _____. *Soultown.* New York: Viking, 1996; rpt. Penguin, 1997. Logan returns where Dogtown left off. She takes Lupe Ramos, released from prison, to Koreatown to get her son, who has been in the care of Kim John Oh, Lupe's brother's girlfriend. At the house, they find an intruder with a gun drawn, holding a gun on Dorothy, Kim's godmother, and Auntie Jin. He makes off with $75,000 after killing Jin Oh. Dorothy hires Logan to catch the killer and retrieve the money.

1027. Lamson, David (Albert). *Whirlpool.* New York: Scribner's, 1937. Lamson based the State of Washington's case against Hannibal Norfolk in his novel on an Alabama case, *People vs. Wilson.* Norfolk is falsely accused of his brother Joel's murder, tried on flimsy circumstantial evidence (his brother has been missing for three years, a grave site containing a skeleton adjoining his property discovered), convicted, and sentenced.

1028. Lancaster, Bruce. *Bright to the Wanderer.* Boston: Little, 1942. Historical novel about the rebellion in Canada, 1836-37. Several bloody and a few legal skirmishes en route to liberty. George Innes is charged "with being a seditious and ill-disposed person," in one instance for contriving "to disturb the peace and tranquility within Upper Canada" (116).

Landels, D. H., pseud. *See* Henderson, Donald. . . .

1029. Landesman, Peter. *Blood Acre.* New York: Viking, 1999. Gritty, well-written novel of a lawyer Nathan Stein and his life collapsing around his ears in two days off Coney Island.

1030. Landon, Christopher. *Dead Men Rise Up Never.* London: Heinemann, 1963. New York: Sloane, 1963. A junior accountant receives a manuscript of a short novel from a deceased writer, a friend of his youth; in it he discovers the real message of the book: the character of Amanda Fane is his wife Lois, with whom the accountant once fantasized as a lover, and the implication is that she poisoned him. Harry Andrews elects to see the book into print and is later sued by the wife's lawyers, but Lois Headly is herself is drawn up on charges of murdering Colin Headly.

1031. Lane, Elinor. *Nancy Stair.* New York: Appleton, 1904.

1032. Langton, Jane. *Divine Inspiration: A Homer Kelly Mystery.* New York and London: Viking-Penguin, 1993. Langton has authored numerous Homer Kelly sleuthing books; this one is interspersed with sheet music and a law firm, Pouch, Heaviside and Sprocket, that tangles with Kelly over a disturbed client's lawsuit in a plot involving arson and switched identities.

1033. Lanham, Edwin. *Six Black Camels.* New York: Harcourt, 1961. Chester Bryan quits his New York law firm after just two cases to go home to a small-town practice in Old Harbor, Connecticut. Besides the usual quirky cases, he reconnects with an old high-school flame and gets involved in a kidnapping-murder case. The title refers to a design by used with the ransom message.

1034. _____. *Thunder on the Earth.* New York: Harcourt, 1941. London: Heinemann, 1942. Rugged and ambitious, Texas wildcatter Cobb Walters builds up a company and loses it through a ruse. With his oil company in receivership, he shoots Jesse Halliday (a man he had won oil leases from in a card game) in a bar in Devant because it was Halliday's perjured testimony in a nuisance lawsuit that distracted him while Cobb was negotiating a large bank loan to build a railroad for his company's expansion. The trial is a few pages in the novel's conclusion.

1035. _____. *The Wind Blew West.* New York: Longman, 1935. London: Heinemann, 1936. Sprawling Texas saga. Book Two ("Satotan's Bugle [1877]") includes the arrest and trial of Kiowa chief Satotan and two others for "depradations on Texas soil" (210); their trial at Fort Rutherford is prosecuted by one of the book's major characters, Amon Hall, a Tennessee lawyer lured to

Texas by its openness.

1036. La Plante, Lynda. *Trial and Retribution.* CBC [Canada], 1998. Orig. Yorkshire TV, 1997. Dir. Aisling Walsh. Devised and prod. Lynda La Plante. Written by La Plante and Vaughan Kingham. Starring David Hayman (Det. Supt. Walker); Kate Buffery (DI North); and Rhys Ifans (Michael Dunne). The creator of the *Prime Suspect* series--and author of 3 of the 5 novelizations of Jane Tennison on *PBS Mystery!*--strikes gold again with outstanding performances from a sterling cast and lean script in this multipart series which aired in the US via cable (TVO, Windsor, Canada). The tension to find and bring to trial a child-killer from a low-income housing project has multiple impacts on the persons involved--principally, the single mother and her live-in boyfriend, the constable who finds the little girl's body stuffed in a sewerage pipe, the lead detectives handling the investigation. The tension mounts right up to the courtroom verdict as the two suspects (the boyfriend and Michael Dunne, an alcoholic resident near the little girl's apartment) are played off against each other. La Plante has written several other bestselling novels in the mystery or suspense genre with powerful characterizations. She is as comfortable with creating a burnout female ex-LA detective as the brilliantly complex English Midlands Tennison. Her stage career with the National Theatre and the Royal Shakespeare was followed by a writing coup when she produced *Widows*, showcasing young widow Dolly Rawlins, altogether a highly successful TV series.

1037. Larner, Jeremy. *The Candidate.* (Warner, 1972). Larner received an Oscar for his scripting of this film, starring Robert Redford as an idealistic California lawyer persuaded to run for senator, compromises and obscures his beliefs to win election. Dir. Michael Ritchie. Perf. Peter Boyle, Melvyn Douglas, and Karen Carlson (as Redford's alienated wife).

1038. Larsen, Jodi. *Deadly Silence.* New York: Onyx, 1997. Attorney Nick Hunter lands a job at prestigious Kellars & Kellars, one of Oklahoma City's premier law firms. But when he and Angela Anderson, public-relations director, collaborate on a case, they suspect the firm is involved in a series of child abductions. Threats against their lives confirm their fears, and when the Attorney General's grandchild disappears, the kidnapping ring they are about to expose could destroy them first.

1039. Lashner, William. *Hostile Witness.* New York: HarperPaperbacks, 1995. Philadelphia attorney Lashner was a trial attorney for the Justice Department during the Reagan administration; he also has experience in the Narcotic and Dangerous Drug Section and the Office of Special investigations. He graduated from the New York University School of Law. This is the second outing for Victor Carl in which the burned-out, luckless lawyer hired by a senior partner from Talbott, Kittredge, and Chase to assist in an extortion and racketeering case. Without realizing he is the patsy of their patsy, Carl succumbs to the lure of fat fees, sexy women, flash cars, and rich clients--that is, if he goes along with the program set by William Prescott III, counsel for the indicted councilman. Between a Southside mafioso and a Northside drug czar, Carl is kept busy dodging bullets and sating his lust with the councilman's mistress, Veronica Ashland.

1040. _____. *Veritas.* New York: ReganBooks, 1997. Victor is hired by rich Caroline Shaw to prove her sister Jackie Redmann's suicide hanging actually a mob hit. Carl would like to cut himself a slice of the Redmann family's pickle-retailing fortune. The title refers to the name of the decaying mansion where the family's buried secrets are kept.

1041. Latreille, Stan. *Perjury.* New York: Crown, 1998. Burned-out Chicago public defender settles in small town of Kirtley, Michigan. His office assigns him the perjury case of Davey (Mrs. Joel) Alden, a woman who lied about her husband's molestation of their daughter during his trial. It seems hopeless because of lawyer's Jack Brenner's attraction to her, the inconsistencies in her story that make this more than an ugly divorce action, and the fact that Alden is the most powerful man around. Latreille is a circuit-court judge.

1042. Latsis, Mary, and Martha Henissart. R. B. Dominic, pseud. *The Attending Physician.* New York: Harper; London: Macmillan, 1980. Another well-known pseudonym is Emma Lathen of the 20-book John Putnam Thatcher series. Latsis, who died in 1996, was a Harvard-educated economist and Henissart is a former corporate attorney; they reside in Massachusetts. There are 7 books in the Ben Safford series, one of the most recent being *A Flaw in the System* (London: Macmillan, 1980; retitled *Unexpected Developments*, New York: St. Martin's, 1984). Ben is a rumpled Ohio congressman whose activities on various subcommittees put him in harm's way and, if nothing else, embroil him with lawyers and lobbyists and various legal issues before the House.

Ben is on a subcommittee investigating Medicaid abuse by doctors, which in investigation is in HEW headquarters near his homestead in Newburg; the investigation leads from missing files through a prominent doctor and a pending malpractice suit to a murdered attorney named Anthony Karras. Another Ben Safford tale is *There Is No Justice* (Doubleday, 1971; retitled as *Murder Out of Court*, London: Macmillan, 1971), in which he is pressured to vote for a former Ohio law professor for a Supreme Court vacancy, but another Ohio colleague believes there is something hidden in Coleman Ives' past.

1043. _____. *Epitaph for a Lobbyist.* Garden City, NY: Doubleday; London: Macmillan, 1974. A woman lobbyist is linked to a bribe in behalf of power companies seeking to avoid pollution control; an unnamed congressman is alleged to have take a $50,000 bribe to change his vote.

1044. Latt, Mimi [Lavenda]. *Powers of Attorney.* New York: Simon, 1993. Critics are divided: execrable or blockbuster, depending on how you like your legal convolutions, with or without twisted bedsheets and groping bodies. Lavenda is not much on sleuthing or the law (she is a prominent LA lawyer like her protagonist) but is very keen on interpersonal relationships, especially where sexy, ambitious women are concerned. Three are featured here (not counting one young adulterous wife). Kate Alexander is an LA lawyer at Manning & Anderson who agrees to defend Sandra D'Arcy when the billionaire husband is murdered and her working-class lover's footprint is found at the scene. Alexander is also competing with two law-school classmates: Madeline Gould is Assistant DA determined to win a conviction and Lauren Cunningham is after the vacant partnership at Kate's firm.

1045. _____. *Pursuit of Justice.* New York: Simon, 1998 . Rebecca Morland and her husband Ryan make plans to start a family; then her husband disappears from a party on a yacht during a fundraiser. His law firm and the cops call it suicide by citing an enigmatic note. The set up and exposure of the killer is unconvincing and clichéd, according to Amazon.com's rabid amateur critics, but their wrath is warranted. When Rebecca fears her husband has disappeared over the side, she politely asks the captain of the yacht if someone would fetch her pants and a top before she joins in a rescue search at sea.

1046. _____. *Ultimate Justice.* New York: Simon, 1999. Alexandra Locke leaves New York to be near her dying mother in LA. She takes a job with her father, Thomas Kendall, who happens to be DA of LA County. Soon she is embroiled in a dark family secret implicating her own father in a sordid family history involving incest, rape, a murder cover-up, and bribery. Worse yet, someone is trying to stop her from investigating.

1047. Lawrence, Jerome, and Robert E. Lee. *Inherit the Wind* . New York: Bantam, 1955. Based on the Lawrence-Lee play, Stanley Kramer's 1960 film (UA/Lomitas) features Spencer Tracy (as Henry Drummond--Clarence Darrow) and Fredric March as the Bible-thumping attorney, a portrayal of William Jennings Bryan. It is a thinly disguised version of the famous 1925 Monkey Trial, as it would come to be known, in which a Dayton, Tennessee schoolteacher named Scopes was brought up on charges for teaching evolutionary theory rather than creationism. Writers Harold Jacob Smith and Nedrick Young worked the script (with Kramer associate Frederic Knudtson editing), but to Kramer must go the accolades for the vision of the Darrow-Bryan clash in its stark and simple passion; the Oscar-nominated camera work by gifted Ernest Laszlo is so confined to zooms and a few artful tilts to the jurors and spectators that you feel this sweltering heat along with the courtroom combatants. The stage version was first performed at Dallas Theatre '55 on 10 January 1955 and directed by Margo Jones. It went to Broadway's National Theatre on 21 April 1955. Melvin Douglas replaced Paul Muni as Drummond.

It has been translated into 31 languages including Urdu.

1048. Lebowitz, Albert. *Laban's Will.* New York: Random, 1966. Laban is an nonconformist, wealthy Jewish lawyer, the father of two twin daughters Rachel and Leah (one doats, the other despises), and a son named Bernie, who purely reviles his father. Laban calls everybody "Baby," and leaves a will tantalizing his offspring with how much his will provides for each of his offspring. The will's revelation in the end is no surprise.

1049. Lee, Elsie. *Sam Benedict: Cast the First Stone.* New York: Lancer, 1963. Novelization of the Sam Benedict TV program and based on the career of San Francisco lawyer J. W. Ehrlich. (*See* entries for Ohleck, Howard; Williams, Brad and J. W. Ehrlich).

1050. Lee, Gus. *No Physical Evidence.* New York: Fawcett-Ballantine, 1998. Lee was a supervising Deputy DA, an Army Judge Advocate, a paratrooper, legal counsel to congressional investigations into military misconduct and a winner of the Silk Purse Award for trial advocacy. He has had success in California as a statewide trainer for state prosecutors; as Deputy Director of the California DA's Association and a senior executive for the state bar. Despite his full-time writing career, he trains FBI and Department of Justice personnel. He has followed Amy Tan's successful *Joy Luck Club* with his own version in *China Boy*, 1991, and returns to a Chinatown setting for this legal thriller involving Joshua Jin, an Assistant DA, reeling from his teenaged daughter's death and breakup of his marriage. Then 13-year-old Rachel Farr is raped but remains silent while the police build a flimsy case against an ex-convict. Politics enter when Jin is told to dump the case to salvage the Chinatown vote for his boss. He refuses and prepares to face a brilliant, high-powered opponent, who also happens to be his former lover.

1051. Lee, Harper (Nelle). *To Kill a Mockingbird.* Philadelphia: Lippincott; London: Heinemann, 1960. Lee studied law at the University of Alabama, spent a year as an exchange student in England, and returned to her law studies without taking a degree, yet this single novel is probably responsible for more babyboomers going to law school than any other. Atticus Finch, the principled father of the protagonist daughter of Lee's novel is a portrait of her lawyer-father Francis Finch Lee. The Finches are genteel Southerners in this 1930s setting, reduced to the middle-class from their family's plantation days, but the real poverty in the novel is experienced by the blacks and the white-trash Ewells. Tomboy Scout (Jean Louise) Finch narrates this tale of racism and justice in the small town in Maycomb County. Mayella Ewell claims that the one-armed black handyman, Tom Robinson, raped her, but it is her father who (probably) has raped her as well as beat her; his nastiness is almost over the top as a Negro-hating, drunken redneck and incestuous father. Atticus Finch exposes him in court as the beater and the daughter, more gently, before Judge Taylor and the white jurors to no avail because the guilty verdict is a foregone conclusion. A wonderful coming-of-age story in which a child confronts evil (Jem, the brother, also but his faith is limited to his father's rectitude). Gregory Peck's rigor-mortis style of acting matched the role of Scout's stern but loving father in the 1962 film version scripted by Horton Foote. Christopher Sergel adapted for the stage (Chicago: Dramatic, 1970).

1052. Leib, Franklin Allen. *The House of Pain.* New York: Forge, 1999. Sally Collins is a 15-year-old girl kidnapped from her Connecticut home; the former Vietnam tunnel rat who frees her is brought to trial for his vigilantism in the major portion of the book.

1053. Leon, Henry Cecil. Henry Cecil, pseud. *According to the Evidence.* London: Chapman; New York: Harper, 1954; Chicago: Academy, 1988. Born in Middlesex before WW I, Cecil edited an undergraduate magazine at Cambridge and had his first novel *Full Circle* (1948) rejected 16 times before publication. He is one of the best practitioners of the legal novel, a meticulous craftsman despite the burlesques of the law and those who have infrequent or habitual scrapes with it, but he reserves some of his best lampooning for those who practice it rather than those who flout it. His novels are cleverly and sometimes convolutedly plotted, but ever full of sardonic asides or clever ruminations on the law's interpretation, and always well written. P. G. Wodehouse acclaimed him. In *Just within the Law*, Cecil talks about his "double life"as a jurist and novelist between 1949-1967. A jurist himself, he wrote 7 books on legal issues and aspects of legal practice in Great Britain, such as *Brief to Counsel* (1959) and *Tipping the Scales* (London: Hutchinson, 1964), the latter being a random history of judgeships to show the undergirding of incorruptibility of British jurists. He wrote about famous and infamous trials, such as Lord Cochrane for fraud in 1814 (*A Matter of Speculation*, Hutchinson: 1965) and for the Celebrated Trials Series one of Walter Graham Rowland, executed for the hammer murder of Olive Balchin on a bombed site in Manchester in 1946. Besides his 28 comic courtroom novels, there are three short-story collections, 8 mystery plays, 6 radio plays, several teleplays, including the *Mr. Justice Duncannon* series with Frank Muir and Denis Norden, and an autobiography to round out his prolific writing life.

Sex fiend Gilbert Essex is being tried for the rape-murder of Ellen Wimslow in Cunningham Assize Court after his fourth attack. After his acquittal by the jury, Essex is himself murdered. Ambrose Low, now married to the daughter of the man he saved in *No Bail for the Judge*, is consulted by Jill Whitby because she fears fiancé Alec Morland, the prosecuting counsel, will be accused. In a complicated plot to get him charged and acquitted, Low (with Colonel Brain's help) rescues the pair from the law. This novel, according to Breen, "explores some serious philosophical questions about vigilante justice" (20). It was adapted and updated for the theater, given an espionage spin, and performed at the Savoy in 1967; it was subsequently published the following year as *According to the Evidence: A Comedy*. Felicity Douglas, pseud. [Felicity Royal-Dawson] and Henry Cecil with Basil Dawson. London: French, 1968. Douglas Wilmer played Low (rechristened Adam), and Naunton Wayne played the Colonel.

1054. _____. *Alibi for a Judge*. London: Joseph, 1960. William Burford is convicted and sentenced to ten years for bank robbery when he fails to provide an alibi or convince the jurors that a mysterious fair-haired double named Thompson, with whom he had gone to school and attended a few horse races, is the likely culprit. Mr. Justice Carstairs, one of Cecil's best county court judges, doubts the verdict and later tries to overturn his own verdict by helping Burford's wife Lesley win an appeal.

1055. _____. *The Asking Price*. London: Joseph; New York: Harper, 1966. Darkly witty tale without much legal action or Cecil's usual drollery on the law's finer points. Lazy, affable, fifty-two-year-old bachelor Ronald Holbrook consults a real-estate agent because he wants to move out of his house in Islington. The reason is that his 17-year-old neighbor Jane Doughty, a girl he has watched grow up and regards as a second father, has fallen in love with him and her infatuation is making his life miserable. He next consults solicitor Joseph Plumb for legal advice regarding Jane's intent to get pregnant and claim him as the father of her baby if he does not sleep with her. At the end of the novel after the obsessive Jane dies from a fall, Holbrook is faced with the likelihood of being charged with her murder.

1056. _____. *Brief Tales from the Bench*. London: BBC, 1968. New York: Simon, 1972. These 8 first-person stories were originally BBC radio plays with Andrew Cruikshank in the role of judge-narrator.

1057. _____. *Brothers in Law*. London: Joseph; New York: Harper, 1955. In this first of the Roger Thursby trilogy, Roger ponders the last question of his Bar final exam as a 21-year-old apprentice at the law. His pupilage consists of the divorce case of *Newent v.* Newent and makes a successful Old Bailey debut as well as sixty guineas despite the fact that his own mother is seated on the jury. Ian Carmichael appeared in the film and the novel formed the basis for a BBC series.

1058. _____. *The Buttercup Spell*. London: Joseph, 1971. Cecil has his types like Gardner but he has gears to shift Gardner never dreamed of. In this tale of whimsy (and gentle satire at flower children), the pollen from a field of buttercups near the home of Norman and Belinda Strang makes people so pacific and full of love for humanity that they act completely out of character. The novel opens with Mr. Justice Salisbury, a notoriously hardnosed judge, sentencing a bank robber to a suspended sentence instead of the thirty years everyone expected. The reason: a visit from college friend Norman during adjournment in the trial and a friendly glass of brandy laced with buttercup. Soon the buttercup pollen goes upward to the Prime Minister's office and then abroad.

1059. _____. *Cross Purposes.* London: Joseph, 1976. A case of unprosecuted fraud in this one that opens with a section called "Strange Encounter," in which a young husband Douglas Barton, newly appointed to a library post in Surrey, meets Edward Livermore, an ex-convict with a penchant for check-kiting bank fraud, who says that he will give him a thousand pounds if he can live with him, his wife Sheila and their children for six months. The fraud in this case is a pools win of £100,000 that changes the lives of Douglas and Sheila.

1060. _____. *Daughters in Law.* London: Joseph; New York: Harper, 1961. Major Claude Buttonstep, with a family history of unfavorable litigation, objects to the plans of his twin boys Digby and John to marry the Coombe sisters, one a solicitor and the other a barrister. The feud with a neighbor over a lawnmower goes to court (Jane and Prunella arrive post haste from Copplestone County Court to assist litigation) in *Buttonstep v. Trotter* with Mr. Trotter exposed as a gentleman but a nutter while Judges Crewe and Blake bicker fulsomely at each other.

1061. _____. *Fathers in Law.* London: Joseph, 1965. [Rpt. as *A Child Divided*, New York: Harper, 1966]. An unusual Cecil novel in that it is an altogether serious one over the issue of child custody. A stranger stops by the house of adoptive parents Bill and Mary Woodthorpe and queries them about their 18-month-old adopted baby Hugh. After he attempts to blackmail £ 50,000 from the terrified parents, he is arrested. The mainline of the book is then the custody battle between the biological father (and his wife) and the Woodthorpes over the boy.

1062. _____. *Friends at Court.* London: Joseph, 1956. New York: Harper, 1957. The principal case involves a bribery charge against the owners of the seaside Glorious Hotel at Weslea. Thursby is opposed by friend and mentor Henry Blagrove in a case that is litigated from Magistrate's Court through the Court of Criminal Appeals. This is the second part of the trilogy with Roger having spent nearly 13 years in practice and now contemplating taking silk.

1063. _____. *Full Circle.* London: Chapman, 1948. These 16 stories are adroitly linked by the account of a Harvard law professor who, after falling and bumping his head at a station platform on the way to a lecture at Cambridge, begins to tell his students (whom he now thinks of as "charming children") stories instead of teaching the law more conventionally. Nine have trial sequences. "The Confession," the first tale is a first-person narrative from prison, and "Liberty of the Subject" evince Cecil's clever use of comic legal problems and trick endings in his novels. "On Appeal" uses a kidnapping plot that shows up later in *No Fear or Favour* (US title is *The Blackmailers*, 1968). A few more that go to court are "Advertisement," "The Dream," "The Name," "The Case of Mr. Tinker," about litigation over the invention of a new weapon and "Tell Tale."

1064. _____. *Hunt the Slipper.* London: Joseph, 1977. This final, posthumously published Cecil novel disappoints, according to Jon Breen, because of a strained and unconvincing denouement. A combined divorce and probate suit brought by Harriet Hunt, whose husband had vanished seven years earlier. Graham Hunt reappears as if nothing had happened just as she becomes involved with another man.

1065. _____. *Independent Witness.* London: Joseph, 1963. New York: British Book Centre, 1974. M. P. Michael Barnes goes on trial for leaving the scene of an accident after a motorcycle hits his car, although he later reports the incident. He faces dreaded Mr. Justice Grampion and a slew of witnesses arrayed against him. According to Breen, this Cecil novel includes "some of the author's best and most extensive wigged combat, [and] provides more of the excitement of the law than most 'big' courtroom books" (24). Cecil's jurist experience undoubtedly gave him some of his inspiration for seeing the utter absurdities, illogical statements, and partial truths that issue from the witness box in even the simplest cases before the court. One witness, Mrs. Benson, concludes her testimony with a long appeal to the judge to restore her driving license (87-89).

1066. _____. *Much in Evidence.* London: Joseph, 1957. [Rpt. as *The Long Arm*, New York: Harper, 1957]. A professional horseplayer is burgled of a hundred thousand pounds in cash that he had insured only the day before, which event makes the insurance-claims assessor suspicious. When the company delays payment, the horseplayer brings suit before a garrulous judge. In later proceedings, Mr. Tewkesbury is arraigned on a drunk charge and yet offers the court a brilliant *pro se* defense. Criminal charges in the Old Bailey also follow for Tewkesbury's client, and still another defendant, Arthur Green, tries to use the verdict in the horseplayer's case in his own *pro se* defense before a judge who banters amiably with the old con artist before sentencing him.

1067. _____. *Natural Causes.* London: Chapman, 1953. Alexander Bean is a litigious newspaper publisher; Mr. Justice Beverley embarrasses Bean in court and becomes a target of his paper; and Sidney York, a former comrade of the judge during WW I, who tries to blackmail him about his perjured testimony in a court martial. The major court proceeding is an inquest of the blackmailer, whose death in a fall precipitates the inquest. As Cecil is wont to do, other cases are interspersed throughout the main trial action. Here, these include a libel action involving a Test Match selection and an action for wrongful dismissal against Bean by his former solicitor. Series characters solicitor Tewkesbury and professional witness Colonel Brain appear.

1068. _____. *No Bail for the Judge.* London: Chapman; New York: Harper, 1952. Crusty Sir Edwin Prout, a High Court judge of impeccable moral rectitude, becomes accused through a bizarre series of occurrences of the murder of a streetwalker known as Flossie. Prout's daughter Elizabeth enlists the aid of burglary contractor Ambrose Low to assist; Low recruits thick-headed Colonel Brain to do research among the whores. (Low must face a hearing in Magistrate's Court on a morals charge as a result.) The final case is Sir Edwin's murder trial, but the ending is strictly *deus ex machina.*

1069. _____. *No Fear or Favour.* London: Joseph, 1968. [Rpt. as *The Blackmailers*, New York: Simon, 1968]. Clifford Ledbury is in the Old Bailey dock for conspiracy to commit blackmail. His organization, the Association for the Suppression of Slander, is a blanket for bilking the vulnerable. Presiding judge Mr. Justice Hereford's daughter is kidnapped in an attempt to influence his decision.

1070. _____. *The Painswick Line.* London: Chapman, 1951. New York: British Book Centre, 1974. Two big trial cases. In the first, Lucy Neeson-Smith, daughter of the Reverend Wellsby Meeson-Smith, stands accused of defrauding her bookmaker employers by placing bets after the races. In the other, a libel suit is brought against a Member of Parliament. Cecil's inebriated solicitor makes his first of many appearances when Lucy finds her way to Bogg, Tewkesbury & Co. Mr. Tewekesbury, "whose main pleasure in life was whiskey, had not yet entirely lost other elementary feelings and liked touching pretty women when he got the chance" (19).

1071. _____. *Portrait of a Judge and Other Stories.* London: Joseph, 1964. New York: Harper, 1965. The title piece presents gouty old Judge Pantin being confronted in his garden by a man who says that he murdered Mrs. Blazegrove, not his friend Frank Turner, whom the judge had convicted by his eloquent summation and caused to be hanged years ago. Furthermore, he says he is here to kill the judge. Eight of the 22 stories here see courtroom action: "I Killed Gordon McNaughton," "The Lesson," "The Application," "The Patient," "Striking the Balance," "The Limit," "Mock Trial," and "The Wife in the Train." One non-courtroom tale, "The Wanted Man," became a novel of the same title (Joseph, 1972).

1072. _____. *Settled Out of Court.* London: Joseph; New York: Harper, 1959. Outraged at being convicted of murder on perjured evidence for the murder of a business rival in a takeover scheme, financier Lonsdale Marsh arranges to escape from prison and uses his wealth for an extraordinary purpose: he orchestrates a second trial with new judge and defense barrister; the original witnesses are held prisoner for the retrial. Mr. Tewkesbury appears here to defend a prostitute in Magistrate's Court. The surprise twist is "one of the author's deftest reader bamboozlements" (Breen 22). The author and William Saroyan collaborated on a stage version that played at the Strand.

1073. _____. *Sober as a Judge.* London: Joseph; New York: Harper, 1958. In this lighthearted, final novel of the Thursby trilogy, 13 more years have passed. Now 46-year-old Roger is appointed High Court Judge with the prospects of a Court of Appeal position intimated. His cases include an extraordinary instance of "libel-on-ice" and a blackmail-con game played on a society woman. At novel's end, he meets fledgling barristers as green as he was at the beginning of *Brothers in Law.*

1074. _____. *Tell You What I'll Do.* London: Joseph; New York: Simon, 1969. After watching the courtroom sample his toffee, con artist Harry Woodstock changes his plea to guilty and is convicted, but cannot seem to get *into* prison. The major trial case concerns a group of shoplifting offenses prosecuted in Magistrate's Court by Randall Blower, Q.C.

1075. _____. *Truth with Her Boots On.* London: Joseph, 1974. Each tale plays off a notion of truth-telling versus lying. It opens with Justice Julian Whitehall presiding over a case of a husband abetting his wife's shoplifting and receiving a year's sentence; shortly thereafter the judge feels compelled to resign because of a small fib he told the wife of a straying husband. In between he assists his replacement Justice Rokeby with advice, and in the end, he goes sleuthing for the author of a series of blackmail letters that have various people, including the local vicar of Pendlebury, hopping about in worry that their secrets are out.

1076. _____. *Unlawful Occasions.* London: Joseph, 1962. New York: British Book Centre, 1974. Attractive Margaret Verney asks her neighbor Brian Culsworth, QC, one of England's best silks, for advice in dealing with a Mr. Sampson in what seems to be blackmail. He also briefly represents a man in a dispute over a football pools win. The novel begins in court with a saucy blackmailer instructing the judge during the pre-sentencing moment known as "moving in arrest of judgment," follows the football-pool case through various courts and ends up in Sampson's trial, thus exposing the chicanery that put the Verneys onto Culsworth in a plot to bilk the newspapers for libel.

1077. _____. *The Wanted Man.* London: Joseph, 1972. New York: British Book Centre, 1974. Cecil gets outside the courtroom much more in this tale of identity switching when a popular newcomer to the village of Little Bacon is believed to be an escaped bankrobber named John Gladstone.

1078. _____. *Ways and Means.* London: Chapman; New York: British

Book Centre, 1952. Two strangers come to reside in the prosperous small community of Tapworth Magna: lifelong friends Basil Merridew and Nicholas Drewe are not doing well financially, however. Then they concoct a scheme, with their wives' approval, to have one husband bring an action against the other on the grounds of estrangement with testimonies certain to fuel salacious gossip of the scandalous affair which, once publicized, will ensure that the women will be able to sell their stories to the tabloids for a quick fortune.

1079. _____. *A Woman Named Anne.* London: Joseph; New York: Harper, 1967; Chicago: Academy, 1993. The Anne of the title is named correspondent in the divorce case of *Amberley v. Amberley.* The novel begins and ends with her on the witness stand being cross-examined by Charles Coventry, QC. One of Cecil's wittiest as the repartee between the flippant Anne Preston and of her interrogator breaks down into cocktail-party chat, a happening that keeps Mr. Justice Brace actively intervening. The plot twist is also a Cecil trademark. Another is *Juror in Waiting* (1970).

1080. Leonard, Elmore. *Maximum Bob.* New York: Delacorte, 1991. Although the prolific and popular Detroit crime-fiction writer has a pair of novels in which Frank Ryan is a process server (*Swag*, 1976; *Unknown Man No. 89*, 1977), he enters here with a serio-comic character named "Maximum" Bob, a South Florida jurist known by trial lawyers and cons alike as a hardnosed judge who always gives a felon the maximum sentence.

1081. LeSage, Alain-René. *The Adventures of Gil Blas de Santillana.* Trans. Tobias Smollet. New York: Routledge, 1887. Though Voltaire envied its huge success and claimed Le Sage had lifted it from a Spanish writer, this episodic, picaresque tale is one of the novel's greatest antecedents (1715-35). There are edicts, decrees, banishments, etc. aplenty to justify its inclusion here, for the hero-rascal's journey from adventure to amour and back again. Between imprisonment in the Tower of Segovia and his visits to the great courts of Toledo and Madrid, there are occasions when legality becomes an issue, comically or otherwise--for example, one of the women Santillana is mutually sharing produces a son and by a legal document is adopted by another one of his possible fathers and subsequently made heir to the powerful Guzman family. Gil Blas joins the household as the boy's tutor.

1082. Lescroart, John T. *A Certain Justice.* New York: Fine, 1995. The San Mateo native (he resides in Davis, CA) and Cal-Berkeley grad was a professional singer and guitarist in LA and San Francisco in the early seventies (Johnny Capo and His Real Good Band). Lescroart's legal experiences occurred in the next decade with a consulting firm in Alexandria, VA and then LA with Pettit & Martin law firm as a word processor. His literary heroes, he says, are Hemingway, Lawrence Durrell, and John Fowles. He admires such disparate mystery writers as P. D. James, John D. MacDonald and Elmore Leanard. His fiction belongs less to legal thriller than to police procedural; however, his series character, Dismas Hardy (St. Dismas is the patron saint of murderers) is an ex-Marine, ex-cop, ex-lawyer "steeped in the Irish-Catholic enclave in San Francisco" (Swanson 191). Dismas tends bar at the Little Shamrock where he binges on Guinness Stout with Bass Ale chasers and sleuths for friends, including the Shamrock's owner, Moses Maguire. Lescroart's courtroom scenes, though rare, are never gratuitous, and the author credits lawyer-pal Al Giannini, a San Francisco homicide lawyer, with keeping him honest. Lescroart is a good writer, not content with slick plots or facile characterization, and he has an ear for the way people speak under duress without resorting to rhetorical flourishes or purple passages. *Sunburn* (New York: Pinnacle, 1981) won a California first-novel prize.

San Francisco erupts when a black man is set free by police after allegedly killing a young white man in a drug-related murder. The white man's friends hold a wake in an Irish bar and get drunk. When Arthur Wade's car breaks down outside the bar, the drunks lynch this innocent black man, a lawyer, and riots break out all over the city. A news photographer snaps a photo of the lynching and, although young Kevin Sheah had tried to stop the mob's vigilantism, he starts running for his life with his girlfriend as the entire city, spurred on by huge reward money and fueled by a an ambitious black city prosecutor and her mother, as well as a grandstanding US senator, hunts him. He calls old friend and attorney Wes Farrell for help. Reviewers note the morality tale in this post-Rodney King/O.J. Simpson day and how easy it is for an innocent person to get caught up in the law's vise and nearly crushed.

1083. _____. *Dead Irish.* New York: Fine, 1989. Eddie Cochran's suicide stuns the Irish-American community of San Francisco because he leaves behind a loving family, including a beautiful mother, pregnant wife, hot-headed brothers. McGuire, the Little Shamrock owner, for whom Diz works, and Eddie's brother-in-law, asks Hardy to pull himself out of his alcoholic stupor and investigate what the "something" at his job was that disturbed Eddie before his death.

1084. _____. *Guilt.* New York: Delacorte, 1997. Mark Dooher is a big-shot attorney and prominent advisor of the Archbishop of San Francisco who is charged in the murder of his wife. The state and Lieutenant Glitsky (series character who is a half-Jewish, half-black homicide cop) try to prove Dooher drugged his wife with chloral hydrate in her champagne, alibied himself at a shooting range, and then returned home to stab her in the heart. Boyhood friend Wes Farrell defends Dooher.

1085. _____. *Hard Evidence.* New York: Fine, 1993. Dismas return to the DA's office as a prosecutor and has remarried. Hardy and a friend find a hand sporting a jade ring in a shark's belly, which appendage belongs to Owen Nash, Silicon-Valley billionaire, whose bullet-riddled body washes ashore later.

Nash's girlfriend, a Japanese former call girl, has been charged with the killing. Hardy, however, believes her innocent and gets her cleared, but he is fired by his office. When his own former father-in-law, a judge, is charged with Nash's murder, Hardy becomes his defense counsel.

1086. _____. *The Hearing*. New York: Dutton, 2001. Diz goes up against ambitious DA Sharon Pratt when a dope fiend is accused of murdering Abe Glitsky's daughter.

1087. _____. *The Mercy Rule*. New York: Delacorte, 1998. Sal Russo is found dead in his apartment of a morphine overdose. Because he was already dying from a brain tumor and suffering from Alzheimer's, no one is surprised. The autopsy suggests someone helped him to commit suicide, and Sal's oldest son Graham, "his one good son," a baseball-player-turned-lawyer, comes under suspicion when his fingerprints are found on the morphine vial. A court order opens the son's safety deposit box and cops find $50,000 and a valuable baseball card collection. Dismas wants to plead him down to manslaughter to avoid a vindictive state's AG who wants a first-degree murder conviction.

1088. _____. *Nothing but the Truth*. New York: Delacorte, 2000. The plot is as simple as any Lescroart novel, but the inner complexities between Dismas and his wife Frannie make the reader think of Turow's *Presumed Innocent*. Frannie fails to pick up her kids after school because she is in jail. She is being held in contempt by a grand jury convened in a murder case. She refuses to tell what a man accused of murdering his wife revealed to her, a man whose children attend the same school as her own. When the man disappears, Hardy must find and clear him to get his wife out of jail--a wife who stubbornly refuses to give up the secret entrusted to her.

1089. _____. *The 13th Juror*. New York: Fine, 1994. Jennifer Witt is convicted of killing husband and son. Running her defense, Dismas is hamstrung be her stubborn refusal to help: "The fact is I haven't found a soul who's got something good to say about Jennifer Witt" (411). Witt will not admit to being an abused daughter and battered wife to help Diz defend her on the battered wife syndrome. All his investigative leads take him down various sordid paths into the lives of both victim and client, but none of the leads pan out, and the gas chamber looms ahead for Witt while he contemplates the SODDI defense as a last resort. Worse yet, the ambitious prosecutor claims he can prove she killed her first husband nine years ago for the insurance.

1090. _____. *The Vig*. New York: Fine, 1990. Fading lawyer Rusty Ingraham left behind a murdered woman and a blood-spattered houseboat in China Basin that says Rusty Ingraham is now a floater in San Francisco Bay. Dismas, a friend of Rusty, does not believe it and he must run a gauntlet of mob foot soldiers and renegade cops to prove there is a paroled killer out there loose, someone who once threatened to kill both Rusty and Dismas.

1091. Lester, Seeleg, and Mervin Gerard, writers. *The Witness.* Santa Monica, CA: Rhino Home Video, 1992. The videorecording was originally produced as a motion picture in 1953. Dir. Robert Aldrich. Prod. Dick Powell and Don W. Sharpe. Perf. Charles Bronson, Dick Powell, Marion Carr, and Strother Martin. Frank Dana is facing death row if his lawyer Mike Donnegan does not come up with the beautiful mystery witness needed to clear him from a charge of robbery-murder. The lawyer searches, the judge grows impatient of granting delays, and when the witness is found, her testimony provides the nick-of-time denouement.

1092. Levin, Meyer. *Compulsion.* New York: Simon, 1956. London: Muller, 1957. The book has a grandness to it as is evidenced in its two section titles: *The Crime of the Century* and *The Trial of the Century.* Judd Steiner and Artie Straus are obviously the notorious Chicago cousins Leopold and Loeb, teen murderers of little Bobby Franks; the murdered boy in the novel is Paulie Kessler. The transplanting and fictionalizing are of little consequence because the author himself is obsessed with this crime and these boys' motive; there is, by our standards, a quaintness about some of the psychological testimony. Nietzsche's *Übermensch* via Raskolnikov will explain more about Nathan Leopold-Judd Steiner than the shrinks have managed yet in their VICAP profiles. Levin does justice to Clarence Darrow (Jonathan Wilk) in his impassioned speech for mercy (once the plea has been changed to guilty) is eloquent against capital punishment. Deserves ranking with *Anatomy of a Crime* and *An American Tragedy.*

1093. Levine, Paul. *False Dawn.* New York: Bantam, 1993. Creator of the popular Jake Lassiter series, Levine has wide legal experience in law firms in South Florida, including as a trial and appellate attorney and partner at Bartel, Levine, & Shuford (1977-78). He has served as adjunct faculty in communications law at Miami (he graduated from its law school in 1973); he is moreover a Miami television personality who inspired and wrote for *You & The Law*, which was nationally syndicated. Not only a writer and commentator on legal issues, especially the First Amendment, on which he is a national authority, Levine serves on advisory boards such as Pennsylvania State University Libraries (he also graduated from Penn State University). Jake, on the other hand, is much less successful; he's been described as an ex-Miami trial lawyer, ex-Dolphins linebacker, ex-public defender, ex-a-lot-of-things, who bears comparison to another South Floridian troubleshooter created by John D. MacDonald. Jake, like Travis McGee, is a human salvager with a similar credo, one Levine sums up for his salty protag: "Best is to have a client you like, a cause that is just, and a check that doesn't bounce. Two out of three and you're ahead of the game."

Jake's client is Francisco Crespo, who admits to killing a coworker with a forklift. jake keeps pressing for the truth and finds more than he expected, including blackmarket Fabergé eggs, Fidel Castro, the new Federation of Russian States and the CIA.

1094. _____. *Flesh and Bones.* New York: Morrow, 1997. A stunner of an opener: Jake is sampling single-malt Scotch in an upscale South Florida bar when a leggy model walks in and blows away the man sitting next to him--her own father.

1095. _____. *Fool Me Twice.* New York: Morrow, 1996. Jake helps one of his lowlife clientele beat a fraud rap but is implicated in the murder of the man's business partner. Jake's search for his missing client takes him into the Colorado hills.

1096. _____. *Mortal Sin.* New York: Morrow, 1994. A Jake Lassiter pilot series for 1998 was planned on this fifth Lassiter novel. Jake is hired by a real-estate developer when an environmentalist is found dead of hypothermia in his wine cellar and the wife files a wrongful death lawsuit. Lassiter wins the suit but is convinced the real-estate developer is a murderer when he learns that the developer had plans for an Indian reservation west of Miami.

1097. _____. *Night Vision.* New York: Bantam, 1991. In his second outing, Jake needs ex-coroner Charlie Riggs' help yet again. This time Jake is a special prosecutor on a serial-murder case involving Compu-Mate, an electronic sex hotline service. Lassiter also turns to psychiatrist Pamela Metcalf, British criminal profiler, for help with the investigation. Suspects abound, including Nick Wolf, a state attorney and lover of the first victim, Michelle Diamond, newscaster, who had questioned Wolf about a suspected Vietnam conspiracy.

1098. _____. *Nine* [9] *Scorpions.* New York: Pocket, 1998. Levine stretches implausibility to the snapping point here. Freshman South Carolina Justice Sam Truitt is smitten by his sexy young law clerk, Lisa Fremont, a former teenage stripper in San Francisco and now a *magna cum laude* Stanford Law School grad, whose former lover is the president of Atlantica Airlines, Max Wanaker. Max engineers her clerkship to Truitt because his airline is in the middle of a multimillion-dollar law suit over the deaths of 275 passengers in a crash in the Everglades and Truitt will be the swing vote that determines whether the case can advance to the Supreme Court. The airlines was financially backed by the Japanese crime syndicate and one of the Yakuza's hit men is going to kill Wanaker and Fremont if she does not get the jock-turned-jurist to sway the vote.

1099. _____. *Slashback.* New York: Avon, 1995. Sam Kazdofsky has lost over a million dollars to a thief and wants Jake to recover them, but Lassiter has wearied of clients like Sam; in fact, he has taken up windsurfing, even organizing a competition with Hawaiian windsurf champion Keaka Kealia as one participant--worse, he is in the throes of a midlife crisis, smitten with a young lovely.

1100. _____. *To Speak for the Dead.* New York: Bantam, 1990. In Levine's first novel in the series, Jake searches for a killer in a medical malpractice case against surgeon Roger Lassiter that leads to a murder prosecution when patient Philip Corrigan dies. Melanie Corrigan believes her husband's aorta was deliberately sliced. After the acquittal, the dead man's daughter attempts to prove a conspiracy between Salisbury and Melanie Corrigan. Jake and Charlie Riggs, retired coroner, exhume the body and discover two bodies in the grave. Amusing sidenote: racing-form reading Judge Crane's idea of fairness is to rule "sustained" and "overruled" on alternating objections. Fellow trial attorney-writer Richard North Patterson praises Levine's courtroom scenes in the *Washington Post* for their "bite" and "authority."

1101. Levitsky, Ronald. *The Innocence That Kills.* New York: Scribner's, 1994. Each novel has the civil rights lawyer Nate Rosen journeying to a new locale in behalf of his Committee to Defend the Constitution. In this one Nate frees two guilty murderers in a Chicago courtroom and tries to explain to his 15-year-old daughter why the Constitution matters more than one case; however, his own daughter might have been molested by Martin Bixby, a drama teacher and colleague of his ex-wife, who also killed Nina Melendez, Sarah's best friend, and now Nate sees how uneasily his legal scruples lie within his father's outrage at his daughter's violation. When Nina's body turns up in a ravine, the Evanston police, the employers of Nina's cleaning-woman mother, and even Nate's ex-wife all want the case closed.

1102. _____. *The Love That Kills.* New York: Scribner's, 1991. Militant white supremacist Edison Basehart is arrested for killing a Vietnamese prostitute; his gun is found near her dead body. Nate head to Musket Shoals, Virginia to defend Basehart against a young prosecutor who needs a fast conviction to prove he is worthy of the DA's office. Nate strikes up a friendship with his courtroom antagonist, gets involved with the drugged-out sister of the dead whore and stirs up trouble among the local rednecks and antagonizes State Senator Dick Dickerson.

1103. _____. *The Spirit That Kills.* New York: Scribner's, 1993. Rosen investigates the case of an elderly Native American pressured into selling his land to accommodate gambling interests.

1104. _____. *Stone Boy.* New York: Scribner's, 1993. Set in the Black Hills of South Dakota, Nate travels to defend Saul True Sky, a man who wants to protect his ranch and sacred tribal lands from gambling interests from building an access road across his land. Opposing him is greed in the form of his son and the people of Bear Coat. A body found on his property and his lack of an alibi make for a railroaded trial--unless Nat can intervene.

1105. _____. *The Wisdom of Serpents.* New York: Scribner's, 1992. Rosen is in Earlyville, Tennessee at the request of his friend Jesse Compton, who wants him to defend the Reverend Gideon McCrae, bible-thumping snake-handler, when one of his rattlers bites Lemuel Banks, a congregant, during a ceremony at the Holiness Church. Nate matches wits with the local DA on more than the freedom of religious expression issue and gets involved in a homicide investigation when Ben Hobbes, the furniture king, is poisoned with strychnine the congregation has been drinking.

1106. Levitt, Diane. Diane Bernard, pseud. *Eternally Yours.* New York: Kensington-Zebra, 1996. A bodice-ripper with a musky legal fragrance. Kendall Roberts is a St. Louis attorney who meets IRS agent Drew Hurley during a hostile takeover while acting as legal counsel. She knows him from another life. The inevitable meets the prurient: "His mouth moved along her stomach, torturing her flesh as he approached the dark triangle between her legs" (201).

1107. Levy, Barbara. *Place of Judgment.* Garden City, NY: Doubleday, 1965. Loosely based on the trial of Marie LaFarge in France in 1840, but the plot owes as much to Maupassant and Emma Bovary as the real persona. Marie La Roche, with a head full of romantic notions, is accused of using arsenic to poison her peasant husband. The trial reveals her involvement in another woman's attempt to hide her blackmail by means of selling her diamonds.

1108. Levy, Harry. *Chain of Custody.* New York: Random, 1998. Dr. Michael Malone is a former cardiologist and police surgeon turned med-mal lawyer; now he is the prime suspect in the murder of his estranged wife because his DNA is found at the crime scene.

1109. Lewis, Hilda [Winifred]. *Send Dr. Spendlove.* London: Jarrolds, 1940. [Rpt. *The Case of the Little Doctor*, New York: Random, 1949]. Charlie Spendlove hates his slovenly drunken wife Dixie, a "double-crossing slut . . . [a] filthy bitch" (31). When he kills her with a lethal dosage, he has to hide the crime to protect his newfound love with Elsie, a woman who is bearing his child. One more is *Strange Story* (London: Jarrolds, 1945. New York: Random, 1947).

1110. Lewis, Mary Christianna Milne. Christianna Brand, pseud. *London Particular.* London: Joseph, 1952. [Rpt. as *Fog of Doubt*, New York: Scribner's, 1953]. Malayan-born Lewis was educated in India and sent to a convent Taunton, Somerset, England. Writes *Detecting Women* author Willetta

Heising: "While employed as a salesgirl she developed a strong dislike for one of her coworkers and wrote her first novel . . . to murder the woman on paper" (32). This is one from her Inspector Cockrill series and begins with the murder of Raoul Vernet during a London particular (slang for a dense fog). The crime occurs in the Maida Vale home of Dr. Thomas Evans, who is brought to the Old Bailey for trial.

1111. Lewis, Roy [John Royston]. *A Certain Blindness.* London: Collins; New York: St. Martin's, 1980. The author has written 20 legal or law-related tomes, including *Civil and Criminal Procedure* (London: Sweet, 1968). Lewis is also a prolific novelist with almost a dozen novels for each of three series characters: Arnold Landon (specialist in medieval architecture); Eric Ward, police officer-turned-solicitor in the north of England begun in 1980; and John Crow, another police officer (Inspector). With an output of close to 40 novels, well received by critics and readers, he has yet to establish a strong American audience, although it is inevitable given his talent for plot and characterization. The author lives in Cumbria, England. Ward hires on as a law clerk after his eye ailment becomes too severe for police work. He probes the background of a man convicted of murder decades before and uncovers information affecting two families in the present.

1112. _____. *Dwell in Danger.* London: Collins, 1982. New York: St. Martin's, 1983. Leaning more toward a psychological thriller in this one about Saxby family secrets and internecine warfare between parent and siblings. Ward has recently qualified as solicitor and works for the firm of Francis, Shaw and Elder when a simple legal matter regarding a trust leads to a clash between Ward and senior partner Francis over a conveyance issue and the unethical (to Ward) suggestion that a son sue his father, but that pales soon when Amos Saxby's estranged son Jack dies in a hit-and-run.

1113. _____. *A Limited Vision.* London: Collins; New York: St. Martin's, 1983. Philip Scarn, silky but shady chairman of Euromotor Enterprises, summons unemployed Eric to London to discuss a proposition: he wants the lawyer to act as his front man in the North Country to smooth his way for purchasing sites to become licensed as a string of "entertainment centres,"which are not merely nightclubs. Ward, recovering badly from his glaucoma surgery, ponders the choice before him that can enable him to marry Ann on the retainer fee but make him a shill for a corrupt enterprise.

1114. _____. *Once Dying, Twice Dead: An Eric Ward Novel.* New York: St. Martin's, 1984. Ward is on the mend from his glaucoma operation when Sandra, his first wife from twenty years ago, asks him to help her find her spouse, Charles Crane, missing three years. Ward also assists Eric Stevens, a ballsy and badly beaten investigative reporter after he had exposed illegal badger-baiting and discovered a body half-buried in the scree. The two plots intersect when the missing man is deemed to be Charles Crane, linked to a shadowy figure named Halliday Arthur Lansley.

1115. _____. *Premium on Death: An Eric Ward Novel.* New York: St. Martin's, 1986. Appointed to his rich wife's board of the Tyneside bank's subsidiary, Ward discovers that the bank is about to pay out on a vast claim for a ship sunk off the coast of Spain. Because he knows maritime insurance well, he suspects the claim is fraudulent but must investigate to prove it.

1116. _____. *The Salamander Chill* [: *An Eric Ward Novel*]. London: Collins, 1988; New York: St. Martin's, 1989. Ward's seventh outing follows the pattern of mixing two strands of plot. In the first, he is attempting to keep overzealous executives, financiers, and an arbitrageur on a tightrope of legality as a hostile bid threatens London's Salamander Corporation, and in the second, Jim Edmonds, merger & acquisition advisor to his rich wife's Morcomb Estates wants him to represent him when he is charged in the murder of his fiancée.
Blurred Reality (1985), *A Fool for a Client* (1972), *A Kind of Transaction* (1991), *A Necessary Dealing* (1998), and *A Wolf by the Ears* (1970).

1117. Lewis, Sinclair (Harry Sinclair). *Cass Timberlane.* Staid Judge Timberlane of the Twenty-Second Judicial District, State of Minnesota, is beguiled by Jinny Marshland, when he encounters her in court one day, and later marries the girl known about town as "a tempting little piece"(99). The 1947 MGM film was scripted from the novel by Donald Ogden Stewart. A pair of Lewis novels should be noted here, although it is incidentally about the law. Lewis, who had won the Nobel in 1930, was chagrined by the negative press heaped on him as an undeserving scribbler, so he came out with a female protagonist that would do justice to the modern woman, a Great Woman, he said to his wife Dorothy Thompson, the inspiration for the character of his protagonist, and he achieved that aim with mixed results in the novel *Ann Vickers* published by Doubleday in 1933. (The novel was serialized in *Redbook*, between 1932-33 according to Nan Bauer Maglin, who wrote the introduction to the Bison Books edition published by the Univ. of Nebraska in 1994--but shorn of nearly a thousand controversial paragraphs.). The reader follows Ann's life from age 10 to 30; she is a feminist, a socialist, a sexually liberated woman with close female friendships and a single mother as a result of an adulterous liaison with a married man. Her zeal for prison reform sees vindication in a pair of corrupt judges indicted by a New York grand jury for kickbacks and bribery, one being a major character of the book's second half, Justice Bernard Dolphin. The other is his futuristic It Can't Happen Here, published in 1936, with its portrait of demagogue Senator Berzelius ("Buzz") Windrip spouting inflammatory dialogue and folksy charm out of both sides of his mouth. President Windrip's assaults on freedom encompass the law courts too; he strips the Supreme Court of any integrity by appointing lackeys and nonentities to it and organizes show trials to denounce his enemies as communists. One character, Doremus Jessup, is accused and immediately sentenced to "twenty-five lashes--and the oil" (267).

1118. Lewis, Terry. *Conflict of Interest.* Sarasota, FL: Pineapple, 1997. Ted Stevens is assigned the defense of a man accused of killing a reporter; the trouble is that, if he uses what he knows as evidence to exculpate his client, he will have to reveal his relationship with the victim.

1119. Lewisohn, Ludwig. *Stephen Escott.* New York: Harper, 1930. [Rpt. as *The Memories of Stephen Escott*, London: Butterworth, 1930]. Stilted tale of a youth who grows up to become a lawyer in New York City along with his lifelong friend and partner David Sampson. The pair manage to get a mistrial in the murder case against bohemian poet Paul Glover, but the partnership dissolves when the antisemitic and nativist prosecuting attorney brings disbarment proceedings against Sampson.

1120. Liebeler, Jean Mayer [Virginia Mary Mayer]. Virginia Mather, pseud. *You, the Jury.* New York: Farrar, 1944. [The 1944 issue notes Little & Ives (New York) as "Printed by" beneath the Farrar & Rinehart imprint; also author as Virginia Mather in the 1946 London printing by Skeffington]. Barton Greeley, prominent banker of Madison County, has been stabbed in the back with an Egyptian dagger while using the freight elevator at the Fenick Museum. ten suspects in the museum are winnowed down to the one who is minus an alibi, Tom Warren. The narrative is filtered through juror Holly Phillips, who holds out alone against a conviction.

1121. Lieber, Joel. *How the Fishes Live.* New York: McKay, 1967. London: Allen, 1968. Long after the *Republic* has been sunk by a saboteur, a lifeboat of 6 survivors is rescued from the sea. It turns into a case of a murder trial for two of the survivors, Isaac Wolfe and Byron Holt, who killed fellow passenger Simon Sachs. Silver-haired defense attorney Hamilton Taylor must deal with the sensational issue of anthropophagism and the so-called natural law. The defendants bludgeoned Sachs with an ax and cut up his body for eating to ensure their survival.

1122. Liebman, Ron[ald S.]. *Grand Jury.* New York: Ballantine, 1983. John Silverman, ambitious US Attorney out of the Philadelphia office, is investigating criminal activities of men named Stavaros and Ames, in particular a construction company under their control; then he comes across evidence leading right to the powerful mayor's office. The question becomes whether to indict or not.

1123. Lincoln, Victoria. *A Dangerous Innocence.* New York: Rinehart, 1958. Another Salem witchcraft novel. Roger Evesham and his wife Ann (the narrator) are denounced as witches and brought to speedy trial.

1124. Linington, Elizabeth. Leslie Egan, pseud. *Against the Evidence.* Garden City, NY: Doubleday, 1962. *Detectionary*, *Mystery & Crime*, and *Detecting Women* deliver the goods on the versatile Barbara Elizabeth Linington, who in her writing career produced almost 90 novels. The first source notes of Jesse Falkington, tall, unhandsome LA attorney, that he

> cannot make up his mind about his own religion and waffles between being a Jew and an agnostic. Wife Nell is a Christian. His unmarrried secretary Miss Miller is inefficient but he cannot bring himself to fire her, and he would like to get rid of his mastiff Athelstane because of the enormous quantities of food it consumes. Bach on the stereo and a drink in hand is his idea of relaxation. But he is a good sleuth and so good he rarely has to appear in a courtroom to vindicate his clients. Sergeant Andrew Clock aids him (Clock dates Fran, Jesse's sister). (39)

Linington used other *noms de plume*, such as Anne Blaisdell, Egan O'Neill, and Dell Shannon, the last-named known as the author of Lieutenant Louis Mendoza, whose 1960 debut is *Case Pending* (106). Here, Glendale series cop and Jesse Falkenstein are introduced. Notes *Detecting Women* of the 26 Varallo and Falkenstein novels, the 38 in her Luis Mendoza series and the 13 about Sgt. Ivor Maddox under her real name: "Her cops were always good guys and family issues were always important" (62).

This novel and three others listed below were included in *Four by Egan* (Garden City, NY: Doubleday, n. d.). A slow-witted man who sells newspapers in an office building is accused of the murder of a young dental assistant who worked in the building, whom he was known to admire, although she feared his advances. The mother comes to Jesse's house to beg him to take the case.

1125. _____. *A Case for Appeal.* New York: Harper, 1961. London: Gollancz, 1962. Falkenstein takes a case as a favor to Varallo, a captain for the Contera police department, and meets Nell Varney in the Contera lockup, convicted of second-degree murder for the deaths of two women for whom she had performed abortions.

1126. _____. *Little Boy Lost.* Garden City, NY: Doubleday, 1983. Mrs. Charlene Garland comes to Jesse with an incredible tale of a kidnapping from 20 years ago, the Traxler case, in which her Uncle Tom's son was taken and never recovered after the money was paid out in ransom. Now a young man has shown up and is claiming to be the long-lost son, and he stands to inherit the small fortune left by Mrs. Garland's uncle because the widow, her Aunt Ruth, is completely taken in by the stranger.

1127. _____. *Look Back on Death.* Garden City, NY: Doubleday, 1978. Jesse's newest client is in the Men's Colony at San Louis Obispo doing twenty to thirty for murdering his aunt Lou to get her fortune; the convict's brother Walter Treadgold wants Falkenstein to convince Richard to go for parole, request that he refuses to oblige his family, for it will be seen as a tacit admission of guilt.

1128. _____. *Motive in Shadow.* Garden City, NY: Doubleday, 1980. John G. Manning, President of C. M. R. Management Company, brings Jesse the legal problem: his mother's second will, in which the former president and owner of the company until 5 years ago has left nearly the entire company 's property, worth several millions, to a total stranger named Adam Pollack, specified in the will as a "third cousin."

1129. _____. *My Name Is Death.* Garden City, NY: Doubleday, 1964. Jesse takes on the divorce case of a young man whose wife has a sordid past that leads to a wild youth in Tennessee and an old man murdered for his money.

1130. _____. *Paper Chase.* New York: Harper, 1972. Falkenstein gets involved in a murder investigation close to home when his secretary of the past 9 years, Margaret Williams, is murdered.

1131. _____. *A Serious Investigation.* New York: Harper, 1968. Sgt. Clock calls Jesse with the news that one of his clients has been found dead, possibly murdered, in her bathtub. Margaret Brandon was a decent, eccentric woman, whose will provides $800,000 to a research institute for paranormal psychology and a mere $25,000 to a sole nephew, a boy she had taken in for a few years, but who married a "cheap little tramp." The reason for Alex Roper's small bequest (Jesse, her executor and lawyer, knows from the many codicils to her will) is that too much money would make it harder for him to progress beyond his present "incarnation" (11).

1132. _____. *Some Avenger, Rise.* New York: Doubleday, 1966. A old man's revenge snares Andrew Clock and threatens to destroy the sergeant's career unless Jesse can save his friend; the sergeant has been suspended by Captain Thatcher and stands accused of accepting a bribe in a homicide case.

1133. _____. *Unexpected Developments.* New York: St. Martin's, 1984. Ben Safford tale in which the southern Ohio Congressman is cajoled by his sister into helping a constituent from Newburg. Ben meets Peg Conroy at the Pentagon, where her Air Force captain son has just been told the experimental plane he crashed in a Utah playground that killed his copilot and some children is his fault, thereby destroying his career. Ben intervenes to help the pilot and immediately smells a rat in the lack of publicity generated by the hearing; in fact, it and the rush to judgment have all the earmarks of a coverup with a scapegoat in place.

1134. _____. *The Wine of Life.* Garden City, NY: Doubleday, 1985. New client Robert Kinsolving, a very modest and likeable man with a good estate and shrewd business acumen, requested Falkenstein draw him up a simple will with his only sister as beneficiary now that he is 42 years old. After a busy day with small-fry cases, Jesse meets Clock at the house and learns that he had just come from a suicide case: one Robert Kinsolving.

More by Lesley Egan: *Back on Death* (1978), *The Blind Search* (1977), *In the Death of a Man* (Harper, 1970), and *The Miser* (1981).

1135. Linn, Edward. *The Adversaries.* New York: Saturday Review-Dutton, 1973. Bigshot Chicago attorney Norman Bannerman flies into town defend Samuel Tabor, who shot David Boone Wilcke, the Chief Justice of the United States, dead on live television during a visit. Opposing him in court will be Jim Ambose and Hilliard Nevins of the Lowell DA's Office. It takes almost 300 pages to get all 12 jurors seated before the showdown and Bannerman's strategy with regard to the M'Naughton Rule.

1136. Lipsky, Eleazar. *The Devil's Daughter.* New York: Meredith, 1969. Native New Yorker Lipsky graduated from Columbia and then its Law School. Banker, former US Senator from Nevada Lew Hagerman of San Francisco is a disgusting debauchee with a penchant for nubile flesh. One of his more genteel conquests is Miss Jessie Roux, who brings suit claiming she is the lawful wife of the old fornicator. While San Francisco revels in the salacious gossip, Miss Jessie's shrewd advocate Trumbull pursues her interests in the courts in this entertaining mix of bawdy humor and legal wrangling.

1137. _____. *Lincoln McKeever.* New York: Appleton, 1953. London: Deutsch, 1954. Lincoln McKeever, once a great Eastern trial lawyer, leaves his Denver home to defend a man in the New Mexico Territory accused of murdering Justice Douglas Hanna.

1138. _____. *Malpractice.* New York: Morrow, 1972. Manya Schroeder has infrequent seizures before her surgery; after her brain surgery by Dr. Percy Tatum's team, she is worse--the seizures intensify and she is deathly ill. William Mahler is summoned to sue Lewiston Central Hospital, and his grilling of the black surgeon is a rousing clash of personal and professional animosities between doctors and their natural enemies. What looks to be a case argued on the legal principle of *res ipsa loquitur* intensifies to exciting courtroom combat among various clashing personalities with the denouement revealing the truth.

1139. _____. *Murder One.* Garden City, NY: Doubleday, 1948. Jimmy Madena's body is found in Alice Williston's apartment, and Assistant DA of New York County Esau Frost is convinced of her guilt. She refuses to implicate codefendant Frank Albany, who was alone with her in the room at the time of Madena's death, nor will she accept Frost's manslaughter offer over Murder One.

1140. _____. *The People against O'Hara.* Garden City, NY: Doubleday, 1950. London: Wingate, 1951. Bill Sheffield, owner of a business at the Carney Fish Market, is shot four times by a man as he lay sleeping on his porch with a gun beside him; the man walks away with a traveling case from the house. Before he dies, he names his killer. Defense attorney Jim Curtayne faces off in the preliminary hearing against Assistant DA Louis Barra in the Johnny O'Hara's trial for shooting his employer.

A collaboration with Robert Silverberg (the authors writing as Laurence L. Blaine) is *Frontier Lawyer* (New York: Pocket, 1961) and one more solo by Lipsy is *The Scientists* (New York: Appleton; London: Longman, 1959).

1141. Listfield, Emily. *Acts of Love.* New York: Viking, 1994. Ted Waring is tried for the death of his wife in what the DA's office calls intentional murder based on daughter Julia's eyewitness testimony, but the prosecution's task is to prove that Waring meant to shoot Ann. Julia also reveals to a newspaper reporter that she witnessed her father making love to his own sister-in-law.

1142. Lockridge, Richard. *Something Up a Sleeve.* Philadelphia: Lippincott, 1972. London: Long, 1973. During a noon-hour adjournment in the case of *People of the State of New York v. J. Stanley Martin*, defense counsel Abe Levinsky's skull is crushed by a mugger. Bernie Simmons, Assistant DA leading the opposition in the murder trial, happens upon the body of his adversary and friend. In some series outings, Simmons is paired with others (Nora Curran, for example) as in *Death on the Hour* (1974) or appears solo as in *Twice Retired* (1970). Lockridge and his wife Francis became a husband-wife writing team cranking out more than a couple dozen mysteries with various series characters. *Catch As Catch Can* (1957) is a murder mystery with one of the main characters being Geoffrey ("Jeff") Bowen of the New York City DA's Office. *The Judge Is Reversed* (1960) features sleuthing spouses Pamela and Jerry North.

1143. Lodge, Marc. *Within the Bounds.* New York: Putnam's, 1993. Cliff Nielson, star lawyer at Ramwell and Bosley, a prestigious Southern law firm. Senior partner Lewis Sherwood, renowned, charismatic criminal defense lawyer himself, is going to take the case of a psychopathic killer of young woman known as the Resort Ripper in the media. Cliff must lead the team of lawyers scouting for chinks in the prosecution's armor. The author received his law degree from the University of Virginia., practices in Raleigh, North Carolina.

1144. London, Ephraim, ed. *The World of Law: A Treasury of Great Writings about and in the Law* . . . . 2 vols. New York: Simon, 1960. London's sampling ranges from biblical literature to modern and includes essays, accounts, letters, opinions, and transcripts of testimony in addition to the short narrative and drama (but a single poem). Volume 1, *The Law in Literature*, which emphasizes courtroom action and trial sequences, includes selections from Dickens' *Pickwick Papers* and *Bleak House* (*Bardell v. Pickwick* and *In Chancery*); Terence Rattigan's "The Winslow Boy"; a pair of de Maupassant tales: "Hippolyte's Claim" and "The Assassin"; two comic gems by W. S. Gilbert and Frank O'Connor ("Trial by Jury" and "Counsel for Oedipus"); Christie's "The Witness for the Prosecution," Train's "The Dog Andrew," Twain's "Science vs. Luck" and an early John Mortimer play before Rumpole titled "The Dock Brief." Herman Wouk's court-martial scene from *The Caine Mutiny* ends this section. One other good Continental author represented (Checkov and Shiga Naoya are two of the non-Europeans) is Karl Čapek ("Mr. Havlena's Verdict"). Part 2 of this section is subtitled "Lawyers, Judges, Jurors and a Witness"and is less solid in its choices, although novel choices and classics are mixed in with the once-popular Le Fanu, Robert Benchley, O. Henry, and Ben Hecht. Théobald Mathew is allotted two: "The Blushing Beginner and the Bearded Juryman" and "The Witty Judge and the Bronchial User." Also a pair by Reid Parker. A very fine Auchincloss ("The Legends of Henry Everett") and a mediocre Maugham ("The Happy Couple") typify the uneven balance, but in the classics there is much to applaud: Bret Harte's "Colonel Starbottle for the Plaintiff," Checkov's "Strong Impressions," Faulkner's "Tomorrow," and Twain's "Act of God in Nevada." Balzac and Scott warrant sections from their novels here; the former involves benevolent Judge Popinot from *A Commission in Lunacy* and the latter is a reprint of "Alan Fairford's First Cause" from *Redgauntlet.* The oldest piece is a 15th-century farcical portrait of a lawyer (trans. by Moritz Jagendorf). Vol. 2 is all nonfiction.

1145. Long, Gabrielle Margaret Vere (Campbell). Joseph Shearing, pseud. *Airing in a Closed Carriage.* New York and London: Harper, 1943. Using Marjorie Bowen as a pseudonym, Long wrote a novel based on Nell Gwyn's life (1650-87) and used George Preedy, another pseudonym, for a collection of bagatelle. Because Mrs. Long (if that is indeed her name) might have used as many as 10 pseudonyms, her output is unknown and library records are unreliable (although British by birth, her name is sometimes preceded with a Spanish honorific and includes the surname Costanzo in some records), but Joan Kahn believes the total is around 150 books (see her biographical notes in *Trial and Terror*, 568). It was once widely believed that she and F. T. [Frniwyd Tennyson] Jesse were the same person. The Joseph Shearing novels were historical criminal cases. Besides this, her most popular, are *Angel of the Assassination* (1935), *Lucile Cléry* (1932), *So Evil My Love* (1947), and *To Be at Noon* (1951). She bases this novel on a trial in England in 1889 and used portions of the trial transcript for her novel. American May Tyler goes on trial in the Manchester Assizes for the poison-murder of her husband; the motive: an adulterous love affair and a desire to be rid of her overbearing husband for good.

1146. Loos, Anita. *Gentlemen Prefer Blondes.* New York: Boni, 1925; rpt. New York and London: Penguin, 1989. The polar opposite of Nathaniel West's piercing satire, this American classic was made famous by both Carol Channing's stage performance and Marilyn Monroe's screen portrayal of the ultimate dumb blonde. Born in Little Rock (Loos' friend H. L. Mencken unkindly considered the city the nadir of stupidity, but it was a Ziegfield chorine who bewitched the great critic of American mores), Mabel Winnow will be rechristened Lorelei Lee by a judge, one of many legal figures pilloried in the book that range from DA's susceptible to Lorelei's charms to corrupt prohibition judges. Lorelei's hilarious diary often reads like Ring Lardner; she records her murder trial, in which everyone weeps for her and an acquittal arrives within three minutes for shooting a lawyer named Jennings, a would-be seducer of her virtue: "[W]hen I came out of it, it seems that I had a revolver in my hand and it seems that the revolver had shot Mr. Jennings" (48). She later meets the DA aboard ship on her travels and is talked into playing Mata Hare to obtain secrets from him.

1147. Lord, Gabrielle. *The Whipping Boy.* Melbourne: McPhee; Ringwood, Vic.: Penguin, 1992; Sydney: Hodder, 1998. Adapted for a television movie (starring Sigrid Thornton as the lawyer), this Australian novel concerns prominent people who are closet pedophiles and the lawyer who exposes them.

1148. Lothar, Ernst. *Loom of Justice.* [*Die Muhle der Gerechtigkeit*] Trans. Willa and Edwin Muir. New York: Putnam's, 1935. Since its publication in Vienna the year before, it was followed by this American edition and a British printing under the title *The Mills of God.* Anton Haushofer is Judge of the Criminal Division of the Provincial Court of Salzburg. He deals routinely with ordinary cases like the assault and battery of a woman by a laborer Joseph Swatil because he believes that a defendant charged is always guilty; then he finds himself in the dock when his irretrievably sick wife Pauline dies of a drug overdose because he administered the veronal to put her out of her misery.

1149. Lovett, Sarah. *Acquired Motives.* New York: Ivy, 1996. Santa Fe psychologist Dr. Sylvia Strange's testimony helps release a sex offender. The defendant is later tortured and Strange herself attacked. Soon more violent sex-offenders are released on technicalities and are killed by the vigilante. Lovett has authored almost two dozen nonfiction books, including thirteen children's books in the Extremely Weird animal series. She also worked for a time at the New Mexico State Penitentiary as a forensic researcher, and she notes in an offline interview for Ballantine Books that she writes about violence, "about people crossing the line." "Prison," she adds, "is interesting to me." Her first Sylvia Strange novel is about a psychopathic serial killer with a fixation on the doctor (*Dangerous Attachments*, New York: Ivy, 1995). Lovett's subjects are entertainingly implausible and her protagonist is a pastiche of nineties' career-woman traits as Sylvia waffles between fear of her own aggressive feelings and then reverts to a Harlequin romance heroine. Despite the graphic violence, a wooden style permeates all and characters remain cardboard figures.

1150. Lowrey, Walter B. *Watch Night.* New York: Scribner's, 1953. William Ransom Edward comes home to New Antioch, Mississippi, after being away in the war and then at college in Connecticut; there the 23-year-old stays with his mother, a servant of the Mayfields, and meets his childhood friend Louise, now 18 years old. They renew their friendship with canoe rides and walks, but trouble erupts in violent fashion when William is charged with raping her and faces a death penalty. The verdict is a foregone conclusion because the novel opens with William counting down the final hours of his life on death row.

1151. Luber, Philip. *Deadly Convictions.* New York: Warner, 1986. Luber's series character is Harry Cline, forensic psychologist like his creator and one who practices at the "interface of psychology and the law." In this, his first Cline novel, which is set in a hospital for the criminally insane, Luber writes about a mass murderer who feigns insanity to beat the system, a hospital (he notes in an interview on Internet in 1997) "not unlike the one where [he] spent several years learning about violent mental illness." For every unsavory impulse, he adds, "[he] know[s] someone who has acted it out." Luber also consults with judges and lawyers regarding criminal cases. Kline's career ends with four books, however. Lube told an archived discussion list on the Internet (*DorothyL* 14 Nov. 1999) that he had written 9,000 words of a fifth novel called *Dark Harbor* set in Maine near Arcadia National Park wherein a serial killer dumps "the brutalized bodies of young women into Somes Sound near [Harry's] vacation home."

Luckless, John. *See* Irving, Clifford and Herbert Burkholz. . . .

1152. Lund, Roslyn Rosen. *The Sharing.* New York: Morrow, 1978. The plot and most scenic dialogue revolve around that fact that Bill Mandel's death leaves his fortyish widow Sophie in contention with her rapacious brothers-in-law over their refusal to liquidate the partnership; meanwhile, she appeals to her mother-in-law to stop her sons from stealing money that belongs to her and her children.

1153. Lundquist, Weyman I. *"The Promised Land" and Other Courthouse Adventures.* Illus. Joan Hanley. Chicago: American Bar Assoc., 1987. American trial stories published by the ABA's Section of Litigation. A sample of the 10 include the title story, about the trial initiated by a one-legged fur trapper named Thumper Johnson that leads to *BIA* [Bureau of Indian Affairs] *v. The Wrangell Point Christian Baptist Colony, Reverend Francis Doheny, and DOES 1 through 100.* "Law in the Yukon--1961" about a lawyer's reminiscence of an IRS case against Scandinavian bar owner Harold Nordstrom, who withheld taxes from his employees but failed to remit them to the government. Others: "Trial Number One," "Out East to Back West," and "In Summation."

1154. Lustgarten, Edgar. *A Case to Answer.* London: Eyre, 1947. [Rpt. as *One More Unfortunate*, New York: Scribner's, 1947]. Nervous Arthur Groome is on trial throughout the novel for the slashing murder of second-class Soho tart Kate Heggarty. Others: *Blondie Iscariot* (Scribner's, 1948; London: Museum, 1949), *Defender's Triumph* (1951), *Verdict in Dispute* (1949), and *The Woman in the Case* (1955).

1155. _____. *Game for Three Losers.* London: Museum; New York: Scribner's, 1952. Two of the three characters, or players in a blackmail scheme to incriminate a popular M. P. with his lovely secretary are Oliver Marchant, footloose from the Army and not quite a complete scoundrel and gorgeous Frances Challinor, the newly hired secretary. It ends in Mr. Justice Tree's courtroom. The author was lawyer and criminologist who specialized in fact-crime books like this one.

1156. Lutz, John. *Death by Jury.* New York: St. Martin's, 1995. Lutz is a two-time Shamus winner in the private-eye genre with a couple hundred short stories and more than 30 novels to his credit. St. Louis' Alo Nudger is his series character, a hard-luck but not hard-nosed sleuth. His *SWF Seeks Same* (1990) was turned into a Bridget Fonda-Jennifer Jason Leigh film (Columbia-TriStar, 1992).

1157. Lynde, Francis. *Young Blood.* New York: Scribner's, 1929. A powerful railroad uses its influence to prod Judge Cullam into expediting the trial against the young general manager of a smaller railroad accused of killing Barker Dickson by hitting him on the head with a large bolt. The reason for jailing, indictment, and trial is believed to be part of "Pacific Railway's plot to bludgeon the G. V. & P [Railroad] into the consolidation scheme by the simple process of killing off the one man who stood in the way . . ." (209).

1158. Lysaght, Brian. *Eye of the Beholder.* New York: Simon, 1995. Assistant US Attorney Julie Beck enlists the help of a former lover she put in prison to get Robert Vargo, criminal financier and fugitive from justice.

Lytton, Edward Bulwer-Lytton. *See* Bulwer-Lytton, Edward. . . .

M

1159. Maas, Peter. *China White.* New York: Pinnacle, 1994. Maas is best known for his nonfictional works, such as *Serpico*, *The Valachi Papers*, and the recent true-crime thriller *In a Child's Name.* This novel belongs to the courtroom genre by the slim thread of a major character's professional interest in a New York law firm. China white is grade-4, processed heroin and the means whereby the rival triads of Hong Kong, united by one Deng Yue-Keung, will reestablish their criminal enterprises once Hong Kong reverts to China's control in 1997. A sprawling historical bridge stretches from Mao's China through the poppy fields of the Golden Triangle during the Vietnam War era to the modern street gangs and tongs of New York City and one man's personal history. Five tons of white powder will hit the streets of Chinatown in one shipment to create a Chinese syndicate more powerful than the Cosa Nostra. Tom MacLean, Manhattan lawyer and son of a CIA agent with a Chinese connection to the mysterious Deng, is sucked into the conspiracy's vortex and becomes linked with FBI agent Shannon O'Shea, who must keep the white powder from reaching America's shores.

1160. MacDonald, John D[ann]. *Cape Fear* [former title: *The Executioners*]. New York: Fawcett Gold Medal, 1957; rpt. 1991. Macdonald was a graduate of Syracuse and a Harvard MBA. His private-eye series with Travis McGee is among the best known in detective fiction. Insane, convicted rapist Max Cady returns to Cape Fear after his release to get vengeance on lawyer Sam Bowden, whom he blames for his sentence. Nick Nolte took Gregory Peck's part in the remake by Martin Scorsese and gave to the lawyer's part a greater fallibility (he withheld information that would might have cleared Cady in the days when the victims of rape were tried for sexual promiscuity). Another difference between the 1961 version and the 1991 is that in the former, Robert Mitchum-Max Cady is after the wife; in the latter, De Niro-Cady targets the daughter. Wesley Strick rewrote James R. Webb's screenplay based on *The Executioners*, but the blunt menace in the modern results from the synergy of the de Niro-Scorsese combination. The *New Yorker* called it Scorsese's "worst picture--an ugly, incoherent piece of work" (qtd. in *Halliwell's* 122). Peck, Mitchum, and Martin Balsam all appeared in both versions.

1161. Macdonald, William Colt. *Wheels in the Dust.* Garden City, NY: Doubleday, 1946. London: Hodder, 1949. Colt ground out more than 30 Westerns. Hoyt Murragh is a deputy marshal investigating payroll robberies of a stagecoach company. In the 50-page trial scene in an unusually decorous courtroom scene (for cowboy novels, the aberration from procedure is the norm) presided over by Judge Arnette in the murder trial of the killer of Uncle Jimmy Cochrane, a most unusual event occurs: Murragh, with pioneering ballistics skills, offers bullet casing evidence to the head juryman, who eagerly participates in Murragh's on-the-spot crime-solving--to no one's objections.

1162. MacDougal, Bonnie. *Angle of Impact.* New York: Ballantine, 1998. Mary Carroll in February 1, 1998's *Booklist* notes that MacDougal's niche in the legal-thriller genre is that "borderland where civil liability and criminal conduct overlap." The author once worked with President Clinton in the early 1980s at the same law firm before she relocated to Philadelphia. (*See* Ms. MacDougal's comment in **Craft Notes**.)

After winning a mass tort litigation in LA, Philadelphia lawyer Dana Svenssen is returning home, chatting by phone with her client Vic Sullivan, President of Pennsteel, who had called her his company's helicopter. Suddenly, their conversation breaks up and Dana sees a mid-air explosion as the helicopter carrying her client collides with an airplane directly over the amusement park where Svenssen's two daughters are spending the day. Although they are uninjured, the wreckage of the helicopter and a small plane are balanced atop a roller coaster. Once the girls are safely away, Dana boards the ferris wheel to snap photos; then the two craft explode, killing rescue workers and destroying evidence. Though drug dealers, right wingers, arms dealers and kidnappers add the flair, MacDougal's viewpoint embraces more, including the wretched state of American jurisprudence. Dan Casella (from *Breach of Trust)* appears in a cameo. Inspired by a real midair crash between a corporate helicopter and a small plane.

1163. _____. *Breach of Trust.* New York: Pocket, 1996. MacDougal's debut novel is as much about a romantic triangle as civil and criminal lawyering. Young attorney Jennifer Lodge and her supervisor Dan Casella, a tough South Philly corporate lawyer, have a strong professional and sexual relationship when Harding & McMann hire them to clean up a defalcation mess involving one of their associates guilty of looting the Chapman trust fund of $2 million. Jennifer and Casella part, she quits the firm, falls for the lawyer who may have been set up by the brother and trustee of the fund.

1164. _____. *Out of Order.* New York: Ballantine, 1999. Cam is a newlywed and a family law lawyer with Jackson, Rieders and Clark of Philadelphia. Her husband Doug Alexander is almost a son to Senator Ashton Ramsay. At the reception for the Alexanders in Delaware, Cam is amazed to hear her husband announce his candidacy for election to the House of Representatives. While the crowd is celebrating the merger of families, law firms, and political aspirations, Trey Ramsay, the 13-year-old son of the Senator, has just been kidnapped.

1165. MacGregor, Gregory Michael. *Deadspin.* New York: Bantam, 1997. Christopher Lang is a senior litigator at Devereaux & Brace, and has just been handed the case of his career: an old chum from law school, whose mysterious career sounds like CIA, has suddenly resurfaced with a proposal that Lang try a lawsuit against a company called Arrow Dynamics and its former owner, celebrated tycoon Russell Lindstrom, a man grooming himself as the next US President. Lang must prove that the swashbuckling businessman with his multibillion-dollar war chest is not only selling military hardware to the nation's enemies but he also designed and certified a recreational aircraft built to secret military specs a plane he knew was unsafe in the air.

1166. Mackenzie, Donald. *The Juryman.* London: Elek, 1957. New York:

Houghton-Mifflin, 1958. Gerry Steel is a decorated RAF pilot and a 5-time-convicted burglar in civilian life. Now straight, Steel believes that he can help a friend in trouble, Danny Sullivan, ex-con with a family now coming up for trial, by bribing a juror with the assistance of juror's own amorous wife as conspirator.

1167. MacKintosh, Elizabeth. Josephine Tey, pseud. *The Franchise Affair.* London: Davies, 1948. New York: Macmillan, 1949. Born in Inverness in the Scottish Highlands, and educated at the Royal Academy there, Tey began her writing career with poetry under the pseudonym Gordon Daviot and introduced her series detective Inspector Alan Grant of the Yard in her second novel. Attempting mainstream novels from time to time, Tey would desert the crime novel but return, and in one burst of creativity, produced 6 fine ones in a row in the post-WW II years. Grant's second appearance came in 1936. Her last novel is an historical one, posthumously published. Here, she reprises and updates the 18th-century Canning kidnapping case. (Sidenote: In 1753 young Elizabeth Canning reappeared bedraggled and starved after several days' disappearance and claimed she had been held in a house in London against her will. She was eventually tried and convicted for perjury, transported to America, where her remains lie in a Connecticut graveyard.)

Marion Sharpe and her mother are accused of imprisoning young Betty Kane. Solicitor Robert Blair defends the pair in Norton Assize Court while Grant plays a backup role.

1168. MacPherson, Malcolm C. *Deadlock.* New York: Simon, 1998. Journalist MacPherson's courtroom tale has Judge Daniel Barr presiding over the trial of a Chinese immigrant accused of murdering a socially prominent woman, the granddaughter of a US senator, no less. Midway through the trial, Barr receives word anonymously that the real killer has been empaneled as one of the jurors. Macpherson shrewdly dissects this racially balanced San Francisco jury as an example not only the gap between wealthy and Chinatown poor but also shows, arguably, how vulnerable juries are to being fixed.

1169. Macrae, Travis. *Trial by Slander.* New York: Rinehart; Toronto: Clarke, 1960. Respectable, widowed suburban mother must testify to her lover's innocence in court because she provides her married lover with the perfect alibi; he could not have been committing murder while simultaneously making love to her.

1170. Malamud, Bernard. *The Fixer.* New York: Farrar, 1966. Bellow must be said to have edged out Malamud as the leading Jewish writer of the post-fifties generation, and although both use the Jew as protagonist (the quintessential symbol of, as someone said, the exposed nerve ending of humanity), Malamud's characters are much more introverted and isolated. The trial in this novel is based on a famous case in pre-Bolshevist Russia in which a Jew had been unfairly accused of a crime. B. A. Bibikov, Investigating

Magistrate for Cases of Extraordinary Importance, examines the innocent Yakov Bok for sexual assault on a Russian woman. When Yakov begs him for mercy, protesting innocence, Bibikov utters the ominous words: "Mercy is for God. I depend on the law. The law will protect you" (80). Soon he faces Prosecutor Grubeshov and the charge of luring a boy to his death in a ritual sacrifice. The trial never comes because the purpose is to wring a confession out of him; the terror of the pogroms after his death is made clear by Grubeshov.

1171. Malleson, Lucy Beatrice. Anthony Gilbert, pseud. *The Night of the Fog*. London: Gollancz; New York: Dodd, 1930. Malleson also used the pseudonyms J. Kilmeny Keith and Anne Meredith (under which she wrote 2 and 3 novels respectively; these are additional to the 65 novels published under her Gilbert pseudonym). She is best known for series character Arthur G. Crook, a shrewd, beer-drinking lawyer, addicted to bright brown off-the-rack suits, who occasionally betrays his Cockney origin, an almost lifelong citizen of Brandon Street in London. He bills himself as "The Criminals' Hope and the Judges' Despair." And according to the authors of *Detectionary*, he "compares to Toad of Toad Hall--burly with a bright red face, bright red hair and a bright red car [known as the *Scourge* and later as the *Superb*]. He believes in his clients' innocence, all of them; if he cannot convince the police, he finds the real killer" (28). Crook debuted in 1936 in *Murder by Experts*. Malleson was a founding member of the Detection Club, served as its General Secretary, wrote more than 25 radio plays and dozens of short stories. Some Crook titles: *By Hook or by Crook* (1946; Brit. title *The Spinster's Secret*); *A Case for Mr. Crook* (1952; Brit. title *Miss Pinnegar Disappears*); *Mr. Crook Lifts the Mask* (1970; Brit. title *Death Wears a Mask*); and *A Spy for Mr. Crook* (1944).

1172. Malone, Michael. *Time's Witness*. Boston: Little, 1989. North Carolina Police Chief Cuddy Magnum investigates shenanigans and coverups involving a gubernatorial campaign and a young black man's scheduled execution during his one-month reprieve before execution. Culminates in a big trial scene.

1173. _____. *Uncivil Seasons*. New York: Delacorte, 1983. A high-society murder with a murky Southern ambience set in Hillston, North Carolina off Cape Hatteras brings the lawyer-narrator into a web of complex sexual and familial relationships beginning with the dead woman, his uncle's wife, whose skull is crushed in. Malone is a Harvard ABD, author of a more than a dozen works including plays and nonfiction.

1174. Manchee, William. *Brash Endeavor*. Dallas: Hervey's Booklink, 1998. The second book of the trilogy about Stan Turner. Dallas is a boom town in the seventies, with oil, gas, and real estate deals everywhere. A couple of shady clients get his fledgling practice off to a rough start. It becomes a sleuthing caper when his wife is arrested for murder.

1175. _____. *Second Chair.* Dallas: Hervey's Booklink, 2000. Stan defends Sarah Winters, a college student accused of murdering her own infant; he seeks out his former law prof Harry Hertel to act as second chair in her defense. The trial proves worse than he reckoned because Harry disappears midway through and Stan is stalked by a religious fanatic calling himself Doomsayer.

1176. _____. *Undaunted.* Dallas: Hervey's Booklink, 1997. Young Stan Turner's brush with the law interests him in the legal system, but a twist of fate sends him reporting to the Marine Corps, where he befriends a serial killer on his first day in boot camp.

1177. Mankiewicz, Don M. *The Trial.* New York: Harper; London: Deutsch, 1955. In the summer of 1947, David Blake, a law student befriended by a professor is given a letter of introduction to activist lawyer Barney Castle, working with migrant workers and Mexican-Americans in San Juno; he is expected to gain experience in law, and by means of his journal entries, we see how he assimilates the experiences confronting him. The trial of the title midway through is over the death of Marie Wiltse and the degree to which Angel Chavez is responsible; both Blake and Castle are involved in his cause for justice.

1178. Mann, Abby. (UA/Roxlom, 1961). *Judgment at Nuremberg.* The Academy Award-winning script by Mann and editor Frederic Knudtson deserves mention for its brilliant ensemble performances, thoughtfully rendered by director Stanley Kramer in one of the most probing, if overlong, fictionalized looks at the evil regime spawned by Hitler and Himmler. Notable are Maximilian Schell (Best Actor) as the Nazi defense lawyer; Spencer Tracy as the world-weary judge presiding over the war crimes trial; Montgomery Clift as a deranged concentration camp victim giving the performance of his career; Burt Lancaster playing against type; Judy Garland as *hausfrau*; and Marlene Dietrich as the widow of a German officer.

1179. Mann, Michael, writ. *The Insider.* The Oscar-nominated film was co-written and directed by Mann in this documentary-like and lightly fictionalized account from the headlines of the whistleblower (played by Russell Crowe) and the producer of *Sixty Minutes* (Al Pacino) who together incited tobacco litigation across the US in the late 1990s (Columbia/TriStar, 1999).

1180. Mann, Paul (James). *The Burning Ghats.* New York: Fawcett-Columbine, 1996. The English-born author abandoned his home in Canada to live in Maine. He has traveled the world as a writer for international magazines and newspapers. He told *Contemporary Authors* that he attributes his acute sense of the world's absurdity to having grown up with a working-class father, a Tory and a police officer, and a manic depressive, alcoholic mother who worked as a nurse in an insane asylum. Besides several pulp thrillers, he writes procedurals of an ancient culture with a newfangled obsession with technology and Hollywood. Like Forster before him, Mann is fascinated by the continual clashing of two cultures: the smug, British imperialistic attitude that still prevails in India today and the native culture's open bohemianism. Mann added in his CA interview: "My life of itinerancy has left me virtually stateless, which can be an asset because it spares me any excess of nationalism, though it also undermines any sense of region perspective" (Vol. 43, 259).

The blue-eyed lawyer is a former decorated officer in police services, or as he puts it here, "I had a little fun chasing the Paks [Pakistani Marxist guerillas] around the valley" (27). In a scenario reminiscent of a recent ecological and human tragedy in India, Sansi is hired by the new state minister for the environment, Rupe Seshan, to investigate the Dumont Chemical Corporation of Philadelphia's environmental disaster when its Bombay plant leaks effluent into the Ganges and kills over a thousand.

1181. _____. *The Ganja Coast.* New York: Ivy, 1995. The title refers to the site of a community of mostly American and European Westerners, comprising unreconstructed hippies, dropouts, dopers, and misfits. No longer a police officer but a lawyer, Sansi poses as a tourist with his journalist girlfriend to investigate a young girl's death among these hedonists.

1182. _____. *Season of the Monsoon.* New York: Ivy, 1995. First book in the Bombay series featuring police detective (later lawyer) George Sansi written with a style that fuses wit with a paradoxical look at life in Indian society.

1183. Marcon, David. *Enemy of the State.* (Touchstone, 1999). Only a brief portion of this high-tech espionage film, directed by Tony Scott, concerns a legal bibliography--namely, Will Smith happens to be a DC labor lawyer with Gene Hackman as an ex-National Security Council spook. Both are forced to team up against agency enemies tracking them with ultrasophisticated equipment including spy satellites. Smith's character, Robert Clayton Dean, inadvertently becomes involved in the murder and cover-up of a congressman who won't play ball with the security agency's desire for a bill that would give them *carte blanche* against American privacy. Encountering an old college friend on the run just prior to his murder; Dean becomes the agency's target when the surveillance disk--evidence of the crime implicating the head of a covert spy operation played by Jon Voight--is secreted on his person. Prod. Jerry Bruckheimer.

1184. Margolin, Phillip M. *After Dark.* New York: Doubleday, 1997. Margolin grew up in NYC and Levittown. From 1972 to1996 he was in private practice, specializing in criminal defense. As an appellate attorney he appeared before the Supreme Court. He is qualified in capital felony cases, having defended in more than 30 homicide cases and was the first Oregon attorney to use the Battered Women's Syndrome in defending a client accused of murder. His writing since 1996 has increased steadily and includes non-fiction and short fiction in law journals and magazines. He has an Edgar nomination, his second novel was made into film by HBO (*The Last Innocent Man*), and two recent novels were Main Selections of The Literary Guild. *Gone, but Not Forgotten* went to 25 international publishers. Margolin tends to overload his plots and, as here, mixes romantic intrigue with various subplots involving legal corruption, drug kingpins, and a death-penalty trial. Exciting but uneven and his reviews are steadily mixed. (*See* Mr. Margolin's commentary in **Craft Notes**.)

Fans of John D. Macdonald's *Cape Fear* will recognize part of the plot here: Charlie Deems is a psycho child-killer released on a technicality and returns to the scene of his conviction for revenge against the deputy DA who put him on death row. Abigail Griffen's ex-husband Robert, a justice of the Oregon Supreme Court and car-bomb victim, overturned Deems' sentence. Now she herself stands accused of the crime. Deems, of course, is the prosecution's number-one witness. Young lawyer Tracy Cavanaugh, working for Abbie's counsel, a famous death-penalty defense attorney named Matthew Reynolds, makes a discovery in her research that turns the book's final section ("After Dark") into a reversal and belated recognition of the killer.

1185. _____. *The Burning Man.* New York: Doubleday, 1996. Margolin returns to a plot he used in his first novel. Peter Hale, an associate in a Portland law firm, disobeys his father's orders, which results in the firm's losing a multimillion-dollar lawsuit. Disgraced and fired, he becomes a public defender. This fifth Margolin novel was a Main Selection of The Literary Guild.

1186. _____. *Gone, but Not Forgotten.* New York: Bantam, 1994. This police procedural with a psychotic-murderer twist: A ten-year-old case of torture-murders of Hunter's Point, New York housewives suddenly surfaces in a similar string of grisly murders of housewives in Portland, Oregon. Feminist attorney Betsy Tannenbaum finds herself defending the New York killer who denies he is involved in the current murders and insists a bitter homicide detective from ten years ago is framing him because he was pardoned for those crimes in a scheme to save some victims.

1187. _____. *Heartstone.* New York: Pocket, 1978. Edgar-nominated first novel of a young lawyer whose multimillion-dollar mistake in a lawsuit destroys his reputation and results in his termination and disinheritance by his family; he exiles himself to public-defender work in a small Oregon town, where redemption awaits him in the form of a case involving a cheerleader's alleged murder of her popular boyfriend.

1188. _____. *The Last Innocent Man.* New York: Bantam, 1995. Margolin offers his mix of suspense and the theme of redemption in this tale of defense attorney David Nash, so successful at getting his clients off that he wonders whether he is part of a corrupt system that lets killers and rapists free. However, he sees promise in a client who actually is innocent, but when that client lies to him and uses him, he despairs until circumstances shock him out of his slump and force him to combat a dangerous killer.

1189. _____. *The Undertaker's Widow.* New York: Doubleday, 1998. Judge Richard Quinn, young son of an honorable Portland, Oregon jurist and himself an ethical judge who wants to adjudicate by Lincoln's credo, has puts his career and his marriage into jeopardy during the murder trial of gun-toting, cigar-smoking state legislator and ex-cop Ellen ("Tough-as-Nails") Crease, accused of murdering her wealthy mortician husband in West Hills. Quinn believes she was set up, but in trying to investigate, he sets himself up as a patsy and blackmail victim.

1190. _____. *Wild Justice.* New York: HarperCollins, 2000. Grisly mass murders, bodies discovered in the woods, black-market sales of organs, and a courtroom defense of a despicable surgeon are the prime ingredients, but the plot is more complex than that. Dr. Vincent Cardoni is implicated and tried but acquitted on a technicality. Holding second chair in his trial is Amanda Jaffe, assisting her famous trial-lawyer father. When a similar killing field turns up years later, it is the wife of the surgeon who is now implicated.

1191. Maron, Margaret. *Bloody Kin.* New York: Mysterious, 1985. Margaret Maron has a slew of mystery awards and nominations for her fiction in the last decade that include Best Mystery Novel (1989, 1992, 1993). In 1992 alone, she racked up a Best Mystery, Edgar, Anthony Boucher, Agatha, and Macavity for *Bootlegger's Daughter* alone. She wrote the NYPD procedurals featuring Detective Sigrid Harald but returned to North Carolina for the setting of the Judge Deborah Knott tales. (Applauded for her pitch-perfect dialogue, the author resides in Raleigh and is herself a farm girl from there). Deborah's first appearance is an Agatha-winning short story called "Deborah's Judgment" in *A Woman's Eye* (New York: Delacorte, 1991). (**See** Ms. Maron's commentary in **Craft Notes**.)

In this non-Knott tale, Jake Honeycutt is a New York financier relaxing and hunting near the family homestead in North Carolina when he dies of a shotgun blast that local authorities and even his own lawyer believe to be an accident; however, his pregnant wife Kate knows that her husband's death is more sinister--first, a stranger turns up murdered and then the photo of one of Jake's Vietnam vet buddies is missing.

1192. _____. *Bootlegger's Daughter.* New York: Mysterious, 1992. Lawyer-protagonist Deborah Knott debuts in the novel form in this tale about running for district judge in rural North Carolina while investigating a bizarre, unsolved eighteen-year-old murder. Deborah is an intelligent, capable woman trying to survive on her own terms almost in spit of her large and loving family.

Note Swanson and James in *Killer Books*: "But she has the wit, the intelligence, and the strength it takes for a professional woman to survive in an atmosphere that subtly undermines women like her" (192). They note that this first Knott novel made history by garnering mystery fiction's four most prestigious awards--the Edgar, the Agatha, the Macavity, and the Anthony. A recent Deborah Knott short story, "With This Ring," is included in *Crimes of the Heart*, ed. Carolyn G. Hart (New York: Berkley, 1995).

1193. _____. *Home Fires* [alt. title: *Home Fires Burning*]. New York: Mysterious, 1998. One of Deborah's nine older brothers has a teenaged son with a vandalism charge for defacing a gravestone. A week later a small African-American church burns to the ground on nearby property as a result of what appears to be a hate crime; then a long-dead body is found buried beneath the ashes.

1194. _____. *Killer Market.* New York: Mysterious, 1997. This is fifth appearance of Judge Knott and the first outside her hometown. Once a year the population of High Point, North Carolina doubles as the town hosts the International Home Furnishings Market trade show, and Deborah gets a close look at the overcrowding when she substitutes for a vacationing judge but finds no hotel room available. Elderly Matilda Jernigan invites Knott to stay with hers; then she disappears--along with Deborah's purse. Deborah is questioned by police when her purse is found near the body of Chan Nolan, murder victim, and partners with an old law-school chum, Chan's mother-in-law, to solve the crime.

1195. _____. *Shooting at Loons.* New York: Mysterious, 1994. Sitting in for a judge from Beaufort, Judge Knott looks forward to a restful week on Harkers Island on North Carolina's southern coast, but her first clamming expedition turns ugly when she discovers the corpse of a well-known fisherman.

1196. _____. *Southern Discomfort.* New York: Mysterious, 1993. Deborah loses the election but a bigoted judge's death and a governor's appointment secure her the bench. When she agrees to fulfill a campaign promise to help build a needy single mother a home. Working on the all-woman crew is her niece Annie Sue, there to wire the house as an apprentice electrician; however, before the house is half-built, Annie Sue is found inside beaten and with her clothes ripped and missing.

1197. _____. *Storm Track.* New York: Mysterious, 2000. Judge Knott's good-looking cousin is implicated in the murder of an adulterous wife, found scantily clad and murdered in a motel one calm summer day. As the exposed web of promiscuity among the decent citizens of Colleton County creates its own kind of storm, Hurricane Fran is busy raging toward the Carolina coast.

1198. _____. *Up Jumps the Devil.* New York: Mysterious, 1996. Black sheep of his own redneck clan, Allan Stancil is suspected in the murder of one of his kin. When another Stancil is killed, Judge Knott becomes the prime suspect. She and Allan have a long-buried marriage that yokes her to a killer's past.

1199. Marshall, Arthur Hammond. Archibald Marshall, pseud. *Claimants.* Boston: Houghton, 1934. Young Sir Piers Johnnes is engaged to marry and settle down on his ancestral estate, Shawn Hall, when a visit from his lawyer Kenworthy disrupts his life. He is informed that a man claiming to be his father's elder brother, believed drowned at sea thirty years ago, has turned up to claim the baronetcy, the family fortune and Shawn Hall itself.

1200. _____. *Nothing Hid.* London: Collins, 1934. Boston: Houghton, 1935. Another arsenic poisoning murder with defendant Hubert Barrowdale on trial in Magistrate's Court, in Felminster, for the murder of his best friend, Colonel Cairn.

1201. Marshall, Robert K. *Little Squire Jim.* New York: Duell, 1949. London: Macdonald, 1950. Frontier trial set in the Tateboro Courthouse, Tennessee, in which James Braxton Boyden ("Little Squire" Jim) stands trial for killing Beldie Thomas. Plenty of commentary from the gallery of witnesses and spectators throughout the trial--for example, Davey Crockett speaks up for his young friend, and the wife of the deceased is ordered out of the courtroom by Jusge Spicer for her interruption.

Marston, Edward, pseud. *See* Miles, Keith. . . .

1202. Martel, John S. *The Alternate.* New York: Dutton, 1999. Martel is a partner of the San Francisco firm of Farella, Braun, & Martel. He was a consultant for the LA DA's office during the O. J. Simpson trial and the Menendez brothers' retrial. The dissipated but beautiful Lara Ashford is sliced to death with a shard of glass and her powerful, mobbed-up husband is accused. Courtroom adversaries Grace Harris works for the prosecutor's office; Barrett Dickson for the defense. An awkwardly contrived whodunit and lackluster characterization.

1203. _____. *Conflicts of Interest.* New York: Pocket, 1995. Small-town lawyer Seth ("Cowboy") Cameron lands a grueling but coveted position in a prestigious San Francisco law firm and becomes locked in a power struggle with senior partner Anthony Treadwell during his probationary period. Treadwell sends him the widow of an Air Force pilot with a risky agenda that proves his ruin at the firm but sends him off on a trail of corruption that leads him through a Caicos Islands tax scam to a San Francisco courtroom and conspiracy trial.

1204. _____. *Partners.* Toronto; New York: Bantam, 1988. First, Martel is a much better writer than John Grisham because he can grab a reader with his style and dictional finesse alone, but he sacrifices that strength to pander to readers who care nothing about verisimilitude of plot. Only one founding partner of the trio of Stafford, Parrish, and McAllister, a top-notch San Francisco firm now survives, but Whit Stafford defers to his top associates Austin Barrington and Gradner White. It is chiefly in the firm's premier trial lawyer, 40-something Kevin Stone and his opposition to Barrington's demonic scheme to hold the firm together in the financial crisis that the book enjoys its tension. The plot hinges on a personal-injury lawsuit with stakes in the high millions against North American Chemical Company, a mafia-owned plant, that is responsible for the contamination of drinking water.

1205. Martini, Steve [Steven Paul]. *The Attorney.* New York: Putnam, 2000. Besides criminal and civil lawyering, Martini had been an LA newspaper reporter before entering law and was capitol correspondent at the statehouse in Sacramento, where series character Paul Madriani operates as defense counsel. Martini himself was once special counsel for California Victims of Violent Crimes Program. His minor characters have a certain thinness, perhaps because he orients viewpoint entirely around the soberly introspective Madriani, and his plotlines are sometimes too slickly resolved, but he is generally very sharp with courtroom action and the arcana of legal machinery even when his clunky prose is elsewhere sinking into the murk or wobbling along on a track of cliché--as sampled by Nico Perone taking the witness box in *Undue Influence*: "Perone could work up a good sweat in January on a stroll in the Arctic" (376).

Madriani is hired by a former client, for whom he had won a railroad pension case, and which is altogether moot now that Jonah Hale has won a huge lottery fortune. Now he wants his attorney to get his 8-year-old grandchild back, taken away by his coke-addicted daughter, who lost custody to her father. Discovering that she is being protected by an organization founded to protect women from wealthy husbands, Madriani clashes with its fanatical founder of Vanishing Victims, Zolanda Suade, who threatens him with exposure and a gun. Her death makes that moot, however, and with Hale now surrounded by a frenzied media and the legal system towering over him, Martini has his favorite narrative sequence for display: a media firestorm-cum-trial with the lawyer versus the law's might.

1206. _____. *Compelling Evidence.* New York: Putnam's, 1992. In this sequel to *Prime Witness*, Madriani is fired from Potter, Skarpellos by Ben Potter, mentor and Supreme Court nominee, because of his affair with Potter's wife. When Potter is found dead of a gunshot wound to the head, Talia Potter is implicated. Paul has to abandon his investigation into a call-girl ring involving state legislators and a defalcation case in his private practice out of his office in "Capital City" (Sacramento) to rescue her against what looks to be a set-up by Ben's partner Skarpellos.

1207. _____. *Critical Mass.* New York: Putnam's, 1998. "Joss" Cole is an ex-public defender from LA representing a group of commercial fishermen in the San Juan Islands of Washington State, all of whom appear to be suffering from toxic pollution. Enter Dean Belden, a rich client in search of a lawyer to help him set up a business in the islands. Within days, Belden is subpoenaed to appear before a federal grand jury and after testifying, dies in an explosion.

1208. _____. *The Judge.* New York: Putnam's, 1996. When Madriani is asked by Judge Acosta to help save his career (he has been arrested in a prostitution sting as one of the johns), Madriani reluctantly agrees to defend his old nemesis, now a leper. But when the vice undercover deputy who solicited Acosta is herself murdered, Madriani has to ask himself whether the charge is a frame-up, as Acosta tells him--or whether the judge opted for a more expedient solution to his problem. All in all, less byzantine in plotting than is typical for Martini, but you can see the rogue cop coming from a mile away, and the present tense begins to grate after a while.

1209. _____. *The List.* New York: Putnam's, 1997. Martini abandons Madriani for a slick tale with a typical Hollywood ending. Abby Chandlis is a Seattle attorney-novelist who has penned a bestseller under a *nom de plume* and hires Jack Jermaine to be her persona. Jack is a failed writer and agrees to become this "Gable Cooper," but her skills at a legal makeover boomerang when someone puts her life in danger. Now that she is on the verge of a book-and-film deal worth seven million, it occurs to her she is expendable. Casting an eye on a Grisham formula, Martini sends his protagonist fleeing for her life across the US as she tries to get to the proof she needs to save her own life--before the killer catches up.

1210. _____. *Prime Witness.* New York: Putnam's, 1993. Madriani accepts a stint in the Davenport, CA prosecutor's office and immediately gets involved a series of grisly triple murders known as the Putah Creek Murders, in which the victims are staked to the ground with tent pegs; then executed with a stake through the heart. The police believe that a 27-year-old security guard is the murderer, a Russian immigrant named Iganovich. His attorney is Adrian Chambers, an old enemy of Madriani's from his early prosecutorial days when a sting operation left Chambers suspended from law practice for five years. But Madriani suspects the most recent killings were copycat; furthermore, he believes there was a witness to the last two slayings hiding in a tree, and he has to resist pressure from all sides--Judge Armando Aacosta, wife Nikki, and the town's assistant prosecutor--to pin all crimes on the Russian.

1211. _____. *The Simeon Chamber.* New York: Fine, 1988. His debut novel is a mixed bag of genres featuring art theft, conspiracy, and murder. A young girl's search for her natural father brings Sam Bogardus, lawyer, to her assistance. The search leads to an ancient parchment with pages from Sir

Francis Drake's diary in modern San Francisco and a mysterious WW II "ghost blimp."

1212. _____. *Undue Influence.* New York: Putnam's, 1994. Wife Nikki's deathbed request is that Paul help sister Laurel in what is becoming a vicious custody case against her ex-husband, community leader and slimy politician. However, after the principals are publicly viewed in a corridor spat with a furious, purse-swinging Laurel on the attack, it is clear that she will be the prime suspect when the new wife is found shot to death in her bathtub and infant murdered in another room. Madriani has to fight a ruthless prosecutor and a cop with a vendetta to get justice for a woman he knows is holding out on him. *Kirkus* named Martini's fourth, which became a CBS two-part telefilm in 1996 with Brian Dennehy, "courtroom novel of the year," and the final fourth of the book is set in the courtroom for a climactic finale.

1213. Masefield, John. *Dead Ned: The Autobiography of a Corpse Who Recovered Life within the Coast of Dead Ned and Came to What Fortune You Shall Hear.* London: Heinemann; New York: Macmillan, 1938. Lackluster seafaring tale of a youth falsely accused of murdering an admiral and being sentenced to hang.

1214. Mason, A. E. W. [Alfred Edward Woodley]. *Witness for the Defence.* London and New York: French, 1913. First performed at St. James Theatre in 1911, Mason's play has neither witness nor courtroom, but it is based on what one witness said in a Bombay courtroom prior to the play's opening curtain. Henry Thresk, who once loved Stella Ballantyne before her marriage to an abusive drunkard, fabricates a story to ensure her acquittal of murdering her husband George. Courted by Dick Hazelwood, Stella's prospective father-in-law is spurred by gossip to summon Thresk to his home in Little Beding in the Sussex Downs. Thresk lies again for Stella but later confronts her and orders her to tell her fiancé the truth: that she shot her husband before he could beat her again. Scribner's published the novel version the next year under the tile *The Witness for the Defence.* Another mystery by Mason is *House of the Arrow* (London: Hodder, 1924) featuring Frobisher & Haslitt, solicitors from Russell Square.

1215. Mason, Philip. Philip Woodruff, pseud. *Call the Next Witness.* London: Cape, 1945. New York: Harcourt, 1946. Woodruff used a pseudonym because of his work in Northern India and the feeling that exposure as a writer would hamper him. Cultural differences, their ambiguities and tensions behind Anglo-Indian justice and its impact on native people is the real subject. Pyari Singh's death triggers an investigation, and as British and Indian police collaborate and collide in the investigation, each witness summoned deepens the mystery of her death as suicide or murder. Finally, her husband is drawn up on murder charges and tried.

1216. Masterman, John C[ecil]. *An Oxford Tragedy.* London: Gollancz, 1933 New York: DeMer, 1981. Much-admired whodunit with a Viennese lawyer protagonist. Ernst Brendel is guest lecturer at Oxford discoursing upon the art of murder when an unpopular tutor named Mr. Shirley is murdered. He then puts his theories into action by examining 11 dons as potential killers. A second outing for the lawyer-sleuth was not published until two decades later in *The Case of the Four Friends: Diversion in Pre-Detection* (London: Hodder, 1956; New York: British Book Centre, 1959).

1217. Masters, Edgar Lee. *Kit O'Brien.* New York: Boni, 1927. Better known for his *Spoon River Anthology*, Masters writes a sequel to his *Mitch Miller* (Macmillan, 1920) in which good-natured Kit O'Brien, a Huck Finn-style narrator, tells of his misadventures in Petersburg with two companions George Heigold and Charley King. The narrator is beguiled at times, like Huck, but makes clear by repetition and indirection what happened versus what he believed happened. There is no trial but a recollection of one in which runaways George and Charley are bribed by a lawyer for the railroad to say in court that Mitch Miller slipped and was ground under the wheels of a train; instead, he was knocked under the wheels by "'the brakeman who caught him flippin'"(13); then the boys were framed on a theft charge and sent to reformatory.

1218. Masur, Harold Q. *The Attorney.* New York: Random, 1973. London: Souvenir, 1974. He was once called to the Pentagon to give a workshop on imaginative thinking on international tension areas. He had served in North Africa, Egypt, India, and China during WW II in the Air Force. He attended Bordentown Military Institute and graduated from NYU School of Law. He tried acting and professional tennis before law practice and subsequently writing. His series lawyer-protagonist is Scott Jordan, wisecracking and cool-headed New York City sleuth-attorney. Masur's style is almost always light-*noir* or par-boiled, never tough on the sensibilities because the glib remarks trip from Jordan's tongue as he faces danger, or more often, whenever the glowering police ask him to explain his presence midst the carnage he stumbles upon. Here is Jordan finding a dead body in a bathtub moments after his entrance into a stranger's apartment: "Somebody had rowed him across the River Styx, using a cartridge shell as a paddle" (*You Can't Live Forever* 5). Jordan appears in a collection of stories called *The Name Is Jordan* (Pyramid, 1962). A sampling of the 14 extant Scott Jordans follows.

This one, however, is an exception to the rule because it concerns a sensational sex-murder case in which maverick lawyer Paul Slater represents his wife's cousin, Ken Sheridan, a law student accused of strangling Dolly Wayne, the actress-mother of his pregnant girlfriend and secret wife. Opposing him is tough John Nicoletti of the DA's Office. Slater has to make a tough decision at the end: Knowing what he knows about Sheridan's alibi, will he put him on the stand and let Nicolletti shred him?

1219. _____. *The Big Money.* New York: Simon, 1954; Boardman, 1955. A familiar beginning: Jordan returns from a trip and finds a stranger using the phone in his apartment, but this strange man claims to be Jordan. In the background is a shady investment company called Opportunities Unlimited and a neurotic ex-wife soon to be implicated in murder.

1220. _____. *The Broker.* New York: St. Martin's; London: Souvenir, 1981. Ocala, Florida lawyer Alex Bogart gets involved with adulterous, rapacious Cora Bendiner when her husband hires him to do a simple power of attorney. When the ailing husband succumbs to a heart attack, he conspires with her to dump the body in the Everglades, masquerade as the husband, forge his signature on stock certificates for deposit in a fraudulent account--all in an elaborate scheme involving a proxy fight to gain a film studio. In 1992, the Mystery Writers Association gave him a Raven Award for his years of long service.

1221. _____. *Bury Me Deep.* New York: Simon, 1947; London: Boardman, 1948. The earlier Scott Jordans show a stronger influence of the Hammett-Chandler tradition, and this one in particular reads like a Chandler knockoff with their hurly-burly openings and violent or tawdry encounters in opening chapters. Masur gentrifies him a bit more hereafter but the early ones show some macho swagger; Jordan is a moodier sort, fresh from the war (his resume includes an OSS stint with "Wild Bill" Donovan). Jordan returns early from Miami and finds an almost naked, completely drunk blonde in his apartment at the Drummond. A young couple mysteriously appears at his door looking for Bob Cambreau before he can ascertain the blonde's story (Jordan reads of the stockbroker's death later); he punches the male in the nose after a brief altercation and dumps the drunk blonde, now passed out, in a taxi. She dies from drinking poisoned liquor; he is rousted from bed by Lieutenant Nola and grilled under the hot lights for the death of Verna Ford.

1222. _____. *The Last Gamble* [alt. title: *Murder on Broadway*, New York: Dell, 1959; Brit. title: *The Last Breath*, London: Boardman, 1958]. New York: Simon, 1958. Comic actor Toby Hammond is arrested for felonious assault, and the producer of the Broadway hit in which Hammond is performing awakens Jordan in the middle of the night to get his star bailed out. The complication mixes Masur's favorite ingredients of adulterously seductive women and forged wills.

1223. _____. *The Legacy Lenders.* New York: Random; London: Boardman, 1967. Jordan investigates a scheme in which prospective heirs are lent money in anticipation of their inheritance but often die suspiciously to the financial benefit of the lenders.

1224. _____. *Make a Killing.* New York: Random; London: Boardman, 1964. As the novel opens, Jordan is getting fined and reamed in court by Judge Hamilton Mack for violence against a trespasser, Ben Mornay, caught redhanded by Jordan going through his office files. This businessman's murder, and another that points toward Jordan, are linked to a vicious proxy fight led by Charles Barlow to take over a theater chain.

1225. _____. *The Mourning After.* New York: St. Martin's, 1981; London: Gollancz, 1983. Jordan uncovers a counterfeiting scheme of Impressionists paintings. When a client dies of a heart attack, the estranged wife inherits an art gallery; then, Jordan is almost killed by an exploding bomb boobytrapped to the dead man's safety deposit box where the provenance of a Picasso is to be found.

1226. _____. *Send Another Hearse.* New York: Simon; London: Boardman, 1960. Jordan in a case of police corruption and embezzlement at the literary firm of Coleman & Varney, which has just sold a book to Hollywood for movie rights and made $50,000--until Adam Colema's partner disappeared with it.

1227. _____. *So Rich, So Lovely, and So Dead.* New York: Simon, 1952; London: Boardman, 1953. Rich and flamboyant Linda Franchini-Romanoff will lose her wealth, owing to a slip in her late father's holograph will. She must be married within a month to an "employee," rather than "executive," of her father's company or she will lose her share to a sister and her rapacious husband. Jordan first dismisses her as a rich eccentric but is compelled to find her killer to help a client.

1228. _____. *Tall, Dark and Deadly.* New York: Simon, 1956; London: Boardman, 1957. Jordan is accused of murdering a man named Steve Banton and precisely between 2:45 and 3:00 in the afternoon inside Banton's hotel room; three witnesses saw Jordan go in and heard fighting. Motive, say the cops, is that Banton helped Jordan rig a divorce case two years ago and the new DA is campaigning to put crooked lawyers out of business.

1229. _____. *You Can't Live Forever.* New York: Simon; London: Boardman, 1951. Jordan, with usual luck and aplomb, runs afoul of the police in the first ten pages of the novel. To serve papers for his client on recalcitrant theatrical producer Jonathan Creel, Scott poses as a telephone repair man; he is let into the man's flat by a strange woman and discovers the dead body of Creel's partner in the bathtub. One more: *Suddenly a Corpse* (Simon, 1949; Boardman, 1950).

1230. Matera, Lia. *Designer Crimes.* New York: Simon, 1995. Born in Canada, the Italian-American author is the creator of two San Francisco lawyer-sleuths, flamboyant criminal defender Laura DiPalma and Willa Jansson. She has picked up all the big nominations, including Edgar, Anthony and Macavity, and earned a Shamus for "Dead Drunk," Best Short Story of 1996 (she has stories in 7 recent anthologies). She attended Hastings College of Law and was editor of its law quarterly until graduation in 1981; then she went on to Stanford Law as a teaching fellow. She lives in Santa Cruz, California.

DiPalma is tough, upscale in her practice, while Jansson's constantly trying to overcome the embarrassment of her pink-diaper upbringing and her aging hippie parents. Willa worries about life, matures, stumbles, and casts a sardonic eye over her life and missteps from time to time; she has much irreverence for her chosen profession and sees the flaws in the law's majestic garb. She does, however, succeed in her sleuthing despite the frequent failures in love and in various jobs, and her confusion, so like many a modern professional's, is endearing to her readers. DiPalma, on the other hand, is

> close to being an unlikable character, since she seems so materialistic and blindly ambitious. But as the series progresses, she grows and changes radically. Matera constructs tight plots that interweave character development with fast-movingaction, balanced against thought-provoking analysis of difficult social issues such as assisted suicide, or pornography and computers. (Swanson 194)

Ousted from her lucrative practice as an important associate in one of San Francisco's high-profile law firms, DiPalma is trying to make a go of her solo practice. She agrees to defend a high-school classmate against a charge of murder. When the head of her former firm begins a subtle slanderous campaign to destroy DiPalma, she attempts to engage a labor attorney to sue. In her first meeting she is a horrified witness to the murder of Jocelyn Kinsley, the labor attorney. Convinced that Kinsley's dying words (*designer crimes*) is an important clue, Laura connects with her friend and former lover, private detective Sandy Arkelett to find Kinsley's killer.

1231. _____. *Face Value.* New York: Pocket, 1995. Laura returns to law practice, moves back to San Francisco. her first client is a woman who wants to sue her spiritual advisor, Brother Mike, who videotapes group sex sessions and by means of computer enhancement, reimages the players to protect their identities because he's selling the tapes to porno shops to raise money for his consciousness-raising therapeutic foundation. When Laura responds to a phonecall from another group member, she finds six murdered exotic dancers. Matera's message is more timely today with international sex slavery in the news and sex workers (prostitutes, film actresses, strippers) dehumanized by society.

1232. _____. *The Good Fight: A Laura Di Palma Mystery.* New York: Simon, 1990. Laura is in turmoil with senior partner Doron White over her newly acquired reputation as a hired gun for guilty clients and her current client is giving her worries: legless Vietnam vet Danny Crosetti is thinking of going "underground" and sticking Laura with the bond pending his trial for killing John Lefevre; worse is lover Hal's diagnosis--alexic, aphasic, partially paralyzed, disoriented, and hostile. When Crosetti does bolt, he soon commits suicide, and Laura is faced with clearing his name.

1233. _____. *A Hard Bargain.* New York: Simon, 1992. Laura is retired from her law practice and living in Northern California with her lover-cousin, when she is visited by her former partner Sandy Arkelett, seeking help with a suicide case of chronically depressed Karen McGuinn, whose husband left a loaded gun with her every day.

1234. _____. *Havana Twist: A Willa Janssen Mystery.* New York: Simon, 1998. Willa Jansson's mother heads off to Cuba with a band of gray-haired *brigandistas* ostensibly to attend a conference of the Women's International league for Peace and Freedom. Willa writes it off until the group returns without her. Risking disbarment for "trading with the enemy," Willa rushes to the rescue and discovers a Cuba in disintegration where food is in short supply and the electricity runs a couple hours a day. She accepts help from two countrymen, supposedly in Havana for a film festival, but it appears they have their own agenda. The trail is thin--however, she is suddenly on the run from a ruthless murderer determined to stop her dead in her tracks. Stuart Miller in *Booklist* (15 April 1998) calls it "the best Jansson adventure yet . . ."

1235. _____. *Hidden Agenda.* New York: Bantam, 1988. Willa is working at a low-paying job when her boss is poisoned; she is subsequently offered a high-paying job at a toney law firm, accepts, and her new boss is fatally poisoned at a retreat.

1236. _____. *Irreconcilable Differences.* New York: HarperCollins, 1999. The lawyer's familiar term for innumerable divorce settlements serves also as principle of selection for this collection of 20 stories by mostly mainstream mystery writers, although familiar names from the legal-thriller stable include Margaret Maron, John Lutz, Jeremiah Healy and Matera herself. The only tale with a legal foot in the door is Healy's "Legacy," in which series protagonist John Francis Cuddy gets involved in a messy divorce involving a cunning, tough old Lithuanian woman in South Boston bent on providing for her daughter and grandchildren without permission from the drunken, penniless son-in-law who plays a pivotal role in the scheme to provide a legacy, as does Cuddy.

1237. _____. *Last Chants: A Willa Jansson Mystery.* New York: Simon, 1996. Willa is sidetracked on the way to her job for a firm specializing in multimedia law; she sees a cop about to arrest her parents' best friend Arthur Kenna, a mythology scholar and two-time convicted radical, because he is brandishing a gun in the street (he claims that a passerby pressed the weapon into his hand). Willa knows that he faces life if he is convicted, so she executes a split-second diversion that takes the two of them away from the scene, escaping through San Francisco's financial district and turning them into fugitives. She turns to a former boyfriend, who owns an isolated cabin in the mountains. This tale works on a second level of the supernatural, for Willa must enter the spirit world to extricate herself and Kenna from this harm.

1238. _____. *Prior Conviction.* New York: Simon, 1991. Willa resigns her lucrative job to work for a liberal federal judge, Michael J. Shanna, in what becomes a tangled skein of events commencing with a friend's request to ask Willa to seek out the husband of a 1960's radical and ask him what his intentions are if she files for divorce. Judge Shanna mysteriously recuses himself from a securities fraud case that the estranged husband, a lawyer himself, is arguing. The wife meanwhile has turned state's evidence, and she dies mysteriously.

1239. _____. *A Radical Departure.* New York: Bantam, 1988. First-year associate Willa is working for radical lawyer Julian Warneke. Then Warneke drops dead in front of the entire San Francisco office during his lunch (hemlock poisoning). Her own radical-liberal mother is one of the beneficiaries of his will.

1240. _____. *Smart Money.* New York: Bantam, 1988. Laura Di Palma's first outing. She returns to her hometown for revenge on her ex: she takes the job he wants as a public defender.

1241. _____. *Star Witness.* New York: Simon, 1997. Willa's new case is a favor to a psychiatrist friend, whose client is charged with felonious hit-and-run. Allan Miller states under hypnosis he was not in the car at the time of the accident when his sports car allegedly went over an embankment landing on top of another car and crushed its driver. His wounds are consistent with what he said the aliens did to him and suppressed memories reinforce a tale of alien abduction. Willa rejects a plea bargain, even though she knows a media circus is looming but is unprepared for helicopter chases, vicious reporters, and snipers. Includes a bibliography of UFO literature.

1242. _____. *Where Lawyers Fear to Tread.* New York: Bantam, 1987.; rpt. Ballantine, 1991. Jansson debuts in a murder investigation at Malhousie Law School in San Francisco as a fledgling yuppie-lawyer, a member of the law school and editor of its review, embarrassed by her hippie-Marxist upbringing but destined to become a high-powered San Francisco multimedia litigator. The deaths of editors and a professor begin the mystery.

Matera has also recently published a collection of legal fiction: "*Counsel for the Defense*" *and Other Stories* (Unity, ME: Five Star, 2000).

1243. Mathew, Theobald. *Forensic Fables.* London, Toronto: Butterworth , 1926. Mathew published under the pen name O this miscellanea of satire, facetiae, anecdote, illustrations, etc. A table of cases cited, table of statutes and index accompany the collection, most of which had appeared in various law journals. A 1961 edition by Butterworth (London) includes contributions by Francis Cowper and Hubert Picarda, in 4 vols. of material collected between 1926-32. The moral lessons drawn are in simple English in contrast to the elaborate and Latinate anecdotal fabulae themselves of errant lawyers, judges, plaintiffs, and so forth--a sample: "The Emeritus Professor of International Law and the Police Court Brief" . . . Moral.--*Choose Your Tribunal Wisely* (147-49, rev.ed.).

1244. Matthews, Clayton. *The Power Seekers.* Los Angeles: Pinnacle, 1978. King Hanratty is a Tennessee lawyer, defending Senatorial candidate Adam Starke, accused in the shooting death of his wife. He prepares his case by researching his client's family tree from 1845 onward. The case and family saga run parallel, alternating with each other. Matthews also published a trial-aftermath novel *The Mendoza File* (1969).

1245. Maynard, Joyce. *To Die For.* New York: Dutton, 1992. The novel is inspired by the sensational trial of Pamela Smart of Massachusetts; the petite, thirtyish high-school guidance counselor talked her teenaged lover and his friends into killing her husband. Maynard's narrator becomes TV Weather Girl Suzanne Stone of Little Hope, New Hampshire, played by Nicole Kidman in the excellent spoof adapted from the book by Buck Henry in the 1995 Columbia film. Dir. Gus Van Zant. Perf. Joaquin Phoenix and Matt Dillon.

1246. McBain, Ed. *Beauty and the Beast.* New York: Holt, 1982. Evan Hunter is the legal name of Salvatore A. Lombino, born in New York City and better known to the world since 1956 as Ed McBain, author of dozens of tough police procedurals called the "87th Precinct" novels. McBain served in the Navy in 1944 and worked for the Scott Meredith Literary Agency. Of certain of his characters and their careers, many readers can recite chapter and verse because they are so familiar to his fans. He created "Evan Hunter" from the names of his high school and college. McBain, who has authored more than 80 novels, is a Mystery Writers of America Grand Master. Although the "87th" novels were suspended with the appearance of the Matt Hope series, they have since resumed and (along with other nonseries novels) continue to appear and continue to stretch the chain of one of the most long-running series ever penned. His detectives infrequently see courtroom action, although in *Kiss* (Morrow, 1992), Det. Steve Carella accompanies his mother to court to hear the forensic pathologist give a clinically detailed account of the three bullets that penetrated his father's body and a brief trial segment ensues when a couple witnesses are crossed. Lawyers appear whenever a Q & A is scheduled and then it is mostly merely a state's attorney's name added on as being in attendance. McBain-Hunter uses this device in the Hope novels as well (i.e., *Puss in Boots*, 1987). Though he has had a late start (between 1977 and 1998, he produced 13 novels in this series), Matt Hope has gained a steady following.

In this one, criminal litigator Matthew Hope is ready to begin divorce proceedings for Michelle Harper, who showed up in his one-man office in Calusa, Florida the day before battered and bruised. The next day her body is found burned on Whisper Key and her hulking, inarticulate husband is arrested for the murder. Hope, who won't defend anyone he believes guilty, is convinced he is innocent--even after he breaks out of jail and another woman dies.

1247. _____. *Cinderella.* New York: Mysterious, 1986. While Matt Hope is knocking boots with his ex-wife Joanna, he hears that his private investigator Otto Samalso has been shot dead off US 41. The marital case Otto had been working is connected to a 4-kilo coke ripoff of a Latino bad guy by a hooker.

1248. _____. *Criminal Conversation.* New York: Warner, 1994. Published under his legal name Evan Hunter, this novel deals with an ambitious ADA in a mafia investigation discovering that his wife is the woman seen with a mafioso's son being groomed to take over the family. Using their child as blackmail, he confronts her with the knowledge of her adultery, stipulates the terms of divorce, and threatens to expose her in court if she does not wear a wire to trap her lover.

1249. _____. *Gladly the Cross-Eyed Bear.* New York: Warner, 1996. Matt Hope's twelfth outing opens with what appears to be a simple case of copyright infringement after Lainie Commins, a designer of children's toys, engages him to take on the former employers, Etta and Brett Toland, over the rights to "Gladly," a cross-eyed teddy bear; however, before he can sue, Brett Toland is found shot to death and Lainie is charged.

1250. _____. *Goldilocks.* New York: Bantam, 1977. The only person who does not have a motive is confessing to three brutal murders of a mother and her two daughters.

1251. _____. *The House That Jack Built.* New York: Holt, 1988. Jonathan Parrish is stabbed to death at a party at his house on Whisper Key; his Midwestern brother Ralph, a farmer, is arrested but Hope is convinced of his innocence despite the fact that the dead brother's extravagant South Florida life was supported by his hardworking brother.

1252. _____. *Jack and the Beanstalk.* New York: Holt, 1984. Young Jack McKinney is killed before he completes a South Florida land transaction and Hope is thrust into the middle of a murder investigation as well as between two beautiful McKinney woman, the sister and her mother.

1253. _____. *The Last Best Hope.* New York: Warner, 1998. Matt is recovering from his coma (See *There Was a Little Girl*) when embittered Jill Lawton contacts him to locate her missing husband, who had gone "up north" to look for work but had found another woman, according to the wife, and wasn't going to return. The manhunt barely commences before a body rolls up on Calusa beach with identification that it is Jack Lawton. Hope learns that Jack had been planning to steal a Greek antiquity touring at the city's museum. He also discovers that this Jack and Jill have other dirty secrets, such as Jack's new partner, Melinda Schwartz. The case takes him to New York City, where--to the sheer delight of McBain fans--Hope enlists the help of Det. Steve Carella of the famed Precinct series. Everything converges on the night the antiquity is to be unveiled at the Calusa museum. "This is McBain's best crime novel in years," declares Wes Lukowsky (*Booklist* Jan. 1 & 15, 1998), "and not just because his two series characters interact. The plot, on its surface a simple robbery, is brilliantly complex due to the shifting alliances of the principals . . ."

1254. _____ [*See* also Hunter, Evan]. *Mary, Mary.* New York: Warner, 1992. In this one, Hope tries to clear Mary Barton, a school teacher accused of sexually abusing and murdering three girls. As the trial proceeds, the case for the defense looks hopeless because the eccentric client can't or won't help herself and eyewitnesses place her with the victims, and one even claims to have seen her burying the bodies in her garden.

1255. _____. *A Matter of Conviction.* New York: Simon; London: Constable, 1959. Hank Bell, New York Assistant DA, is assigned the prosecution of three youths accused of the stabbing murder of a Puerto Rican youth from Spanish Harlem. The DA's office wants to crucify the three as an example, but Bell wants the opposite; in fact, he wants an acquittal for two and leniency for the third, but he has to prove that blind Rafael Morrez was a gun-bearer for the Horsemen. In the trial at the end Bell works on juvenile Danny Di Pace a.k.a. "Batman," to get him to confess to fake-stabbing Morrez with the blade reversed.

1256. _____. *The Paper Dragon.* New York: Delacorte, 1966. London: Constable, 1967. Centered around the plagiarism trial of Arthur Nelson Constatine versus James Driscoll, et alia. Arthur's suit contends that he wrote the play *Catchpole* after his release from the Army and that the novel *Paper Dragon* is a direct steal from it. Constantine takes the stand in the beginning of the novel and trial resumes with intercuts and flashbacks to the denouement on page 578 (a typed facsimile of the judge's brief concludes the novel on pp. 579-96). Published as by Evan Hunter.

1257. _____. *Puss in Boots.* New York: Holt, 1987. McBain's gimmicky use of fairy-tale titles proves fortuitous here. Prudence Ann Markham is killed in a Calusa parking lot and her filmmaker husband is charged. Hope realizes that the film she was secretly making is the key to her murder--a film now missing and avidly sought by many, including a South Miami theater owner and two pornographers.

1258. _____. *Rumpelstiltskin.* New York: Viking, 1981. Recording artist Vicky Miller is beaten to death the day after Hope leaves her bed while she's in Calusa on a comeback tour after 12 years out of music as a former rock star. Hope was not only her lover but is named her executor, and he discovers a will that left a huge trust fund to Vicky's missing 6-year-old daughter.

1259. _____. *Snow White and Rose Red.* New York: Holt, 1985. Hope is convinced that Sarah Whittaker's mother, abetted by two bought psychiatrists, have had her committed as insane to get her money. But Hope must confront a mystery when the decayed body of a young woman is fished out of the Sawgrass River, which body will link the bright and beautiful Sarah to a sordid world of call-girl prostitution and topless dancing.

1260. _____. *There Was a Little Girl.* New York: Warner, 1994. Matt takes two bullets outside a seedy Calusa bar and lies in a post-surgery coma while his friends--Toots Kiley, p. i., Morris Bloom, cop, and Warren Chambers--scour the neighborhood to find clues and witnesses that will lead them to the Hope's shooter. They learn that Matt had been near closing a real estate deal for a small, successful circus and that some members of this society shared dangerous secrets that had already cost one woman her life when Hope was shot.

1261. _____. *Three Blind Mice.* New York: Arcade, 1990. Although witnesses place his client at the scene, Hope believes Stephen Leeds is innocent when the three men who raped his wife are found murdered and their corpses defiled.

1262. McCrumb, Sharon. *The Ballad of Frankie Silver.* New York: Dutton, 1998. Descended from Smoky Mountains circuit preachers, Native North Carolinian McCrumb now lives in the Virginia Blue Ridge and writes a popular series based on Appalachian history and folklore; normally, her series character is Elizabeth Macpherson. Here, she weaves fiction and fact in a saga of parallel murder (she calls her books "Appalachian quilts"). Frankie Silver is the first woman in North Carolina to be hanged for murder. Tennessee Sheriff Spencer Arrowood becomes obsessed with the Silver case when he's summoned to attend the execution of Lafayette ("Fate") Harkryder, whom Arrowood helped convict of murdering two college students on the Appalachian Trail decades ago. Now Arrowood, older and less sure of himself, isn't so confident about the guilty verdict and finds striking similarities between Fate, a dirt-poor Tennessean, and Frankie Silver, a Carolina mountain girl hanged for killing and dismembering her husband in 1832. Both pled not guilty but circumstantial evidence convicted in each case. Bill Ott writes: "McCrumb jumps effectively between both stories, interlacing first-person testimony from Frankie and others involved in her trial with a third-person narrative set in the present. The two stories mesh evocatively in the in the defiant refusal to speak of both Frankie and Fate. . . A poignant melding of history, Appalachian folklore, and human emotion" (*Booklist* 15 April 1998).

1263. _____. *If I'd Killed Him When I Met Him . . .* New York: Ballantine, 1995. Edgar, Agatha, and Macavity winner McCrumb features a forensic anthropologist as series character who, in this eighth series novel, crosses over to the legal thriller when she acts as official investigator for her brother's Virginia law firm. Elizabeth MacPherson investigates two bizarre murders, plus finding time for a third that has gone unsolved for over a hundred years.

1264. McDaniel, Ruel. *Vinegarroon: The Saga of Judge Roy Bean, "The Law West of the Pecos."* Kingsport, TN: Southern, 1936. From information gathered at Langtry, Texas, the author records the larger-than-life deeds of the famous outlaw, Justice of the Peace, and Judge of the wild and lawless Trans-Pecos, Roy Bean. Bean kills his first man at 14 and dispenses rough justice from Vinegarroon, his village and site of the bar from which killers and rustlers are sentenced:

> 'The court finds the accused guilty as charged; and as there ain't no worse punishment I know of right handy, I hereby sentence him to be hung. Reb, I'm busy's hell here. You and some of yore *compadres* take him out and tie his neck to some handy limb--some place where his cronies'll be positive to see him; and that's my rulin'. Court's adjourned and what'll it be for you down there, Slim?' (89)

The Paul Newman 1972 film was a messy mix of burlesque and violence, "sporadically entertaining," opines the reviewer of *Halliwell's* (437). Dir. John Huston. Writ. John Milius.

1265. McGivern, William P. *Summitt.* New York: Arbor, 1982. A conspiracy thriller about mind-control with a murder trial in the conclusion. Harry Selby loses his half-brother shortly after being summoned to Summitt City; then his daughter is raped.

1266. MacGowan, Alice, and Perry Newberry. *The Seventh Passenger.* New York: Stokes, 1926. A pulp thriller featuring a San Francisco dockworker and murder fugitive, Jerry Boyne, posing for a lookalike reform candidate for DA, Ross Garrett, who disappears afer a campaign speech. Three days before election, Boyne-Ross implicates the Lamartine gang for a seamstress' murder in the park (the same gang who framed him), during a hasty trial convened in a synagogue.

1267. McGown, Jill. *Verdict Unsafe.* New York: Fawcett, 1997. The Argyll, Scotland native and author of British police procedurals is critically admired for her darkly obsessive novels (she has resided in Corby, England since childhood). McGown features series characters Detective Chief Inspector Lloyd (no first name) and his lover, Detective Inspector Judy Hill working the gritty East Midlands (theirs is a relationship similar to Fyfield's pairing of frustrated lovers in the West-Bailey tandem). Their sleuthing stops short of the courtroom with this exception. A psychopathic serial rapist known as the Stealth Bomber has committed five vicious rapes upon young women. Accused of these crimes is a privileged and arrogant youth from Malworth. One of the shifting points of view is DI Hill, threatened by the rapist and a gallery spectator at the trial.

1268. McGuire, Christine. *Until Death Do Us Part.* New York: Simon-Pocket Star, 1997. McGuire's prosecutorial experience lends a richness of detail to her depictions of homicide investigations even without a courtroom denouement. In addition to heading the Special Prosecutions Unit out of the DA's Office in Northern California, McGuire also has coauthored a nonfictional work, *Perfect Victim* about a sexual-enslavement case, and taught at the FBI Academy in Quantico, Virginia. McGuire sacrifices little verisimilitude in having her protagonist steeped too much in her criminal investigations, although she naturalizes this detail in context well enough by depicting her Assistant DA Kathryn Mackay as having a close personal basis with Dave Granz of the sheriff's department of fictional Santa Rita, a California coastal community. Mackay is a complex but interesting woman, a single professional mother whose occasionally wavering faith in the criminal justice system to effect justice for the victims makes her interesting, credible, and complex.

Mackay has a media-frenzied case on her hands in the Santa Rita Courthouse when the California DA's office charges a defendant with the intentional infliction of the HIV virus. Then a bomb explodes in the courtroom wounding an officer, Kathryn and Dave Granz, lead investigator, connect the bombing and the trial.

1269. _____. *Until the Bough Breaks.* 1998. Lawrence Lancaster is found within the charred remains of his house in Santa Rita County's fashionable Mission Heights district with a .22 slug in his brain. Prosecutor Kathryn Mackay believes it was premeditated murder, not the Battered Women Syndrome that Mackay believes the wife is hiding behind with her high-priced lawyer. A further complication is lover David Granz being accused of raping a former girlfriend.

1270. _____. *Until Justice Is Done.* London: Heinemann, 1994. New York: Pocket Star, 1995. Santa Rita's forensic pathologist Morgan Nelson points out to Kathryn Mackay that the number of autoerotic deaths showing up on his slab lately are highly suspicious for several reasons: they are copycats of a spate of deaths in the county about five years earlier, there are tape marks on the wrists of the victims but no tape at the crime scenes, and all the victims were linked by a criminal past involving serious sex crimes. The subplot dovetails neatly as Kathryn's office, meanwhile, is on the track of the worst serial rapist in recent history--a vicious, sadistic male who beats, sodomizes, and leaves sexual and psychic wounding in his victims whom he picks out from society-page photos. Now it is Kathryn herself who has attracted the rapist, the next "little pig" who will experience his psychotic wrath.

1271. _____. *Until Proven Guilty.* New York: Pocket, 1993. A series of sexual mutilation killings involving young Hispanic women embroil Karthryn in a case of a serial murderer who sends taunting messages to the cops and then to Mackay.

1272. _____. *Until We Meet Again.* New York: Pocket, 1999. MacKay's boss Harold Benton dies abruptly of a heart attack. Kate and Robert Simmons, the physician attending Benton at the moment of his death, begin a relationship. When a couple drives off a cliff in a suicide pact, the survivor is subject to prosecution by Kathryn's office; however, it becomes apparent that a rapist is at work in Simmons' Department of Public Health. The pregnant female in the suicide pact is added to two more teenaged girls who had visited the clinic and afterward committed suicide.

1273. McGuire, William Anthony, writ. *A Kiss before the Mirror.* Scriptwriter McGuire adapted László Fodor's play for the first film version (Universal, 1933). Dir. James Whale. Perf. Frank Morgan, Nancy Carroll, and Gloria Stuart. A lawyer defends a man accused of murdering his wife out of jealousy; then he discovers that the same thing is happening to him. Surprisingly, this once-stylish film became a ripe piece of cinematic cheese when it was remade in 1938 as *Wives under Suspicion*, same plot, also by Universal, also directed by James Whale, but with the counsel table reversed to recast the lawyer's lead as the DA prosecuting the case.

1274. McInerny, Ralph M. *Body and Soil: An Andrew Broom Mystery.* New York: Atheneum, 1989. The author is a medieval scholar and authority on St. Thomas Aquinas, with, most recently, a biography of the early church father published in 1999. He has taught at the University of Notre Dame for 4 decades (as Michael P. Grace Professor of Medieval Studies) and published widely on Christian ethics, Christianity, and the priesthood. Moreover, he is the creator and inspiration of an ABC television series featuring Fox River parish priest Father Roger Dowling. Author of more than 40 mysteries, 17 of which feature Wyler (South Bend), Indiana series attorney Andrew Broom (a Sister Mary Theresa series, a Chicago nun, is written under the pseudonym Monica Quill.) Here, Broom defends Pauline Stanfield, a socialite wife in Wyler, Indiana, accused of killing her husband because he had refused her request for a divorce, fearing exposure of his financial and extramarital affairs.

1275. _____. *Cause and Effect: An Andrew Broom Mystery.* New York:

Atheneum, 1987. Broom is a different man from his later appearances here, all naïveté and *gravitas*, and it is not evident from this novel that he will grow into a series character with moral rectitude, a little wit and humor, and decency. The wealthy lawyer is surrounded by unsympathetic family as well: his ungrateful nephew Gerald, fresh out of law school, is given a berth in his Wyler law offices; and his adulterous wife tells him, at her doctor-lover's instigation and doctoring of Broom's physical chart, that he is dying of leukemia so they can tryst while he is seeing specialists in Chicago. In the interim between extracurricular events, the Brooms are working on a case that parallels Andrew's ongoing domestic life: Agnes Walz was convicted of conspiracy to hire a hit man to kill her husband (he is killed later), but her lover was killed instead.

1276. _____. *Frigor Mortis.* New York: Atheneum, 1989. Thriller about the execution-style killing of a widow in a tornado shelter; the culprits are indicted and tried at the end.

1277. _____. *Heirs and Parents.* New York- St. Martin's-Minotaur, 2000. The sixth Broom mystery begins with a body found in a car inside the Resurrection section of Overlook Cemetery. The victim is the once-lovely Helga Bjornsen, a college student-intern in Broom's law office.

1278. _____. *Law and Ardor.* New York: Scribner's, 1995. Edgar Bissonet is found dead on the seventh fairway of the Wyler Country Club, and Matthew Bissonet is charged with his father's murder, Andrew defending against courtroom nemesis Cecil Quarles.

1279. _____. *Mom and Dead.* New York: Atheneum, 1994. One of Andrew's business clients, Jerome Blatz, attempting to shaft him in a property deal, plans to meet with two partners on the banks of the river, but he discovers the body of Louise Long instead.

1280. _____. *Savings and Loam.* New York: Atheneum, 1990. Broom is called by the concerned New York agent of artist Willard Palmer, who had returned to visit his old homestead in the country. Broom discovers the body outside, partially eaten by animals, but the cause of death is shot twice with an M1, an antique WW II rifle.

1281. McMahon, Thomas Patrick. *The Hubschmann Effect.* New York: Simon, 1973. [Rpt. as *The Little Victims*, London: Constable, 1974]. The case involves the terrible side effects of an oral contraceptive known as Panesterol; the manufacturers are charged with selling a dangerous product. "This is a science-fiction mystery with a fascinating theme rich in legal and moral ramifications," writes Jon Breen (131). The narrative structures assumes the shape of grand-jury testimony.

1282. McMorrow, Thomas. *The Sinister History of Ambrose Hinkle.* New York: Sears, 1929. Rise and fall of a successful criminal lawyer in New York City as narrated by a fellow lawyer and witness to the successful events of his career; he is, however, hardly "one of the most sinister characters that ever afflicted New York" (3) as the opening chapter purports. Little Amby, as he becomes known to the courts and gangsters about town, begins his career as a fledgling lawyer, not by practicing before the judge in the murder trial of an alderman accused of murder, but as a spectator at the trial. He exposes the perjured testimony of two men who claimed to have witnessed the shooting through a skylight that Amby proves was not yet in place on the day of the killing.

1283. McNeish, James. *The Glass Zoo.* London: Hodder; New York: St. Martin's, 1976. Fourteen-year-old John Marsh is tried for the murder of schoolmaster Douglas Page by a piece of masonry dislodged from the roof at a school building. The narrator is New Zealander Ralph Stanton, Page's replacement at the Coldstream Park School, a South London slum.

1284. Meek, M. R. D. [Margaret Reid Duncan]. *Hang the Consequences.* London: Collins, 1984; New York: Scribner's, 1985. Meek of Cornwall, England is a rarity in mystery fiction but not merely because she did not begin her writing career until she was in her sixties. She told an interviewer for *Contemporary Authors* that she was delayed "by marriage, children, and following [her] doctor-husband to post-war Germany." After his death, she pursued a law career (graduating with honors from the College of Law, Lancaster Gate, with her LL. B. from London University, which career lasted until 1978. She possesses the unusual dexterity in alternating between the two contrasting styles of the Chandler-Hammett American school with its emphasis on a hardboiled detective and the bloodless British standard whodunit of Christie and Sayers, always, as she says, aiming for a "high standard" in her fiction. (She professes to be "astonished" by her American success.) Her series character is dryly sardonic Lennox Kemp, who made his American debut in this novel, disbarred and working for a detective agency. (*With Flowers That Fell*, published two years earlier, without US publication, is the story behind Kemp's disbarment.) Whether for her crisply elegant prose in the one book or her clever puzzle in the other, she is lauded by critics.

Kemp, in the employ of McCready Detective Agency of Walthamstow, meets a client who wants him to find her husband; he has run off with another woman. We learn in subsequent novels why he has been struck from the Law Society roster; these are his six years in the "wilderness," although he is essentially unchanged in temperament from novel to novel, and all his cases, like Lew Archer's in California, evolve from tangled familial relationships while seeming obvious on the surface--make out a will, find a runaway husband, etc.

1285. _____. *A House to Die For.* London: Severn House, 1999. Kemp and new wife Mary move into old Mrs. Channing's house in Newtown. When Grace Juniper, one of the lodgers next door is found strangled in the woods, another lodger is the prime suspect, whom Kemp reluctantly agrees to defend.

1286. _____. *In Remembrance of Rose.* London: Collins, 1986; New York: Scribner's, 1988. Escorted by her daughter, Rose Amaury of Castleton House is a 70-year-old woman of grace and tact who comes to Lennox's firm to make out a will. Kemp is shocked when the woman abruptly announces on departing that someone is trying to kill her. A week later, her fear is a reality.

1287. _____. *A Loose Connection.* London: Collins; New York: Scribner's, 1989. Kemp, now restored to full respectability, is plagued by a problem of a 20-year-old case of bribery in the Newtown law office of Gillhorns, Solicitors he is managing. Dorothea Copeland, wife of colleague Charles, discovers something odd in her friend Amanda's suicide besides the fact that she loved life too much: someone sent lilies to Mandy's funeral from Queenie Mangan, now living with her husband in the Cotswolds. What is odd is that Queenie died in a fire twenty years ago.

1288. _____. *A Mouthful of Sand.* London: Collins, 1988; New York: Scribner's, 1989. Lauded as her most complex novel, Kemp is undecided about marriage to penelope Marsden, companion of many years, and the seductively mysterious Mirabel Snape.

1289. _____. *Postscript to Murder: A Lennox Kemp Mystery.* London: Collins, 1996. Newlywed Lennox is married to the Irish-American Mary Blane. He is receiving a series of threatening, unsigned letters lately. When a member of his firm is killed beside his car, wearing a coat similar to his, Kemp is convinced the killer mistook Tony Lambert for him. His cop friend Detective Inspector John Upshire is stymied, Kemp becomes depressed, so Mary swings into action as a sleuth and actually makes progress. Tony Lambert bequeathed his entire estate to Anita Allardyce, his Australian fiancée.

1290. _____. *The Split Second.* London: Collins, 1985; New York: Scribner's, 1987. Kemp is also an "enquiry agent" for McCready's detective firm in this one.

1291. _____. *This Blessed Plot.* London: Collins, 1990; New York: Scribner's, 1991. Lennox is involved with two cases that connect insidiously: Venetia and Vivian Courtenay are a twin brother and sister with plans for the estate they have finally inherited from a miserly uncle. Bedraggled and slovenly Julie Sorrento wants Kemp to file papers on her missing husband so she can go on the dole.

1292. _____. *Touch and Go.* New York: Scribner's, 1993. Lennox's past is opened when an American lawyer presents him with a special difficulty: one of their wealthy client's hastily wrote a second will leaving all her possessions to her ex-husband, but the will, dictated to a new associate of the firm, was neither Xeroxed nor recorded in the firm's archives; as a result, the missing will might prove difficult to validate in probate. The testator is none other than Kemp's former wife, she whose gambling addiction twenty years ago (and his subsequent embezzlement of a trust to save her) cost him six years of his career.

1293. _____. *A Worm of Doubt.* London: Collins, 1987; New York: Scribner's, 1988. Kemp's latest client is Frelis Lorimer, a woman seeking divorce from her adulterous husband, a garage-owner in Newton. Faced with no alimony settlement suitable to punish him, she tries to blackmail the solicitor into helping her have his paramour murdered; the leverage is the fact that Lennox once saved a client from having acid thrown in her face by embezzling money to pay off the thugs, and the scandal could destroy his career. Two more by Meek are *Sitting Ducks* (1983) and *With Flowers That Fell* (1982).

1294. Megahey, Leslie. *The Advocate.* Droll, witty screenplay and clever direction by Leslie Megahey made this courtroom thriller (Miramax-BBC, 1993) one of the very best. It is set in the late Middle Ages at the time just before the outbreak of the Black Death that would sweep across Europe. Amazingly, the classic situation of a big-city lawyer on the threshold of burnout works here, too, as Colin Firth's character, the advocate of the title, comes to a small town to practice law. Everything seems simple and rustic at first, but he is the one deceived by a complex web of murder, witchcraft, superstition and religious hypocrisy alongside the machinations of a secret society bent on maintaining its power. Ian Holm and Nicol Williamson add luster in their roles.

1295. Mehling, Harold. *Assumption of Guilt.* New York: Carroll, 1993. Laurie Coles, a teacher at the Snug Arms Nursery School, is accused of molesting 4- and 5-year-olds; her attorney Henry Hull adopts a trial strategy that pits him against Judge Mathes (the Hangman). Opponent Peter Harmon, Harvard Law School grad and his housemate-lawyer Serena Wiley are also major characters. Mehling's focus, however, is how the community of Hudson Ferry reacts to the charges rather than to the question of innocence or guilt.

1296. Meltzer, Brad. *Dead Even.* New York: Weisbach, 1998. Meltzer's second legal thriller takes implausibility to a new level. Trying to jump-start her career after six months of unemployment, NYC Assistant DA Sara Tate literally steals a case file intended for a senior prosecutor to prove she should not be laid off by the city's falling budget axe; however, her opponent is to be Jared Lynch, her husband, who assumes he is merely bringing a new client into the firm in his bid to make partner with a prestigious New York law firm, the very same defendant in his wife's burglary case. When he attempts to withdraw, the burglar tells him he will kill his wife.

1297. _____. *The Tenth Justice.* New York: Morrow, 1997. Ben Addison, Yale Law School graduate, is clerking for Supreme Court Justice Hollis when he reveals a pending decision that will make millions for one of the litigants--worse, the blackmailer is demanding more insider information. Ben recruits several friends to help him but puts them all in danger. Lev Raphael slams it in a *DorothyL* posting, the Internet discussion group: "Dull writing, thin suspense, silly dialogue, weak description . . . Imagine a particularly smarmy episode of *Friends*, say, after they've seen *Mission Impossible* and they're all keyed up about spies and espionage" (14 May 1997, 2 paras.) But Meltzer once asked a Supreme Court justice if the plot were plausible: "What the scariest thing is," Meltzer recalled her saying, "is that it could happen."

1298. Melville, Herman. *Billy Budd, Foretopman [Melville's Billy Budd].* Cambridge: Harvard U P, 1948. Ed. F. Barron Freeman. Melville's death in 1891 was barely noted by the *New York Times* on September 29, 1891: "He was the author of *Typee*, *Omoo*, *Mobie* [sic] *Dick*, and other sea-faring tales, written in earlier years." Only the United States Book Company/American Publishers Corporation and Dana Estes & Company issued limited reprints of his works. Variously retitled from a short story Melville had called "Baby Budd, Sailor" (*Billy Bud* or *Billy Budd, Sailor; Billy Budd, Foretopman*), this short novel was an expanded but unproofed version that went unpublished because it had lain undiscovered with Melville's papers in neat bundles stored in a small attic trunk until 1921. The 12,000-word short story was itself buried within the 36,000-word novel in a jumble of confused, smudged, and canceled pagination that scholars pieced together from the bundle left to writer Paul Metcalf's mother (Melville's granddaughter). It is both a seafaring tale and philosophical novel about an illiterate, illegitimate so-called Handsome Sailor--a stuttering, good-natured youth impressed aboard the *Indomitable*, an H.M.S. warship, who is tormented without reason by master-at-arms John Claggart, a figure who represents the evil side of humanity. Billy kills his tormentor in a rage, repents his rash deed, is tried by benevolent Captain Vere, nicknamed "Starry" Vere (from Andrew Marvell's "Appleton House," referring to the "discipline severe" of a child's raising)--and hanged by the yardarm. The work is widely reprinted and been adapted for opera by Benjamin Britten (1913-1976) for the BBC. Cond. David Atherton. Libretto E. M. Forster and Eric Crozier. Perf. Thomas Allen, Philip Langridge, and Richard van Allan. (Long Beach, CA: Pioneer Artists, 1988). Louis O. Coxe and Robert Chapman adapted for the stage (*Billy Budd: A Play in Three Acts*, Princeton, NJ: Princeton U P, 1951).

Two of Melville's brothers were lawyers. Allan Melville (1823-72) had an office on Wall Street that the novelist frequently visited. The long short story "Bartleby the Scrivener: A Story of Wall Street" features a lawyer-protagonist and the character of the scrivener (a copier of legal documents) who works in his New York City law office at first furiously copying manuscripts and then abruptly subsiding into motionless refusal to do any work at all, "I prefer not to" becomes his laconic and maddening refrain. His character is so widely interpreted that he symbolizes a modern, almost existentialist figure rebelling against the soul-killing capitalism of Wall Street (however, we never learn why his inertia reverses itself) and the Christian soul withdrawing into death because of the failure of Christianity to triumph in a world that blasphemes the spiritual. Bartleby wanders from Dead Letter Office to empty, money-mad Wall Street to, finally, the enclosure of the Tombs prison. The seemingly benevolent narrator is his brother, in a sense, whose life is just as lost as his employee's albeit he is successful in his capacity as Master in Chancery (a position abolished by New York State in the 1840's). Published by *Putnam's* in two parts in November and December 1853.

1299. Meredith, D. R. [Doris R.]. *Murder by Deception.* New York: Ballantine, 1989.

1300. Mergendahl, Charles. *The Bramble Bush.* New York: Putnam's; London: Muller, 1958. A euthanasia case set in Pelham, Massachusetts. Lawrence McFie was injected with a fatal dose of morphine by a doctor who disdained to inject air bubbles into the dying man's heart and so cover his deed of mercy killing. The defense attorneys worry about the seven Catholics empaneled for the trial.

1301. Merritt, Miriam. *By Lions Eaten Gladly.* New York: Harcourt, 1965. London: Gollancz, 1966. Texas saga of the Camerons. When Gaylen Cameron's wife is killed after a road accident with a farm truck driven by Joe Peru, the farm worker is charged with negligent homicide because of the broken taillight and the fog conditions. His defense by Martin Fairchild is secondary to another, bigger worry by John Horne, Joe's employer, who fears a civil-action trial and consults Lobo City's single attorney Lester Chad for advice.

1302. Mickelbury, Penny. *Where to Choose.* New York: Simon, 1999. The Decatur, Georgia native was the first black reporter for the Athens *Banner-Herald* and has covered politics for the *Washington Post.* Lawyer Carole Ann Gibson's clients ranged from white-collar computer thieves to lowlife hoods until she walked away from her practice because of Ricky Ball, a vicious killer now loose because she convinced the prosecutor to try him as a juvenile instead of as an adult. Then news from home sends her back to her ethnic neighborhood in Los Angeles, now being plagued by attacks as was experienced by her mother's best friend. Gibson must find out why the police are indifferent and who is behind the attacks before she herself becomes the next victim. Her first outing was *One Must Wait* (Simon, 1998) and her most recent is *The Step Between* (2000). She also has a pair of novels about a lesbian police lieutenant.

1303. Miedan, Terrel. *The Soul of Anna Klane.* New York: Coward, 1977. London: NEL, 1979. Madison, Wisconsin defense attorney Jason Hunt must prove the existence of the soul to save his client, Anatol Klane, accused of being "an accessory to the premeditated death" of his daughter Anna, a crime that carries the same penalty as murder. Believing Anna lost her soul during brain surgery, Klane has provided her with a revolver and urged her to kill herself. The novel presents serious legal, religious, and philosophical arguments. (*See* De Felitta, Frank; Thompson, Gene)

1304. Miles, Keith. Edward Marston, pseud. *The Dragons of Archenfield.* New York: St. Martin's, 1995. Playwright and critical biographer Miles has created a colorful Elizabethan mystery series about Lord Westfield's Men, a sixteenth-century acting troupe. He also has a Domesday series set during the reign of William the Conqueror (1066-1154). Faced with plague, near-starvation, and onslaughts of Danes, the king required money to maintain an army and repel attacks. He sent royal tribunals out to survey the countryside, assess landholdings, levy taxes, and investigate criminal activities. Their reports were compiled into a massive record of eleventh-century English life known as the Domesday Book. Each novel in his series draws upon an entry in the Domesday Book and features series characters Ralph Delchard, a soldier, and Gervase Bret, a lawyer, two of the king's men who lead such a tribunal. While conducting their official investigations, Ralph and Gervase enter communities full of antagonism between Normans and Saxons and feuding landowners.
In this outing Delchard and Bret are sent to Hereford to settle a land dispute in Archenfeld. Then a wealthy landowner is murdered, his home burned, and a carved red dragon left behind as a clue. Others in this Domesday series: *The Lions of the North* (1996), *The Ravens of Blackwater* (1994), *The Serpents of Harbledown* (1996), *The Wolves of Savernake* (Random, 1993).

1305. Millar, Margaret [née Sturm]. *Ask for Me Tomorrow.* New York: Random, 1976. The first of three Tom Aragon novels by the author of three series, two of which were set in Toronto. (The author was born in Kichener, Ontario, educated at the University of Toronto in the thirties, and a screenwriter for Warner Brother in the mid-forties.) Inspector Sands is a cop while Dr. Paul Prye is a psychiatrist, and Aragon is a California attorney of Hispanic descent.

Young lawyer Tom Aragon ventures through Mexico seeking a wealthy woman's first husband with scenes, including a murder, set in Baja California and a Mexican prison. Reminiscent of her famous author-husband's plottings with their hint of malice and long-buried secrets forcing their way into the light.

1306. _____. *Beyond This Point Are Monsters.* New York: Random, 1970. London: Gollancz, 1971. Devon Osborne files a non-adversarial probate action to have her missing husband, a wealthy San Diego fruitgrower declared legally dead and herself declared administrator of his estate. Her lawyer argues that he was murdered the night he left their ranch house in search of his dog; a famous case in California (L. Ewing Scott) is used as precedent for proving death in the absence of a body.

1307. _____. *Mermaid.* New York: Morrow, 1982. The final Aragon novel with the lawyer hired to find a retarded woman.

1308. _____. *The Murder of Miranda.* New York: Random, 1979. The second Tom Aragon novel but a mix of humor with murder in a case involving the head lifeguard of Santa Felicia's ritzy Penguin Club and rich Miranda Shaw of the title.

1309. _____. *Spider Webs.* New York: Morrow, 1986; London: Gollancz, 1987. Defense attorney Charles Donnelly defends Cully King, the African-American captain of the *Bewitched*, a private yacht, accused of murdering Madeline Ruth Pherson, a white woman for her jewelry. She is last seen boarding the yacht in a tipsy condition but missing upon its return to dock. King was seen pawning her diamond stud earrings that day. The novel opens with "All rise" (15) in the Superior Court of Santa Felicia and follows the case from Judge George Hazeltine's entrance to the jury verdict.

1310. _____. *Vanish in an Instant.* New York: Random, 1952; London: Musuem, 1953. Features Tom Aragon's predecessor in legal fiction, attorney Eric Meecham.

1311. Miller, Alice Duer. *Manslaughter.* New York: Dodd,1921. London: Parsons, 1922. The Grosset edition includes scenes from the Claudette Colbert-Frederic March film ((Paramount, 1921). *Halliwell's* notes that Cecil B. de Mille was testing out his format for his *Ten Commandments* because of the long flashback sequence (DA's speech traverses to the idle rich of ancient Rome). Jeanie McPherson adapted Duer's novel for de Mille. Director Gere Abbot later cut the flashback in a 1930 remake without updating the film in Paramount's sound version (479). A rich, spoiled girl kills a man out driving and is sent to prison, yet she falls in love with the DA who convicted her.

1312. Miller, Arthur. *The Crucible.* New York: Viking, 1953. Miller is the preeminent American playwright of our times, and *Death of a Salesman* is one of a few great plays of this past century. *The Crucible* is another look at the Salem witchcraft trials; yet on another level it is more profound, more so even than the allegorical implications of Communist witch-hunting in the McCarthy era (Miller was also one subpoenaed to testify before the infamous House UnAmerican Activities Committee). In his autobiography, he states: "The political question . . . of whether witches and Communists should be equated was no longer to the point. What was manifestly parallel was was the guilt, two centuries apart, of holding illicit, suppressed feelings of alienation toward standard, daylight society . . ." (qtd. in *CA*). In his screenplay for Nicholas Hytner's the film starring Daniel Day-Lewis and Winona Ryder, the then 81-year-old playwright noted: "There's less dialogue because the camera is doing so much of the work" (*Plain Dealer* 5 Jan. 1997, sec I2). Besides the screenplay (Penguin, 1996), there is a four-act opera by Robert Ward based on the play: *Crucible. Piano-Vocal Score* (London: Highgate, 1962). Librettist Bernard Stambler.

1313. Miller, John A. *Causes of Action: A Claude McCutcheon Novel.* New York: Pocket, 1999. Lawyer Claude McCutcheon in a San Francisco case involving business intelligence and intellectual property rights issues. One more McCutcheon outing is *Cutdown* (1997).

1314. Mills, James. *The Hearing.* New York: Warner, 1998. Mills, prolific author and researcher, puts knowledge gleaned from nonfiction works on the drug trade to service in this tale of a Supreme Court nominee, Alabama Judge Gus Parham, selected by the President, a college friend, for the high position. Soon Parham is besieged by enemies seeking to oust him that include a militant pro-choice action committee trying to exploit the scandal of a daughter he never knew he had (who comes to his aid), Columbian drug kingpin Ernesto Vicaro, seeking revenge for his conviction by Parham, who--if he cannot smear the Judge's good name with a drug-money scandal--will try to smear him across the pavement with a car bomb.

1315. _____. *One Just Man.* New York: Simon, 1974. The life and despairing times of a Manhattan public defender; the novel's intercalary chapters add an unnecessary gothic touch because the protagonist's insights about the structure of New York's criminal justice system is gothic enough for anyone.

1316. Mitchell, S[ilas]. Weir. *Constance Trescot.* New York: Century, 1905. Known to every reader of Charlotte Perkins Gilman's "The Yellow Wall-Paper," the physician and discoverer of the cure for "nervous depression." Domestic fiction with the title heroine's husband George arguing a case of disputed land in behalf of a pettifogging and wealthy Rufus Hood, uncle and guardian of his wife and her sister Susan, against a widow with three orphans.

1317. Molloy, Robert. *An Afternoon in March.* Garden City, NY: Doubleday, 1958. An autodidact who worked mostly manual-laboring jobs (except for a stint at Columbia teaching creative writing), Molloy translated French, Italian, and Spanish writers. This novel is based on a scandal that may have originated in Charleston high society. Dr. Fairchild is attracted to the beautiful governess of Colonel Devere. One afternoon, as the title goes, he is confronted with an accusation by the colonel; the result is a *crime passionel* and a murder trial with black jurors. One of whom comments to the narrator years later: "[The white jurors] told us they wouldn't have any colored jury condemning a white man" (240).

1318. Monhollon, Michael L. *Criminal Intent.* New York: Signet, 1992.

Attorney David Loring has a lot on his plate: a class-A liar in prison for a client, the man's faithless girlfriend, a mission million dollars from the firm vanished with his firm's partner, and an art swindle that moves beyond South Texas into the international criminal arena.

1319. Moore, Robin, with Henry Rothblatt. *Court-Martial.* Garden City, NY: Doubleday, 1971. London: Harrap, 1972. Vietnam Commander General Zachary Taylor Flint despises the Green Berets for their secret operations and when Tran Van Troc (a civilian secretly working for the NVA) is murdered (the Prologue's torture-execution scene makes clear Moore's propaganda effort in behalf of Special Forces and their now-familiar black ops), Major Richard Becker and Captain Lew Marone, two of five Green Beret officers accused of the murder, are defended by Hank McEwan, a non-JAG lawyer. The long trial sequence takes place at the Pentagon amid demonstrations. Rothblatt has lent his legal knowledge to Robert L. Fish's *A Handy Death* and coauthored with F. Lee Bailey four texts on successful criminal trial techniques.

1320. Morgan, Mary. *Willful Neglect.* New York: St. Martin's, 1997. In this medical-legal thriller, lawyer Noah Richards is engaged by a young black couple to institute malpractice charges against the lone hospital in their depressed logging town in Washington State. The Ambroses are convinced that the death of their 5-year-old son was due to neglect on the part of the medical staff. At first reluctant, Richards discovers what actually went on in Jordan Ambrose's treatment or lack of it. Morgan, a nurse married to a surgeon, possesses the verisimilitude of her background in this, her first novel.

1321. Morris, Jean. *Man and Two Gods.* London: Cassell, 1953. New York: Viking, 1954. A cold-war novel with a frontier incident and a court martial. The countries are disguised with Slavic and Germanic nomenclature, whereas the laws invoked are British. The incident that warrants a court martial is over a disputed shooting by a former pacifist-turned-professional soldier. The Advocate General accuses him of succoring a professed seditionist (the woman being also a pacifist) and then shooting Julian Radaev, in "an ecstasy of patriotism," killing a man he deems an enemy of his country (120).

1322. Morrow, Honoré Willsie. *The Devonshers.* London: Hodder; New York: Stokes, 1924. A Wyoming wife finds her husband dead in his corral, his mouth a bloody pulp, in the first chapter. Toward the end of the book she is on trial for Angus Duncan's murder, and the prosecuting attorney scoffs at the mitigating circumstances offered by her lawyer in his impassioned appeal for mercy: "She killed an unarmed man, not in fear or panic or in an overwhelming brainstorm, because he had insulted her or her family or was pursuing her with intentions that were loathsome to her. She shot him because he kicked a horse!" (309).

1323. Mortimer, John [Clifford]. *The First Rumpole Omnibus.* London: Penguin, 1983. Himself the son of a barrister, Mortimer attended Harrow, Brasenose College, Oxford (1940-42; B. A. 1947), practiced in London before taking silk in 1966 and was appointed Master of the Bench, Inner Temple, 1975. Although he quit his legal practice 12 years ago, his fame exceeds the Rumpole series, for he is a novelist, a playwright of distinction, author of dozens of radio and televison plays, and screenplays and has been drama critic for three London dailies. His play *The Dock Brief* won the Italia Prize (broadcast in 1957, produced in London in 1958 and in New York in 1961 (in *Three Plays*, London: Elek, 1958; New York: Grove, 1962). It was also filmed in 1982 with Peter Sellers and Richard Attenborough (US title *Trial and Error*). It is about Morgenhall, an aging barrister who accepts a brief and the traditional one-guinea fee to defend a murderer. *A Voyage round My Father* was best original teleplay in 1969, a Golden Globe nomination followed the next year for the screenplay *John and Mary.* (He had served with the Crown Film Units as scriptwriter during the war.) To his three honorary doctorates bestowed in the 1980s, there is his C. B. E. (Commander of the British Empire) in 1986. In 1975 *Rumpole of the Bailey* first aired on British television. Leo McKern did for disheveled Horace Rumpole what David Suchet did for the immaculate Hercule Poirot and Helen Mirren would soon after do for the feisty Jane Tennison (the award-winning *Prime Suspect* series by Lynda La Plante). So successful were these teleplays that Mortimer converted many into short stories. Rich with eccentrics and series characters--perhaps none better than his own stern wife Hilda ("She Who Must Be Obeyed"). As bedraggled, rumpled as his name, bewigged in a dirty horsehair article he purchased from the Chief Justice of Tonga, celebrating with his favorite champagne, any available supermarket plonk ("Chateau de Thames Embankment"), Rumpole never casts his eye on the main chance (in his late sixties, he has all but given up on being understood), and because he takes every case that comes his way, he is without a hope of rising to become what Hilda's father, "Daddy," old C. H. Wystan had been--Head of Chambers. Popular on both sides of the Atlantic, the novels and plays about Rumpole are skilful commentaries on the British system of justice, although it must be noted that Rumpole stretches the law to suit his purpose and that biased jurists (like Judge Bullingham), ineffective QCs like Moreton Colefax, and ambitious prosecutors are every bit as common on this side of the Atlantic too.

Although first-time American readers struggle with British (East End) slang, French legalese, and literary quotes that tumble from the supple dialogue, Rumpole's creator provides with wit, charm, and subtlety (Mortimer said in an interview from San Francisco this year that he has turned down a lot of money for refusing to Americanize his aging barrister to accommodate the large US audience). The portly barrister was first introduced in a short-story series later produced by BBC and starred Leo McKern. The US Rumpole TV series aired on the PBS series *Mystery!* via WGBH-TV, Boston. American audiences were targeted for *The Best of Rumpole*, a Penguin USA rpt. in 1994, featuring a collection of 7 tales including Rumpole's first appearance.

As is now true of almost every author, many fictional characters, and hordes of self-published authors, there are homepages galore for the discerning fan. The authors of *Killer Books* ascribe their success to Mortimer's "mordant wit" and insightful commentary filtered through his remarkable creation: "With his courtroom theatrics, larger-than-life personality, and buoyant air, Rumpole remains a thorough original" (195). This omnibus comprises *Rumpole of the Bailey*, *The Trials of Rumpole*, and *Rumpole's Return*.

1324. _____. *The Judge.* London: Methuen, 1967. First performed in hamburg at the Deutsches Schauspielhaus on 29 January 1967; then Michael Codron produced the first English version at the Cambridge Theatre on 1 March 1967. A High Court judge returns to his small cathedral town to make restitution to a local girl he believes he wronged in his youth, troubled by an old, confused memory of "[a] child helpless, wounded, unprotected. A life, dying, dead. A girl screaming in a back room in Chamber Pot Alley, touched with steel" (Act 2.sc.1, 61). She is now the slatternly owner of an antique shop.

1325. _____. *Regina v. Rumpole* [Rpt. as *Rumpole for the Defence*, New York: Penguin, 1984] . London: Lane, 1981. . Of the stories here, three are of detection involving career criminals and 3 concern nonviolent capers, such as a landscaper working for a college accused of blackmailing a professor and a policeman accused of entrapment. "Rumpole and the Expert Witness" is about a doctor accused of murdering his wife. "Rumpole and the Dear Departed" is about a will contest. "Rumpole and the Boat People" is another title from this collection of six.

1326. _____. *Rumpole à la Carte.* London: Viking, 1990. in the title piece, Rumpole is dining at La Maison Jean-Pierre when he spies Claude Erskine Brown, "opera buff, hopeless cross-examiner," dining with a woman clearly not his wife Phillida (an effective QC dubbed "the Portia of our group"by Horace); the resulting case evolves out of a mouse in the restaurant and Soapy Sam Ballard's brief to prosecute the fatuous French-Irish cook for his rodent-infested establishment. Except for "Rumpole and the Summer of Discontent," the remaining 4 are Rumpolian triumphs, full of his anecdotal wit and reveries of triumph and riposte--the exception being the occasional wifely nagging, especially about his weight. One of the best is "Rumpole at Sea." "Rumpole and the Quacks," in which Rumpole exposes another put-up job intended to dislodge an Indian doctor from his practice. Unique in the Rumpole lexicon is "Rumpole for the Prosecution," a murder trial before Justice Oliver ("Ollie") Oliphant, Rumpole virtually changes sides in the middle of the case. In his only prosecution, he has been hired by the wealthy Fabians, estate agents, to prosecute another agent named Jago for the murder of their daughter; it is even better because Soapy Sam Ballard is defending Jago. Enjoying the reversal of roles to the hilt, Rumpole utters a famous line from *Twelfth Night*: "thus the whirligig of time brings in his revenges" (more subtle is the name Fabian, the clown Rumpole quotes (5.1.85-86). Rumpole's favorite subject to quote is Wordsworth--that is, if H. Ryder Haggard's adventure novel *She* is excluded ("She Who Must Be Obeyed" is Ayesha, Queen of Kor).

1327. _____. *Rumpole and the Angel of Death.* New York: Viking, 1995. Six stories: "Rumpole and the Model Prisoner," "Rumpole and the Way through the Woods," "Hilda's Story," "Rumpole and the Little Boy Lost," "Rumpole and the Rights of Man,"and "Rumpole and the Angel of Death." The barrister's subjects and cases range from an animal-rights activist accused of murder and a wife-killer with a passion for teaching.

1328. _____. *Rumpole and the Golden Thread.* Harmondsworth, Eng; New York: Penguin, 1983. Rumpole is summoned to Africa to defend a former pupil, but he learns that he is expected to fail. Junior barrister Fiona Allways takes over the narration toward the end as Rumpole's situation becomes dire.

1329. _____. *Rumpole of the Bailey.* Harmondsworth, Eng: Penguin, 1978; New York: Penguin, 1980. Six tales including one of the best Rumpoles: "Rumpole and the Honourable Member" in which he defends a Labour M. P. on a rape charge and (in chambers) senior clerk Albert on charges of fiddling the accounts to embezzle the petty cash. "Rumpole and the Married Lady" is a divorce case. Other cases concern robbery, marijuana possession, and murder.

1330. _____. *Rumpole on Trial.* London: New York: Viking, 1992. The title story is the final one in this collection of 7 because Rumpole, defending loquacious bore Henry Sebastian Tong in a manslaughter case, contravenes Justice Oliphant's instructions not to talk to his client during adjournment and with several skirmishes with the judge during the trial, the end result is Rumpole hauled up before the Disciplinary Tribunal. The others: "Rumpole and the Children of the Devil," "Rumpole and the Eternal Triangle," "Rumpole and the Miscarriage of Justice," "Rumpole and the Family Pride," "Rumpole and the Soothsayer," and "Rumpole and the Reform of Joby Johnson."

1331. _____. *Rumpole's Last Case.* London: Penguin, 1987; New York: Penguin, 1988. Six of the 7 cases here were featured on *Mystery!*. Rumpole is involved in the theft of a case of wine, puts his vast knowledge of bloodstains and typewriters to work elsewhere, entertains himself with three stories of battles with Judge Bullingham, "the Mad Bull of the Old Bailey." One of the "old darlings" whom Rumpole refers to as an endearment for the judges he practices before in the amusing case of "Rumpole and the Judge's Elbow," which leads to a courtroom triumph before indiscreet Judge Guthrie Featherstone but also and thereby to another thwarted ambition to become a sitting judge in a case of a spiritual doctor who operates massage parlors.

1332. _____. *Rumpole's Return.* Harmondsworth, Eng: Penguin, 1981;

New York: Penguin, 1982. The first Rumpole novel is set in Florida, where he and Hilda will try to live with their son's family because of his continual hammering in the court of hostile Judge Roger ("Mad Dog") Bullingham. However, he soon flees retirement to return to London and reestablishes himself back in chambers. The old warhorse dons armor for two more actions--firstly, in an obscenity trial (a novelization results from its televising), then, and worse, it is back inside the courtroom of the obnoxious Bullingham for a murder trial. He also deals with a mysterious letter written in blood, a fanatical religious cult, and the Pornographer-in-Chief to the town of Grimble.

1333. _____. *The Second Rumpole Omnibus.* London: Viking, 1987; New York: Penguin, 1988. Includes *Rumpole for the Defence*, *Rumpole and the Golden Thread*, and *Rumpole's Last Case.*

1334. _____. *The Third Rumpole Omnibus.* London: Penguin, 1998. This collection of 19 Rumpole stories includes 6 from *Rumpole and Age of Miracles*, 6 from *Rumpole à la Carte*, and 7 from *Rumpole and the Angel of Death.* The final section includes the delightful "Hilda's Story" in epistolary form, written to Dodo (Dorothy Mackintosh) and tells about her husband's case involving Michael Skelton. Besides devil worshipers, Horace must fend off a mysterious vamp looking for a barrister to defend her husband--for a murder to be committed. There is, as ever, Horace's rapier wit applied to the justice system's foibles and a few favorite types.

1335. _____. *The Trials of Rumpole.* Harmondsworth, Eng: Penguin, 1979; New York: Penguin, 1981. Six Rumpole tales in the second collection. "Rumpole and the Fascist Beast" about a rightwinger charged for inciting a crowd under the Race Relations Act, and an Indian barrister is welcomed into Chambers as Rumpole's pupil. "Rumpole and the Age for Retirement" concerns Rumpole's retirement to America under the pressure of family and friends. Other cases involve a vicar accused of shoplifting, murder in an acting troupe, and a schoolmaster charged with a sex crime.

Two more titles *Rumpole* (London: Lane, 1980) and *Rumpole and the Age of Miracles* (London: Penguin, 1988; New York: Penguin, 1989). Mortimer began with a pseudonym, writing as Geoffrey Lincoln, pseud., *No Moaning of the Bar* (London: Bles, 1957).

1336. Mosley, Walter. *Always Outnumbered, Always Outgunned.* New York: Norton, 1998. The Detroit author of the Easy Rawlins series creates a contemporary character and LA setting. Socrates Fortlow is an ex-con who has been released after 27 years in an Indiana pen for rape-murder conviction. He takes a job in a Watts grocery store and tries to help a young wannabe gangbanger named Darryl to a better life but winds up in court on assault charges.

1337. Motley, Willard. *Knock on Any Door.* New York: Appleton, 1947. London: Collins, 1948. Motley spent six years in the preparation of this sweeping panorama of big-city life as focused around several high and low characters. Among the former is Judge Drake, who presides over Nick ("Pretty Boy") Romano's murder trial for a policeman's shooting murder. In the latter category is prosecutor Kerman.

1338. Murfree, Mary Noailles. Charles Egbert Craddock, pseud. *The Prophet of the Great Smoky Mountains.* Boston: Houghton, 1885; New York: AMS, 1970. Murfree's once-popular, thick novels are regional tales told mainly by the characters themselves in their dialects and concern the denizens the Tennessee hills and vales. Here, the lives of Parson Kelsey, Dorinda Cayce, and Rick Taylor of a community in the Smoky Mountains of Tennessee intersect. The preacher is taken off by the sheriff to a settlement to be tried for helping Taylor, operator of a still, to escape from revenuers. His trial is summarized in a couple pages and a judgment of *nolle prosequi* results.

Murphy, Haughton P., pseud. *See* Duffy, James. . . .

1339. Murphy, Warren B. *Leonardo's Law.* New York: Carlyle, 1978. Brilliant David Vincent Leonardo teaches college math and is requested by Lt. Jezail of the Walton, CT police to look into the locked-room murder mystery of writer Barry Dawson.

1340. Myers, Walter Dean. *Monster.* New York: HarperCollins, 1999. Young-adult and children's novelist, a frequent award winner, and a writer whose fiction often features African-American protagonists; this one comes with a crime and a courtroom denouement.

N

1341. Nava , Michael. *The Burning Plain.* New York: Bantam, 1998. The growing number of gay/lesbian sleuths in the marketplace ranges from closet-bound to out, from reticent to unabashedly gay or lesbian, as in most of society. It is both a literary and social phenomenon marking mystery writing's changing times; some excellent writers are making their mark. One of the best, if not the sole attorney-sleuth in this field, is Nava's Henry Rios. Like his creator, Nava is a gay man and a Mexican-American, a combination that, he says in a recent *CA* interview, entails a certain "challenge" but not, he asserts, "preaching or apologizing." Nava's award-winning series is set in California and most recently, in Los Angeles. Nava's fiction explores gay life and sex with understatement, for his characters experience the prejudices of mainstream American/Latino societies, the ravages of AIDS on the gay population, the ensuing deaths and suffering, dysfunctionalism in drug/alcohol addiction as well as the emotional and bittersweet sides of love. Nava received his *juris doctore* from Stanford Law in 1981.

Rios falls for a young actor he had defended on burglary charges, and when the man is killed immediately after a night out with Rios, the cops come calling. However, a second and third victim follow and Rios, to save himself, follows a trail of murder to a conspiracy that leads him from the LA court house through the studios of Hollywood to the mayor's office.

1342. _____. *The Death of Friends.* New York: Putnam's, 1996; rpt. Bantam, 1998]. Zack Bowen shows up one day claiming to be the lover of Rios' longtime friend Chris Chandler, a man with a son and a career who preferred the closet. Although Rios believes his client, when Bowen suspect disappears, Rios tracks him through the earthquake-ravaged Valley.

1343. _____. *Goldenboy.* Boston: Alyson, 1988. Josh Mandel becomes Henry's lover; after their relationship collapses, Rios discovers Josh has become HIV-positive.

1344. _____. *The Hidden Law.* New York: HarperCollins, 1992. Rios, struggling with the loss of his HIV+ lover to another man, takes on the case of a young man who had threatened to kill an important Chicano politician running for mayor. Rios' client had made the threat during a therapy session in a drug-rehab clinic. Plots are secondary to Nava's strength in characterization. The homosexual factor shadows another and original strength of the writer: his ability to portray tensions and conflicts in upwardly mobile Hispanics.

1345. _____. *How Town.* New York: Harper 1990. Rios takes on the case of a man known to be a child molester; he must fight his own repugnance to defend him in the case.

1346. _____. *The Little Death.* Boston: Alyson, 1986. Rios is in the public defender's office at work on the case of Hugh Paris, arrested on charges of drug possession, resisting arrest, and assaulting police. Henry discovers that Paris comes from a troubled family, and he becomes intimately involved with him against his better judgment.

1347. Nelson, Truman. *The Sin of the Prophet.* Boston: Little, 1952. Set in Boston in the days prior to the rupture between North and South over the Dred Scott case. Colonel Suttle comes north looking for a runaway slave and sets the novel in motion, but the panorama widens to include numerous local and state--even nationally significant--events surrounding abolitionist politics. One of the large cast of characters, real and fictional brought in to play a role is Benjamin Franklin Hallett, the US DA for the Commonwealth, a local satrap with subsequent events occurring in the state courtroom.

1348. Nevins, Francis M[ichael]., Jr. *Corrupt and Ensnare.* New York:

Putnam's, 1978. Nevins is a two-time Edgar winner with a pair of series sleuth and a biographer of Ellery Queen (1974) and *noir*ist Cornell Woolrich (1988). He has edited numerous editions of crime fiction. he is a cum laude New York University law School graduate (admitted to the New Jersey Bar in 1976), and in 1978 became a full professor of law at St. Louis University.

Loren Mensing is a St. Louis law-school professor who had once practiced for his father's law firm of Mensing & Nalbin until he realized he hated it, and thanks to Judge Ben Richmond, he found his escape in a law school professorship. Richmond, dying of cancer, utters his last words to Mensing which mention a tape; this tape mysteriously shows up in his possession long after the funeral but not before a couple of goons claiming to be CIA threaten him in the basement of the law school library. On it, Mensing hears the Judge speak of a beloved paramour, a child born out of wedlock, and his dying wish to give this unnamed woman money. Mensing must find her and restore the Judge's reputation against a charge of bribery over the discovery of a shoebox containing $49,000 in cash.

1349. _____. *Into the Same River Twice.* New York: Carroll, 1996. Mensing is in New York City as a visiting professor at NYU when a phonecall from Kim Hale, an old girlfriend from law school whom he had once intended to marry, asks for help because someone is trying to kill her, yet she disappears before the rendezvous. Assisted by a current girlfriend and private sleuth, Mensing investigates her second disappearance form his life.

1350. _____. *Publish and Perish.* New York: Putnam's, 1975. Years ago Mensing rewrote the wills for a popular and financially lucrative husband-and-wife pair of writers, she of smarmy romances and he of historical sagas. When the husband dies in a mountain cabin fire, Loren must attends a probate hearing over Section 349 (b), enabling the inheritors of the estate to expedite the will into probate because his father and the senior secretary, the will's witnesses, are deceased. He discovers that Judge Collison is an old flame and then later learns that the writer's death by fire might not have been an accident.

1351. Nicholson, Margaret Beda Larminie. Margaret Yorke, pseud. *Almost the Truth.* New York: Mysterious, 1994. British author Yorke is lauded as a psychological suspense writer of high talent. She is a former librarian at Christ's Church, Oxford, and past chair of the Crime Writer's Association with over 30 novels, including the Dr. Patrick Grant series. Bicklebury is a tiny village and the scene of a brutal crime. Mild-mannered accountant and family man Derek Jarvis is blamed by his wife and daughter for the rape of his daughter in his own home. The two men are caught, but the law's punishment is not enough for Jarvis, whose family has disintegrated.

1352. Niederman, Andrew. *The Devil's Advocate.* New York: Pocket, 1990. The novel about a small-town Florida lawyer with big ambitions blends courtroom fiction with horror. First scouted, then duped, by Lucifer into selling his soul, the lawyer in the film confronts the firm's charismatic founder--his actual biological father, in a silly subplot--with queries, such as Why choose the law as a base for a global takeover of souls? Satan adroitly explains that the law is wired into everything. Chortles Pacino-as-Lucifer: "The law is the new priesthood!" Dir. Taylor Hackford. Writ. Jonathan Lemkin and Tony Leroy. Perf. Al Pacino, Keanu Reeves, and Charleen Theron (Warner, 1997).

1353. Niles, Blair. *East by Day.* New York: Farrar, 1941. The *Amistad* case and its effect on certain citizens of Hartford, especially young Lucy Giles and her two different grandfathers, one a skipper and the other, Grandfather Giles, a lawyer. However, there is no court action except indirectly as characters report the ongoing events of Cinque, the slave rebel, and rumors of the trial and aftermath.

1354. Niven, Larry. *The Patchwork Girl.* New York: Ace, 1980. London: Orbit-Futura, 1982. A science-fiction novel with courtroom action that concerns the attempted murder of a delegate to a Lunar Law Conference being held on the moon. As a detective story, the novel is less successful, says Jon Breen, than "the novelette collection *The Long ARM of Gil Hamilton* (1976)"(137).

1355. Nordan, Lewis. *Wolf Whistle.* Chapel Hill, NC: Algonquin, 1993. Nordon already had a Ph. D. in English from Ole Miss when he joined the M.F.A. writing program at the University of Arkansas, under the celebrated tutelage of three outstanding writers-in-residence (novelist William Harrison, poet and novelist Jim Whitehead, and *Prix de Rome* winner poet Miller Williams). Having grown up in Itta Bena, Mississippi, near the town where the incident occurred, his novel reprises and fictionalizes the infamous 1955 Emmett Till case, in which a black Chicago teenager was lynched for whistling at a white woman in Mississippi and two white men were acquitted for his murder. In an e-mail interview with the compiler, Richard ("Lindy") Lindell, Buddy's fellow student in the M.F.A. program, English adjunct professor, Detroit matchmaker and author of a book on the history of Detroit boxing, echoes the committee's verdict that awarded it the Southern Book Critics Circle Award for fiction by praising its mix of hilarity and horror: "It is one of the finest works to come out of a program that has produced several nationally recognized writers" (20 Oct. 2000).

1356. Nordhoff, Charles, and James Robert Hall. *Mutiny on the Bounty.* Boston: Little, 1932. [Rpt. as *Mutiny!*, London: Chapman, 1933]. The *Bounty* trilogy of novels covers the original voyage of His Majesty's ship en route to Tahiti for a cargo of breadfruit trees before the intolerable conditions imposed by Captain Bligh resulted in mutiny led by Fletcher Christian. The narrator is Roger Byam, an old man recollecting the events, based on Midshipman Peter Heywood. The trial of the mutineers, rounded up by H. M. S. *Pandora* on Tahiti, occurs in the first tale. The second book is *Men against the Sea* with Bligh and his crew of 18 loyal men set adrift on a 3,600-mile voyage to safety. *Pitcairn's Island* rounds out the trilogy with the discovery in 1808 of the progeny of the final voyage of Christian and a few followers. Sole survivor "Alexander Smith" benevolently rules Pitcairn's Island with his score of mixed-blood children.

1357. North , Darian. *Criminal Seduction.* New York: Dutton, 1993. While researching a true-crime book, Kansas cowboy-writer Owen Byrne falls in love with the prime suspect, an Southeast Asian woman, Lenore, accused of murdering her famous artist husband. Digging for background on the murdered man, Byrne offers a key fact to the defense in exchange for an interview with Lenore.

1358. Nyswaner, John. *Mrs. Soffel.* Nyswaner's script is based on a sensational true case in 1901 Pittsburgh, in which the wife of a prison warden falls in love with a convicted killer, but the film fizzled badly (MGM-UA, 1984). According to one reviewer: "A basis in truth does not prevent this from being both glum and dull from beginning to end . . . " (qtd. in *Halliwell's* 504). Dir. Gillian Armstrong. Perf. Diane Keaton, Mel Gibson, and Matthew Modine.

O

1359. Oates, Joyce Carol. *Do with Me What You Will.* New York: Vanguard, 1973. London: Gollancz, 1974. Oates' sixth novel about Elena Howe's faithless marriage to an older, brilliant lawyer.

1360. O'Hara, John. *Ten North Frederick.* New York: Grosset, 1955. Domestic drama about the life of lawyer and Gibbsville politico Joseph Benjamin Chapin, told backwards in classic whodunit style from his early days as a young man at Yale to his rise as senior partner of McHenry & Chapin and the part played by Kate Drummond. The film (TCF, 1958) by writer-director Philip Dunne starred Gary Cooper, Geraldine Fitzgerald, and Diane Varsi.

1361. Olander, Joseph D., and Martin Harry Greenberg, eds. *Criminal Justice through Science Fiction.* New York: New Viewpoints-Watts, 1977. The title shows varying amounts of courtroom action within the sci-fi genre. Among the stories in the collection, thematically divided into three sections, are Dean R. Koontz' "The Undercity"and Arthur Porges' "Guilty as Charged" about a 1956 time-travel researcher able to view the trial of *State v. Frances Wills* in Massachusetts in the 2180s. J. Francis McComas' "Shock Treatment" concerns a court system "extremely enlightened" developed by settlers on a distant planet (25). Pg Wyal's "A Jury Not of Peers" also gives a different and simpler judicial system from ours, in which a "judging machine" is employed. Alexander B. Malec's "10:01 A. M." involves a hit-and-run killing of a child by two "null-vehicle" hotrodders. Others: Cynthia Bunn's "And Keep Us from Our Castles,"

Steve Allen's much anthologized "The Public Hating," about Professor Arthur Kettridge's execution via mind-over-matter in a stadium and Hayden Howard's "The Modern Penitentiary." (*See* Harness, Charles L.; McMahon, Thomas P.; and Niven, Larry.)

1362. Oleck, Howard. *A Singular Fury.* Cleveland: World, 1968. Jon Breen tracks down the history of the lawyer whose first hardcover novel appeared several years after the program left the air. Oleck, himself an attorney, never produced another in what what is intended to be a series for Sam Benedict. The model for Benedict is lawyer J. W. Ehrlich who, along with Brad Williams, co-authored two more outings of the San Francisco lawyer. In one of the two cases here, Benedict defends the daughter of a famous legal scholar; she is accused of bludgeoning her lawyer-husband to death with a bronze statue of justice. Contains several oddities, notes Breen, among which is a "risible" courtroom climax (139).

1363. Oliansky, Joel, and William Sackheim. *The Law.* Veteran trial attorney John Wesley hall of Little Rock calls this 1974 television film his favorite courtroom film, and it is superbly scripted and acted. Oliansky and Sackheim collaborated on the original story from an original idea. (*See* the entry for Ballard, Bill S. for the storyline.) Dir. John Badham. Perf. Judd Hirsch (as the criminal defense attorney), John Beck, Bonnie Franklin, and Gary Busey.

1364. Orczy, Emmuska [Baroness]. "*The Dublin Mystery*" in *The Old Man in the Corner: Twelve Mysteries/The Baroness Orczy.* New York: Dover, 1980. Baroness Orczy will be remembered as the creator of the swashbuckling Scarlet Pimpernel series. One of her tales of detection from a collection of 12 edited with introd. by E. F. Bleiler falls within purview of the legal tale. "The Dublin Mystery" (1909) concerns the will of "Millionaire Brooks," a rich Irishman with two sons: Murray, the favorite, and Percival, a wastrel enamored of a dance-hall girl. Brooks dies of a stroke; Patrick Wethered, his lawyer, is murdered. the will left behind provides £100,000 per year to Percival but Murray is to receive a £300. Everyone is sure that Percival forged his father's will.

1365. Ornitz, Samuel. *Haunch, Paunch and Jowl.* New York: Boni, 1927. A coming-of-age tale of a young Jewish-American youth in New York City. In the fourth period of his life's adventures, he narrates his becoming a lawyer for gangsters. In one brief murder trial three of his clients are found guilty and sentenced to die because the jury was too high-classed to be fixed. He becomes a politically connected lawyer and co-founder of Hirsch & Freund with clients who speak Yiddish, English, and Russian.

1366. Osborn, John Jay, Jr. *The Associates.* Boston: Houghton, 1979. Harvard Law School grad Osborn clerked for a federal circuit court judge, worked in a Wall Street law firm, and became a law prof himself. His *Paper*

Chase became a bestseller, an Oscar-winning film for John Housman, and a popular TV series. Samuel Weston joins the Wall Street firm of Bass and Marshall, falls in love with associate Camilla Newman, works 16 hours per day (sometimes with speed) on multimillion-dollar deals, and worries about being fired by octogenarian Cosmo Bass, the firm's legendary founder.

1367. _____. *The Paper Chase.* Boston: Houghton,1971. Tribulations of a Harvard One L. In the film John Housman, as Professor Kingsfield, dominates the milquetoast students for his role as Hart's hardnosed contract law prof and the father of the girl (Lindsay Wagner) he is having sex with; otherwise, it remains another ho-hum youth movie, the difference being that these are the spoiled darlings selected for Harvard (the one older, married student fails to go on)--by writer-director James Bridges with Timothy Bottoms as the protag (TCF, 1973).

1368. _____. *Inadmissible Evidence.* (Paramount/Woodfall, 1968). The British film of Osborne's play (New York: Grove, 1965) and script about a solicitor on the verge of mental collapse is "surprisingly successful," notes *Halliwell's*, because the play itself begins surrealistically as a dream, "virtually an anti-humanity soliloquy" (375). Osborne and Alan Sillitoe were two of the leading members of the post-WW II Angry Young Men movement in Great Britain. Noted drama critic Stanley Kauffmann called it a "grittily detailed naturalistic film" (qtd. in *Halliwell's* 375). The English Stage Company production opened at the Belasco Theatre in New York on 30 November 1965; it was directed by Anthony Page with Nicol Williamson as Bill Maitland (also the film role).

1369. O'Shaughnessy, Mary, and Pamela O'Shaughnessy. Perri O'Shaughnessy, pseud. *Acts of Malice.* New York: Delacorte, 1999. California sisters Pamela and Mary combined lawyerly and writing talents to create the Nina Reilly lawyer-sleuth mysteries. Pamela, born in Missouri but grew up in LA, is a Harvard Law grad with 16 years of trial experience; Mary graduated from the University of California at Santa Barbara, moved to Boston as a writer and editor of multimedia projects. Protagonist Nina is a transplanted Lake Tahoe attorney, a scrapper for her clients, and even though she wants out of criminal practice, an intrepid and intelligent woman with worries about raising a son alone yet suspicious of commitment and one whose inner thoughts are marked by a droll self-awareness. Though detection is paramount, the sisters are sharp with details regarding courtrooms and juries.

The manager of one of Tahoe's largest ski resorts is accused of murdering his brother. Nina agrees to defend but must face Collier Hallowell as both courtroom adversary and the man who dumped her a year ago.

1370. _____. *Breach of Promise.* New York: Delacorte, 1998. It's a high-stakes *Court TV* palimony case that the authors integrate into a love-*cum*-murder courtroom thriller. Nina's client Lindy Markov has helped her husband Mike, an ex-boxer and nightclub bouncer, build a $200 million business together--the biggest employer in Reno. But Mike wants a divorce because he loves Rachel, a younger woman who works for the company. Mike's claim is that, because he never formally married Lindy, he owes her nothing. Nina must oppose archrival Jeffrey Riesner in the suit. Male-midlife crisis as the plot avoids being hackneyed because the authors look objectively at the way men and women have come to define commitment versus business in the climate of the nineties.

1371. _____. *Invasion of Privacy.* New York: Delacorte, 1996. The sequel to *Motion to Suppress* has Theresa London, filmmaker of a documentary about the twelve-year-old disappearance of a young girl, imploring Nina to help defend her against the family's charges of invasion of privacy. The novel loads up on melodrama when London is murdered, leaving behind a videotape implicating Nina's first lover and father of her son as the killer of the sleazy filmmaker.

1372. _____. *Motion to Suppress.* New York: Delacorte, 1995. In the first Nina Reilly adventure, Nina is running from terminal burnout and a failed second marriage by fleeing San Francisco to Lake Tahoe, where she hopes to begin a quiet civil practice and raise her young son. However, among her first clients is Misty Patterson, a cocktail waitress who tells Nina an incredible story of falling asleep after bashing her husband over the head with a statue of a polar bear after a violent quarrel. When his body is recovered at the bottom of Lake Tahoe, she is charged with murder.

1373. _____. *Move to Strike.* New York: Delacorte, 2000. Nina, widowed, agrees to take on a case for her son's friend Nikki Zack, accused of murdering her uncle with his samurai sword; the motive: Dr. William Sykes was a prominent Lake Tahoe plastic surgeon with a fortune, and Nikki broke into his home to steal money she believed was rightfully her mother's.

1374. _____. *Obstruction of Justice.* New York: Delacorte, 1997. This one might be styled a trequel, for it takes up just days after *Invasion of Privacy:* Deputy DA Collier Hallowell takes Nina Reilly on a romantic climb to the summit of Mount Tallac, when a storm brews. They are partial witnesses to the death of another climber, disreputable businessman Raymond de Beers, who is struck by lightning and falls off the cliff. Reilly is then approached by the family patriarch Quentin, who believes this was no accidental death despite the inquest ruling. When his grandson Jason is brought to trial, Nina must find the connection between this death and the hit-and-run death of Hallowell's own wife three years earlier.

O'Shaughnessy, Perri, pseud. *See* O'Shaughnessy, Mary, and Pamela O'Shaughnessy. . . .

1375. Ostlere, Gordon. Richard Gordon, pseud. *The Medical Witness.* London: Heinemann, 1971. [As *Witness for the Crown*, New York: Simon, 1971]. Cambridge-educated Ostlere was qualified as a doctor at St. Bartholomew's, London. He gave up medicine in 1952 and authored numerous books of fiction and nonfiction. This one concerns the rise and fall of a monstrously arrogant pathologist, John Rumbelow, whose expert testimony from the witness stand sends many to the gallows altogether on the strength of his reputation.

1376. Oursler, Will (William Charles). *The Trial of Vincent Doon.* New York: Simon, 1941. London: Museum, 1943. The trial is told via trial transcripts (including annotations and Doon's artist sketches) provided by James Mathews, the lesser partner of Strong and Matthews, the firm engaged to defend the title character. The novel features the artist Doon accused in the Court of General Sessions, County of New York, of the knife-stabbing murder of Edwin Hallett; the murder occurred in the home of the powerful Van Eyck family (the victim was the fiancé of Betty Van Eyck, whom Doon wanted to marry). The novel's sequel, *Folio on Florence White* (1942), is also told in edited-transcript format from Matthews' files (with partner Philip Strong's approval).

P

1377. Page, Elizabeth. *The Tree of Liberty.* New York: Farrar, 1939. Overlong historical opus mostly set in Albermarle Hall in Virginia and built around important national events from the days of Washington and Jefferson. A trial occurs in Part 6 in which federalist lawyer Elisha Cortwright watches a young colleague make a series of blunders that raise Judge Chase's hackles and set his nostril to quivering and cause the so-called accused, the "traverser" Peyton Howard, to rise to his own defense; he is accused of publishing "a false, slanderous and malicious writing with intent to defame the President of the United States" (731).

1378. Page, Thomas Nelson. *Red Rock: A Chronicle of Reconstruction.* New York: Scribner's, 1898; rpt. and ed. Lucas Carpenter. Albany, NY: NCUP [formerly New College and University Press], 1991. Page authored numerous novels of Virginia in the pre- and post-Civil War era. Once celebrated for his realism and use of dialect, his novels are quaint backward glances through the misty lens of Southern gentility; if he portrays the local influence of the Ku Klux Klan without rancor, he does so without a modern bias. Page considered blacks inferior and in 1904 wrote *The Negro: The Southerner's Problem.* In this his last major novel, he presents a brief, overblown trial scene over a plantation and a fraudulent claim between Captain Stevenson Allen and Jacquelin Gray with much ranting from the aggrieved defendant, opposing counsel, and judge. Lawyer Hiram Still is attempting to sell part of Red Rock to a Major Welch, all of which becomes "clear" in the garbled testimony of a former slave, whose eyewitness recollection exposes the chicanery to all in court, despite the fact that the judge ignores the testimony.

1379. Pairo, Preston A., III. *The Angel's Crime.* New York: Onyx, 1998. Pairo has two series characters, one an attorney--actually, Dallas Henry is a motel owner in Ocean City, Maryland, and sometimes lawyer. When he's sleuthing, he is assisted by a couple eccentrics named Herbie and Susan (she is a lawyer, too). The author is a practicing criminal defense attorney and lifelong Maryland resident. He graduated from the University of Baltimore School of Law and has authored hundreds of short stories under various *noms de plume*. This one concerns an investigator for the prosecutor's office. Jimmy Griffen is an ex-cop retired to Juno Beach, Florida, hired to find a brilliant high-schooler who had gone on a family-killing rampage and then put the grisly videotape on the Internet. Griffen had appeared in a previous serial-killer novel set in Baltimore called *Bright Eyes* (Onyx, 1996).

1380. _____. *Breach of Trust.* New York: St. Martin's, 1995. Harry Walsh has an undeserved reputation as a mafia lawyer. When his brother Tucker is murdered in a mob-style hit, Harry asks benefactor Sam Giardino for information but is warned off. Harry discovers his brother was a federal snitch and was coerced into working undercover because of a counterfeit money scam the feds were holding over him.

1381. _____. *One Dead Judge.* New York: Walker, 1993. Dallas Henry returns from *Beach Money* to lawyering because an old friend asks him to keep a package for him in the event of his death. When Judge Crenshaw is a hit-and-run victim, Henry discovers he has been left $50,000 and therefore becomes prime suspect in the Judge's death. But the potential killers are legion and include a zany lot of characters Crenshaw was suing, blackmailing, or being threatened by. One more Pairo is *Beach Money* (New York: Walker, 1991).

1382. Palmer, John Leslie, and Hilary Adam St. George. Francis Beeding, pseud. *Death Walks in Eastrepps.* London: Hodder; New York: Mystery League, 1931. The Francis Beeding pseudonym was made famous over the course of 50 detective and suspense novels by these authors, this being generally acknowledged as their best effort.

1383. Palmer, Stuart. *The Penguin Pool Murder.* New York: Brentano's, 1931. London: Long, 1932. Schoolteacher-sleuth Hildegarde Withers' first caper about a hatpin murder in the New York City Aquarium's penguin pool. Palmer has a collaboration with Craig Rice, pseud. in a collection of short novels entitled *People vs. Withers & Malone: Six Inner Sanctum Mystery Novelettes by Stuart Palmer and Craig Rice* (Simon, 1963). Introd. Ellery

Queen. Pref. Stuart Palmer. Palmer and Rice began their friendship at RKO some 20 years earlier and this collaboration collection teaming up Hildegarde Withers and John J. Malone results in the following: "Once upon a Train," "Cherchez la Frame," "Autopsy and Eva," "Rift in the Loot," "People vs. Withers & Malone," and "Withers and Malone, Brain-Stormers."

1384. Pangborn, Edgar. *The Trial of Callista Blake.* New York: St. Martin's; London: Davies, 1961. Convoluted tale of a courtroom case based on a hackneyed plot long before Amy Fisher drew down on Joey Buttafuoco's wife. In *The People of the State of New Essex* [an unfixed New England state] *v. Callista Blake* is tried for killing (via a combination of poisoning and drowning) her lover James Doherty's wife. Because Callista remains an enigma despite the novel's deep inward plunges of Judge Terence Mann's psyche and other tatterdemalion techniques of narration, the book does not succeed in creating sympathy for a teenaged girl carried away in a passion murder.

1385. Paretsky, Sara. *Bitter Medicine.* New York: Morrow; London: Gollancz, 1987. Paretsky has a Ph. D. in medieval history and an MBA from the University of Chicago. Her popular private-eye series is about an ex-lawyer turned sleuth named V. I. [Victoria Iphegenia] Warshawski is the daughter of a Polish cop and an Italian-Jewish opera singer, who left the public defender's office to become a private investigator with a special talent for bagging white-collar criminal. She occupies a niche above the darker extremes of the hardboiled p. i., but the streets are mean enough to satisfy fans that she is resilient and tough without sacrificing her femininity. In every novel, "Vic" Warshawski attacks the entrenched institutions that protect the criminal from the police (*Burn Marks* [Brit. title *Toxic Shock*], 1990) through corporations (*Deadlock*,1984; *Blood Shot* 1988) to the unsuspected power structures like unions (*Indemnity Only*, 1982), the Catholic Church (*Killing Orders*, 1985) and, as here, the medical establishment. Sometimes, as in *Burn Marks*, law enforcement (or the Cook County political machine) is the criminal. She has a collection of short stories, published in 1995, entitled *Windy City Blues*, also featuring Warshawski.

1386. _____. *Guardian Angel.* New York: Delacorte, 1992. Hattie Frizzell is an elderly neighbor on Racine Avenue with a litter of dogs being pressured by a block group to yuppify her premises when she falls in the bathtub and is taken unconscious to the hospital; subsequent events see two other neighbors, lawyer Todd Pilchea and his wife Chrissie, go to court to get appointed the old lady's guardians. Irked by the husband's pushiness, Vic investigates the Pilcheas. She also probes the disappearance of a downstairs neighbor, all of which leads to union fraud and a politically-connected bank.

1387. _____. *Indemnity Only.* New York: Dial; London: Gollancz, 1982. Andrew McGrath, union leader, hires a V. I. Warshowski, believing he is hiring a former cop friend's son to investigate his fiancé's death.

1388. Parker, Barbara [J.]. *Blood Relations.* New York: Dutton, 1996. Parker's novels and protagonists with their troubled families and domestic crises generally involve more of the soaps than the law or the courtroom, for she emphasizes personal relationships above courtroom dramas and legal technicalities. She is, nonetheless, a former county prosecutor for Dade County and attends to the legal details as necessary. She resides in Fort Lauderdale.

Sam Hagen, head of Major Crimes for Dade County, wants to be Florida's next AG, but he has a hard call coming up, one complicated by memories of his son's recent death: a 17-year-old model claims she was raped in the VIP room of a South Beach nightclub by three rich, high-profile men. When a key witness is found brutally murdered, Hagen is forced past his reluctance and even suspects his own devastated family.

1389. _____. *Criminal Justice.* New York: Dutton, 1997. Dan Galindo was once a bright young lawyer in the US Attorney's Office before he refused to suborn a witness in a high-profile drug case, lost the case and then his job over it, and practices out of a seedy Miami law office. The plot is ambitious, stuffed with characters with connections to one another and Dan, including dangerous Miguel Salazar with his money-laundering scheme; Martha Cruz, rocker and client; Dan's ex-brother-in-law, a desperate music promoter; an ex-wife and 7-year-old son that Dan is trying to appease; and a ruthless DEA agent Vincent Hooper with a score to settle with Galindo. Finally, a federal prosecutor, Elaine McHale, a former colleague and friend is his sole ally.

1390. _____. *Suspicion of Betrayal.* New York: Dutton, 1999. Gail Connor's domestic life is in turmoil, despite her engagement to Anthony Quintana, when a threatening phonecall comes out of nowhere, and what had seemed a crank call mushrooms into a waking nightmare as she finds herself terrorized and stalked by an anonymous phonecaller who begins sending her crude drawings, each more violent than the last.

1391. _____. *Suspicion of Deceit.* New York: Dutton, 1998. Attorney Gail Connor's newest client is the Miami Opera House, and a young tenor becomes the focus of a potential problem with Miami's South Florida Cuban community because he gave recitals for Castro. When her fiancé Anthony Quintana's brother-in-law, a radio talk-show host lathering up anti-Castro sentiment, is about to debate one of the Opera House's directors, Gail intercedes and is wounded while the director is assassinated by a sniper. Connor now comes to wonder about her Cuban-born lover Quintana, who had defended her in a murder trial. His past is full of mystery and Marxist doings in Latin America with links to the deaths of more people who all have ties Cuba. A *Kirkus* reviewer calls the climax "too silly for words" and the book full of "politically correct palaver about Miami's misunderstood Cuban exiles."

1392. _____. *Suspicion of Guilt.* New York: Dutton, 1995. Connor takes a case that could mean millions for her firm and a partnership at Hartwell Black and Robineau--if she wins. But a suspected will forgery becomes murder as Gail pulls the lid off a secret society of powerful Miamians looting the dead woman's estate.

1393. _____. *Suspicion of Innocence.* New York: Dutton, 1994. Edgar-nominated first book in which Gail Connor is a defense attorney who works for a big Miami firm; she has a failing marriage, a financial tightrope to walk, custody battle looming over her young daughter's head, and too much ongoing litigation. When her sister Renee Pettis is found dead in the Everglades, she turns to her future heartthrob--Cuban-born attorney Anthony Luis Quintana for help.

1394. _____. *Suspicion of Malice.* New York: Dutton, 2000. Quintana and O'Connor are estranged when Gail meets his daughter and agrees to take on her boyfriend, Bobby Gonzales, as a client. He is suspected of killing Roger Cresswell, the owner of the Cresswell Yacht Company, who had fired him for stealing. The boy's alibi is Judge Nathan Harris, whose lawyer is Anthony Quintana.

1395. Parker, Gilbert. *The Right of Way.* New York and London: Harper, 1901. In a French Canadian province, lawyer Charley Steele practices his craft and pursues his love interest with the same zeal. A scoundrel named Joseph Nadeau is save in a murder trial in the opening pages (this act will haunt Steele later), and he returns to court midway through this turgid tome in a case involving shoplifting.

1396. Parker, James Reid. *Attorneys at Law--Forbes, Hathaway, Bryan, and Devore.* New York: Doubleday, 1940. Not much goes on at the firm despite grandiloquent chapter titles, such as "Guide, Philosopher, and Friend." Office gossip, liabilities, patent infringements, office flirtations (mainly junior partner Stafford Latimer and a secretary). The senior partners are interchangeable albeit each has a specialty--Devore, for example, in corporate law but he resembles a "village idiot" because of the pouches under his eyes. One liability case involving a faulty fire extinguisher gets briefly into court in "Expert Witness" when a case young Latimer prepares for trial attorney Breitstein backfires with the academic on the stand inadvertently destroying the firm's case with his superior technical and chemical knowledge.

1397. Parrish, Richard. *Abandoned Heart.* New York: Dutton, 1997. Born in Brooklyn, Parrish has experience in both prosecution and defense. He has even worked as an articled clerk for the Israeli Attorney General's Office. He began his Arizona law practice in 1971. Six years later he created the

Economic/Organized Crime Unit of the Pima County Attorney's office. He maintains a private practice in Tucson and remains one of the state's best white-collar crime lawyers. His series character is attorney Joshua Rabb, who scratches out a living as a lawyer working the divide between widely separate cultures in 1947 Arizona, that between the Papago Indian Reservation and the Anglo community of Tucson. *Abandoned Heart*, however, is his first legal thriller about the 3-year-old daughter of Kate O'Dwyer, beginning a new life in Scottsdale, Arizona, who is raped and infected with the HIV virus. When the rapist gets acquitted, O'Dwyer and her boyfriend-lawyer Mike Fallon plot revenge.

1398. _____. *Defending the Truth.* New York: Onyx, 1998. Rabb takes the case of a Tucson professor accused of traitorous activities during the red-scare years preceding the McCarthy hearings. The plot entwines the suspicious death of a trusted friend and Rabb's own daughter's arrest on a charge of murdering of a US marshal. As always, there is good courtroom action in a Parrish novel within primeval themes of greed, treachery, and betrayal.

1399. _____. *The Dividing Line.* New York: Dutton, 1993. Josh is recovering from his war wounds and the psychological horror of the Holocaust when he takes a job with the Bureau of Indian Affairs as the legal representative of the Papago tribe. Powerful US Senator Jake Lukis wants the mineral rights to the reservation. When Indian children and a nun turn up dead in an irrigation ditch, Rabb defends a tribesman accused of the crimes.

1400. _____. *Nothing but the Truth.* New York: Dutton, 1995. When the flamboyant Benjamin ("Bugsy") Siegel draws heat down on himself for his public exposure and cost overruns in building the Flamingo casino and hotel in Las Vegas, his friend Meyer Lansky, Jewish dealmaker and gangster, comes to see Joshua in his office to retain his services. It isn't so much the government heat and the IRS that worries Lansky, who must remain discreetly in the background despite his admission that he owns "a big piece" of the hotel-casino, but certain associates of the pair, including "Lucky" Luciano, are getting irritated with the publicity and the costs of building Bugsy's dream in the desert. Now, Lansky has been given a subpoena *duces tecum* along with his pal Siegel for the Flamingo's construction records and Lansky wants Rabb to accompany him to Phoenix when he testifies before the grand jury.

1401. _____. *Versions of the Truth.* New York: Dutton, 1994. The lungshot, one-armed war vet Rabb takes the case of a psychotic, sadistic baby-raper and murderer, although in his heart he knows the man is guilty. In the main plot, as Bureau of Indian Affairs agent, he solicits bids for a big government contract that involves greed on both sides of the border, especially in Mexico where corrupt police and officials are the rule. Before long, he is having an affair with the Diana Thurber, niece of the man to whom he awards the $20-million contract but who has sweetheart deals south of the border with the shakedown artists and thugs who threatened Rabb.

1402. _____. *Wind and Lies.* New York: Onyx, 1997. When evidence suggests Ed Hendly of the Bureau of Indian Affairs is guilty of the sex-murder of a young Indian woman, Rabb rushes to his best friend's defense, desperately wanting to believe him innocent, but to get proof, he must follow a trail into a lawless Mexican border town.

1403. Patterson, Richard North. *Dark Lady.* New York: Knopf, 1999. The author graduated in 1968 from Ohio Wesleyan University and serves on its board of trustees. He is also a 1971 graduate of Case Western Reserve University's School of Law and served as Assistant Attorney General for the State of Ohio. A trial attorney for the Securities and Exchange Commission in Washington, DC, and San Francisco (like his character Christopher Paget), he was SEC's liaison to the Watergate Special Prosecutor and a former partner in the Birmingham, Alabama firm of Berkowitz, Lefkovitz & Patrick; more recently, a partner in San Francisco's office of McCutchen, Doyle, Brown & Enerson until his retirement in 1993 to devote himself to full-time writing. He grew up in the fifties reading westerns, liking their black-and-white simplicity; he calls courtroom novels "easterns" because, he says, they "reflect all that we've learned about the moral complexity of questions." He credits *noir* author Ross Macdonald as having crystallized an urge to write fiction. Besides novels, Patterson publishes articles on contemporary society in *USA Today*, *The Times* (London), and the *Washington Post.* Patterson is recent to the bestseller lists, but he has been writing courtroom mysteries while he practiced law for over twenty years. He attends to characterization with the same precision and skill he brings to the law's technicalities in his plots. He spends time between San Francisco and Martha's Vineyard with his wife Laurie and family. This, his most recent novel, involves the cops, mobsters, and lawyers in a tale of small-town Midwestern corruption.

1404. _____. *Degree of Guilt.* New York: Knopf, 1992. Patterson broke an eight-year hiatus in fiction with this novel, which was combined with *Eyes of a Child* (1995) to become a miniseries by NBC-TV. It also won the French Grand Prix de Litterateur Policiere in 1995. A San Francisco murder trial caught up in the whirlwind of publicity, as Christopher Paget, famed for his work in a Watergate-type scandal of a decade past, finds himself defending the estranged mother of his teenaged son Carlo from a murder charge, TV journalist Mary Carelli, for the murder of famed author Mark Ransom. Carelli was to interview literary celebrity Ransom in his hotel room, but when he attempts to rape her, she shoots him. Problems unfold during the trial when evidence suggests Mary lied about Ransom being a sexual predator. Patterson's theme here is a long-familiar one nowadays: rape victims do not fare well in US courtrooms. David James Elliott and Daphne Zuniga had the major roles in the 1995 two-part TV movie.

1405. _____. *Escape the Night.* New York: Random, 1983. Patterson eschews the law and its courtroom in his third novel about an heir to a prominent publishing fortune, a result of the protagonist Peter Carey's parents' violent death, which he had witnessed--but had been so traumatized by--that he blocked its memory and is haunted by guilt. One the day before his inheritance, he realizes he is being followed and closely monitored.

1406. _____. *Eyes of a Child.* New York: Knopf, 1994/1995. The estranged wife of Ricardo Arias Terri Peralta, becomes Paget's lover. Arias plots revenge to get Terri back by alleging sexual abuse against Paget's son to discredit both him and his son. Then Arias is found dead, "the gun still wedged in his mouth," which makes Paget the prime suspect, and it soon turns out his alibi is threadbare. Worse, the police investigation uncovers an ugly custody battle over the couple's 6-year-old daughter; worst of all: an eyewitness claims to have seen Paget leaving Arias' house.

1407. _____. *The Final Judgment.* New York: Knopf, 1995. Patterson's seventh novel, and third consecutive bestseller, features the return of Caroline Masters, a judge from *Degree of Guilt.* Masters has received a presidential nomination to the Court of Appeals hours before she learns that her niece has been charged with the murder of a boyfriend and that her family in New Hampshire wants her to return to defend the girl she has not seen since she escaped her domineering father to make her own way in the world. The scandal of a sensational murder case involving a prominent family, dope, and sex could destroy her nomination chances altogether, but Caroline goes home to help and face the bitter past and the secret she thought she left behind.

1408. _____. *The Lasko Tangent.* New York: Norton, 1975. This first novel, an Edgar Award winner, introduces series character Christopher Paget, a troubleshooting attorney working for the US Economic Crimes Commission. Paget goes after the powerful and unscrupulous William Lasko, close friend of the President, after he witnesses the murder of a key witness in the investigation of fraud and stock manipulation.

1409. _____. *No Safe Place.* New York: Knopf, 1998. Twelve years ago, James Kilcannon was making a strong run for the presidency when he was assassinated in California (see *Private Screening*). In the 2000 election is James' younger brother Kerry, an idealistic but calculating US Senator making a strong bid despite being hounded by the religious right for his stand on abortion. Worse, he has an adulterous secret that an ambitious reporter is ferreting out, a secret that would destroy his presidential chances if the media uncovers it. Worst of all, an unknown assailant, who has murdered three people at a women's clinic, is stalking Kerry. Patterson traveled with a 1996 campaigner, talked to everyone from George Bush to George Stephanopoulos of Clinton's team to do the necessary research for the background and said in an online interview that he had wanted to write this book ever since he was inspired by Allen Drury's *Advise and Consent.*

1410. _____. *The Outside Man.* Boston: Little, 1981. Lawyer Adam Shaw is a transplanted Northerner seeking the murderer of his best friend's wife in a genteel, closed-minded Alabama town.

1411. _____. *Private Screening.* New York: Villard, 1985. Patterson turns to the question of technology and terrorism when a terrorist uses a satellite linkup to poll his audience over whether he should kill his hostages. Tony Lord, fresh from his successful defense of a Vietnam vet accused of assassinating presidential hopeful James Kilcannon, is the too-good-to-be-true protagonist. The televised murder trial of a celebrity proved prophetic.

1412. _____. *Silent Witness.* New York: Knopf, 1997. This bestseller features San Francisco attorney Tony Lord, who returns to his hometown of Lake City, Ohio to defend a childhood friend, Sam Robb, vice principal of their old high school, accused of murdering Marcie Calder, a 16-year-old high-school track star and one of his female students. More a psychological thriller about the male friendship between Tony and Sam, the past's demand upon the present, and a plunge into the murky recesses of love.

1413. Paul, Raymond. *The Bond Street Burlesque.* New York and London: Norton, 1987. His first book examines the murder of Mary Rogers (1820-41), famous in the Poe story "The Mystery of Marie Rogêt," which story is fully annotated in *Who Murdered Mary Rogers?* (Englewood Cliffs, NJ: Prentice, 1971). Dr. Harvey Burdell, at home in his apartment in the heart of the medical district, is stabbed in his apartment by an intruder leaping from a closet. The first third of this book is "Portrait of the Attorney as a Young Man" dated the April prior to the murder and introduces series sleuth Lon Quincannon, maverick lawyer, who comes to the aid of young lawyer Tobias Brendon, carrying letters of reference for the firm that brings Quincannon to his aid.

1414. _____. *The Thomas Street Horror.* New York: Viking, 1982. Beautiful Helen Jewett, a notoriously witty and self-educated New York City streetwalker, was murdered in 1836 with an axe, her body set ablaze in bed. A cub reporter for the *Sun* teams up with Quincannon defending the accused, Richard P. Robinson. Paul's book is based on courtroom testimony and newspaper accounts of the crime with lavish quoting of the lurid purple prose commonplace in accounts at the time. Paul's theory of the crime is revealed in the final chapter, "The Third Whore," when Maria Stevens takes the stand. Paul's other historical crime novel is *Tragedy at Tiverton* (1984).

1415. Peak, John A. *Mortal Judgments: A Legal-Medical Mystery.* New York: St. Martin's-Dunne, 1999. Peak's third novel is about a malpractice lawsuit against a surgeon in San Francisco. Someone is attempting to stop his attorney.

1416. Pearl, Jack. *A Jury of His Peers.* Englewood Cliffs, NJ: Prentice, 1975. Stephen Walker, a sexually frustrated seminarian, is tried for attempted rape and beating of Marie Koestler, a girl he had propositioned in the park. Right after defense lawyer John Devlin cross-examines the young woman on the stand, her lawyer serves him papers for libel and defamation of character.

1417. _____. *Stockade.* New York: Simon, 1965. Lawrence Kass, a "pretty fair" lawyer in civilian life by his own admission, is a Pfc in the Army and content to remain that until he is coerced into taking on the role of defense counsel in the court martial of Ed Remington for shooting Lieutenant Allen Price Black. His strategy, he tells his co-counselers, is simply to put the deadman on trial: "That's precisely what we we're going to do--put Lieutenant Allen Price Black on trial. Place the guilt where it properly belongs" (214).

1418. Pearson, William. *A Fever in the Blood.* New York: St. Martin's, 1959. Political novel in which a murder trial, Norman Hart for killing his wife, occurs two months before the state democratic convention in this fictionalized state capital. It culminates in an adversarial relationship between Judge Hoffman and ambitious Dan Callahan, Rowton 's DA, with his eye on a political prize, and an allegation of manufactured evidence in the Hart case.

1419. _____. *Trial of Honor.* New York: NAL, 1967. Jub Tesper, a remorseless animal, is on trial for murdering the 7-year-old son of Ted Vernal during the night he held the family captive; although he had threatened to kill lawyer Vernal for a wrongful conviction 4 years prior, it was the son who is accidentally shot in a struggle. Two big problems: Judge Probst is a buffoon throughout the trial and counsel Jake Osborn peels off on a double-jeopardy tangent--in effect arguing a Constitutional point that never seems to be clear in the public's mind (i.e., you do not have a license to kill if, say, you escape from prison and commit the crime you were already convicted of.)

1420. Pease, William D. *Playing the Dozens.* New York: Viking, 1990. An Assistant US Attorney in Washington, DC investigates charges of corruption in the criminal justice system.

1421. _____. *The Rage of Innocence.* New York: Viking, 1993. Det. Sgt. Christine Boland, a Maryland state cop, is convinced the prosecutor's office wants to convict husband Cooper rather than get the truth behind the killing of Marian Avery, daughter of one of the nation's biggest construction firms. The sole witness is her traumatized 10-year-old son.

1422. Philips, Judson Pentecost. Hugh Pentecost, pseud. *Around Dark Corners.* 1970. George Crowder, once a renowned criminal lawyer and prosecutor, sent an innocent man to the electric chair. In despair he gives up his practice and moves to a small house in Lakewood, Connecticut, where he hunts, fishes, and walks through the woods; sometimes he helps his neighbors. He also spends time with his 12-year-old nephew Joey Trimble, whose father does not approve of his shiftless brother-in-law, but Joey learns a great deal from his "dear Uncle Sherlock" . . . . "In the Middle of Nowhere," one of the stories form this collection, is outstanding (*Detectionary* 29; 159).

1423. Phillips, Steven. *Civil Actions.* Garden City, NY: Doubleday, 1983. Four former law-school classmates are each variously involved in a controversial case over a Vietnam vet who wants to collect damages from the army for giving him pills to prevent tropical diseases but which, he alleges, caused his terminal cancer.

1424. Phillpotts, Eden. *The Jury.* London: Hutchinson; New York: Macmillan, 1927. To Phillpotts goes the distinction of concentrating action in the jury room. After the trial in Redchester Assize Court, ten men and two women consider the evidence against Lady Heron, a Spanish fencing champion accused of the stabbing murder of her husband Sir Philip. The jurors behave in a way that 12 strangers, even small-town folk who know one another and something about the trial personages, would not, but it nonetheless compares well to Reginald Rose's famous TV play *Twelve Angry Men* and Goodchild and Roberts' *The Jury Disagree.*

1425. Picoult, Jodi. *The Pact.* New York: Morrow, 1998. Two affluent New Hampshire families, the Hartes and the Golds, professionals and close friends, have children, the Hartes' son Chris and Emily Gold, born just weeks apart, who are inseparable through childhood, and fall in love in high school, a transition their parents welcomed. But Emily is secretly appalled by the incestuous nature of her relationship with Chris. When she discovers she is pregnant, she attempts a drastic solution to the problem. Chris is with her when she dies and is subsequently charged with her murder. Donna Seaman praises this novel for its tragic dimensions in *Booklist* (April 1, 1998): "[T]his psychologically shrewd tale is as suspenseful as any best-selling legal thriller. . . . As Picoult takes us through the nightmare that follows, examining each character's struggle with guilt and sorrow, she forges a finely honed, commanding, and cathartic drama."

1426. Pierce, William L. Andrew Macdonald, pseud. *The Turner Diaries.* Hillsboro, WV: National Vanguard, 1980. The fly page reveals a skewed history of printing and editions but a "second" edition, sixth printing of February 1995 shows that a continual updating of the novel's recorded chronology has been occurring since its first printing in 1978. Widely distributed at gun shows across the US, its popularity among hard-core bigots is legendary. The novel's blueprint for war against ZOG (Zionist Occupied Government) is believed by many people to have inspired Timothy McVeigh's plot to blow up the Murrah Building in Oklahoma City. In a futuristic world, Earl Turner, LA citizen born in 1991, becomes a guerilla fighter when the Supreme Court approves passage of the Cohen Act, outlawing privately owned firearms. The Equality Police then enforce Jewish-mandated laws to give Jews, blacks, and Hispanics complete control over society and sanction abuse of the white majority. Turner and his mates organize themselves into militias to take back the country city by city, street by street, herding the American *Untermenschen* into camps in the East and hanging race traitors from lampposts (especially white women who cohabit with blacks).

1427. Piesman, Marissa. *Alternate Sides.* New York: Delacorte, 1995. This Manhattan prosecuting attorney co-wrote *The Yuppie Handbook.* Thirtyish Nina Fischman works for the Legal Services Project for Seniors as Housing Court advocate and *kvetches* with her mother about everything from fashion styles and religion to real-estate prices and suitable beaus among her acquaintances, as here, casting a glance at boyfriend Jonathan, a *schlemiel* except in bed: "Her entire life as an adult sexual being could be summed up in a single freeze frame of some guy looking over his shoulder, waving good-bye" (10). Jonathan's doorman is found shot to death in his car. Nina's sleuthing takes her to an unlikely source: Public Advocate Henry Carr, professional politician and WASP with a connection to the dead man.

1428. _____. *Close Quarters: A Nina Fischman Mystery.* New York: Delacorte, 1994. Nina, wrapped in her usual emotional cocoon over a boyfriend she believes is about to dump her, stoically utters her Yiddish mantra *nicht gefaitlach* [It is not so bad] and agrees to go on a summer weekend vacation to an island beach house with lawyer-pal Cheryl; she is present when fellow guest and sex-addict Barry Adelman is discovered dead from poisoning in a bedroom.

1429. _____. *Heading Uptown: A Nina Fischman Mystery.* New York: Delacorte, 1993. Nina is executor of one of Ida's childless acquaintances. However, the son of Helen Hirsch was a severe diabetic and had an intolerance for alcohol, yet the accident report from Lake Placid reports an alcohol-related car crash. Ever-observant Nina scopes out the wife's black leather miniskirt of the wife at the funeral and believes she has her prime suspect in this suspicious death.

1430. _____. *Personal Effects: A Nina Fischman Mystery.* New York: Pocket, 1991. Nina investigates a murderous date when her best friend is murdered shortly after answering one of those personal classifieds.

1431. _____. *Survival Instincts.* New York: Delacorte, 1997. Forty-year-old Nina is back from LA and living with her mother in Manhattan again. She agrees to help clear her sister's husband under suspicion of murdering a friend. The widow believes animal-rights activists killed him for his mice experiments.

1432. _____. *Unorthodox Practices.* New York: Pocket, 1989. Harassed and romantically entangled as usual, Nina has two elderly women on West End Avenue with apartments undergoing million-dollar co-op conversions suddenly die. She tries to convince Judeh Lev, orthodox prosecuting attorney in the DA's office, that these women were murdered for their property.

1433. Pileggi, Nicholas. *City Hall (Rank/Castle Rock, 1996).* Pileggi, investigative reporter and author of wiseguy novels and exposés, co-scripted with Paul Schrader and Ken Lipper a tale of politics and disillusionment in the New York mayoral office. Harold Becker's direction is interestingly episodic, the script literate, yet it has what film critic Roger Ebert castigates as "a shamelessly upbeat ending." Al Pacino is Mayor Pappas, John Cusack his idealistic assistant, Bridget Fonda is the lawyer for the policeman's association defending a widow's right to her husband's pension, although it turns out he was a dirty cop killed at a meeting with a mafioso in the opening scene in which a six-year-old boy is killed in the crossfire. Other perf. Danny Aiello as political boss of Brooklyn and Tony Franciosa as a Mafia boss.

1434. Plum, Mary. *The Killing of Judge MacFarlane.* New York: Collier, 1930. First, a murdered low-level gangster wearing a chain-metal jacket is found stabbed to death in an Englishman's Chicago apartment. While dining, he meets Judge MacFarlane, a civic hero to the people working under menacing threats from the underworld to convene a grand jury to clean up the city's gangsters, asks to meet with the Englishman at his house to discuss the killing. When Gerald Gillespie, or "G," as he is called throughout, arrives at the house, he finds Judge MacFarlane's body.

1435. Podrug, Junius. *Presumed Guilty.* New York: Forge, 1997. Podrug's first novel, *Frost of Heaven* (Arlington Heights, IL: Dark Harvest, 1992), is a curious mix of Shangri-La mysticism and gritty realism. The title of his second refers to the Russian court system's presumption of a person's guilt. San Francisco prosecutor Lara Patrick refuses to believe that her Russian mother's death had been an accident precipitated by LSD; she returns to post-Communist Moscow to uncover the truth, bribes various bizarre individuals who all perish after muttering dark hints about her mother's demise and eventually finds herself framed for the slasher-murder of a wealthy sexual partner's lover. A detective named Yuri Kirov comes to her rescue, but the consensus of *Kirkus*' unforgiving reviewer stands: "campy melodrama, kinky theatrics, and cartoon violence."

1436. Ponicsan, Darryl. *The Accomplice.* New York: Harper; London: Joseph, 1975. Ralph Ferguson, DA of Pueblo County, Colorado, is prosecuting a woman for the murder of pregnant Maria Delgado Wynn in a case the media sensationalizes as "the Silver Cord Murder Case." The book includes several accomplices to the murder but not in the legal sense that they abetted the crime; the narrative is focused through (and hampered by) the viewpoint of bovine, rootless drifter Beef Buddusky. Defense attorney Sally Ryan bristles with Triple-I objections in the brief courtroom segment; afterward, three clients will be sentenced to death.

1437. Pope, Dudley. *Ramage.* London: Weidenfeld; Philadelphia: Lippincott, 1965. Lieutenant Nicholas Ramage faces a court martial for his actions at the end of the eighteenth century when the British frigate *Sibella* is sunk by a larger French warship.

1438. Popkin, Zelda. *A Death of Innocence.* Philadelphia, Lippincott, 1971. London: Allen, 1972. Marvin Hirsch of Hirsch, Markwell and Seelig obsesses over a murder case involving accused Elizabeth Cameron and Joseph La Cosset, her married lover, of the murder of Mrs. Sherman, a woman they intended to rob for her jewels to bankroll their romance.

1439. Porter, Katherine Anne. *Noon Wine.* Detroit: Schuman's, 1937. Porter authored two of the best ten short novels written by an American, one of them is about a farmer's interceding to save his hired man from a bounty hunter, who is looking to return him to his asylum after killing his brother; in the confrontation between good and evil, the bounty hunter dies from a blow to the head with an ax in the moment his friend is running to his aid. Although her novella has no actual trial--Thompson refers to his recent acquittal by a jury--in the blurring of good and evil within the concept of justice and retribution is a quiet masterpiece by a great and neglected American writer.

1440. Porter, Monica E. *The Mercy of the Court.* New York: Norton: 1955. Surprisingly good tale of a small-town judge and the human personalities that revolve about him. This takes a Monday-to-Monday look at the court docket of Judge Andrew Evans of Elm City, Michigan. The big case, hence the title, is how the hard-nosed judge will treat youthful offender Robert J. Heberman, number 17995, when he comes up for sentencing after a plea of guilty to armed robbery.

1441. Post, Melville Davisson. *The Complete Uncle Abner.* San Diego: U of California P, 1977. Born in Romines Mills, West Virginia, educated at Buckhannon Academy, and a graduate of West Virginia University Law School, Post practiced both criminal and corporate law in Wheeling. Post's Uncle Abner is a bible-reading sleuth with enough moral fiber for a dozen wild and lawless backwoods communities. He first featured, however, the villainous Randolph Mason, astute at finding those legal loopholes for his clients to duck through. In fact, the author's brilliance at finding such points was cause for rebuke, for it was argued that he was enabling would-be criminals to circumvent justice. (See the collections below.)

1442. _____. *The Corrector of Destinies: Being Tales of Randolph Mason As Related by His Private Secretary, Courtlandt Parks.* New York: Clode, 1908; rpt. Freeport, NY: Books for Libraries, 1971. originally the third volume of the Randolph Mason stories with the long title shortened to *Randolph Mason: Corrector of Destinies* in the modern reprint. Thirteen stories with the first "My Friend at Bridge,"citing precedent from a case against a bank to help a young seeming spendthrift secure a vast amount of cash from the very man who had swindled his own father and put him into debt. One of the best is "The District Attorney," in which a St. Louis judge orders the release of defendant Jeremiah Patton, president of a bank that crashed, against the DA's outrage because introduction of evidence and discharge of a jury constitutes a trial and a postponement does not negate that fact (only one of two to get into court). The ending is poetically good, too: as Courtlandt Parks rushes into Mason's office with a cablegram to tell his cold, unemotional master how the defendant and the bank's arch-swindler fared: Patton is dead in his hotel of pneumonia, Belmont Lane shot himself in his Berlin hotel when faced with Mason's writ of extradition. Except for a tale of divorce in "The Danseuse" and "The Virgin of the Mountain," a murder involving an Italian marquis, the remainder deal with the staple of legal chicanery involving trust funds, conveyances, deeds, and stock manipulation in which a tricked person will have something restored to him or her. In "The Pennsylvania Pirate," the laconic Mason utters a wonderful line in his new role as avenger of iniquities: "Gratitude, . . . like regret, annoys me"(199).

1443. _____. *The Man of Last Resort; or, The Clients of Randolph Mason.* New York: Putnam's, 1897. The lawyer makes few appearances in this second collection and does not appear at all in the final one. "The Governor's Machine" is the lead story with Mason working behind the scenes. One is the often-anthologized locked-room mystery "The Doomdorf Mystery," about a European settler in Virginia. Doomdorf whose devilish brew wreaks havoc on the rural community because it attracts the idle and vicious for miles around. Uncle Abner and Squire Randolph set out to destroy the still and evict the moonshiner, but they find him in his cabin murdered, in a room with a bolted door, window frames secured, and layers of dust on the sills. Two people confess, but Uncle Abner lays a stratagem for the killer that exposes the real culprit. Other tales: "Mrs. Van Barten," "The Grazier,"and "The Rule against Carver."

1444. _____. *The Methods of Uncle Abner.* New York: Curtis, 1927; Boulder, CO: Aspen, 1974 . After abandoning the formerly unscrupulous Randolph Mason, Post created his Uncle Abner series of stories with their strong emphasis on plot. A whiff of Old Testament majesty leavened with Uncle Abner's joyful sense of life is the sum of his characterization. Here are 4 tales beginning with the first reprint of "The Mystery at Hillhouse." "The God of the Hills," "The Dark Night," and "The Devil's Track"complete the collection.

1445. _____. *The Silent Witness.* New York: Farrar, 1930. Thirteen stories of the dashing, nineteenth-century Virginia attorney Colonel Braxton, able to quote the King James version or Blackstone with equal aplomb. "The Metal Box," the first tale, shows Braxton's ability to pose the irrelevant question on cross-examination that will prove crucial in this contest over a will. Other tales include "The Survivor," "The Cross-Examination," "The Guilty Man," and "The Leading Case."

1446. _____. *The Strange Schemes of Randolph Mason.* New York: Putnam's, 1896. Collection of 7 tales featuring the cunning lawyer with the long white hands. "Corpus Delecti" is a blackmail-exposure case: Samuel Walcott, for years impersonating the real man of that name (he killed him in a drunken brawl), has enjoyed the inheritance of his estate and built a good name for himself. Now that he is a pillar of the community, and about to marry Nina San Croix, the dead man's wife he did not want tries blackmail. Amazingly but typically for this sneering archfiend of amoral lawyers, Mason "advises" his client to kill the woman. Note the compilers of *Detectionary*: "The publication of this story helped to bring about much-needed reforms in criminal jurisprudence" (174).

1447. _____. *Uncle Abner, Master of Mysteries.* New York: Appleton, 1918; London: Stacey, 1972. Arguably the best Uncle Abner collection. "The Doomdorf Mystery" leads off the 18 and "Naboth's Vineyard" concludes it. A weak attempt at Poe and gothic retribution occurs in "The Riddle," but the best in between are "An Act of God," "The House of the Dead Man," "The Tenth Commandment," "The Hidden Law," "The Straw Man," "The Mystery of Chance," "The Edge of the Shadow," and "The Adopted Daughter."

1448. Postgate, Raymond [William]. *Verdict of Twelve.* London: Collins; Garden City, NY: Doubleday, 1940. Educated at Perse School, Cambridge and St. John's College, Oxford, Postgate pursued journalism mainly as a social historian and wrote over 20 books on socialism, unions, and biographies of labor and social leaders; he was a close associate of George Lansbury, whose biography he would publish in 1951. He also wrote a biography of Karl Marx. He worked for the Board of Trade and Ministry of Supply in the forties; he was named a Fellow of Trinity College.

We open with the Clerk of Assize swearing in jurors (6 of the 12 are given very detailed biographies via flashbacks). Rosalie van Beer has been accused of murdering her own nephew, Philip Arkwright. What makes Postgate's use of the technique is his ability to fit the jurors into a socialist scheme in which class and personality are subsumed. Because the reader knows each juror intimately (ratiocination is cast aside for emotionalism in their responses), we know how they will vote at the end of the trial. Postgate subtly shows the interplay of power in a Marxist microcosm in the jury room and here, too, the strong overwhelm the weak. The conclusion is vivid and memorable nonetheless. (For novels built around the jury room, see George Bullett's *The Jury*, Goodchild and Roberts' *The Jury Disagree*, Michael Underwood's *Hand of Fate*, Harvey Jacobs' *The Juror*, and John Wainwright's *The Jury People*.)

1449. Pottinger, Stanley. *The Fourth Procedure.* New York: Ballantine, 1995. Thriller with sex, violence, and medical technology. An emergency hearing at the end in an incognito case *John Doe I v. John Doe II* argues a pregnancy termination in front of Judge Francis X. McCarthy, "the severest antiabortion district court judge east of the Mississippi" (490). Pottinger graduated from Harvard Law and practiced in California. As a civil rights lawyer for the Attorney General's Office, he has argued before the Supreme Court.

1450. Powell, Richard. *The Philadelphian.* New York: Scribner's, 1956. A family saga of Irish immigrants whose branch begins with a servant girl and culminates in Anthony J. Lawrence, lawyer for the big corporations and the Social Register. He takes on a murder trial in defiance of his position at Morris, Clayton, Biddle and Wharton, however, in defending lowlife client Chesley A. Gwynne alias Howard Jones.

1451. Probst, Mark. *Winter Losses.* New York: Farrar, 1989. Pointless, meandering *Big Chill* kind of novel with a smaller cast. The protag is a 56-year-old corporate lawyer named Kreg with a largely absent son Adam, who gets mixed up in a white-collar criminal enterprise.

1452. Pyper, Andrew. *Lost Girls.* New York: Delacorte, 2000. More psychological than legal, this thriller is set in the town of Murdoch on the shores of Lake St. Christopher in Canada, the lawyer-narrator from the disreputable firm Lyle, Gederov & Associate is asked to defend Thomas Tripp, a teacher accused of murdering two schoolgirls, whose bodies are never found. The teacher's guilt or innocence is not an issue for young, arrogant Bartholomew Crane in his first murder trial, but not long after arriving in this depressed little town of mud and rain, with locals clamoring for a conviction, he becomes unnerved by the bizarre past of Murdoch, his own nightmares, the incessant ringing of the phone in his seedy motel and the events of twenty years ago from his own past. First published in Canada.

Q

Queen, Ellery. *See* Dannay, Frederic, and Manfred B. Lee. . . .

1453. Quick, Herbert. *Invisible Woman.* Indianapolis: Bobbs, 1924.

London: Brentano's, 1925. Christina Thorkelson, the self-effacing title character, begins a new life in Monterey after her homestead in New Hampshire is defrayed by a tornado. A love interest leaves for Albuquerque meanwhile; it is all centered around the law offices of Creede, Silverthorn & Boyd. One case over a testator's desire to legitimize a young man for inheritance occurs with Creede, Silverthorn arguing in court.

Quill, Monica, pseud. *See* McInerny, Ralph. . . .

1454. Quindlen, Anna. *One True Thing.* New York: Random, 1994. Pulitzer-Prize winning columnist (1992) for the elite Op-Ed pages of *The New York Times*, essayist on personal, political, and social subjects, Quindlen is also a bestselling novelist. Meryl Streep plays the title role in the film version of this legal thriller.

R

1455. Racina, Thom. *Snow Angel.* New York: Dutton, 1996. TV journalist finds her parents brutally murdered on Christmas morning and her best friend is charged with the crime.

1456. Radin, Max. *Day of Reckoning.* New York: Knopf, 1943. Post-war trial of Hitler (*See* van Rjndt, Philippe.)

1457. Ramos, Manuel. *The Ballad of Gato Guerrero.* New York: St. Martin's, 1994. Creator of the Luis Montez series, Ramos is an attorney with the Denver Legal Aid Society and a professor of Hispanic literature at Metropolitan State College of Denver. Chicano attorney Montez narrates these atmospheric novels, commended for their style and details of Mexican-American life in the way that Walter Mosley mixes politics and race in the Detroit of the Easy Rawlins series. Notes the authors of *Killer Books*: "The novels are told in a flowing narrative style . . . and they recount many small details of Chicano [sic] history, politics, and culture, and about the discrimination and racism that Chicanos still face" (200). Here, Felix ("Gato") Guerrero and his girlfriend are on the lam from a crime boss and need Montez' help.

1458. _____. *The Ballad of Rocky Ruiz.* New York: St. Martin's, 1993. In the first book of the series, nominated for an Edgar for Best First Novel, Montez is a middle-aged lawyer with a patina of rust on his idealism but still a true believer; it is just that he must pay bills, and the Chicano Movement of his youth seems far away. His first murder case introduces him to Teresa Fuentes, pretty daughter of an old amigo who died for the cause. His attempts to help her take him through Colorado and Texas.

1459. _____. *Blues for the Buffalo.* New York: St. Martin's, 1997. Luis is recuperating on a Mexican beach from the bullet wound in his knee on his last outing. he speaks briefly to a freelance writer named Rachel and returns home. Back home in Denver, a p. i. named Flores confronts Montez and demands to know the details of this meeting because Rachel Espinoza is missing and her well-heeled family wants to know whether he is involved in her disappearance.

1460. _____. *The Last Client of Luis Montez.* New York: St. Martin's, 1996. Jimmy Esch is a charming coke addict from a powerful Denver family and Luis' client, charged with narcotics possession; he is also dead one day after Montez earns his acquittal. Montez is then charged with the murder, but earns an acquittal despite the fact his alibi is missing (Jimmy's sister). With cops looking for him, Montez flees across the Rockies all the way to San Diego's barrios in search of the reason why Esch is murdered and his sister missing.

1461. Rawlinson, Peter. *The Caverel Claim.* New York: St. Martin's, 1998. The 3-year-old son of the deceased 16th Baron Caverel cannot claim his father's estate because a mysterious woman raised in America claims to be the legal descendant of the elder brother and is therefore legal heir to the family inheritance. South Carolinian Fleur Caverel, a black, travels to London to stake her claim by insisting she is the rightful heir and legal descendant of the fifteenth baron, who died in 1978. Replete with facts about the British court system and English peerage.

1462. Raymond, Ernest. *We, the Accused.* London: Cassell; New York: Stokes, 1935. A grim kind of fatalism pervades this overlong story of an ordinary man who finds himself the subject of a police investigation because of his wife's death. Paul Presset's wife dies, a buried tin of arsenic becomes the focal point of the case. QC Sir Hayman Drewer gently lets Paul condemn himself to the gallows with a few admissions about his unhappy home life and his mistress.

1463. Read, Opie Percival. *Judge Elbridge.* Chicago: Rand, 1899. Judge John Elbridge and George Bodney's father were law partners. Bodney is the Judge's foster son and a lawyer too, whose gambling addiction and alliance with an "adventurer" named Goyle lead him to steal from the Judge's safe. Two more courtroom thrillers are : *The Jucklins* (Chicago: Laird, 1896) and *A Tennessee Judge* (Chicago: Laird, 1893).

1464. Reade, Charles. *Griffith Gaunt Or, Jealousy.* London: Chapman, 1866; Boston: Estes, n.d. Reade is best-known for the historical *The Cloister and the Hearth* (1861), first serialized in 1859 under the title *A Good Fight. Griffith Gaunt* became a 5-act drama adapted by Augustin Daly (New York: Wemyss, 1868). Imperious Catherine Gaunt is on trial for her life. The accusation is that, "being moved by the instigation of the devil," she aided Thomas Leicester in an assault upon her husband Griffith and that so provoked, he killed his foe. Catherine at her arraignment points out a discrepancy of law courts in the time of this indeterminate historical novel: "So, then, if I be sued for a small sum of money, I may have skilled orators to defend me against their like. But, if I be sued for my life and honor, I may not oppose skill to skill" (406). Another with legal action is *It Is Never Too Late to Mend: A Matter-of-Fact Romance* (New York: Century, 1904).

1465. _____. *Hard Cash.* London: Chatto, 1913; New York: Colonial, n. d. Reade's magpie style can irk, but he is powerful at times and can be even drolly humorous *a la* Dickens when it comes to the law's delays in righting wrongs. His madhouse scenes are as grimly painted. Published in 1868, it was derided as another "Sensation Novel," but could not be as easily dismissed; moreover, like the realism of the later George Borrow, Reade's gritty fiction is an important stepping stone from the wank of late-Victorian schmaltz and a precursor to the naturalism to come. Here, he exposes the madhouses and the lunacy laws behind them. The protracted trial of *Hardie v. Hardie* owes something to *Bleak House.* Alfred Hardie sues Thomas for imprisoning him in an asylum, but it will never come to trial. The narrator explains:

> In theory every Englishman has a right to be tried by a jury of his peers: but in fact there are five gentlemen in every court, each of whom has by precedent the power to refuse him a jury, by simply postponing the trial, term after term, until the death of one of the parties, when the action, if a personal one, dies too . . . (557)

The end result, as in *Jarndyce v. Jarndyce*, is justice baffled, and in this novel, its delaying effect is risibly to have "cooled the ardent Alfred and sickened him of law" (537).

1466. Rechy, John. *This Day's Death.* New York: Grove, 1969. Jim Girard, a law student in an El Paso, Texas, law office is facing two grim realities: his mother seems to be dying of an unspecified illness and he is facing a trial on a sex charge in Los Angeles. The courtroom scene interspersed with sometimes long flashbacks that slowly release the pent-up sexual guilt haunting the protagonist to reveal the truth of what happened in the park.

1467. Reed, Barry. *The Choice.* New York: Crown, 1991. The author is a Boston trial lawyer, a graduate of Holy Cross and Boston College Law School, who specializes in legal-medical cases. His $5.8 million settlement in a malpractice suit in 1978 was at the time the highest jury verdict of its time in the country. Reed is also a member of the Board of Governors of the Massachusetts Trial Attorneys and a past Treasurer of the American Society of Law and Medicine. Reed's staple plot element comes to the fore in his second novel concerning a medical malpractice suit over a miracle drug that causes birth defects.

1468. _____. *The Deception.* New York: Crown/St. Martin's, 1997. Attorney Dan Sheridan's fourth outing calls on him to sue St. Anne's Hospital in behalf of the parents of a dead tennis star after the patient leapt from a sixth-floor balustrade, resulting in paralysis and near death. The unusual circumstance is that the patient's death, a suicide, must be proven the result of negligence on the hospital's part, and it happens to be owned by the all-powerful Archdiocese of Boston.

1469. _____. *The Indictment.* New York: Crown, 1994. A prominent surgeon is indicted for murder. Trial attorney Dan Sheridan is being watched by the FBI: his phones are tapped and his new legal secretary is an undercover federal agent.

1470. _____. *The Verdict.* New York: Simon, 1980. London: Granada, 1982. Brilliant courtroom give-and-take in this account of a boozy maverick lawyer, Frank Galvin, taking on the establishment in the form of the Catholic Church of Boston in a medical malpractice suit for millions. Paul Newman's performance in the Academy-Award nominated film by Sidney Lumet is memorable as Galvin on the brink of destruction (Newman, James Mason, and Lumet all nominated as well as the script). David Mamet adapted for the film (TCF Zanuck-Brown, 1982). Trial attorney Dan Sheridan makes a first appearance.

1471. Reeve, Arthur B. [Arthur Benjamin]. *The Dream Doctor: The New Adventures of Craig Kennedy, Scientific Detective.* New York: Van Rees, 1914. Dubbed the American version of Sherlock Holmes, Craig Kennedy shares Holmes' avocation for science in his şleuthing, especially chemistry (Kennedy's other profession is Columbia professor). The chapter titles themselves reveal the escapism and Kennedy's bipolar interests of chemistry and gadgetry in these tales: "The Detectaphone," "The Elixir of Life," "The Toxin of Death," "[T]he Crimeometer," etc. In this part-espionage tale, Kennedy receives a letter from the wife of a man on death row in Ossining. Sanford Godwin has been tried and convicted of murdering his adoptive parents. A will was discovered after the old man's death leaving a small annuity to her husband. "I am only a woman," she writes, "but about some things I know more than all the lawyers and scientists" (348). One more with a brief legal case is *Atavar: A Craig Kennedy Novel* (Harper, 1924; cover title *Atavar, the Dream Dancer*).

1472. Reinken, Pat. *Judgment Day.* New York: Simon, 1996. Legal-medical novel involving AIDS research.

1473. Reizenstein, Elmer L. *On Trial: A Dramatic Composition in Four Acts.* New York: French, 1919. First performed at Candler Theatre, New York City, 19 August 1914. Robert Strickland is being tried for the murder of Gerald

Trask, his friend and a prominent baker, over a $10,000 loan. The prosecuting attorney alleges that Strickland paid the money in cash with the express purpose of stealing it back from Trask's safe in his home; when discovered in the burglary, he killed Trask in cold blood.

1474. Rhodes, Eugene Manlove. *Stepsons of Light.* Boston: Houghton, 1921. London: Hodder, 1922. Rhodes' cowboy novel was curtly dismissed by New York's literary nabobs of the day--H. S. Canby, Christopher Morley, and William Rose Benét--but there is a certain charm to his style--that is, if you can imagine a collaboration between Rudyard Kipling and O. Henry. The courtroom scene in the novel's finale is amusing in the tall-tale, unrealistic fashion as all principals in the murder trial are caricatures. Prosecutor Benjamin Attlebury Wade bursts into more Triple-I objections than Hamilton Burger. Accused of murdering while apprehended rustling cattle is cowboy Johnny Dine, who offers an effective *pro se* defense and even calls his horse to the stand over eye-witness testimony regarding his height. Judge Hinkle is a buffoon and parody of a jurist, of course, but he belongs to all those eccentric, wise, cranky, drunken, uneducated, bible-quoting judges across the plains of western fiction.

1475. Rhodes, James A., and Dean Jauchius. *Trial of Mary Todd Lincoln.* Indianapolis: Bobbs, 1959. The authors have a specific agenda--to resurrect Mary Todd Lincoln as an anguished, but not insane, woman who protected her great husband and deliberately let herself appear in unfavorable lights. They do not let this agenda conflict with the presentation of facts; in fact, they are spare and all the more effective for stifling any impulses toward hagiography. Witness the opening paragraph:

> A little more than ten years after the death of her martyred husband, Mrs. Abraham Lincoln was placed under arrest, taken into custody under threat of violence, hailed summarily into a courtroom--before a jury already impaneled, sworn and waiting--tried, found insane, ordered confined in an institution and stripped of approximately $56,000 in cash and securities. (9)

Rice, Craig, pseud. *See* Craig, Georgiana Ann Randolph . . . .

1476. Rice, Craig, pseud., and Ed McBain, pseud. [Georgiana Ann Randolph and Evan Hunter]. *The April Robin Murders.* New York: Random, 1958. Craig Rice is the pseudonym of Georgiana Randolph (Mrs. Laurence Lipton) and Ed McBain's legal name of Evan Hunter replaced his birth name Salvatore A. Lombino (who also used pseudonyms early on, such as Richard Marsten and Hunt Collins). She and McBain collaborated on three novels, although he had to complete the third after her death.

1477. Rice, Elmer L. *Imperial City.* New York: Coward; London:

Gollancz, 1937. Sprawling saga of New Yorkers that concludes with the murder trial of Gregory Coleman, accused of stage actor Perry Kane's murder. While he languishes in the Tombs awaiting his trial, and various characters pertinent to the sensational trial move in and out, his defense attorney Bresnahan sleeps with the actress he loves, a witness named Ruby the lawyer has secreted in an apartment--after coaching her with a fictitious narrative for her part on the stand.

1478. Richler, Mordecai. *St. Urbain's Horseman.* London: Weidenfeld; New York: Knopf, 1971. Satirical novel about a Canadian film and TV director named Jake Hersh, who grows up in Montreal's Jewish community and then immigrates to London, marries, and becomes rich and famous. His dealings with a sleazy accountant and his search for his cousin, the symbolic horseman of the title, almost undoes him. He finds himself on trial in the Old Bailey on multiple charges that include aiding and abetting, sodomy, indecent assault, and possession of marijuana.

1479. Richter, Conrad. *Sea of Grass.* New York: Knopf, 1936. Narrated by the nephew of Colonel Brewton, a Texas rancher with a hundred-miles square acreage of range. The trial involves the shooting of Andrew Boggs by two cowhands of the Colonel because he had attempted to file a claim on 160 acres for a homestead. The Colonel's wrath for "that worthless granger" seems like a stacked deck to lovers of *Shane*, but the cattle baron's point would prove true throughout Texas Hill Country when hundreds of real "nesters," after a couple plantings, stripped the thin soil of its nutrients.

1480. Rinehart, Mary Roberts. *The Case of Jennie Brice.* Indianapolis: Bobbs, 1913. London: Hodder, 1919. Elizabeth Pittman runs a theatrical boarding school in Pittsburgh and narrates the case of Philip Ladley, accused of the murder of his wife, actress Jennie Brice. A body washed ashore during a recent flood is believed hers.

Roberts, Bechhofer. *See* Goodchild, George . . . .

1481. Roberts, Les. *Cleveland Local.* New York: St. Martin's-Dunne, 1997. Roberts' series character is Milan Jacovich in straightforward crime novels set in Cleveland's environs with a little quirky humor added. This one features the murder of a labor lawyer's son.

1482. Robin, Robert. *Above the Law.* New York: Pocket, 1992. Harvard law graduate, lecturer at the John F. Kennedy School of Government and other universities, Robin practices corporate law in Chicago. His novel is centered around dealmaker Sam Yones, the grieving father of a son killed in Miami under mysterious circumstances, and the IRS and US Attorney's Office investigation into his finances led by Assistant DA Spencer Pelcheck.

1483. Rodgers, M. J. *Beauty v. the Beast.* New York: Harlequin, 1995. This and a second Harlequin romance by the author (*Baby v. the Bar*) feature the Seattle law firm of Justice, Inc.

1484. Roeburt, John. *Jigger Moran.* New York: Mystery House, 1946. Captain A'hearn of Homicide and Jigger lock horns in a case when bookie Dixie Travers hires Moran to help get evidence to clear Blaine Fowler, on trial for murdering a middle-aged shopkeeper he was romancing. Fowler owes the bookie "50 G's," and doesn't want him fried in the electric chair. He has authored legal books on censorship and sex-life and the law. Roeburt's hackdriving, polyglot Irishman, and ex-lawyer with a *de Jure* and a doctorate is all sleuth similar to Paretsky's V. I. Warshawski's or Neil Albert's Dave Garrett. Although the State of Illinois dropped charges of criminal extortion against Moran, his law career ended.

1485. _____. *Wine, Women, and Murder.* New York: Avon, 1958. Its orig. title is *Jigger Moran* (New York: Greenberg, 1944). In this espionage caper, Moran takes a Broadway numbers runner's money to look for the murderer of one of his former customers, a man whose face was smashed in right after he collected $12,000 from a bet that Little Joey says his man paid up to the deceased.

1486. _____. *There Are Dead Men in Manhattan: A Jigger Moran Story.* New York: Dagger, House, 1947. A revised edition was published under a different title: *Murder in Manhattan* (Avon, 1946).

1487. Roffey, Jack. *Hostile Witness.* London: Arrow, 1968. *Halliwell*'s critique includes this memorable line from the film version of based on Roffey's play and script (New York: French, 1965): "If you'd hit me and given me orders on our wedding night, I would have kissed your hand!" (481). Though "boring" in its flat cinematography, says that source, it is "a complex courtroom thriller," starring Ray Milland (UA/Caralan, 1968) in which a barrister succumbs to a nervous breakdown after his daughter's death; he is accused of the murder. Roffey's two-act drama was first performed at the Music Box Theatre in New York, after a run in London, on 17 Feb. 1966 and directed by Reginald Denham. Milland also played Simon Crawford on stage with all the action occurring in the chambers of Crawford, QC, and in a consultation cell in the Old Bailey. The play opens with Crawford announcing to his staff that he is about to be arrested for the murder of a judge on the information supplied to the police by a man named Armitage. The motive is the hit-and run death of his daughter.

1488. Rogers, Garet. *Scandal in Eden.* New York: Dial, 1963. London: Putnam's, 1964. Clearly based on the notorious Fatty Arbuckle case (the book uses a different time and locale, LA circa 1930), motion-picture comic Archibald Forbes is accused of raping and causing the death of Muffin

Naismith. Mark D'Andor defends the obnoxious actor, even though Muffin was once his mistress. Prosecutor T. Amos Slake is the oft-inebriated D'Andor's courtroom combatant.

1489. Rollins, William, Jr. *The Shadow Before.* New York: McBride, 1934. When the Baumann-Jones mill at Fullerton goes on strike, 30,000 textile workers are in conflict with management over lowered wages. Picket-line violence leads to beatings and deaths and a trial for the strike leaders in the conclusion, much Q & A interspersed throughout and a semblance of the techniques employed in John Dos Passos' *USA* trilogy. The forces against the workers are many besides the owners--judges, police, prosecutors, and solid citizenry whip up anti-Bolshevist sentiment against the workers and the six labor organizers on trial.

Rolls, Anthony, pseud. *See* Vulliamy, C. E. [Colwyn Edward]. . . .

1490. Ronco, Neil. *Elevator Symphonies.* Greensboro, NC: Tudor, 1999. Dark-humored tale of about former screenwriter Ed Smith arrested in his Atlanta home on charges of molesting his own children; charges are filed by his wife Wendy. While awaiting trial, he writes a novel under a female pseudonym about sex in the nineties but is fearful it might prejudice his case when he comes up for trial, so he attempts to talk his sexually attractive neighbor into assuming authorship.

1491. Roscoe, Theodore. *Only in New England.* New York: Scribner's, 1959. Based on a real but heavily disguised, turn-of-the-century trial, the author sets the case in 1911 New England and even interjects himself as narrator. He researches the clubbing-murder of family matriarch Abby Bridewell of Quahog Point. The accused is her own son, a state senator who was always at odds with his mother over money.

1492. _____. *To Live and Die in Dixie.* New York: Scribner's, 1961. Full of vivid details of social history and everyday affairs as was his previous period novel, this one is set in 1902 Amityburg, Virginia. The story begins with New York journalist Sherman Grant accepting an assignment to cover the trial of Wade B. Brodie, a notorious seducer but a model of propriety on the surface. he is on trial for the murder of his wife Effie May Brodie, battered with an Indian club and dumped in a boiling tub of water.

1493. Rose, Reginald. *Twelve Angry Men.* Teleplay, *Studio One,* 1954. It is not well known that Rose's first Emmy-winning teleplay for *Studio One* was a live telecast on September 20, 1954 with Robert Cummings three years prior to the film's release with Henry Fonda in the celebrated role of the impassioned but reasonable juror. In August 1997 *Showtime* aired a remake of the United Artist 1957 classic with Jack Lemmon in Henry Fonda's role along with veteran performers Ossie Davis and George C. Scott as jurors and directed by William Friedkin. Although its screenplay was never novelized, *Twelve Angry Men* is still one of the most impressive of works centered upon what happens in the social microcosm of the jury room. Here, a murder trial climaxes in one reasonable man's arguing against his peers in which the eleven have assumed guilt on the defendant's part. He steadily, if improbably, exposes the flawed evidence against the boy accused of a savage, knife-murdering parricide. By the time the unanimous verdict of innocence is reached, the dynamics of the jury process and the fallible nature of humanity have been satisfyingly if melodramatically intermingled. Some of the portraits are dated but it is the universality of human emotions and types that remain constant because it is not the youth on trial for parricide that fascinates but the jurors themselves who are on trial. Friedkin added four blacks to the jury but told *TV Guide* ("Jack in the Jury Box," 16 August 1997) that you could not add women to the jury without changing the title. The older film version was directed by Sidney Lumet (his debut as director) and co-produced by Henry Fonda and Rose. All three received Academy Award nominations in 1957 including best picture. The cast, besides Fonda as the holdout juror, included E. G. Marshall, Ed Begley (superb as the bigot), Jack Warden, Lee J. Cobb, and Jack Klugman. Boris Kaufman's gritty black-and-white direction puts us right into the sweaty, claustrophobic jury room, all but two minutes of which was filmed in a 16-foot by 24-foot room. It is a vital work still, recently adapted, albeit streamlined, and produced by British playwright Harold Pinter for the London stage.

1494. Rosen, Norma Stahl. *Touching Evil.* New York: Harcourt, 1969; Detroit: Wayne State U P, 1990. There is no real trial in Rosen's unusual Holocaust novel but yet there is one that anchors the novel and these characters' lives to one another all living within proximity of one another in New York City. Brief references and bits of dialogue from a nearby TV of moments from the Eichmann trial telecast live to the world intrude upon the lives of immigrants, survivors, and "safe"Americans.

1495. Rosenberg, Nancy Taylor. *Abuse of Power.* New York: Dutton-Signet, 1997. Rosenberg is a former model, an ex-cop with experience in Arizona and New Mexico, a police officer for the Dallas and Ventura, CA, departments, a probation officer, a criminal investigator, and a vice president and owner of a video wholesale company. All these experiences, she says, have contributed to her courtroom fiction. She is also the mother of five who began her writing career at the age of 45 by studying writing at UCLA. Her first novel, written a year later, hit the jackpot and earned her a four-book contract with NAL/Dutton and was spotlighted for a future Jonathan Demme film project. Rosenberg allows that she packages herself commercially as a fictional writer attractive to prospects and some of this is borne out in the sensationalism of her later plotlines and lack of depth in characterization, but her protagonists--judges, lawyers, and probation officers--share the common fear of the impending breakdown of the criminal justice system and imply that escalating violence is a major threat to society.

Idealistic, 34-four-year-old Rachel Simmons is a widow with two children; she joins the Oak Grove, California, police force for personal as well as financial reasons. Once, she had been kidnapped and never forgot the policeman who saved her. When Rachel observes a vicious abuse of police authority--and reports it--she finds herself confronting the blue wall of silence; moreover, she is slandered, her children threatened, and frame-up in a shooting is put on her. Finally, faced with the prospect of a real killer hunting her, she takes help from an attorney with dubious motives.

1496. _____. *Buried Evidence.* New York: Hyperion, 2000. In the sequel to *Mitigating Circumstances*, Santa Barbara DA Lily Forrester has made progress with her life since taking the law into her own hands; however, her ex-husband, now facing trial on a vehicular homicide charge, blackmails her with the threat of revealing her past deed if she does not get him a top-notch defense attorney; on the personal front, love interest Richard Fowler, defense attorney, is demanding a commitment.

1497. _____. *California Angel.* New York: Dutton, 1995. Rosenberg catches the infectious angel-craze sweeping the nation at this time. Toy Johnson is a teacher in Southern California married to a surgeon and leading a normal life until a near-death experience leaves her with psychic visions. On two occasions of cardiac arrest, she sees children about to die--notably in a Kansas schoolhouse fire. When she is arrested on kidnapping-murder charges, her dapper attorney Miles Spencer assumes it is an open-and-shut case because she was in a New York City emergency room at the time of the fire--until he learns that she insists she was in Kansas during the fire.

1498. _____. *First Offense.* New York: Dutton, 1994. Ann Carlisle is a tough-minded, overworked probation officer (and ex-cop), who is shot and nearly raped for no apparent reason--except for the coincidence that one of her cases, Jimmy Sawyer, a rich-kid drug dealer, is out on bail. Her 12-year-old son, already giving her fits because of his father's disappearance, is receiving threats. Now she must find the strength to discover why she is in jeopardy and why anonymous phonecalls to her house sound like her presumably dead husband's voice. Note the authors of *Killer Books*: "Rosenberg's talent lies in creating an atmosphere of menace lying in wait for the average person" (201).

1499. _____. *Interest of Justice.* New York: Dutton, 1993. Judge Lara Sanderstone is deeply affected by violence in her family; when her sister and brother-in-law are killed, she takes in her nephew and determines to find out who killed her sister. This novel, like Avery Corman's 1977 *Kramer vs. Kramer*, shows the self-obsessed personality struggling to become human again and walking a tightrope between raising children and maintaining a pressure-cooker career.

1500. _____. *Mitigating Circumstances.* New York: Dutton, 1993. Lily Forrester is a mother with a troublesome teen, a sour marriage, and is yet a success as a Southern California Assistant DA, who will turn vigilante after she and her 13-year-old daughter are raped at knifepoint on their first night in their new house. Rosenberg, never the most graceful stylist, does explore the emotional trauma of Lily and her daughter with sensitivity.

1501. _____. *Trial by Fire.* New York: Dutton, 1996. Rosenberg's fifth novel has all the earmarks of an overwritten first novel that misses on all counts because it tries to do too much. Stella Cataloni is the major character who is either a sensitive, beautiful woman, rising star of the Dallas District Attorney's Office, or a woman with terrible scars and a violent temper. Her rival in political ambition is Holly Oppenheimer, vamp or ruthless schemer. A bloated effort, teeming with description of every character's attire and dialogue so stilted that the courtroom legalese sounds natural by contrast. The female histrionics between Stella and Holly call this novel's intent into serious doubt, for Stella is arraigned on murder charges by the grandstanding Holly from the Houston DA's Office for the murder of her returning ex-boyfriend and accuser. Making least sense of all, however, is the plot, which involves a fire that killed Stella's parents when she was a vapid, seventeen-year-old cheerleader sleeping with the boy she is accused of killing, shortly after his return to Dallas as her accuser; this same loutish hunk had impregnated her and fled the tragedy--only to resurface sixteen years later to accuse Stella of setting the fire that killed her parents and scarred her as she heroically carried her sleeping brother to safety. The plot seems to be an excuse to highlight Stella as the fulcrum for male rivalry between a taciturn Jewish colleague, who happens to be her divorce lawyer, and Brad, the husband. This latter character, like the two leading females, has the same dual-sided portraiture: he's either a vile-tempered, aging drugstore cowboy with a past shady business connection to Stella's father or a nurturing male who took pity on her, married her, saw her through plastic surgery and raised her younger brother.

1502. Rosmond, Babette. *The Lawyers.* New York and Toronto: Walker, 1962. Portrait of the lawyers who would eventually become the partners of Adams, Tree, Potter and Harrington, a New York firm specializing in (ho-hum) corporate law. Some real cases are cited--for example, Judge Parton's decision on Gallivant Oil Company (Standard Oil of New Jersey) on pp. 283-84.

Ross, Barnaby, pseud. *See* Queen, Ellery . . . .

1503. Rossiter, John. *The Villains.* London: Cassell, 1974. New York: Walker, 1976. Rossiter is a former Detective and head of Wiltshire CD. He left England for Spain and a career as a writer of espionage and mystery. This is a well-written, well-characterized procedural that begins with a badly beaten Det.

Sgt. William Gault giving evidence against Edward Toffler, the malicious thug who beat him. Although it is clear that Toffler is guilty, and that gaunt is not the noble cop, Toffler's exoneration through legal manipulation is a masterpiece of justice circumvented.

Rothblatt, Henry. *See* Fish, Robert L. and Robin Moore. . . .

1504. Royde-Smith, Naomi Gwladys. *For Us in the Dark.* London and New York: Macmillan, 1937. Based on a real trial, young Violet Comer comes into an inheritance worth as much as £250,000 by the time she comes of age; it ends in a quadruple murder and the trial of two defendants with scene-shifting between Cornwall and London in the years 1917 to 1933.

1505. Ryan, James H. *Suffer the Little Ones.* Nashville: Aurora, 1972. The author is a pediatrician and expert in battered child syndrome. Dr. Patrick Brennan is *amicus curiae* during the trial of Mrs. Jacqueline Teal, charged with beating her 3-year-old infant to death. Brennan then finds himself the victim of a blackmail attempt initiated by a major pharmaceutical house anxious to keep him from testifying before a congressional committee to protect a highly profitable patented drug.

1506. Rylee, Robert. *Deep Dark River.* New York: Farrar; London: Heinemann, 1935. Rambling tale of Clarksville, Mississippi, and lawyer Mary Winston trying to find her place as a woman attorney. The novel finally settles into a court case as Mary defends black Mose Southwick for the murder of Willie Stubb. The semiliterate black speech of the characters throughout the novel is obtrusive.

S

1507. Sabatini, Rafael. *Captain Blood.* London: Hutchinson; Boston: Houghton, 1922. The life of buccaneer Captain Peter Blood, who began his career as a surgeon put on trial before Judge Jeffreys for helping rebels. The film of the same title (Warner, 1935) made a star of Erroll Flynn despite its many anachronisms and cheap production values. Dir. Michael Curtiz. Writ. Casey Robinson. Perf. Olivia de Havilland and Basil Rathbone.

1508. _____.. *The Minion.* London: Hutchinson, 1930. [Rpt. as *King's Minion*, Boston: Houghton, 1930]. The full title is *The King's Minion, Being the Rise and Fall of Robert Carr of Ferniehurst, Earl of Somerset, Viscount Rochester, Baron Winwick, Baron Brancepeth, Knight of the Most Noble Order of the Garter, A Member of His Majesty's Most Honorable Privy Council & c., & c., &c.*

1509. _____. *Sea-Hawk.* London: Secker; Boston: Houghton, 1915.

Another piffling swashbuckler with the obligatory trial scene in which the hero will either save himself with more jurisprudence than his opposition or by means of a nick-of-time *deus ex machina.* Sir Oliver Tressilian surrenders himself to a court within his enemy Lord Henry Goade's jurisdiction to be charged on charges of piracy, abduction, and murder. The instrument of his salvation is his secret wife Rosamund, present at the tribunal, and able to convince the justices that a ne'er-do-well brother is behind the calumny.

1510. Salter, Anna. *Shiny Water.* New York: Pocket, 1997. Michael Stone, a forensic psychologist, is asked by the guardian *ad litem* of two children to evaluate 3-year-old Adrienne and 6-year-old Andrew in a child-custody case to see if symptoms of sexual abuse exist; her findings convince her that the children have been abused and she makes this declaration in court despite the fact that father is an esteemed surgeon and community leader. The day after the children are restored to the father, the mother (deemed incompetent) is in prison charged with double homicide for their murder.

1511. Sanders, Lawrence. *McNally's Trial.* New York: Putnam's, 1995. Sanders has cranked out 19 mystery bestsellers that fall more or less under the rubric of thrillers. This one is serio-comic piffle about a roguish son who plays at being an investigator for his father's prestigious Miami law firm. A client who is the comptroller of a chain of mortuary establishments in Florida asks the firm to investigate why the business of Whitcomb Funeral Homes is enjoying a drastic upswing in business when the advertising campaign and the referrals have remained constant, and unless the citizens of South Florida are dying at an unwarranted pace, flunky-son Archie McNally is assigned to undertake the riddle.

1512. Sariola, Mauri. *The Helsinki Affair.* Trans. Alan Blair. New York: Curtis, 1970; Walker, 1972 [Trans. of *Lavean tien laki, oikeudenkayntiromanni*]. The jacket blurb reads: "Blackmail, murder, and three attractive women turn a struggling young lawyer into a detective and then advocate for the accused murderer in a tense courtroom climax." The reality is less exciting, but there is not much one wants to argue against his chauvinism regarding the exquisite beauty of Finnish women with their "delicious blend" of high cheekbones and blue eyes. Sariola served as an officer in Finnish Lapland, studied at the Law Faculty of Helsinki University and became editor of Helsingen Sanomat, Finland's largest daily, for which he was chief editor of the crime section. Given the pedestrian translation, one can speculate whether his mysteries fare better with a Swedish or French version, but this is his first translation into English. The advocate in question is Osmo Kilpi and he is a cross between Len Deighton's Harry Palmer and Bernard Malamud's archetypal schlemiel. In the courtroom sequence, however, when he trips up the murderer, he is all Perry Mason.

1513. Sartre, Jean-Paul. *No Exit [Huis Clos], a Play in One Act & The Flies [Les Mouches], a Play in Three Acts.* Trans. Stuart Gilbert. New York: Knopf, 1952. Lifelong Parisian, France's post-WW II leading intellectual, a philosopher (refused the Nobel in 1964), playwright, and a novelist of great distinction. He taught at the Ecole Normale Supérieure in 1929--also at Le Havre, Lyon, and Paris--he studied with philosophers Husserl and Heidegger in 1933-34 in Germany. Like Camus, with whom he would later quarrel, he wrote for the Resistance after his return from a German prisoner-of-war camp; in fact, *The Flies* was produced during the German Occupation. *No Exit* was first performed at Théâtre du Vieux-Colombier, Paris, in May 1944. Purists will quibble, but this is the ultimate book in judgment and justice by the arch-Hanging Judge of all time. As Sartre's Garcin says in the play: "Hell is--other people" 45).

1514. Sayers, Dorothy L[eigh]. *Clouds of Witness.* London: Unwin, 1926. New York: Dial, 1927. One of the first women to obtain an Oxford degree, Sayers had a first in medieval literature, and when her mystery afforded her the leisure, she returned to scholarly and religious writing; she translated Dante. Lord Peter Wimsey's second outing sees his elder brother, the Duke of Denver, accused of the murder of his sister's fiancé, Denis Cathcart. Wimsey obtains evidence that will convince brilliant barrister Sir Impey Biggs to try the case before the House of Lords.

1515. _____. *Strong Poison.* London: Gollancz; New York: Brewer, 1930. Her famed gentleman-detective Lord Peter Wimsey meets Harriet Vane, on trial for the murder of her lover, Philip Boyes. Sayers disinterestedly outlines the case against Vane in the opening chapters, commencing with the presiding judge's charge to the jury. The hung jury enables Wimsey to sleuth about for the killer.

1516. Saylor, Steven. *Roman Blood.* New York: St. Martin's, 1991. Set in Rome in the first century B.C., several Saylor novels of ancient Rome feature the likeable Gordianus the Finder and on occasion, the sleuthing gives way to the courtroom as the litigious Romans of the First Triumvirate (60-53 BC) argue cases, such as Clodius' trial (and acquittal for the Good Goddess scandal) and Marcus Caelius' prosecution of Antonius (Cicero defending)--a plethora of conspiracies, culprits, and assassinations before the senate. This novel, in fact, is based on the first case Cicero argued in the Roman Senate. Others: *Catalina's Riddle* (1993), *A Murder on the Appian Way* (1997), and *The Venus Throw* (1995). In the last-named, a "prim, dyspeptic" Cicero defends again in a poison-plot against Clodia, the allegation being that he attempted to bribe Clodia's slaves to poison him. Saylor also has 9 stories collected *The House of the Vestals: The Investigations of Gordianus the Finder* (St. Martin's, 1997), all of which were previously published in *Ellery Queen's Mystery Magazine* and *Armchair Detective.*

1517. Schanker, D. R. *A Criminal Appeal.* New York: St. Martin's, 1998. Newly minted lawyer Nora Lunsey is working as a legal clerk for Indiana Court of Appeals Judge Albertson. She writes the opinion that helps to convict a deaf African-American boy, Dexter Hinton, of slaying a white woman. Later, doubting Dexter's confession, she begins an investigation that could cost not only end her career but her life.

1518. Schier, Norma. *Death Goes Skiing.* New York: 1979. Schier's series character is Colorado DA Kay Barth. She also edited *The Anagram Detectives* (New York: Mysterious, 1979). Others: *Death on the Slopes* (1978), *Demon at the Opera* (1980), and *Murder by the Book* (1979).

Schoonover, Winston P., pseud. *See* Sevilla, Charles. . . .

1519. Schweitzer, Gertrude. *Born.* Garden City, NY: Doubleday, 1960. The second half involves a court case over a child's religious welfare. Adoptive parents professing a Unitarian faith (mocked by opposing counsel as "pagan") are being sued to force the child's return to the natural mother, a devout Catholic, on the grounds that her child's religious rights are being denied. Lawyers for both sides cite precedents, but the plaintiff stresses the human rather than the theoretical.

1520. Scott, Walter [Sir][Bart.]. *The Antiquary.* By the Author of "Waverley" and "Guy Mannering." 3 vols. Edinburgh: Ballantyne, 1815; London: var. pubs.; New York: Van Winkle, 1816. 2 vols. For all that he is out of favor or dismissed as a romanticizer or merely the exponent of the antiquarian interest of the English Romantic Movement, Scott is an exciting writer and a remarkable storyteller. He is not the first lawyer to find more excitement in literature than in his Edinburgh law books, but he had an irrational fixation with the medieval atmosphere, including Abbotsford, his castle on the banks of the Tweed that became a financial sinkhole when his printing establishments failed and he had to drive his pen more furiously than ever to pay off debts. His first novel *Waverley*, published anonymously in 1814, began the sequence of Waverley Novels that Scott would produce at an extraordinary pace of two per year (largely driven by debt). Among the best and most realistic besides *The Antiquary* are *Guy Mannering, Old Mortality, Rob Roy*, and *The Heart of Midlothian.* These were all published between 1815-18 and set in Scotland. Though *Ivanhoe* (1819) is one of his most popular, it is largely inferior to these and remains an exciting novel of Richard the Lion-Heart's reign.

Others with legal issues and conflicts or with lawyers and courtrooms are *Anne of Geierstein, The Fair Maid of Perth, The Fortunes of Nigel, Ivanhoe, Peveril of the Peak*, and *Quentin Durward* (1823).

(Sidenote on publication: Because Scott's novels exist in many modern editions, original publishing information is cited for two of the three novels below. Scott's success enabled him to be his own publisher (Ballantyne and

Company). At the height of his personal success, Scott's publishing firm went under as a result of a domino effect once banks stopped bankrolling financial speculators. Ballantyne was deeply financially involved with Constable's, as well as his two literary agents, Hurst and Robinson. When Messrs. Archibald Constable and James Ballantyne failed, Ballantyne & Co.'s liabilities--perhaps owing to the speculations of Hurst and Robinson just prior to the banks shutting off loans in 1825-26--amounted to £117,000.)

1521. _____. *The Heart of Midlothian* [orig. *Mid Lothian*]. Edinburgh: Black, 1886; New York: Macmillan, 1893; rpt. New York: Oxford U P, 1982. The title is derived from the name for Old Tolbooth, Edinburgh's version of Newgate Gaol. Scott records a great trial scene (Effie Dean before the Edinburgh magistrates) in this 1818 novel, if not his best, his most unified work of fiction. Beginning with the authentic Porteus Riot of 1736, the in which crowds assembled at the hanging of a condemned robber named Wilson resulted in the Captain of the Guards, John Porteus, firing on the crowd after the reprieve was announced. An associate of Wilson led a mob into Tolbooth; they carried out John Porteus and hanged him. Robertson, whose real name was George Staunton, is the lover of Effie Dean, in Tolbooth for child-murder, and she refuses to escape during the chaos. Her half-sister Jeanie refuses to give perjured testimony to clear her, and Effie is sentenced to death at a trial. Her devoted sister walks on foot to London to see Queen Caroline, an interview having been arranged by the powerful Duke of Argyll.

It was also adapted for the stage and produced in Covent Garden on 17 April 1819 by Daniel Terry, an actor-friend of the writer. William Brough performed a comedy version of the trial scene in *The Great Sensation Trial, or, Circumstantial Effie-Dean: A Burlesque Extravaganza* (London: Dramatic Author's Soc., 1863). Two opera versions were performed at the Paris Opéra Cornique in 1833, *La Prison d'Édimbourg*. The Edinburgh Theatre also performed a version titled *Jeanie Deans*, with libretto by Joseph Bennett and music by Hamish MacCunn (1894). Jerome Mitchell published an analysis of Scott's adaptations into operatic form (Lanham, MD: University Press of America, 1996).

1522. _____. *Redgauntlet: A Tale of the Eighteenth Century.* By the author of "Waverley." 3 vols. Edinburgh: Constable; Edinburgh, and Hurst, Robinson, London, 1824. Philadelphia: Carey, 1824. 2 vols. A tale of the Jacobites and Charles Edward, Prince, grandson of James II, King of Scotland, 1720-88.

1523. _____. *Rob Roy.* Introd. Andrew Lang. Edinburgh: Ballantyne for Constable, Edinburgh; London: Longman, Hurst, et al., 1818; New York: Eastburn. 2 vols. Philadelphia: Thomas, 1818. 2 vols. The history of a very notorious rogue of one of the Scottish Highlands most famous clans, the MacGregors, published . Set during the civil wars of the eighteenth century, Rob Roy Campbell (of the name-banished MacGregors) breaks most of the laws of

England and a large number of his own in the pursuit of his livelihood, whether other men's cattle or person or property.

1524. Scottoline, Lisa. *Everywhere That Mary Went.* New York: Harper, 1993. This former trial lawyer and native Philadelphian graduated *magna cum laude* from of the University of Pennsylvania and its law school, where she was associate editor of the Law Review. She credits novelist Philip Roth's contemporary American novels course as beneficial to her post-law writing career. Her web site lists an apprenticeship for the prestigious Philadelphia firm of Dechert, Price & Rhoads. When her marriage collapsed, and having a daughter to care for, she took the heady risk of becoming a novelist and says that, while her daughter slept, she turned her experiences as an associate into fiction and supported herself along the way with a part-time clerkship for a federal appellate judge. Her first novel earned an Edgar nomination; her second won. With a steady output of starred reviews for the subsequent three novels, she hasn't looked back. Praises Anita Manning in a 1998 *USA Today's Bookshelf* review of her first hardcover novel, *Running from the Law:* "Scottoline's writing is sharp, intelligent, funny and hip." *Moment of Truth* was a *New York Times* bestseller.

Nominated for an Edgar, Scottoline's first novel features Mary DiNunzio, a widowed lawyer, is practicing in the court of her former law professor Judge Bitterman. She is being stalked at the very time she is trying to become partner in her law firm. She fears notifying police because an investigation will jeopardize her chances. The mystery element is pure melodrama--the author will do better--but the glib, wisecracking, woman-in-a-man's world humor that laces the novel is pure Scottoline.

1525. _____. *Final Appeal.* New York: Harper, 1994. Grace Rossi left high-powered corporate law career behind to raise her daughter; her husband, another high-powered lawyer, loses interest in her and they divorce. When the alimony runs out, she takes a part-time job as clerk to Chief Judge Armen Gregorian in the Third Circuit Court of Appeals. They fall in love. He goes home to tell his wife he wants a divorce, and then apparently uses his wife's handgun to commit suicide. Forensic evidence supports a judgment of suicide, but Grace is not buying it. Edgar Award for Best Original Paperback in 1995.

1526. _____. *Legal Tender.* New York: HarperCollins, 1996. The day after her partner Mark Biscardi announces that he wishes to dissolve Rosato & Biscardi, Bennie becomes the prime suspect when Biscardi is found dead. Her latest client is Bill Kleeb, an activist roughed up by police during a demonstration at a pharmaceutical company, Furstman Dunn. It's an open-and-shut case for her until Kleeb confesses that the protests are only a part of the story. Kleeb's group was planning a far more violent punishment of the company just before Biscardi's death. Bennie has no alibi, the evidence mounts, and the cops are eager for revenge. To prove her innocence, Bennie probes the murder with her only ally, her lawyer Grady Wells, until she discovers secret meetings that make her suspect him. Just as she closes in, a second murder occurs and she is framed for that. Now it's double homicide, she is indicted, and it is death row if she is convicted; with nothing to lose, Bennie goes on the lam, not to flee but to find the killer.

1527. _____. *Mistaken Identity.* New York: HarperCollins, 1999. Hers is far from being the first book to take advantage of computer technology in the creative process, but she might well have a unique accomplishment in legal-fiction publishing. The rough draft of the first chapter of the novel was put on her web page in a dynamic text format for readers to edit online and make changes, some of which survived into the published version, a fact she acknowledges by acknowledging her many contributors—"from all sorts of people and professions." Galley proofs were sent to various magazines and journals, including the *Wall Street Journal*, and the consensus is praise for the experiment.

Bennie Rosato, reappearing from *Legal Tender*, is summoned to see a prisoner in Philadelphia's Central Corrections lockup about a cop killing and a possible police cover-up. To her stunned amazement, there is her double staring back at her in prison togs claiming to be her own twin sister. Alice Connolly is accused of murdering her cop boyfriend Anthony Della Porta but claims a police coverup involving drug-dealing is behind the frame-up. With inmates trying to kill her and her defense already botched, Bennie, intrigued by her double, takes the case. The defendant had become the lawyer; the twins had traded places.

1528. _____. *Moment of Truth.* New York: HarperCollins, 2000. Mary DiNunzio, working for Bennie Rosato's Philadelphia firm, returns for her second outing in a case that opens with estates lawyer Jack Newlin arriving home to see his wife Honor butchered on the floor. Knowing the killer's identity, he incriminates himself, calls the police, confesses to doubtful detectives, and hires rookie DiNunzio to ensure he loses.

1529. _____. *Rough Justice.* New York: HarperCollins, 1997. One of Philadelphia's top defense attorneys, Marta Richter, has brilliantly defended her client millionaire Elliot Steere, accused of killing Heb Darnton, a homeless man who tried to carjack him. Marta builds her case around self-defense, proving that the victim was shot while coming after her client with a knife. While waiting for the jury verdict, Steere coldbloodedly states that he deliberately murdered Heb. Marta is stunned by his confession, and has only hours before the expected acquittal while the city is paralyzed in a blizzard. Series character Benedetta ("Bennie") Rosato, Scottoline's brainiest, fastest in repartee, and savviest lawyer yet, enters the fray from Rosatto & Associates, Steere's own firm, to assist the cause of justice.

1530. _____. *Running from the Law.* New York: HarperCollins, 1995.

Trial lawyer Rita Morrone agrees to defend her live-in lover's father, a respected judge, against a sexual harassment charge brought by his secretary. Rita finds herself at the center of a murder case instead when the Honorable Fiske Hamilton becomes the prime suspect. Wisecracking and ruminating all the way, she uncovers a secret life and more suspects than she needs--especially when she brings the killer's attention right to her.

1531. _____. *The Vendetta Defense.* New York: HarperCollins, 2001. Elderly pigeon racer Anthony ("Pigeon Tony") Lucia carries out murderous revenge for a blood crime committed half a century earlier on another continent by his enemy Angelo Coluzzi. The powerful South Philly crime family now plans a vendetta of its own. Lawyer Judy Carrier is the latest protag from the formidable Rosato & Associates stable of women lawyers.

1532. Seaman, Donald. *The Defector.* London: Hamilton, 1975. [Rpt. as *The Chameleon Course*, New York: Coward, 1976). Although an espionage novel, it comprises three days of trial and a verdict; the denouement restores it to its spy-fiction genre. The case is ordinary enough: a nondescript householder in Saddlers Hills shoots a housebreaker in self-defense. The trouble that, when asked his name by the Crown prosecutor, he does not admit to the cover name ("John Stevens") but to his real name: Alexandrei Petrovitch Geria, a name familiar to the KGB but until then not the whereabouts.

1533. Seton, Anya. *My Theodosia.* Boston: Houghton, 1941. Saccharine novelization of the famous father-daughter relationship with the trial itself a mere chapter. Sidenote: The author's research claims an answer to the mystery of Theodosia's end in a storm off Cape Hatteras that sunk ship, crew, and passengers, including the 30-year-old daughter of Aaron Burr.

1534. Sevilla, Charles M. Winston P. Schoonover, pseud. *Wilkes: His Life and Crimes.* 1990. San Diego attorney Sevilla authored the nonfictional, hilarious *Disorder in the Court: Great Fractured Moments in Courtroom History* (Norton, 1992). Reissued in 1999 with additional selections by another prominent name brought to the fore via the Simpson trial, Gerald F. Uelmen. He has a wonderful series character in John Wilkes, the cunning and buffoonish defense attorney, whose clients are on a treadmill between the Tombs and the court. One peeps through the sardonically tinged eyes of colleague "Schoon" (Sevilla) as he surrounds Wilkes with a myriad of personalities from the criminal justice system and the New York streets in bite-sized vignettes heralded by quotations from Ovid through Pascal to Charlie Chan. The majesty of the law takes a real pummeling and the ire toward eccentric, irrational, and black-hearted judges will warm the deepest cockels of a defense attorney's heart.

1535. _____. *Wilkes on Trial.* New York: Ballantine, 1993. Wilkes locks horns with one of his most-hated NYC jurists in Judge Y[ulburton] Knott in a case that ought to be a slam-dunk for the prosecution: black street thug and gang leader Diderot (Sevilla's naming is droll and Dickensian) sends his soldiers to Wilkes to get him released on bail and acquitted of his charge; it seems a petite, white blind woman was mugged and she identified Diderot from the feel of his jewelry and the smell of his clothes.

Shakespeare, William, pseud. *See* de Vere, Edward. . . .

1536. Shannon, Doris. E. X. Giroux, pseud. *A Death for Adonis.* New York: Ballantine, 1986. Canadian author Shannon lives in British Columbia but was born in Elmira, New York. Her mystery series features barrister Robert Forsythe and his secretary Abigail ("Sandy") Sanderson. Forsyth does not practice law. In this one, he is drawn out of retirement to investigate the 25-year-old conviction of sculptor Sebastian Calvert, committed to an asylum for the murder of his daughter.

1537. _____. *A Death for a Dietician.* New York: St. Martin's, 1988. Sandy is invited to play detective at a fashionable island resort for a murder weekend when the chef and his wife are murdered and the guests stranded.

1538. _____. *A Death for a Dilettante.* New York: St. Martin's, 1986. New York: Ballantine, 1987. The dilettante is Winslow Maxwell Penndragon, who asks Robby to investigate after two attempts on his life. Hobbled by a skiing accident, Robby arrives too late.

1539. _____. *A Death for a Doctor.* New York: St. Martin's, 1986. Sandy is recruited by Chief Inspector Adam Kepesake to impersonate a cousin of murder victim Gillian Foster, whom she resembles.

1540. _____. *A Death for a Double.* New York: St. Martin's, 1990. Forsythe is called by Anthony Funicelli, who has just returned with his very young bride to his family homestead in England because of threats against his life. Others by St. Martin's in the series include: *A Death for a Dancer* (1986), *A Death for a Dancing Doll* (1991), *A Death for a Darling* (1985), *A Death for a Dodo* (1993), and *A Death for a Dreamer* (1989).

1541. Shapiro, Fred R., and Jane Garry, eds. *Trial and Error: An Oxford Anthology of Legal Stories.* New York: Oxford UP, 1998. Outstanding collection of 19th- and 20th-century legal fiction by British, Irish and American authors including novel excerpts and dramas. Excerpted novels include Scott's *The Two Drovers*, Dickens' *Bleak House*, Trollope's *Lady Anna*, Melville's novella *Billy Budd* and Stevenson's *Weir of Hermiston.* Modern novels include Lee's *To Kill a Mockingbird* and John Fowles' *The French Lieutenant's Woman*, and Tom Wolfe's *The Bonfire of the Vanities.* The modern short fiction is well varied also: O. Henry, pseud. [William S. Porter], "The Cop and the Anthem";

Maugham "The Letter"; Frank O'Connor, "The Majesty of the Law"; Faulkner, "Tomorrow"; Philip Roth, "Eli, the Fanatic"; Auchincloss' "The Senior Partner's Ghosts"; also sel. from Oates' *American Appetites*; and Gaines' *A Lesson before Dying*. Other pieces include Christie's *The Witness for the Prosecution* and Glaspell's "A Jury of Her Peers." As seen from the preceding selections and others--particularly Quentin Crisp's *The Naked Civil Servant*, Nadine Gordimer's "Happy Event," and especially George Orwell's "Shooting an Elephant"--this eclectic anthology takes the domain of "legal stories" well beyond the traditional courtroom's pale.

1542. Shapiro, L. S. B. [Lionel S. B.]. *The Sealed Verdict.* Garden City, NY: Doubleday, 1947. London: Jarrolds, 1950. For many years a roving European correspondent, Shapiro writes about the successful prosecution of a German war criminal and the doubts that American prosecutor Major Robert Lashley has after the verdict.

1543. Sharp, Paula. *Crows over a Wheatfield.* New York: Hyperion, 1996. A judge gets involved with a woman who kidnaps her own child to protect him from an abusive father.

1544. Sheldon, Sidney. *Rage of Angels.* New York: Morrow; London: Collins, 1980. Manhattan DA Robert Di Silva is prosecuting Mafia capo Michael Moretti in a high-profile murder case sure to provide him a stepping-stone to the gubernatorial mansion when a young Assistant DA named Jennifer Parks is tricked by Moretti into delivering a package containing a dead canary to Camillo Stela, a Moretti underling-turned-informer helping build the DA's case. The canary message is sufficient to cow Stela and derail the Moretti case; moreover, di Silva starts a file on Parks and her clientele while Moretti attempts to entice her into defending his friends.

1545. _____. *Tell Me Your Dreams.* New York: Morrow, 1998. *The People of the State of California versus Ashley Patterson*. She is the beautiful daughter of a famous, overbearing father and on trial for three bloody murders. committed under an alias (says the state). Her defense team argues she suffers from MPD (Multiple Personality Disorder). Once a definite "thriller" ingredient, the split-personality gambit is dying out in legal fiction as the courts--and psychiatrists themselves--disallow this dubious disease of the mind.

1546. Sherry, Edna. *Call the Witness.* New York: Dodd, 1961. London: Hodder, 1962. This is a variation of the infamous Julia Wallace case, updated and transplanted to a small American town. Bartley French, a social climber and lawyer, married to a prominent wife is accused of her murder.

1547. Sherwood, Robert E[mmet]. *Abe Lincoln in Illinois.* Fwd. Carl Sandburg. New York: Scribner's, 1939. First presented at the National Theatre in Washington, DC, on 3 October 1938 with Raymond Massey as Lincoln. Act One opens in New Salem, Illinois, in the 1830s, Act Two in Springfield a decade later in the law office of Stuart and Lincoln. The play won the Pulitzer and Massey reprised his role in the RKO film (1940).

1548. Siegel, Barry. *Actual Innocence.* New York: Ballantine, 1999. Siegel is an award-winning *Los Angeles Times* journalist with two nonfiction books, including an Edgar-nominated true-crime. Series character Gregg Monarch reluctantly returns in this one to defend his ex-lover Sarah Trant, on death row for killing an elderly geologist in El Nido Valley; he soon discovers via forensic evidence that the victim's throat was severed, making it impossible for him to name Sarah as his killer. Not only do the sheriff and the DA refuse to cooperate but Sarah's appointed attorney also refuses to assist Gregg's inquiries. Time is running out, Gregg finds himself stonewalled by a town intent on hiding its secret.

1549. _____. *The Perfect Witness.* New York: St. Martin's, 1997. Siegel's tale is about a ruthless DA and fading attorney Greg Monarch, resigned to estates and wills for a practice, squaring off in fictional La Graciosa, CA. Bested in court by unscrupulous Dennis Taylor in the past, Monarch agrees to defend his former partner Ira against a charge of murder. To succeed, he must go after the prosecution's star witness, Paul Platt, a pathological liar and Taylor's puppet, and figure out his case's connection to a jury verdict against nearby Devil's Peak nuclear power facility.

1550. Siegel, Benjamin. *The Jurors.* New York: Delacorte; London: Hale, 1973. The trial of Clement Jefferson for the murder of his lover Theresa, a prostitute. The jury, despite the title, is not the focus. Much revolves around the defense team of Lester Proude and Timothy Joley. It begins in *voir dire* with a few jurors developed via flashback, but the investigation during trial occurs in the midst of dialogues between adversarial counsel, the sheriff, and Proude's investigation as evidence comes to light. The twenty days of trial are succinct, but what is best is Siegel's ability to put all these jigsaw pieces of justice together; the verdict is anticlimactic because, in this manslaughter case, the truth is impossible to know.

1551. Siegel, Robert Anthony. *All the Money in the World.* New York: Random, 1997. Louis Glasser is in his sixties and a defense attorney with a lucrative practice built upon hookers, dopers, lower echelon goodfellows, and pornographers. He revels in his role as a defender of such clients. One of his biggest clients, Brian Brianson, is a pusher who has over the years provided Glasser with a sizeable portion of his hefty income; now he calls to inform his lawyer that he has just been bagged by the authorities, a worrisome fact to Glasser because the smoothie dope dealer has always managed to evade the law.

1552. Siegel, Sheldon M. *Special Circumstances.* New York: Bantam, 2000. Debut novel about two murders in a big San Franciscan law firm with an ex-priest-turned-lawyer Mike Daley. Daley did a 7-year stint as a San Francisco PD before joining a big, money-making law firm downtown and acts as "father confessor to the entire firm" (92). His client Joel Mark Friedman is arraigned for the double homicide of two colleagues. Siegel himself is a corporate securities lawyer for the San Francisco branch of Sheppard, Mullin, Richter & Hampton of LA. He took creative writing from legal author Michael Nava, and though he has never witnessed a criminal trial, he was once very close to a murderous rampage when gunman Gian Luigi Ferri shot his way though the 34th floor of Pettit & Martin in 1993. Siegel was working on the 36th floor at the time. Siegel is a graduate of Boalt Hall School of Law at University of California at Berkeley and been in private practice for 15 years in San Francisco.

1553. Sienkiewicz, Henryk. *Western Septet: Seven Stories of the American West.* Trans., ed., and annotat. Marion M. Coleman. Fwd. Maria Kornilowicz. Cheshire, CT: Cherry Hill, 1973. Of the 7 stories collected and translated by the Polish author of *Quo Vadis?* and a trilogy of novels with sweeping canvases, such as the Cossacks uprising in 1648-51 in *Fire and Sword*, one qualifies as legal: "A Comedy of Errors." A judge in the tiny town of Struck-Oil cannot understand what either of the two rival grocers, a constantly spatting German man and woman, are saying in their broken English, but thinking he understands, he speaks and then signs a paper declaring them man and wife, which brings an end to their feud.

1554. Signore, Robert. "*Juridic Park: Traps and Illusions of Harmonization (A Work of Legal Fiction).*" *Journal of the Patent and Trademark Office Society* 77 (1995): 699-707. This futuristic, uncollected short story is told from the perspective of a French narrator assessing the results of the new treaty between the US and France that has opened America to the European system of awarding patent rights to a "first filer" rather than to an inventor. The US, however, has kept its patent protectionism during a grace period; thus, he opines, a "Pyrrhic victory" is all the French have for "imposing our principles on the other side of the Atlantic" (707).

1555. Silberstang, Edwin. *Sweet Land of Liberty.* New York: Putnam's, 1972. Messy novel of radical chic. At the end indictments are handed down by a federal grand jury charging Dean Curtis Stillman and Arno Svenson with kidnapping; they and two others with conspiracy to commit kidnapping (the President's daughter). A New York grand jury also charges Stillman and Svenson with two murders. Another by the author is *Rapt in Glory* (Pocket, 1964).

1556. Simenon, Georges. *The Strangers in the House* [*Les Inconnus dans le Maison*] Trans. Geoffrey Sainsbury. Garden City, NY: Doubleday, 1954. A lawyer in a small French town has been living in an alcoholic stupor since his wife left him twenty years earlier. He awakens one night to the sound of a pistol shot from an upstairs room and finds a dying man. His 20-year-old daughter is accused of murder, and as he defends her to find the real murderer, he discovers her involvement in a gang of thieves (his house is used to hide the swag). (*See* Clouzot, Georges.)

1557. Simon, Leonard. *Dissociated States.* New York: Bantam, 1994. Ludicrously posited novel on the MPD angle. Ruthless stockbroker Felix Kiehl pleads (via his attorney Mary Buchanan) that he performed illegal acts--that is, he acquired great wealth through insider trading as a result of several personalities inhabiting his mind. Dr. Claire Baxter testifies on multiple personality disorders for the defense. The jury never gets to decide because Kiehl, presumably in a dissociated state, attacks Buchanan and virtually kills her in the courtroom. The mistrial results in his being sent upstate. Later, he attempts to abscond with his stashed wealth, but Baxter and another clinical psychologist, romantically involved, intervene.

Simpson, Helen. *See* Dane, Clemence . . . .

1558. Sinclair, Upton. *Boston: A Documentary Novel of the Sacco-Vanzetti Case.* Long Beach, CA: Sinclair, 1928. London: Laurie, 1929. Cambridge, MA: Bentley, 1978. A quote from Howard Zinn's introduction in the modern reprint remarks upon the clear feminist impulse, a pioneer work in this sense, in Sinclair's choice to make Cornelia Thorwell, born a Brahmin in a banker family, abandon her life to live and work with the poor Italians and walk a picket line with them. The trial of anarchists Nicola Sacco and Bartolomeo Vanzetti for the shoe-factory robbery in South Braintree which sent them to Charlestown Prison and death by electrocution on 27 August 1927 is one of the infamous trials of American history. The story cries for the political passion of a Steinbeck, and though Sinclair cannot achieve that elevation, his doggedness, despite a pedantic approach, is a very worthy effort to make this disgraceful trial as rank and black in American jurisprudence as the Salem witchcraft trials or the McCarthy-Cohn hearings of the fifties.

1559. Slaughter, Frank G[ill]. *Sword and Scalpel.* Garden City, NY: Doubleday, 1957; London: Jarrolds, 1968. After two years of heroic endurance in a Chinese prisoner-of-war camp, Captain Paul Scott of the Army Medical Corps faces a court martial in San Francisco's Presidio on a charge of treason.

1560. Sloan, Susan R. *Guilt by Association.* New York: Warner, 1995. Former lawyer Sloan has a psychological suspense thriller, which takes a serious look at rape laws. In 1962 undergraduate Karen Kern is viciously beaten and raped by a Harvard law student who takes her home from a party. Years later, as Karen Doniger she comes forward to accuse the man of the crime just as he receives his party's nomination for US President. After a preliminary hearing, Robert Drayton Willmont is bound over for trial on sex charges.

1561. Smith, Edgar. *A Reasonable Doubt.* New York: Coward, 1970. Death-row convict Smith told his case in his non-fiction book *Brief against Death* (1968) and was championed by celebrities like William F. Buckley, Jr. His novel has the slight stink of the lamp common to jailhouse lawyers and yet he resists attacking the judicial process that nearly took his life. The story is about the rape-murder of a young New Jersey girl and the two youths accused of the crime.

1562. Smith, H[arry]. *Allen.* Rhubarb. Garden City, NY: Doubleday, 1946. Comedic novel in which the title character, a cat, inherits the New York Loons baseball team from his eccentric millionaire owner. The deceased's daughter challenges the will, providing a burlesque courtroom battle between opposing lawyers Orlando Dill and P. Duncan Munk; no less eccentric is Judge Phidias Loudermilk, a screwball himself with a penchant for translating Faith Baldwin novels into Greek. Rhubarb works for the clients of the law firm Meriwether Cockburn & Son, entitled under contractual law to use Rhubarb in their advertising work *Son of Rhubarb* (1967) also entails courtroom hijinks.

1563. Smith, Janet L. *Practice to Deceive.* New York: Fawcett-Columbine, 1992. MacPherson's past and present intertwine as she suspects her father might have been supporting an illegitimate son; meanwhile, her near-bankrupt, two-person law office is on the verge of being incorporated by a powerful Seattle firm in which Gordon Barclay, an old acquaintance of her father and senior partner, is receiving anonymous death threats. One possible motive: Barclay is planning to leave his firm and take his clients with him.

1564. _____. *Sea of Troubles.* Menlo Park, CA: Perseverance, 1990. Like her creator, Annie MacPherson is a Seattle attorney; her first case involves a murder trial at an island resort in Puget Sound. Notes *Detecting Women* compiler Willetta Heisling of Smith's MacPherson trio: "If you enjoy law firm politics, this series delivers . . ." (178). Smith was born and raised in Southern California but has lived for the past 20 years in Seattle. She graduated from law school at the University of Washington and worked for 5 years as a trial attorney and several years as an administrative law judge for the state and has returned to trial work with a small firm. Annie and Joel Feinstein, her partner, are open for business. In San Juan on business for a client, she is involved in a kidnapping when her client's girlfriend is abducted.

1565. _____. *A Vintage Murder.* New York: Fawcett-Columbine, 1994. The third book in the series featuring Seattle lawyer Annie McPherson. here, she comes to the rescue of a friend from her high-school days, although she and Taylor North have not spoken in seventeen years. Taylor's estranged husband, a violent brute, is believed to be harassing his ex-wife by sabotaging her vineyards with various malicious acts.

1566. Smith, Julie. *Crescent City Kill.* New York: Fawcett, 1998. Born in Annapolis, raised in Savannah, and educated at Ole Miss, Smith worked in New Orleans for the *Times-Picayune.* She earned an Edgar Best Novel for *New Orleans Mourning* (St. Martin's, 1990), a first for a woman author since 1956. Of her three concurrent series, attorney Rebecca Schwartz belongs here. Although she and Tony Dunbar work the same New Orleans streets and bring out the bawdy festivity of Mardi Gras season, Smith takes a darker view of murder and mayhem in the other series novels.

A vigilante group calling itself The Jury is assassinating high-profile killers who have escaped the justice system. The first victim is an acquitted defendant who resembles O. J. Simpson; the second is the honest Afro-American New Orleans police chief. Series character Detective Skip Langdon suspects that her old nemesis Errol Jacomine is behind the killings. In *Murder on the Internet,* Smith says that she based the Jacomine character on the archetype of the fallen angel, "the Satan character in Milton as well as in our culture" as well as on Jim Jones, a real demonic character she met as a cub reporter in San Francisco. The idea for her vigilante group, Smith adds, is based on the infamously articulate Unabomber, with whose ideas as a social critic--not methods--she approves.

1567. _____. *Dead in the Water.* New York: Ballantine, 1991. Rebecca is visiting her friend Marty at the aquarium in Monterey when the kelp-shrouded body of Marty's supervisor surfaces in one tank with a knife sticking out of its eye socket. The woman has been having an affair with Marty's husband. Rebecca agrees to defend her when the police arrest Marty.

1568. _____. *Death Turns a Trick.* New York: Walker, 1982. Before she transformed herself into a Jewish feminist lawyer, nice girl Rebecca Schwartz begins her series career as a piano player "in a feminist bordello" (Heisling 179). During the raid by police, Rebecca escapes in friend Ellen Mooney's Mustang--but not for long. She is pulled over by a cop and taken to the slammer. Bailed out and back home, she finds a dead hooker on her Flokati rug. Sleuthing uncovers a Mob-controlled stooge and a corrupt senator in a plot to legalize prostitution.

1569. _____. *Other People's Skeletons.* New York: Ballantine-Ivy, 1993. Rebecca's law partner and best friend is accused of the hit-and-run murder of a well-known San Francisco critic, Jason McKendrick. To help her, Rebecca pries loose from her friend the secret that Chris Nicholson possesses psychic abilities, was in fact attending a session on the night of the killing, but has no solid alibi to explain to police how her car came to end life. Soon Rebecca is awash in suspects, especially castoff mistresses, all of whom could have had a serious grudge against the celebrity critic including a local gangster and

Tenderloin restaurateur named Tommy La Barre, who served up women to select clientele, McKendrick among them.

1570. _____. *The Sourdough Wars.* New York: Walker, 1984. Partner Chris' new love interest is Peter Martinelli, scion of a family bakery famous for its sourdough loaf produced by the unique *Lactobacillus sanfrancisco.* A cryogenics firm has frozen the sourdough starter and Martinelli has put it up for auction. The competition, including two local rival brothers, a New Yorker named Clayton Thomas as well as Martinelli's own sister who is contesting the will, are vying for the valuable equipment, but before it can be auctioned, he is shot to death in his apartment.

1571. _____. *Tourist Trap: A Rebecca Schwartz Mystery.* New York: Mysterious, 1986. British crime fiction author Lesley Grant-Adamson writes of her fondness for Smith's other series character, calling Rebecca Schwartz "[a] nice Jewish girl with an office across the bridge and the whole of San Francisco to play in. She's intelligent, loving, courageous, female. No grim 'exercise in role reversal,' no masculine hero in drag" (qtd. in Jakubowsky 183). Smith, says Grant-Adamson, likes to send Rebecca into "mean rooms," [which is] a way of saying that women writers deal with the serious pain in life, the kind you can't leave behind you when you go home after adventures on the streets because the pain is too deep, too personal" (Jakubowsky 184). In this one, Rebecca has to face a mad man destroying San Francisco's economy by fear through terroristic acts, such as the crucifixion of a tourist on Easter, poisonings, and sabotage. Her own client is framed as a suspect.

1572. Smith, Kay Nolte. *The Watcher.* New York: Coward, 1980. London: Gollancz, 1981. Nolte's first novel garnered an Edgar and earned praise for its "absorbing, if unbelievable, tale." The murder victim is Dr. Martin Granger is a renowned social scientist with a sadistic bent; he is also a murder victim. The defendant is a journalist, the wife of one of Granger's subjects. Also involved is a former lover of the defendant, a cop with a law degree. "The finale is a decidedly soggy one," laments Jon Breen, but he finds it possible to praise this for its "interest and readability" (155).

1573. Smith, Martin J. *Shadow Image.* New York: Jove, 1998. Brenna Christensen is hired by a prominent Pittsburgh family to provide legal advice in the suspicious death of a family member with Alzheimer's.

1574. Smith, William. *The Drunkard: or, The Fallen Saved!.* Boston: Jones, 1847; Boston: Gregg, 1972. Very much as its title expresses, a Temperance play was a visual sermon against the demons of drink with a dose of theatricality and melodrama that generally included a scene of *delirium tremens* and family distress caused by the alcoholic member of the family, a husband or father. The authorship is open to question, perhaps owing to its subject, but a William H. Smith purportedly rewrote the manuscript given him by an autobiographical source, directed the 140 performances of its first-year run in Boston in 1844. The audiences wept, especially when the drunkard Edward Middleton raved in the fourth scene of Act II: "Unloose me; leave me; why fasten me down on fire? [M]adness is my strength; my brain is liquid flame!" Lawyer Cribbs adds salt to the mush by attempting to fleece a widow and her child out of their property.

1575. Snow, C. P. [Charles Percy]. *Strangers and Brothers.* London: Faber, 1940. New York: Macmillan, 1958. Physicist, scientific consultant, don, government minister, and novelist of an 11-book sequence on life in modern Britain. The first novel of STRANGERS AND BROTHERS, as the series came to be known, by its first novel's title. The major events occur from 1925 to 1933 and are set in a Midland town. George Passant, chief clerk in a law office and charismatic leader of a group of rebellious freethinkers, is tried, along with two others from the group, on charges of conspiracy to defraud and obtaining money by false pretense in seeking investors in the Passant group's farm and advertising agency. Barrister Lewis Eliot (the author's alter ego, born in the same year, and narrator of the series) defends his friend Passant (this one was republished in 1970 as *George Passant*). The novel was followed by *The Light and the Dark* (1947) with events occurring from 1935 to 1943 and focusing on manic-depressive Roy Calvert. The third book is *Time of Hope* (1949), in which Eliot's sexually frustrated marriage is the subject, one that ends in wife Sheila's suicide in the 1956 *Homecomings* (rpt. as *Homecoming*, Scribner's, 1956). Two more novels from the sequence ought to be mentioned because of their courtroom procedures: *The Affair* (London: Macmillan; New York: Scribner's 1960) takes place in 1953-54. Donald Howard is a fellow of Cambridge, a militant Marxist dismissed because of a scientific fraud. Martin Eliot, Lewis' brother and a don himself, brings his barrister brother back to defend the obnoxious Howard in an academic dismissal hearing. Finally, in *The Sleep of Reason* (London: Macmillan, 1968; New York: Scribner's, 1969), Eliot returns to the provincial town for the trial of Cora Ross (George Passant's niece) and Kitty Pateman, accused of torturing, then murdering, an 8-year-old boy. Their attorneys offer a diminished-responsibility defense. "Snow's trial scenes are extremely effective," says Jon Breen (156), but he enjoys "an inflated reputation," argues Seymour-Smith, yet the latter critic praises this novel for its "doggedness, honesty of purpose, industry and a certain sympathetic insight into the difficulties encountered by gifted provincials when they make social progress" (479).

1576. Snow, Donald Clifford. Thomas Fall, pseud. *The Justicer.* New York: Rinehart, 1959. London: World Distributors, 1962. Courtroom western set in 1889 in Ridgefield just north of the Kansas border. Young lawyer Angus DeWolfe gets a new trial for an Indian accused of murdering a family. Wolfe must face the hostilities of the people of the plains region of this time and, especially, the federal district judge assigned, a jurist known as a hanging judge.

1577. Solmssen, Arthur G. *The Comfort Letter.* Boston: Little, 1975. Solmssen is a graduate of Harvard and the Law School of the University of Pennsylvania. A resident of Bryn Mawr, he practiced law in Philadelphia. The novel's title pertains to the underwriters' letters that update a stock's prospectus on offer--i.e., a "cold comfort" letter. The same firm as in his previous two novels, Conyers & Dean, but like Auchincloss he shifts to different lawyers and partners. For example, Graham Anders narrates *Alexander's Feast* (Boston: Little, 1971) but the book quickly moves from a boardroom vote of proxies in Philadelphia to to the Eurpoean theater of pre-war Spain. Unlike Auchincloss, Solmssen will work in courtroom scenarios as in *Alexander's Feast.* Here, clubman and socialite Ordway Smith, a firm partner, is no great shakes as a lawyer, but he finds himself in a real predicament when the firm's securities specialist is in the hospital. He must broker an incredibly complex deal, a debenture issue involving a $1000 million bond for a recalcitrant client, rough-hewn Charlie Conroy, who has grown too big too fast, and needs some legal help to keep his vast conglomerate from imploding and destroying the firm's reputation.

1578. _____. *Rittenhouse Square.* Boston: Little, 1968. London: Hodder, 1969. Ben Butler is volunteered by Conyers & Dean to spend a month doing *pro bono* work for the Philadelphia Public Defender's Office, but his experience causes him to question his career goals. His first jury case involves the theft of diamonds by an exclusive call girl's by a maid.

1579. Solomita, Stephen. *Last Chance for Glory.* New York: Penzler, 1994. Solomita is a former New York City cabbie. Melody Mitchell leaves her Gramercy Park apartment early in the a.m. to walk her dog and sees a nude, bloody woman in the back of a parked car. A retarded, homeless man named billy Sowell is browbeaten by cops to confess. Two years later Maxwell Steinberg, flashy criminal lawyer, looking about for a challenging case fastens on this one and begins to make the legal and extra-legal moves to get Sowell freed.

1580. Sorkin, Aaron. *A Few Good Men.* New York: French, 1990. This military courtroom drama proved a showcase piece for both Tom Cruise and Jack Nicholson's over-the-top performance as blustering Colonel Jessep about the hazing death of one of the men at the US military base at Guantánamo Bay, Cuba (Columbia TriStar/Castle Rock, 1992), directed by Rob Reiner. But it is Kevin Bacon who gives the surprising performance as the competitive counsel for the prosecution. Demi Moore is Cruise's special counsel; Kevin Pollack, Cuba Gooding, Jr., and a gung-ho jarhead played well by Kiefer Sutherland round out the cast.

1581. Sorrells, Walter. *Cry for Justice.* New York: Avon, 1996. Garrett

Brock III has been framed, accused of bribery, and facing disbarment in Georgia. He is accused of bribing a witness on a case in which he is the complainant's lawyer. Worst of all, a serial killer known as "Shakespeare" has targeted him and four lawyers have already been murdered. When Shakespeare makes contact with his daughter, Garrett flees to his in-laws.

1582. _____. *Will to Murder.* New York: Avon, 1996. Tax lawyer Mae-Mae Cosgrove works a probate matter for the widow of a printer killed for $117, but her paperwork leads to serious sleuthing as she uncovers forgery, pornography, and premeditated murder. One other by Sorrells is *Power of Attorney* (1996).

1583. Spark, Muriel. *The Bachelors.* London: Macmillan, 1960. Philadelphia: Lippincott, 1961. The main character is graphologist Ronald Bridges, whose epileptic seizures is mistaken for the beginning of a psychic trance in this comic novel that culminates in the trial of a spiritualist.

1584. Sparks, Dorothy. *Nothing as Before.* New York: Harper, 1944. John Matthews flees the turmoil of New York City for the haven of Danfield, Illinois and is befriended by three citizens of the town, including a love interest; however, when one of the three is murdered, he discovers, during his trial for murder, that New York City and Danfield are not much different in human nature.

1585. Spicer, Bart. *Act of Anger.* New York: Atheneum, 1962. London: Barker, 1963. Benson Kellogg is a lawyer with a quiet practice in a desert town in Rincon County on the Mexican border until the sensational murder trial of Arturo Campeón propels him into the limelight.

1586. Sprague, Gretchen. *Death in Good Company.* New York: St. Martin's, 1997. A slender but superbly written tome which gives both insight into an overwhelmed and underpaid public defender's office but offers up realistic, complex and non-Hollywood characters. The main character is transplanted New Yorker, Martha Patterson, a paralegal doing *pro bono* work as a second career. She is so involved in a variety of cases at West Brooklyn Legal Services, including murder, that another character, Carlos Quinones, summarizes her two weeks' service in a letter to her, apologizing for stealing her money: "[You got] an extremely raw deal, getting ripped off and fired and half strangled . . ." (213).

1587. St. Johns, Adela Rogers. *Final Verdict.* Garden City, NY: Doubleday, 1962. The author's fictionalized homage to her lawyer-father. A journalist daughter tells the story of her famous, hard-drinking father, legendary in legal circles as much for his courtroom panache as his legal and learned witticisms and triumphs--a cross between a celebrity lawyer like Jerry Geisler and Clarence

Darrow. At the end, the daughter must take the stand against her beloved father, who acts *pro se*, in a courtroom battle to have him institutionalized for his alcoholism.

1588. Stabenow, Dana. *A Cold Day for Murder.* New York: Berkley, 1992. Stabenow writes primarily mystery fiction with a series character, Kate Shugak, formerly of the Anchorage DA's office, as detective. She is an Aleut who was so badly injured (her throat was cut) trying to save a daughter from a sexually abusive father that she has retreated to the wilderness. Three series characters are Mutt, her half-wolf dog, Jack Morgan, sometime lover, and Bobby Clark, a wheelchair-bound Vietnam vet with an attitude. In this one, Kate investigates a park ranger's murder and the disappearance of the investigator sent in after the crime.

1589. _____. *Dead in the* Water. New York: Berkely, 1993. Kate goes to work undercover aboard a fishing boat to investigate the deaths of two crewmen.

1590. _____. *A Fatal Thaw.* New York: Berkley, 1993. In another typical adventure in the Gulf of Alaska region, Kate investigates a series of murders linked to the slaughter and smuggling of endangered species. Others in the Prime Crime series (unless otherwise noted) include *Blood Will Tell* (1996), *Breakup* (Putnam's, 1997), A *Cold-Blooded Business* (1994*), Midnight Come Again* (2000), *Killing Grounds* (Putnam's, 1998), and *Play with Fire* (1995).

1591. Stapleton, Douglas, and Helen A. Carey. *The Corpse Is Indignant.* New York: Five-Star Mysteries, 1946. Sample of series sleuth Judge Massie.

1592. Stegner, Wallace. *The Preacher and the Slave* [alt. title: *Joe Hill, Autobiographical Novel*, Garden City, NY: Doubleday, 1969]. Boston: Houghton, 1950. London: Hammond, 1951. Fictional life of Joe Hill, IWW organizer, between 1879-1915. from a birthing in 1905 to a rise in the late teens and early twenties until its back was broken in the 1920s by frame-ups and antisyndacalism trials, and by alienating socialist unions with its credo of strike-and-sabotage, the IWW was a strong force among migrant workers and had certain areas of labor earmarked as power bases. Stegner's life of the Swedish immigrant, Joe Hillstrom, a sailor and stevedore-turned-labor organizer, is essentially recreation of that turbulent era; it includes Hill's murder trial on trumped-up charges and execution in Utah.

1593. Stein, Sol. *The Magician.* New York: Delacorte; London: Joseph, 1971. In his acknowledgments, Stein gives thanks to Leslie A. Fiedler, "a friend whose trial gave me first-hand evidence of the disparity between the practice of law and the administration of justice." The plot is notably thin: a 16-year-old boy wh practices magic tricks is severely beaten by the school bully after he embarrasses him during a school performance; the rest of the novel follows the grinding of the law to its unsurprising jury verdict--and *deus ex machina* conclusion. Stein avoids a dry, objective narration by interjecting points of view, "comments," from all the characters involved in the case except the bully, who is a mindless thug of whom the psychiatrist Dr. Koch evinces his portrait of a "category three" personality (sociopath). What is fascinating is, in fact, the exposure of the workings of the law at its clinically worst so that the disparity between justice and law that Stein made mention of at the beginning acquires its Kafkaesque surreality.

1594. Stern, Mark. *Inadmissible.* New York: Carroll, 1994. Stern's novel concerns a rape trial in Washington, DC.

1595. Stern, Richard Martin. *The Will.* Garden City, NY: Doubleday; London: Secker, 1976. A will contest with a courtroom protocol violation so egregious that Jon Breen amusingly laments, "Is it naive to believe that at least *some* of the jurors would observe the judge's charge not to discuss the case?" (157).

1596. Steven, Daniel. *Clinical Trials.* New York: HarperPaperbacks, 1998. Dylan Ice is an ambitious African-American attorney at a St. Louis law firm. He wins a case for a hospitalized patient deemed mentally unfit by her parents, who sought guardianship. When the girl disappears, he investigates and uncovers a medical establishment conspiracy.

1597. _____. *Final Remedy.* New York: HarperCollins, 1996. This suspense thriller cannot make up its mind as to what it wants to be because it is equal parts medical thriller, legal thriller, and espionage tale. The unsavory plot involves an ongoing secret project with access to genetic splicing techniques that will enable them to create a snake-venom toxin which will work on black Americans only. This retrovirus, called V-5, is stockpiled, shipped to South Africa (to an intact Afrikaaner government). However, its real purpose is to be burst over the heads of rioting blacks in Washington, D.C., sparking a race war that will end in the American version of the final solution. The whole conspiracy is the brainchild of a sexually wounded general, fragged in Vietnam by a black soldier; when his plot is discovered by the Secretary of the Army--a black career soldier--the secretary's death is arranged with the DNA-altered venom. He is brought, barely alive, to the emergency room of a public hospital and treated for drug overdose--until his identity is discovered and the public furor over the racist assumption that a comatose black male in a jogging outfit must be a drug addict results in the misdiagnosis by the white emergency-room staff. The intern is subsequently sued by the widow and that brings the two leading characters together. Elliot Roth, plaintiff's attorney, is himself a Vietnam vet wracked by war memories of guilt and plagued by a former cocaine addiction. To this skein of improbability add another: a romance blossoms between the two antagonist-protagonists--the doctor and the lawyer suing her for malpractice.

1598. Stevenson, Robert Louis. *Kidnapped.* Chicago: Foresman, 1920. Young David Balfour's uncle Ebenezer arranges to have his nephew abducted and sent to sea to deprive him of his inheritance. The lad experiences many adventures before returning to Scotland to reclaim his inheritance under the law known as heir of entail. He finds a lawyer, Mr. Rankeillor, who uses his skills to effect justice. Scribner's published the first American edition as *David Balfour, a Sequel, to Kidnapped* in 1895.

1599. _____. *Weir of Hermiston.* London: Penguin, 1996. This definitive Penguin Classics edition comes with introd. and notes by Karl Miller as well as a much-needed glossary of the broad Scots dialect spoken by Stevenson's characters. Miller calls this unfinished work (Stevenson died of his tuberculosis in Samoa in 1894). It is a conflict of father and son--young Archie refuses to heel to his stern Presbyterian father's edicts. The story is infused with Scotland's richly complex religious and political strife that sprang from the Reformation, which produced the Covenanters. The fictional Lord Hermiston's portrait is based on Stevenson's avid reading of Henry Cockburn's 1865 biography of one of the "bloodiest" of Scotland's judiciary of the rabid Scottish eighteenth-century--namely, Robert MacQueen, Lord Braxton. We meet Archie's father on the bench, clad in red robes of criminal jurisdiction; a notoriously repressive hanging judge, he glowers from beneath black eyebrows at the "whey-colored, misbegotten caitiff" Duncan Jopp, standing in the prisoner's dock: "Honest all through, he did not affect the virtue of impartiality, this was no case for refinement; there was a man to be hanged, he would have said, and he was hanging him" (26).

1600. Stewart, Edward. *Jury Double.* New York: Island, 1996. New York murder trial centering on a pair of women jurors.

1601. Stewart, J. I. M. [John Innes Mackintosh]. Michael Innes, pseud. *Silence Observed.* London: Gollancz, 1961. The former Yorkshire author and Oxford don was a Reader in English Literature who published many novels under his own name, including the quintet *A Staircase in Surrey*, but he is known largely as a writer of classical whodunits, especially for his Sir John Appleby series. In this typical and polished work, Sir John is summoned from a quiet dinner party at home to a murder scene; the dinner guest who failed to appear is standing over the body. The MacGuffin is a missing Rembrandt.

1602. Stewart, Mike. *Sins of the Brother.* New York: Putnam's, 1999. Mobile, Alabama lawyer Tom McInnes grew fed up with the billable-hours marathon at Higgins & Thompson and set up a solo practice. Six months later, he learns from his mother's phonecall that his estranged brother Hall was found dead in the river, murdered while fishing. He goes home to investigate and immediately discovers his brother's involvement with drugs and money.

1603. Stillwell, Hart. *Border City.* Garden City, NY: Doubleday, 1945; London: Hurst, 1948; rpt. New York: AMS, 1977. Jim Billings is a political boss in a border town between Mexico and the US. The book opens with Chelo Moreno in the court house demanding justice; she is a 17-year-old girl raped by Billings. Journalist Dave Atwood take sup her case and becomes involved in the social causes of exploited Mexican workers after her father is killed and another is beaten by a policeman.

1604. Stimson, Frederic J. *The Residuary Legatee Or, The Posthumous Jest of the Late John Austin.* New York: Scribner's, 1888. Barely a legal tale and ponderous with classical allusions in its chapter epithets, it contains a Thurber-like plot twist. Five sections beginning with the will, passing through the codicil, the administration, final accounts, and the residuary bequest. Austin May is in receipt of a bequest of some 20,000 a year from the estate of the uncle of the title with a restraint against his marriage until he attains the age of 35 else the residuary legatee inherits.

1605. Stockley, Grif. *Blind Judgment: A Gideon Page Novel.* New York: Simon, 1997. Stockley is an Arkansas lawyer like his series character Gideon Page; he has worked the past 25 years for the Arkansas Legal Services, a nonprofit corporation funded by the government to provide legal services to indigent clients. His awards are numerous and include Citizen of the Year by the Arkansas Social Workers Association, the Jim Miles Advocacy Award from the Arkansas Foster Parents Association, and in 1994 the Pulaski County Bar Association named him its Citizen of the Year. Stockley offers readers an unvarnished and nonglamorous portrait of a blue-collar lawyer with depth, character, but not ironic detachment, for Page is at heart a good man, if prone to self-doubt about his profession and his clients' motives. He is a workhorse for his clients but no legal whiz at the law, and will on occasion take a punch (or give one). His responsibilities to his daughter show the less ironical side of him because she has her father's number. (*See* Mr. Stockley's commentary in **Craft Notes**.)

Gideon Page must decide between giving his client the full benefit of his legal skills or exacting revenge on old enemies. He leaves Little Rock to defend African-American Doss Bledsoe, indicted for killing his employer, Chinese-American Willie Ting. The case is being held in Bear Creek, his birthplace and a town where the Taylor family cheated Page's family out of property. The prosecutor offers to plea bargain with Page and Bledsoe. The state would lighten his sentence in return for Doss' testimony against Paul Taylor.

1606. _____. *Expert Testimony.* New York: Summit, 1991. Arkansas State Senator Hart Anderson is murdered and deputy public defender Gideon Page has to lock horns with prominent people in the state to defend the accused murderer, a schizophrenic. named Perry Sarver. The defendant is also a patient of the dead man's wife. Page must overcome his own serious depression over the death of his wife to discover whether the expert psychological testimony of Jerry Kerner is motivated by blackmail.

1607. _____. *Illegal Motion: A Gideon Page Mystery.* New York: Simon, 1995. Stockley undoubtedly took his plot from the notorious past of the Arkansas Razorbacks football team, but he should have taken the morals of one of its coaches as well (Lou Holtz suspended most of his offensive backfield before an Orange Bowl game on the mere *allegation* of rape). Page agrees to defend a black star receiver for the University of Arkansas Razorbacks against the charge of raping a white, wealthy cheerleader, but his anti-feminism is too close to misogyny. Says a reviewer: "Only when he thinks about his daughter being raped does Page even see the remote possibility of outrage."

1608. _____. *Probable Cause.* New York: Simon, 1992. Page has been gone from Blackwell County Public Defender's Office for a year and is doing the unglamorous but profitable brief writing and corporate work expected of an associate at Mays & Burton--until he is shocked to be told that his employment is terminated; the call he had received earlier that day from Dr. Andrew Chapman at the city jail returns him to the kind of lawyering and sleuthing he prefers. Chapman as director of the Human Development center was charged with manslaughter when a mentally retarded girl died while staff were attempting to stop her self-mutilation.

1609. _____. *Religious Conviction.* New York: Simon, 1994. Gideon's murder case here takes on a rural born-again fundamentalist group when he agrees to take on the defense of Leigh Wallace, the beautiful daughter of Shane Norman, a big-time minister, accused of murdering her wealthy husband. It is personally complicated when his daughter joins Norman's Christian Life group.

1610. Stockton, Frank R[ichard]. *The Late Mrs. Null.* New York: Scribner's, 1887; rpt. 1907. Lawrence Croft searches for a man previously affianced to Roberta March, a woman he is attracted to for purposes of marriage, then later, wishes to extricate himself from to marry Annie Peyton. It is not Jane Austen here, but there is a whiff of it in the confusion that results and largely because of a matchmaking aunt and Annie's sham marriage (i.e., Mrs. Null or Mrs. Nothing)--all to avoid a marriage to cousin Junius Keswick, the very man Croft had sought out. When the aunt is informed, a threat of prosecution is made for breach of promise.

1611. Stoker, Bram. *Dracula.* New York: Doubleday, 1927. Stoker's 1897 classic inspired by Vlad the Impaler (1431-76) is worth an entry for the part played by solicitor Jonathan Harker, a minor figure, sent to transact business with Count Dracula in Transylvania, but finds himself a prisoner of phantom-women, growing ever weaker, while the Count moves to London. As all know, when victims begin to turn up with tiny punctures on their necks, Dr. Van Helsing, symbol of all that is masculine and rational, in the Freudian sense, warns that the attacks are the work of a vampire able to live for centuries on the blood of its victims.

1612. Stone, Irving. *Adversary in the House.* Garden City, NY: Doubleday, 1947. London: Falcon, 1949. Stone authored a biography of Clarence Darrow (*Clarence Darrow for the Defense*, Doubleday, 1941). Based on the life of Eugene V. (Eugene Victor) Debs, labor organizer and Socialist leader, 1855-1926. Darrow's and Debs' careers intersected most notably in the murder trial of Charles Moyer and William D. Haywood of the Western Federation of Miners; they were charged with the assassination of ex-Governor Frank Stuenenberg of Idaho, mostly on perjured testimony. If convicted and hanged, Debs threatened authorities in a manifesto, he would put "a million revolutionists will meet them with guns" (359).

1613. _____. *False Witness.* Garden City, NY: Doubleday, 1940. Quiet Mission Valley erupts into two camps: those who believe Mary Shoemaker stole Widow Smithers $50 and those who believe in John Annister's defense of her. Two trials occur; in the first subornation of perjury occurs, which results in Mary's excommunication from her church, and in a Los Angeles trial before a judge in a juryless courtroom, Annister's name is cleared of slander.

1614. _____. *Immortal Wife.* Garden City, NY: Doubleday, 1944. London: Falcon, 1950. Novelized biography of Jessie Benton Fremont, feisty chatelaine of explorer John Charles Fremont, which includes Fremont's court martial.

1615. Stout, Rex. *Where There's a Will.* New York: Farrar, 1940. Nero Wolf gains admittance by his title (a contested will) rather than Stout's overrated talent but the porcine gourmand and orchid-growing dilettante does have his followers. A condensed version appeared in *American* magazine under the title *Sisters in Trouble*. The Hawthorne sisters and their lawyer Prescot ask Wolfe to investigate the will of their deceased brother, who died suddenly at age 49. In the will he left appropriate, token amounts to friends and ample bequests to family, but to his sisters the multimillionaire left, respectively, "[a]n apple to his sister June, a pear to his sister May, and a peach to his sister April" (14).

1616. Stowe, Harriet Beecher. *Dred; A Tale of the Great Dismal Swamp.* Boston: Phillips, 1856. 2 vols. Grosse Pointe, MI: Scholarly, 1968. Stowe's reprising of the story of slave Dred Scott, who sued for liberty after living in a territory where slavery had been banned by the Missouri Compromise, is behind the important judicial decision named for him that furthered the split between the North and the South in the decade prior to the American Civil War. The famed abolitionist author of *Uncle Tom's Cabin* acknowledges liberties with the times of sessions of court for the narrative and "placed in the mouth of one of her leading characters a judicial decision of Judge Ruffin, of North Carolina, the boldness, clearness, and solemn eloquence of which have excited admiration both in the Old World and the New" (iv).

1617. Street, Cecil John Charles. John Rhode, pseud. *The Davidson Case.* London: Bles, 1929. [Rpt. as *Murder at Bratton Grange*, New York: Dodd, 1929]. Rhode authored dozens of mysteries between the late 1920s and 1950s featuring Dr. Lancelot Priestley and Inspector James Waghorn.

1618. Strindberg, August. *The Scapegoat.* Trans. Arvid Paulson. Introd. Richard B. Vowles. New York: Eriksson, 1967. The great Scandinavian playwright who anticipated expressionism in his oneiric plays also wrote 150 stories and a dozen novels, mostly realistic urban studies like The Natives of Hemsö, influenced by Balzac, whom he had met during his wanderlust during the mid-1890s ("Inferno Period").

Written in 1906, with a plot similar to Mann's *The Magic Mountain*, a small, down-at-heels Swedish village inhabited by pensioners replaces a sanatorium as microcosm of human venality, comedy, suicide, and failed dreams. The protagonist lawyer, notes Vowles, is much like the Lawyer in *A Dream Play*, for Edvard Libotz is also prematurely aged by a profession that forces him to deal with the ills, not the good, of humanity (x-xiii). There is more action in the local restaurant than in the Magistrate's Court although Libotz accuses his law clerk of embezzling funds and absconding.

1619. Stuart, Francis. *Julie.* London: Collins; New York: Knopf, 1938. A corrupt businessman and seducer of the title character is charged with twelve counts in the Old Bailey; among the charges are arson, conspiracy to defraud, attempted arson, and bribery.

1620. Stuart, Jesse. *Trees of Heaven.* New York: Dutton, 1940; rpt. Lexington: U of Kentucky P, 1980. Stuart writes of the same hill people as John Fox, Jr. and Mary Noailles Murfree; however, his kinship is the Snopes clan of Faulkner or the poor-white trash of *Tobacco Road.* Writing in the foreword of the modern reprint, Wade Hall compares the feuding Boliver Tussie and Anse Bushman and the shiftless denizens of Ragweed Hollow in the Eastern Kentucky hills to A. B. Longstreet's Ransy Sniffle and Faulkner's Flem Snopes (10). Anse kicks the lazy Tussie off his property and a court case ensues in Judge Whittlecomb's court, but it ends in a screaming, swearing mêlée as Anse denounces Tussie from the stand as "a thief on my farm" (313) and Lawyer Wadell has to hold back the irate sharecropper by the coatsleeves.

1621. Styron, William. *The Confessions of Nat Turner.* New York: Random, 1966. America's greatest living novelist writes "a meditation on history" in the form of the actual slave insurrection led by the infamous preacher

Nathaniel Turner in southeastern Virginia in 1831. Styron's poetic novel is filtered through the reminiscences of 30-year-old Turner (initially begun as a criminal confession elicited by attorney Thomas R. Gray's for the prosecution, not the defense). Nat confesses his life, in effect, while awaiting execution in jail for the slaughter of more than 60 people including women and children. The novel opens after the summary trials and executions of his followers (some were acquitted, more than a dozen transported, and 17, including Turner, hanged). Turner's trial itself is technically over at the outset with the official transcript of the death sentence partially incorporated as a preface.

1622. Swanson, Doug J. *Big Town.* New York: HarperCollins, 1994. Jack Flippo is a Dallas private eye with a law degree and a former prosecutor, who once worked for his brother Jefferson, one of the best criminal defense lawyers in Dallas, until the day they found him in his office dead of cocaine-induced coronary occlusion. Jack now works for a law firm when it needs some tough investigating work done fast; his current case starts as a routine spy-on-the-cheating husband job. A second outing is *Dreamboat* (1995).

1623. Swinnerton, Frank. *A Woman in Sunshine.* London: Hutchinson, 1944. Garden City, NY: Doubleday, 1945. Novel of manners in the style of Jane Austen but without her repartee or irony of situation. Letitia's husband Monty, now in his fifties, is a lesser judicial light, not likely to make the judgeship that would redeem his unimpressive career as a barrister. There is one sensational case at the end, viewed from alternating points of view, but it fizzles to an abrupt dismissal of the charge. One more is *The Two Wives* (London: Hutchinson, 1939. Garden City, NY: Doubleday, 1940).

1624. Symons, Julian [Gustave]. *The Blackheath Poisonings.* London: Collins; New York: Harper, 1978. Symons is one of the great practitioners of the modern crime novel. His nonfiction has added an invaluable footnote to the genre and although he is a high-brow writer in the best sense, he does not overvalue intellection as the criterion of good crime fiction; a writer, he argues, must be an entertainer foremost. In a 1966 omnibus volume, he wrote:

> The thing that absorbs me most in our age is violence behind respectable faces. . . the judge speaking with passion about the need for capital punishment, the quiet obedient boy who kills for fun. (qtd. in *Crime and Mystery Writers* 1000)

An upper-class Victorian murder case involving two households in Blackheath. Isabel Collard is tried for only one of several murders: the arsenic poisoning of Roger Vandervent.

1625. _____. *The End of Solomon Grundy.* London: Collins; New York: Harper, 1964. The Dells, a suburban London community, is hostile to the presence in their midst of a new black neighbor. There is an Old Bailey for the strangulation-murder of Sylvia Gresham, the white mistress.

1626. _____. *The Man Whose Dreams Came True.* London: Collins, 1968. New York: Harper, 1969. Tony Jones, who also uses a pair of aliases, is a charming rascal; his lover, Jenny Foster, concocts a plot to kill her wealthy husband and flee to Venezuela with Tony; in a double-cross, it is Tony who finds himself in Magistrate's Court.

1627. _____. *The Progress of a Crime.* London: Collins; New York: Harper, 1960. Reporter Hugh Bennett investigates the Guy Fawkes Night stabbing of a pub owner who had a beef with a motorcycle gang. John Garney and Leslie Winter, two of the lowriders are charged in Assize Court.

1628. _____. *Sweet Adelaide.* London: Collins; New York: Harper, 1980. Symons fictionalizes the life of Adelaide Bartlett, tried in the Old Bailey in 1866 for the chloroform poisoning of her grocer husband George. Trial action derives from transcripts and Notes Jon Breen in admiration: "The postscript, in which Symons spells out exactly what is real and what is invented in the novel, should be obligatory reading for all writers of 'faction'" (159).One more Symons with trial action in the book's second half is *The Color of Murder* (Harper, 1957; rpt. 1978). A man with a frigid wife fantasizes over a librarian; he has blackouts that could be from mental disease or booze, but when he learns she is engaged, his blackout is more severe, and when the mental fog lifts, she is dead and he wonders if he is the killer.

T

1629. Tanenbaum, Robert K. *Act of Revenge.* New York: HarperCollins, 2000. Brooklyn-born Tanenbaum worked his way into the New York City District Attorney's Office as Assistant DA, 1968-73, and was promoted to Chief of the Homicide Division. He worked for the Congressional Committee on Investigations in Washington, DC, as deputy chief counsel and between 1978 and 1981, he maintained a private law practice in Beverly Hills, CA, where he also served two terms as mayor from 1988-96. His writing career opened with a pair of collaborations based on sensational killings and real killers in *Badge of the Assassin* with Philip Rosenberg (Dutton, 1979 and later as TV movie) and *The Piano Teacher* with Peter S. Greenberg (New York: NAL, 1988). Since then, he has drawn upon his wide experience as a DA in the seventies to create the Butch Karp series. Like his hero Karp, Tanenbaum is a college basketball player sidelined with a twisted knee that led him to law school. He is widely admired by readers and critics for the gritty feel of his courtroom novels. He was expert commentator during the O. J. Simpson trial and appeared frequently on CNN and KCAL-TV in LA. Cops, lawyers, and bad guys talk their own distinct languages. He has one of the rockiest marriages in popular fiction.

Lawyer Marlene Ciampi heads the rape unit of the prosecutor's office and advances from friend to lover to wife, and will eventually open her own detective agency to help battered women, but she and Butch clash as career-driven professionals as often as lovers over the course of the novels to make this unfinished relationship as irritatingly fascinating as the Tracy-Hepburn films of the forties.

Tanenbaum's single weakness is as plotmaker: he believes that the more strings a writer throws out there to be tied off at the end, the better an excuse to use repartee to cover up the tangled lines. His latest is so flawed. Two gangs offset his team of Karp-Ciampi when Butch's investigation of a Bollano family *capo*'s killing involves the Ghost Dragons, and Marlene's investigation into a mafia lawyer's killing makes her a target, but are the Chinese gangs now cooperating with the Cosa Nostra, or about to launch an all-out war with them? Add yet an additional worry for the pair when their 12-year-old daughter witnesses a killing in Chinatown that puts her under a death threat.

1630. _____. *Corruption of Blood.* New York: Dutton, 1995. Karp reopens the Kennedy assassination for the Select Committee with assistants Clay Fulton and attorney V. T. Newbury. Tanenbaum was Deputy Chief Counsel to retired Congressman Louis Stokes' congressional committee investigating the assassinations of both JFK and Dr. King.

1631. _____. *Depraved Indifference.* New York: NAL, 1989. The trial in this one is over the hijacking of an aircraft by terrorists. It is proof that Tanenbaum is frequently able to call in his many plotlines without undue stress on the book's structure in the terminal sections of his novels.

1632. _____. *Falsely Accused.* New York: Dutton, 1996. Fellow author Walter Sorrells admires Tanenbaum but considers the *Unlikely Coincidence Quotient* in this novel to be off the charts--undoubtedly because of the series of shocking crimes that bring Karp and Ciampi's path together from their widely separate investigations. "Butch" is in private practice defending Murray Selig, fired as NYC's chief coroner, in a wrongful termination suit; he is weary of being the only courtroom litigator in a firm of papershufflers. A plausible suspect in his firing is Karp's old foe, DA Sanford ("Sandy") Bloom. Meanwhile, Marlene has grown bored of taking care of their daughter Lucy (she is former head of the DA's rape unit) and becomes a private investigator with a specialty for taking on stalkers.

1633. _____. *Immoral Certainty.* New York: Dutton, 1991. Karp's Criminal Courts Bureau is investigating a series of trash-bag murders when Marlene and he engage in one of their bitter professional conflicts. Her excessive number of cases involving child rape and homicide in the past year has given her the "black screamers" and now St. Michaels, a posh Manhattan daycare center, is implicated in a ring of pedophiles with worse to follow, including Marlene's own kidnapping by a homicidal psychopath.

1634. _____. *Irresistible Impulse.* New York: Dutton, 1997. Butch's and Marlene's paths intersect as he prepares to prosecute the Rohbling case--a series of brutal murders of elderly black women--against brilliant courtroom foe Lionel T. Waley. Her new detective agency, which specializes in helping women in domestic abuse cases, confronts her with a stalker known as the Music Lover and Vincent Robinson, an uppercrust Harvard doctor and a sexual sadist, who may be one and the same.

1635. _____. *Justice Denied.* New York: Dutton, 1994. The edgy relationship between reckless Marlene and by-the-book Karp continues in a plot centered around the assassination of a Turkish diplomat by Armenian terrorists, the murder of his wife's yuppie friend, and a Jane-Doe killing in the East Village. The melange of terrorists, shysters, New York scum, etc. shows the NYC justice system rotten to the Apple's core.

1636. _____. *Material Witness.* New York: Dutton, 1993. Karp gets involved in the political investigation of a professional basketball star's death. Marion Simmons is found dead in a parking lot in Queens. Butch resigns from office when a procedural error of one of his staff results in the death of a woman (Marlene is eight months pregnant but manages to straighten out alcoholic cop Harry Bello and set up a meet with a Jamaican drug lord). Aside from the personal issues Karp and Marlene face, they uncover a vast conspiracy scandal that the star's death exposes, one involving drugs, arson, and laundered mob money.

1637. _____. *No Lesser Plea.* New York: Watts, 1987. Ex-basketball jock and current ADA Roger ("Butch") Karp makes his debut. Tanenbaum also sketches in the beginnings of the Ciampi-Karp duet here. The first half of the novel is overwritten with Karp's philosophizing about the flaws of the criminal justice system, his daily grind of a dozen cases and the politics and infighting that go with it, and the macho atmosphere of the New York City DA's office. The second half settles around the case of Mandeville Louis, a psychopath who plays the system and especially its stooge psychiatric profession for his own vicious ends.

1638. _____. *Reckless Endangerment.* New York: Dutton, 1998. Marlene has become a one-eyed, gun-packing woman and part owner of the Bello & Ciampi detective agency specializing in protecting women from stalkers, and as a partner in the Karp-Ciampi tandem adventures as adversaries-lovers-lawyers, she now equals Butch in characterization. This time, the Karps' linguistically talented daughter Lucy is important to the plot as her parents work the same case following a double homicide in Manhattan. A bloody message scrawled above the murdered couple pits the Jewish community against the city's Arab population; meanwhile, there is a sadistic Mexican child-killer named El Chivato on the loose.

1639. _____. *Reversible Error.* New York: Dutton, 1992. Butch and Ciampi work separate cases of a killer and a serial rapist (she enrages him for going out as a decoy despite her pregnancy to trap the killer). His case involves corrupt cops and murder.

1640. _____. *True Justice.* New York: Pocket, 2000. A series of infanticides, indigent mothers killing newborns, brings Karp into action because his supervisor Jack Keegan wants to set an example; a similar case hooks Marlene resulting from a headline shocker about a middle-class college girl and her boyfriend are indicted for murdering their child after a concealed pregnancy.

1641. Tapply, William G[eorge]. *Client Privilege.* New York: Delacorte, 1990. Newgate Callendar once praised Brady L. Coyne, a whiskey-drinking, fly-fishing, discreet sleuth with a well-healed Boston clientele (less work, more money) and a Yale law degree, because of Tapply's "assured," "graceful" style. Brady is a successful mix of frivolity and seriousness, sometimes to the point of physical action. Brady's creator has lived in New England all his life, taught history, and written articles for *Field and Stream* (his father was longtime columnist H. G. ("Tap") Tapply) as well as books on the art of fly fishing, which happens to be Brady's real love as well. His first Coyne novel, *Death at Charity's Point* in 1984 earned the Scribner Crime Novel Award. Some essays on reminiscing and fly fishing (with a sideways smirk at the animal-rights "fanatics" of PETA) are found in the 1997 *A Fly Fishing Life.* In 1995, he and collaborator Linda Barlow produced a romantic suspense novel, *Thicker Than Water.* The biggest rap? Brady lacks fire in his belly. He drifts through life like an overgrown teenager taking people and cases without letting anything touch him. Yet some readers crave this aloofness and read more into him than he possesses.

Judge Chester "Pops" Popowski summons his friend and lawyer Brady Coyne to ask him to meet a man in a bar called Skeeter's because of a phonecall from a man named Wayne Churchill and his note that said: "I know about Karen Lavoie." Churchill's threat to expose the judge's adulterous affair could destroy his chances of a Supreme Court nomination. Brady gets Churchill's offer to be bought off for ten thousand dollars, but when the man is murdered later that night, the police and the press become interested in talking to Brady, who was the last person to see him alive.

1642. _____. *Close to the Bone.* New York: St. Martin's, 1998. Coyne enlists Paul Cizek to defend a client's son in a drunk-driving charge that resulted in an innocent woman's death, even though the verdict looks like a no-brainer for the prosecution. The young man, clearly guilty, gets off, a victory that, for Cizek, seems to precipitate a midlife crisis; he is tired of defending mobbed-up clients and guilty scum. Months later, his fishing boat is found adrift off Plum Island near Newburyport, commencing Brady's investigation into what could be a murder case or a willful disappearance of a man from his own life.

1643. _____. *Cutter's Run.* New York: St. Martin's, 1998. Brady's fifteenth outing of the series begins with an African-American woman's dog being poisoned en route to Alexandria's house. He later gets an urgent message from her, but when he goes to Charlotte Gillespie's cabin, she is gone but he finds red swastikas spray-painted on the walls. The idyllic town hides some clannish secrets.

1644. _____. *Dead Meat.* New York: Scribner's, 1987. Tapply's fifth Brady Coyne caper sees him in northern Maine combining business and pleasure when Vern Wheeler asks Brady to go to Raven Lake Lodge, owned by brother Anthony ("Tiny"), who lives there with family, because Indian lawyers are threatening a suit, demanding he sell the place to them by claiming it to be a sacred burial site. Brady then finds the corpse of a man named Rolando floating in the lake, someone who had disappeared from Tiny's camp five days ago, and now the danger is more than litigation and land-settlement rights.

1645. _____. *Dead Winter.* New York: Delacorte, 1989. Retired Unitarian minister Desmond Winter calls Coyne in the middle of the night about the murder of his daughter-in-law Maggie, found dead in a boat.

1646. _____. *Death at Charity's Point.* New York: Delacorte, 1984. Wealthy, elderly Florence Gresham has lost a husband to suicide a son to Vietnam, but when younger, scholarly son steps off a cliff, she wants answers the inquest cannot provide. Brady Coyne's first outing as Boston lawyer-sleuth to the Brahmins was reissued by Poisoned Pen Press (Tucson, AZ) in 1997 with a new introduction by Tapply.

1647. _____. *The Dutch Blue Error.* New York: Scribner's, 1984. As a rule, mayhem in Tapply occurs offstage but there is a whiff of Fleming in the opening every now and then, as here, in 1967 San Juan, where Guillaume Lundi, on instructions to pick up a packet of documents, is throttled from behind by his contact on the mission. Cut to present: aristocratic client Oliver Hazard Perry Weston is showing Brady his Dutch Blue Error, the philatelic prize of the stamp world, a Netherlands 15-cent 1852 imperforate. Weston wants Brady to investigate the authenticity of a letter from a claimant in possession of another Dutch Blue--for $250,000 because, if a second stamp is known to exist, the value of Weston's greatly diminishes.

1648. _____. *Follow the Sharks.* New York: Scribner's, 1985. The daughter of a wealth attorney contacts Brady about her missing son. Soon Coyne is involved in the delivery of ransom to secure her 10-year-old boy. The boy's father is an ex-Bosox pitcher named Eddie Donagan, reduced to shilling tennis shoes at a shopping mall, and he too disappears after the $150,000 has been paid.

1649. _____. *The Marine Corpse* [British title: *A Rodent of Doubt*]. New York: Scribner's, 1986. International politics come to Faneuil Hall when an attempt is made on the life of the Deputy Assistant Secretary of State for Latin American Affairs, although the would-be assassin is killed. Felix Guerrero's death confirms the government's claim that Cuba is involved in the Haitian revolution. Connecting these events is Brady's client's death a month later: "[Stuart Richmond Carver] got no headlines at all--partly because of the intercessions of his uncle, former United States Senator Benjamin Woodhouse" (6).

1650. _____. *Muscle Memory.* New York: St. Martin's, 1999. Brady's sixteenth outing a divorce case, reluctantly taken on for a drinking buddy and former NBA power forward--until it turns into homicide when the man's wife is murdered. Mick Fallon is a compulsive gambler who might have tried to stiff a loan shark, but dead wife Kaye was not the ideal of a devoted schoolteacher and homemaker, as Brady discovers.

1651. _____. *Scar Tissue.* New York: St. Martin's-Minotaur, 2000. Brady is called on a cold February by old friend and client Jacob Gold; his son Brian and the boy's girlfriend were in a fatal accident when the car went off the road and into the river.

1652. _____. *The Seventh Enemy.* 1994. Coyne's childhood friend Wally Kinnick is a host on a sportsman TV show who is scheduled to testify in opposition to Massachusetts gun-control legislation on an assault-weapons control bill pending before the legislature. When he reverses his testimony, a radical pro-gun lobby called SAFE (Second Amendment for Ever) puts him on an enemies list (Brady, being his lawyer, makes the seventh spot). Then Kinnick is shot and wounded fishing with Brady along the Deerfield River, Coyne is reluctant to believe local authorities calling it an accidental shooting.

1653. _____. *The Snake Eater.* New York: Penzler, 1993. Coyne, on referral from a friend, comes to the defense of a Vietnam vet whose homegrown supply of 70 pounds of cannabis is raided by a rogue cop. Though not one of his usual well-healed clients, Coyne takes a liking to Daniel McCloud (the dope is to relieve the aftereffects of Agent Orange) and his girlfriend Cammie Russell. When the charges are dropped, Brady sends McCloud's manuscript to a New York literary agent he knows. Then McCloud is killed shortly after Coyne's friend Al Coleman is murdered; the answer lies in a file McCloud had labeled "Insurance," in which particulars about the deaths or disappearances of 8 men are recorded.

1654. _____. *The Spotted Cats.* New York: Delacorte, 1991. Jeff Newton, a professional hunter, has been savaged by an African jungle cat. While he lies near death, Coyne investigates the disappearance of Newton's pre-Columbian treasure.

1655. _____. *Tight Lines.* New York: Delacorte, 1992. Wealthy Susan Ames is dying and asks Brady, her friend and lawyer, to find her estranged daughter Mary Ellen, who had run off with a married man twenty-five years older a dozen years earlier. The trail leads Coyne to a psychiatrist and sexual partners of both genders--and, ultimately, to murder when her drowned corpse turns up in a New England pond.

1656. _____. *A Void in Hearts.* New York: Scribner's, 1988 . Private eye Les Katz becomes a Brady client for a ten-dollar fee and tells him a story about cheating a spouse-client and blackmailing her adulterous husband. Brady tells him to return the money to the husband and tell the wife the truth. Before that can happen, Les is killed in a hit-and-run. Brady's new client becomes the wife and the husband is suspect number-one.

1657. _____. *The Vulgar Boatman.* New York: Scribner's, 1987. Gubernatorial candidate Tom Baron asks Brady to look for his missing son who disappeared after his girlfriend was murdered.

1658. Tarkington, Booth. *Conquest of Canaan.* London and New York: Harper, 1905; Upper Saddle River, NJ: Literature, 1970. One of Tarkington's formulaic poor-boy-makes-good tales. Joe Louden is the object of young Ariel Tabor's campaign to save him from his drinking problem in the town that rejected him and from which he once fled. Tarkington's father served as advisor for the book's legal issues, involving a first-degree murder in the shadows of the town's courthouse cupola, causing the author to say afterward, "Never again a lawyer hero for me."

1659. Taylor, Geoff. *Court of Honor.* New York: Simon, 1966. Although kangaroo courts and vigilance committees are beyond the pale of this bibliography, exception is made to accommodate an unofficial but intriguing court comprised of Nazi officers still holding fealty to Adolph Hitler in the aftermath of Berlin's fall. Aristocratic, blind Panzer General Dietrich von Bluckau convenes the court in April of 1945 to try some German soldiers for disloyalty in the dungeon of his family estate; the second section is a flashback that ends brings the novel to the news of Hitler's death in the bunker and culminates in a lenient sentence for Pastor Schillinger for violating "German honor" (323). Taylor, a journalist in peacetime, was an RAF pilot shot down over Germany and prisoner until the Russian liberation.

1660. Taylor, Joan. *Asking for It.* New York: Congdon, 1980. Kate Bianchi is visiting Nauset Island when a local professional man named Purdy breaks into her cottage and rapes her; she reluctantly brings charges against him, but the pre-trial proceedings favor the accused, a respectable family man with two children and a pregnant wife. Midway through the trial, the narrator, and the entire courtroom, learns that she is not the only victim.

1661. Terrot, Charles. *Miss Nightingale's Ladies.* London: Collins, 1948. [Rpt. as *Passionate Pilgrim*, New York: Harper, 1949]. Historical novelization of Sarah Anne Terrot's diary and observations on the life of Florence Nightingale (1820-1910) and her nurses at the base hospital at Scutari in 1854 during the Crimean conflict. One of the nurses who signed a letter highly critical of the medical doctor's competence to *The Times*, accusing Dr. D'Arcey of criminal negligence among other things, is formally "examined" by the Duke of Newcastle's Commission.

1662. Thackeray, William Makepeace. *The History of Pendennis*[:] *His Fortunes and Misfortunes, His Friends and His Greatest Enemy.* New York: Harper, 1850; London: Smith, 1868; Harmondsworth, Eng.: Penguin, 1972 [*Pendennis*. 2 vols. London: Dent; New York: Dutton, 1959. Introd. M. R. Ridley.]. Thackeray was the equal of Dickens in one book at least (*Vanity Fair*, 1847-48) and if his novels lacked the flair of Dickens in characterization, he nonetheless had a more sincere hatred of sham and snobbery than his greater contemporary. The first installments began in 1848 after his triumph with *Vanity Fair*, but in September 1849 the production of monthly issues stalled because of his serious illness. The novel's first part thinly veils the author's experiences at Charterhouse and Trinity College in the the later years of George IV. (After Cambridge, Thackeray abandoned law for journalism in 1832.) Arthur Pendennis struggles with worldly successs. The character of Warrington is drawn from a barrister that the author had known, the Paris correspondent of the *Daily News* for 30 years. Some action and characters, such as barrister Stunning Warrington, derive from the "dismal old flower-pot of a Shepherd's Inn" (95) in the environs of the prestigious Temple and Lincoln Inn.

1663. Thanet, Octave. Alice French, pseud. *The Missionary Sheriff, Being Incidents in the Life of a Plain Man Who Tried to Do His Duty.* New York: Harper, 1897. Little legal action, albeit a town judge exists for the malefactors; it is mostly a tale of Sheriff Amos Wickliff's physical and moral courage. He shows a heart in collaring a wanted fugitive, compassion for an elderly widow and her cat, and resourcefulness in poisoning the whiskey to kill attacking Redskins.

1664. Thayer, Lee. *The Prisoner Pleads "Not Guilty."* New York: Dodd, 1953. London: Hurst, 1954. Writing mysteries well into her nineties, Thayer introduces some courtroom action with a pair of Americans, one helping the other out of a jam. Peter Clancy--a private eye with a valet, no less--finds a drowning victim at a Bermuda resort hotel; then the death is determined to result from a croquet mallet. Dennis Macilroy will stand trial before the Supreme Court.

1665. Thompson, Gene. *Lupe.* New York: Random, 1977. London: Raven, 1978. Described by one reviewer as "an occult courtroom mystery, describing a witchcraft trial in the incongruous atmosphere of contemporary San Francisco."

1666. Thompson, Maurice. *A Banker of Bankersville.* New York: Cassell, 1886. Two young lawyers open a partnership in Bankersville, Indiana, and prosper. The town benefits from their business, especially because of the more aggressive of the two men; however, his speculation with town funds makes him a fugitive on the lam. Apprehended, he is brought back to town and pacifies an angry mob with a speech that exonerates his innocent partner.

1667. Thompson, Thomas. *Celebrity.* Garden City, NY: Doubleday; London: Lane, 1982. Three Texas high-school seniors calling themselves the Three Princes are responsible for the death of a 16-year-old girl. Mack Crawford later becomes an athlete and Hollywood leading man disguising his homosexuality; Kleber Cantrell becomes a journalist, and the reckless T. J. Luther becomes a religious convert known as The Chosen and defendant on trial for murdering one of the trio. The novel jumps between 1950 and the seventies with the main, present-day character DA Calvin Sledge, who is secretly building a case.

1668. Tillett, Dorothy Stockbridge. John Stephen Strange, pseud. *All Men Are Liars.* Garden City, NY: Doubleday, 1948. [Rpt. as *Come to Judgment*, London: Collins, 1949]. Strange wrote novels of detection in a long career that extended from 1928 to 1976, and in her later writing centered more of them in trial action with courtroom scenes. Her series character is a cop, George Honegger. A dying garage owner names a playboy as his killer with eyewitnesses to back up accusation.

1669. _____. *Let the Dead Past.* Garden City, NY: Doubleday, 1953. [Rpt. as *Dead End*, London: Collins, 1953]. Although he does not recuse himself, Judge Bardoley once loved the defendant Valentina Abbott, an often-married woman accused of killing her ex-husband 17 years before her trial.

1670. _____. *Reasonable Doubt.* Garden City, NY: Doubleday; London: Collins, 1951. Ruth Purdy is a children's book author-illustrator tried for the murder of her husband. Her lawyer marries her after the acquittal, but he is unable to forget the case.

1671. Topor, Tom. *The Codicil.* New York: Hyperion, 1995. Well-written tale of a lawyer-turned-private investigator named Bruno hired by a top New York City law firm to investigate the background of a strange codicil that had somehow slipped past the senior associates. Wealthy Matt Marshall changed his will just months before his death and cut one-half of his estate (approximately $150 million) from the main will to go to a child he fathered on a Vietnamese girl named Cricket or to endow a foundation for, literally, Vietnamese-American Bastards if the child he fathered is proved to be dead or since returned to Vietnam. Bruno's job is to find the child if it exists.

1672. Torres, Edwin. *Q & A.* New York: Dial, 1977. Former cop, now Assistant DA Al Reilly is assigned to take Q & A from Lieutenant Guido Brennan after the shooting of a small-time Puerto Rican crook in Spanish Harlem. The Homicide Bureau wants the inexperienced Reilly to clear the shooting for the DA's Office, but Reilly's suspicions about Brennan pan out when Bobby Texidor convinces him that Tony Roman was executed by the rogue cop. Reilly, fighting departmental corruption and cover-up, is led back to Nancy Bosch, Texidor's woman, who was once the love of his life when he was a beat cop. Torres himself grew up in the barrio of East Harlem, became an Assistant DA and a criminal court judge. Sidney Lumet directed faithfully from Judge Torres' gritty novel and Nick Nolte is chilling as the psychopathic Brennan (Virgin/Regency, 1990). Torres authored two other action novels including Puerto Rican gang life, including *Carlito's Way*, starring Al Pacino in the Brian de Palma film (Universal, 1993).

1673. Touster, Irwin, and Richard Curtis. *The Perez Arson Mystery.* New York: Dial, 1972. A young-adult courtroom novel designed to teach how the criminal justice system works. An unpopular Puerto Rican, Antonio Perez, is accused of arson by his former employer; teenage science whizkid Vernon Stevenson offers expert testimony.

1674. Train, Arthur. *Ambition.* New York: Scribner's; London: Nash, 1928. Attorney Ephraim Tutt, with frock coat, stogie, and stove pipe is Lincoln reincarnated in New York City, although side trips to upstate Pottsville occur infrequently; he is the creation for whom Train will be remembered, and the long-running *Saturday Evening Post* did much to ensure that fame, albeit faded now. Mr. Tutt has a younger partner, Samuel Tutt, known simply as Tutt, who is no relation. The firm of Tutt and Tutt specializes in criminal law and many plots revolve about a particular abuse of the justice system. Critics like Jon Breen note that sometimes Mr. Tutt skates over thin ethical ice without falling through. Train was born and educated in Boston (received his LL. B. from Harvard in 1899) and became Assistant DA for New York County. From 1904 on he produced volumes of short stories and novels about Tutt and at his death in 1945 had been President of the National Institute of Arts and Letters since 1941. He had a number of legal miscellanea as well as fiction, including his autobiography *My Day in Court* (Curtis, 1938; Scribner's, 1939); he even had one for Mr. Tutt (*Yankee Lawyer: Autobiography of Ephraim Tutt*, Scribner's, 1943) in which the memoirist offers many a wry comment on how Train had gently exploited him "in these yarns," including a *Saturday Evening Post* cartoon (405) parodying his courtroom dress.

1675. _____. *By Advice of Counsel.* New York: Scribner's, 1921. In the title story, Mr. Tutt gets client Theophilus Higgleby off in a bigamy case on a technicality. "The Shyster" is exposes abuses by lawyers. An accused young murderer's confession in "Contempt of Court" to proud Althea Beekman the reason why she refuses to testify. In "Beyond a Reasonable Doubt" (old Danny Lowry is a defendant practicing veterinary medicine without a license); "You're Another!" features the complainant Mrs. Pierpont (Edna) Pumpelly seeking to have her equally snobbish neighbor arrested for blocking her driveway.

1676. _____. *The Confessions of Artemas Quibble.* New York: Scribner's, 1911. Rpt. 1923. In the manner of Defoe, Fielding, and Dickens, Train's fictionalized autobiography of a scalawag lawyer, born in Lynnn, Massachusetts in 1855, reads true to its own delightful subtitle: *Being the Ingenious and Unvarnished History of Artemus Quibble, Esquire, One-Time Practitioner in the New York Criminal Courts, Together with an Account of the Divers Wiles, Tricks, Sophistries, Technicalities, and Sundry Artifices of Himself and Others of the Fraternity, Commonly Yclept "Shysters" or "Shyster Lawyers," As Edited by Arthur Train.* Early on in life Quibble sees "criminal" lawyer Gottlieb in action swindling a friend and decides to take up the law profession himself. Late in the novel, the firm of Gottlieb and Quibble go on trial themselves.

1677. _____. *The Hermit of Turkey Hollow.* New York: Scribner's, 1921. The title character is murdered and "Skinny the Tramp" (born James Hawkins) is accused of the murder of his hermit friend; the action occurs near Pottsville. Hezekiah Mason is the newly appointed prosecutor; The Squire sees this case as a stepping-stone to the governor's mansion despite an overwhelming conflict of interest in that he is trustee of the tramp's money.

1678. _____. *McAllister and His Double.* New York: Scribner's; London: Newnes, 1905. Train's first book of 11 stories show nothing about Mr. Tutt, although the last 4 ("The Jailbird," "The Course of Justice," "The Maximilian Diamond," and "Extradition") concern young Assistant DA John Dockbridge, Ephraim Tutt's precursor. The first 7 feature "Chubby" McAllister, an obnoxious rich man and frequenter of night spots; in the title story the clubman has a resemblance to larcenous Fatty Welch, a former valet named Wilkens.

1679. _____. *Mr. Tutt at His Best: A Collection of His Most Famous Cases.* Sel. and introd. Harold R. Medina. New York: Scribner's, 1961. Judge Medina introduces the collection of 16 stories with a testimonial about Train's apprenticeship days as Assistant DA for the County of New York "under a

Tammany regime" (ix). Samples: "The Shyster," "The Hand Is Quicker Than the Eye," "'Mr. Tutt, Take the Stand!'" (Tutt takes the stand in behalf of a pathetic burglar knocked cold by his housekeeper Miranda and presents the prosecutor with a legal knot: if Gogarty avails himself of Tutt's eyewitness testimony, he deprives the defendant the right of cross-examination). "Saving His Face," "Contempt of Court, "In Witness Thereof," and "His Honor, the Judge."

1680. _____. *Mr. Tutt Comes Home.* New York: Scribner's, 1941. A good mix of travel and law stories by the now-aged lawyer. The legal points range from matters on probate law to the human drama of confronting a lynch mob in "The King's Whisker." Mr. Tutt travels across several states from Butte, Montana to the salmon rivers of Canada and home to Bangor, Maine in this collection of 11 tales. Back in Bangor, he saves as niece from penury in a case involving a holographic will in "A Salmon for the White House."

1681. _____. *Mr. Tutt Finds a Way.* New York: Scribner's, 1945. Thirteen tales including "The Best Tutt Story of All," "The Camels Are Coming," in which Squire Mason, angry at being rejected again by the Sacred Camel lodge, orders his building destroyed so that the adjacent Camel lodge hall will fall and leave him legally blameless. "Mr. Tutt Pleads Not Guilty" is a narrative defense of his craft brought on by a citizen of Philadelphia, who caused a summons to be served against the author of *Yankee Lawyer* because Mr. Linet had purchased the volume under the assumption that it was biography, not fiction.

Other omnibus collections: *The Adventures of Ephraim Tutt* gathers 27 stories (Scribner's, 1930; rpt. 1946 with two more tales) along with a preface by Train; *Mr. Tutt's Case Book* repeats nearly half the stories along with Train's preface, an introduction by John Henry Wigmore, and scholarly annotations by Ferdinand J. Wolf (Scribner's, 1936). When in "The Bloodhound," for example, after Tutt has allowed a client and Gas House Gang member to take the stand, Wolf punctuates the tale with a scholarly disquisition on self-incrimination under the New York rule (513-16). *Mr. Tutt at His Best* gathers 16 stories from earlier collections and includes an introduction about Train and his creation by Judge Harold R. Medina (Scribner's, 1961).

1682. _____. *Mr. Tutt Takes the Stand.* New York: Scribner's, 1936. Of the 10 stories, one is noteworthy for its narrative structure: "Take the Witness" is a breach-of-promise action against a wealthy client of Mr. Tutt brought by a chorine that is almost entirely cross-examination of the plaintiff. In "Life in the Old Dog Yet" Tutt uses semantics of a law's wording to save a youth from felony murder.

1683. _____. *No Matter Where.* New York: Scribner's, 1933. Wall Street investment banker Donald Lee turns over everything he owns to recompense the investors who lost money with his firm and follows his grandfather's quit-claim deed to Dorrsport, Maine to begin a new life, but he ends up accused of murder.

1684. _____. *Old Man Tutt.* New York: Scribner's, 1938. Breen calls "Tootle" the most unusual tale in this collection of 11 because Train plays games with Mr. Tutt's "dual citizenship"as real person and fictional lawyer, foreshadowing the mock-autobiography, *Yankee Lawyer* (Scribner's, 1943). Hack journalist Jasper Gilchrist publishes a short story in *Whiz-Bang Monthly*, a tale of the death of Tutt in a style like Train's, which event immediately results in Tutt, Train, the *Saturday Evening Post*, and illustrator Arthur William Brown bringing suit over the issue of one author killing off another's fictional character. Series characters "Bloodhound" O'Brion (spelled O'Brien in some editions) and Squire Mason appear in "Jefferson Was Right," "Tit, Tat, Tutt," and "Mr. Tutt Goes Fishing." Two others "Black Salmon" and "Mr. Tutt Takes the Count." In the last-named Tutt attempts to forestall a grasping Count von Gryr-Staz from collecting on his breach of contract against an old family friend and client.

1685. _____. *Page Mr. Tutt.* New York: Scribner's, 1926. Nine tales in this collection. "The Acid Test" takes place in court in which Tutt does a seeming *volte-face* to pursue an aged man onfessing to check forgery against Tutt's company and the employer willing to forgive him.

1686. _____. *Tutt and Mr. Tutt.* New York: Scribner's, 1920. Five of the 7 in the first Tutt collection (nicely illustrated) get inside the courtroom. In one of the best-known tales, "The Dog Andrew," a beachfront boundary dispute results in litigation when Mr. Appleboy is accused of assaulting neighbor Tunneygate by siccing on him a newly acquired dog. "The Human Element" gets defendant off in an airtight case and without legal tricks; "The Hepplewhite Tramp," with much interesting talk about the relationship of crime to progress. In "Lallapaloosa Limited," an expose of stock manipulation, Mr. Tutt tries in Federal District Court to halt the reorganization of the Horse's Neck Mining Company. "Mock Hen and Mock Turtle" concerns a Tong War slaying .

1687. _____. *Tutt for Tutt.* New York: Scribner's, 1934. A collection of 10 stories. Mr. Tutt locks horns with foe Squire Mason twice in "Mr. Tutt Swandangles the Squire" and "Mr. Tutt Takes a Chance."

1688. _____. *Tut, Tut! Mr. Tutt: Being Adventures of the Celebrated* Firm *of Tutt & Tutt*[,] *Attorneys and Counsellors at Law.* New York: Scribner's, 1923. London: Nash, 1924. Cleveland: World, 1945. Five out of 8 stories involve courtroom action. The title story returns snobbish matron Edna Pumpelly to form in a tale involving her husband's valet Beaton, whom she accuses of stealing her jewels. Mr. Tutt exonerates the decent Englishman. In "Hocus-Pocus," Mr. Tutt mislays a will. Others: "The Bloodhound," "The Liberty of the Mail," "Hocus-Pocus," and "In Witness Whereof," a wife seeks to have a codicil included in her husband's will.

1689. _____. *When Tutt Meets Tutt.* New York: Scribner's, 1927. Of the 5 tales, the best is when the Tutts oppose each other over old Commodore Lithgow's will with J. Waterbird Maloon presiding. "The Meanest Man" is a Pottsville tale showing ignomimnious Hezekiah ("Stinker" by the locals) Mason still conniving to get into the Sacred Camels of King Menelik lodge and trying to undermine a hard-working widow's sudden good fortune.

Legal nonfictions of Train include *Blind Goddess* (Scribner's, 1926), *Courts, Criminals, and the Camorra* (Scribner's; London: Chapman, 1912), and *The Prisoner at the Bar: Sidelights on the Administration of Criminal Justice* (New York: Scribner's, 1906; London: Laurie, 1907; rev. ed. 1908; retitled *From the District Attorney's Office: A Popular Account of Criminal Justice* (Scribner's, 1939).

Traver, Robert, pseud. *See* Voelker, John Donaldson. . . .

Tree, Gregory, pseud. *See* Bardin, John Franklin. . . .

Tremayne, Peter, pseud. *See* Ellis, Peter Berresford. . . .

1690. Trimble, Barbara Margaret. B. M. Gill, pseud. *The Twelfth Juror.* New York: Scribner's, 1984. Gill is a popular Welsh novelist, who once wrote romance novels under a pair of pseudonyms. In this one (a Gold Dagger winner) she explores the psychological motivations behind two characters in the manner of contemporaries P. D. James and Ruth Rendell. A popular TV presenter is on trial for the murder of his wife. One of the jurors, a former *Times* journalist, does not want to serve on the jury panel for a reason he keeps to himself, yet his life and the defendant's cross in and out of the courtroom. He narrates and so underscores the differences between American and British justice systems.

1691. Trollope, Anthony. *Phineas Finn: The Irish Member and Phineas Redux.* London: Chapman; New York: Dodd, 1893. 3 vols.; London: Trollope Soc., 1990. Introd. Robin Gilmour. Trollope should endure for his Barsetshire novels, especially *Barchester Towers* (3 vols., 1857) and *The Last Chronicles of Barset* (32 weekly parts, 1867). Another series of interconnected novels, known as Palliser or Political or the Parliamentary Novels, involve some legal issues, characters, and trials.

Volume one (*Phineas Finn*) was first published in 2 vols. (London: Virtue, 1869) and contains a chapter on the Duke of Omnium's will and bequest to headstrong Lady Glencora Palliser, now Duchess of Omnium of Omnium Gatherum Castle and wife of Plantagenet, the humble Chancellor of the Exchequer. The title character is an impecunious but good-hearted Irish lad with enough luck to enter politics While the aged duke perishes, Phineas Finn is busy with various legal and other matters; first, he has been shot at over the provocation resulting from M. P. Robert Kennedy and his libelous letter. Kennedy, a dour Scot is a former friend but insanely jealous of wife Laura, formerly Lady Laura Standish because she loves Finn from an earlier courtship before she made a marriage of convenience; then he files Vice-Chancellor Pickering's affidavit enjoining the *People's Banner*, a Fleet Street newspaper, from publishing the slanderous letter about his own wife, the Lady Laura Kennedy as "being under the influence of Mr. Phineas Finn" (vol. 1, 256).

Nearly half the third volume of *Phineas Redux* in this edition--covering Finn's languishing in Newgate Gaol through high-society tittletattle over the case to the verdict--is a wry portrait of English law in action by one of the nineteenth-century's great novelists; it was originally published in 1874 in both America and England. He is on trial for murdering Mr. Bonteen, a man with whom he had quarreled. A host of characters take the stand, none so accusingly as Lord Fawn. Some of the characters are Dickensian in their portraits as well as their names: Serjeant [sic] Birdbott, Lady Cantrip, Lord Chiltern, Sir Gregory Grogam (attorney-general), Quintias Slide (publisher and archenemy of Phineas), Mr. Low, QC, Mr. Slope (the Crown prosecutor), Bouncer (the novelist), Mr. Rattler and Mrs. Bunce (witnesses), and Chaffanbrass (the defense barrister), etc. Volume two includes a chapter unrelated to Phineas on the Browborough trial, in which Mr. Browborough, member for Tankerville, was tried for bribery. Sir Gregory Grogam, who also sits for Clovelly borough, appears here on behalf of the prosecuting House of Commons.

Two more novels with trials are *Orley Farm* (20 monthly parts, London: Chapman, 1862; pirated Am. ed. Harper, 1862) and *The Vicar of Bullhampton* (completed in 1868 for serialization; New York: Harper, 1870; London: Ward, 1880). In *Orley Farm* Lady Mason forges a codicil to her husband's will to provide for her son Lucius.

1692. Troutt, David Dante. *The Monkey Suit and Other Short Fiction on African-Americans and Justice.* New York: New-Norton, 1998. Bonnie Smothers extolls this collection: "None of the 10 stories mentions the doctrines they represent; most of them posit a viewpoint on racial equality that will not soon be forgotten by readers" (*Booklist* Feb. 15, 1998). In tracing the brutal history of the Middle Passage and the African-American struggle for civil rights, Troutt follows the practice of "legal storytelling" practiced by Derrick Bell and Richard Delgado in allowing characterization, not legality, shape his narratives as he assumes the role of writer disguised as a law professor. He is obviously familiar with past masters like Wright and Baldwin, who knew how to relate experiences from within a character's psyche and thereby reveal the full scope of the brutality that character experiences. Four of the stories contain Supreme Court cases: the Scottsboro Boys in "For Love of Trains"; warrantless searches in "Bitch, Son of a Bitch"; segregation ordinances in "The Bargain"; and the constitutionality of a Reconstruction-era statute in "Never Was." Other tales: "Glow in the Dark," "The Tale of Almost," "The Bargain," "Junius Dogman and the Mischief," "Tell about Tellin'," "Love Space," and the final story, a real delight, "Monkey Suit."

1693. Truman, Margaret. *Murder on the Potomac.* New York: Random, 1994. Actress, singer, mystery writer Truman's eleventh novel in her series features two protagonists who have appeared in two prior novels. Mackenzie ("Mac") Smith is a Georgetown University law professor and Annabel Reed is his attorney wife turned art gallery owner. In this one, Mac finds a weed-covered body in the Potomac; he and Annabel discover that the corpse was once the confidante of a wealthy Washingtonian, a fact which leads them to the sinister Scarlet Sin Society, a theatrical group that reenacts historical murders from Washington's past--with dangerous verisimilitude.

Others in the *Capital Crimes* series: *Murder at the FBI* (Arbor, 1986), *Murder at the Kennedy Center* (Ballantine, 1989), *Murder at the National Cathedral* (Random, 1990), *Murder at the National Gallery* (Random, 1996), *Murder at the Pentagon* (Random, 1992), *Murder in the CIA* (Random, 1987), *Murder in the House* (Random, 1997), *Murder in the Smithsonian* (Arbor, 1993), *Murder in the Supreme Court* (Arbor, 1982), *Murder in the White House* (Arbor, 1980), *Murder on Capitol Hill* (Arbor, 1981), and *Murder on Embassy Row* (Arbor, 1984).

1694. Trumbo, Dalton. *The Remarkable Andrew, Being the Chronicle of a Literal Man.* Philadelphia: Lippincott; London: Lane, 1941. Trumbo's later blackballing by Hollywood would ironically keep his name alive after his screenwriting and novels were laid to rest. In Shale City, Colorado, "our Hero" Andrew Long goes about his citizenly ways in time present surrounded by a cast that includes the likes of General Andrew Jackson, Mr. George Washington, Mr. Thomas Jefferson, Dr. Benjamin Franklin and his betrothed Peggy Tobin. The aristocratic bad guys are Chief Justice John Marshall, Orville Beamish, DA for Shale County, and Ormond Krebbs, a District Magistrate and presiding judge in Andrew's bizarre and allegorical trial (reminiscent of the kangaroo-court House UnAmerican Activities Committee proceedings), in which his actual crime is less significant than the fact that he would be denounced as "an agitator and a Communist and an atheist and a pacifist and a believer in free love and a fifth columnist and a drunkard" (312).

1695. Truscott IV, Lucian K. *Heart of War.* New York: Signet, 1998. Truscott burst onto the thriller-writing scene with *Dress Gray* (1979) about the murder of a gay West Point cadet in 1969. He returned to West Point and the microcosm of military justice in *Full Dress Gray* (1998) in which feminism and the politics of women at the Point are mixed with a plot involving a cabal of highly placed chauvinists and conservatives. A female cadet dies during parade ostensibly of heat stroke; yet her autopsy reveals she had recently had sex with three men. *The New York Times Book Review* lauds *Heart of War* as "a fascinating peek behind the olive drab curtain, blending a solid plot with a piercing critique of hypocrisy, power, politics, and sexual misconduct in today's armed forces." Lieutenant Sheila Worthy's murder rocks Fort Benning, Georgia. Finding her killer is the responsibility of Major Kara Guidry from JAG (Judge Advocate General's Office). Guidry follows a trail of suspicion all the way to Washington, DC in a race with a courtroom disclosure that will blow the lid off the military establishment.

1696. Turnbull, Agnes Sligh. *The Wedding Bargain.* Boston: Houghton, 1966. London: Collins, 1967. Daniel Morgan, President of Morgan Coal Company of Connecticut, is tried for the murder of socialite Paula Ruston, wife of a famous polo player.

1697. Turnbull, Dora Amy Elles Dillon. Patricia Wentworth, pseud. *Silence in Court.* Philadelphia: Lippincott, 1945. London: Hodder, 1947. Whodunit that opens in court as Carey Silence hears Sir Wilbury Fossett, QC, read the charge of feloniously administering a fatal dose of sleeping medicine to her cousin Honoria Maquisten. Wentworth debuted her sleuth Miss Silver in *The Case Is Closed* in 1937.

1698. Turow, Scott. *The Burden of Proof.* New York: Farrar, 1990. Chicagoan Turow should be credited for revitalizing the courtroom thriller in recent times, but he did not revolutionize it, as his most ardent admirers say. He simply writes better than most, regardless of genre--and as any first-class writer would do, he attends to all aspects of the craft of writing. With a canny lawyer's mind for winkling out corruption in urban justice, Turow imposes an ethos of "old-fashioned" sensibility that, according to Paul Gray of *Time*, seems to "revolve around a nexus of . . . values: honesty, loyalty, trust." His characterizations are superbly drawn; his plots evolve out of the press of conflicts his characters bring to their storyworlds, rather than the superimposed puzzles or clichés of the second-rate writer. *Presumed Innocent* was one of the most stunning first-novel debuts in recent times, and its film success with Harrison Ford as "Rusty" Sabich was the blockbuster complement to the bestseller. It spawned imitators by the score--more importantly perhaps, it sent the legal thriller back into the courtroom with a new purpose and helped to distinguish the new breed of lawyer-sleuths from mysteries featuring sleuths who happen to be lawyers on the side. The law mattered once again. Born in 1949 into a Chicago family of psychiatrists, although his own father was a driven, often-absent obstetrician, Scott Turow says that law school was, in fact, his second choice after writing. He graduated from Amherst in 1970, receiving a Stanford scholarship from its Creative Writing Center. In 1975, he became a "One L" (see **Lawyers' Lexicon**) at Harvard Law School. From 1978 to 1986, he was an Assistant US Attorney in Chicago; as lead prosecuting attorney (like protagonist Rusty Sabich), he had an active role in investigations of corruption in the Illinois judiciary known as Operation Greylord. Unlike John Grisham, whose return to the courtroom was an interruption of his writing, Turow maintains both careers at a high level. He is a partner in the Chicago firm of

Sonnenschein, Nath & Rosenthal, an international firm; his own specialty is white-collar crime. In a celebrated 1995 *pro bono* case in Illinois, he won a reversal in the murder conviction of a death-row convict who had spent almost 11 years in prison. He is married to painter Annette (Weisberg) Turow and maintains a daunting 60-hour work schedule. He told the *New York Times Magazine* that he is driven by "a combination of fear, anxiety, and compulsion. I have to control my habit to work all the time." A quote from his web page is axiomatic to the issue of justice in the courtroom vs. justice in fiction: "One of the ironies is that this poor genre, the mystery, is so looked down upon, yet it enthralls people. It delivers answers that life and certainly the courtroom cannot." That is quintessential Turow: the drama between that search for justice and the terrifying realization, even from his most in his philosophical narrators, that human beings can never claim to achieve or know justice, can never in fact understand the darker machinations of the human heart. Perhaps it is hyperbole to call him the Dostoevsky of legal fiction in our time, but he is a serious novelist who scours the consiences of his characters across the abrasive surfaces of their lives.

Middle-aged (and menopausal) Alejandro ("Sandy") Stern, Rusty's lawyer in *Presumed Innocent*, is the main character of Turow's second novel. He returns from a business trip to find his wife Clara dead, a presumed suicide. As he mourns her, Sandy comes to learn more about her and himself as the details of Clara's life are reconstructed and hard truths that range from sexual to business through legal to medical (Clara had genital herpes, for example) that lead to many other unanswered questions emerge about her private life, long-buried family scandals and an insider stock-trading scheme involving a commodities-broker brother-in-law. Hector Elizondo played Stern in a 1992 made-for-TV movie.

1699. _____. *Guilty As Charged: A Mystery Writers of America Anthology.* New York: Pocket, 1996. Turow has written the introduction to this collection of 16 legal tales in which he comments about the art of the contemporary legal thriller and how much it differs from the slick Perry Masons of the past. However, the short-story form itself would preclude most of what Turow argues for: pre-trial research, a study of the opposing counsel, the pseudoscience of jury selection, courtroom dynamics, etc. In fact, only two stories collected from his fellow members of the Mystery Writers of America involve the courtroom (by Marcia Muller's "Knives at Midnight," and Jeremiah Healey's "Turning the Witness"), whereas the others are more akin to straight mystery or hardboiled fiction. Others by Andrew Klavan, "Lou Monahan, County Prosecutor"; Stuart Kaminsky, "Justice"; John Jakes, "Celebrity and Justice for All"; Lia Matera, "Dead Drunk"; Jay Brandon, "The Grip"; and Carolyn Wheat's "Cruel and Unusual."

1700. _____. *The Laws of Our Fathers.* New York: Farrar, 1996. His most ambitious effort yet, this novel's alternating chapters depict both a 1995 murder trial in Kindle County and a background story of anti-Vietnam activism set near Cal-Berkeley and the San Francisco Bay area of the late 1960s and early seventies. Turow has promoted Sonia ("Sonny") Klonsky from a minor role in *The Burden of Proof* (1990) to center stage as a newcomer to the bench after the district cleans house of corrupt justices in the latest sting. She is presiding judge in a bench trial that brings the two tracks together, for she knows all the characters but will not recuse herself. Nile Eddgar, a young probation officer, is accused of plotting the murder of his father, Loyell, a state senator and religion professor with a radical activist past. Loyell, meant to die in a drive-by, is not killed; instead, the victim is Nile's mother (Loyell's ex-wife), a ghetto-activist sent to a housing project plagued by the Black Saints Disciples with a message from Loyell to a drug dealer. The late sixties-seventies sections center on the commune-like relationship and radical politics among all the principals: Eddgar's militant politics, Sonny's eroding love affair with Seth Weissman, and Weissman's tortured relations with his Holocaust-survivor parents while he ponders fleeing to Canada to avoid the draft. Loyell is a charismatic Maoist (and Christian) expelled from his university teaching post for inciting a riot. His wife will stoop to anything to advance her radical agenda. Seth's moral dilemma on Vietnam gets swept up in a phony kidnapping scheme that requires him to assume the name of his neighbor, Michael Frain, graduate student who may have bombed his own chemistry lab. It is as Michael Frain that Seth turns up at the 1995 trial (now he is a confident, middle-aged journalist). He is present not only to observe Nile, whom he knew as a child, but to rekindle romance with Sonny. Lifelong buddy Hobie Tuttle, ex-Black Panther, has resurfaced as Nile's defense lawyer. As the trial proceeds, it becomes clear that Nile's relationship with ex-con gang leader Ordell ("Hardcore") Trent has gone way past the professional. Is he, however, guilty of murder? Until the end, Turow keeps Nile silent and out of the witness stand. Writes Cryer, "In its musings on time's ravages, [the book] is a baby boomer's legal thriller. It ponders whether the flower children of the '60s are becoming their own parents. It speaks in the language of rue and regret, of marriages and careers gone strangely awry."

1701. _____. *Personal Injuries.* New York: Farrar, 1999. Three agents of the IRS's Criminal Intelligence Division coerce Robbie Feaver, a womanizing, wisecracking personal injury lawyer who for years has been bribing judges in the Dickensianly venal world of Chicago/Kindle county politics, to work undercover for an FBI investigation of judicial bribery by disclosing knowledge of his secret account along with partner Mort Dinnerstein. He and Robbie have been bilking client accounts and depositing the money at the River National Bank without paying taxes. Evon Miller, FBI agent, is planted in his office as a paralegal to keep an eye on him. Robbie agrees to wear a wire to implicate five judges who have been fixing cases. As always with Turow, the human motives and aspirations that conflict with ethics and the law matter most. Robbie's personal situation is aggravated by a wife dying of ALS ("Lou Gehrig's disease") and a sick mother.

1702. _____. *Pleading Guilty.* New York: Farrar, 1993. The author told *Newsweek* reviewer Dan Cryer that he was blocked working on *The Laws of Our Fathers* and turned to writing this novel instead. Mack Malloy is a former policeman and burnout lawyer made responsible for locating a missing colleague--law partner Bert Kamin, the eccentric partner in Mack's big Midwestern law firm, Gage & Griswell, who disappeared one day with $5.6 million of a client's insurance profits. The other partners fear a scandal and loss of income, and decide to minimize exposure by assigning Mack the task of finding the man and the money, and so, eager to be useful, he ventures forth, a shabby, alcoholic knight errant. Along the way, he finds a body in a refrigerator, an old nemesis, a still-closeted gay lawyer, a mafia character, a corrupt corporate lawyer, a fixer of college games. Little happens inside the courtroom because this is one of those Célinesque journeys-to-the-end-of-night--that is, the book is a transcript of a recording to be "listened" to a later date. This straightjacket does not suit Turow's zeal for extended introspective moments, yet it is always that terrain his narrating characters inhabit so movingly. Swanson and James write: "[It] is a literate, thoughtful novel. . . It's a detailed, loving characterization of a man whose personality has been formed by his Catholicism and his parents' congenital meanness" (203). Turow himself wryly observes of colleagues like Mack in a 1993 *Playboy* interview that "sometimes lawyers can try the hell out of a case when they're drunk. When they sober up, they're lost, they can't go near a courtroom."

1703. _____. *Presumed Innocent.* New York: Warner, 1987. Literary icon Wallace Stegner called *Presumed Innocent* an "achievement of a high order." Even by Grisham standards, this was a blockbuster cresting a wave of 43 weeks on the bestseller list, through 16 hardcover printings, and grossing $4 million in paperback sales. Turow's novel indeed excels for its stunning psychological self-profile of the narrator's mind. When Rusty Sabich becomes suspected of having murdered the woman with whom he was having an affair, he attempts to stave off the forces he himself set in motion with his passion. All the characters resist stereotypes and breathe life; many have their own dark secrets or secret ambitions beginning with the victim, Carolyn Polhemus, Rusty's adulterous, ambitious partner in Raymond Horgan's office. Rusty's own nascent designs to replace Horgan as chief prosecuting attorney of Kindle County embroils him in the internal politics of a major homicide investigation and a sensational trial. The novel teems with characters drawn to power, such as Nico Della Guardia, who also covets Horgan's office and who will find himself in court pitted against the suave and unflappable Sandy Stern, assigned to defend Rusty from the very investigation he once headed. Even minor characters like Judge Larren Lyttle, Tommy Molto, and Barbara, Rusty's aloof mathematician wife expand this novel beyond the confines of the traditional courtroom thriller. What drives Rusty's angst is memory: himself as husband, attorney, father, and son--and the facts surrounding his tawdry midlife crisis with a beautiful colleague. In his too-calm recountal of the affair that shook him loose from his comfortable existence, we hear the genuine voice of a man to whom something as bizarre as a savage murder has knocked the underpinnings from his entire life. Turow adapts the confessional style without sensationalizing emotion or diluting passion as Rusty weaves between cool rationality amid the ongoing investigation's progress, for all the arrows of guilt are pointing at him, and a brooding introspection of a life he thought he had under control. It ultimately proves one of the most satisfying courtroom thrillers in recent years. The film (Warner, 1990) starred Harrison Ford, Bonnie Bedelia (as Barbara), and Raul Julia as Sandy Stern. Alan J. Pakula directed and scripted Turow's novel.

1704. Tuttiett, Mary Gleed. Maxwell Gray, pseud. [variant sp. Grey]. *The Silence of Dean Maitland.* New York: Allison, n. d. Henry Oswald Everard faces a hanging judge midway through this apprenticeship novel when he is on trial for the murder of aged Benjamin Lee. Although the evidence is entirely weak and circumstantial, the brief trial is mostly summarized except for Mr. Justice Manby's stern rebuke of the youth found not guilty of first-degree murder but guilty of manslaughter. Says the tongue-in-cheek narrator of Judge Manby, preparing to sum up Everard's "murderous character," "He had once given a wife-killer . . . five years and people had been aghast; precisely similar cases in other parts of the country had got six weeks or a twelvemonth, or even two years" (179).

Twain, Mark, pseud. *See* Clemens, Samuel Langhorne. . . .

U

1705. Uhnak, Dorothy. *False Witness.* New York: Simon, 1981; London: Hodder, 1982 . Bronx-born, CUNY-educated Uhnak served 14 years as an NYC cop (12 as detective) and saw all the raw material that city provides for her outstanding police procedurals. She turned these experiences into nonfictional as well: *Policewoman: A Young Woman's Initiation into the Realities of Justice* (New York: Simon, 1964; London: Star, 1978). Her fame rests on two series: the Irish-Catholic family of cops (O'Malleys) she introduced in *Law and Order* (1973) and the Christie Opara series that began in 1968. This one presents a second, white protagonist and counterpart to her ethnic Sanderalee Dawson character, a black woman and media celebrity, who is attacked in her own apartment by a male-unknown, invited for consensual sex. The report reads rape, sodomy, a dismembered hand, and a bitten off lower lip. New York County DA's Office Bureau Chief Lynn Jacobi, with similar obstacles in her career path, fights for justice for the victim when the perp is deliberately misidentified as Dr. David Cohen.

Underwood, Michael, pseud. *See* Evelyn, John Michael. . . .

1706. Uris, Leon. *QB VII.* Garden City, NY: Doubleday, 1970. A naturalized British citizen, knighted for his contributions to medicine, brings a libel action against Abraham Cady, an American novelist because his book on the Holocaust alleges that Dr. Adam Kelno committed war crimes while working in a Nazi concentration camp. The trial is in the second half with a considerable amount of testimony.

V

1707. Van Gieson, Judith. *Ditch Rider.* New York: HarperCollins, 1998. The author graduated from Northwestern University. Her series character is Neil Hamel, a lawyer with a languishing practice in Albuquerque, passionate about tequila and her environment. She handles mostly run-of-the-mill divorce cases and real-estate closings. Her partner Brink is lazy and ineffectual and she is saddled with an incompetent secretary to boot. Van Gieson's powers of description highlight the American Southwest in its harsh beauty and especially when it comes to the terrific heat of New Mexico and the desert region. She lives in Albuquerque. She has a style described in *Killer Books* as "spare, economical, and often sardonic" (204). Nominated for a Shamus Award for Best Private Eye Novel. She has begun a new series with another detective called Claire Reynier (*The Stolen Blue*, NAL, 2000).

In her eighth outing, Neil has relocated to North Valley in Albuquerque, crisscrossed by irrigation ditches and patrolled by teenaged gangs. She defends 13-year-old Cheyanne Morales in a gang slaying, although Hamel is not convinced the girl's confession is valid. She also fears retaliation by the victim's family.

1708. _____. *The Lies That Bind.* New York: HarperCollins, 1993. Neil just returns from a successful custody case when the mother of a high-school friend calls on her about being arrested for a hit-and-run killing of a girl who used to date her grandson. Neil disapproves of snobbish Martha Conover but takes the case.

1709. _____. *The Other Side of Death.* New York: HarperCollins, 1991. Her social cause in this one is opposition to urban development.

1710. _____. *Parrot Blues.* New York: HarperCollins, 1995. Brilliant parrot researcher Deborah Dumaine and a rare macaw have been kidnapped. The husband plays Neil a tape of the kidnapping and asks for her help. Like Scottoline's lawyers, Neil combines fun, sexiness, and seriousness in her sleuthings.

1711. _____. *Raptor.* New York: Harper, 1990. Neil's Aunt Joan dies of a sudden heart attack; inspired by her aunt's love of rare birds, she takes the offer of her aunt's acquaintance Avery, a wilderness guide, to go to Montana. She is soon involved in the plight of falcon poaching: "I'd been in Montana long enough to know what there was to get angry about . . . poachers who illegally took raptors from the wild for money, poachers who did it for the federal government; people who were imprisoned for crimes they didn't commit, people who committed crimes and went free" (169).

1712. _____. *The Wolf Path.* New York: HarperCollins, 1992. Hamel's cause in this novel is reintroducing the wolf to its former habitat. Neil agrees to keep an eye on hot-tempered Juan Sololobo and his wolf Sirius, newly come to the border country of New Mexico to campaign for the reintroduction of wolves. Ranchers are immediately hostile. When Juan threatens a government agent over a cattle-killing incident (someone let Sirius out of his pen), and that agent mysteriously dies in the desert, Juan is framed to take the fall. One more Neil Hamel is *Hotshots* (1996). The first Neil Hamel novel is *North of the Border* (New York: Walker, 1988).

1713. Van Gulik, Robert [Han]. *The Celebrated Cases of Judge Dee.* New York: Dover, 1976. As the subtitles of van Gulik's novels go, these are "Chinese detective stor[ies]." Judge Dee's legal status as the highest-ranking representative of the T'ang court in his region makes him both administrator and criminal investigator. Dutch diplomat and Orientalist scholar van Gulik, while a prisoner of the Japanese in WW II, found a 1940 copy of a Ming-dynasty translation of the real Judge Dee's career in ancient China (1,000 years after the T'ang dynasty's collapse). His translation of that book notes in a postscript that the real Judge Dee (often given as Ti Jen-chieh but transliterated in *pinyin* as Di-Ren-jie) lived between 630 and 700 A.D. and served as a Minister at Court with considerable influence in the foreign and domestic policies of the T'ang Empire (his stories borrow from medieval Chinese rather than this late period, according to *Twentieth-Century Crime and Mystery Writers* 1139). His fictional namesake, however, is a worldly but modest functionary from provincial Chang-Ping with Holmesian powers of deduction (if one allows for both ghostly premonitions and torturing of prisoners to assist investigations). Van Gulik reveals the Chinese court in action throughout his Dee novels, such as the protocol of district magistrates and tribunals with their clerks, assessors, and a sinister factotum known as a headman who faces kneeling witnesses with instruments of torture ready to help prevaricating or recalcitrant witnesses recall their misdeeds. The accused are assumed guilty, by the way, until they prove themselves innocent. His tales are invariably based on plot twists with major and minor characters mere stereotypes. The Judge has depth, however, and counsels his headman to keep himself free of emotional involvement in the investigations they undertake. "I have never learned it," says the Judge at the conclusion of *The Morning of the Monkey* in a rare glimpse of his emotional side. Hoong Liang is a trusted advisor.

Dee Jen-djieh is a young, capable magistrate who is involved in three cases (*see The Jade Screen* below): the first involves the murder of silk merchants;

the second is a young husband's death with suspicion falling on the wife, and then third involves a bride's poisoning in her chambers.

1714. _____. *The Chinese Bell Murders.* New York: Harper, 1958. Judge Dee confronts mystery in the forms of a Buddhist temple with a well-kept secret, a hideous rape-murder and a skeleton in the Pooyang district. The reprint in 1983 includes 15 plates "in Chinese style" drawn by van Gulik.

1715. _____. *The Chinese Gold Murders.* New York: Dell, 1959. Judge Dee's new appointment as magistrate of the Peng-lai district of China begins with problems involving a murdered predecessor, a disappearing bride, and a butchered village ruffian. A modern reprint includes an introduction by Donald F. Lach (Chicago, U of Chicago P, 1979).

1716. _____. *The Lacquer Screen.* New York: Scribner's, 1970. The Judge and assistant Chiao Tai, ex-highwayman, are on a trip to another district when Dee becomes involved in another magistrate's case involving a wealthy silk merchant's presumed suicide. Events get complicated as one crime overlaps another when the magistrate's wife is found raped and murdered in a swamp outside town; the judge goes incognito to mingle with unsavory characters and various rogues implicated in the killing.

1717. _____. *The Monkey and the Tiger.* New York: Scribner's, 1965. Two short novels containing *The Morning of the Monkey* and *The Afternoon of the Tiger.* In the former, a gibbon swinging through the trees near the magistrate's veranda drops an emerald ring which sparks an investigation into a murdered vagabond found on the slope above with four fingers of one hand chopped off. The latter tale has Judge Dee traveling from fictional Pei-chow to the capital where he is to have his new post conferred upon him. The flooding of the Yellow River isolates him with other refugees at the estate of a dying old man's country house. A vast band of highwaymen calling themselves the Flying Tigers intend to ransack the estate in the morning and kills the inhabitants unless they are bought off with two hundred gold pieces; meanwhile, Dee has uncovered a mystery involving the death of the man's daughter and the disappearance of his gold.

1718. _____. *Murder in Canton.* Chicago: U of Chicago P, 1993. First published in 1966, the novel has the Judge arriving in Canton to investigate first the disappearance, and then the death, of the Imperial Censor. This edition also includes a dozen illustrations by the author. Two other outstanding Judge Dee mysteries are *The Chinese Lake Murders* (London: Joseph, 1960) and *The Chinese Nail Murders* (London: Joseph, 1961).

Others by title and year include: *The Chinese Maze Murders* (1952), *The Emperor's Pearl* (1963), *The Haunted Monastery* (1961), *Judge Dee at Work* (1967), *Necklace and Calabash* (1964), *The Phantom of the Temple*

(1966), *Poets and Murder* (1968), *The Red Pavilion* (1961), *Murder in Canton* (1966), and *The Willow Pattern* (1965).

1719. Van Rjndt, Philippe. *The Trial of Adolph Hitler.* New York: Summit, 1978. The author is primarily known among espionage fiction buffs as a writer of high caliber who scrupulously researches his backgrounds.

1720. Van Wormer, Judith. *Jury Duty.* New York: 1996. Van Wormer's service as juror in a sequestered murder trial that sounds very much like the Preppy Murder Trial prosecuted by Linda Fairstein seems to be the inspiration for her fifth novel. James Bennett Layton, Jr., son of a wealthy tycoon, has been charged with the murder of a beautiful model he could not seduce. The press dubs it the "Poor Little Rich Boy Case" and plays up the sex and drugs involved. The novel has almost no trial action despite the plot. Two jurors become enamored of a third, who is also the focal character of the piece, a novelist Libby Winslow.

1721. Veiller, Bayard. *Within the Law.* New York and London: French, 1917. Bayard's 4-act drama was first performed at New York City's Eltinge Theatre on 11 September 1912. Typical of popular theater of its time, this melodrama is full of mouth-filling sentiments, g about wealth and poverty, the plight of the shop girl, etc. and built around unrealistic coincidences and lurid murders--in this case, the gunplay is postponed until the end, but it all begins with the young son of an emporium falls in love with a girl convicted of shoplifting. Mary Turner is innocent of the crime of stealing from her emporium, but that does not prevent her from receiving a three-year sentence. Years later, she returns to Gramercy Park, a very cynical woman yet financially expert in the ways of the world. Here is Mary's view of lawyers in a capitalist society: "[The richest men] made up their minds what they wanted to do and they engaged lawyers clever enough to show them how they could do it and still stay inside the law. Anyone with brains can get rich in this country if he'll engage the right lawyer" (2. 1. 30).

1722. Vern, David. David V. Reed, pseud. *I Thought I'd Die.* New York: Green Dragon, 1946. This is a fantasy novel with documentary elements within a detective story; it includes excerpts from the transcripts of Elliott Hammond's trial for the murdering three women. His diary blames the ,mutilations on a metallic swamp thing, which lives in a scrapyard occupied by a writer-friend. (Rpt. as *The Thing That Made Love,* New York: Unibook, 1951). Another sci-fi/fantasy with trial action is *Murder in Space* (New York: Galaxy, 1954).

1723. Victor, Metta Victoria Fuller. *The Senator's Son; or, The Maine Law: A Last Refuge: A Story Dedicated to the Law-Makers.* Cleveland: Tooker, 1853. The author's preface shows her principle of writing that only reform writing matters: "But it is only when some effort at human improvement is robed in its captivating garb that fiction should be tolerated" (vi). Written in the purple ink of Temperance fervor and in the wake of the Maine Liquor Law, the sole character worth his salt, or his cup of wine in this case, is the young bounder Parke Madison, impervious to his crusading mother and goody-goody sister, an imbiber and reprobate who pretends to the study of law and even steals from his best friend.

1724. Vidal, Gore. *Burr.* New York: Random, 1973. London: Heinemann, 1974. The fictionalized biography of Aaron Burr includes ten pages on his trial for treason in the US Circuit Court, District of Virginia, and the proceedings of the grand jury that brought the indictment. Other trials including Richard Robinson's for the murder of Helen Jewett (Vidal creates a character, Burr's biographer Charles Schuyler, to attend).

1725. Voelker, John Donaldson. Robert Traver, pseud. *Anatomy of a Murder.* New York: St. Martin's; London: Faber, 1958. Judge Harlan Weaver is, according to Jon Breen, "one of the most nearly perfect jurists in fiction" and Claude Dancer "one of its most memorable prosecuting attorneys" (170). There is nothing to dispute in the assertion. Traver's trial sequence (nearly 200 pages) still holds fascination because of its authenticity in the give-and-take of opposing counsel--especially good is the calculated histrionics of Biegler succumbing to well-timed pique to get the word *rape* interjected over the court's ruling. The book was an enormous bestseller of its time and rejuvenated the legal thriller in the wake of the dying Gardner behemoth. Paul Biegler is the narrator, a chagrined ex-DA of Iron Cliffs County in Michigan's Upper Peninsula, whose replacement is Mitch Lodwick, the handsome, local football hero. Biegler misses the courtroom action in his private practice and has his appetite whetted by a phonecall from Laura Manion, wife of Lieutenant Frederick Manion, a decorated war hero stationed in the U. P. Laura claims that a notorious resort lodge proprietor and local sportsman named Barney Quill raped and beat her one night after she left Quill's establishment without her husband. Manion found Quill that night and emptied a German Lüger into him. Biegler despises the cool insouciance of the war veteran and learns of his jealous rage over a wife who radiates sex but finally opts for a defense based on temporary insanity. Biegler must convince jurors to believe Manion was not acting out of the "natural law" for revenge but was in the grip of an "irresistible impulse." The author is a former DA and Michigan Supreme Court Justice. Jimmy Stewart exudes his boyish charm in the Otto Preminger's film (Columbia, 1959) but George C. Scott captured Dancer's grating exasperation to perfection. Lee Remick played Laura to Ben Gazzara's soldier-husband. Traver's preface to the 1982 edition mentions six legal tales in his short story collection; his first published efforts include two works on his experiences as a DA in Upper Michigan. Two legal novels have appeared since *Anatomy*: *People Versus Kirk* and *Laughing Whitefish* (New York: McGraw, 1965; London: Allen, 1967) about a nineteenth-century Michigan case.

1726. _____. *People versus Kirk.* New York: St. Martin's, 1981. Lawyer Frederic Ludlow defends Randall Kirk, who claims to have no memory of killing his lover, the heiress Constance Spurrier. Dr. Hugh Salter provides expert testimony on hypnosis. Notes Breen wryly: "Outside the courtroom, Traver is the dullest novelist imaginable, but in it he can still be fascinating" (171).

1727. Von Elsner, Don. *Don't Just Stand There, Do Someone.* New York: Signet, 1962. Lawyer-sleuth David Danning is consulted by the founder of a cosmetics firm, who informs him her husband will be murdered and she accused. He becomes her codefendant. This is a "messy" novel according to Jon Breen because it is "outrageously fast-moving, overpopulated, excessively eventful. . ." (182).

1728. _____. *Pour a Swindle through a Loophole.* New York: Belmont, 1964. Vehicular homicide trial of truck driver Luigi Ramazetti.

1729. Vulliamy, C. E. [Colwyn Edward]. *Cakes for Your Birthday.* London: Joseph; New York: British Book Centre, 1959. The Liquidation Committee comprises a retired headmaster, a lawyer, and an engineer-poet who have identified 27 methods of elimination, but their attempts at actual murder misfire. They fail to kill gossip Millicent Euphonia Peaswillow of Raddlesgate with poisoned cakes. It culminates in a trial at Waldringham Assizes in a Dickensian match before Mr. Justice Ambledew between Sir Patcham Claydaw and Robert Lumjaw-Puddleboy, KC.

1730. _____. *Don among the Dead Men.* London: Joseph, 1952; Baltimore, MD: Penguin, 1955. Subtitled "A Satirical Thriller," it features a research chemist at the University of Ockham, who practices what he calls "Social service through Selective Elimination." His potion for providing a pleasant euthanasia for people the world is better off without is DGX. Professor Kerris Bowles-Ottery is tried in Ockham Assizes murdering his former student and mistress. Vulliamy's scholarly side included editions of Mary Granville (Pendarves) (1700-88), Lord Byron, and the Crimean campaign.

1731. _____. *Floral Tribute.* London: Joseph, 1963. Weatherblow House is a nursing home operated by Dr. Theophilus Phudd and the setting for a strangulation murder in which victim and accused are equally despised.

1732. _____. *Tea at the Abbey.* London: Joseph, 1961. Violet Oskinlowe is stabbed to death while a guest at Stathering Abbey, her fiancé's aunt's home. Bruce Westerman is charged with the murder at Mansterbridge Magistrate's court.

1733. _____. *The Vicar's Experiments.* London: Bles, 1932. [Rpt. as *Clerical Error,* Boston: Little, 1932]. The Reverend Gregory Virgil Pardicott, vicar in the village of Lower Pydal, decides to become a murderer; one of his victims is the irritating parishioner Colonel Cargoy. Two more novels under the Anthony Rolls pseudonym are *Lobelia Grove* (1932) and *Family Matters* (1933). Two other Vulliamy titles are *Body in the Boudoir* (1956) and *Justice for Judy* (1960).

W

1734. Waddell, C. C. [Charles Carey]. *Juror No. 17.* New York: King, 1931. New York grand jury convenes for a big murder trial.

1735. Wainwright, John. *Acquittal.* London: Macmillan; New York: St. Martin's, 1976. Wainwright, a retired Yorkshire policeman with 20 years on the force began his prolific writing career with pieces for legal and academic journals (he has an external LL. B. from London University). Amazingly, since 1965 he has authored over 100 novels about the British police and legal systems; furthermore, as Jon Breen notes, Wainwright is uncommitted to a preset novel formula (187). His policemen are not types of one another and his character Rucker is one of the vilest fictional villains extant. Many of his series characters cross over one another's novels, and one series protagonist, Charles Ripley, Chief Superintendent, is widely popular. In this novel, a building contractor is surprised to be acquitted of his wife's murder. The narrative employs flashback and trial transcript in Harvey Russell's search for the truth.

1736. _____. *The Jury People.* London: Macmillan; New York: St. Martin's, 1978. The murder trial of a Pakistani youth through the twelve jurors' viewpoints.

1737. _____. *Man of Law.* London: Macmillan, 1980; New York: St. Martin's, 1981. Simon Whitehouse, QC, and Dr. Martin Webb, professor of criminal psychiatry from Lessford University, are college friends from way back who now find themselves adversaries in court in a murder case involving Gerald Patsold and the death of his wife and the part played by the other woman.

1738. _____. *An Urge for Justice.* London: Macmillan, 1981; New York: St. Martin's, 1982. Annie Miller, aging recluse is found village home, hanged with piano wire. The crime is revealed to have its roots in the Holocaust. Barrister Whitehouse defends a Jew and Nazi hunter charged with the crime. "Trial action is relatively brief," writes Breen, an admirer of Wainwright's plot-twisting skills, but there are some interesting observations about the relationships between barristers and solicitors, and Wainwright "delivers his usual knockout punch at the end" (187).

Wakefield, Hannah, pseud. *See* Burton, Sara, and Judith Holland. . . .

1739. Wakefield, H[erbert]. Russell. *Hearken to the Evidence.* London: Bles, 1933. Garden City, NY: Doubleday, 1934. Sandra Tarnhorn is on trial for the poison-murder of her invalid husband; her co-conspirator is writer Noel Carroll with delicate sensibilities that the Crown prosecution will argue made him susceptible to Sandra's enticements.

1740. Walker, Walter. *The Immediate Prospect of Being Hanged.* New York: Viking, 1989. A murder case involving old money and family scandal in a small New England town and the DA's Office.

1741. Wallace, Irving. *The Seven Minutes.* New York: Simon; London: NEL, 1969. A bookstore owner is charged with selling an obscene novel, *The Seven Minutes* by the pseudonymously J. J. Jadway. Defense lawyer Michael Barrett is the protag-hero. The identity of the mysterious Jadway is one of the novel's plot concerns while Wallace lugubriously ponders the censorship and the First Amendment.

1742. Wallace, Rangeley. *No Defense.* New York: St. Martin's, 1997. The frontrunner in Alabama's gubernatorial election becomes the prime suspect in a racial killing. The investigator probing the old civil rights case is the daughter.

1743. Wallace, Robert. *Seven [7] Men Are Murdered.* New York: Fiction League, 1930. DA Martin and Det. Sgt. Doyle investigate a dope ring responsible for the title's mayhem, shot with a .32 caliber through the back or heart.

1744. Wallach, Anne Tolstoi. *Trials.* New York: Dutton, 1996. Pax Peyton Ford and Rosa Macario are two women judges in Manhattan competing not only for the same seat on the state's appellate court but also for the same man. The flashpoint of their rivalry is Leonard Scholer, the defense attorney whose involvement in a bitter child-custody case causes presiding Judge Ford to break off her relationship with him. The author is married to a New York State appellate judge.

1745. Wallis, James Harold. *The Niece of Abraham Pein.* New York: Dutton, 1943. London: Jarrolds, 1944. A Jewish man and his niece settle in the tiny village of Varak in New Hampshire attempting to find a life safe from the German terror, but they meet anti-Semitism. When the unhappy niece disappears with money stolen from her uncle's hiding spot, he is immediately suspected of killing her and is arrested and charged.

1746. Walsh, William Thomas. *Out of the Whirlwind.* New York: McBride, 1935. [Rpt. as *A Murder Makes a Man*, London: Longman, 1935]. Portrait of a young man, Stephen West, and his foe Scanlon, a man who rises to fame and glory in Little Dublin as a lawyer and prosecutor (he puts Stephen in prison for 5 years in the Pine Tree Murder), gets his girl Janina convicted, then intercedes for her release, rises to become a congressman and local hero.

1747. Walz, Jay, and Audrey. *The Bizarre Sisters.* New York: Duell, 1950. London: Gollancz, 1951. "Bizarre" is the name of Richard Randolph's Appomattox plantation, where the scandal of illicit sex and infanticide produced one of America's most salacious trials with celebrities like John Marshall and Patrick Henry acting as the accused pair's co-counsels. In 1792 rumors fly that Richard and his sister-in-law Nancy (more blood relationship than otherwise, for his wife was also his cousin) had a child never seen. They were both tried and acquitted. The authors do their research and even follow up the record with the principals' lives after the notorious trial. Except for Nancy and her fortunate marriage to the rich and distinguished Gouvernour Morris, the remainder of this side of the famous Randolph clan reads like something from Faulkner.

1748. Ward, Edmund. *The Main Chance.* London: Weidenfeld, 1976. New York: Coward, 1977. Ward has written plays for Yorkshire TV (*The Challengers*, London: Elek, 1972) and this novel was turned into a serial about an aggressive solicitor, David Main, seeking to recover custody of his two children.

1749. Warfield, Gallatin. *Silent Son.* New York: Warner, 1994. Maryland States Attorney Gardner Lawson is Warfield's series character. In a convoluted plot that goes back to WW II and the rescue of one soldier by another, a family secret between a rich man and a poor man comes down to a grandson's malevolent desire to eradicate the shame of his low birth. Although Warfield normally maintains good pacing and a realistic decorum in his courtroom scenes--he is superb with characterization and motive--he fumbles the end of this one in a courtroom denouement that depends upon a nick-of-time resolution with more pandemonium in a courtroom than any judge would tolerate.

1750. _____. *Raising Cain.* New York: Warner, 1996. Lawson's friend and colleague, state cop Brownie (Sergeant Joe Brown) suspects his father's death on a deserted country road is not a natural passing, but foul play. When the prime suspect is found dead, Brown finds himself charged with the man's murder.

1751. _____. *State v. Justice.* New York: Warner, 1992. Gardner Lawson is in the middle of a sensational murder case with international implications because the youthful victim was a Soviet citizen [1989] allegedly murdered by one T. J. Justice. During *voir dire*, hostile media publicize accusations of influence-peddling with licensing agents to get him unseated from the proceedings.

1752. Warren, J[ohn]. Russell. *Gas-Mask Murder.* London: Heinemann, 1939. [Rpt. as *Murder in the Blackout*, New York: Sheridan, 1940] Topical whodunit in which a girl from Trenton, England is found dead after a practice Air Raid Precaution drill; she is bandaged, labeled and wearing a gas mask like a simulated victim. A brief trial at the end. One more by Warren is *This Mortal Coil* (London: Melrose, 1947. [Rpt. as *This Inward Horror*, New York: Dutton, 1948]).

1753. Warren, Robert Penn. *All the King's Men.* New York: Harcourt, 1946. Pulitzer-prize winning fictionalized life of the Kingfish, Louisiana Governor Huey Long, is a deservedly much praised novel of a politician's rise and fall. Jack Burden plays a soulful Nick Carraway to the Gatsby-like Willie Stark. Amid the scoundrels behind Willie--Jack, Sadie, Tiny, and Sugar-Boy--and the corrupted is Judge Irwin, the novel's one idealized man, but he holds a terrible secret for Jack, the Boss' factotum and fixer, in the days following the bloody aftermath of the assassination. Born in Guthrie, Kentucky and a *summa cum laude* graduate of Vanderbilt, Warren was a Rhodes Scholar (B. Litt., 1930).

Lesser books with legal-thriller ingredients are *Meet Me in the Green Glen* (Random, 1971; London: Secker, 1972) and *World Enough and Time* (New York: Random, 1950. London: Eyre, 1951). The latter is both a biographical and historical novel which includes Jeremiah Beaumont's trial in Frankfort, Kentucky in 1827.

1754. _____. *Night Rider.* Boston: Houghton, 1939. Percy Munn is a lawyer in turn-of-the-century Kentucky; he gets involved in the struggle of tobacco farmers against the men who buy and control tobacco.

1755. Warren, Samuel. *The Experiences of a Barrister, and Confessions of an Attorney.* Edinburgh: Blackwood's, 1845; rev. Boston: Estes, 1880. Some third-person stories infiltrate this volume of loosely connected, first-person narratives from a young lawyer-narrator of Flint & Sharpe, mostly revolving around crimes of property or crimes against persons in various degrees. The stories themselves are often interesting for their views of the rascality and decency in human nature, with or without the law's contrivance, but the style is excessively florid. Warren's collection of legal comic tales *Ten Thousand a Year* was frequently in print on both sides of the Atlantic and adapted for stage by Richard Brinsley Peake (London: Cumberland, 1842). The US version had been printed by the American Publishing Corporation probably the year prior. Its popularity is unfathomable, the volume itself weighs in at 1,086 pages, and the author seems to share an indulgence of his greater contemporaries in the flippant naming of characters and, unfortunately, a worse characteristic in the emulation of accents and brogues. The law firm of Quirk, Gammon, and Snap, solicitors, of Saffron Hill acquire client Tittlebat Titmouse, who has great expectations when he reads a newspaper notice announcing the death of a possibly related and wealthy heir. Later he will aspire to parliament and be befriended by the likes of Smirk Mudflint and Swindle O'Gibbett. Warren's zest for interjecting law cases resulting from insolvency laws or bribery cases and bubble companies is profoundly tiresome, but Titmouse and his solicitors will be embroiled throughout this turgid narrative.

1756. Waugh, Hillary. *A Madman at My Door.* Garden City, NY: Doubleday, 1978. London: Gollancz, 1979. The novel opens with a sanity hearing in the Superior Court of New Haven County, Connecticut. Orville Elliot, found to be insane when he raped and murdered three women several years before, is about to be released. Elliot has a score to settle with high-school teacher Herbert Murdoch because the rapist's genitals were shot off by Murdoch in the act of raping his wife.

1757. _____. *Parrish for the Defense.* Garden City, NY: Doubleday, 1974. London: Gollancz, 1975. "This defense attorney is interesting for being so thoroughly despicable a character in the fictional world of heroic defense attorneys," argues Breen (188-89). Cleveland Parrish comes to Connecticut to defend Dr. Gerald Whittaker, accused of the murder of his wife. Parrish's first action is to offer his client a paperback book contract for the ghost-written story; his second is to seduce the defendant's mistress.

1758. Webster, Bill. *One by One.* Garden City, NY: Doubleday, 1972. The first black prosecutor on Bay City's DA staff, Ben Waddell, former lieutenant and pilot in Korea's integrated Air Force, now has to face the resentment of the black community when he prosecutes activist Vernon Peel for the murder of three police officers. His opponent is a crack trial attorney Leonard Weinstein with a national reputation.

1759. Weidman, Jerome. *Counselors-at-Law.* Garden City, NY: Doubleday, 1980. Weidman is a prolific novelist and short-story writer. The counselors in the title are many and often act acrimoniously toward one another, but they engage in courtroom battles as a team. Among them: Ira Bodmer and Salvatore Guidice are the youngsters of a prestigious New York law firm on Madison Avenue. Hugh F. X. Kelly, Jr., J. C. Taunton and T. L. Lichine are three others; managing clerk is Mr. Tessitore. As the novel opens, Lichine is down in Alabama on a *pro bono* death-penalty case involving a 15-year-old black youth.

1760. Weisberg, David, and Douglas S. Cook, writ. *Double Jeopardy.* (Paramount, 1999). Libby Parsons is contentedly living the good life in a fine house off the coast of Washington when she is framed by her husband for his murder. She is tried, convicted, sentenced, and while on parole from a halfway house run by an alcoholic ex-lawyer, she tracks him to New Orleans and threatens to kill him--with impunity--based on the title's Constitutional safeguard. Dir. Bruce Beresford. Perf. Ashley Judd and Tommy Lee Jones. Not the first time, of course, Hollywood bollixes the law. Harvard law professor

Adam Harris Kurland finds the film's legal premise frighteningly aberrant:

> The double jeopardy clause provides no protection where a different state . . . seeks to prosecute an individual based on the same act or transaction that has already been subject to prosecution in a different state. This is the 'dual sovereignty' exception to double jeopardy.

He concludes by citing New York and Louisiana laws of criminal estoppel that Libby cannot hide behind so flimsy a premise (*Legal Times* 11 Oct. 1999: 62).

1761. Weiss, Philip. *Cock-a-doodle-doo.* New York: St. Martin's-Griffen, 1996. Political campaign novel with a lawyer protagonist, Jack Gould, as the inside man, convention whip, confidant and yet essentially a loner.

1762. Weiss, Steve. *The Farewell Principle.* Pittsburg, PA: Sterling House, 1998. The author, a Michigan civil litigation attorney, opens his debut novel with a young black male waiting in a downpour for a ride; a car pulls up and shoots him in what appears another senseless driveby killing. Author Robert C. Wilson notes: "[The novel] is a tale of murder and retribution, of courtroom strategies and personal awakenings." Maurice ("Mo") Robinson is a black Oakland County, Michigan prosecutor who takes on a white supremacist organization.

1763. Wellman, Manly Wade. *Not at These Hands.* New York: Putnam's, 1962. Most people in Lawson County believe that George Cobbett would be found guilty of first-degree murder of Ira Drumm and sentenced to death in the electric chair.

1764. Wellman, Paul I[selin]. *Walls of Jericho.* Philadelphia: Lippincott, 1947. Portrait of the fictional city of Jericho and its denizens with a stress on the gentler, low comedic vignettes of human nature. The budding love interest between the title character, hoydenish daughter of lawyer Jefferson Norman, a "soak"and attorney Dave Constable, newly arrived from St. Louis, is the plot mainstay. Low-keyed humor occurs in the Constable's light sentence (as county prosecutor) for the town drunk. Judge Hutto is the other legal luminary of Jericho. Constable becomes Special Counsel to the Attorney General and pleads before the Supreme Court in Topeka against "brilliant, eloquent, and high-priced corporation attorneys" in behalf of the challenged rate-regulated act (325).

1765. Wesson, Marianne. *Render Up the Body.* New York: HarperCollins, 1997; UK: Headline, 1997. Mimi Wesson is a Vassar grad, University of Texas Law School product, and a former federal prosecutor with trial experience in violent and white-collar crimes. In the early 1980s, she returned to teaching as a law professor at the University of Colorado. She has published articles about pornography in feminism and law. Her character Lucinda ("Cinda") Hayes is fed up with the big egos, machismo, and lack of decency in the Boulder County DA's Office and decides to resign as chief sex-crimes prosecutor. The title is a loose translation of *habeus corpus*, a legal maneuver Cinda uses when her old mentor, a Colorado Supreme Court Justice, urges her to make a final appeal for death-row inmate Jason Smiley, convicted of the rape-murder of girlfriend Nicole Caswell. Mimi Wesson dedicated her novel to Jerry Grant Frye, a San Quentin death-row convict whom she is representing before the California Supreme Court. An excellent debut novel, according to the reviewers, and more than one has compared its promise to Turow: "*Render Up the Body* is among the few which matches the impact . . ." (*The London Telegraph*, December 18, 1998).

1766. _____. *A Suggestion of Death.* New York: Pocket, 2000. The daughter of Colorado senatorial candidate Harrison McKay calls makes a radio talk show call-in to claim she was molested by her father. Cinda Hayes investigates and discovers that the woman is living with a neo-Nazi militia headed by a dangerously charismatic leader "Judge" Pike Sayers, who presides over an illegal courtroom of vigilantes. Wesson explores the murky area between the law and repressed memories as evidentiary testimony.

Cinda Hayes joins a phone-in radio program in *An Unconcerned Condition* (1999).

1767. West, Jessamyn. *The Massacre at Fall Creek.* New York: Harcourt; London: Macmillan, 1975. The Pendleton trial and aftermath of the men who massacred three Indian women and four children at a sugar camp. Lone Fawn, a Miami chief, and Bent Arrow, a Seneca brave, are present as representatives throughout the trial to see white justice done. The trial, despite Judge McGowan's need to gavel down the outbursts and interruptions, is well handled. Reverend Caleb Cape helps one of the "unironed" (unfettered by iron) men escape from the jail after the verdict.

1768. West, Morris L. *Daughter of Silence.* New York: Morrow, 1961. Anna Albertini exits a taxi in the piazza of San Steffano and pumps several bullets into the village mayor, a popular bachelor. Although the why is made clear, the book through its characters play off the secular and spiritual chords of the crime and responsibility. Lawyer Carlo Rienzo argues this early on with a concerned spectator, Fra Bonifacio, who sees the murder as revenge, bringing closure to a crime 16 years ago. Says Rienzi: "Let me show you first a little of the law. Murder was done here today. . . . The defense has only two pleas: insanity or mitigation. If we plead mitigation we have a choice of two grounds: provocation or partial mental infirmity. . . . A court is not a confessional. The law takes only a limited cognizance of the moral guilt of an act" (41).

1769. West, Pamela Elizabeth. *Madeleine.* New York: St. Martin's, 1983. Fictionalized account of the trial of Madeleine Hamilton Smith of Scotland. Lord Advocate Moncrief reads the charge to her: "You are charged with two counts of attempted murder and one count of murder, in that: one, on February 19th or 20th, of the year 1857, anno Domini, you did administer arsenic or other poison to Pierre Emile L'Angelier; two, on February 22nd or 23rd, you did again administer arsenic or other poison to the same; three, on the third occasion, on or about Sunday, March 22nd, you did, by means of arsenic, murder the aforesaid Pierre Emile L'Angelier" (5).

1770. Weyman, Stanley. *The Man in Black.* New York: Cassell, n. d. Swashbuckler set in Paris. In a late chapter, there is an examination and brief trial over the poisoning of the Prince of Condé by his servant, Brillaut, at the instigation of Madame la Princesse.

1771. _____. *My Lady Rotha.* New York: Longman, 1894. A romance of the Thirty Years' War with a brief courtroom scene in besieged Nuremberg in which the title heroine pleads before five magistrates for the incapacitated, absent hero, Waldgrave Rupert of Weimar, her kinsman. Weyman was once held in high esteem for his historical novels but they are pale imitations of Scott or Thackeray. Another with a trial scene is *The Story of Francis Cludde* (Cassell, 1891).

1772. Wheat, Carolyn. *Dead Man's Thoughts.* New York: St. Martin's, 1983; rpt. Berkley Prime Crime, 1994. Wheat spent years as a staff attorney for the New York City Police department and is a former defense attorney with the Legal Aid Society in Brooklyn, New York. She has taught both mystery and legal writing in New York (New School and Brooklyn Law). She relocated from Brooklyn to Southern California and is currently teaching writing in Oklahoma. Her protagonist Cassandra ("Cass") Jameson is a tough, principled fighter for the underdog whose sixties idealism (Wheat puts her on the Kent State University Campus on 4 May 1970 when the National Guard killed 4 students) is steadily eroded by the realities of crime and the drudgery of her caseload, yet in her persistence and faith in a dodgy system that purports to be about justice for all, not the well-off or rich, her very lack of glamor, she strikes the reader as more interesting and worthy of our time than many of her fictional colleagues who breeze through their cases and lives with aplomb. She is versatile with the sentence and has flair. Cass' doubts about her role in the system and doubts about the system itself (she's trying to develop another profession and isn't sure about that, either) make her believable and sympathetic.

Borrowing its title from the sixth line of a sardonic poem by Sandburg "The Lawyers Know Too Much" ("The lawyers know a dead man's thoughts too well"), Wheat entwines a pair of plotlines in this Edgar-nominated Best First Novel about the discounted criminal justice system and its plague of quick-fix plea-bargains. The second plot evolves out of that. When lover Nathan

Wasserstein is murdered in what looks like a gay killing by a beautiful Puerto Rican boy named Paco he had picked up--the night after making love to her--Cass investigates and discovers a Mob-connected case Nathan had been working on. When stoolie Charlie Blackwell, Nathan's client, dies in his cell, she knows she is on the right track.

1773. _____. *Fresh Kills.* New York: Berkley, 1994. Cass' dilemma begins with what should be a routine adoption case that she takes on for an old acquaintance. Wheat told *CA*: "I'm fascinated by legal issues that create a large impact on the lives of ordinary people, issues such as adoption . . ."

1774. _____. *Mean Streak.* New York: Berkley, 1996. The man who dumped Cass wants her to defend him on a bribery charge. Cass believes him innocent--the pawn of an ambitious DA--but when witnesses start dying off, she has to convince herself that the man she loves is not a coldblooded killer.

1775. _____. *Sworn to Defend.* New York: Berkley Prime Crime, 1998. Believing she finally has an innocent client, Cass proves Keith Jernigan could not have committed the robbery and gets him off. Next, her tenant Nellis Cartwright wants Cass to renegotiate her divorce settlement because, she claims, it was botched by Cass' lawyer-friend. An angry ex-husband warns her not to take his ex-wife's case. The cases merge when the son of her secretary is soon arrested after befriending Keith Jernigan, but when Cass investigates Jernigan, she discovers he had once stalked a former girlfriend and threw acid in her face. Now, he might well be stalking that girlfriend for the charges that got him arrested. Then Nellis is murdered in her office, and Cass suspects she died from the bullet meant for her.

1776. _____. *Troubled Waters.* New York: Berkley, 1997. The summer of 1969: Cass Jameson and brother Ron are organizing migrant farm workers into unions. Because of this idealistic activity, Ron foregoes conscientious-objector status and winds up a quadriplegic Vietnam vet in a wheelchair. In 1982 Ron is driving his specially built van with Jan Gebhardt, one of the sixties idealists, and several illegal aliens as part of the sanctuary movement. This trip goes bad, a federal agent dies. Jan flees underground, charges against Ron are held in abeyance. Cut to 1997: Jan decides to surrender to FBI officials in Kansas City. Both she and Ron will face murder charges in Toledo. Cass leaves Brooklyn to return home to represent Ron at his trial, determined to assuage her guilt and save her brother.

1777. _____. *Where Nobody Dies.* New York: St. Martin's, 1986. Cass leaves Legal Aid in this second outing to establish her own practice; however, she finds herself visiting the same familiar places as before. Mainly, the Brad Ritchie case is preoccupying her, even though he had been her opponent in the ugly custody battle for the 12-year-old daughter preceding his wife's murder.

Cass believes him innocent when she discovers that Linda Ritchie was blackmailing a number of people in Brooklyn.

1778. White, Stephen (Walsh). *Cold Case.* New York: Dutton, 2000. The eighth outing for these series characters has psychologist Alan Gregory and his wife, Assistant DA of boulder, Colorado, Laura Crowder being asked to investigate a cold case by a group known as Locard, a team of forensic specialists, law-enforcement officers, and former prosecutors. The mutilated bodies of two young girls are exposed in the melting snow, missing since 1988. The case becomes complicated the girls were visitors of the nearby ranch of talk-show celebrity psychotherapist Raymond Welles, now a US Congressman, whose own wife was kidnaped and murdered by a psychopathic former patient.

1779. _____. *Manner of Death.* New York: Dutton, 1999. Clinical psychiatrist Dr. Alan Gregory's sixth outing opens with his mentor, Dr. Arnold Dresser's funeral. The legal half of the marriage is largely absent from this outing, although Laura provides some crucial observations about the killer's identity in this tale that mixes the legendary hijacker D. B. Cooper with Alan Gregory's past, an old flame, and a bizarre set of deaths of people he once new and all of whom are linked by one common factor: they all worked the 1982 Orange Unit on Eight East of the University of Colorado's Health Sciences Center.

1780. _____. *Privileged Information.* New York: Viking, 1991. White's first novel introduces his protagonist--not a lawyer but a Boulder, Colorado clinical psychologist (White's own profession and locale where he was a staff psychologist at Children's Hospital in Denver and author of Barney books.). It is Dr. Alan Gregory's sidekick and spouse who involves him in the legal profession, although both he and Lauren Crowder take turns bailing each other out of dilemmas and life-threatening situations. Gregory's debut concerns a beautiful but tormented patient who had a sexual obsession for him--and so records it as well as his willing participation. The discovery is made by the police after her murder and now Gregory must clear his name or face prison and the ruin of his reputation. When more patients die, his place as prime suspect in all the murders is assured. What can he reveal without betraying, in the legal parlance, privileged information?

1781. _____. *Remote Control.* New York: Dutton, 1997. The fifth novel of series characters Gregory and Crowder. The latter is here Assistant DA in Boulder. Lauren's multiple sclerosis and the blinding snow affect her vision as she stands behind Emma Stiles' house to fire a warning shot at an intruder, but the police find a dead body in the middle of the street--alive, but run over twice besides shot in the back. The police arrest and process Lauren while Gregory and her lawyers try to find Emma's stalker. Others in the series: *Harm's Way* (1996), *Higher Authority* (1994), and *Private Practices* (1994).

1782. White, William Allen. *In the Heart of a Fool.* New York: Macmillan, 1918. Soporific tale of a youth growing up to found a radical labor organization but told in an unruly style that attempts to marry the picturesque to the picaresque, for White is no Fielding and Grant Adams, martyr-hero, is no lovable Tom Jones. One of the major characters is Judge Van Dorn, who gives Grant the opportunity in court to proselytize after his arrest. The author once enjoyed a high reputation for his novels of Kansas life.

1783. Whitney, Janet. *Jennifer.* New York: Morrow, 1940. London: Harrap, 1941. Set in England in the early days of the Industrial Revolution, young Jennifer Carey is falsely charged with attempting to poison the wife of Sir Thomas Gresham, the aristocratic brute who exploits child labor and throws men out of work, and her own physician father.

1784. Wickware, Francis Sill. *Dangerous Ground.* Garden City, NY: Doubleday, 1946. A young psychiatrist finds himself involved in the affairs of unstable Charles Wilson, important citizen of Fairbridge. When he dies of arsenic poisoning, lovely wife Serena is indicted and tried for murder with Rawley and the Forbstein, the lawyer he hires, working in the background to get her cleared.

1785. Wilder, Thornton. *The Eighth Day.* New York: Harper, 1967. Wilder novelizes a famous case in Illinois in 1902. John Barrington Ashley of Coalton, a small southern Illinois mining town, was tried for the murder of Breckenridge Lansing. He was found guilty and sentenced to death. He escaped and vanished from a prison train carrying him to his execution five days later. What made the case notorious was not the shooting (Asley claimed it was an accident while they were practice shooting) but the trial. Judge Crittenden was alleged to be senile, and the town (and jury) believed it was because of Asley was in love with Lansing's wife, although no evidence was admitted into the record proving that was the motive. Five years later the State's Attorney's Office announced that evidence existed to affirm Ashley's innocence.

1786. Wilhelm, Kate. *The Best Defense.* New York: St. Martin's, 1994. Born in Toledo, Ohio, the author grew up in Kentucky. She published her first novel in 1963 and has now written more than 3 dozen novels and story collections. Of her scores of popular novels, many in the science fiction series deservedly praised for avoiding the clotted prose of most sci-fi, including a series about a husband-and-wife sleuths (the psychologist-and-arson investigating team of the *Constance and Charlie* mysteries, popularized in *A Flush of Shadows: Five Short Novels Featuring Constance Leidl and Charlie Meiklejohn* (New York: St. Martin's, 1995--and, of course, the legal mysteries noted here. She sometimes overwrites, and yet her trial scenes and her courtroom material are widely admired. The main rap against her fiction is that some of her characters are often wooden or are indiscriminately involved in plots where they serve no purpose--for example, Holloway's father fancies himself a gourmet cook and provides the comic relief whenever his dishes are served. Barbara marries her geologist beau, and much interplay between the newlyweds centers around Holloway's dangerous habit of becoming the focus of attention of the criminal element. Her plots are sometimes contrived, and often the fusion of her speculative fiction with gothic thriller or science fiction with mystery ends up annoying some readers. Her cautionary themes of imminent environmental collapse, the chaos theory, and the future that technology brings to civilization, however, are sophisticated in their ambivalence and despite the quibbles here and there, she is one of the better producers of courtroom drama around. her latest book is *The Deepest Water* (St. Martin's-Minotaur, 2000). "Rousing trial scenes," sings a *Kirkus* reviewer of this one in which Barbara is in another high-profile case, this time involving a woman, Paula Kennerman, accused of setting fire to a shelter for abused women and killing her young daughter to be free for a sexual liaison with a wealthy local man. Barbara must defend her client in the face of right-wing fundamentalists and anti-feminist politics in the Pacific Northwest.

1787. _____. *Death Qualified: A Mystery of Chaos.* New York: St. Martin's, 1991. Holloway, a "death qualified" attorney when she had given up the law five years previous to the events of the story, finds herself summoned home to Oregon by her father, a retired judge. She agrees to help defend his neighbor, Nell Kendricks, a woman who has been indicted for the murder of her estranged husband Lucas, a fugitive computer scientist who had escaped sedation at his research facility. Barbara's research into Lucas' whereabouts for the past seven years exposes the core of this legal mystery in which "some rather strange research [is] being conducted into the perception of reality" (Swanson and James 206). A *New York Times* Notable Book of the Year.

1788. _____. *Defense for the Devil.* New York: St. Martin's, 1999. Lowlife Mitch Arno returns to Folsum, Oregon after seventeen years away. Now the former wife-abuser is sporting a suitcase of money and stolen software but he is killed just hours after his return. Abused wife Maggie is suspected first; then attention focuses upon Mitch's brother. Because of a conflict with brother Ray, Barbara cannot take his case, but unofficially she decides she must help out the lackluster defense to make sure that Maggie, not the IRS, gets to keep the money.

1789. _____. *Justice for Some.* New York: St. Martin's, 1993. Sarah Drexler is introduced as a lonely, widowed, middle-aged county judge in Pendleton, Oregon, who has stepped into her late husband's shoes. She has aspirations of a federal judgeship but she wants first a reunion with her children at the family home near Shasta, California. A lost son Vergil, a daughter Winnie, who is pregnant by a disreputable professional athlete, and aging Uncle

Peter, who is a biochemist concerned only with the reputation of the family name and particularly his own, for his college is planning to endow a chair in his honor. The mystery commences with an overheard conversation on the telephone between Sarah's father shortly before his death with a private investigator, who is soon after discovered shot to death near the family homestead.

1790. _____. *Malice Prepense* [retitled *For the Defense* for pbk release by Fawcett, 1977]. New York: St. Martin's, 1996. One of Oregon's important politicians is murdered; is it a coincidence that he led the field trip during which Teddy Wendover's accident occurred almost twenty years ago which left Teddy with the mind of a little boy? The killer left rocks strewn about the murder site just like the ones Teddy plays with.

1791. _____. *No Defense.* New York: St. Martin's, 2000. Thirty-three-year-old nurse Lara Jessup is the prime suspect when her older husband, a well-known lawyer dying of bone cancer, is found dead in his van on a dangerous road and she is the beneficiary of a large insurance policy. Barbara Holloway investigates but finds much resistance in the community of Salt Creek, especially from Judge Harris McReady, who is in line for a Supreme Court nomination and does not want his reputation sullied by scandal if certain facts come to light, such as the fact that Vinny Jessup believed him responsible for framing his son for murder 20 years ago.

1792. Willett, Sabin. *The Deal.* New York: Random, 1996. Boston lawyers and bankers are fighting a deadline to close a $840,000,000 leveraged buy-out. Under the pressure of the crowded agenda, no one notices that a zero has been dropped from the mortgage document. The papers are signed, applause roar from the boardroom--and somebody lights the fuse of a time bomb. Later, the partners of Freer, Motley, the presiding law firm, discover that each of them is personally liable to their client to make up the multimillion-dollar shortfall. When a senior partner is found dead, the firm's brightest young associate is arrested for the murder and its most arrogant defends him.

1793. Williams, Ben Ames. *Crucible.* New York: Dutton, 1937. Arthur Sentry is tried for the murder of Agnes Wines; he claims he fired a shot at a burglar he surprised in his office and tried to cover up the shooting by burning the money from the safe in his furnace. On the stand during Q & A, he reveals casual infidelity. His family also gives incriminating evidence on the stand.

1794. _____. *Death on Scurvy Street.* New York: Dutton, 1929. A junior reporter follows a murder case, a seeming gangland hit on this derelict street, from investigation through trial and verdict.

1795. _____. *Leave Her to Heaven.* Boston: Houghton, 1944. London:

Hale, 1946. High melodrama about a deeply unhappy woman married to a Bar Harbor writer whose suicide by arsenic attempts revenge from the grave on a rival by means of an accusatory suicide note, which becomes crucial evidence in the trial. Jo Swerling adapted Williams' novel (TCF, 1946), and although James Agee hated the technicolor glare, it earned an Oscar for Leon Shamroy's camera work. Dir. John M. Stahl. Perf. Gene Tierney, Cornell Wilde, and Jeanne Crain.

1796. Williams, Brad, and J. W. [Jacob Wilburn] Ehrlich. *A Conflict of Interest.* New York: Holt, 1971. Jon Breen tracks down the brief history of series character Sam Benedict, San Francisco detective-lawyer modeled on lawyer Ehrlich in the two extant hardcover novels (first being Howard Oleck's *A Single Fury*) and poses an interesting legal question based on the antiquated phrasing of a testator's reference to the "heirs of my body" on the issuing of offspring conceived by artificial insemination. Eccentric millionaire Cyrus Thurman posing as a hippie returns from Mexico to see Benedict but is murdered--possibly by Zodiac-like killer dubbed the "Astro Killer." Benedict bests Dredge, a tax lawyer in probate after he himself is nearly killed by a sniper. Breen notes that Ehrlich's autobiography professes the author's scriptwriting for many of the Benedict TV scripts. (*See* Lee, Elsie.)

1797. _____. *A Matter of Confidence.* New York: Holt, 1973. Two seemingly unrelated incidents connect and involve Benedict in two murders: the first occurs over pieces of a stolen jade chess set delivered to a wealthy San Francisco collector; the second is over a man's wife in *flagrante delicto* with a Chinese tong leader. Writes Jon Breen: "[T]he Chinatown background and chess lore are interesting, but this is the lesser of the two Benedict cases by these authors. It was published after the death of Ehrlich, and no further novels in the series appeared" (191).

1798. Williams, Nicola. *Without Prejudice.* New York: St. Martin's, 1998. Successful barrister Lee Michell is a black woman from a working-class background working in the British legal system, a real anomaly. Solicitor Brendan Donnelly asks her to take on a fraud case in behalf of a rich playboy client. Reluctantly at first, she does so and finds financier Clive Omartian a difficult case because of his drugs and young girls and the way he imposes upon her. Moreover, someone is sabotaging her legal efforts, someone who could be as close as her own firm.

1799. Williamson, [Mr.]. *The Lawyer, or a Suit for the Season.* N. p.: n. pub., 1783. The application for the license to perform the play is dated 12 August 1783, but it is uncertain whether George Colman, then manager of the Theatre Royal in the Haymarket, where the play was produced one week later, took out the license or if the attribution to the "Mr. Williamson" is correct.

1800. Wilson, C. M. [Charles Morrow]. *A Man's Reach.* New York: Holt,

1944. Fictionalized tale of Arkansas Governor Archibald Yell and his early association with Andrew Jackson in the frontier wars when he was Captain Yell. Yell becomes a Tennessee lawyer by dint of studying Blackstone's volumes and a treatise on land transaction abetted by a hunchbacked mentor, also a lawyer.

1801. Winer, Elihu. *Anatomy of a Murder: A Court-Drama in Three Acts.* New York and London: French, 1964. Based on *Anatomy of a Murder* by Robert Traver, pseud.

1802. Winterton, Paul. Andrew Garve, pseud. *Death and the Sky Above.* London: Collins; New York: Harper, 1953. Louise Hilary, a dissipated and adulterous wife, refuses her husband's request for a divorce so that he can marry a beautiful younger woman. When she is murdered, Charles is arrested, tried, and sentenced to death.

1803. Winwar, Frances. *Gallows Hill.* New York: Holt, 1937. Another picture of Salem, Massachusetts during the witchcraft persecutions in the late seventeenth century.

1804. Wishman, Seymour. *Anatomy of a Jury*. New York: Times, 1986; New York and Harmondsworth, Eng.: Penguin, 1987. Wishman practiced criminal law in New York and New Jersey for both sides, but in 1977, he left his practice for a year to become Deputy Assistant to the President. His memoirs as a trial attorney in *Confessions of a Criminal Lawyer* (Penguin, 1981) is an extraordinary book. With brutal honesty, he talks about defending murderers, muggers, and rapists and getting them off by using his skills to traduce witnesses, distort facts, and distract victims on the stand; it is a searing look at the professional responsibilities of a trial lawyer as well as a ghoulish look at the criminal justice system itself.

This book takes a murder case (fictionalized, a composite case, says the author) of a black man accused of the rape-murder of the white wife of a doctor. He follows the case from *voir dire* through verdict (half the book is over before the first witness is sworn) interjecting his own observations and commentary, replete with jurors' gossip before the trial. The mixture is not obtrusive and the commentary is welcome; fortunately, for those with an appetite for legal scholarship, copious notes are relegated to an appendix. Another thriller is *A Question of Consent* (New York: Jove, 1995).

1805. Wolfe, Carson. *Murder at La Marimba.* New York: St. Martin's, 1984. Puerto Rican and Dominican teenagers mix it up at a South Bronx disco. Ricky Betancourt is accused of Pablo Alvorado's murder. Attorney Carlita Rivera, called in by Ricky's girlfriend's mother, investigates.

1806. Wolfe, Susan. *The Last Billable Hour.* New York: St. Martin's, 1989. Wolf practices law in Palo Alto, California. *Detecting Women* quotes Stanford's

Law Dean: "[A] diverting tale of legal skullduggery" about high-tech and law in the Silicon Valley.

1807. Wolfe, Tom. *A Man in Full.* New York: Farrar, 1998. Wolfe began as a journalist who reported on popular culture, especially the Ken Kesey phenomenon (*The Kandy-Kolored Tangerine-Flake Streamline Baby*, 1965; *The Electric Cool- Aid Acid Test*, 1969), but has since become a bestselling novelist and sharp critic of American mores (*The Bonfire of the Vanities*, 1987). This one, a massive 700+ page tome, involves one character, a rich Atlanta banker named Peepgass, in a paternity suit; he goes on trial for seducing a blonde Finnish girl named Sirja. Defending him from the woman he "seduced, impregnated, and abandoned" (325) is Alexander ("Sandy") Dickens from the downtown firm delightfully named Tripp, Snayer & Billings.

1808. Wolff, William Almon. *The Trial of Mary Dugan.* Garden City, NY: Doubleday; London: Heinemann, 1928. Novelization of the play by Veiller (1869-1943). (*See* Veiller, Bayard).

1809. Wood, [Mrs. Henry]. *East Lynne.* London: Bentley; New York: Fitzgerald, n.d.; rpt. New York: Dick, 1961. The earliest extant dating exists in microform (1864). Mrs. Wood herself is shrouded in anonymity, but she seems to have produced some popular novels that transformed to gaslight melodramas on stage, if one can infer from the number of surviving but undated American copies of her novels. This one had a long life as a novel and is subtitled *Or, the Earl's Daughter.* Chicago's Rand, McNally published an edition in the 1890s. The play's synopsis is full of the usual characters from the theater of the time and surrounded by lurid events and murky pasts. Archibald Carlyle is a lawyer who marries the only surviving daughter of the deceased earl, Lord Mount Severn, whose county seat is in East Lynne. There are domestic difficulties, a secret attachment to the lawyer, a brother who is a fugitive from a murder accusation, an "unprincipled villain" named Levison, who whispers Iago-like things into Lady Isabel's shell-like ear, causing her to elope with him and later return after his cruel desertion, impoverished as a governess, before dying pathetically in the final act--along with the son she deserted.

1810. Wood, William P. *Court of Honor.* New York: Pocket, 1991. Paul Roemer, Assistant US Attorney, approves an ill-conceived sting operation to target corrupt judges, the plan of which is turn one judge to inform on the others. The target is Judge Timothy Nash of Santa Maria County, California. Husband-wife writing team Joan Didion and John Gregory Dunne adapted Woods' novel for a feature film titled Broken Trust (Turner, 1995). Dir. Geoffrey Sax. Perf. Tom Selleck, Elizabeth McGovern, and William Atherton.

1811. _____. *Quicksand.* New York: Kensington, 1998. Wood has a true-crime book on the San Diego boardinghouse murders committed by Dorothea

Montalvo Puente (*The Bone Garden*, 1994). In this one, a prosecutor uncovers federal protection of a potential terrorist in order to use him as bait to catch more terrorists.

1812. _____. *Rampage.* New York: St. Martin's, 1985. A liberal DA assigned to prosecute a serial killer fights his conscience on the death-penalty conviction he seeks. The film (Paramount, 1993) starred Michael Biehn as the prosecutor and novelist, writer-director William Friedkin adapted the script. A straight tale involving the prosecutor's office, this time in LA, is *Stay of Execution* (Pocket, 1994).

1813. Woods, Stuart. *Dead in the Water* . New York: HarperCollins, 1997. Woods, a former advertising director, transatlantic sailor and restaurant critic, has over 20 novels and one series character: Stone Barrington, former NYPD cop-turned-lawyer. Barrington is for all intents and purposes still a sleuth in a police procedural. He is vacationing in Antigua when he gets involved with a woman whose rich husband is missing and she is convicted for the presumed crime.

1814. _____. *Grass Roots.* New York: Simon, 1989. Will Lee is chief aide to Senator Ben Carr, whose stroke forces him to quit office but catapults Ben into a campaign to replace him; besides a scandal and rivals, he must contend with a white supremacist group that has made him a target.

1815. _____. *Santa Fe Rules.* New York: HarperCollins, 1992. When a Hollywood producer reads about a triple murder occurring in his Santa Fe home, he goes on the lam to clear his name; assisting him is a hotshot lawyer.

1816. _____. *Swimming to Catalonia.* New York: HarperCollins, 1998. Barrington's former girlfriend marries his friend, an actor, who calls Barrington for help when his new wife is kidnaped by *mafiosi.* Two previous Barrington novels: *Dirt* (1996), and *New York Dead* (1991).

1817. Wooley, Marilyn. *Jackpot Justice.* New York: St. Martin's, 2000. Psychological thriller set in Northern California with Cassandra Ringwald, psychologist, hired to do an evaluation for a lawyer's client, a skinhead on trial for murder.

1818. Woolfolk, William. *Opinion of the Court.* Garden City, NY: Doubleday, 1966. Although it is chiefly a Washington, DC political novel, albeit the central character is Nebraska Governor Paul Lincoln Lowe, the Supreme Court cases and discussions are vastly more sophisticated and interesting than either Lowe or Chief Justice Charles Edmundson, the aging, once-brilliant jurist whose time on the nation's highest bench is almost up. Cases range from a passport denial to a former pacifist attempting to exit the country to a well-argued, multi-page debate on capital punishment before the court.

1819. Woolrich, Cornell. William Irish, pseud. *Phantom Lady.* Philadelphia: Lippincott, 1942. London: Hale, 1945. Woolrich wrote excellent *noir*; he was born in New York City, partially raised in South America as well, and educated at Columbia University. He used a pair of *noms de plume* but principally that of William Irish after his *Black Mask* days of the thirties. There is a wonderful story that he saw *Madame Butterfly* at a tender age and became a doom-haunted man forever after. He is not fully recognized as the inspiration behind the French *roman noir* and *noir* cinema but a scholarly work is needed to take him out from Cain's shadow. The Hitchcock classic *Rear Window* is also based on his short story. In *Phantom Lady*, Scott Henderson meets a pretty girl by chance and takes her to the theater. When he returns home he finds cops and his wife of five years dead in her bedroom, not of suicide as he thinks. He is charged with her murder, and when he fails to produce the mystery woman to alibi him, he is sentenced to die. A pair of courtroom sequences of the prosecutor's summation and the judge addressing him at the bar comprise the trial.

1820. Wouk, Herman. *The Caine Mutiny.* Garden City, NY: Doubleday; London: Cape, 1951. Lt. Commander Steve Maryk's court-martial for "conduct to the prejudice of good order and discipline" is one of the most famous trials in fiction. As executive officer of the destroyer USS *Caine*, Maryk relieves neurotic Philip Queeg of command during a typhoon, by applying Article 184 of *Naval Regulations*. Lt. Barney Greenwald is defense advocate, and he attacks, not Maryk, but Tom Keefer, third-in-command, because he goaded Maryk to act. Henry Fonda and José Ferrar alternated between screen and stage versions of Barney Greenwald. (Columbia, 1954) Van Johnson was Maryk and Fred MacMurray as the novelist and amateur psychiatrist Keefer. Humphrey Bogart's Queeg was an Oscar-nominated performance ("Ah, but the strawberries! That's where I had them. . . ."). Wouk's successful play version, *The Caine Mutiny Court-Martial* (Doubleday, 1954) allows the characters to learn about themselves through the courtroom revelations without the distractions of the film's action sequences.

1821. Wright, Richard. *Native Son.* New York: Harper; London: Gollancz, 1940. (Subtitled *The Biography of a Young American*, the play was adapted by Southerner Paul Green, originator of outdoor theater with patriotic themes, and Richard Wright. According to Green's daughter Janet, an English professor living in Ohio, Wright and Green disagreed "violently" about the ending: "[Green] insisted on this positive ending [as performed and published (New York: French, 1941)] . . . Paul Green believed in the goodness of life--that we've all got to have a good dream or perish").

1822. Wright, Williard Huntington. S. S. Van Dine, pseud. *The Benson*

Murder Case. New York: Burt, 1926. Debonair sleuth Philo Vance made his debut in this novel. One of that breed of dilettante sleuth who be excluded here were it not for his DA John F. X. Markham. In fact, Van Dine's introduction attempts to slip Philo past the bar of verisimilitude on the pretext of his being "*amicus curiæ* in Markham's investigations" (viii). Sergeant Heath is the typical cop who cannot solve a case without the superior amateur's help. Vance frequently pauses in mid-investigation to lecture his auditors on esoteric subjects while they politely listen; his foppish speech is spiked with Latin, French, and desiccated British slang and colloquialisms like *y'know, what?* and *silly buggar.* Markham, on the other hand, is a good lawyer, serious and high-minded, honest and hard-working. When Alvin Benson is discovered murdered in his West 48th Street apartment, Vance deduces the murderer immediately but lets Markham and Sgt. Heath fumble through incriminating evidence against five other suspects. A sample of Vance's drollery in lecture form occurs in Chapter 19:

> 'You see how silly the confession is, what? Our pure and lofty Captain is an incredibly poor Munchausen. No one could lie as badly as he did who hadn't been born into the world that way. . . . And he did so want us to think him guilty. Very affectin'. He prob'bly imagined you'd merely stick the confession in your shirt-front and send him to the hangman. You noticed, he hadn't even decided how he got into Benson's house that night. [Suspect Leander] Pfyfe's admitted presence outside almost spoiled his impromptu explanation of having entered *bras dessus bras dessous* with his intended victim. And he didn't recall Benson's semi-négligé attire.' (249-50)

Another Vance novel where Markham plays a supporting role is *The Greene Murder Case* (New York: Scribner's, 1927; rpt. Introd. Chris Steinbrunner. Boston: Gregg, 1980). Several actors played the role in a series of Philo Vance films from 1929 to 1947. Among them were William Powell, Warren William, Edmund Lowe, William Wright, and Alan Curtis.

1823. Wright, Sydney Fowler. Sydney Fowler, pseud. *The King against Anne Bickerton.* London: Harrap, 1930. [Rpt. as *The Case of Anne Bickerton*, New York: Boni, 1930; author noted as by S. Fowler Wright]. A coroner's inquest attempts to determine whether the weed-killer ingested by Mrs. Belle Hackett of Liverpool was by misadventure, suicide, or introduced into her tea by someone close to her. The exposure of the relationship between husband James and the nanny, Rose Dorling, and theirs to the title character, the sister of the deceased, Anne Bickerton, result in a jury trial for the latter.

1824. Wyrick, E. L. [Edward L.]. *Power in the Blood.* New York: St. Martin's, 1996. Born in New Orleans, and resident of Athens, Georgia, Wyrick has a doctorate in counseling; he is the creator of Tammi Randall, a legal aid attorney. She investigates the murder of a Hollywood celebrity who wanted to "buy" the small Georgia town of Warrendale by taking on the defense of the local youthful offender accused and seeks the killer in the sex-drenched byways of Los Angeles and New Orleans.

1825. _____. *A Strange and Bitter Crop.* New York: St. Martin's, 1994. Randall debuts and defends a black teen accused of murder in a stereotypical plot.

Y

1826. Yaffe, James. *Nothing but the Night.* Boston: Atlantic-Little, 1957. London: Cape, 1958. Paul King and Barry Morris are 1950s New Yorkers and literary knockoffs of the infamous Chicagoans Leopold and Loeb of the 1920s. Defense lawyer Brennan's closing argument does not bear comparison to Darrow's defense of young killers in Meyer Levin's *Compulsion.*

1827. Yarbro, Chelsea Quinn [as by C. Q. Yarbro]. *Cat's Claw.* New York: Jove, 1992. Berkeley native and San Francisco State graduate Yarbro has achieved success in the horror genre with female vampire series beginning in 1987 (*A Flame in Byzantium*) and most recently in *Angry Angel* in 1998. Her male version is popularly known as the Saint-Germain Chronicles for le Comte de St. Germain, who died in 1784. She has over 40 books spanning children's stories and westerns, suspense thrillers, romance, sci-fi, and fantasy to a well-received legal thriller series starring Charles Spotted Moon, who practices law in San Francisco, but one who is never far from his Ojibway roots as a shaman and sometimes goes on spirit walks to communicate with the dead to find out how they were murdered. His associate in practice is Morgan Studevant, who acts as sounding board for Charlie's spiritual disquisitions.

The lawyer in Charlie could easily defends handsome, easy-going Jared Eden, charged with the grisly serial murders of wealthy women, whose bodies are dumped on doorsteps of the elite of San Francisco's houses, but the shaman must know, and so he uses a sauna as a sweat lodge for his vision with Eden's Rolex attached to a leather thong about his neck.

1828. _____. *Music When Sweet Voices Die* [alt title: *False Notes*, New York: Jove, 1991]. New York: Putnam's, 1979. Charlie investigates the murder of a famous and hated French tenor at the San Francisco Opera House.

1829. _____. *Ogilvie, Tallant & Moon/Bad Medicine.* New York: Putnam's, 1976. Moon takes a malpractice case for a woman friend being sued because their son died of a seizure during treatment for Parkinson's Disease. The autopsy showed the boy had milk in his system, although he was highly allergic to lactose in any form and would not have taken it willingly.

1830. _____. *Poison Fruit.* New York: Jove, 1991. Charlie believes his client Frank Girouard, a schoolteacher accused of molesting 5 female students, is innocent, but when Susan Lake, another female student from Sutro Glen Junior High, is found dead, the investigation tightens around Charlie's client.

1831. Yastrow, Shelby. *Under Oath.* New York: Diamond, 1994. Chicago Charlie Mayfield is representing a divorced couple in a multimillion-dollar malpractice suit against Dr. Steven Sinclair for the irreversible damage to their unborn child, now four years old.

1832. _____. *Undue Influence.* Chicago: Contemporary, 1990. The bland, elderly client that Chicago attorney Philip Ogden met once to draft a will turns out to be millionaire Benjamin Stillman, who left his fortune to Beth Zion Synagogue--despite the fact that he was a Catholic and received last rites as such. A rush to find relatives and corroborate accusations of embezzlement ensues in the will contest. Another is *Under Oath* (Diamond, 1990). Yastrow is a former senior vice president and general counsel of McDonald's Corporation and a graduate of Northwestern University Law School.

1833. Yates, Alan G. Carter Brown, pseud. *Loving and Dead.* Sydney: Horwitz; New York: NAL, 1959. "Carter Brown" was the pseudonym of Australian pulp-thriller writer Yates, whose best-known character is a dumb blonde from a dozen paperback novels of the 1950s to the early 1970s named Mavis Seidlitz, a partner in Hollywood-based Rio Investigations. In this one, the contested will Randolph Ebhart is featured in which family members must spend 72 hours at the deceased's estate to inherit. Mavis is hired to play the role of Clare Ebhart, the eldest son's late wife.

1834. Yglesias, Helen. *Sweetsir.* New York: Simon; London: Hodder, 1981. Sally Sweetsir, a 32-year-old housewife in the New England town of Eatonville, stabs her abusive husband Morgan with a kitchen knife. "This," lauds Jon Breen, "is an immensely powerful novel, offering a hard and uncompromising depiction of male-female relationships at their worst. It is a feminist book but not a black-and-white one--feminists are not spared a jaundiced look, and few of the men are pure villains" (202-03).

Yorke, Margaret, pseud. *See* Nicholson, Margaret Beda Larminie. . . .

1835. Youmans, Claire. *Rough Justice.* Huntington Station, NY: Rising Tide, 1996. Lawyer and sailing enthusiast Youmans combines both skills in her protag Janet Schilling, an ambitious Chief Deputy Prosecutor for Sacajawea County, who launches an investigation into the death at sea of Glen Lowry, a man not much missed by anyone in the quiet coastal town of Salmon Bay near Seattle. Among several suspects is Catherine Adams, Janet's former lover.

1836. Young, Francis Brett. *Mr. and Mrs. Pennington.* London: Heinemann; New York: Harper, 1931. Young authored more than 16 forgettable novels and other works. Here, a very brief coroner's inquest appears in the conclusion. Dick and Susan Pennington are torn apart when she falls for the charms of Henry Levinson, and her husband discovers the treachery. Pennington appears in the offices of the stockbroker Magnus, uncle to the caddish seducer to confront him, and when the uncle offers him a check to "compensate" him, the indignant young husband throws over a chair and storms off. Magnus' sudden death shortly after gets Pennington arrested, but nobly, he refuses at the inquest to say why the check was offered.

1837. Young, Phyllis Brett. *A Question of Judgment.* New York: Putnam's, 1969. London: Allen, 1970. This is an apprenticeship novel built around the young narrator's early interest in a law career. Her friendship with a girl named Doreen leads to a courtroom denouement when she is drowned and two males she had been drinking with in the cottage give conflicting stories before one of the perjurers recants.

1838. Yurick, Sol. *Fertig.* New York: Trident, 1966. An ordinary, middle-aged accountant goes on a murder spree, killing seven people one year after his child dies because, he believes, of the callous indifference of the emergency room staff at Mercy Hospital, where he had begged for help and was told to fill out forms and wait his turn. Yurick is a former investigator for the New York Department of Welfare, who turned his experiences into another novel about Brooklyn street gangs in *The Warriors.* (*See* Black, David for the film version.)

Z

1839. Zangwill, I[srael]. *The Big Bow Mystery.* Chicago: Rand, 1895. Old-style whodunit with the body found in bed with his throat slashed. When boarder Arthur Constant's body is discovered by Mrs. Drabdump, proprietor, the coroner's inquest comes to the erroneous conclusion that a fellow-lodger and friend is guilty despite "the almost superhuman ingenuity of Mr. Edward Wimp, of the Scotland Yard Detective Department" (167). Mr. Spigot, QC, prepares the case for trial.

1840. Zinberg, Leonard S. Ed Lacy, pseud. *Breathe No More, My Lady.* New York: Avon, 1958. Zinberg-as-Lacy created black detective Toussant Moore, scoring an Edgar for *Room to Swing* (1957).

1841. Ziran, Goland. *The Counsellor.* New York: Arbor, 1982. Trial lawyer Saul Belinsky abandons his youthful idealism to become a mob lawyer.

1842. Zubro, Mark [Richard]. *The Truth Can Get You Killed.* New York: St. Martin's, 1997. Zubro, an openly gay high-school teacher, authors two series of homosexual sleuths: Tom Mason is an English teacher and amateur detective in suburban Chicago whose lover Scott Carpenter, is a pro baseball pitcher. The other features Chicago police detective Paul Turner, a father of two sons and a quiet gay man, who in this novel discovers that the shooting death of a rabidly homophobic federal judge is fraught with loose ends. The judge was a supporter of anti-gay legislation--not surprisingly Paul finds little help among his own friends (readers should question the ease with which he moves between disparate worlds). One big loose end: the judge was supposed to be out of Chicago the day of his murder, yet he was witnessed in a notorious gay night club.

Supplemental Bibliography

Barnes, Glenn M. *Lawyers Don't Hang*. New York: Mercury, 1953.
Bechdolt, Frederick R[itchie]. *Mutiny: An Adventure Story*. New York: Chelsea, 1927.
Becker, Stephen D. *A Covenant with Death*. New York: Atheneum, 1964.
Canter, Mackenzie. *The Indictment*. New York: Carroll, 1994.
Carlisle, Henry. *Voyage to the First of December*. New York: Putnam's, 1972.
---. *Voyage to the First of December: A Play in Two Acts*. New York: Intern'l Famous Agency, n.d.
Cassidy, Carla Bracale. *Passsion in the First Degree*. New York: Harlequin, 1996.
Conners, Bernard F. *Dancehall*. Indianapolis: Bobbs, 1983.
Cooper, Natasha. *Creeping Ivy*. New York: St. Martin's, 1999.
Dibner, Martin. *The Trouble with Heroes*. Garden City, NY: Doubleday, 1971.
Dinneen, Joseph. *Anatomy of a Crime*. New York: Scribner's, 1954. London: Cassell, 1955.
Dunning, Philip. *Sequel to a Verdict*. New York: Dramatist's Play, 1962.
Ellis, Kenneth M. *Dolores Divine: Guilty or Innocent?*. New York: Grosset, 1931.
Frasure, Caro. *A Hallowed Place*. London: Orion, 1999.
Friedman, Donald. *The Hand before the Eye*. Minneapolis, MN: Mid-List, 2000.
Goldman. R. L. [Raymond Leslie]. *Death Plays Solitaire*. New York: McCann, 1939.
Gore, Trevor. *The Juryman's Tale*. London: Bloomsbury, 2000.
Green, Vincent S. *The Price of Victory*. New York: Walker, 1992.
Greene, F. N. [Frances Nimmo]. *The Devil to Pay*. New York: Scribner's, 1918.
Gross, Ken. *The Talk Show Defense*. New York: Forge, 1997.
Hale, Edward Everett. *Philip Nolan's Friends*. New York: Scribner's, Armstrong, 1877.
Hayes, Ralph. *A Sudden Madness*. New York: Tower, 1981.

Henderson, Donald. [D. H. Landels, pseud.]. *His Lordship the Judge.* London: Paul, 1936.
Henriques [David Quixano] Robert. *No Arms, No Armour.* New York: Farrar; London: Nicholson, 1939.
Hinkemeyer, Michael T. *The Fields of Eden.* New York: Putnam's, 1977. London: Futura, 1980.
Howard, B. *Leary: A Portrait of an Alcoholic.* Santa Barbara, CA: Fithian, 1996.
Hunter, Evan. [Ed McBain, pseud.] *Nocturne.* New York: Warner, 1997.
Johnston, Myrtle. *A Robin Redbreast in a Cage* London: Heinemann, 1950. Boston: Houghton, 1951.
Kaye-Smith, Sheila. *Rose Deeprose.* London: Cassell; New York: Harper, 1936.
Kelton, Elmer. *Medicine Hill.* Garden City, NY: Doubleday, 1984.
Kennedy, John de N. *Crime in Reverse.* London: Nelson, 1939.
Large, Mary Harriott. *The Twelfth Juror.* Boston: Clark, 1908.
Lichfield, Richard. *Diana K.C.* London: Walker, 1930.
Lowe, Shirley. *Kavanagh K. C.: Blood Money.* London: Coronet, 1998.
Lowndes, Marie Belloc. *Letty Lynton* London: Heinemann; New York: Cape, 1931.
Lyon, Winston. *Criminal Court.* New York: Pocket, 1966.
Marcum, Robert. *The Orlov Legacy.* Salt Lake City: Deseret, 1996.
Masterman, Walter S. *The Perjured Alibi.* London: Methuen; New York: Dutton, 1935.
Mavity, Nancy Barr. The State Versus Elna Jepson. Garden City, NY: Doubleday, 1937.
Menen, Aubrey. *Prevalence of Witches.* London: Chatto, 1947. New York: Scribner's, 1948.
Page, Elizabeth. *Tree of Liberty.* New York: Farrar; London: Collins, 1939.
Parsons, Helen Beal. *The Trial of Helen McLeod.* New York: Funk, 1938.
Pearce, Dick. *The Darby Trial.* Philadelphia: Lippincott, 1954. London: Hodder, 1955
Petersen, Herman. *The D. A.'s Daughter.* New York: Duell, 1943.
Pillsbury, Samuel H. *Conviction.* New York: Walker, 1992.
Porter, Rebecca N. *The Rest Hollow Mystery.* New York: Century, 1922. London: Long, 1924.
Poyer, David. *Winter in the Heart.* New York: TOR, 1993.
Reach, James. *Late Last Night.* New York: Morrow, 1949. London: Heinemann, 1950.
Reywall, John. *The Trial of Alvin Boaker.* New York: Random, 1948.
Robinson, Lewis. *The General Goes Too Far.* London: Nicholson, 1935. New York: Putnam's, 1936.

Robson, Ruthann. *Another Mother.* New York: St. Martin's-Griffen, 1995.
Roth, Holly. *Shadow of a Lady.* New York: Simon; London: Hamilton, 1957.
Sheldon, Richard. *Poor Prisoner's Defense.* London: Hutchinson; New York: Simon, 1949.
---. *Harsh Evidence.* London: Hutchinson, 1950.
Spicer, Bart. *The Adversary.* New York: Putnam's; London: Hart-Davis, 1974.
Steen, Marguerite. *The Sun Is My Undoing.* London: Collins; New York: Viking, 1941.
Stubbs, Jean. *My Grand Enemy.* London: Macmillan, 1967. New York: Stein, 1968.
Thompson, Estelle. *The Lawyer and the Carpenter.* London: Hodder, 1963. New York: Washburn, 1964.
Treat, Lawrence. *Trial and Terror.* New York: Morrow, 1949. London: Boardman, 1958.
Trell, Max. *Lawyer Man.* New York: Macaulay, 1932.
Upward, Allen. *The Queen against Owen.* London: Chatto, 1894.
Wambaugh, Joseph. *The Blue Knight.* Boston: Little, 1972. London: Joseph, 1973.
Watterson, George. *The Lawyer, or Man As He Ought to Be.* Pittsburgh: Cramer, 1808.
Wetlaufer, Suzy. *Judgment Call.* New York: Morrow, 1992.
Winslow, Walker. *Man in Paradise.* New York: Smith, 1941.
Woolson, Constance Fenimore. *Anne.* New York: Harper, 1882. Rpt. New York: Arno, 1977. Introd. Elizabeth Hardwick.

References and Recommended Reading

Books

Alford, John A., and Dennis P. Seniff. *Literature and Law in the Middle Ages: A Bibliography of Scholarship*. New York: Garland, 1984.

Auchincloss, Louis. *A Writer's Capital*. Minneapolis: U of Minnesota P, 1974.

---. *Life, Law and Letters: Essays and Sketches*. Boston: Houghton, 1979.

Barnard, Robert. *A Talent to Deceive: An Appreciation of Agatha Christie*. London: Collins; New York: Dodd, 1980.

Barnes, Melvyn. *Best Detective Fiction*. London: Bingley; Hamden, CT: Linnet, 1975.

Boot, Max. *Out of Order*. Foreword Robert H. Bork. New York: Basic, 1998.

Bounds, J. Dennis. *Perry Mason: Authorship and Reproduction of a Popular Hero*. Contributions to the Study of Popular Culture. No. 56. Westport, CT: Greenwood, 1996.

Breen, Jon L. *What about Murder? A Guide to Books about Mystery and Detective Fiction*. Metuchen, NJ: Scarecrow, 1981.

---. *Novel Verdicts: A Guide to Courtroom Fiction*. Metuchen, NJ: Scarecrow, 1984.

Brodsky, Louis Daniel, and Robert W. Hamblin, eds. "*Country Lawyer*" *and Other Stories for the Screen by William Faulkner*. Jackson: U P of Mississippi, 1987.

Bugliosi, Vincent. *Outrage: The Five Reasons Why O.J. Simpson Got Away with Murder*. New York: Norton, 1997.

Curiae, Amicus, pseud. ed. *Law in Action: An Anthology of the Law in Literature*. New York: Crown, 1947.

Davis, David Brion. *Homicide in American Fiction, 1798-1860: A Study in Social Values*. Ithaca, NY: Cornell U P, 1957.

Douglas, John, and mark Olshaker. *Mind Hunter: Inside the FBI's Elite Serial Crime Unit*. New York: Simon, 1995.

Dunne, Dominick. *Another City, Not My Own*. New York: Crown, 1997.

Eden, Kathy. *Poetic and Legal Fiction in the Aristotelian Tradition*. Princeton: Princeton UP, 1986.

Elias, Robert H. *Theodore Dreiser: Apostle of Nature*. Ithaca: Cornell U P, 1970.

Fabre, Michel. *The Unfinished Quest of Richard Wright*. New York: Morrow, 1973.

Ferguson, Robert A. *Law and Letters in American Culture*. Cambridge: Harvard UP, 1984.

Frank, Jerome. *Law and the Modern Mind*. 6th ed. New York: Tudor, 1949.

Frankel, Marvin. *Criminal Sentences: Law Without Order*. New York: Hill, 1973.

Friedman, Lawrence M. *A History of American Law*. New York: Simon, 1973.

Fugate, Francis L., and Roberta B. *Secrets of the World's Best-Selling Writer: The Storytelling Techniques of Erle Stanley Gardner*. New York: Morrow, 1980.

Gelderman, Carol W. *Louis Auchincloss: A Writer's Life*. New York: Crown, 1993.

Gest, John Marshall. *The Lawyer in Literature*. Intro. John H. Wigmore. Boston: Boston Book, 1913. Rpt. Holmes Beach, FL: Gaunt, 1982.

Glover, Dorothy, and Graham Greene. *Victorian Detective Fiction: A Catalogue of the Collection Made by Dorothy Glover and Graham Greene*. Bibliog. Eric Osborne. Intro. John Carter. London: Bodley Head, 1966.

Goldstein, A. S., and Goldstein, J., eds. *Crime, Law and Society*. New York: Free, 1971.

Goodrich, Peter. *Legal Discourse: Studies in Linguistics, Rhetoric and Legal Analysis*. New York: St. Martin's, 1987.

Grape, Jan, Dean James, and Ellen Nehr, eds. *Deadly Women: The Woman Mystery Reader's Indispensable Companion*. New York: Carroll, 1998.

Green, Adwin W. *Inns of Court and Early English Drama*. New Haven: Yale UP, 1931.

Grossman, James. *James Fenimore Cooper*. Stanford: Stanford U P, 1967.

Hagen, Ordean A. *Who Done It?: A Guide to Detective, Mystery and Suspense Fiction*. New York: Bowker, 1969.

Harr, Jonathan. *A Civil Action*. New York: Random, 1995.

Haycraft, Howard, ed. *Murder for Pleasure: The Life and Times of the Detective Story*. New York: Appleton, 1941.

Heising, Willetta L. *Detecting Men: A Reader's Guide and Checklist for Mystery Series Written by Men*. Dearborn, MI: Purple Moon, 1998.

---. *Detecting Women 2: A Reader's Guide and Checklist for Mystery Series Written by Women*. Dearborn, MI: Purple Moon, 1996.

Henderson, Lesley, ed. *Twentieth-Century Crime & Mystery Writers*. 3rd ed. Pref. Kathleen G. Klein. Chicago: St. James, 1991.

Herald, Diana Tixier. Genreflecting: *A Guide to Reading Interests in Genre Fiction*. 4th ed. Englewood, CO: Libraries Unlimited, 1995.

Hinz, E.J., T. Anderson, and A. McGillivray, eds. *Adversaria: Literature and Law*. Winnipeg: U of Manitoba P, 1994. [Special issue of *Mosaic: A Journal for the Interdisciplinary Study of Literature* 27.4 (1994)].

Holdsworth, William S. *Charles Dickens as a Legal Historian*. New Haven: Yale UP, 1928.

Hubin, Allen J. *The Bibliography of Crime Fiction, 1749-1975*. Del Mar, CA: University Extension. U of California, San Diego. 1979.

Hughes, Dorothy B. *Erle Stanley Gardner: The Case of the Real Perry Mason*. New York: Morrow, 1978.

Jakubowsky, Maxim, ed. *100 Great Detectives or the Detective Directory*. New York: Carroll, 1991.

Johnson, Timothy, and Julia Johnson. *Crime Fiction Criticism*. New York: Garland, 1981.

Kane, Patricia. *Legal Fictions: The Lawyer in the American Novel*. Diss. University of Minnesota, 1961.

Kent, James. *Commentaries on American Law*. Boston: Little, 1873.

Landrum, Larry N., Pat Browne, and Ray Browne, eds. *Dimensions of Detective Fiction*. Bowling Green, OH: Bowling Green U Popular P, 1976.

Ledwon, Lenora, ed. *Law and Literature: Text and Theory*. New York: Garland, 1996.

Leonard Maltin's 1997 Movie & Video Guide. Ed. Leonard Maltin. New York: Penguin, 1997.

Levinson, Sanford, and Steven Mailloux, eds. *Interpreting Law and Literature*. Evanston, IL: Northwestern U P, 1988.

Levy, Leonard. *The Law of the Commonwealth and Chief Justice Shaw*. New York: Harper, 1967.

Lewis, Anthony. *Gideon's Trumpet*. New York: Vintage, 1964.

Loncar, Kathleen. *Legal Fiction: Law in the Novels of Nineteenth Century Women Novelists*. London: Minerva, 1995.

London, Ephraim, ed. *The World of Law: A Treasury of Great Writing about and in the Law, Short Stories, Plays, Essays, Accounts, Letters, Opinions, Pleas, Transcripts of Testimony from Biblical Times to the Present.* 2 vols. New York: Simon, 1960.

Malin, Irving. *Truman Capote's In Cold Blood.* Belmont, CA: Wadsworth, 1968.

McCart, Samuel W. *Trial by Jury.* Philadelphia: Chilton, 1964.

McCleary, G. F. *On Detective Fiction and Other Things.* London: Hollis and Carter, 1960.

Mellinkoff, David. *Legal Writing: Sense and Nonsense.* New York: Scribner's, 1982.

Melville, Herman. *White-Jacket or The World in a Man of War.* Ed Hennig Cohen. New York: Holt, 1967.

Melvin, David, and Ann Skene. *Crime, Espionage, Mystery, and Thriller Fiction and Film: A Comprehensive Bibliography of Critical Writing Through 1979.* Westport, CT: Greenwood, 1980.

Moley, Raymond. *Our Criminal Courts.* New York: Minton, 1930.

Mundell, E. H., Jr., and G. Jay Rausch. *The Detective Short Story: A Bibliography and Index.* Bibliographic Ser. 14. Manhattan: Kansas State U Library, 1974.

---. *Erle Stanley Gardner: A Checklist.* The Serif Ser: Bibliographies and Checklists. 6. Kent, OH: Kent State UP, 1968.

Nevins, Francis M.., Jr. *Royal Bloodline: Ellery Queen, Author and Detective.* Bowling Green, OH: Bowling Green U Popular P, 1974.

Nieminski, John. *EQMM 350: An Author/Title Index to Ellery Queen's Mystery Magazine, Fall 1941 Through January 1973.* White Bear Lake, MN: The Armchair Detective, 1974.

Norton, Charles A. *Melville Davisson Post: Man of Many Mysteries.* Bowling Green, OH: Bowling Green U Popular P, 1973.

Pearsall, Jay. *Mystery & Crime: The New York Public Library Book of Answers.* New York: Stonesong, 1995.

Penzler, Otto, comp. et al. Eds. Otto Penzler et al. *Detectionary: A Biographical Dictionary of Leading Characters in Mystery Fiction.* Woodstock, NY: Overloook, 1977.

Petrocelli, Daniel, with Peter Knobler. *Triumph of Justice: The Final Judgment on the Simpson Saga.* New York: Crown, 1998.

Posner, Richard A. *Law and Literature: A Misunderstood Relation.* Cambrideg: Harvard UP, 1988.

Queen, Ellery, pseud. [Frederic Dannay and Manfred B. Lee]. *The Detective Short Story: A Bibliography.* Boston: Little, 1942.

Reilly, John M., ed. *Twentieth-Century Crime and Mystery Writers.* Twentieth

Century Writers of the English Language Ser. New York: St. Martin's, 1980.

Roy, Sandra. *Josephine Tey*. Twayne's English Authors Ser. 277. Boston: Twayne, 1980.

St. James Guide to Crime and Mystery Writers. 4th ed. Ed. Jon L. Breen. Detroit: St. James, 1996.

Seymour-Smith, Martin. *Who's Who in Twentieth Century Literature*. New York: Holt, 1976.

Smith, Carl S., John P. McWilliams, and Maxwell Bloomfield. *Law and American Literature: A Collection of Essays*. New York: Knopf, 1983.

Smith, Myron, J., Jr., and Terry White. *Cloak and Dagger Fiction: An Annotated Guide to Spy Thrillers*. 3rd ed. Westport, CT: Greenwood, 1995.

Sonnenschein, Hugo, ed. *New Webster's Law for Everyone*. New York: Avenel-Crown, 1982.

Steinbrunner, Chris, and Otto Penzler. *Encyclopedia of Mystery and Detection*. Marvin Lachman and Charles Shibuk, Senior Eds. New York: McGraw, 1976.

Stilwell, Steven A. *The Armchair Detective Index (Vols. 1-10) 1967-1977*. Intro. Allen J. Hubin. New York: Armchair Detective, 1979.

Swanson, Jean, and Dean James. *By a Woman's Hand: A Guide to Mystery Fiction by Women*. Pref. Nancy Pickard. New York: Berkley, 1994.

---. *Killer Books: A Reader's Guide to Exploring the Popular World of Mystery and Suspense*. Foreword Anne Perry, pseud. New York: Berkley, 1998.

Symons, Julian. *Bloody Murder: From the Detective Story to the Crime Novel*. London: Faber, 1972. [American title: *Mortal Consequences: A History: From the Detective Story to the Crime Novel*. New York: Harper, 1972.]

Talburt, Nancy Ellen, and Lyna Lee Montgomery. *A Mystery Reader: Stories of Detection, Adventure, and Horror*. New York: Scribner's, 1975.

Thacker, Cathy Gillen. *Guilty as Sin*. New York: Harlequin, 1994.

Thomas, Brook. *Cross-Examination of Law and Literature: Cooper, Hawthorne, Stowe, and Melville*. Cambridge: Cambridge UP, 1987.

Turow, Scott. *One L: An Inside Account of Life in the First Year of Harvard Law School*. [Warner's 1997 pbk subtitle: *The Turbulent True Story of a First Year at Harvard Law School*] New York: Putnam's, 1977.

Van Dover, J. Kenneth. *Murder in the Millions: Erle Stanley Gardner, Mickey Spillane, Ian Fleming*. New York: Ungar, 1984.

Walker, Samuel. *Popular Justice: A History of American Criminal Justice*. New York: Oxford U P, 1980.

Watson, Jay. *Forensic Fictions: The Lawyer Figure in Faulkner*. Athens: U of Georgia P, 1993.

Weiner, Susan. *Law in Art: Melville's Major Fiction and Nineteenth-Century*

American Law. New York: Lang, 1992.
White, G. Edward. *The American Judicial Tradition.* New York: Oxford U P, 1976.
White, James Boyd. *Heracles 'Bow: Essays on the Rhetoric and Poetics of the Law.* Madison: U of Wisconsin P, 1985.
---. *Legal Imagination: Studies in the Nature of Legal Thought and Expression.* Boston: Little, 1973.
Wright, Benjamin Fletcher. *American Interpretations of Natural Law.* Cambridge: Harvard U P, 1931.

Articles & Essays

Allen, Bruce. Rev. of *The House of Cards*, by Leon Garfield. *Christian Science Monitor* Eastern ed. 9 Feb. 1983: 15.

Bridges, Phyllis. "First Thing We Do, Let's Kill All the Lawyers." Ed. Francis Edward Abernethy. *Publications of the Texas Folklore Society 1993: 295.*
Bruzzi, Stella. "Court Etiquette." *Sight and Sound* Feb. 1993: 4.

Cohen, Morris Raphael. "Moral Aspects of the Criminal Law." *Yale Law Journal* 49 (1940): 987-1026.

DiNizo, Alice. Rev. of *The Final Judgment*, by Richard North Patterson. *Library Journal* 120 (1995): 100.
Dreiser, Theodore. "I Find the Real American Tragedy." *Mystery Magazine* 11 (1935): 11+.
Duncan, Laura. "'Hot' Trials, Fiction Being Used as Teaching Tool." *Chicago Daily Law Bulletin* 4 Nov. 1994: 3+.
Dunlop, C. R. B. "Literature Studies in Law Schools." *Cardozo Studies in Law and Literature* 3.1 (1991): 63-110.

Emerson, Andrew C. "Legal Fictions." *Res Gestae* 37 (1994): 555+.

Gemmette, Elizabeth Villiers. "Law and Literature: An Unnecessarily Suspect Class in the Liberal Arts Component of the Law School Curriculum." *Valparaiso University Law Review* 23 (1989): 267-321.
---. "Law and Literature: Joining the Class Action." *Valparaiso University Law Review* 29 (1995): 665-859.
Goldberg, Stephanie B. "Who's Afraid of Derrick Bell? A Conversation on Harvard, Storytelling and the Meaning of Color." *ABA Journal* 78 (1992): 56-58.
Grisham, John. "The Rise of the Legal Thriller: Why Lawyers Are Throwing the Books at Us." *New York Times Book Review* 18 Oct. 1992, sec. 7: 33 .

Hall, Jerome. "The Basic Dilemma of Criminal Procedure." *Yale Law Journal* 51 (1942): 723-34.
Harmon, Louise. "Falling Off the Vine: Legal Fictions and the Doctrine of Substituted Judgment." *Yale Law Journal* 100 (1990): 1-71.

Jones, Malcolm. "Grisham's Gospel." *Newsweek* 15 Feb. 1999: 65+.

Kane, Patricia. "Lawyers at the Top: The Fiction of Louis Auchincloss." *Critique: Studies in Modern Fiction* 7.2 (1965): 36-46.
---. "Perry Mason: Modern Cultural Hero." *Heroes of Popular Culture*. Ed. Ray B. Browne. Bowling Green, OH: Bowling Green U Popular P, 1972. 125-33.
Kevles, Daniel J. "Darwin and Dayton." Rev. of *Summer for the Gods: The Scopes Trial and America's Continuing Debate over Science and Religion* by Edward J. Larson. Norman: U of Oklahoma P, 1999. *The New York Review of Books* 19 Nov. 1998: 61-63.

Moore, Steven. Rev. of *A Frolic of His Own*, by William Gaddis. *The Nation* 258 (1994): 569.
Morton, Charles W. "The World of Erle Stanley Gardner." *Atlantic* January 1967: 79-91.

Packer, Herbert L. "Two Models of the Criminal Process." *The Limits of the Criminal Sanction.* Stanford: Stanford U P, 1968: .
Paul, Joseph, and Sharon Carton. "The Law of the Federation: Images of Law, Lawyers, and the Legal System in *Star Trek: The Next Generation*." *The University of Toledo Law Review* 24 (1992): 43-85.

Reilly, Elaine. "'Hollywood 101': What Does Legal Fiction 'Teach' Law Students?" *Delaware Lawyer* 14.2 (1996): 36+.
Robbins, Frank. "The Firm of Cool and Lam." *The Mystery Writer's Art*. Ed. Francis M. Nevins, Jr. Bowling Green, OH: Bowling Green U Popular P, 1970. 136-48.
---. "The World of Perry Mason." *Michigan Alumnus Quarterly Review Summer* 1950: 349-52.
Rodriguez, J. Rafael. "Attempted Felony Murder: An Improbable Legal Fiction Meets Its Demise." *Florida Bar Journal* 69.9 (1995): 63-66.

Steinberg, Sybil. "Fiction: Legal Fictions: Short Stories about Lawyers and the Law." Ed. Jay Wishingrad. *Publisher's Weekly* 20 July 1992: 226.
Sreitfeld, David. "Writing Fiction from the Legal Trenches." *The Los Angeles Daily Journal* 21 Sept. 1990: 7.
Suretsky, Harold. "Search for a Theory: An Annotated Bibliography of Writings on the Relation of Law to Literature and the Humanities." *Rutgers Law*

Review 32 (1979): 727-40.

Tanenbaum, Robert K. "I Believe in the American Dream." *Publisher's Weekly* 12 Sept. 1994: 71-72.

Thomas, Brook. "The House of the Seven Gables: Hawthorne's Legal Story." *The University of Mississippi Studies in English* 5 (1985).

---. "The Legal Fiction of Herman Melville and Lemuel Shaw." *Critical Enquiry* 11 (1984): 24-51.

---. "*The Pioneers*, Or the Sources of American Legal History: A Critical Tale." *American Quarterly* 36 (1984): 86-111.

Ward, Ian. Rev. of *Legal Fiction: Law in the Novels of Nineteenth Century Women Novelists,* by Kathleen Loncar. *Journal of Legal History* 17.2 (1996): 191-92.

---. Rev. of *Adversaria: Literature and the Law*, by E.J. Hintz, et al., eds. Winnipeg: U of Manitoba P, 1994.

Zorn, Jean G. Rev. of *Final Argument*, by Clifford Irving. *The New York Times Book Review* 9 May 1993: 11.

Internet Publications & Archived Group Lists

DorothyL Listserv@Listserv.Kent.Edu. Owners: Kara L. Robinson & Diane K. Kovacs. Kent State Univ., Kent, OH

Murder on the Internet (Mystery News from the Ballantine Publishing Group). MOTI-DIST@cruises.randomhouse.com

Law-Related Media Sites

Internet Sites

From: Legal Links column by Erik J. Heels list of Top 10 Legal Periodical Web Sites:

Law Journal EXTRA!
http://www.ljx.com/indexhigh.html

Cal Law
http://www.callaw.com/

ABA's Law Practice Management Magazine
http://www.abanet.org/lpm/magazine/intro.html

Lawyers Weekly Publications

http://www.Lweekly.com

PaLaw Online
http://www.legalcom.com/

ABA's Business Law Today Magazine
http://www.abanet.org/buslaw/buslawtoday.html

ABA Journal
http://www.abanet.org/journal/

ABA Law Practice Management Section's Network 2d Newsletter
http://www.abanet.org/lpm/newsletters/home.html#net

Law Bulletin Publishing Company
http://www.lawbulletin.com

From: Legal List *Research on the Internet*
http://www.lcp.com/The-Legal-List/ch9b2.html

CourtTV
http://www.courttv.com

Federal News Service
http://www.fednews.com

Federal Register (daily contents)
gopher://gopher.counterpoint.com:2002/00/Tod ay/toc

Intellectual Property Magazine
http://www.ipmag.com

LawMagZine
http://www.islandnet.com/~wwlia/news.htm

National Law Journal
http://www.ljx.com/nlj

NetWatchers
http://www.ionet.net/~mdyer/netwatch.shtml

New York Law Journal
http://www.ljx.com/nylj

TexLaw
http://www.texlaw.com

Villanova Information Law Chronicle
http://ming.law.vill.edu/vill.info.1.chron

West's Legal News Top Stories
http://www.westpub.com/wlntop/front.htm

Appendix 1: LAWYERS' LEXICON

Scott Turow's autobiographical record of his first year as a "One L," a freshman Harvard law student, records the common experience ("a physical, emotional, intellectual combat zone," writes a reviewer) of lawyers-in-training discovering the semantics of legal language. It is worth a verbatim rendering:

> It's obvious, in looking back, that one of the things which made me feel most at sea was the fact that I barely understood much of what I was reading . . . What we were going through seemed like a kind of Berlioz assault in 'Legal,' a language I didn't speak and in which I was forced to read and think sixteen hours a day. Of course Legal bore some relation to English--it was more a dialect than a second tongue--but it was very peculiar. It was full of impossible French and Latin terms--*assize, assumpsit, demurrer, quare clausem fregit*--thousands more. Moreover, throughout Legal I noted the an effort to avoid the normal ambiguities of a word. 'Judgment' for instance has a variety of senses in ordinary speech. 'What's your judgment of him?' 'I think he has good judgment.' 'He'll come out right on the Judgment Day.' In Legal, 'judgment' means only the final and determinative utterance by a court on a lawsuit. (*One L*, 46-47)

Many terms below are likely to be familiar to readers of courtroom fiction due to their frequency of usage. Generally, a writer will take pains to couch the term as naturally as possible in plot or dialogue so that it does not catch the reader by surprise--this, as all readers know, does not always succeed and one sees the efforts many writers take to winch the term into a more or less natural context without baffling the reader. Is it because human meaning is so various and ambiguous relative to language that the language of law has both a stark simplicity and an onion-skinned kind of historical layering? Or is it a combination of the complexities of human behavior and semantics? Just as a homicide detective takes most pride in building a circumstantial case that the jury may not approve of, a courtroom thriller can pivot upon a technicality of law that leaves the reader befuddled in the denouement, and it is in this fascinating yet mystifying area that readers feel most at a serious disadvantage.

Most terms are given in laypersons' language and not all terms are legal (lawyers like their slang too). Despite frequent usage, some terms will retain that slipperiness or ambiguity that Mr. Turow decries above. Concepts like *beyond a reasonable doubt* and *guilt* or *innocence* will continue to defy adequate definition because they lie at the heart of our very notions of moral justice and fair play, and so I willingly risk the reader's patience by their inclusion. Sometimes commonality of usage is no barrier to ignorance--for example, to be *indicted* for a crime is often still confused with being guilty of that crime in the public's collective memory. Where a term or expression has special significance to a novel or writer, I have noted such in parentheses after the definition. A final disclaimer applies to fans who move easily between British courts and the American system: although American jurisprudence is obviously based on English law, almost everyone knows that barristers and solicitors hew to different tasks from their American counterparts in the formal rendering of justice; fortunately for American readers, the customs of English courtroom procedures are very familiar. For the most part, any term that shares both countries' legal traditions or procedures has been given an American bias. Latinate terms are italicized, and of course, a good many have entered the public domain as a result of frequency of usage and that inevitable purveyor of modern culture: television. Lawyers will please excuse the imprecision of some terms either misappropriated or perhaps wrenched too awkwardly into common parlance. I plead guilty to two charges: defining terms every reader will consider obvious and on several occasions of using the term with others from the list for purposes of context. The language of the law is a magnificent blend of borrowings from French and Latin, metaphor and euphemism, everyday colloquialisms and Anglo-Saxon English; the interrelationships among language levels can be a rich semantic experience of its own, and the rap against lawyers for using their legalese against lay persons is often both trite and unfair. Whether in the pages of a legal thriller or in the courtroom itself, the use of legal jargon is unmatched by any profession except espionage agents. One must recall that David J. M. Cornwell, better known by his pseudonym John le Carré, often invented words in his fiction--who today does not know of the sinister connotations of *mole* and *witch-hunt*? Many such coinages have entered the professional intelligence agent's domain and the same is true of legal terms and common vernacular. On a more mundane level, repetition will acclimate the reader to the fuller sense of the word's relationship to other terms of its kind--for example, those that apply to questioning of witnesses in court--*direct, cross, re-direct*--are the soul of exciting courtroom theater. I do split hairs in some cases because I believe lawyers and readers alike appreciate the distinctions drawn among *attorney, counselor*, *counsel*, and *solicitor*--not to mention the transatlantic confusion between *barrister* and *solicitor*.

Readers gluttonous for more punishment of this kind may wallow to their heart's content in *Court TV's Glossary of Legal Terms* on the Internet. Finally, I am again indebted to my friend David M. Fuqua of Hilburn & Calhoon in North Little Rock for casting his lawyer's eye over this section. Errors that exist, regardless, are mine alone.

A to Z

Absente reo	Latin, "in the absence of the accused."
Access before the fact	Someone who incites, orders, or counsels another to commit a crime.
Acting in concert	As explained by Susan Wittig Albert's lawyer-herbalist China Bayles in *Witches' Bane*, "When two people plan something illegal--the law calls it 'acting in concert'--each person is responsible not only for what he or she does and what the two do together, but also what the other does alone" (231).
Adjournment in contemplation of a dismissal	*See* **pre-trial diversion**.
Admissible (evidence)	Evidence ruled by the court to be entered into the proceedings; the opposite is inadmissible evidence.
Adverse ("hostile") witness	A witness so denoted, a trial attorney may ask leading, yes-no questions.
Affidavit	Statement taken under oath.
Amicus curiae	"Friend of the court." A disinterested party allowed to provide information to the court, but the person has no direct involvement in the case being heard.
Answer	The defendant's written response to the plaintiff in a civil case.
Appeal	Formal request to a higher court, usually a panel of judges, to overturn the ruling of a lower court.

Arcane law — Law that has been superseded or become obsolete; also Roman law, Anglo-Saxon law.

Arraignment — The first appearance before the judge in a criminal case; the charges are read, a lawyer appointed, if not present, and a plea to the charges is entered.

Articles of incorporation — States require corporations to file papers listing owners, purpose of corporation and kind of stock to be issued.

Article 32 — The legal military protocol of establishing sufficient evidence to warrant trial from the Uniform Code of Military Justice. (*See* Finder's 1998 *High Crimes*.)

Attorney — Lawyers are variously referred to by several nouns that denote persons who practice law or give legal advice; however, some terms retain a distinction. The *American Heritage Dictionary*, 3rd edition, provides these: "*Lawyer* is the general and most comprehensive term for one authorized to give legal advice to clients and to plead cases in a court of law. . . *Attorney* is often used interchangeably with *lawyer*, but in a narrower sense it denotes a legal agent for a client in the transaction of business. . . *Counselor* and counsel are terms for persons who give legal advice and serve as trial lawyers; *counsel* also applies to a team of lawyers employed in conducting a case. (*See* **barrister** and **solicitor**.)

Bad faith — Knowingly misrepresenting in a transaction.

Bail — The amount set by a judge during **arraignment** that a defendant must pay is usually reserved for serious crimes (*see* **bail schedule**). This is the guarantee that the **Defendant** will show up for trial later.

Bailiff — The term has a long history in British law. Formerly one who oversaw an estate and, later, one who worked along with the district sheriff and who executed writs and mad arrests; nowadays, in the American usage chiefly, one who maintains order in the courtroom. Often an appointee of the US Marshall's Office.

Barrister — The English equivalent of a trial lawyer who is engaged by the **solicitor** to try the case in court. Mortimer's Rumpole is one of many examples.

Bench trial — A trial before a judge but without a jury.

Beyond a reasonable doubt — *See* **reasonable doubt**.

Bifurcation — Splitting the trial into two phases, one to determine guilt or liability; the other to deliberate the penalty. A new jury can be empaneled for the second phase.

Booking, Booked into evidence — The former term refers to the actual process of arrest in which the charges are detailed and state why the person was arrested; the latter refers to the investigation's determining of evidence to support the charge or its formal recognition

	as such in court. (*See* **chain of evidence**.)
Bound over	Held for trial.
Brief	The written document outlining one party's legal arguments.
Burden of proof	Not an absolute standard but its variousness makes for all the art and drama of courtroom theater. Different levels of **burden of proof** exist in order to persuade judge and jury that the allegations are true enough and supported by sufficient factual evidence to convict the defendant as charged in a lawsuit. (*See* **guilt or innocence**; **reasonable doubt**.)
Capias ad respondendum	In **common law** the commencement of a suit for debt under which the debtor was arrested and obliged to give **bail**. If the judgment were recovered and the person being sued unable to pay (the common fate of several famous Dickens' debtors like Mr. Pickwick or Mr. Micawber, for examples), a companion term would be invoked--*capias ad satisfaciendum*--and that person would be committed to the Fleet or to Marshalsea prison until the debt was paid.
Capital case	Death-penalty case. Segmented into two phases, such as a "guilt phase," in which the jury must decide whether the accused committed the crime and whether there exist **special circumstances** justifying the death penalty; the second part is the "**penalty phase**," in which the jury must weigh the circumstances of the

crime with any mitigating factors of the defendant's record or character.

Case law — *See* **common law**.

Caveat emptor — Latin, "buyer beware." Refers to a buyer's, not a seller's, responsibility for the quality of goods in a transaction.

Certoriari — Latin, "to be informed of or about." A court is said to grant *certoriari*, or a writ of *certoriari*, when it chooses to review proceedings in a lower court to determine irregularities.

Chain of evidence — In fictional usage, both lawyers and detectives mean the same thing when they refer to the progress evidence makes from a crime scene to the courtroom with its various stops in between and the multiple, inevitable handling by the many disinterested forensics experts evidence endures. Its value to courtrooms real and fictional is in the arrival into court records as having been uncontaminated by the various hands that have tagged its progress in examination and so becomes entered into evidence. (*See* **circumstantial evidence**.)

Champerty — A charge brought against an attorney who is representing a client and defraying that client's bills with disbursements from the firm (Auchincloss' "Power in Trust" from *Powers of Attorney*).

Chapter 7 bankruptcy — The liquidation of a person's assets to pay off creditors.

Chapter 13 bankruptcy — In this type of bankruptcy, a person keeps his/her assets and pays off creditors according to a plan approved by all parties.

Change of venue — Relocating the trial to avoid prejudicing one of the parties in a case.

Character defense — A psychological truism co-opted by defense attorneys that insists that people do not suddenly change in character--that is, they will behave as they have always acted.

Charging lien — Often a lawyer's first order of business in a lawsuit; it entitles an attorney to be paid in behalf of the client filing suit before the client can receive any money out of the proceedings.

Circumstantial (evidence) — *See* **corpus delicti**. Circumstantial evidence is indirect evidence--the soul of good criminal investigation and successful prosecution. Because jurors often have an unfounded faith in eyewitness testimony and a concomitant resistance to **circumstantial evidence**, the state's case must be proven **beyond a reasonable doubt** to gain a conviction. Its origins are rooted in criminal law beginning with an infamous murder trial in Boston in 1850. Until that time, no one had ever prosecuted a case where no body existed. Judge Lemuel Shaw instructed jurors that they could consider circumstantial evidence--further, that they need only conclude beyond a **reasonable doubt**. (They did. John Webster was hanged for the murder of George Parkman.) (*See* **trial**.)

Civil case (trial)

The crucial difference is that only the state, not the victim or the victim's family, may bring an individual to trial in a criminal proceeding. In a civil case, it is the individual's prerogative to seek justice in the courts. One may be guilty of murder in a civil case and serve no time, as for example in the not-guilty verdict of O.J. Simpson in the **criminal** trial of 1995 and the subsequent guilty verdict of the civil in 1997. (*See* **trial** and Higgins' *Sandra Nichols Found Dead*, 1996.)

Class action suit

A complaint or lawsuit filed in behalf of one or more parties who are "similarly situated"; used for comparable claims of large numbers of persons.

Clear and convincing evidence

For a plaintiff to prevail in a civil suit, the proof required is more than a **preponderance of the evidence** but less than **beyond a reasonable doubt**. (*See* **Trial**.)

Codicil

Supplement to a will.

Cohabitation agreement

Also known as a living-together contract and similar to a pre-nuptial agreement. This document makes clear to both parties how property and finances will be divided if the relationship ends.

Comity

The code of conduct or etiquette among courts that governs interactions in different states and applies to international jurisdictional matters. For instance, a court would agree to defer scheduling a trial if identical issues are being tried elsewhere; moreover, contracts and court orders issued in other countries are recognized and enforced in the US. **Comity** resolves the plot in Michael A. Kahn's short story "Cook County Redemption" (*See* Bernhardt, William, ed. *Legal Briefs*).

Common law

All law, theoretically, and its history of case-by-case decision-making as established by judges, a heritage from ninth-century Anglo-Saxon times to the most recent jurisprudence manifested on Court TV. Also known as **case law**.

Comparative negligence

A concept treated variously among states and known also as comparative fault. A person suing another may recover partial damages for negligence, even though the party suing may be partially at fault for causing damage or responsible for injury.

Complainant

One who brings an action against another. In a criminal matter, the police or the state would be the complaining party.

Complaint

The document initiating the lawsuit, which would allege the facts and the remedy being sought. It is also the preliminary charge filed by the police or the court in a criminal action.

Concurrent sentence

Sentences served simultaneously rather than one after another. The opposite of consecutive sentence.

Conditional dismissal

See **pre-trial diversion**.

Conservator

Someone appointed to oversee the property or finances of another. (*See* **guardian**.)

Contempt of court

Any insult to the court's dignity, anything that obstructs the court from proceeding in its business of administering justice. Actions that elicit contempt may range from disparaging remarks to the presiding judge or failure to testify. Jail and/or fines can be levied against individuals in contempt.

Continuance

Postponement of proceedings; the presiding judge's nightmare. On occasion a stalling tactic, sometimes a litigator's trademark.

Count

As in "felony-murder count"; each distinct charge in a **true bill** or an **indictment**.

Court witness

Witness called by the judge in a trial and open to questions by both sides. (*See* Roy Flannagan's *County Court* (1938).)

Criminal trial

Opposed to **civil** trial. The state's apparatus for ensuring public peace and probity by all its **officers of the court** depends upon the sanctity of this cornerstone of our rights and freedoms in a Jeffersonian democracy. In general, this is what happens after an individual violates a section of the penal code who does not wish to **plea bargain**.

Corpus delicti

"Body of crime." Sometimes misunderstood by lay persons to mean a "no body" case. In Melville Davisson Post's short story entitled "The Corpus Delicti" (in Blaustein's *Fiction Goes to Court*, 3-30), Randolph Mason abets a grisly murder and subsequently frees the

	murderer in court by citing the New York statute that precludes both "components of the *corpus delicti* [from being] established by circumstantial evidence" (25). In this particularly gruesome murder, the body is disposed of in an acid bath, and the murderer cannot be linked as the criminal agent of the woman's death.
Crimen falsi	"Crime of falsifying," which in Roman law meant every kind of **dishonesty** but today refers primarily to forgery and (less often) **perjury**.
Crimen laesae majestatis	"Crime of lese majesty"; high treason.
Cross (examination)	The middle of a three-part sequence of questioning witnesses that begins with the **Q & A** outside court (coaching the witness to get the desired response to the questions to be asked in court); that testimony, or direct examination, is then "crossed" by the opposing attorney who will attempt to undermine it or expose its flaws or untruth; the capstone of this triad is the **redirect** of that witness as more evidence or testimony dictates its need. *See* also **recross (examination)**.
Death qualified	A trial attorney certified for capital punishment cases, such as Barbara Holloway in Wilhelm's *Death Qualified* (1991) or Matt Fielder in Klempner's *Flat Lake in Winter* (1999).
Defamation	Publishing a statement injurious to a person's reputation.

Default — Failure to meet a legal or binding commitment.

Defendant — One who has been charged with a **complaint** by another person in a civil matter or by the police or courts in a criminal one. Generally, the person accused of the crime.

Defense attorney — A trial lawyer, generally. One of a minute number of the total number of licensed attorneys who prefer defending to prosecuting or litigating.

Deposition — Questions asked of witnesses under oath by lawyers in pre-trial **discovery**, which answers or responses constitute evidence. The opposite of a police interrogation.

Direct evidence — Evidence that stands alone to substantiate a charge, such as eyewitness testimony of a crime.

Directed verdict — The specified verdict of a judge to a jury when one party has failed to prove its case.

Direct examination — The first round of questioning of a witness during trial. (*See* **cross (examination)**).

Discovery — Previous to trial, each party requests information and documents relevant to the case from the other; the burden is greater on the prosecution than the defense for the defense does not have to release incriminating information, but the prosecution must release any evidence or testimony that would exculpate the accused.

Discovery file — Police reports and all paperwork related to a case, such as Crime-scene logs, witness statements, test results, photographic evidence, bloody clothing, etc. that constitute the results of the investigation. The level of the adversarial relationship between prosecution and defense can be seen in how tidy are the boxes of evidence given to the other side; "discovery" can be obfuscation when unsorted and untyped boxes of evidence are merely handed over.

Dismissal with prejudice — The formal dismissing of a case and the barring of the plaintiff from bringing similar action against the defendant. (*See* Bentley's *Mistress Nancy*, 1980).

Doctrine of substituted judgment — The state may invade the "bodily integrity" of the incompetent without justifying its invasion (Harmon 61).

Double jeopardy — No person can be tried twice for the same offense.

Due process — The constitutional guarantee of everyone's civil rights that laws and their administration will be even-handed.

Duty to warn — The legal obligation to warn people of a danger in a product's use.

En banc — French, "by the full court." The entire membership of an appellate court hearing an argument brought before it is sitting **en banc**.

Encumbrance — Any restriction or claim made on the title of a property.

Entrapment — The premise that a crime would not have occurred were it not for the

	luring of a previously uncontemplated action.
Evidence	Almost anything usable in any form that proves alleged facts ranging from eyewitness testimony through documents to video tapes.
Executor, -trix	Person named in a will to oversee the estate.
Exigent circumstance	Legal euphemism for an emergency.
Ex parte	Latin, "by or for one party." One of the parties appearing before the judge during litigation without the opposition; a legal taboo often violated when one side wishes to convey privileged information.
Federal rules of evidence	Judicial guidelines for admitting evidence in federal trials as distinct from state courts.
Felony	Any serious crime punishable by a year of imprisonment.
Felony murder rule	Subject to much recent criticism, the felony-murder rule applies if a murder is committed during the perpetration of a felony crime, such as robbery, even though robbery, not murder, was the sole intent of the perpetrator. According to J. Rafael Rodriguez, Florida trial attorney, the rule "stands as an exception to the general rule that murder is homicide with the specific intent of malice aforethought. . . . [so that] the perpetrator of a particular felony, as a matter of law, necessarily acts with the culpability from which the **mens rea** requisite to a murder conviction may be inferred" (63).

Fiduciary duty

The code or standard of conduct that stipulates one party is obligated to act in the best interest of another, such as the attorney-client relationship.

First-degree murder

Usually but depending upon state statutes (murder is not a federal crime), this refers to the willful, deliberate, and premeditated taking of life. Much depends upon prosecutorial vs. defense attorneys' abilities to prove those three traits qualify in murder cases. If, for instance, an attorney for the defendant can successfully intimate a killing occurs because his or her client was wallowing in a "heat-of-passion" moment, then he or she will have the jury leaning toward second,- third-degree convictions--possibly even manslaughter. This "stepping down" of the bill is, of course, what plea-bargaining without trial is all about.

Force majeure

Unexpected or uncontrollable event. (*See* **exigent circumstances**.)

Fruit of the poisoned tree

Evidence "tainted" and therefore inadmissible because its source may have been contaminated, such as evidence obtained without a search warrant or extracted from a confession under false pretenses. (*See* **chain of evidence**.)

Garnishment

Court-mandated debt collection. One of the first legal terms a young man careless with his spermic exudate will learn, right after *paternity*.

GAL (guardian *ad litem*)

For or during a legal process, a nonpartisan party is selected to represent an individual because of that person's incapacity for reasons of extreme youth, age, mental competence or physical incapacity.

Good faith — Opposite of **bad faith**. If one party enters into an agreement with intent to defraud, bad faith, if proven, nullifies the agreement.

Grand jury — Citizens convened to hear prosecutorial evidence that **probable cause** exists to indict a suspect for a **felony** crime.

Grantor — One who sets up a trust.

Gross negligence — Willful and reckless disregard for the safety of others.

Guardian — Person assigned by the court to care for minor children or incompetent adults. Also called a **conservator**.

Guilt/Innocence — Two of the most seemingly simple, yet profound, terms in law for which legal pro and author Vincent Bugliosi provides this definition in the footnotes to his successful prosecution of two killers in 1987 as recounted in his and Bruce B. Henderson's *And the Sea Will Tell*: "To the words 'convinced of the defendant's guilt' are appended the words 'beyond a reasonable doubt.' It would seem we have now jettisoned the inferential 'innocence' . . . for a verdict of not guilty. In other words, when jurors are instructed that to convict, they have to be convinced *not only* [author's emphasis]of guilt, but of guilt beyond a reasonable doubt, they are clearly being told that *a mere belief in guilt is not enough to convict.*"

Citing the 1981 US Supreme Court case of *Bullington v. Missouri*, Bugliosi reveals his prosecutorial bias in lamenting the shift of Justice's balance from equilibrium toward the defendant's side of the courtroom, especially in what has come to be seen as empowering of the jury's sensibilities toward the defendant: "It is pure folly to expect a lay jury to be less confused than the U. S. Supreme Court." In his condemnation of the verdict in the O. J. Simpson trial (*Outrage*), Mr. Bugliosi refers to his 1981 article "Not Guilty or Innocent," the subtitle of which is "The Problem Children of Reasonable Doubt." "Not guilty" is confused with "innocent"; however, it should be akin to the Scots' verdict, as an Alan Dershowitz lawyer-protagonist argues in *The Advocate's Devil* to mean "not proven."

Habeus corpus

Latin, "You have the body." A writ of *habeus corpus* is a judicial mandate to a prison official ordering that an inmate appear before a judge to determine whether imprisonment was lawful. Two examples: the 1939 Gardner novel *They Bigger They Come* [alt. title: *Lam to the Slaughter,* A.A. Fair, pseud.], in which disbarred attorney Donald Lam explains the term to an Arizona judge and in Marianne Wesson's 1997 *Render Up the Body*, in which defense counsel Cinda Hayes uses it to try to save a man from execution.

Hearsay

Hearsay has a specific meaning in law not often appreciated by lay people; it is, of course, second-hand (and therefore inadmissible) evidence in its general sense; however, it also refers to a statement made **outside of court** offered into evidence as both having been made and, more importantly, true.

Heat of passion — A concomitant of a murder charge that is less than first-degree or premeditated--that is, manslaughter.

Holographic will — Unwitnessed handwritten will (Masur's *So Rich, So Lovely, and So Dead*, 1952).

Immunity — Exemption from prosecution, a prosecutor's best bargaining chip.

Implied (express) consent laws — Laws adopted throughout the US that apply to testing for alcohol in the breath, urine, or blood. The "implied" in the consent means that all vehicle operators on state roads have given consent to be tested for intoxication.

In camera — Latin, "in chambers." Usually, any hearing that occurs in a judge's private chambers.

Incompetent, irrelevant, and immaterial! — The frequent Triple-I objection so often heard in novels and so seldom in real courtroom action. Its legal usage, according to Jon L. Breen, is dubious but it has a novelistic heritage eight years before the Perry Mason novels in Dreiser's great novel *An American Tragedy* "albeit with the three *I*'s in different order." Breen further notes: "Gardner probably did the most to popularize it, though, and other writers picked it up in subsequent novels (52). A side note to "**incompetent**": a defendant who files on appeal for retrial based on incompetence of representation is bucking the odds because real courts disapprove of such attempts owing to the fine line between a sub-par legal performance as defense counsel and bad strategy, especially true as lawyers must often do their clients' bidding against advice of counsel.

Indictment — Formal accusation of a felony once a grand jury has convened and considered in favor of the evidence.

Indigent — The legal euphemism for "poor," the precondition for having the judge appoint an attorney for representation.

In flagrante delicto — A well-trod Latin euphemism for lovers caught up in the "heat of passion"; the part that matters to law is that when such lovers are discovered by one of their spouses in the throes of passion, it can beget bloodshed.

Information — The predecessor to an **indictment**--the formal accusation by the prosecutor that a crime has been committed.

Informed consent — The stipulation that doctors must inform patients of any course of treatment except in emergencies.

Injunction — Loosely, a court order to cease an activity.

Interrogatories — Witnesses' formal responses to questions posed during pre-trial **discovery**.

Intestate — To die intestate means to die without a will. Lawrence Kasdan's script for

Warner's 1981 film *noir Body Heat* has Kathryn Turner rewriting her murdered husband's will and signing her lover's name, lawyer Ned Racine, to it. She knew that Florida probate law would the new will void, his death **intestate**, and the state would give her all, instead of half, the money.

Irrevocable living trust — A trust that cannot be emended during the maker's lifetime.

Johnson letter — According to Martini's *Prime Witness*, it is based on *People v. Johnson* that says a prosecutor, if requested in a letter by a defendant, must give to a grand jury evidence deemed exculpatory (175).

Judgment — The court's official **decision** on the matter before it.

Judgment *non obstante verdicto* — **Judgment** "notwithstanding the verdict"; the judge's prerogative of overruling a **jury verdict** and deciding for the loser when the facts of the case do not support it.

Jurisdiction — Two factors determine the court's authority to arbitrate: geographical locale and the kind of case to be presented.

Jury — Twelve people of average ignorance.

Jury charge — The judge's instructions to jurors on laws and legal definitions applicable to the case. (*See* **guilt or innocence**.)

"Jury nullification" argument — To argue that the jury should correct a glaring social wrong with its verdict despite the evidence.

Just cause	"Legal reasons," for instance, why someone is terminated from employment.
Latches	Concept that says, basically, rights long neglected cease to be rights and cannot later be invoked. (Tapply's *Dead Meat*, 1987, applies the term to Indian settlement rights.)
Legatee	Beneficiary.
Lesser included offenses	Charges below that of the most serious charge, such as second-degree murder (killing without premeditation) would include a lesser charge of manslaughter (killing in the **heat of passion**).
Liability	Legal responsibility.
Libel	Defamatory written statements against someone's character, an interpretation widened by recent court rulings to include photographs and films.
Lien	A claim against property to secure repayment like the common mortgage on a house.
Limited partnership	Limited partners provide financial backing but generally do not participate in a firm's management, and unlike their opposites in a **general partnership**, have no liability.
Lord Chancellor	England's highest legal authority.
LWOP	Life without parole.
Maintenance	Modern euphemism for old-fashioned alimony.

Majority — *See* **minor**.

Malpractice — Negligent behavior by a professional such as a lawyer or doctor.

Mandatory sentence — A pre-set sentence that limits the judge's discretion in sentencing; it sets a minimum time that must be served for a specific crime.

Manslaughter — An intentional killing that, but for mitigating circumstances such as provocation, would be murder. The phrase **"heat of passion"** often surfaces in trials where the difference between a second-degree conviction or manslaughter is arguable.

McNaughten Rule — (Var. sp. M'Naghten; McNaghten) This nineteenth-century insanity definition is named for Daniel M'Naughten, who attempted to kill Prime Minister Robert Peel. The McNaughten Rule of 1843 is not the first record of insanity as a defense tactic because William Lambard's *Eirenarcha* predates it by more than three centuries as an organized statement of insanity in Anglo-Saxon jurisprudence. It states that a person is innocent of a crime if that person did not know right from wrong at the time of the crime's commission. According to John Douglas, of the famed FBI's VICAP program, this defense has evolved into the "irresistible impulse test" of today, in which a defendant is so mentally ill that that person cannot control his actions or "conform his conduct to the law." McNaughten's acquittal so outraged the British public that the Lord Chief Justice had to explain its "logic" before the House. (*See* Curtis Bok's *Star Wormwood*, 1959.)

Mediation — Alternative dispute resolution by a neutral third party.

Mens rea — Latin, "concerning the [state of] mind." The question of deliberation or premeditation in the commission of a crime. In Moore's *The Court-Martial* (1971) a defense lawyer arguing for Green Beret officers accused of murdering a double agent: "If the agent was eliminated, he was not eliminated with any criminal or evil intent or what we lawyers call *mens rea*" (314). (*See* also Wainwright's *Man of Law* (1980).

Miranda Warning (Rule) — The statement recited to an individual at the time of arrest by a police officer which speaks to the accused person's right to be silent and have an attorney.

Misdemeanor — Crimes punishable by less than a year. The opposite of **felony**.

Mistrial — One of two possibilities for making a trial invalid: either the **jury** are in disagreement (*see* **hung jury**) or there is a basic prejudicial error in procedure.

Mitigating factors — Information helpful to a defendant at sentencing or information about the circumstances of the crime that may cause the judge to lessen the sentence.

Motion — A request from counsel asking the judge to rule on a procedure or a legal matter.

Motion for a new trial	Losing counsel requests a new trial because of prejudicial errors.
Motion for a directed verdict	The **defendant** in a civil trial may request the judge to rule in his or her favor on the grounds that the **plaintiff** has no valid case to argue nor have genuine legal issues been raised to warrant a continuation of trial.
Motion for a summary judgment	Similar to a **motion for a directed verdict** except that the request is made before trial.
Motion to dismiss	The **defendant** in a civil trial may request a judge's ruling to dismiss the case on the grounds that the **plaintiff** has no right to seek legal reward even if the charges are proven true.
Motion to suppress evidence	Requested of the judge to keep evidence out of the trial because it may have been illegally obtained. (*See* **fruit of the poisoned tree**.)
Negative evidence	Evidence that something did not happen--for example, in a disappearance case, if the friends of the missing individual have not heard from him or her, that is evidence is significant.
Negligence	Failure to use the caution or the degree of care that a reasonable person would be expected to use in a given circumstance.
Nol-pros	Abbreviation of *nolle prosequi.* The plaintiff in a civil case or the prosecutor in a criminal enters a ***nolle prosequi*** in court records and thereby drops all or part of a suit or

an **indictment**.

Nolle prosequi — Latin, "I am unwilling to pursue." (*See* **nol-pros**.)

Nolo contendere — Latin, "I do not wish to contend." The plea in a criminal action that is an all but technical admission of guilt; it subjects the **defendant** to punishment in present proceedings but allows for denial of alleged facts in others.

Non compos mentis — Latin, "of unsound mind." In Gardner's *The Case of the Beautiful Beggar*, 1974, elderly but sane Horace Shelby is faced with this charge by covetous relatives.

No process to issue — No **disposition** results when a **complainant** refuses **to press charges**. In Tapply's *Client Privilege*, such paperwork is filed alphabetically in the Clerk's Office.

Notice of appeal — The document filed with the court to pursue an appeal.

Old Bailey — A street in the western part of the City of London, where the Central Criminal Court is located. The CCC gets its common name from the English custom of referring to buildings by their street location.

AOpening the door@ — Lawyers' slang for getting favorable but seemingly irrelevant testimony into the proceedings.

OR — [Released on] Own Recognizance.

Outside of court — Not from the witness stand at the present proceeding.

Overrule, -ed	The court's decision to rule against an objection by counsel on a proceeding. (*See* **sustain**, **-ed**.)
Own recognizance	A person released without bail who promises to appear at trial date to answer criminal charges.
Palimony	*See* **maintenance**.
Parens patriae	Latin, "parent of his country." Applied to the state when asserting control for the welfare of mentally incompetent adults and children.
Parole	The supervised release of convicts prior to their sentences' terminating; the system whereby "good time" in prison yields time off a sentence and makes a convict eligible to meet a **parole** board to plea for early release. Does not apply to federal crimes.
Partition	Court-ordered division of property.
Penalty phase	The second part of a **bifurcated** trial in which the penalty or damages are imposed by the jury.
Peremptory challenge	*See* **Important Judicial Hearings and Challenges** below.
Perjury	Lying under oath, a crime; or making false statements on a document (in some jurisdictions).
Personal recognizance	*See* **OR**, **own recognizance**.
Per stirpes	Latin, "through the stem [lineage]." A line of common ancestry or persons from whom a family is descended. (Auchincloss' *The Lady of Situations*).

Petit jury	Jurors empaneled to hear civil or criminal cases.
Petition for probate	The will as summarized and entered into **probate**.
Plea-bargain	Negotiated settlement between prosecution and defense to lower the sentence by having the accused plead guilty to a lesser charge. A much-maligned practice that ensures court dockets will not be overloaded with cases nor public funds exhausted by getting the accused to plea-bargain, which practice does achieve those ends, although it may sacrifice justice to economy or expediency.
Pleading, -s	In civil cases only, this refers to allegations and or defenses from both sides concerning their legal positions.
Power of attorney	The legal authority to act for someone.
Precedent	A case citation from **common law**. A decision from a past case will be considered binding for that court and apply to all lower courts in that jurisdiction.
Preliminary hearing, prelim	States will differ, but a preliminary hearing means that the prosecution will present the charges and try to show **probable cause** that the accused person did commit a crime; if the judge agrees, the person is bound over for trial; if not, the accused is released.
Presentence report	Often prepared by a parole officer, a judge will use this document in considering sentence; it contains both good and bad information (prior

arrests, convictions, spotty work history, etc.) about a defendant's life.

Preponderance of evidence

Applicable to **civil** cases only in which a "sufficient" level of proof is required for the **plaintiff** to win. (*See* **beyond a reasonable doubt**, **probable cause**).

Presumption of death

In a disappearance, the law assumes that if someone has been missing for seven years and has not been heard from, that person is presumed dead (Neil Albert's *The January Corpse*).

Pre-trial diversion

Also referred to as **adjournment in contemplation of a dismissal** or **conditional dismissal**. If the court believes in the accused person's integrity, it may offer this program; it means that a person will not have to go to trial if the probationary period is observed or the court's condition is met during this time of abeyance.

Pre-trial writ petition

Example: a judge who does not let a lawyer confer with his client at pretrial exposes the court's later verdict to the Court of Appeal to being overturned on the ground that a defendant's right to counsel was denied.

Prima facie

Latin, "at first view." Minimal evidence needed to avoid having a case dismissed.

Privileged communication

Not only is the conversation between a lawyer and client privileged but almost all states recognize similar "protected" relationships, such as wife-husband, doctor-patient, and priest-penitent. *See* Stephen White's *Privileged Communication*.

Probable cause — A reasonable belief that a person has committed a crime.

Probate — The legal process of overseeing the inheritances of wills.

Probation — Release of a convict prior to the full sentence imposed by the court as long as certain conditions, such as drug treatment, community service, avoiding contact with criminal associates, etc., are met. Failure to satisfy the stipulations for probation can mean return to prison; however, mammoth case loads prevent strict guidance once a person is released into the community.

Pro bono [*publico*] — Latin, "for the public good." The legal practice of donating service **indigent** to clients.

Pro-per — *Propria persona* (to act as one's own defense counsel)

Pro se — Latin, "for oneself"; to appear *pro se* in court is to act as your own lawyer (Ex. Gardner's *The Buried Clock*, 1943). Not recommended.

Prosecutor — A government lawyer with the rank to try cases in behalf of the public's interest. Basically, one who works out of the district (or state's) attorney's office, whose chief duty in representing *the People* is to do justice, not garner convictions. Also called district attorney or state's attorney.

Prejudicial error — Legal euphemism for a miscarriage of justice.

Premeditated murder	Differs from felony murder. *See* **First-degree murder**.
Probable cause	The responsibility of the judge during preliminary hearing is to determine whether the state's witnesses and evidence prove sufficiently credible to commit the defendant to a superior court for trial.
Public defender	A lawyer who works for the state defending **indigent** clients.
Punitive damages	Money awarded a victim intended to deter a person or business from repeating that action.
Q & A	Question and answer. One of the best examples of incisive questioning on the witness-stand Q & A in Gardner's career canon is the 1944 *Give 'Em the Ax* (not, however, a Mason novel; its British title is *An Axe to Grind*, 1951).
QC	Queen's Counsel. A QC may appear for any person, not just the Crown, in either civil or criminal jurisdictions, but it is actually a means toward appointing senior barristers. Barristers permanently employed to appear for the Crown in criminal proceedings are called Crown Prosecutors ("Crowns," for short).
QC MP	Queen's Counsel, Member of Parliament. About one-eighth of Members of Parliament are lawyers, and the majority of those are **barristers**.
Quash	To declare void.

Quid pro quo — Latin, "something for something." Applies to contracts.

Quid pro quo sexual harassment — Applies to litigation involving workplace situations where an employee is expected to return sexual favors for promotion or under threats of demotion.

Rainmaker — Lawyer slang for a moneymaker, usually said of a partner with great earning potential like Sandy Lord in *Absolute Power* (*See* also John Grisham's *The Rainmaker).*

Reasonable doubt — That level of certainty needed to convict in a criminal case. *See* **beyond a reasonable doubt**, **probable cause**, and **preponderance of the evidence**.

Reason of insanity — A plea that asks a jury in a criminal case to find the defendant not guilty because of mental incompetence at the time of the crime; in other words, the defendant could not have told right from wrong during the commission of the crime and is therefore innocent. *See* **McNaughten Rule**.

Rebuttal witness — A witness brought forward by either side to refute crucial testimony. *See* **cross**, **recross** (**examination**).

Recross (examination) — Questioning of a witness about statements made during **redirect**. *See* **cross** (**examination**).

Redirect (examination) — Questioning of a witness about statements made during **cross**.

Recuse, -ing — To except oneself, another or challenge a party as interested--that

	is, "biased" in the proceedings.
Remand	An appellate court sends or returns a case to a lower court.
Res judicata	L., "things judged." A matter once decided in a court of law remains decided.
Residuary legatee	One who is to receive what is left over from a will after bequests.
Res ipsa loquitur	Latin, "It [the thing] speaks for itself." A legal presumption that a thing could not have occurred--say, an accident--were it not for the negligence of another party.
Retainer	A lawyer's money paid up front to retain the lawyer's services.
Right against self-incrimination	The Fifth Amendment.
Right of eminent domain	The government's right to take property for public use.
Right of survivorship	The co-owner, or survivor, of a jointly held property is the automatic beneficiary.
Sacred goods	Human body parts sold as commodities (Aubert's *Free Reign*, 1997).
SC	Senior Counsel. Australian equivalent of a Crown Prosecutor. *See* **QC**.
Scraping a defendant's conscience	Early nineteenth-century English legal practice of adding to the **bill** after fresh interrogatories reveal more. Sometimes a **plaintiff** would file what was called a "fishing bill," and then, after answers or averments

	come in, amendments would be added.
Self-proving will	A will signed by witnesses before a notary public.
Sentencing guidelines	Judges are obliged to follow these in assessing prison time; however, it matters greatly whether the guidelines are for the federal or the state system because the federal guidelines are considered much more stringent and do not allow a judge much latitude in sentencing. A less well- known difference between the federal and the state systems is the fact that there is no parole in the federal penal system and "good time" sentence reductions are generally much less compared to the state.
Sequestration	Two meanings in legal parlance: less commonly, a writ for seizing property or isolating a jury during deliberation.
Service of process	Formal notification to another party that an action has begun and what must be done to comply or respond.
Settlement	Resolution (or compromise) of an action in a civil lawsuit.
Settlement agreement	The document of an out-of-court **settlement**.
Sidebar	Said of private conferences traditionally held at the side of the court among judges and attorneys over anything any party deems necessary to be discussed out of the jury's hearing and off the record.

Silk, to "take silk"

Silks are appointed by the Lord Chancellor. To "take silk," a junior barrister must first serve with distinction at the Bar for ten years. John Mortimer, though a Silk himself, has Rumpole disdain the entire old-boy network of favoritism in the appointment process. Henry Cecil's Roger Thursby considers taking silk in the second novel of his trilogy.

Slander

False, defamatory, and injurious oral statements.

Solicitor

An attorney who is not a member of the bar and who may be heard by lower courts only. In the British sense, the solicitor is largely a legal agent who prepares cases for the **barrister**; in the US the solicitor is the chief law-enforcement officer of a town or governmental department. (*See* **lawyer**.)

SODDI

Jocularly known among trial attorneys as a desperate lawyer's last defense tactic, the idea is that Some Other Dude Did It. (*See* **Twinkie defense**.)

Special circumstance

After the Supreme Court abolished capital punishment in the 1970s because of its haphazard administration across the country, state legislatures were sent scrambling to write new laws in a language that could not be overturned on appeal and one of the byproducts of that effort is the wording that pertains to certain kinds of heinous murders that would justify a death penalty. In California, for instance, Section 190.2 of the Penal Code covers 19 possible **special circumstances** that warrant capital punishment--for example, 190.2 (7) is the killing of a police officer in the performance of his or her duties.

Spendthrift trust	A trust meant to keep money out of creditors' hands.
Spousal rights	Alimony. (*See* **maintenance**.)
Stalking	Nowadays a legal term in many states. Variously defined in the lawbooks, it usually requires two parts: there must be a pattern of wilful, malicious conduct; secondly, this conduct must cause a reasonable person to be fearful of her or his welfare.
Standing	The legal right to initiate a lawsuit.
Stare decisis	Latin, "to stand by that which is decided." The principle of adhering to **precedent**.
State-of-mind exception	A time-honored premise attached to the **hearsay** objection rule that prohibits lawyers from using third-party evidence. Normally, what a person said someone else had said outside of court is mere speculation, but a witness may often be induced to get that testimony into the record by careful questioning.
Stationhouse bail	**Bail** paid at the precinct for **misdemeanors**.
Statute of limitation	Any one of various time limits for filing lawsuits.
Stipulate, Astip@	To enter a witness, such as a professional expert's testimony without having that person testify in

court--say, for instance, at a **preliminary hearing** with a ballistics expert on the weapon or a coroner's report.

Strict liability — Liability without proof of **negligence**.

Strike from the record — A ruling from the judge to the court reporter to delete material that is generally followed by an admonition to the jury to disregard what it has just heard uttered. According to Bill Blum's *Prejudicial Error,* it is tantamount to a "circus ringmaster telling the crowd not to think of an elephant after the house lights go down in the big top" (119).

Subpoena — From Medieval Latin, "under penalty," the first words of the traditional writ requiring appearance in court to give testimony.

Subpoena *duces tecum* — A formal order to bring "with you" documents or specified materials to a deposition hearing.

Summation — The closing argument in a **trial**.

Summons — The document that notifies a party a lawsuit has been initiated and states the time and place for the recipient to answer the charges. (*See* **subpoena**.)

Superior court — The place where defendants accused of felonies go for jury trial.

Sustain, -ed — The judge's ruling in favor of an objection by counsel on a procedural matter. (*See* **overrule**, **-ed**).

Testator — One who makes a will.

Title search — Review of land records to determine ownership of property.

Tort law — Laws that pertain to civil wrongs resulting in injuries to persons or property.

Totten trust — A bank account trust naming a beneficiary.

Trial (by judge vs. jury) — Juries need **reasonable doubt** to convict but a judge needs merely a preponderance of evidence. Comparable to civil cases (unlike criminal) in which it is necessary to determine only that it is *more likely than not* a person is guilty of the crime. Juries, for better or worse reasons, traditionally demand absolute, unconditional evidence of guilt before they will convict.

True bill — A bill of **indictment** endorsed by a **grand jury**.

Trust — Property given to a **trustee** to manage for the benefit of a third person for, usually, a specified number of years.

Trustee — Person or institution that manages a **trust**.

Twinkie defense — Originally , a journalistic tag for the defense of Dan White, slayer of San Francisco mayor George Moscone and gay- rights activist Harvey Milk, who in the weekend preceding the murders, claimed to have been agitated by stress and a diet of junk food. Nowadays, a generic term for any such strategy of defendant self-victimization. A recent example: "black rage," a strategy proposed by court-appointed counsel to Colin

	Ferguson, the Long Island Express killer of 1993.
Uniform Reciprocal Enforcement	The law of reciprocity among states regarding the enforcing of Support Act of child support.
Unjust taking	Unfair seizure of property by the government without adequate compensation.
Valid claim	Legal grievance.
Verdict	The formal decision of a jury after deliberation.
Vicarious liability	The liability of one person for another, such as a parent for a child.
Victim confrontation laws	Many states allow for "victim impact statements" to be read by survivors during the penalty phase of a criminal case. This new legal concept borrows from psychology more than law and is akin to the sociological pap that speaks of "closure" rather than justice. Writes brilliant crime-novelist James Ellroy in *My Dark Places*, a memoir of his search for the killer of his mother when he was ten (New York: Knopf, 1996): "The confrontation law was passed by morons hooked on daytime TV" (314).
Vi et armis	A centuries-old term of the common law to describe acts of violence. Rusty Sabich in *Presumed Innocent* reflects upon this term's heritage: "The phrase is archaic, long abandoned in most jurisdictions. . . " (148).

Void marriage	A marriage that is invalid from the beginning and can therefore be annulled. (*See* **voidable marriage**.)
Voir dire	Formal process of jury seating a panel of twelve jurors to try a case. First, eligible jurors, usually registered voters, are summoned to the courthouse on the basis of a lottery; after this first rough cut, the presiding judge will excuse those potential jurors who may be ineligible or disadvantaged or openly unfit as jurors. Afterward, it becomes as much psychological chess match as crapshoot between defense and prosecution in determining through carefully crafted questions whether a prospective juror is likely to be receptive to one side or the other. (*See* **challenge for cause**.) In high-profile cases, trial lawyers seek psychological profiles and demographic statistical analyses to determine how jurors might vote.
Warrant	A judicial **writ** authorizing an officer to make an arrest, a search, a seizure, or execute an order of the court.
Witness	One who swears under oath to give truthful evidence in court.
Writ of *certoriari*	*See* ***certoriari***.

Important Judicial Hearings & Challenges:

Due process hearing	The hearing that determines whether a person's rights have been infringed.

402 hearing — An **in camera** hearing in which the judge rules on the admissibility of evidence.

Griffin hearing — So named for the first challenge of its kind in which defense counsel requests a splitting of the evidence with prosecution.

Kelly-Frye hearing — From two court cases--*People v. Kelly* and *Frye v. United States*. In the latter, the court ruled against admitting lie detector tests, and thereafter the scientific credibility of any scientific procedure became known as the Frye test; the California precedent in the former is the same issue.

Challenge for cause — The elimination of a prospective juror during **voir dire** on the grounds that his or her responses to counsel's questions suggest an inability to be objective about the case.

Rule 11 proceeding — Jonathan Harr's *A Civil Action* (1996) mentions this 1938 rule of Civil Procedure that, once revised, allows for harsh penalties against lawyers for "sham and false" claims. Based on a highly publicized Massachusetts torts case involving a failed lawsuit against two companies, W. R. Grace and Beatrice Foods, for allegedly polluting the town of Woburn's groundwater with a toxic chemical that resulted in eight cases of leukemia and the subsequent deaths of five local children. The 1998 film version pitted John Travolta as Jan Schlictmann, who represented the eight families, and Robert Duvall as his courtroom nemesis from Beatrice, Jerome Facher.

Peremptory challenge	The limited number of potential jurors each side may dismiss without giving reasons, reasons which must not be used to eliminate for racial or gender motives.
Wheeler challenge	In precedent-setting *People v. Wheeler* (1978), the state singled out and removed prospective jurors based on race.

Appendix 2: SERIES CHARACTERS

CHARACTER & Related Characters	**AUTHOR & Pseudonym**	**Practice &/or Locale**
A	**A**	**A**
Acosta, Armando [Judge]	*See* **Madriani**, Paul	
Adams, Doc	*See* **Coyne**, Brady	
Amerotke [Judge]	Paul C. Doherty	Thebes, Egypt
Antonelli, Joseph	D. W. Buffa	Portland, OR
Aragon, Tom	Margaret Millar	"Santa Felicia," CA
Attwell, Clare	Michael Underwood, pseud.	London
Attwell, Nick	*See* **Attwell**, Clare	
Austen, Kate	Jonnie Jacobs	"Walnut Hills," CA
Bailey, Geoffrey [Det. Sup.]	*See* **West**, Helen	
Ballard, Sam ("Soapy")	*See* **Rumpole**	
Bard, Jack S.	Warwick Downing	Denver, CO
Barlow, Hannah	Carroll Lachnit	Orange County, CA
Barrett, Lynda	Terri Blackstock	"St. Clair," FL
Barrington, Stone	Stuart Woods	New York City
Barron, Peter	Michael Farris	Spokane, WA
Barth, Kay	Norma Schier	Colorado
Bayles, China	Susan Wittig Albert	"Pecan Springs," TX

Retired from law practice, she advises clients in trouble while enjoying her avocation as herbalist. Romantically active with Mike **McQuaid**, ex-cop turned professor at the nearby college.

Bean, Roy [Judge]	Ruel McDaniel	Texas, "West of the Pecos"

The judge's title is self-awarded and like much Tennesseean Davy Crockett's lore, is part-fiction, part-truth.

Bencolin, Henri		Paris
Benedict, Sam	Elsie Lee/Brad Williams, and J. W. Ehrlich	San Francisco
Blackwell, Mark	Jay Brandon	San Antonio
Bloom, Sanford ("Sandy")	*See* **Karp**, "Butch"	
Bradley, Bill	Gregory Tree, pseud.	New York City
Brain [Colonel]	*See* **Thursby**, Roger	
Branson, John Lloyd	D. R. Meredith	Canadian, TX
Braxton [Colonel]	Melville Davisson Post	Virginia
Brendel, Ernst	John C. Masterman	St. Thomas College, Oxford
Bret, Gervase	Marston, Edward, pseud.	England

Lawyer Bret and soldier-sidekick Ralph **Delchard** are two of King William's men who represent the law of 11th-century England settling disputes between Normans and Saxons as well as conducting criminal investigations.

Broom, Andrew	Ralph McInerney	Wyler, IN
Brown, ("Brownie") Joe [Sgt.]	*See* **Lawson**, Gardner	
Burger, Hamilton	*See* **Mason**, Perry	
Butler, Patrick	John Dickson Carr	London
Cain, Harry	D. Kincaid, pseud.	Los Angeles
Cape, Adam	Michael Underwood, pseud.	London
Carl, Victor	William Lashner	Philadelphia
Carr, A. B.	*See* **Selby**, Doug	
Carstairs, Gerald [Mr. Justice]	Henry Cecil, pseud.	London
Cellini, Emmanuel [Dr.]	John Creasey	London
Chambers, Adrian	*See* **Madriani**, Paul	
Chastain, Laura	Lelia Kelly	Atlanta
Chew, Enoch	Leslie Ford, pseud.	Baltimore
Chirke, Nicholas	P[aul]. C. Doherty	Midlands England
Ciampi, Marlene	*See* **Karp**, Butch	
Clunk, Joshua	H. C. Bailey	London
Cohen, David	Richard Berman	Brooklyn
Cole, Harlan	Jack Donahue	Houston
Connor, Gail	Barbara Parker	Miami
Cooper, Alexandra ("Alex")	Linda Fairstein	New York City.

Alex is the Manhattan D.A.'s Director of Sex Crimes Unit.

Coyne, Brady William G. Tapply Boston
Brady's law office is in Copley Square and his practice includes mostly the well-off clientele of the Boston area. Xerxes **Garrett** is barely more than a mention in the Tapply books. He once clerked with Coyne and later declined a partnership offer because he didn't want to help "rich white folks get richer." Two other non-lawyers in the Brady Coyne circle deserve mention: first is Mickey **Gillis**, columnist for the Boston *Globe*. Coyne likens her in *Client Privilege* thusly: "She has the tenacity of an angry pit bull, the eclectic knowledge of a *Jeopardy* champion, the commonsense smarts of a downeast lobsterman, and the mistrust of human nature of a maximum-security prison guard." His divorced wife Gloria and two boys occasionally provide a wistful recollection of guilt. Sidenote: Doc **Adams** is a good friend, and in his other fictional life is the protagonist of a series of mysteries by by Rick Boyer. Les **Katz**, a private eye, dies in *A Void in Hearts* (1988). Hungarian-American girlfriend Silvie **Szabo** once provided sexual companionship. In the later outings, Brady lives with "virtual spouse," Alexandria Shaw, a writer in Maine.
Crang Jack Batten Toronto, Ontario
Crook, Arthur G. Anthony Gilbert, pseud. London
Crowder, Lauren Stephen White Boulder, CO
Lauren is the Assistant DA of Boulder; her husband Alan is a clinical psychologist.

Darwin, Jack Gaylord Dold San Francisco
Daley, Mike Sheldon Siegel San Francisco
Dee Jen-djieh [**Judge Dee**] Robert [Hans] van Gulick China, Shantung Province Judge Dee is a magistrate of the Peng-lai district during the Tang dynasty. **Chiao** Tai is one of his lieutenants, an ex-highwayman. **Tao** Gan, the Judge's headman, and **Ma** Joong are two more. Dee's confidential advisor is Sergeant of the Tribunal **Hoong** Liang, killed in service aiding the Judge.
Delchard, Ralph *See* **Bret**, Gervase
Devlin, Harry Martin Edwards Liverpool, England
DiNunzio, Mary Lisa Scottoline Philadelphia
Di Palma, Laura Lia Matera San Francisco
Dockbridge, John Arthur Train New York City
The young Assistant DA is featured in the final four stories of Train's first collection of courtroom fiction, *McAllister and His Double* (1905).
Dobbs-Frisco, Hunter Michael C. Eberhardt
Drake, Paul *See* **Mason**, Perry
Drake, Simon Helen Nielson Southern CA via Chicago
Drexler, Sarah Kate Wilhelm Oregon
Drumm, Claude *See* **Mason**, Perry
Dubonnet, Tubby Tony Dunbar, pseud. New Orleans

Eliot, Lewis C. P. Snow England

Epton, Rosa	Michael Underwood, pseud.	London
Everly, Frank	*See* **Mason**, Perry	
Fairchild, Lydia	*See* **Branson**, John Lloyd	
Fairr, Melville	Michael Venning	New York City
Falkenstein, Jesse	Lesley Egan, pseud.	"Contera," Southern CA
Farrell, Wes	John T. Lescroart	San Francisco
Fell, Gideon [Dr.]	*See* **Butler**, Patrick	
Fischman, Nina	Marissa Piesman	New York City
Fleming, James	Ann C. Fallon	Dublin, Ireland
Flippo, Jack	Doug J. Swanson	Dallas
Flynn, Arlene	H. Paul Jeffers	New York City
Forrester, Lily	Nancy Taylor Rosenberg	Santa Barbara, CA
Forsythe, Robert	E. X. Giroux, pseud.	London
Fortune, Sarah	Francis Fyfield, pseud.	London

Sarah will never make partner at the firm Ernest Matthewson founded, although she is allowed a generous salary; it is because of her clientele; she "filled a gap: she took on the duffers, the no-hope clients related to other clients" (*Staring at the Light*, 1999, 19).

Frost, Reuben	Haughton Murphy	New York City
Furnshill, Baldwin [Sir]	*See* **Puttock**, Simon	
Garrett, David	Neil Albert	Philadelphia

Disbarred for taking his wife's law exam in *The January Corpse* (1991).

Garrett, Xerxes	*See* **Coyne**, Brady	
Garrison, Luke	J. F. Freedman	Santa Barbara, CA
Gillis, Sue [Det.]	*See* **Sloan**, Charley	
Glitsky, Abe [Det.]	*See* **Hardy**, Dismas	
Gold, Rachel	Michael A. Kahn	Chicago-St. Louis

Associate at a firm in Chicago who later opens a private practice in St. Louis, her home. Benny **Goldberg** is her best friend from her time there, but leaves to become a law professor at De Paul University's law school.

Grant, Alan [Inspector]	Josephine Tey, pseud.	London

The Yard's Inspector Grant is the Yard's brilliant young Scots detective with keen powers of deduction; for example, he has an "unerring instinct for spotting the one dishonest face in a lineup of a dozen men," so note the compilers of *Detectionary* (46). London actress Marta **Hallard** is the love of his bachelor life.

Gregory, Alan [Dr.]	*See* **Crowder**, Lauren	
Gryce, Ebenezer	Anna Katherine Green	
Gulling, Harry	*See* **Mason**, Perry	

Hallard, Marta — *See* **Grant**, Alan
Halloran, Bruce — *See* **Maitland**, Antony
Hamel, Neil — Judith Van Gieson — Albuquerque, NM
She has a lazy partner **Brink** and a younger, Argentine-born lover she calls "The Kid."
Hamilton, Rita Morrone — Lisa Scottoline — Philadelphia
Hanson, ("Bomber") Derrick — David Champion — "Angleton," CA
Hardy, Dismas — John T. Lescroart — San Francisco
Half-Jewish, half-black homicide detective Abe **Glitsky** occurs in several books.
Harrington — Mel Arrighi — New York City
Hastings, Stanley [p. i.] — Parnell Hall — New York City
Hayes, Cinda — Marianne Wesson — Boulder, CO
Hays, Sharon — Sarah Gregory, pseud. — Dallas
Henry, Dallas — Preston Pairo, III — Ocean City, MD
Hill, Judy [Detective] — Jill McGown — Stansfield, England
Hill is partnered sexually and professionally with Inspector **Lloyd** (no first name).
Hill, ("Nikki") Nicolette — Los Angeles
Holcomb [Sgt.] — *See* **Mason**, Perry
Holden, Vicky — Margaret Coel — Lander, WY
Vicky is an Arapaho lawyer who works for the tribe on Wyoming's Wind River Reservation.
Holland, Billy Bob — James Lee Burke — Deaf Smith, TX
Billy Bob is an ex-Texas Ranger, former city cop, and US Attorney now with a small practice in the Hill Country.
Holloway, Barbara — Kate Wilhelm — Eugene, OR
Hope, Matthew — Evan Hunter — "Calusa," FL

Jacomine, Errol — *See* **Langdon**, Skip
Jameson, Cassandra ("Cass") — Carolyn Wheat — Brooklyn, NY
Jansson, Willa — Lia Matera — San Francisco
Jordan, Scott — Harold Q. Masur — New York City

Kale, Steven — Montague Jon — London
Kardon, Don — Jamie Katz — Boston
Karp, Roger ("Butch") — Robert K. Tanenbaum — New York City
Butch's wife Marlene **Ciampi** heads up the DA's rape unit. Karp's courtroom nemesis is DA Sandy **Bloom**.
Keane, Owen — Terence Faherty — Boston
Owen is a former seminarian who works as a law-firm research assistant.
Kemp, Lennox — M. R. D. Meek — London
Kemp worked for a detective agency in Walthamstow when he was disbarred and later was reinstated to become a branch manager of a law firm in Newton; when he left the agency, he took secretary **Elvira** with him. Love interest Penelope **Marsden** appears in the later novels.

Kennedy, Jeremiah ("Jerry") — George V. Higgins — Boston

Full name: Jeremiah Francis X[avier]. Kennedy. Higgins' creation is one part sleaze like most of his clients and two parts tough-minded, crafty defense lawyer.

Kincaid, Ben — William Bernhardt — Tulsa, OK

Klonsky, Sonia ("Sonny") — Scott Turow — "Kindle County" [Chicago]

Knott, Deborah [Judge] — Margaret Maron — North Carolina

Langdon, Skip [Det.] — Julie Smith — New Orleans

Skip's nemesis in this series of police whodunits is cult leader Errol **Jacomine**.

Lassiter, Jake — Paul Levine — Miami

Lassiter is an on- again, off-again lawyer, ex-Dolphins linebacker and South Florida denizen with a motley crew of colorful characters in his wake: offbeat secretary **Cindy**, **Doc Riggs**, the former Dade County M.E., and courtroom-cum-jury expert "**Marvin the Maven**."

Lathen, Emma — R. B. Dominic, pseud.

Latterly, Hester [Nurse] — *See* **Monk**, William

Lawson, Gardner — Gallatin Warfield — Baltimore, MD

Lewis, Wynsome ("Wyn") — David A. Kaufelt — "Waggs Neck Harbor," NY

Locke, Jeremy — Mary Challis — England

Logan, Whitney — Mercedes Lambert — Los Angeles

Low, Ambrose — Henry Cecil, pseud. — London

McCain, Sam — Edward Gorman — BlackRiver Falls, IA

McCutcheon, Claude — John A. Miller — San Francisco

McDevitt, Charlie — *See* **Coyne**, Brady

Mackay, Kathryn — Christine McGuire — "Santa Rita," CA

Mackenzie ("Mac"), Smith — Margaret Truman — Washington, DC

Mac is a law prof who teams with Annabel **Reed**, gallery owner.

MacPherson, Annie — Janet L. Smith — Seattle

MacPherson, Elizabeth — Sharon McCrumb — Eastern Kentucky

McQuaid — *See* **Bayles**, China

Madriani, Paul — Steve Martini — "Capital City" (Sacramento)

Adrian **Chambers** is a defense attorney with a grudge for having been barred; he took a bribe in a sting operation directed by Madriani.

Maitland, Antony — Sara Woods, pseud. — Kempenfeldt Square, London

Woods' British barrister was introduced in 1962. **Jenny**, wife of Antony, resides with her husband in her husband's uncle's house in Kempenfeldt Square. She and two other inhabitants of the house along with some Scotland Yard detectives form the nucleus of Woods' characters surrounding her protagonist. Sir Nicholas

Harding is a famous and surly barrister who opened his house to his nephew and his wife, a temporary arrangement owing to Antony Maitland's war wound that lasted well into the seventies; a butler named **Gibbs**; and Meg **Hamilton**, actress and visitor. Lady Harding enters the family circle from Chedcombe, West Midlands; she is barrister Vera **Langhorne**. Detective-Inspector **Sykes** and Superintendent **Briggs** represent the friendly and unfriendly forces from theYard and Derek **Stringer** performs mainly as junior counsel and office factotum. Finally, there is Bruce **Halloran**, QC, performs as courtroom antagonist to Antony Maitland much as Mason has his Hamilton Burger.

Mallet, Inspector	*See* **Pettigrew**, Francis	
Malone, John J.	Craig Rice, pseud.	Chicago
Manton, Simon [Chief Inspector]	Michael Underwood, pseud.	London

Scotland Yard's youngest Detective Chief Inspector is here enrolled among lawyers because of his creator's successful bridging of the mystery with the courtroom thriller, even though most trial action in Underwood's fiction is light. Manton comes to the assistance of numerous barristers and solicitors to spring his traps once the action has left the Old Bailey.

Markham, John F. X.	S. S. Van Dine, pseud.	New York City
Marryat, Stephen	Margaret Leek	London
Mason, Hezekiah [Esq.]	*See* **Tutt** [Mr.]	
Mason, Perry	Erle Stanley Gardner	Los Angeles

The world's most recognized fictional lawyer, originally named Ed Stark, is renowned for solving his cases in the final moments of courtroom denouement (85 cases with a single loss). Born in 1891, Mason is believed to hail from Fayette County, PA. His team is almost as well known: plucky secretary Della **Street**, private investigator Paul **Drake**, a tall bachelor with a queasy stomach, who has LA offices in the same bank building in the Central Utilities Building at Central and Clark Streets, and courtroom nemesis Hamilton **Burger**, LA County DA, who has matched wits with Mason in fifty cases and lost. Some early characters failed to find permanent places in the Mason saga and were cast off or replaced--for example, young assistant Frank **Everly**, who appears in *The Case of the Sulky Girl* and *The Case of the Howling Dog* (1934); the same occurs to early police antagonist Sgt. Holcomb, replaced by a friendlier Lt.**Tragg**, Judge **Markham** and Claude **Drumm**, Assistant DA and forerunner of Burger. **Jackson**, his seldom seen meticulous researcher, makes an extended appearance in *The Case of the Half-Wakened Wife* (1945) before he disappears. Another low-key character is Burger's assistant, Harry **Gulling**, who receives one of the most dubious compliments in the entire Mason saga when Perry himself in *The Case of the Borrowed Brunette* (1951) calls Gulling "the shrewd legal mind that guides the policy of the district attorney's office." Actor Raymond Burr--big, broad of shoulder and wavy-haired as Mason is said to be--played the redoubtable criminal lawyer and bachelor in the TV series (1957-1966) and throughout the mid-1980s starred in several made-for-television films based on the Mason novels.

Mason, Randolph	Melville Davisson Post	Virginia
Masters, Caroline	Richard North Patterson	Washington, DC/ New Hampshire
Matheson, Garrett [Major]	Julian Prescot, pseud.	England, a small town

Prescot does not refer to specific locales, except to locate the county court house and Matheson's law office on "South Kemp Street," but it appears an indefinable locale with each court case, sometimes sounding more like London than a small city of, say, the Midlands, where the locals would betray an accent. The Major, as viewed by **Prescot**, the lawyer-narrator, is a rich, vain, and vainglorious barrister who is bested in the courtroom by a young, capable solicitor named **Weld** in the courtroom action of *Case for Court* (1964).

Mayberry, Noel	*See* **Bradley**, Bill	
Mellanby, Hugh	*See* **Warrington-Reeve**, Claude	
Mensing, Loren	Francis M. Nevins, Jr.	St. Louis
Merrivale, Henry [Sir]		London
Middleton-Brown, David		London
Milholland, Katherine Prescott	Gini Hartzmark	Chicago

Kate is that rare corporate attorney (securities expert) whose sleuthing is as violent as her career is tame.

Monk, William	Anne Perry, pseud.	London
Montez, Luis	Manuel Ramos	Denver
Moran, J. ("Jigger") Howard	John Roeburt	Manhattan

O'Brien, Kali	Jonnie Jacobs	San Francisco
O'Brien, Kevin	*See* **Maitland**, Antony	
O'Brion, William Francis	Arthur Train	New York City/Pottsville, NY

Mr. Tutt's second-most villainous opponent in court, after Squire Mason, is Assistant DA O'Brion.

Page, Gideon	Grif Stockley	Little Rock, AR
Paget, Christopher	Richard North Patterson	Washington, DC
Perry-Mondori, Karen	Catherine Arnold	Florida
Pettigrew, Francis	Cyril Hare, pseud.	London
Peck, Ephraim [Judge]	August Derleth	Sac Prairie, WI
Perry-Mondori, Karen	Catherine Arnold	Tampa, FL
Pettigrew, ("Frank") Francis	Cyril Hare, pseud.	London
Phillips, Wendell Arthur ("Bino")	A. W. Gray	Dallas

Bino's investigator is "Half-a-Point" **Harrison** and Dodie **Peterson** is his sexy secretary. US Attorney Marvin **Goldman** is his courtroom nemesis.

Portal, Ellis	Rosemary Aubert	Toronto
Prescot	*See* **Matheson**, Garrett	
Priest, William Pitman [Judge]	Irvin S. Cobb	Kentucky

Presiding judge of the First Judicial District of Kentucky, Civil War veteran, and much like another log-cabin lawyer born in that state, he has a folksy but discerning wisdom to dispense.

Pugh, Percival [Sir]	Robert L. Fish	London
Puttock, Simon	Michael Jecks	Devon, England

Puttock is appointed bailiff of Lyndford Castle in 1316.

Queen, Ellery	Ellery Queen, pseud.	New York City
Quincannon, Lon	Raymond Paul	New York City
Quintana, Anthony	*See* **Connor**, Gail	

Rabb, Joshua	Richard Parrish	Tucson, AZ
Reeder, J[ohn] G.	Edgar Wallace	London
Reilly, Nina	Perri O'Shaughnessy, pseud.	Lake Tahoe, NV/CA

Nina's team consists of private investigator Paul von Waggoner, a former lover, and a Native-American secretary-assistant, Sandy.

Riordan, Matt	Frederick Huebner	Seattle, WA
Rios, Henry	Michael Nava	"Los Robles," CA/Los Angeles

Rios began his practice in Palo Alto but by *How Town* had moved to LA.

Robak, Donald	Joe L. Hensley	"Bington," IN

Hensley borrows scenic descriptions from northern and southern Indiana for Mojeff County. In any event, Donald acquires partners in the later books: Sam **King** and Jake **Bornstein**. Circuit Court Judge **Steinmetz** continues as Donald's alter ego and acts, according to the sign outside the office as "of counsel" in his semi-retirement.

Robinson, Nan	Taffy Cannon	Los Angeles
Rosato, Benedetta ("Bennie")	Lisa Scottoline	Philadelphia
Rosen, Nate	Ronald Levitsky	Washington, DC

Nate is a civil-rights lawyer who takes on constitutional and civil rights cases for the Committee for the Defense of the Constitution; his courtrooms range from Chicago to the Black Hills of South Dakota to Musket Shoals, VA.

Rosenberg, Richard	*See* **Hastings**, Stanley	
Rossi, Grace	Lisa Scottoline	Philadelphia
Ruggles, Danny	Louis Auchincloss	Manhattan
Rumpole	John Mortimer	London

The barrister practices in the City of London along with his head of chambers, Sam **Ballard**. Wife **Hilda** is "She who must be obeyed!"

Sabich, Ro⟩at ("Rusty")	Scott Turow	"Kindle County" (Chicago)
Safford, Benton (ABen@)	R. B. Dominic, pseud.	Washington, DC/ "Newburg," OH

Safford is a Democratic congressman from this fictional Ohio southern district. His sister Janet **Lundgren** and office scecretary-deputy Mag **Anderson** provide support.

Sanderson, Abigail	*See* Forsyth, Robert	
Sansi, George	Paul Mann	Bombay, Gao, India
Schwartz, Rebecca	Julie Smith	San Francisco

Rebecca runs a private law firm with partner Chris **Nicholson**.

Selby, Doug	Erle Stanley Gardner	"Madison County," CA

Selby was elected in a close vote in 1936 with the goal of ending local corruption. Selby's courtroom foe is famed, unscrupulous trial lawyer A.B. **Carr**. Sheriff Rex **Brandon** is friendly; police chief Otto **Larkin** is not. Reporter Sylvia **Martin** and trial lawyer Inez **Stapleton** form the other two ends of the romantic triangle with the handsome DA.

Sheridan, Dan	Barry Reed	Boston
Shugak, Kate	Dana Stabenow	Anchorage, AS
Simmons, Bernie	Richard Lockridge	New York City
Sinclair, Mark	Jay Brandon	San Antonio
Sloan, Charley	William J. Coughlin	Detroit
Smith, Annabel	*See* **Smith**, Mac	
Smith, ("Mac") Mackenzie	Margaret Truman	Washington, DC
Spotted Moon, Charles	Chelsea Quinn Yarbro	San Francisco

Charles is equal parts attorney and Ojibway tribal shaman.

St. Clair	*See* **Vail**, Martin	
Stampler, Aaron	*See* **Vail**, Martin	
Stern, Alejandro ("Sandy")	Scott Turow	"Kindle County" (Chicago)

Defends Rusty **Sabich** in *Presumed Innocent* and is featured in *The Burden of Proof.* The author's record of his experiences at Harvard law school in *One L* mentions a Sandy Stern among his study group: an MIT graduate in engineering with "precise analytic skills" that he expressed in a measured "dry, almost toneless, voice" which may have inspired part of the description of the fictional Stern (59).

Stevens, Gavin	William Faulkner	"Yoknapatawpha County," MS

Private defender and public prosecutor (in the later cycle of Yoknapatawpha novels of Mississippi life, he is Judge Stevens). This Harvard and Heidelberg-educated lawyer is one of the few but memorable Faulkerian characters whose universe is completely ordered and driven by language. In "Tomorrow" from *Knight's Gambit* young Stevens fresh from law school loses his case to a hung jury.

Strange, Sylvia [Dr.]	Sarah Lovett	Santa Fe, NM
Street, Dee	Hannah Wakefield, pseud.	London

American attorney.

Street, Della — *See* **Mason**, Perry

Tamar, Hilary — Sarah Caudwell — Oxford, England
Gender indeterminate Tamar, an Oxford don, presides over a group of like-minded barristers and sophisticates from the office at 62 New Square or in coffeehouses and pubs: Selena **Jardine**, Desmond **Ragwort**, Michael **Cantrip**, and Timothy **Shepherd** (uncouth because he hails from Cambridge).

Tanner, John ("Marsh") Marshall — Stephen Greenleaf — San Francisco

Tewkesbury [Mr.] — *See* **Thursby**, Roger

Thorndyke, John Evelyn [Dr.] — R. Austin Freeman — London

Thursby, Roger — Henry Cecil, pseud. — London
Thursby, a barrister who ends a High Court Judge, is featured in a mid-1950s trilogy by Cecil: *Brothers in Law*, *Friends at Court*, and *Sober as a Judge*. Other Cecil series characters come and go with frequency throughout his other novels, such as the comically dim Colonel **Brain** and the frequently inebriated Mr. **Tewkesbury**.

Tilney, Clitus — Louis Auchincloss — New York City
Clitus is the senior partner of Manhattan's Tower, Tilney & Webb and its benevolent driving force. Rutherford **Tower** is an associate and bloodless relative of the founding Tower; another senior partner is the ambitious Chambers **Todd**. Waldron **Webb** is the principal trial attorney of the firm. Assorted minor characters of the firm--associates, staff, and clients--recur throughout the works much like a Faulkner saga. Clarence **Cup** is an attorney from a rival firm.

Tragg [Lt.] — *See* **Mason**, Perry

Turner, Stan — William Manchee — Dallas

Turntide, Reggie — *See* **Dubonnet**, Tubby

Tutt, Ephraim — Arthur Train — New York City
Train's flinty advocate has Lincolnesque traits, is always called *Mr.* Tutt in the *Saturday Evening Post* stories to distinguish him from his younger partner Samuel--who is just **Tutt**, but no kin--and maintains a spartan office in Manhattan. Occasionally, he makes business calls upstate to Pottsville. His courtroom opponent is Hezekiah **Mason**.

Ulen [Judge] — Curtis Bok — Philadelphia

Vail, Martin — William Diehl — Chicago
Defense attorney in *Primal Fear* who becomes acting DA for Cook County in *Show of Evil*. Vail's group takes on the tough cases (he refers to them as the Wild Bunch) and includes some regulars like investigator **St. Clair**.

Venable, Linda — William Diehl — Chicago
She left the DA's office in *Primal Fear* to become a corporate lawyer in *Show of Evil*.

Von Waggoner, Paul — *See* **Reilly**, Nina

Ward, Eric | Roy Lewis | Newcastle, England

The lawyer's office in Newcastle at the Quayside in the Northumberland hills includes a young assistant Ted **Grainger**, responsible for the commercial side of Ward's business.

Ward, Peter	David St. John, pseud.	Washington, DC
Warrington-Reeve, Claude	Josephine Bell	London
West, Helen	Francis Fyfield, pseud.	London

Helen is a Crown Prosecutor who teams with her sometimes lover, Inspector Geoffrey Bailey.

Westcott, Peter	Auchincloss, Louis	New York City
Whitehouse, Simon [QC]	John Wainwright	London
Wilkes, John	Schoonover, W.	NYC
Wilson, Lisa	*See* **Garrett**, David	
Winslow, Steve	J. P. Hailey, pseud.	NYC

Some Literary Law Firms:

Abbott & Windsor = Firm where Michael Kahn's Rachel Gold began practicing and which occasionally retains her services (*The Canaan Legacy*, 1988; *Death Benefits*, 1992).

Andrew Broom, Atty-at-Law = Ralph McInerny's law office for Andrew Broom. Located on the 12th floor of Hoosier Towers, the tallest building in Wyler, Indiana. Secretary and wife Susannah manages the office while nephew Gerald helps with the caseload.

Arnold & Degener = Auchincloss' Danny Ruggles begins his law career here (*Fellow Passengers*, 1989).

Bendini, Lambert & Locke = John Grisham. The firm from hell in *The Firm* (1991).

Bogg, Tewkesbury & Co. = Henry Cecil's law office for his drunken solicitor in the vicinity of Marlborough Street.

Callahan Ross = Kate Milholland's law firm (*Principal Defense*, 1992).

Chase & Ward = Manhattan's prestigious law firm which provides a former partner, Reuben Frost, with most of his sleuthing cases.

Clunk & Clunk = H. C. Bailey's disreputable solicitor Joushua Clunk has an office (no partner but a clerk named Hopley) in Covent Garden, "denounced by its many enemies as the shadiest practice in London" (*Orphan Ann*, 1941).

Conyers & Dean = Arthur R. G. Solmssen's Philadelphia firm for three of his novels: *Rittenhouse Square* (1968), *Alexander's Feast* (1975), and *The Comfort Letter* (1975).

Dodson & Fogg = Charles Dickens (*Bleak House*, 1852-53). Some of the most disreputable, pettifogging lawyers Dickens ever created, based on his brief experience as an office boy at 15 in Lincoln's Inn and, later, Gray's Inn for the firm of Ellis & Blackmore, reside in *Bleak House*: Solicitor Vholes and the Dedlock family solicitor, Mr. Tulkinghorn. Perhaps worst of all Dickens lawyers is Sampson Brass, Daniel Quilp's attorney, in *The Old Curiosity Shop* (1841). The Court of Chancery, which contains the never-ending case of *Jarndyce v. Jarndyce*, concerning a contest over a will in which the legatees are reduced to poverty or who, like Tom Jarndyce, commit suicide from despair or exhaustion awaiting a verdict that never comes. "For," said he, "it's being roasted at a slow fire, it's being stung to death by single bees, it's going mad by grains."

Everett & Coates = Law firm of Louis Auchincloss' idealistic young attorney and alter ego in "The Legend of Henry Everett" and "The Great World and Timothy Colt."

Forbes, Hathaway, Brian & Devore = James Reid Parker. Law partners of this mythical firm appear with various other characters in the collected short stories.

Francis, Shaw and Elder = Eric Ward's blue-chip firm in Newcastle before his resignation brought on by a charge of professional negligence (dismissed by the Master at preliminary hearings); after glaucoma surgery, he sets up a solo practice.

Gillorns, Solicitors = Lennox Kemp's legal firm in Newtown, England. Its main branch is in Clement's Inn, London.

Gottlieb & Quibble = Artemas Quibble and partner Gottlieb are two thoroughly disreputable lawyers brought to trial toward the end of Arthur Train's episodic novel *The Confessions of Artemas Quibble* (1911).

Hartwell Black and Robineau = Barbara Parker's law firm where series character Gail Connor practices along with 67 other attorneys, hoping to become the eighteenth partner.

Hewitt, Sinclair, Smith and Perri-Mondori = Tampa law firm of feisty Karen Perry-Mondori, youngest of four partners.

Jaggers, Attorney at Law = Charles Dickens (*Great Expectations*, 1860-61). Mr. Wemmick is satellite to the compulsively handwashing criminal lawyer, whose offices are close to infamous Newgate Prison. The law office of Jaggers is not named in the book, but David Lean's outstanding film (Rank/Cineguild, 1946) with John Mills and Alec Guinness shows Pip reading this sign on his arrival in London from the marshes of Chatham. Francis L. Sullivan, who played Jaggers in the 1934 Universal version, reprises his role in the later film.

J. Lymon Stone = "Bruiser" Stone is young Rudy Baylor's first employer, under FBI investigation throughout John Grisham's *The Rainmaker* (1995), as he fights a corrupt insurance company in *Black v. Great Benefits*.

Justice, Inc. = Harlequin Romance's contribution to the legal-thriller genre in its Seattle law firm.

Kenge & Carboy = Charles Dickens (*Bleak House*, 1852-53). "Conversation" Kenge employs Mr. Guppy in his law offices.

Legal Services for the Elderly = Nina Fischman, Manhattan housing & social services lawyer.

MacPherson and Feinstein = Near-bankrupt Seattle firm of Annie MacPherson and partner. In *Practice to Deceive* (1992), the firm is bought up by Kemble, Lawton, Mercer and Duff.

Matheson & Co. = One-man law firm of Garrett ("Major") Matheson, as viewed by solicitor Prescot, himself one of the "Prescot Partners" noted in the authorial disclaimer of Julian Prescot, pseud.

Matthewson & Co. = The London law firm founded by Ernest Matthewson, where Fyfield's Sarah Fortune works.

Mensing & Nalbin = Loren Mensing's St. Louis law firm for a time before he chose to leave it and become a law professor; it was founded by his father Stephen and Stanford Nalbin.

Ogilvie, Tallant & Moon = Chelsea Quinn Yarbro's San Francisco law office for Charles Moon.

Patton, Shaw & Lord = David Baldacci's Washington, DC blue-chip law firm dominated by Sandy Lord in *Absolute Power* (1996).

Pomeroy, Macarthur, Brovak and Sage = Brian Pomeroy's law firm in *Dance of*

Shiva (1984) and *Kill All the Lawyers* (1994) by William H. Deverell.

Prendergrast & Crawley = Lelia Kelly's white-shoe Atlanta firm for Laura Chastain.

Raven, Tucker & Tubb = Ben Kincaid's former employer (*Primary Justice*, 1991) and recent courtroom nemesis in *Silent Justice* (2000).

Robinovich, Barr, Barr, Tchobanian = William H. Deverell's Vancouver, British Columbia law firm with the two Barrs husband and wife and popularized on CBC-TV's *Street Legal.*

Rosato & Biscardi = Lisa Scottoline's Benedetta ("Bennie") Rosato's firm in *Legal Tender* (1996) expands as she becomes a managing partner of Rosato & Associates, an all-female Philadelphia firm, in the 1998 *Rough Justice.* In *Moment of Truth* (2000), Mary DiNunzio goes to work for the firm to be followed by Judy Carrier in *The Vendetta Def*ense (2001).

Schaffer, Powell and Briggs = Kendall Roberts' law firm (Diane Bernard, pseud.).

Simpson & Gates = Siegel's name for his ex-priest lawyer Mike Daley's firm plays upon a Los Angeles odd couple (O. J. Simpson and Police Chief Daryl Gates), albeit the firm is in San Francisco.

Small, Weston & Burke = Erle Stanley Gardner.

Snaith & Epton = Michael Underwood, pseud. Rosa Epton graduates to partner in the 1981 *Crime upon Crime.*

Snitchey & Craggs = Charles Dickens ("The Battle of Life," London: Bradbury, 1846). One of Dickens' most amusing fictional cases is *Bumple v. Sludberry* in his first work, *Sketches by* Boz, 1836. Another is *Bardell v. Pickwick* in *The Pickwick Papers*, 1836-37 (Rpt. Adams, A. K. *Favorite Trial Stories* (New York: Dodd, 1966). Dickens was probably influenced by the adultery trial of Lord Melbourne and the wife of the Hon. George Norton, a case he covered for his paper, *The Morning Chronicle* in June of 1836.

Spenlow & Jorkins = Charles Dickens (*David Copperfield*, 1849-50*).*

Strong and Matthews = Will Oursler's New York State firm which provides the trial transcripts for two documentary-style novels in the 1940s.

Sweeney & Drake = Michael Brock's law firm in Grisham's *The Street Lawyer*

(1998).

Tower, Tilney, & Webb = Louis Auchincloss. Occupies two floors of a vast office building on Wall Street.

Appendix 3: CRAFT NOTES

Among the novelists (often both practicing attorneys and writers) who returned a survey form with commentary, the following were chosen for their commentary on the craft of writing fiction or on the distinctions they drew between courtroom justice in fiction and in fact. The second part consists of a sampling of trial attorneys, and again, as is the case here, many are distinguished in both fields. [Author's note: George V. Higgins would have been represented in both sections; his recent death is a great loss for literature and law both. His friends will appreciate his response to number three of the Trial Attorney survey: Do you have a favorite courtroom lawyer? Why? Response: *Several because they've either beaten me or taught me, and become my cherished friends.*]

Novelist/Lawyer Surveys

Neil Albert

1. Who are the writers of fiction that you read? Do you read other writers of legal fiction?

   I read very widely in modern fiction; in no particular order, Robert Stone, John Updike, John Ford, Isabel Allende, Robertson Davies, Harry Crews, Norman Mailer, Ellen Gilchrist, and Dianne Johnson, just to give you a few off the top of my head. No, I do not read any legal fiction on a regular basis.

2. Do you have a favorite novel about courtroom drama? A favorite short fiction?

Hands down, the best courtroom book I have ever read is by Cornelius

Grafton, *The Presumption of Innocence.* It is a wonderful, human document, cleverly plotted, intelligent, and highly realistic in terms of what a trial lawyer really thinks about. All the more surprising because it is my understanding he was an office lawyer. I have also enjoyed several of Jay Brandon's books, chiefly because he holds the jury system in almost as much contempt as I do.

3. Do you have a favorite courtroom lawyer or stereotype that you model your protagonist upon? Is there a "history" to your character's creation?

My protagonist, Dave Garrett, is a disbarred lawyer, modeled on myself. He ekes out a living as a private eye. In my third book he has a chapter in which he winds up trying a case after a friend of his becomes too drunk to handle the second day of trial. It is one of the darkest things I have ever written.

4. How close is your version of courtroom justice in your fiction to courtroom justice as you know it in life?

Courtroom justice in fiction is far more precise and certain than what happens in real courtrooms. Real cases, as George Orwell once said about war, involve intense preparation, but are actually won or lost by luck and muddle. In fiction, the workings of the courtroom must always fit into the logic of the story; real life isn't so tidy.

5. How do you get your ideas for novels? What does your creative process involve from incubation of the concept through the actual writing process?

My ideas for my books come from a variety of sources; my first book was based on a real case; my second was based on an episode in my own life; the third and fourth were conscious exercises in writing books about a particular topic; the fifth just came to me in the writing; and the sixth was, again, based on something that happened to me. As far as what my own creative process really involves, I subscribe to the "vivid dream" theory: I find that if I can concentrate sufficiently to visualize the world in the book, and hear the characters speak, writing the book (to borrow from Annie Dillard) is simply remembering something you once knew and then forgot for a while.

6. What do you consider to be most significant about the way you portray courtroom law, juries, trial attorneys, etc.?

I have been a trial lawyer for 22 years and I've tried misdemeanors, felonies, and a wide variety of civil cases. I would say that the most important thing I bring to my portrayals of courtroom law is my utter distrust of juries. I am personally a strong liberal and I appreciate that the jury system is an important institution in a political sense; but the idea that twelve people off the street with an average of a 10th-grade education can, without taking notes or being allowed to ask questions of their own, decide contested issues of medicine or engineering or other technical matters, is utter nonsense--and yet in this country we do it every day.

William Bernhardt

1. Who are the writers of fiction that you read? Do you read other writers of legal fiction?

   I read and enjoy many of them. In fact, I'm editing an anthology of short fiction by lawyer writers, including Grisham, Martini, Patterson, Friedman, Margolin and others. It will be published by Doubleday next year.

2. Do you have a favorite novel about courtroom drama? A favorite short fiction?

   To Kill a Mockingbird -- one of the most influential books I read as a teenager.

3. Do you have a favorite courtroom lawyer or stereotype that you model your protagonist upon? Is there a "history" to your character's creation?

   I can't really explain this in the limited space provided. I wanted a hero who was not perfect, not "Perry Mason"--but was endearing and likeable as a result. I also wanted to reflect the ambiguities and disillusionment most law students and lawyers experience.

4. How close is your version of courtroom justice in your fiction to courtroom justice as you know it in life?

   I usually have to tone things down -- to make them seem "realistic" in a novel. People have no idea what really goes on in courtrooms!

5. How do you get your ideas for novels? What does your creative process involve from incubation of the concept through the actual writing process?

   A lot of work. Many drafts, much revision, and taking my wife out to dinner, so I can drain her much smarter brain.

6. What do you consider to be most significant about the way you portray courtroom law, juries, trial attorneys, etc.?

   I try not to get so consumed by the easy cynicism that pervades most treatments of the American justice system that I forget what good is and can be done.

Bill Deverell

Most of my ten published books can fairly be described as involving court dramas: *Needles*, *The Dance of Shiva*, *Platinum Blues*, and *Trial of Passion*, but others feature lawyers in dramatic situations: *Kill All the Lawyers*, *Street Legal: The Betrayal*. And *High Crimes* was drawn from a trial in which I was counsel.

My books may be best described as literary dramas, and though I have sampled writers of the courtroom genre (Turow, good; Grisham, awful), my library contains more Updike and Atwood and Irving, etc. than crime fiction of any kind.

My protagonists vary, from young civil libertarian to 63-year-old alcoholic, and often these are indeed drawn from real-life figures. My courtrooms are portrayed as accurately as possible - though usually as found in Canada. I rely on strong characterization and hard-paced plot with twists and a high degree of humor. Ideas come from incidents in my former practice, or just straight from my head.

Linda A. Fairstein

1. Who are the writers of fiction that you read? Do you read other writers of legal fiction?

   In current fiction, I read Patricia Cornwell, Susan Isaacs, Richard North Patterson, Scott Turow, and just about every mystery I can get my hands on. In between those, I reread a lot of the classics (like Trollope), which I had studied as an English literature major in college - I love the use of language in 18th- and 19th-century classics. Other recent reads, which I've enjoyed immensely, were John Banville's *The Untouchable* and David Freeman's *One of Us*.

2. Do you have a favorite novel about courtroom drama?

   Presumed Innocent by Scott Turow.

3. Do you have a favorite courtroom lawyer or stereotype that you model your protagonist upon? Is there a "history" to your character's creation?

The protagonist in my series, Alexandra Cooper, does have a history. Her professional role, as Chief of the Sex Crimes Unit in the New York County District Attorney's Office, is based directly on my own experience, since I have served in that office for 26 years. I've taken far greater liberties with her personal portrayal - making her younger, thinner, blonder and endowing her with a trust fund, to allow her the freedom to do some things most prosecutors wouldn't be able to afford.

4. How close is your version of courtroom justice in your fiction to courtroom justice as you know it in life?

   One of the things I thought I would be able to bring to this genre is the authenticity of my experience. So most of the courtroom events I portray are based on actual situations.

5. How do you get your ideas for novels? What does your creative process involve from incubation of the concept through the actual writing process?

   My original idea to create a series was based on my admiration of Cornwell's early work. I like the idea of a strong woman character in a non-traditional role, and felt that the fascination my prosecutorial position holds would make an excellent vehicle for a mystery series. In more than two decades as an assistant district attorney, I have worked on the prosecution of some of the most interesting and challenging cases imaginable. Generally, I use concepts from real cases, and create a fictional murder in which to display classic procedural techniques.

6. What do you consider to be most significant about the way you portray courtroom law, juries, trial attorneys, etc.?

   I think what is most significant about my series is the fact that it gives an accurate depiction of the criminal justice system in the area of speciality in which I have worked.

Frances Fyfield

1. Who are the writers that you read? Do you read other writers of legal fiction?

   I read all kinds of fiction, avoiding legal fiction if I can.

2. Do you have a favorite novel about courtroom drama?

   Tragedy at Law by Cyril Hare.

3. Do you have a favorite courtroom lawyer or stereotype that you model your protagonist upon?

   I have lawyers in some but not all of my novels. One lawyer, Helen West, is based on myself. Another, Sarah Fortune, is based on the person I'd like to be. The history of their creation is nothing but accident.

4. How close is your version of courtroom justice in your fiction to courtroom justice as you know it in life?

   Uncomfortably close and unglamorous.

5. How do you get your ideas for novels? What does your creative process involve from incubation of the concept through the actual writing process?

   Ideas come from overheard conversations at bus stops, newspaper headlines turned upside down and my own morbid imagination. The creative process is one long, hellish muddle without much of a plan.

6. What do you consider to be most significant about the way you portray courtroom law, juries, trial attorneys, etc.?

   I try to portray them as decent but flawed, as most of us are.

Parnell Hall

I grew up on Erle Stanley Gardner. My parents were both lit teachers, and after a hard day of slogging through the classics, they would rush home, put their feet up, and whip out the latest Perry Mason murder mystery. As a ten-year-old child, I was intrigued by this phenomenon, so I read one. It was fantastic. Since then I have read all of them, many times.

When Gardner died, it was like a personal blow. In 1973 I began writing a Perry Mason book, and applied to Gardner's widow for permission to use the characters. She refused, saying no one but her husband could ever write Perry Mason. Unfortunately, by the time she got back to me, I was already 150 pages into The "Case of the Anonymous Client," but I complied with her wishes, set the manuscript aside, and did not think of it again.

Until I got published. Then it occurred to me I could finish the book. But not as Perry Mason, since I still couldn't use the characters. And it could be the first book in a series, since the plot required that the lawyer be an established character when the book began. But I had a screenplay called The Baxter Trust about a young hippie lawyer named Steve Winslow left over from my screen-writing days. I wrote that up as novel, got a two-book deal, and the second book in the series, *The Anonymous Client*, was the Perry Mason book I had started 15 years before. It came out in 1989 and sat on the shelf in Barnes & Noble right next to *The Case of Too Many Murders*, a Perry Mason mystery by Thomas Chastain, published with the consent of Gardner's widow.

While my book got criminally good reviews, not one reviewer noticed it was basically a Perry Mason novel and compared it to the Chastain book, or even reviewed it in the same column. The one person who would have noticed, never got the chance. Years later, Jon L. Breen, noted reviewer of courtroom fiction, walked up to me at an Edgar Awards dinner and said, "I want to shake your hand. You're the only man I've ever read who can write like Erle Stanley Gardner." I said, "I beg your pardon, but why didn't you ever review me?" He said, "Your publisher never sent me the books." I was devastated–at the time, my series had folded after five novels.

My knowledge of legal proceedings comes from reading Gardner. Because he was a lawyer, his books are pretty accurate. After my first Steve Winslow, *The Baxter Trust*, I spent three months in a courtroom in the Bronx watching a murder trial, before completing *The Anonymous Client*. The defendant, Larry Davis, was charged with killing four drug dealers. The defense counsel was William Kuntzler. After three months of watching the trial, the only changes I made in my second book was that I would sometimes have the lawyers argue objections at the sidebar instead of in front of the jury.

As for my other series, Stanley Hastings is a private investigator who works for a negligence lawyer, but occasionally winds up in court. In *Juror*, he's tapped for jury duty, and put on a rather boring civil case that heats up when one of the jurors gets killed. In *Trial*, Richard Rosenberg, the negligence lawyer, gets a murder case, and Stanley plays Paul Drake to his Perry Mason. And in *Shot*, Stanley is called before a grand jury to tell who shot him, but he is terrified and lies.

Jonnie Jacobs

1. Who are the writers of fiction that you read? Do you read other writers of legal fiction?

   I read mystery and legal fiction, but I read mainstream books as well.

2. Do you have a favorite novel about courtroom drama?

   Both *Presumed Innocent* and *Anatomy of a Murder* are classics in the genre and excellent books.

3. Do you have a favorite courtroom lawyer or stereotype that you model your protagonist upon? Is there a "history" to your character's creation?

   My protagonist, Kali O'Brien, is a mix of many people, including myself. She's a person first, and an attorney second - at least that's how she appeared to me initially. I didn't create her to be a series character. When I wrote *Shadow of Doubt* (first in that series) I thought I was writing a single-title book about a San Francisco fast-track attorney who returns home to the small town where she grew up. It was the contrast of environments and the conflicts inherent in "coming home" that were my starting points.

   But the other thing I'm struck by is how rarely real-life issues are clearly black and white. The many shades of gray fascinate me and I try to incorporate that into my novels. While I write for entertainment, I'd like to leave the reader thinking about something a little differently than he or she had before.

4. How close is your version of courtroom justice in your fiction to courtroom justice as you know it in life?

   One of the reasons mystery and courtroom fiction is so popular is that it provides a sense of closure in which the loose ends are wrapped up, the questions answered and justice prevails. This isn't always true in real life. As both a writer and reader, I like fiction because I like knowing what actually happened and how the seemingly inconsistent bits of evidence are explained by the end of the novel. In that sense, novels aren't like real life. In real life we may feel that justice isn't always served and we rarely have all our questions answered. For all its flaws (and there are many) I'm still a great believer in and defender of our judicial system. I usually try to work some of that passion into the books as well.

5. How do you get your ideas for novels? What does your creative process involve from
   incubation of the concept through the actual writing process?

   Ideas come from many places - the news, friends' stories, my own "supposing," I have folders full of ideas. The problem comes in trying to work those ideas into full-blown stories. I usually start with one or two ideas that have some emotional impact on me at the moment and then I brainstorm how I might structure the story. It's a real process for me, one that evolves only over time and with a fair amount of pain.

   When I start writing, I generally know the broad brush strokes of the story and a few of the major plot points I want to pass along the way, but I don't outline in much detail. I wish that I could because I think the writing would then be so much easier. But any plot I try to outline is wooden and bland. For me, the story comes alive in the writing of it. It's the only way I can see connections, possible plot twists, character motivation etc. I don't outline but I do re-write, constantly.

6. What do you consider to be most significant about the way you portray courtroom law, juries, trial attorneys, etc.?

I don't know that there's anything significant about my portrayal. I try to make both "sides" seem real, and I try to capture some of the personal tensions and conflicts felt by the parties. Portraying courtroom scenes is always tricky because the reality of what goes on in most courtrooms is very dull. Even with a trial that is fascinating in the abstract, much of the questioning is slow, repetitive and bland. So the trick as a writer is to make the scenes feel real, but also keep the pace moving so that you don't bore your reader to tears.

Roderic Jeffries

Trial scenes should always make for a sense of growing drama, but I frequently introduce them into a book because it enables me to highlight something which has intrigued me from the day I was called to the Bar in England - the difference between law and justice.

If the average person is asked "What are criminal trials for?" it's odds on that the answer will be "They are held to determine whether the accused are innocent or guilty." In English law this is only partially true. A trial is held in order to determine whether, within the evidence which is allowed to be given in court, the accused is innocent or guilty. The difference, in broad terms meant to defend a person's right to the initial assumption of innocence, has the paradoxical effect of allowing many a guilty man to go free. In such cases, the law is honoured, justice is not. Can the two ever be combined? Probably not. Has anyone ever satisfactorily answered the question, Is a starving man who takes a loaf of bread from a rich man's table guilty of theft?

With practical knowledge of the courts, though gathered many years ago, I try to make my courtroom scenes as factual as possible, allowing for the fact that repetition and inconsequences do not sit easily in a work of fiction (Who'd bother to read a book in which all the dialogue is completely lifelike?).

I enjoy reading any book with a courtroom scene provided that is sufficiently accurate to be reasonably authentic - Erle Stanley Gardener was a past master at that.

I have no idea where the ideas for a book come from, but wherever, I wish they'd come more readily. As someone once said, "Who would write for a living if he could earn an honest penny sweeping the streets?" Or a dishonest one, for that much, provided only he could guarantee that the law caught up with him, but justice did not.

Michael A. Kahn

1. Who are the writers of fiction that you read? Do you read other writers of legal fiction?

I have fairly eclectic reading tastes. My last four books read were *Our Man In Havana*, *Get Shorty*, *Cold Mountain*, and *Anna Karenina*. My favorite authors are Jane Austen, Joseph Conrad, William Faulkner, Elmore Leonard and Carl Hiassen. My favorite novels (besides those by the above-listed authors) include Matthiesson's *At Play in the Fields of the Lord*, Eliot's *Middlemarch*, Chandler's *The Long Goodbye*, *The Great Gatsby*, and *Moby Dick.*

2. Do you have a favorite novel about courtroom drama?

My all-time favorite "legal thriller" is *Bleak House* by Dickens. Contemporary legal thrillers that I like include Scott Turow's *Presumed Innocent* and several by Phillip Margolin. My definition of a good legal thriller, in addition to the basic prerequisites of any good novel (i.e., strong writing, arresting characters, compelling plot), is a solid feel for the lawyer's life. Although experience as a trial lawyer is not mandatory for an author of legal fictions, I have to believe that Turow's and Margolin's courtroom experience plays an important role in the effectiveness of their fiction.

3. Do you have a favorite courtroom lawyer or stereotype that you model your protagonist upon? Is there a "history" to your character's creation?

My protagonist, Rachel Gold, is not based on anyone I have ever known or read about. Nor are any other lawyers or judges in my books. At least not consciously.

The creation of Rachel gold was a convoluted process. When I first decided to try writing a novel, I was a young associate in a large Chicago law firm. In the beginning, all I had was a wonderful premise: a powerful senior partner in the firm dies, and the firm discovers a secret codicil to his will that establishes a trust fund for the care and maintenance of a grave in a pet cemetery. The hitch: neither the partner nor his family has ever owned a pet.

I decided that my protagonist/detective would be a young male associate at the firm assigned to find out what was in the grave (which is robbed early on). The book would be structured as a mystery and narrated in the first person by the protagonist. I didn't realize that a first-person narrator would be a problem for someone writing his first novel. My protagonist was a young male associate in the litigation department of a large law firm. So was I. Before long, the book was veering off the plot expressway onto long, dull, autobiographical dirt roads. Disappointed, I set the manuscript aside after about seventy pages.

About a year later, I realized that the basic flaw in my manuscript was the protagonist. It dawned on me that the detective hero in many of the best mystery novels is an outsider--someone who was once part of the mainstream (say, a homicide cop) but is now on his own (say, a private investigator who has occasional run-ins with his former colleagues). Thus, my novel would work better if my hero were a *former* litigation associate who left the fancy digs of a big firm for the life of a solo practitioner. Moreover, I realized, that former associate should be a woman, not a man. That would make her even more of an outsider in a world of litigation still dominated by men. Thus, Rachel Gold came to life.

By the way, when I wrote the first novel--published in hardcover as *The Canaan Legacy* and in paperback as *Grave Designs*--I had no idea that I was writing the first of several Rachel Gold novels. Not until my agent told me that she had a publisher who wanted the second and third books in the "series" did I even consider writing another one.

4. How close is your version of courtroom justice in your fiction to courtroom justice as you know it in life?

Courtroom justice in the real world generally lacks an essential ingredient of courtroom justice in the fictional world, namely, a strong sense of closure. Real cases drag on for years and are often settled before trial. Those that do go to trial frequently end in verdicts that satisfy none of the litigants. Moreover, whatever closure is achieved at the trial level is often undone months or years later by the court of appeals. And even where the jury verdict is upheld--as in the O. J. Simpson civil trial--other facts (such as the defendant's inability to pay the judgment coupled with his ability to shield his pension funds from garnishment) conspire to reveal the illusory nature of what had originally appeared to be closure. It takes a writer of special talent--say, Franz Kafka in *The Trial*--to write a satisfying "legal thriller" that is set in a fictional world without closure.

Sometimes I think we lawyer-authors enjoy writing legal fictions because it finally gives us a chance to control all of the courtroom variables. We can finally make witnesses say what we want them to say, judges rule the way we want them to rule, and juries reach the verdicts we want them to reach. We totally control the outcome. It's the ultimate dream scenario for any trial lawyer.

5. How do you get your ideas for novels? What does your creative process involve from incubation of the concept through the actual writing process? I have absolutely no idea where I get my ideas. I've spoken with some authors of legal thrillers who tell me that they borrow heavily from their own cases, but I haven't done that yet.

The incubation process is a mystery to me. I usually start with the fairly basic premise--a dead lawyer with the secret pet cemetery trust fund (*The Canaan Legacy*), a mysterious suicide (*Death Benefits*), a divorce client accused of murdering a sexy aerobics instructor (*Firm Ambitions*), the illegal trade in weird animal parts (*Sheer Gall*).

A good premise has to not only set up a decent mystery plot but provide me with an opportunity for fun--say, a chance to spoof life in a pretentious law firm (*The Canaan Legacy*) or poke fun at the spandex world of high society aerobics classes (*Firm Ambitions*).

From there, I try to come up with a few interesting characters. Once the characters are in place, I start doing my research (sometimes in the library, sometimes "on location") during the day while working out the plot during long, late-night walks of my dog. Eventually, I write a 10- to 20-page synopsis of the novel, and that becomes the rough outline for the book.

6. What do you consider to be most significant about the way you portray courtroom law, juries, trial attorneys, etc.?

I try to do two different law-related things in my novels: (1) convey a true sense of the life of a trial lawyer, and (2) illuminate an interesting area of the law. Examples of areas of the law explained include the insurance law (*Death Benefits*), and the Dead Man's Statute (*Sheer Gall*).

Bonnie MacDougal

1. Who are the writers of fiction that you read? Do you read other writers of legal fiction?

I read both literary fiction and "the lowbrow stuff." In the past month or two, for example, I've read Cormac McCarthy, Jane Smiley, James Lee Burke and John Sandford. Among current mystery/thriller writers, I particularly enjoy Michael Connolly.

2. Do you have a favorite novel about courtroom drama?

Scott Turow's *Presumed Innocent* set the standard, I think, by which all courtroom dramas should be measured. Steve Martini's Paul Madriani novels are also first-rate.

3. Do you have a favorite courtroom lawyer or stereotype that you model your protagonist upon? Is there a "history" to your character's creation?

This question touches upon an issue which is both an advantage and disadvantage to me and the handful of other women who write in this field. Until recently there were so few women trial lawyers that there was a dearth of real-life models. That's the disadvantage; the advantage is that there are no stereotypes to avoid. When I was a young lawyer, all my mentors and all my heroes were men. I learned from them, yet I knew it would be a mistake to use them as role models. Now my characters struggle with the same problem. Jennifer Lodge in *Breach of Trust* is a novice lawyer stumbling to find a style, while Dana Svenssen in *Angle of Impact* is a more experienced lawyer, at the top of her form professionally, though her personal life has suffered for it.

4. How close is your version of courtroom justice in your fiction to courtroom justice as you know it in life?

Dead on. In terms of atmosphere and procedure, my courtroom scenes are faithfully authentic to my real-life experiences. And in terms of achieving justice? I'm afraid my fiction mirrors my reality here, too. In *Breach of Trust*, the entire trial is a charade, manipulated to obscure the truth and obtain an unjust result. It's the action *outside* the courtroom that finally reveals the truth and leads to the way to justice. The same is true of the custody battle in *Out of Order* [1999]. In my own jaded view, a trial, with all its arcane rules and often mismatched advocates, is the least likely route to truth and justice.

5. How do you get your ideas for novels? What does your creative process involve from incubation of the concept through the actual writing process?

Breach of Trust and *Angle of Impact* were inspired by actual cases I was involved in as a lawyer. The germ of the idea for my next novel came from an amalgamation of news stories as well as a private family experience. *Out of Order* bubbled up from some wellspring in my mind.

More important than where the idea comes from, I think, is what the author does with it. A lot of books start off with a killer premise, but then flounder around until finally they whimper and die. The books I enjoy most and strive to write myself are those that get better as the pages turn.

My creative process? First comes the premise, which I think of as the essential conflict of the story. Next I think of the characters who could best populate that story, the ones who will bring the most interesting dynamic. A few key scenes come to life in my imagination, and finally I undertake the most laborious process: planning the plot and subplots that will string together those scenes and provide the framework for the execution and resolution of the essential conflict. Sometimes I do this final step only in the roughest outline before I start writing, and the plot takes on its form as I go.

6. What do you consider to be most significant about the way you portray courtroom law, juries, trial attorneys, etc.?

The personalities of the key players. The courtroom is one of the few places outside show business where the participants are really called upon to perform. What makes it interesting is how they do it.

Phillip Michael Margolin

I graduated from New York University School of Law in 1970 and I stopped practicing law in 1996, although I am still a member of the Oregon State Bar. When I was in the seventh grade, as a result of an overdose of Perry Mason novels, I decided that I wanted to be a criminal defense lawyer when I grew up and that is what I have been for the majority of my legal career. As a trial attorney, in state and federal court, I handled every type of criminal case from traffic tickets to murder cases. I was the attorney of record in 30 homicide cases, including 12 death penalty cases. At the appellate level, I was the attorney of record in approximately 80 appeals. I have appeared before the United States Supreme Court, the Oregon Supreme Courts, the Oregon Court of Appeals and the United States Court of Appeals for the Ninth Circuit. I was the first attorney in Oregon to use the battered-woman's syndrome as a defense in a homicide case involving a wife who had killed her abusive husband.

I have always been a voracious reader and reading the works of Conrad, Shakespeare, Hemingway, etc., convinced me that I could not possibly write publishable fiction. In my last semester of law school, I decided to try to write a novel simply to figure out how people wrote books that were 400 pages long. I was never able to write anything more than 25 pages and this was a great mystery to me. My first two novels were terrible and I did not try to get them published. In 1974, *Mike Shayne Mystery Magazine* published a short story I had written. This gave me self-confidence to try to write a publishable novel. My first job after law school was working as the clerk for the Chief Judge of the Oregon Court of Appeals. While serving in that capacity I came in contact with the Peyton-Allen murders, which were Oregon's most famous murder cases at that time. In my opinion, this is the single most complex and amazing murder case in American history. Fortunately for me, it was an Oregon case and few people knew about it outside of the state. I decided to try to write a novel based on the Peyton-Allen murders. That book was published as *Heartstone* in 1978 and was nominated for an Edgar Award.

As a practicing criminal attorney, I am frequently asked how I can represent a person who I know is guilty. I decided to explore that ethical and moral dilemma in the context of a novel. My second book, *The Last Innocent Man*, which was originally published in 1981, is a thriller that centers around what happens when a criminal defense lawyer decides to base the way he represents a client on his own personal view of the client's guilt or innocence rather than being an adversary for his client, the way he is supposed to in the American criminal justice system.

The idea for *Gone, But Not Forgotten* came from a cocktail party conversation I had with a friend. It led me to think about what I would do if Adolf Hitler asked me to be his attorney. In *Gone, But Not Forgotten*, I have a heroine who is nationally known for representing women in cases involving women's issues. She is hired by a mysterious multi-millionaire who may be the Rose Killer, a horrifying serial killer who dehumanizes women before he kills them. This puts the heroine's personal ethics and morals at odds with her duty as a defense attorney to represent anyone no matter who they are or what crime they have committed.

The Burning Man is very loosely based on a real murder case that I handled in the mid-1980's.

I do not have a continuing character in my books. I try to have my fictional lawyers act as closely as possible to the way real people act, although I take liberties to make the books entertaining. I try to confront my fictional lawyers with moral and ethical problems that are faced by lawyers in real life to show some of the ethical and moral pressures that criminal defense lawyers are under. For instance, in one of my books, an attorney discovers that evidence that was introduced in court to help his client has been fabricated. However, the attorney is not certain that the client is behind the creation of the false evidence. The lawyer has a clear ethical duty to inform the court that the evidence is fabricated, but the prosecutor could then use this information to try to convince the jury that the client is behind the fabrication and this could lead to death sentence. What should the lawyer do? I include this type of intellectual conflict in many of my books so that the reader can get a chance to try to figure out what he or she would do if he or she was an attorney in this situation. In addition to the ethical and moral problems, all of my books have complex plots with twists and turns, and surprise endings. I love to be fooled when I read mysteries, so I write the type of book I like to read.

My fictional cases are similar in many ways to real trials, but they are also very different. I have handled 30 homicide cases and only two of them had mystery elements in them. Most real-life cases are fascinating for the lawyer trying them, but pretty dull for anyone sitting through them. When I write about a trial in one of my books, I make sure that only the exciting parts are included. If I wrote about a trial the way it is in real life, most readers would fall asleep after a few pages.

I also try to stay away from the Perry Mason type of legal character, even though I really enjoy the Perry Mason novels. My characters have real problems and are not perfect. Most of my fictional lawyers have character flaws. However, I do not buy into lawyer-bashing. I think most lawyers are decent people. So, the lawyers in my books are normal, decent people who may act heroically or badly in specific circumstances.

It usually takes me a few years between the time I get an idea for a book and the time I actually finish a novel. I usually get an idea, but cannot figure out how to create a complete book from it. I forget about the idea for a while. Usually a second idea comes into my head and I realize at some point that I can put it together with the first idea and create a whole book. I will not start writing until I have figured out the ending of the book. I have to know who the bad guy is and what clues trip him up. Once I have my ending, I write an extensive outline that details all the plot twists and where the clues and red herrings are going to be inserted in the plot. It then takes me six to eight months to write a first draft of the book. My first draft is usually pretty bad. I spend four to six months of intense editing getting the book into final shape.

I do believe that the denouement in a legal thriller should be a resolution or vindication of justice. With a few exceptions, I do not like books where the bad guy gets away with his crime. This is usually a sign that the author was too lazy to try to figure out a clever way of trapping the bad guy.

There are several excellent courtroom thrillers. Among my favorites are Agatha Christie's *Witness for the Prosecution*, Turow's *Presumed Innocent* and *Anatomy of a Murder*.

Margaret Maron

1. Who are the writers of fiction that you read? Do you read other writers of legal fiction?

   I grew up reading all Erle Stanley Gardner's Perry Mason books; loved Christie's *Witness for the Prosecution* and Robert Travers' *Anatomy of a Murder* and was enthralled by the movie *12 Angry Men*; but I don't find myself seeking out legal fiction just because it has a courtroom setting.

3. Do you have a favorite courtroom lawyer or stereotype that you model your protagonist upon? Is there a "history" to your character's creation?
   I wanted a protagonist who would be "of the law" without being a professional police detective. As a rule, judges (especially small-town judges) are respected and given more leeway than the average amateur sleuth might be, which makes it a perfect profession for Deborah Knott, who often sticks her nose in where it doesn't properly belong. District court judges do not sit on capital cases in NC, so she'll never have to recuse herself for meddling.

4. How close is your version of courtroom justice in your fiction to courtroom justice as you know it in life?

   In my case, very close since many of Deborah Knott's cases are things I've either witnessed myself or been told by judge friends.

5. How do you get your ideas for novels? What does your creative process involve from incubation of the concept through the actual writing process?

   I usually start with the setting, throw in some local characters appropriate for that setting, figure out what the conflicts would be, add my protagonist and then play "what if--?" until a plot springs into being.

6. What do you consider to be most significant about the way you portray courtroom law, juries, trial attorneys, etc.?

   The cases where Deborah Knott sits in judgment are not the focus of the book. I use her courtroom sessions either to reveal more about her character and/or mindset or to counterpoint the main plot. Sometimes they're just there for comic relief since so many funny things do come before a district court judge.

Lisa Scottoline

1. Who are the writers of fiction that you read? Do you read other writers of legal fiction?

I read all sorts of fiction, mainly literary fiction and crime fiction. In the high-brow department I like Philip Roth, a former writing professor of mine at Penn, and Barbara Kingsolver. I still love P. G. Wodehouse and S. J. Perelman, for fun, and because they are complete masters of character and dialogue. Wodehouse, in particular, can show character *through* dialogue, with his eyes closed. For crime fiction, I have a soft spot for the Spenser series by Robert Parker, the 87th Precinct Series by Ed McBain, and the Thorn series by James Hall. I read almost all of the other legal-thriller writers, and my favorites are Richard North Patterson, Phil Margolin, Philip Friedman, Barbara Parker and Linda Fairstein. Martin Edwards and Frances Fyfield, from England, are also quite good.

2. Do you have a favorite novel about courtroom drama? A favorite short fiction?

Anatomy of a Murder by Roberts Travers is my favorite book of all-time. The voice is at once compelling and familiar, and the writing is so subtle it's breathtaking.

3. Do you have a favorite courtroom lawyer or stereotype that you model your protagonist upon? Is there a "history" to your character's creation?

I don't model any of my fictional characters on anybody real. That's the fun part of fiction--you get to make it up. In my fiction, there is a history to every character's creation. I just give them a personal history--familial, professional, and romantic--and keep it in my head.

4. How close is your version of courtroom justice in your fiction to courtroom justice as you know it in life?

My fictional version of courtroom justice is as real as I can possibly make it. I think that it's vital, especially for lawyers-turned-authors, to keep things realistic and legally accurate. My readers, because I'm not shy about saying that I'm a former trial lawyer, implicitly assume that what they're reading could happen, so I make sure that it really could, or even has, to me. I try to show them the behind-the-scenes stuff--and the way a lawyer thinks--that only an insider could know, since I think they should understand that our system of civil and criminal justice belongs to all of us, equally.

5. How do you get your ideas for novels? What does your creative process involve from incubation of the concept through the actual writing process?

I don't know where I get my ideas. They just come to me, and remarkably, on time. I use them if they sound really intriguing to me and to others. I am a pretty active sponge of the popular culture and rely on the faith that if an idea interests me, it will interest other people, too. Each of my books contains some central question of legal ethics--oh-so-cleverly disguised--and that will play into the plot. Often the issue arises naturally, as the lawyer-characters conflict over the resolution to a certain issue. I never preach. Or lecture. Except in surveys like this.

As for the creative process, as soon as the idea arrives, I start writing. I go start to finish. I just proceed from the premise--for example, in *Rough Justice*, a lawyer finds out her client is guilty while the jury's out, and in *Mistaken Identity*, a lawyer represents a client who may be her twin. After the premise is established--usually in the first five or seven pages, since my books keep the pace moving--I just keep asking what the characters would do next, given who they are, in the predicament in which they find themselves. I have no outline; I have no concept of what will happen next. I don't know who-did-it or why-did-it. I don't even know who will win the case. When I get to the end I find out the murderer. It is a dangerous way to make a living. Anxiety is my middle name.

6. What do you consider to be most significant about the way you portray courtroom law, juries, trial attorneys, etc.?

If I may say so, *Publishers Weekly* raved that my book *Legal Tender* "may change the way people think about lawyers." That pleased me no end. It wasn't my intent, as I said I don't preach, but if I am portraying a realistic character, fully realized and appealing in some way, who also happened to be a lawyer, then logically, I will be changing the way people think about lawyers. That they're human, too, which would be a significant step up from the way people think of them now.

Grif Stockley

1. Who are the writers of fiction that you read? Do you read other writers of legal fiction?

John Updike, William Styron, Jane Smiley.

2. Do you have a favorite novel about courtroom drama? A favorite short fiction?

Turow's *Presumed Innocent.*

3. Do you have a favorite courtroom lawyer or stereotype that you model your protagonist upon? Is there a "history" to your character's creation?

   I do not have a model. My main character, Gideon Page, has been the chief protagonist and is a series. He began as a public defender and now is in private practice.

4. How close is your version of courtroom justice in your fiction to courtroom justice as you know it in life?

   My version is as close as I can make it. Gideon makes mistakes and is not the smartest lawyer in town.

5. How do you get your ideas for novels? What does your creative process involve from incubation of the concept through the actual writing process?

   Some are derived from things close to my own practice. My creative process is very fluid. I change many things as I go along.

6. What do you consider to be most significant about the way you portray courtroom law, juries, trial attorneys, etc.?

   My novels are told in the first person and allow the reader to know as much as Gideon does. He knows painfully little.

Trial Attorney Surveys

***Harland W. Braun**, Atty.*
Los Angeles, CA

2. Do you have a favorite courtroom drama? A favorite short fiction about lawyers, courtroom theater, justice?

   Man for All Seasons, *My Cousin Vinnie*, and *Judgement at Nuremberg.*

4. How close is courtroom justice in fiction to courtroom justice as you know it in life?

   Much more rational and less biased. In general an idealized version of reality.

6. What is the best (or worst) stereotype (or generalization) about the way

writers portray courtroom law, juries, trial attorneys, lawyers in general?

Writers do not understand how totally biased and irrational the trial process is.

Paul DePasquale, Atty.
Los Angeles, CA

1. Who are your favorite writers of legal fiction? Why?

   None, actually. None of the legal fiction with which I have become familiar is realistic enough.

2. Do you have a favorite courtroom drama? A favorite short fiction about lawyers, courtroom theater, justice?

   12 Angry Men and *The Verdict*--pretty good dramatically, and sufficiently realistic.

3. Do you have a favorite courtroom lawyer? Why?

   No. Why? Modesty forbids . . .

4. How close is courtroom justice in fiction to courtroom justice as you know it in life?

   Not at all, as a rule. In fiction there are surprises, behaviors and issues discussed in front of juries that are never (or very rarely) tolerated in real courtrooms.

5. Do you agree with the statement that the denouement in a legal thriller must be a resolution or vindication of justice, whereas real justice in real courts is about, as one lawyer said, the "fixing of blame"?

   No. Neither is true. Neither in the thriller nor in the courtroom does the resolution "have to" be just, or to involve attribution of blame.

6. What is the best (or worst) stereotype (or generalization) about the way writers portray courtroom law, juries, trial attorneys, lawyers in general?

   Best Stereotype--(some) judges who are arrogant, biased, lazy and/or stupid. The exceptional, better judges make it much easier and more pleasant to practice law. I appeared before one of the best this morning. Stands out like a beacon of justice.

Linda A. Fairstein, Deputy Chief of Trial Division
New York County DA's Office

1. Who are your favorite writers of legal fiction? Why?

   My favorite writers of legal fiction are Richard North Patterson, Scott Turow, David Baldacci, and Lisa Scottoline. All of them start with an excellent knowledge of the law and legal issues, and all of them write well. I find that the authenticity of their professional experience adds a great deal to the entertainment that they provide for the reader.

2. Do you have a favorite courtroom drama? A favorite short fiction about lawyers, courtroom theater, justice?

   My favorite courtroom dramas are *Presumed Innocent, To Kill a Mockingbird, Anatomy of a Murder* and *Inherit the Wind.*

3. Do you have a favorite courtroom lawyer? Why?

   My favorite fictional courtroom lawyer is Atticus Finch, in *Mockingbird.* I think his intelligence, judgement, integrity and decency represent the best of our profession.

4. How close is courtroom justice in fiction to courtroom justice as you know it in life?

   With few exceptions, I don't think that fictional courtroom justice is very close to the real life experience. And most of the time, despite all the dramatic efforts of fine writers, what happens every day in our courts of law is far more fascinating than fictional portrayals.

5. Do you agree with the statement that the denouement in a legal thriller must be a resolution or vindication of justice, whereas real justice in real courts is about, as one lawyer said, the "fixing of blame"?

   I don't agree with the statement about fictional justice vs. real justice to which you refer. It's too pat a description of either process. Many fine writers, like Patricia Cornwell, do not neatly tie up the legal ends of a story, any more than usually happens in the real world. And I don't agree that trials are about the "fixing of blame" - it is generally far more complex than that.

6. What is the best (or worst) stereotype (or generalization) about the way writers portray courtroom law, juries, trial attorneys, lawyers in general?

Although I devoured Erle Stanley Gardner from my adolescence on, I think that his stereotypical development of courtroom law remains one of the worst - because the prosecutor was always wrong! It didn't bother me--until I became one.

David Fuqua, Atty.
Hilburn, Calhoon, Harper, Pruniski & Calhoun, Ltd.
Little Rock, AR

1. Who are your favorite writers of legal fiction? Why?

   John Mortimer. He focuses the legal with the personal lives of the clients and lawyers and clearly shows the pretensions of the profession and of individual lawyers while pointing out that justice requires dedicated, qualified trial lawyers who apply reason and common sense to solve a problem.

2. Do you have a favorite courtroom drama? A favorite short fiction about lawyers, courtroom theater, justice?

3. Do you have a favorite courtroom lawyer? Why?

   Horace Rumpole. He loves the law and could do nothing else. He abhors pretension. His method requires use of instinct for the truth and logic to disclose the truth through his presentation of evidence. Also, he relies upon learned skills in cross-examination and trial skills, not upon rhetoric, flash, and technology (a trend in trial work now).

4. How close is courtroom justice in fiction to courtroom justice as you know it in life?

   Good fiction captures much of the real dynamic of a good trial. A good trial requires that lawyers be good story tellers. Fiction can write its own ending while trials remain unpredictable at every turn. A seasonal lawyer knows that the pre-trial expectations of the trial lawyer are rarely met once the witnesses are sworn and face a jury.

5. Do you agree with the statement that the denouement in a legal thriller must be a resolution or vindication of justice, whereas real justice in real courts is about, as one lawyer said, the "fixing of blame"?

   Yes. Unfortunately lawyers have learned that jurors are more skilled at fixing blame than doing justice. True justice often wears a gray mask while blame is black or white.

6. What is the best (or worst) stereotype (or generalization) about the way writers portray courtroom law, juries, trial attorneys, lawyers in general?

   Win at any cost. Unfortunately, enough lawyers act this way for the stereotype to ring true more often than not.

John Gerald Gleeson*, Director of Litigation*
Strobl & Borda
Bloomfield Hills, MI

I have been a litigator for 27 years. I have tried in excess of 100 cases to jury verdict. I am also a voracious reader. I have a substantial library dedicated, in the main, to two subject areas: the study of military history and fiction.

My tastes in fiction run from the classic works of Dickens through the historical fiction of such authors as Kenneth Roberts and Bernard Cornwell and the thrillers of Jack Higgins, Robert Parker, and Frederick Forsyth. I even enjoy the fantasy fiction of David Eddings and Terry Brooks, as well as books by Dean Koontz and Stephen King. While working on my MA (English Literature), I think I was the only graduate student whose private library included the complete works of Zane Grey and Edgar Rice Burroughs.

What I abstain from totally in my reading are books about lawyers, unless the profession is incidental to the plot. In a similar manner, although I watch little television, I do *not* watch fictional portrayals of my profession.

The American public had a huge dose of bad courtroom advocacy in the form of the O. J. Simpson trial. In my opinion, to make "legal fiction" interesting to the general public, the authors, to avoid boring the reader to tears, must deviate from the reality of the practice.

No trial lawyer of my acquaintance ever had a "courtroom confession" like Perry Mason does in every trial. No successful female lawyer in any firm I have been associated with has ever "slept her way to the top", as I understand happened regularly in *LA Law*. Although I am a practiced good shot with both pistol and rifle, I have had the consistent good fortune of never having to shoot my way out of a difficult situation.

I have published over 20 articles dealing with various aspects of the trial process. Successful litigators work hard, work late, and work smart. I have never found it possible to apply Coleridge's "willing suspension of disbelief" to legal fiction, when I know the reality of the practice so well.

John Wesley Hall, Jr., Atty.
Little Rock, AR

1. Who are your favorite writers of legal fiction? Why?

John Clifford Mortimer, creator of the Rumpole of the Bailey series; Charles Sevilla, creator of John Wilkes and "Wilkesworld"; and, of the mass market, Scott Turow, J. F. Freedman, and Steve Martini–at least until his last book. The Rumpole series has interesting twists that are never fully telegraphed, but they are short stories so it is hard to do. Sevilla's are essentially a collection of short stories, too. Turow's example of the cross-examination of the coroner in *Presumed Innocent* is actually used by a friend of mine (with Turow's permission) who teaches cross-examination techniques in Chicago.

Rumpole and Wilkes share my distrust for prosecutors, judges, and clients. While their stories are not all that real, their descriptions of prosecutors, judges, other criminal defense lawyers, clients, and witnesses are uncanny and usually humorous. Turow's novels are remarkably real and believable.

2. Do you have a favorite courtroom drama? A favorite short fiction about lawyers?

My favorite short fiction is Sevilla's stuff about Wilkes. Mortimer's is a close second. My favorite courtroom drama is the 1974 made-for-TV movie *The Law* [*see* Oliansky, Joel in the Bibliography]. A close second is *The Verdict* [*see* Reed, Barry].

3. Do you have a favorite courtroom lawyer? Why?
Fictional: Wilkes (for zealousness) and Rumpole (for finesse).
Real: Any defense lawyer willing to stand up to the prosecution machine and take it on. Ninety percent
of those who call themselves criminal defense lawyers are not zealous enough and do not know how to cross-examine worth a damn. I closely observed a lawyer in a case, and I was sorely disappointed in him, yet he was written up in *The Best Lawyers in America*.

A criminal trial in America is the closest thing to civilized war, and the combatants need to be representing their clients to the best of their ability, especially in criminal cases. The prosecuting authority is trying to put your client in jail, and it is the defense counsel's sworn duty to prevent that at all costs within the limits of the law. After all, it is the prosecutor's sworn political "duty" to put everybody in jail. Canon 9 of the lawyers' *Code of Professional Responsibility* says, "A lawyer should represent a client zealously within the bounds of the law." It is a command to me. I think that criminal defense lawyers that are not vigorous, creative, and zealous advocates are in the wrong line of work and should quit before they hurt somebody.

4. How close is courtroom justice in fiction to courtroom justice as you know it in life?

   Generally, it is bad and full of errors. Bad writing is bad writing, and need not be tolerated. Errors, however, will have to be tolerated because of literary license and the need to compress time and events and to make the story come out the way the writer wants. Few real trials have any great moments as courtroom dramas portray. In 200 jury trials, I have had maybe one great moment where there was a look of revelation on a witness' face that he had identified the wrong man for a murder repeatedly in seven courtroom proceedings and actually once caused the defendant's wrongful conviction.

5. Do you agree with the statement that the denouement in a legal thriller must be a resolution or vindication of justice, whereas real justice in real courts is about, as one lawyer said, the "fixing of blame"?

   True justice is an accident, something not contemplated by either side. As Percy Foreman said, "You don't approach a case with the philosophy of applying abstract justice. You go into it to win." Sometimes justice is the last thing I want because my client likely is guilty. And, maybe two-thirds of the truth makes it to the courtroom.

6. What is the best (or worst) stereotype (or generalization) about the way writers portray courtroom law, juries, trial attorneys, lawyers in general?

   Most lawyers in the real world do not care for their clients beyond the case or take any personal interest in their case or clients. That hurts both of them. On the other hand, we have to remain objective and detached, so a proper balance must be found and maintained.

   Juries are a complete unknown quantity. One never knows from one case to the next what will happen with a jury because each is different. What I hate most about juries is their ability to accept plausible explanations from a prosecutor that have no foundation in fact because juries usually just want to convict and go home.

   As for trial attorneys, the only real generalization I see is the lonely lawyer battling against and beating the prosecution machine the public calls the criminal justice system. Prosecutors and their cops just want to win and convict as many people as possible. . . . Once they [the government prosecutors] make a decision to charge and later see how bad their case is, they usually don't have the *cojones* to admit that they were wrong in charging in the first place. Take the prosecutor in the JonBenet Ramsey case. I personally think that he is acting in the best interest of the system without rushing to personal judgment.

And trial judges? State trial judges are usually: (a) elected, and therefore, politically sensitive to not holding in favor of the accused; (b) shills for the prosecutor; (c) stupid; (d) intellectually dishonest, or (e) all of any combination of the above.

Defense lawyers? We fantasize about outwitting, out-preparing, and out-maneuvering the machine and pulling off a victory in cases we feared we would lose where we went before the jury scared to death that a guilty client would be treated unfairly by the system or, worse yet, an innocent client convicted. I've had that happen, and there is no worse feeling for a lawyer to experience.

Believing in "justice" is a true escape from reality.

Stephen Jones, Atty.
Jones, Wyatt & Roberts
Enid, OK

1. Who are your favorite writers of legal fiction? Why?

   (1) James Gould Cozzens because of the intricate plot, careful eye for detail and elegance of language; (2) Robert Travers for a realistic description of what the practice of criminal law is really about.

2. Do you have a favorite courtroom drama? A favorite short fiction about lawyers, courtroom theater, justice?

   Anatomy of a Murder, *Inherit the Wind*, and *Compulsion.*

3. Do you have a favorite courtroom lawyer? Why?

   John W. Davis and Edward Bennett Williams in this country, and Lord Birkett and Sir Edward Marshall Hall in Great Britain.

4. How close is courtroom justice in fiction to courtroom justice as you know it in life?

   Sometimes very close, as in *Anatomy of a Murder*, and sometimes miles away.

5. Do you agree with the statement that the denouement in a legal thriller must be a resolution or vindication of justice, whereas real justice in real courts is about, as one lawyer said, the "fixing of blame"?

   Yes.

6. What is the best (or worst) stereotype (or generalization) about the way writers portray courtroom law, juries, trial attorneys, lawyers in general?

   The Perry Mason syndrome.

Nancy Kopp, Commissioner, Supreme Court
Wisconsin

As an author of three legal thrillers, I think courtroom justice in fiction is fairly close to real-life courtroom justice, although I have the perception that fictional "bad guys" are convicted more often than their real counterparts. This perception is consistent with the statement that in order to satisfy the reader's sensibilities, the denouement in a legal thriller must be a resolution or vindication of justice, whereas real-life justice is more about "fixing the blame."

Moving beyond actual courtroom scenes, I think most modern legal fiction fairly accurately captures the spirit of our legal system. The timeline for fictional cases, however, is generally much shorter than real-life cases, and individual proceedings (depositions, court hearings, etc.) Depicted in legal fiction are also greatly condensed over their real-life counterparts. This is not meant to be a criticism of writers since, if authors did not take some liberties and streamline the cases they're writing about, their books could easily run to 2,000 pages and readers would be so bored that they would lose interest after the first few chapters. Most authors of legal fiction have a good feel for when to cut to the chase and describe only the high points of the case.

My favorite writers of modern legal fiction are Linda Fairstein and Barbara Parker. Both these authors do a fine job capturing the essence of what it is to work on a troubling case. My favorite all-time legal novel is *To Kill a Mockingbird* and Atticus Finch, with his intelligence and humanity, is my favorite lawyer. My favorite courtroom drama is *Inherit the Wind.*

The stereotypes and generalizations of the legal profession found in fiction pretty closely mirror the stereotypes that society has in general of the profession--i.e., lawyers (especially trial lawyers are grandstanding, money-grubbing crooks; jurors are stupid; judges are either dumb or corrupt, or both.

There are, of course, some people who do fit the stereotypes and it is much more entertaining to read about the characters who are a bit out of the mainstream (whether good, bad or just plain eccentric) than to read about the rather bland life of the average lawyer/judge/juror.

Albert J. Krieger, Atty.
Albert J. Krieger, P. A.
Miami, FL

1. Who are your favorite writers of legal fiction? Why?

I know this sounds rather churlish, but I have no favorite writers of legal fiction for the simple reason that I dislike fiction so far divorced from fundamental reality of life as I know it. Misunderstanding of the role of the lawyer within our society is promoted. Conversations with jurors almost invariably have shown me that they either come into the courtroom with a bias or a misunderstanding of the system that is directly attributable to the popular misrepresentation of the lawyer, professionally or personally. There are exceptions, of course. Atticus Finch in *To Kill a Mockingbird* portrays much of the humanity that exists in the average trial lawyer.

2. Do you have a favorite courtroom drama? A favorite short fiction about lawyers, courtroom theater, justice?

Because of the depth of the feeling that I have exhibited in my response to question #1, I do not have anything faintly resembling a favorite courtroom drama. I cannot think of one that exhibited the reality that it pretended to portray, and yet I feel that each has left a residue with the public which taints the work I have to do on behalf of citizens accused. In spite of what may appear to be my continuing irritability, I have seen *My Cousin Vinny* perhaps a dozen times and enjoyed it more on each viewing than I had the time before.

3. Do you have a favorite courtroom lawyer? Why?

I assume that you are referring to lawyers currently practicing. I have no favorite, but I can think of a number of lawyers who are truly superb in their craft. To place one above the other creates erroneous results, as each case and each courtroom experience is different. I think that among the best courtroom lawyers in this country today are Neal R. Sonnett of Miami, Gerry Spence of Wyoming, and Paul Luvera of Washington. Each one brings intelligence, integrity, and an honest and honorable concern for the client that he represents into the courtroom. Therefore, each fulfills the role of the lawyer that enhances our constitutional process. Though each may enjoy public notice, such notice does not become the be-all and end-all of their representation. Each has represented clients in cases of extreme notoriety and each has done so without necessarily resorting to sickening self-glorification.

4. How close is courtroom justice in fiction to courtroom justice as you know it in life?

Courtroom justice and fictional courtroom justice are so disparate that no comparison is fair. Courtroom justice in real life is a totally different. Similarly, judges, at least in my experience, by and large, are dedicated to their duties and obligations. Misconduct by prosecutors can occur but it, too, is, in the overall scheme of things, rare. Most seek to do a difficult job within the law. Conflict is an integral part of the adversary system and the responsible lawyer or judge does not drink to excess, nor pack a gun, nor pretend to be an educated Rambo. Our system is quite healthy without booze, drugs, or guns.

What sells books or fills theater seats is not the stuff of which the real courtroom experience is made. Frankly, I wonder at the imagination that goes into these portrayals. I know that witnesses very rarely break down and confess to being the perpetrator in real life. I also know that most lawyers are honorable, ethical and hard-working to a fault. Their devotion may be the stuff of a dull book or a dull movie, but it is real life. The bizarre trial, such as O. J. Simpson's, is–I thank the powers that be–not the rule.

5. Do you agree with the statement that the denouement in a legal thriller must be a resolution or vindication of justice, whereas real justice in real courts is about, as one lawyer said, the "fixing of blame"?

I disagree with both clauses of this question. Whatever drives a legal thriller to its conclusion, should dictate what that conclusion should be. To begin with a preconception that a legal thriller should have one conclusion or another restricts the creativity of the author and more likely than not will further distort the appearance of reality in the fictional piece. The lawyer who said that real justice is "fixing of blame" apparently is inexperienced in criminal defense. The fixing of blame "in a civil case" is not an empirical fact but rather a tipping of scales. In criminal cases we seek empirical truth when the prosecution attempts to prove a certain set of circumstances "beyond a reasonable doubt." A verdict of not guilty does not of necessity state a factual truth in innocence, but more often than not is a response to a failure of proof.

6. What is the best (or worst) stereotype (or generalization) about the way writers portray courtroom law, juries, trial attorneys, lawyers in general?

If writers of today would show judges functioning as tolerant individuals applying the law dispassionately but with concern and consideration, the public would gain an insight into the workings of our system that they do not get now. Showing trial lawyers to be drunkards, thieves, and cheats is as destructive to our system of justice as anything can conceivably be. In the minds of those who produce theater it may fill seats. There should be, however, some concern for what the patron takes from the theater. I have no objection to, and vigorously support, truth-telling. On the other hand, I object to the stereotype. No one of us should be so idealized as to create a picture that grossly distorts the honest and selfless efforts on the part of the lawyers and the courts in thousands of cases in thousands of courtrooms across our country on a daily basis. Unfortunately we see little in the media of recognition of that type of effort or conduct.

Mary Grace O'Brien, Judge, Juvenile Domestic Relations/Assist. Commonwealth *Attorney*
Prince William County, Manassas, VA

George V. Higgins' novels featuring Jerry Kennedy, the Boston-area criminal defense attorney, are excellent. Higgins captured the humor inherent in trial practice and his short, snappy dialogue rings true. He managed to convey realistically the tedium involved in trial preparation without being tedious himself. His knowledge of trial law and human nature served him well.

Scott Turow's *Presumed Innocent* was one of the best courtroom dramas (and his best novel, I think) that I have read. Turow effectively conveyed the intensity, focus and mental flexibility required to successfully prosecute (or defend) a major case.

Both authors also recognized common personality traits of courtroom characters (the occasional disorganized defense attorney, arrogant prosecutor and lazy judge) which have been encountered by practicing attorneys everywhere. It is with a smile of recognition that we recognize our colleagues and adversaries in Higgins' and Turow's books.

Most courtroom fiction relies on melodrama and *deus ex machina* resolutions which are unrealistic and far more black and white than the shades of gray which color the courtrooms of my experience. Succinct, concrete resolutions are less common in real life than in courtroom thrillers. Killers generally don't unexpectedly confess on the witness stand and criminals often are convicted of lesser-included offenses.

Other favorite fictional attorneys of mine include Rumpole, Portia of *Merchant of Venice* and Sir Thomas More as conveyed in Robert Bolt's *A*

Man for All Seasons. All of these attorneys display the wit, intelligence and economy of language which the rest of us strive for, generally unsuccessfully.

Wendy Putnam Park, Atty.
Avalon, CA

3. Do you have a favorite courtroom lawyer? Why?

   Yes. I get paid.

Mark Seiden, Atty.
Mark Seiden, P. A.
Miami, FL

1. Who are your favorite writers of legal fiction? Why?

   John Grisham--well researched, entertaining, very readable, good story lines.

2. Do you have a favorite courtroom drama? A favorite short fiction about lawyers, courtroom theater, justice?

   My favorite courtroom dramas are *The Caine Mutiny*, *Anatomy of a Murder*, *Rumpole of the Bailey*, *Witness for the Prosecution*, and *A Time to Kill*. And, of course, *To Kill a Mockingbird*.

3. Do you have a favorite courtroom lawyer? Why?

   Roy Black. Simply the best criminal defense lawyer in the country and a real gentleman.

4. How close is courtroom justice in fiction to courtroom justice as you know it in life?

   Any similarities are pure coincidence.

5. Do you agree with the statement that the denouement in a legal thriller must be a resolution or vindication of justice, whereas real justice in real courts is about, as one lawyer said, the "fixing of blame"?

   Disagree. Real justice in real courts is ofttimes related to the amount of justice the defendant can afford.

Robert L. Shapiro, Atty.
Christensen, Miller, Fink, Jacobs, Glaser, Weil & Shapiro, LLP

Attorney, Los Angeles

1. Who are your favorite writers of legal fiction? Why?

   Scott Turow, John Grisham and David Balducci.

2. Do you have a favorite courtroom drama? A favorite short fiction about lawyers, courtroom theater, justice?

   Twelve Angry Men.

3. Do you have a favorite courtroom lawyer? Why?

   Gerry Spence and Roy Black because they bring intelligence, psychology and drama to the courtroom and make it all real. Those who have left a lifelong impression include Clarence Darrow, Edward Bennett Williams, Melvin Belli and Frank Rothman.

4. How close is courtroom justice in fiction to courtroom justice as you know it in life?

   Depending on the author, courtroom justice in fiction rarely comes close to reality. Most authors unnecessarily take dramatic license in an attempt to portray characters in a way that is much different from courtroom presentation. With rare exception, the majority of court cases are dry, with the exception of the occasional searing cross-examination or mesmerizing closing argument.

5. Do you agree with the statement that the denouement in a legal thriller must be a resolution or vindication of justice, whereas real justice in real courts is about, as one lawyer said, the "fixing of blame"?

   Although most legal fiction I have read ends in a resolution or vindication of justice, it is not a necessary element. I think a reader's interest could be greatly piqued with a story that ends with jury deliberations, leaving the reader to reach his or her own conclusion. However, most readers are not satisfied or fulfilled without a resolution, and so, in my novel [*Misconception*], there is a resolution.

6. What is the best (or worst) stereotype (or generalization) about the way writers portray courtroom law, juries, trial attorneys, lawyers in general?

   The most typical stereotype that I find offensive is painting prosecutors as the personification of good and defense attorneys as the personification of evil. Further, the stereotype of trial lawyers being alcoholics or drug users is not what occurs in today's courtrooms. Although there is much room for criticism of some sitting judges, the overwhelming majority perform their functions in an exemplary manner. Fictionally, they are generally depicted as megalomaniacs who are psychologically imbalanced.

David L. Strauss, law professor
Univ. of Chicago

1. Who are your favorite writers of legal fiction? Why?

   Grisham is weak. *The Rainmaker* (the movie) was horrible. I find many more flaws than truths in legal fiction.

2. Do you have a favorite courtroom drama? A favorite short fiction about lawyers, courtroom theater, justice?

   Among the best are some TV writing (i.e., *Murder One*). *Twelve Angry Men* is a classic. But, again, most are very painful to watch.

4. How close is courtroom justice in fiction to courtroom justice as you know it in life?

   Real life messes up much more than fiction. It is also much less sexy.

6. What is the best (or worst) stereotype (or generalization) about the way writers portray courtroom law, juries, trial attorneys, lawyers in general?

   Horribly simplistic and inaccurate.

Michael E. Tigar, Atty.
Haddon, Morgan & Foreman, P. C.

2. Do you have a favorite courtroom drama? A favorite short fiction about lawyers, courtroom theater, justice?

   I don't have a favorite short fiction about lawyers, although I did enjoy reading the collection by Ephraim London, *The Law as Literature*. The companion volume is *The Law in Literature*.

3. Do you have a favorite courtroom lawyer? Why?

   My favorite courtroom lawyer was Edward Bennett Williams, my mentor. I don't have a single favorite among advocates of the past, although Cicero, Lord Erskine, and Clarence Darrow would certainly be at the top of my list.

4. How close is courtroom justice in fiction to courtroom justice, as you know it in life?

   Most writing about courtroom justice is filled with nonsense. I think the work of Scott Turow and John Grisham is particularly trashy.

5. Do you agree with the statement that the denouement in a legal thriller must be a resolution or vindication of justice, whereas real justice in real courts is about, as one lawyer said, the "fixing of blame"?

   Is there a difference between vindication of justice and "fixing of blame"? The purpose of a legal system, at least since the time of Exodus, is to fix responsibility in a way consistent with our deepest values about fairness and justice.

Charles Alan Wright, former Chair, Federal Courts
The University of Texas School of Law

[Author's note: Charles Alan Wright died in July of 2000. His was one of the great legal minds of America. The Dean of Texas Law School, Mike Sharlot, said, "He was the greatest legal scholar of my lifetime and perhaps of our century." Wright's 54-volume *Federal Practice and Procedure* is a landmark of legal scholarship. His national recognition came during the Watergate years when his arguments against releasing the Nixon tapes in federal and district courts earned him national exposure as a Constitutional authority and wide respect for his argumentation. He once said in 1973 after being the target of acrimonious attacks from all across the United States: "If tarnishing my reputation is the price for saving the presidency and this president, then so be it."]

I can answer the first of your questions--at least within my own limitation to crime novels--by quoting something I wrote in a review published in a 1996 issue of *The Practical Lawyer*:

> When people hear that I review crime novels, they regularly ask me 'Who is your favorite author?' That is not really an answerable question. There are a handful of writers whose books are so consistently good that when I see that they have a new book coming out I arrange to get a copy as soon as possible. Sarah Caudwell, Michael Gilbert, P. D. James, Margaret Maron, Lia Matera, and Stephen Saylor come immediately in mind.

You asked me "Why?" There is no single answer to a question of that kind because the seven writers are very different in their styles and approaches. Saylor's books are set in Rome in the first century B.C. and there is a substantial historical basis for every one of them. All of the others set their books in the present time. Lia Matera's books feature people who are or come close to being what 25 years ago I would have called "hippies" although they have outgrown some of those characteristics. P. D. James and Margaret Maron write about mainstream people. Sarah Caudwell wrote in a highly stylized, even arch, manner. I think her books are splendid but I have a friend who shares my love of the language who finds them unreadable. Amanda Cross combines highly sophisticated writing with a strong feminist point of view. Michael Gilbert simply cannot be categorized. His books for the most part have no series character or similar setting. The one thing that the Gilbert books have in common is really splendid writing.

I suppose the reason I single out these writers is that I know that whatever they write I will enjoy reading. Though the writing styles be different the writing will be good in all of them, the characters will be different, but they will be interesting and the plot compelling. My life is so busy that I have little opportunity to read fiction and I do not want to waste that time reading something that is not worth my attention. Of course, these are not the only writers of crime fiction who produce good books well worth reading. These are simply seven who stand out for their consistent excellence.

In question 5 you ask if I agree that the denouement of a legal thriller must be a vindication of justice. I do not agree. In Wesson's *Render Up the Body*, the book begins and ends with the narrator attending the execution of her client, who almost certainly is not guilty of the crime for which he is sentenced to death. I do not think our legal system blunders that badly often, but it certainly does happen. And it can, as it did in the Wesson book, make for a splendid novel.

Title Index

Author Index

About the Compiler

TERRY WHITE is Assistant Professor of English at Kent State Ashtabula. In addition to scholarly articles, detective fiction stories, and a one-act play, Professor White has authored or edited such works as *Cloak and Dagger: An Annotated Guide to Spy Fiction*, with Myron J. Smith, Jr. (Greenwood, 1995) and *The Sibling Society*.